# ANDES

# ANDES

MICHAEL JACOBS

GRANTA

Granta Publications, 12 Addison Avenue, London W11 4QR

First published in Great Britain by Granta Books 2010

A CIP catalogue record for this book
is available from the British Library.

1 3 5 7 9 10 8 6 4 2

ISBN 978 1 84708 170 4

Typeset by M Rules
Printed and bound in Great Britain by
MPG Books Ltd, Bodmin, Cornwall

For my brother Francis;
and for the bus drivers of the Andes,
the true heroes of this book

# CONTENTS

## PART THREE: THE CENTRE

## PART FOUR: THE SOUTH

# LIST OF MAPS

## NOTE

Maps appearing on the chapter openings
do not show *graphically* the continuous
mountain (Andean) chain running the
entire length of South America, but it is
indicated wherever space permits. Specific
mountains and volcanoes are named and
shown with a symbol.

Mountain  ▲  *Mte.*

Volcano  △  *Vol.*

Archaeological site  ∴

Salt lake  . . . . . .  *Salar*

Lake shore and coast  ▒▒▒

# LIST OF ILLUSTRATIONS

# LONG AGO AND FAR AWAY

Across unending grassland, towards evening. In a dented old taxi whose bonnet does not close properly. A tall man, squeezed next to the driver's seat, is being taken along an interminable straight road. In the middle of the Argentinean pampas, the Atlantic a three hours' drive to the east, the Andes a day to the west. No other cars in sight, no other people.

The driver is talking incessantly, about everything: his daughter, Argentina's economic crisis, the exceptional cold, the country estate to which the taxi is now heading. His passenger, of European appearance, grey-haired, white-bearded, intensely blue-eyed, smiles, nods, scans the landscape distractedly, and lends his full attention only when the driver talks about the area they are travelling through, its history, its geography, the estate at the end of their journey.

As he listens, the passenger records the name of the estate's aristocratic owners, the Anchorenas. He notes that the driver's daughter is an aspiring crime writer. He imagines himself in one of her novels, a tall, blue-eyed detective being driven in a taxi towards an isolated country house, the light fading, the clouds darkening, gusts of wind building up over the endlessly flat pampas.

Suddenly the monotony is interrupted. There is a silvery break in the threatening sky, a line of hills, a crown of rocks. The Sierra de Tandil, says the driver, swerving towards this unexpected apparition. Then the clouds close in and the first drops of sleety rain spatter the windscreen. They enter a wooded park. Night falls and the rain begins to pour. A white house, eerily luminous, lies ahead, surrounded by cypresses, like a mausoleum.

I have arrived in mid-winter at the Estancia Siempreverde. A man has come to the main door to greet me, dressed in an immaculate grey woollen poncho, traditional garment of the pampas. He introduces himself as Horacio Forster. Everything about him suggests British forebears made rich from the encircling infinity of cattle-grazing land.

His wife Susanna is of even grander pedigree. She is from one of Argentina's oldest families, the Anchorenas, who still own much of the Sierra de Tandil. Tall and blonde, she stands waiting for me in the living-room. At her command a smiling maid brings a pot of tea and home-made shortbread in a Harrods tin. Susanna hopes these might help me recover from my long journey, then shows me up to my room. I absorb a world of sporting prints, hunting trophies and British-made grandfather clocks. After half an hour I hear my name being called out from downstairs.

My hosts appear keen to talk to someone from the Old World. I am an oddity in their environment. Six months of continuous travelling has left me with a handful of frayed clothes, a leathery complexion, chapped hands, and – as I now self-consciously realize – long fingernails ingrained with dirt. When they invite me for a 'pre-supper drink' in the sitting-room, I come not in a jacket and tie but with the worn North Face fleece of the ageing backpacker.

They praise such British pleasures as salmon-fishing in the Scottish Highlands and window-shopping in London's Knightsbridge. I tell them then that I have been living in recent years more in Spain than in Britain. The stiff conversation shifts accordingly. We move on into a candle-lit dining-room, where Susanna outlines a family connection linking her in some obscure way with Fernan Gómez, first king of Castile. There are also Anchorenas who took part in the wars against the Moors; others who came to the New World with the conquistadors; still others who appear to have bought up half the pampas and risen to extraordinary political heights. Then Susanna says something that makes me hold back for a moment my knife and fork. A nineteenth-century relative of hers, Aarón Anchorena, was a friend and patron of Perito Moreno, the great Andean explorer in whose footsteps I have been following in southern Patagonia.

I blurt out that I have just travelled the entire length of the Andes, inspired by the example of a long line of visionaries that includes Humboldt, Bolívar, Darwin and Perito Moreno himself. My hosts assume benevolent smiles, encouraging me to describe my journey in greater detail, like Stanley regaling an astonished Victorian dinner-party with his exploits.

Breathlessly I outline to my hosts my journey south from the tropics: from summer to winter; by bus and boat; on foot and horse; through jungles and moorland; under volcanoes; beyond the snow level; across deserts and high plateaus; down giant canyons; into forests of pines and oaks; over lakes and fjords; alongside an ice-field as large as a small country; between glaciers and icebergs; to the southernmost community on earth. And now here, to this most unexpected of final destinations, a country estate extending over a range of low hills in the middle of one of the flattest landscapes on earth.

Sentiment has brought me here. I am about to explain why, when Horacio brusquely gets up from the table and beckons me to follow him outside. The rain has stopped and a full moon is rising through a patch of brilliant starlit sky. He takes me across a lawn to what seems like a gardener's shed, but which is his study. He wants to show me a gleaming white stone, displayed in an alcove like some massive diamond.

'It's quartz,' he says, 'from the Sierra de Tandil, the hills behind the house. The hills are made of quartz. That's why there's all this energy around,' he adds, repeating something I had been told at various points along the Andes.

Seated at Horacio's writing desk, I am back to my role as detective, jotting down names and observations. He is talking about geology's central mystery: how are mountain ranges formed? 'How,' he asks, 'does a range such as the Sierra de Tandil appear out of the surrounding flatness?' Then he loses me in a wealth of detail involving this sierra's geological make-up. I start to drift, and soon I am imagining I am already dead, stranded on a rock in a horizontal limbo, separated from the world I have known by an immensity of time and distance. I find myself staring at the spine of W.H. Hudson's famous memoir of childhood in the Argentinean pampas, *Far Away and Long Ago*. The words repeat themselves in my head.

'As I'm sure you're aware,' interrupts Horacio, disturbing me in my reverie, 'the Sierra de Tandil is one of the world's oldest ranges. So shouldn't you have come here at the start rather than the end of your journey?'

And then he confirms what I had first heard several months ago from an Ecuadorian naturalist and which had made me vow that I would visit the Sierra de Tandil, should I ever come out of the Andes alive, if indeed I am still alive.

'This,' he explains, his hand now resting on the stone, 'is where the Andes begin.'

# PART ONE

# THE VIEW FROM AFAR

# 1

# HOW IT ALL BEGAN

In the case of Charles Empson, an Englishman of the early nine-teenth century, it all began with a climb up a Yorkshire hill with the homely name of Roseberry Topping. The view from the summit, seen at sunrise as an adolescent, kindled in him an early desire to 'tread the lofty steps of the Andean range, and ascend the yet-untrodden summits of the snow-clad Cordilleras'.

There was no Roseberry Topping in my London childhood, but I travelled widely when I was very young and acquired my elder brother's obsession with snow-capped mountains. We felt no attrac-tion towards skiing or even mountaineering, yet we loved mountain walks and the distant sight of snowy peaks. My brother's response to a spectacular mountain panorama was to stand with hands on hips and shout 'Wow! Wow! Wow!' His love of mountains was stimulated by our mother's ancestral homeland in the Italian Alps. Mine was fuelled more by dreams of the Andes, where our English grandfather Bethel had worked as a railway engineer immediately before the First World War. Though Bethel had died when I was only three, his tales of the Andes were relayed to me by my grand-mother. I was taken by the idea of the longest continuous mountain range in the world. I found it incredible that a single range could stretch from the tropics almost to Antarctica. I was filled with a desire to go there.

In my early teens, I developed what would become a life-long passion for Spain and the Spanish world. I was also becoming addicted to books about travel and exploration. The first travelogue I ever read was *Tschiffely's Ride*, a gripping account of 'ten thousand miles in the saddle' from Buenos Aires to Washington DC. Later I received a heavily illustrated book called *The Age of Discovery*, which introduced me to the German scientist and explorer of South America, Alexander von Humboldt. The engravings and paintings showing Humboldt sketching beneath volcanoes and giant tropical trees mysteriously excited me. So too did the captions. These stressed how Humboldt's constant sense of wonder in the face of nature had inspired hundreds of travellers to come to South America in his wake.

One of these travellers was Empson himself, whose vague longing for the Andes had crystallized after a reading of Humboldt. 'The glorious descriptions of Humboldt,' he wrote, 'had induced many persons who had no other motive beyond that of beholding Nature in all her majesty, to explore those regions so gorgeously clothed in primeval vegetation, and so abundant in every production interesting to mankind.'

In the 1830s the young Empson had rushed off to the Andes at the first opportunity. I did not follow his example. Other passions and interests intervened. I would not visit the Andes until many years later, after confounding family and friends by moving in my late forties to a remote village in the mountainous interior of southern Spain.

By then little in my life had turned out as I had once expected. I had always thought of myself as a city man, and had never imagined wanting one day to live in the Spanish countryside. I eventually bought the predictable whitewashed old house, and was soon tied to this by the gift of a gentle and endearing Spanish mastiff. For the first time in my life I felt as if I was settling down.

Though the village was not conventionally attractive, it was beautifully situated, between oak-covered slopes and olive fields, within sight of faraway mountains. My isolated house, dominating the village, backed onto a steep wooded hill which I used to climb every day towards sunset. The views, extensive enough from the terrace of my house, became progressively grander until soon the long snowy crest of the Sierra Nevada could be seen in its entirety, sometimes so sharply that every crag and crevice of the range was highlighted by the pink evening light.

The views from behind my Andalusian house were perhaps the catalyst that drove me to the Andes. My yearning for the Andes had by now merged with a deeper curiosity about my grandfather's travels through the wilder parts of Chile and Bolivia. I finally had access to all his letters from that period. They were fuelled by a belief both in progress and in the redemptive power of a single all-consuming love. He had left his native city of Hull after having just become engaged to a woman whom he would barely see again for the next eight years.

In the winter of 2003 I went off to the Andes to follow in my grandfather's footsteps. I travelled from the Atacama Desert down to the icebergs of Patagonia. The Andean scenery terrified and exhilarated me in a way not even my grandfather's letters had prepared me for. On my return to Andalusia, the landscape surrounding my village seemed tame in comparison. I was hooked on the sublime. I wanted to go back to the Andes at the soonest possible opportunity. I made a brief return visit to Bolivia the following year, and was almost caught up in a bloodbath. But I was undeterred in my ambition to travel ever further into the Andes.

In the meantime, back in my Andalusian village, I prepared myself for this by reading as widely as I could. My new rural existence allowed me to become absorbed by books on natural history to a degree inconceivable in my earlier, urban days. For the first time in my life I took an interest in geology. I wanted to understand how the Andes began.

The world expanded in my imagination. I read about the rapid evolution of geology itself and how it had moved away from the mere collecting of rocks, minerals and fossils to become, from the eighteenth century onwards, ever more dedicated to the explanation of the Earth's origins. Charles Lyell, in his *Principles of Geology* of 1842, wrote: 'Never perhaps did any science, with the exception of astronomy, unfold, in an equally brief period, so many novel and unexpected truths, and overturn so many preconceived opinions.'

This radical transformation of geology changed attitudes towards mountains. Once associated with what the Victorian geologist Sir Archibald Geikie called 'ideas of horror, danger, and repulsion', mountains now inspired the most rapturous prose, such as that of the pioneering Swiss scientist Horace-Benedict Saussure, who, in 1775, memorably evoked the thoughts and sensations of someone who 'standing as it were above the globe, seems to discover the forces that move it, or at least to recognize the principal agents that effect its revolutions'.

Mountains became the main focus of geological studies from the time of Saussure, and the Andes – as the highest known mountains in the world until British engineers started surveying the Himalyas from the 1840s omwards – began to attract scientific expeditions seeking answers to fundamental questions about the planet. In 1731 a group of French scientists including La Condamine travelled to present-day Ecuador to pursue their studies of geodesy, the measurement and representation of the Earth. After 1800 the German Alexander von Humboldt stimulated scientific interest in the Andes as never before in an epic journey which would serve as the basis of a great, unfinished study of the cosmos.

Slowly I assimilated geology's endlessly changing and conflicting theories. With each theory I became gradually more aware of geology as a successive process involving ever greater and more unimaginable lengths of time.

I learnt about the seventeenth-century archbishop who had dated the world to 4004 BC on the basis of the life spans of Adam's descendants; about the 'Catastrophists', who viewed the Earth as having been brought into being by single, cataclysmic events; about those scientists who continued to reconcile geology and the scriptures to the extent of claiming maritime fossils as evidence of Noah's flood; about the 'Neptunists', who believed that almost all rocks were 'sedimentary', or formed by water; about their rivals the 'Vulcanists', who argued that heat was as important as water in the Earth's creation; and about 'Hutton's unconformity', named after the pioneering Scottish Vulcanist James Hutton, whose discovery of differently tilted sequences of earth and rock had led him famously to say of the history of this planet that he could find 'no traces of a beginning, no prospect of an end'.

I reached the twentieth century and terms such as 'Panagea', 'isostasy', 'continental drift' and 'plate tectonics'; the idea of a giant continent that had drifted apart; and the subsequent theory that the uppermost part of the Earth or 'lithosphere' was made up of seven major and numerous minor tectonic plates which floated on the 'astheonosphere', and created colliding boundaries that produced not just mountains, but also earthquakes, volcanic activity and oceanic trenches.

With this last theory, formulated in the 1960s, I thought that little more could be said about the Andes' origins other than that these were to be found in the collision of the Nazca and South American plates, and that the former and younger of the two plates had been pushed downwards into the ocean bed to create what was known as a 'subduction zone.' But, of course, nothing in geology is definitive. I had failed to take into account how bored geologists would soon become of a world in which 'plate tectonics' provided answers for everything.

As I delved into more recent geological research, I was riveted by one theory in particular: the theory that mountains, contrary to all appearances, behave more like a fluid than a rigid plate, and that they are ephemeral things that are born and die just like human beings. This simple idea of mountains as human set my mind wandering. I was starting to conceive a journey far more ambitious than any I had ever undertaken. I wanted to travel the whole length of the Andes and, in so doing, observe these mountains as I would the unfolding story of a human life.

I would begin in those tropical areas of the north where Humboldt had located the life force and finish up in winter in the islands off Tierra del Fuego, where Humboldt's passionate admirer Charles Darwin had concluded that there was barely life at all. On the way, I would trace the Andean journeys not only of Humboldt and Darwin but also of those many others whose lives had became so tied to the Andes that they had often come to perceive the mountains as near deities, capable one moment of inflicting natural catastrophes on a near-unprecedented scale and the next of inspiring the most lucid intellectual insights and the loftiest political and spiritual aspirations.

My vague plans for an Andean odyssey slowly took on a more concrete and practical shape, and as they did so, something curious happened. The Andes started encroaching more on the European consciousness.

The election in December 2005 of Bolivia's first indigenous president, Evo Morales, and his subsequent inauguration in an archaic Indian ceremony at the ancient site of Tiawanako, broke through the time-honoured western indifference to events in the Andean world. This election was seen as symptomatic not just of an indigenous revival but also of the great social revolution initiated by Castro in Cuba, taken up in Venezuela by Morales' mentor Hugo Chávez, and now surely spreading soon to Peru and Ecuador. European socialist commentators were already referring to an Andean 'axis of good' that would balance decades of North American intervention in South America. There was even talk of the resurgent spirit of the nineteenth-century liberator Simón Bolívar, whose crazed Andean march in pursuit of a free and unified South America was very much on my mind as I planned my own journey.

Meanwhile, in Spain itself I witnessed the arrival of thousands of Andean citizens who did not share the optimism of the liberal West towards their countries' futures. They came principally from Bolivia, Peru, Colombia and above all Ecuador, a reputed quarter of whose population was settling in Madrid, Barcelona and – for some reason – eastern Andalusia and the adjoining region of Murcia. My own small village of Frailes, where I had been for years the sole foreign resident, was a testimony to these demographic changes.

I would have liked to have thought that a lifetime of travelling had banished the fears I used to have before embarking on any long trip. But South America remained for me a daunting continent; and I recalled a phrase that Christopher Isherwood had used on the point of going from Colombia to Argentina to research his book *The Condor and the Cows*. 'South America,' he confessed to a friend, filled him with 'an increasing and quite serious uncampy horror.'

I even had a recurrence of a specific anxiety I had not had since my mid-teens, before wandering off on my own around Franco's Spain: that I was starting on a journey from which I was not going to return. This morbid premonition was not entirely irrational. My first childhood friend to have died had been killed after being overtaken by a storm in the Patagonian Andes, and my brother had almost been stoned to death by Andean villagers while camping in Peru. My own two previous journeys to the Andes had seen some of the more terrifying moments of my life, the first while negotiating precipices and landslides along my grandfather's abandoned Bolivian railway line, the second when I witnessed a dynamite-fuelled demonstration in which a miner was killed.

Reading about the Andes was itself not encouraging, and not just the warning sections in guidebooks and foreign office web pages, or the newspaper articles drawing attention to South America's having overtaken Africa as the world's most violent continent. The whole history of travelling in the Andes was so tinged with tragedy that the mountains now appeared to me at times as they had done to the thousands who had been irresistibly drawn to them by tales of incalculable hidden treasures: as a Herculean challenge whose vast potential rewards were balanced by barely endurable hardships. And I was no longer so young. I could no longer say, as Humboldt had done, that I had reached the age 'when our life seems to open before us like a limitless horizon in which nothing attracts us more than intense mental thrills and images of positive danger'.

My worries about the journey were certainly not helped by my setting off from a traditional Spanish village, where to go anywhere too far beyond the confines of the pueblo was considered a risky undertaking. 'Where the body goes, danger goes,' said an elderly village friend whose entire experience of travelling was limited to a couple of trips to Granada. Others in Frailes, hearing about what I planned to do, looked at me as if offering their condolences.

But there was also something touching about the villagers' concern for my well-being; and it had its practical benefits. The woman who tailored the costumes for the local passion play insisted on sewing into my trousers an array of hidden pockets. This inspired another woman to make for me something which she said had been worn by the village men when returning by train from the grape harvest in France, 'during the years of hunger'. It was a cloth pouch in which the men used to place all their earnings. The problem was that it had to be tied to one of the shoulder straps of a hideous nylon string vest, with which I was also presented. 'Anyone robbing you could easily take away your trousers, but they would never strip you of your shirt.' I was clearly unconvinced, for she added that I could always use the pouch for keeping condoms. I did not want to point out that my wearing of the vest would make it unlikely that I would ever have need of one.

Less than a month before my departure, my close friend Merce, the village social worker, proposed that her husband Manolo should accompany me for the first few weeks of the journey to see me safely across Venezuela and into Colombia. She reckoned he would be the perfect companion, as well as a necessary bodyguard.

Manolo, a local maths teacher, had hardly travelled outside the area but was passionately keen to see lands that had played such a large part in Spanish history. And he thought he might never have the opportunity again.

He had two young children, a wife from whom he had never been apart in more than twenty years of marriage and a job that would allow him to go only on condition he took unpaid leave. But he was still determined to come. I sensed he would be a great asset to the journey: he was easy-going, undemanding, street-wise and had an attitude of calm resignation towards the possibility of disaster.

Manolo bought his air ticket as Christmas approached. The days were now unfailingly clear and sunny, enhancing my affection for the Andalusia I was about to leave. My emotions came to the surface when the time came to go. I stroked my dog Chumberry, and gave her a tin of her favourite meat in the hope of distracting her. She buried her head in her tin for a few seconds, before pausing to look at me with an expression of disbelief, sadness, anger and bewilderment. I left the property, locked the gate and gave her a final glance intended to convey that my kind friend Merce would be looking after her now and that I would be back soon. I continued walking down the hill, still unsure whether I would be back at all.

The village taxi driver was waiting for me outside the town hall. Manolo emerged from the building, accompanied by Merce, their two sons and others who had come to wish us goodbye. They waved as the car started, and were joined by others as the car drove through the village, passing women taking their children to school.

Looking towards the Sierra Nevada I could see the first rays of the sun touching its crest of snow. Outside the village a sense of elation competed with other emotions. Then we left Andalusia on a train bound for Madrid and entered the dusty plains of La Mancha. Manolo fell slowly asleep and I took out a copy of the paperback I had brought to read on the journey – an abridged edition of

Alexander von Humboldt's snappily titled *Personal Narrative of a Journey to the Equinoctial Regions of the New Continent.*

I got as far as the paragraph describing Humboldt's emotions on leaving Europe for the first time. Modern means of communication, he reflected, had made the world seem a smaller place than before. 'Yet,' he continued, 'what we feel when we begin our first long-distance voyage is none the less accompanied by a deep emotion, unlike any we may have felt in our youth. Separated from the objects of our deepest affections, and entering into a new life, we are forced to fall back on ourselves, and we feel more isolated than we have ever felt before.'

## 2

# CABINETS OF
# CURIOSITIES

In Madrid, with just a couple of hours to spare, I persuaded Manolo to indulge a sudden whim to visit the city's Museum of Natural Sciences. So we jumped on a bus outside the railway station at Chamartín and soon we were coursing down the multi-lane avenue of the Castellana. The bus continued hurriedly south towards the Paseo del Prado, sweeping us back in time, from the tinted glass towers of the twenty-first century to the eighteenth, to the Madrid endowed by Spain's Bourbon rulers with street lighting, a proper sewage system, museums, a massive hospital, an observatory, an art academy, a botanical garden and one of Europe's most elegant promenades. This was the Madrid that Humboldt had got to know shortly before his departure for South America in June 1799 – a city whose Enlightenment beliefs encouraged westerners to travel to the Andes for no better reason than mere curiosity.

Before the eighteenth century most Europeans would have found it almost impossible even to imagine the Andes. The Incas and their predecessors had no proper written language, so that there were no descriptions of the mountains until after the arrival of the Spaniards in 1507. And the Spanish chronicles that did appear were barely concerned at first with the physical attributes of the mountains,

17

only with their mineral and metallic wealth, the customs of those who lived there and such quirky features as llamas and potatoes. The accompanying illustrations were generally so crude and schematic that the Andes were reduced to fantastically tapering mounds a child might have fashioned out of plasticine.

Conscious perhaps of the desire to view Spain's newly conquered lands in a more vivid light, the controversial Viceroy of Peru, Francisco de Toledo, proposed in 1572 sending a collection of Inca and other indigenous artefacts to Madrid's Royal Palace. These and other objects from America fuelled the growing curiosity about the continent. Americana began featuring ever more prominently in Spain's royal inventories; and though many of these objects were probably lost in the fire that destroyed the Hapsburg palace in 1734, many more would arrive in Spain over the following decades. By then the Bourbons had come to power, and the royal seal of approval had been given to a young generation of scientific explorers.

In the same year that his palace burnt down, Philip V gave permission to the surveyor and mathematician Charles-Marie La Condamine to travel with a team of fellow French scientists to the equatorial regions of South America. For the first time a major scientific expedition had set its sights on that continent. For the first time, too, a group of foreign scientists had been allowed to travel freely through lands the Spaniards had always jealously guarded. Few other foreigners before Humboldt would enjoy this privilege again. Nonetheless a growing number of expeditions were mounted in the second half of the eighteenth century, including major botanical and geological ones to Colombia, Chile and Peru, and a more general survey carried out along the continent's western coast by Spain's answer to Captain Cook, Alejandro Malaspina.

Whereas Francisco de Toledo had envisaged sending to Spain only objects of anthropological value, the collections of Spain's Bourbon kings reflected the encyclopaedic approach of the Enlightenment, with curiosities illustrating equally the mineral, vegetal and animal spheres into which the world was now classified.

Interest in 'natural history' continued to grow and Spain's first museum dedicated to the subject opened in 1752. The director was Antonio Ulloa, one of the two Spanish scientists sent by Philip V to keep an eye on the activities of La Condamine and the 'Geodesics'.

Ulloa resigned as the museum's director just three years later, and the establishment fell into neglect. But a second 'Royal Cabinet of Natural History' was founded in 1771 by the 'enlightened despot' Charles III. The impetus this time was a collection of rocks, stuffed animals and Egyptian, classical and other antiques donated to the Spanish Crown by an Ecuadorian-born merchant who had lived in Paris, Pedro Franco Dávila. This second museum, occupying relatively modest premises in the middle of the old town, was intended to complement the Royal Botanical Garden, which was also heavily dependent on what was brought back from America.

In 1776 the young and as yet barely tested architect Juan de Villanueva was commissioned by Charles III to create a new botanical garden alongside the showpiece promenade of the Paseo del Prado. After successfully completing this garden, Villanueva was given the go-ahead to build next to it a museum virtually unrivalled in its scale and architectural boldness in Europe. It is certainly telling of the priorities of Enlightenment Spain that this extraordinary building – focus of today's tourism to Madrid, and filled with a sensational collection of works by Titian, Velázquez, Goya and other old masters – should originally have been intended as a celebration of the natural world.

Manolo and I got off the bus well before the Castellana turns into the shaded Paseo del Prado. The Royal Cabinet of Natural History was never moved to Villanueva's purpose-built museum. Instead it was renamed the Museum of Natural Sciences, and eventually transferred to a late-nineteenth-century industrial pavilion within sight of the fascist arcades of Franco's Nuevos Ministerios. My desire to visit the musuem was connected with Humboldt. I was keen to see the geological specimens the great scientist had acquired in the Andes before I set off in his footsteps.

When the 29-year-old Humboldt arrived in Spain in January 1799 he had no real idea of where ultimately he was heading. Nothing had turned out as he had planned over the past three years. Ever since his mother had died from breast cancer in 1796, this life-long bachelor, already famed in his native Prussia as one of the great prodigies of his age, had been devising some ambitious journey that would bring together his remarkably wide-ranging gifts as a scientist. His mother's death had freed him emotionally and provided him with the financial means to give up his first and only job, as Chief Inspector of Prussia's mines.

His initial idea had been to go with a large group of family and friends to Italy, where he would study volcanoes, and then set off on his own to Paris, London and the West Indies. But he never made it to Italy, delayed as he was by the illness of his sister-in-law, and by the military activities in that country of his exact contemporary Napoleon. Then he received an invitation to accompany the eccentric Lord Bristol ('half mad and half genius') on a journey to Egypt that promised to be one of the most lavishly sponsored scientific expeditions of the age. Excitedly he had gone off to Paris to equip himself for this with the latest scientific instruments. But again Napoleon put an end to these plans, this time with his Egyptian campaign.

At the same time, while in Paris, Humboldt had a chance meeting with a great hero of his, Louis Antoine de Bougainville, whose account of his voyage of discovery in the Pacific Ocean had been one of his favourite childhood books. When Lord Bristol's expedition fell through, the septuagenarian Bougainville made a proposal that more than made up for it: he wanted the young German to accompany him on a five-year circumnavigation of the world. Humboldt was later disappointed when the French authorities decided to replace Bougainville with the younger and less appealing Captain Baudin, but he quickly regained his enthusiasm for the enterprise, and had completed his hurried preparations for it, when political circumstances intervened yet again. A new war with Austria had broken out, and the French government felt that under the circumstances it would be unwise to finance the trip.

Meanwhile Humboldt had become close friends with the French scientist who was going to be the expedition's botanist, Aimé Bonpland. Five years younger than Humbolt, Bonpland had studied medicine during the Revolution and had already served in the navy as a ship's doctor under Baudin. Brave, physically robust, passionate about science and restless to travel, he was as depressed as Humboldt was by being stuck in Paris. The two of them decided to join forces and organize their own private expedition, which Humboldt himself would finance.

Despite their similarities, the two men would later be perceived as a pair of opposites, most recently by the German writer Daniel Kehlmann in his best-selling novel *Measuring the World*. Bonpland would go down in history as a Sancho Panza figure, level-headed, down-to-earth and lustily heterosexual. Humboldt meanwhile, if not exactly a Don Quixote, would acquire an image as a lofty dreamer who hid his personality in his narrative writings and sublimated his homosexual impulses in what he described as 'hard work and the pursuit of nature'.

The two men set off from Paris in October 1798 for the French coast, from where they hoped to sail to Algiers and meet up with the scientific retinue in the rear of Napoleon's conquering army in Egypt. However, after waiting in vain for a boat, they opted instead to go to Tunis, and then changed their minds again on hearing that all French travellers were being thrown into prison on arrival.

They ended up walking to Spain with their plans vaguer than ever, unable to choose between Africa and America. They reached Madrid on 23 February 1799, whereupon their fortunes changed for the better.

Within days they had established a footing within Madrid's scientific community. They made useful contacts with the soon-to-be director of the Royal Botanical Garden, Antonio José Cavanilles, and the natural historian who had taken over from Dávila at the Royal Cabinet of Natural History, José Clavijo y Fajardo.

But the most useful encounter of all would be with the Baron Phillipe de Forrell, whose brother Humboldt had met in Dresden. Not only was Forrell a distinguished mineralogist, he was also the Saxon ambassador to Madrid and well placed to help Humboldt and Bonpland with travel problems. When the two men were finally persuaded to set their sights on America, it was Forrell who offered to assist them in the difficult task of obtaining permits.

Though foreign scientists, such as the Flemish geologists Cristian and Conrad Heuland, had recently been allowed to work in America, the Spaniards were becoming obsessed by the notion of spies and dissidents infiltrating a continent growing increasingly restless under Spanish rule. Such suspicion was directed not just towards foreigners but even towards Spanish visitors such as Malaspina, who was accused of political intrigue on returning to Spain in 1795, thrown into prison and never heard of again.

Humboldt's application to travel with Bonpland to South America would in fact proceed with surprising ease. On 11 March Forrell wrote to enlist the support of the newly appointed Secretary of State Mariano Luis de Urquijo, who was asked to ensure that Charles IV would receive two short documents Humboldt had written. One of these was a summary of the German's intentions in America (none other than the study of 'the Earth's Formation'), and the other an account of his career to date.

The latter must surely be one of the most impressive *curricula vitae* ever written, with references to such diverse aspects of Humboldt's life as his first book (an 'undeservedly successful' work on the Basalt mountains of the Rhine); his renewal of the Prussian salt mines; his discovery of abandoned seams of cobalt, alum and gold; his invention of safety lamps and breathing equipment for miners; his seminal publication on the chemical make-up of plants; his extensive geological wanderings around the Alps; his pioneering experiments on the nervous system; his travels around Holland, England and France in the company of Captain Cook's botanist George Forster; his devising of what he called an Antracometer to measure the quantity of carbonic acid in the atmosphere; and his studies of magnetic force, barometric pressure, the elasticity of the air, electrical charges in the environment, the colour of the sky and the temperature of the sea at great depths.

The extent to which Charles IV took all this in is difficult to know. He had not inherited the intelligence of his father. Portrayed by Goya with a mindless expression likened by one of his contemporaries to that of a 'contented grocer', he was not the person to appreciate the finer qualities of Humboldt's mind. But he would have been impressed that the German had immeasurably increased the yield of the Prussian mines and had become such an invaluable asset to his country that he had been offered a vastly improved salary to try and stop him resigning from his job. The potential usefulness of such a person in South America must have been noted.

Only four days after Humboldt's documents had been left at the Court of Aranjuez, Forrell was informed by Urquijo that the German's request had been granted. It took almost a further month for the actual issuing of the passport – an extremely concise document allowing 'Sr. Hunlbald' to travel with 'his Secretary' to America with a view to continue 'the study of Mines and perfect himself in the knowledge of other discoveries'.

In the last days before his departure, Humboldt passed his time calculating the exact position of the Aranjuez Royal Palace and by reading the works of the mountain-loving Saussure. On 5 June he and Bonpland set sail from La Coruña in a frigate named, ironically, after a man who was Humboldt's antithesis, the conquistador Pizarro.

All I was looking for in the Museum of Natural Sciences were eight stones with handwritten labels in sepia ink. The sole request made of Humboldt in return for his passport had been to make donations to Madrid's natural history museum and botanical garden. Humboldt, a man of honour, had immediately complied. For most of his stay in America he would continue supplying Clavijo and Cavanilles with rocks, minerals and seeds.

But his letters revealed his mounting concern about the fate of these donations: not a single one of them had been acknowledged. For his first three years abroad, he claimed to have received only two communications from Spain. Was it just that the replies were not getting to him? Or had everything he had sent been lost? Or had he been completely forgotten? 'Why,' he wrote to Cavanilles from Mexico in April 1803, 'are you all punishing me with your silence?'

Humboldt never went back to Spain. Nonetheless at least eight of his stones made their way into the present Museum of Natural Sciences. I had seen them reproduced in an exhibition catalogue and I had assumed they were still on regular display. However, an attendant proudly told me, 'Over the past three months the museum has been completely changed.' He thought I might find one or two of the stones in a new basement section devoted to a re-creation of the original Royal Cabinet of Natural History.

An area of greying concrete, like some corner of an underground car park, was partially cordoned off for the benefit of a group of young children. Their teacher stole the occasional worried glance towards me as I moved manically around the room to try and assimilate its jumbled contents. After a while my eyes settled on an amateurishly printed notice. This revealed that what I was seeing had little historical authenticity, but was in fact a work ('inspired by an eighteenth-century Cabinet of Curiosities') by a Canadian installation artist.

Human skeletons, butterflies, beetles, a stuffed armadillo, fossils, a snake coiled up in a jar and a row of bottled fetuses were among the miscellany of exhibits whose overall effect was somehow to underline the futility of knowledge. I inspected the fifteen or so rocks and minerals, one of which was a piece of azurite discovered in Chile in 1797. But none bore any mention of Humboldt, whose memory was invoked only in the Latin name of a Patagonian sea bird resembling an albatross.

As a last resort, I decided to search the museum's annex. Muttering to an uncharacteristically impatient Manolo that I needed only a few more minutes, I left the building by its main entrance, re-entered it by a side door, and ran up a couple of flights of steps. Yet all I found was the Hall of Experiences, which I experienced as fast as my feet allowed, conscious only of the sounds of videos echoing in a darkened empty space.

Manolo quickly handed me my rucksack, we hailed a taxi and then we were heading towards the airport and Venezuela's perpetual summer.

# PART TWO

# THE TROPICS

Caribbean Sea

CARTAGENA ■

PANAMA

Pacific Ocean

Serranía de Perijá

Lago de
Maracaibo

CARACAS

Trujillo
VALERA ●

MERIDA ●     ● BARINAS

de Mérida

Sierra Nevada

VENEZUELA

CÚCUTA ■   ● SAN
CRISTÓBAL

Río Magdalena

Santa Fe de
Antioquia
●
MEDELLÍN ■

Villa de
Leiva ●

Oriental

Honda   TUNJA ■

Central

■ BOGOTA

IBAGUE ■

C O L O M B I A

Occidental

CALI ■

POPAYÁN ■

Cordillera

Cordillera
de
los Andes

∴ Parc Arqueológico
San Agustín

Cordillera

PASTO ■

Tulcán ●
IBARRA ■
Vol. Cayambe △

Equator

● ■ QUITO
Santo Domingo de     △ Vol. Cotopaxi
los Colorados
● Latacunga     E C U A D O R
AMBATO ■   Vol. Tungurahua
Vol. Chimborazo △   △ ● Baños  P. Nac. Llanganates
■ RIOBAMBA

GUAYAQUIL ●   ● Alausí

Cordillera
de
los Andes

∴ Ingapirca
■ CUENCA

P E R U

● LOJA

# 3

# HOTEL HUMBOLDT

The Caribbean sky was a translucent blue. The coastline was green and mountainous, with clusters of giant, swaying palms set against thickets of cassia, capers and arborescent mimosa. The light was dazzling when the *Pizarro* sailed at midday into the Venezuelan port of Cumaná, a place Humboldt would later recall more vividly than all the 'glories of the Andes'.

For his first few days there, Humboldt had been unable to settle on anything. He and Bonpland were in a state of sensory intoxication, excited by absolutely everything, almost incapable of taking in so many new phenomena: the climate, the natural abundance, the unusualness of the plants, the tigers, the monkeys, the armadillos, the parrots, the electric eels, the 'semi-savage' natives ('beautiful and interesting'), the colours of the birds and the fish, the overwhelming sensuality of a world in which even the crabs were sky-blue and yellow. They rented a white wooden house, unpacked their scientific instruments and found them miraculously unharmed by their journey. Within days they were measuring the atmospheric tide, observing the tropical night skies, recording the effects of galvanism on a frog, peering at the spots on the moon, even magnifying the remarkable variety of lice to be found in the curly hairstyles of

Cumaná's fashionable women. And, in their few spare moments, they danced. Seduced and liberated by their new environment, Humboldt briefly cast aside his scientific obsessions and gave in to the infectiously vibrant African rhythms of the Congo minuet, the *animalito*, the samba.

They had not intended to be in Cumaná at all. They had been on their way to the Andes by way of Cuba. But typhoid had broken out aboard the *Pizarro* and the unaffected passengers had demanded to be let off at the nearest port. However, neither Humboldt nor Bonpland was in any hurry to move on. Having found themselves by chance in this region so little known to naturalists, they thought it their duty to explore it. They decided to acclimatize themselves on the coast and then move on into the interior. On 4 September 1799, after seven weeks at Cumaná, they felt finally ready to make an incursion into the barely accessible mountains to the south of the town.

Thus Fate (in the form of typhoid) temporarily diverted the two men away from the Andes and into the South American rainforest, for which – despite all their reading – they were not properly prepared: for the intensity of the solitude, for the constant shrieking of the birds, or for the sheer freshness, multiplicity, strangeness and size of all the trees and plants that prevented any clear view of the sky. Eventually, on much more prolonged exposure to this 'living nature', they would come to the realization ('both odd and sad') of how inessential was man to the natural order.

Stunned by this world, they returned to the coast with their minds already set on spending many more months in the jungle. They remained six more weeks in Cumaná, enough time to experience a near-fatal attack by a deranged mulatto, their first earthquake and a meteor shower. Then, in mid-November, they sailed off towards La Guaira, the nearest port to Caracas, capital of the future Venezuela. Humboldt said goodbye to the 'first land we had reached in a world I had longed to know since childhood'. As the town receded, and Cape Arenas approached, there were further natural wonders to distract him. He stared endlessly at the bands of dolphins trailing behind the boat, their bodies like flames as they leapt into the brilliant sunlight.

I glanced out of the plane window and spotted the tiny speck of a boat sailing on an uninterrupted expanse of water. The video panel in front of me indicated that we were flying at an altitude of 8563 metres, and that three hours and seven minutes remained before our arrival at Caracas. The once-empty seat between me and Manolo had been occupied while I was asleep by a burly man in his early sixties. He had yellowing matted hair, and was breathing heavily. He had evidently moved next to us in search of conversation.

He said he was of Bulgarian origin but had immigrated as a boy to Venezuela. When I told him my plans, he could not understand why I should want to leave such a green and beautiful country as England. He could understand even less why anyone should want to travel down the Andes, or indeed travel at all. 'I'm too old for adventure,' he admitted. I asked him what he did for a living. 'I'm a private detective.' He told me to be careful in Venezuela. 'The security is very bad. Caracas is now the world's most dangerous city. Few tourists get away without getting mugged. More and more get killed each year. For the silliest reasons. For a mobile phone. For a good watch. For a few dollars. You must never resist an armed hold-up.' And with those words he got up and disappeared towards the back of the plane.

What I needed was someone to reassure me about present-day Caracas, not to confirm my image of a place on the verge of anarchy. Everything I had heard about the city suggested that you were constantly under such threats as being held up at knife or gun point, becoming a victim of 'express kidnappings', having your drinks spiked, or even – according to the characteristically grim travel advice provided by the British Foreign Office – innocently accepting pamphlets and flyers that turn out to 'be impregnated with potent and disorienting drugs, which permeate the skin'. The dangers of a Caracas visit were said to begin at the airport to which I was now heading, situated at the coastal village of Maiquetia, a few kilometres from La Guaira.

We began our descent to the coast. The rainy season was supposedly over, but dark clouds hung over mountains that had been likened by an English traveller of 1878, James Mudie Spence, to 'cruel giants' at whose feet La Guaira clasped like a 'pleading supplicant'. The town today was a mess of apartment blocks tapering upwards into slums. Our plane flew parallel to it as we descended sharply into Maiquetia, swerving slightly after landing to face an intensely blue sunlit sea. It was late afternoon.

The arrivals hall was rather less daunting than I had been led to imagine. Beyond the barrier officially marking our entry into 'The Bolivarian Republic of Venezuela', we were not besieged by vociferous, demanding porters, or by unofficial taxi drivers in cahoots with criminals, or by bogus uniformed officials insisting we accompany them to quiet corners of the airport where we could be planted with drugs, fleeced, sodomized or worse. Instead we were met by a smiling, mustachioed young man called Richard. He had been sent by the cousin of a close Spanish friend of mine, Elena Arenas, who had lived in Venezuela until the age of eighteen. Elena's cousin, Federico, was a second-generation Venezuelan who had made a fortune in property. Richard telephoned him once we had been led into the car park and shown into a sturdy four-wheel drive.

The journey from the airport took on the quality of a military operation. Less than ten minutes after leaving Maiquetia, Federico was making the first of several calls to Richard to try and find out where exactly we were, and to see if there had not been any hold-up.

The motorway link between the airport and Caracas had become notorious in recent years, particularly after the collapse eighteen months before of a bridge outside La Guaira. Repairs to the bridge had yet to be completed, resulting in a long detour and traffic conditions that often made the journey last up to four hours. Late at night, when the traffic finally dwindled, the road was to be avoided at all costs. It was then that the criminals emerged from slums that had grown up alongside it, doing everything they could to make cars stop, ramming them from the back, blocking them from the front, driving them off into side-roads, shooting anyone who resisted. 'We won't be taking the motorway,' Richard announced as we made our way through La Guaira. 'Federico has asked me to take the Galipán road. It'll be quicker. Few other drivers do it.' I wondered why. 'Because you need a car like this.'

No one in La Guaira seemed to bother with traffic lights. The place, under a greying humid sky, was menacing and uninviting, with desultory palms, graffiti-daubed walls, tattered posters and damp-stained plasterwork in pastel colours. We turned off on to a narrow track paved with concrete. 'We're beginning to climb,' Richard relayed to Federico on the phone just before we began ascending the mountain in steep zigzags. Caracas was barely twenty kilometres away, but a pass of over a thousand metres had to be negotiated before getting there. As we climbed up into the clouds, the sea, with its distant strip of sunshine, was turning into a hazy blur until finally all visibility was lost in enveloping fog and drizzle.

And then we appeared to be rising above the clouds, for there were ever greater breaks in the sky, revealing patches of vivid green forest. Through one of the breaks, we could see far below another vertiginous road, apparently narrower, rougher and steeper still. 'El Camino de los Españoles,' muttered Richard, the Spanish Route. 'We also call it *La culebrilla*' ('the little snake'). I realized that it was the road featured in every travel account I had read of Venezuela. The Spaniards had built it shortly after founding Caracas in 1589. Until modern times it had been the main link between the city and the sea. I recalled how nineteenth-century travellers, such as Bolívar's American follower Colonel William Duane, were impressed by the survival of so many of the original Spanish stones, 'laid out with the blood of Indians'.

As the sky continued to clear, further descriptions of the Spanish Route came back to me. I remembered them because they were among the earliest impressions of South America formed by such first-time visitors to the continent as the future 'discoverer' of Macchu Pichu, Hiram Bingham, who came here in 1906 while undertaking a journey in Bolívar's footsteps. Bingham was particularly attracted by the road's 'many curves' and by its 'inspiring views of the Caribbean'. It was also notorious for fatal accidents. Rudolph Messel, a German who travelled to Colombia in the 1930s in search of some missing compatriots, had been shown the many places along the road where vehicles had fallen off the cliff.

With every new vista created by the dispersing clouds, I found it difficult to believe that the modern road was any less dramatic than the celebrated Camino de los Españoles. My mood had changed as rapidly as the sky. Earlier worries about entering a hostile and dangerous world had suddenly vanished. I was dazzled by the sunlit patches of dense tropical vegetation, with their lianas, giant ferns and multitude of completely unfamiliar trees, some resembling Mediterranean pines, others covered in yellow blossom, some streaked with silvery white leaves.

With the gradual disappearance of the clouds, and the ever sharper early evening light, other details of the panorama caught my attention: sheer cliffs of rock, clusters of tiny houses, outcrops of red stone, palm-shaded farms, near-vertical glimpses down to the sea, views towards an ever expanding horizon of mountains. And as we neared the scattered village of Galipán, close to the summit of the pass, I noticed how Richard waved at almost everyone we passed. They were all, he revealed, relatives or friends, for though he went every day into Caracas, he was a native of tranquil Galipán, where he had always lived. Being from Galipán, he said, and not from the 'madhouse' Caracas, gave him a saner outlook on life.

But when we reached the pass and stopped to admire the view down the other side of the mountain, the Caracas that stretched out below us had the idyllic appearance that had been conveyed to me in the childhood memories of my friend Elena Arenas. The forested slopes below us were free of all houses and cultivated fields and extended without a break down to a faraway line of skyscrapers ringed by further mountains. The excitement of approaching a capital city in such an unusual and theatrical way was matched by a sense of relief on seeing a serene, sunset Caracas fringed by exuberant greenery.

Manolo nudged me. He was pointing to our left, where the last of the clouds was slowly rising to reveal what Richard identified as Mount Ávila. At its highest point an immensely tall round building came into sight.

'That's the Hotel Humboldt,' said Richard. 'It's named after the German explorer. He spent some time in these mountains.'

Humboldt had stared longingly at the Galipán range from the isolated house he had rented in one of the higher zones of Caracas. Eventually, he and Bonpland decided to make the first recorded ascent of the highest peak in the area, La Silla. The climb took them fifteen hours, almost without stopping and with barely any food or drink. Afterwards they disappointed their Caracas friends by concluding that the city's surrounding mountains were lower than Spain's Sierra Nevada.

'The hotel,' continued Richard, 'was built in the 1950s, at the same time as the funicular leading up to it.' With its bold shape, fourteen floors and lonely position at a height of over two thousand metres, this former state-run hotel must have struck contemporaries as the ultimate in cosmopolitan sophistication. But the later fortunes of the hotel reflected the country's changes of government. Once famous for its lavish banquets and parties, it was allowed to deteriorate, a victim of humidity and high winds. Turned into a catering school, and then closed down completely, it was privatized in 1998. The private consortium that bought the hotel intended it as the centrepiece of a 'Magical Ávila Tourist Complex', complete with restaurants, an ice-skating rink and a square supporting 'the tallest flag in the world'.

'And what happened?' I asked.

'There were lots of protests from ecologists and the villagers of Galipán. The hotel is still closed, though I think there are daily guided tours of the place, if you're interested.'

I took a last look at the grand folly bearing Humboldt's name and got back into the car. Within moments an anxious Federico was ringing again. 'We'll be there in about forty minutes,' Richard replied, as we began winding our way down from the heights of the sublime towards the uncertainty of a city.

4

# DISTANT MOUNTAINS

'He's been running up and down the mountain ever since I can remember,' said Richard, as we passed an ancient jogger heading downwards through the darkening, empty forest, towards the point where virgin nature ended and the track gave way to a sloping sub-urban street, with half-functioning lights, cubical concrete homes, brightly coloured corner shops, people sitting around on steps and a growing congestion of traffic.

'The Venezuelans are the happiest people in the world,' contin-ued Richard. 'I was reading about it today in this survey conducted by one of the newspapers. The Colombians came second. The British were quite low down. But not as low as the Chileans. The Chileans were almost at the bottom.' In South America, apparently, people become progressively unhappier the further south you go.

We had left the highway and were crawling along the city's central avenue. The last patch of daylight shone behind a distant dark-green slope covered with a sinister rash of interconnected, end-lessly spreading brickwork and breezeblock dwellings, roofed in corrugated iron. 'The *Barrios*,' muttered Richard.

'And we have the world's most beautiful women,' he declared in a more cheerful tone of voice. I scanned the motley types walking along sidewalks that were fast emptying as the night set in, as if obeying some unspoken curfew. Soon the entire population of Caracas seemed to be squeezed into barely moving cars. I started taking in the names of the streets and the signposts. The avenue we were on was called El Libertador, after Simón Bolívar. The airport at which we had arrived was known officially as the Aeropuerto Simón Bolívar. The highway to which we had descended was named after Bolívar's great victory at Boyacá. A sign pointed to a park commemorating the battle which finally brought independence to Venezuela, Carabobo. There were streets and squares referring to Bolívar's fellow generals, to the 'Precursor Francisco de Miranda' whom he ignominiously betrayed, and to the courageous, intellectual mistress of his last years, Manuela Saenz. The whole of Caracas seemed like a series of prompts reminding you of the life of the man whose dream of an independent and unified South America had been nurtured here.

'It's Federico again,' announced Richard, handing me his mobile phone. 'Tell him we're already in sight of the hotel.' We were aiming directly towards an island-like mound bristling with palms, carpeted by lush floodlit lawns. On top of this loomed an enormously long, tiered apparition whose white walls shone at night as brightly as the moon. We had navigated through the urban chaos to approach what could have been Hollywood.

The Hotel Tamanaco Intercontinental was not the sort of hotel I would ever have chosen. But Federico was in charge of every detail of our stay in Caracas. He would have put us up in his own apartment, but he and his family were going away the next day to the coast. Caracas was not like other world cities. You had to think of security. In this respect the Hotel Tamanaco was for him the perfect choice; and, in any case, it was one of the 'oldest and most beautiful' of the city's hotels. It dated from the days of the dictatorship of Pérez Jiménez, the man responsible for the Hotel Humboldt.

The eponymous Tamanaco was a sixteenth-century Indian chief who had repeatedly tried to destroy the newly founded Caracas.

When he was eventually captured by the Spaniards, he was given the choice of being hanged or fighting a dog that had been specially trained by the Spanish commander. He chose to battle with the dog, which soon managed to tear open his throat. I wondered how he would have reacted had he known that he would later be commemorated in the Caracas branch of the Intercontinental hotel group.

Federico arrived over half an hour late, apologizing profusely. I had a sudden rush of memories of his cousin Elena, as well as a vague sensation of having embarked this time in South America on a journey into my past. Federico, a nervously excitable man, asked about her and her family before looking anxiously at his watch and rushing us outside into his imposingly sturdy car.

We drove back onto the Avenida del Libertador and then off into an exclusive residential area, quiet, verdant and spacious, with chalets, low-lying apartment blocks, swimming pools, walls and fences fringed by barbed wire and security cameras, and guards with machine guns. We pulled up outside an ivy-coloured brick wall marked Bodega La Mancha. In the large car park were an unusual number of tank-like vehicles, marked in huge letters HUMMER. 'That's the new Venezuelan status symbol,' said Federico. 'There's a waiting list of at least two or three years. They're much sought after by the *Boliburgeses*.' Manolo and I looked puzzled. Federico explained that these were government supporters who had made their wealth during Venezuela's past three years as a 'Bolivarian Republic'.

The Bodega La Mancha was a cavernous establishment attempting to combine the look of an old Spanish bodega and casual, Californian-style chic. A smartly jacketed waiter took us to Federico's favourite table, in an exposed-brick room lined with wine barrels. Seated around us were the elements of a Latin American soap opera – ridiculously glamorous couples, immaculately groomed elderly businessmen with gold cufflinks, hard-bodied young males in T-shirts tapping on their mobiles and a predominance of women of sensational if studied beauty. While Federico looked at the menu, Manolo and I exchanged amused looks, as if half-awaiting the scenes of declared passion, revelations of jealousy, cheeks being slapped, abrupt departures from tables and evil scheming that were routine in the overblown Latin dramas on Spanish television.

After describing with engaging enthusiasm the copious and 'typically Venezuelan' food presented on a series of wooden platters (corn, chicken and cheese-filled pastries, and char-grilled meats served with chili and coriander sauces), Federico brought out a large album of photos he had taken of Venezuela's renowned beauty spots, from its jungles and Caribbean beaches to the Andean peaks near Mérida where Manolo and I would soon be travelling.

Then, as we neared the end of a second bottle of a Rioja Gran Reserva, Federico confessed how much he loved his country. 'Elena's parents loved it too. They still do. They always talk about their Venezuelan years as the best in their life. They had arrived here as socialist refugees from Franco's Spain, just like my own parents. They were hugely optimistic. They saw Venezuela as the land of the future. Then democracy was restored to Spain, while corruption and chaos came back to Venezuela. Elena's parents returned to Andalusia.

'Many people wonder now why I don't do the same. I've got the money. I love Andalusia every time I go there. My roots are there, after all. But I love Venezuela even more. I'll never leave this country. The Spanish members of my family don't understand, and sometimes I don't. The way things are going, the present government could nationalize my company at any moment. I worry every day about whether I'm going to be shot at in the streets or kidnapped. Worse still, I worry about whether something's going to happen to my children.'

He asked us if we had heard about a notorious recent crime. Three brothers and their bodyguard had been kidnapped on the way home from school. A huge ransom had been paid by their desperate family, but the three children had been killed all the same, together with the bodyguard. There had been a massive protest in the streets of Caracas, calling for an end to violence. 'It was a wonderful gesture. But of course it achieved nothing.'

'You really must try a vintage Venezuelan rum, it's the best there is,' he added, anxious to change the subject. 'Or if you want a whisky . . . But don't ask for an eighteen-year-old malt. That's what the *Boliburgeses* always order.'

'Now, what do you want to do in Caracas?' he asked in a friendly but business-like manner. I mumbled apologetically about not having much time to do justice to his city, in fact not more than a day. Manolo had to get back to Spain in just over a month, and the two of us were keen to move on to the Andes as soon as we could. But I said that in the little time we had I wanted to see all the key places relating to Simón Bolívar.

'Unfortunately,' he responded, 'tomorrow might not be the best day to do so. Much of the city centre is going to be cordoned off, at least until the late afternoon. It's the official inauguration of our president, Hugo Chávez.'

Through a blur of tiredness, Rioja, vintage rum and confused first impressions, I assimilated the news that our attempt to follow in Bolívar's footsteps was being thwarted from the start by the man many consider his reincarnation.

Back in the hotel, I slumped fully clothed on top of my bed and Manolo did likewise on his, though with the television's remote control in his hand. As he flicked from channel to channel, I took in half-consciously a variety of Latin American chat shows, news programmes and game shows. But then Manolo's attention stayed fixed on a man with a red beret giving a speech. He had darkish skin, tightly curled hair, the face of a typical Venezuelan of European, African and indigenous blood, a *zambo*. Even with sleep in my eyes and no glasses, the face of Hugo Chávez, progressively rounder over the years, was unmistakable. I sat up and put my glasses back on, and observed Chávez's famous skills as a communicator, his actor's

Hugo Chávez with a portrait of Simón Bolívar

sense of timing, the generous lips that burst into a frequent winning smile, the inspiring decisiveness of manner that left me nonetheless unsure whether I was in the presence of a hero or a messianic demagogue.

Manolo turned up the volume, just as the image on the screen switched to a dusty village surrounded by grassy marshlands. In honour of tomorrow's inaugural ceremony, a programme was being shown about Chávez's life. The narrator described how the future president was born, like Abraham Lincoln, into poverty. He was one of seven boys whose parents were schoolteachers from the impoverished state of Barinas, in the middle of the flat cowboy land of Los Llanos. The camera panned to a characteristic mud-and-straw-walled hut of the region, with a dirt floor and a roof made from palm leaves. We discovered that Chávez was brought up in such a house under the care of a grandmother to whom he would

42

always be deeply attached. 'We were very poor children but very happy,' said the voice of Chávez himself. I felt as if I were being told a fairy tale.

During his idyllically simple childhood in the lowland village of Sabaneta, the young Hugo Chávez loved days when the heat haze lifted to expose a snowcapped crest rising above the forested tropical slopes of the distant Andes. Slowly he would direct his gaze to a peak noticeably higher than the others, and, for him, nobler and more dramatic in its shape. Already he was imposing on the mountain his romantic preconceptions of the man after whom it was named, Simón Bolívar, his first and most enduring love.

Chávez's grandmother Rosa was the one who had ignited his early interest in Bolívar and in Venezuela's history in general – a history in which his own family had been deeply involved. He was raised on tales of a great-great-grandfather, Colonel Pedro Pérez Pérez, who had fought alongside Bolívar's revolutionary follower Ezequiel Zamora, many of whose battles against the landowning oligarchy had taken place around Sabaneta. His imagination was fired, too, by the story of his great-grandfather 'Maisanta', whom he had originally thought of as a cold-blooded assassin capable of decapitating his enemies in front of their children. Later, after coming across a revisionist biography of Maisanta, Chávez would appreciate this ancestor as another maligned freedom fighter.

But the young Hugo had another and even greater obsession – with the Venezuelan national sport of baseball. It is ironic that the man later renowned for his virulent anti-Americanism should be so taken by a sport introduced into his country by North American oil prospectors. More ironically still, had it not been for his huge talent for the game, he might never have got into the army, which in turn allowed him to embark on a political career.

As a cadet in Venezuela's most prestigious military academy, Chávez was able to hone his baseball skills to the extent that he could have ended up as a professional player for his country.

However, his developing fascination with Bolívar and his progressive social views made him eventually see a way of helping Venezuela that had nothing to do with sport. He grew into a visionary Bolivarian who, when only nineteen, could express the wish 'to assume one day the responsibility of an entire country, the country of the great Bolívar'. In that same year, 1974, he was among the cadets selected to go to Peru to witness the 150th anniversary celebrations of Bolívar's victory at Ayacucho. Several years later, as a married paratrooper, he started giving his three young children Christmas cards featuring Bolívar's image. Later still, when his self-identification with the Liberator had reached new heights, he took on as mistress someone whom he could compare with Bolívar's Manuela Saenz. This woman, Herma Marksman, was both his intellectual equal and a person who shared his ideals in the more dangerous phase when he allied himself to a clandestine Bolivarian revolutionary movement that had as its figureheads not just the great general himself but also Ezequiel Zamora and Bolívar's idiosyncratic mentor when younger, an educationalist called Simon Rodríguez.

That someone from Chávez's background could grow up with a profound sense of social injustice was understandable in view of Venezuela's typically South American history of volatile and corrupt leadership dominated by a white elite. From the time of Bolívar right up to Chávez's early childhood in the 1950s, Venezuela had been almost uninterruptedly under the control of brutal dictators. The last three of these were from the Andean state of Táchira, including General Marcos Pérez Jiménez, whose progressive building schemes, such as the Hotel Humboldt and its funicular, have to be seen against his ruthless suppression of dissidents and a playboy lifestyle funded by the public treasury. An additional element of corruption in Venezuelan politics stemmed from the discovery in 1914 of vast oil deposits under Lake Maracaibo. By 1928 Venezuela was the second-largest oil producer in the world and its top exporter. But much of the profits were taken by foreign companies and untold future damage done to a rural economy based on cocoa and coffee.

Democracy came to Venezuela in 1959, and in 1976 President Carlos Andrés Pérez took the popular step of nationalizing the oil industry. The huge wealth derived from this industry might not have filtered down to the lower levels of society, but it gave Venezuela a higher standard of living than most other South American countries. Unfortunately Pérez's years as Venezuelan ruler were a lesson in the fragility of political popularity. Voted in for a second time as president in December 1988, he succumbed to Andean delusions of grandeur. Only a few weeks after an inaugural ceremony described by the *New York Times* as 'one of the grandest celebrations Latin America has ever known', he contradicted his previous public denouncements of foreign capital by announcing a 'shock package' which effectively meant giving in to the emerging 'neo-liberal' free-market policies to which his continent was increasingly resorting in response to its debt crisis. Believing that short-term suffering was necessary to achieve long-term prosperity, he proposed doubling the cost of petrol. This measure, in a country whose inhabitants had come to expect among the lowest petrol prices in the world, proved especially inflammatory. It was the immediate cause of the revolt in February 1989 which came to be known as the 'Caracazo'.

The Caracazo was exactly what the inhabitants of Caracas's privileged residential districts had always feared, and continue to fear – a popular uprising originating in the city's slums. Looters and rioters streamed down into the centre, where they were finally quelled by the army with a violence that completely shattered Venezuela's recently acquired reputation as a model Latin American democracy. Chávez, with his usual luck, was ill at the time with chickenpox, which prevented him from having to bloody his hands with the suppression of a revolt with which he was wholly in sympathy. Pérez's government managed to recover, as did the country's economy. But there remained a mood of deep underlying dissatisfaction, which Chávez and his fellow revolutionary Bolivarians would soon exploit.

The turning point for Chávez, and his entry into a realm somewhere between reality and myth, was the 1992 coup soon to be characterized as the 'Rebellion of the Angels'. The coup failed, but government forces made the fatal mistake of allowing Chávez to broadcast his surrender on radio, thus transforming him overnight into a media star. Such instant celebrity distracted attention from Chávez's failure to come to the aid of his fellow conspirators, who had taken control of the presidential palace. Best forgotten, too, was the radio statement he later made in prison insisting that he was a happily married man and disowning any relationship with 'Manuela Saenz' Marksman. The person who would not forget was Marksman herself. She saw his prison broadcast as the death of the brilliant, caring man she had known and the emergence of a mega-lomaniac opportunist.

Even before being released from prison in 1994 Chávez was idol-ized as a true man of the people; and though, four years later, his main rival as presidential candidate was a blonde six-foot-one former Miss Universe (a not-to-be-underestimated factor in this beauty-obsessed country), there was no doubt who would win. For sheer charisma, style, wit and lack of stuffiness, Chávez was unequalled in South American and perhaps even world politics. When he was finally made president in February 1999 he lived up to expectations. Referring to his country's 'moribund constitution' at the moment of being sworn in, he later called for a referendum allowing him to change it. In the meantime his popularity as a people's man and media figure went from strength to strength: he played baseball with his new friend Fidel Castro and was reassur-ingly visible when heavy rains caused a horrific mudslide to hit Caracas from Mount Ávila.

Of course, Chávez faced mounting opposition from all sides. But he maintained a remarkable degree of popular support, helped by his enormously successful weekly live television show, *Aló Presidente*, and the rising price of oil on the world market. Best of all for his image was the coup in early 2002, when he was briefly deposed, only to be reinstated in triumph. Whether or not George

Bush and the American government were involved in the coup, Chávez's insistence that they were greatly boosted his heroic status at a time when Bush's activities in the Middle East were fanning virulent anti-Americanism.

The coup and its aftermath also aggravated Chavez's paranoia, tetchiness and dogmatism. For the first time, he openly declared himself to be a communist. He railed against his opponents in increasingly extreme terms. Believing, like Bush, that those who did not wholeheartedly support him were his enemies, he pressed ahead impetuously with what he called '21st Century Socialism'. To his detractors his 'Bolivarian Revolution' was completely unsustainable, too heavily reliant on oil revenue, on the loan of doctors and nurses from Cuba, on buying the support of a large proportion of the electorate and on reforms and improvements that were purely cosmetic. Yet, to politically committed western intellectuals, Chávez and his acolytes represented almost the last hope of a truly socialist world. They flocked to Venezuela to see him and were unfailingly seduced. In December 2006 Chávez was voted back in as president but with a considerably diminished majority. His future was not as certain as he would have liked.

# 5

# BOLÍVAR'S DREAM

I woke up with all my clothes on, at around six in the morning. Through a gap in the curtain I could see it was already full daylight. I got up to peep at a view of worn office blocks silhouetted against Mount Ávila. I had optimistically envisaged a brilliant tropical dawn, but the sky was heavy with dark clouds and pollution. On the television a young blonde turned to face a screen featuring the presidential palace. A reporter was standing microphone in hand outside the building, towards which were heading a crowd of red-shirted Chávez supporters.

We had arranged an early meeting with Federico in his office. He had offered us the use of his chauffeur for the day, to prevent us from doing anything so silly as going on public transport or, more suicidal still, walking on our own down a street.

Walter, the chauffeur, called at the hotel at eight o'clock. He was elderly, black and dignified, with jacket and tie and neatly trimmed moustache. The sprawling incoherent city, with its constant views of the *Barrios* through which he drove us, was more threatening than ever in the grey daylight.

Federico, on the point of leaving for the coast, greeted us in his office with guidebooks and a mountain of tourist leaflets. 'It's not going to be the best day for sightseeing,' he confessed. He asked his secretary to ring up and check what if any of the city's monuments were going to be open. After a series of calls, she told us that we would be able to visit the museums of contemporary art. But all the places in the historic centre, including Bolívar's birthplace and the Pantheon, where he was buried, would not be open until after the president had finished his inaugural address. 'That could take the rest of the day,' Walter commented with a soft smile. Chávez, like Castro, was famous for speeches that could last up to seven hours. 'And what about the Quinta de San Mateo?' I asked plaintively, referring to the now urban-engulfed country estate where Bolívar had spent much of his childhood. 'Closed today for fumigation,' came the response to a telephone enquiry.

That left us with the Quinta de Anauco as the one building with Bolivarian associations that we would certainly be able to visit. We set off with Walter, his car radio playing President Chávez's speech at a soothingly low volume. The house, a late-eighteenth-century building in the middle of a residential district deemed by Walter 'only relatively unsafe', was now the Museum of Colonial Art and could be visited only on a guided tour. While Walter waited in the car, listening to the President, Manolo and I climbed some shaded steps to hear a young man explain the history of the estate to a group of housewives and grandmothers. The place, once the residence of 'the leaders of Venezuelan independence', was not the most appropriate starting point for a Bolivarian tour of Caracas. Bolívar himself had stayed here only towards the end of his life, in January and July 1827, immediately after another of his triumphant entrances into Caracas and immediately before leaving the city for ever on his road to exile.

We woke Walter from his sleep. Chávez was still talking on the radio. We bided our time by going off to see the city's Museum of Contemporary Art, reputed to have one of the finest collections of modern art in Latin America. We returned to a business area of the city, 'very dangerous at night', with brutalist towers randomly arranged around bleak empty spaces and unkempt parkland.

The museum was a labyrinth, with no indications of where anything was. I was looking forward to seeing canvases by Picasso, Matisse, Léger, Miró and other world masters, but what interested me more than anything were the works by the Venezuelan artist Jesús Soto, a pioneer of kinetic art who had helped put Venezuela at the forefront of the twentieth-century avant-garde. However, out of what I took to be respect for Bolivarian socialist principles, the main floors of the museum had been given over entirely to a display of works by staff and students from every art school in the country. Eventually we came across some steps to a poorly lit basement. What little was left of the permanent collection was in hiding there, as if escaping from the revolution above.

'*Socialismo o muerte!*' shouted Chávez over the car radio. The speech gave little sign of nearing its end, allowing us to move on to the National Gallery of Art, where I hoped we would have better luck. The mounds of sand and cement laid beyond the entrance to the public park which enclosed it were not promising and, sure enough, the classical-style 1930s museum, with its collections tracing the history of Venezuelan art from the pre-Columbian period onwards, was a half-empty shell awaiting renovation. Inside, however, we discovered a small exhibition of contemporary works inspired by the life of Bolívar's mistress Manuela Saenz, as well as a scattering of academic nineteenth-century works of Bolivarian inspiration, such as *The Battle of Ayacucho*, and *The Crossing of the Andes*.

There was now little option but to take a long lunch in a restaurant vetted over the phone by Federico, who continued to exert a controlling hand even from the coast. We invited Walter to join us, but he insisted, as always, on remaining in the car. He said with a touch of irony that he had Chávez for company. Chávez stayed with us too, speaking now from a television set to which no one in our dining-room paid the slightest attention.

Walter came into the dining-room to tell us that the city centre was open again to traffic, but that we would be better off starting our afternoon's homage to Bolívar at the National Pantheon, to allow more time for the area around the presidential palace to clear.

Within half an hour we were standing in the middle of an enormous square, staring towards a soaring neo-baroque building set against a backcloth of mountains. To my surprise, the exterior of Venezuela's most hallowed monument, the burial place of Bolívar and other visionaries, was painted a shocking pink. The interior, more suitably solemn, betrayed the building's origins as a church, except that the nave, lined by flags of the countries liberated by Bolívar, led the eye not to a high altar but to the angel-flanked tomb of Bolívar himself.

One hundred years earlier, almost to the day, the American Hiram Bingham had studied the same marble and bronze tomb in front of us, searching perhaps for the Liberator's blessing before following his victorious march of 1819 into Colombia. Hiram, the son and grandson of missionaries, was about to perpetuate this family tradition when he married someone who freed him from the influence of his parents. The subsequent unhappiness of the marriage encouraged his urge to escape. Having got himself a job building up a library of South American works for Harvard University, he came across some papers relating to Simón Bolívar and thought he had the ideal subject for a biography. He also had an excuse for satisfying his love of travel. While studying Bolívar's march of 1819, he found it 'almost impossible to form an intelligent estimate of the actual obstacles that were overcome by the Liberating Army'. The only solution, he concluded, would be to do the route himself. The book resulting from this would throw little light on Bolívar himself, but the journey would enable Hiram to find his true vocation – as an adventurer.

Absentmindedly making the sign of the cross, I turned away from the tomb to walk out into the greying, rain-spattered afternoon. Walter drove us further into the historic centre, into an area of congested streets and pavements, crammed with tiny shops, bags of uncollected rubbish and old plasterwork buildings that had survived the encroaching concrete. Alerted to our being in an 'exceptionally dangerous area at all times of day', where not even Walter would stray after nightfall, we prepared to leave the car as if we were soldiers taking part in the Normandy landings. Walter's quiet and understated manner made us take seriously his warning that there would be people on the busy streets who would immediately register with interest the presence of two gringos. But this sense of vulnerability soon changed to a wonderful sensation of freedom as we mingled happily with a crowd speckled with red T-shirted Chávez supporters, or *Chavistas*.

What I did not feel was any of the profound emotion a South American visitor might have felt on nearing the famous statue of Bolívar in the square next to his birthplace. I thought of the anonymous traveller described by the Cuban poet and revolutionary of the late nineteenth century, José Marti – the traveller whose initial concern, on arriving at Caracas after dusk, was not about where he could sleep or eat, but about how he could get to the statue at the centre of the verdant Plaza Bolívar. 'They say that, alone beside the tall, fragrant trees of the square, the traveller stood in front of the statue as tears ran down his cheeks; the statue seemed to move, like a father when his son draws close to him.' Instead I studied the monument with the dispassionate eye of an art historian and questioned the appropriateness of commemorating the Liberator with an equestrian statue inspired by that of the Spanish King Philip III rearing towards the Madrid royal palace. And would a father approach a son in this way? On top of a rearing horse? Had Marti actually seen the statue?

We continued walking towards the Liberator's birthplace, a single-storied neoclassical building incongruous against a soaring office block behind. The house, half open, scantily furnished and drastically restored in a way that lent it an atmosphere of cold, marbled grandeur, was decorated all over with modern wall paintings of scenes from Bolívar's life, one of which was of 'Bolívar's delirium at the summit of Chimborazo'. The building seemed as unlikely as the delirium. No one of flesh and blood could possibly have been born there. It was not the birthplace of Bolívar the man, but of Bolívar the myth.

The supernatural was supposedly attendant even at Bolívar's christening in 1783. The parents, according to a popular version of the Liberator's life, wanted to call their son Pedro José, but the officiating priest insisted they should change the name to Simón. He explained that an inner voice had told him that the child would grow up to become the 'Simon Macabee of America', a religious revolutionary.

That the Church should wish to claim as one of their own an atheist frequently in dispute with the ecclesiastical authorities is a mark of the almost desperate need to mythologize Bolívar. He was the first major native hero in a continent whose epic and empty landscapes cry out for larger-than-life figures to populate them. Bolívar, a man as short as Napoleon, began the process of his own mythical aggrandizement. Extremely conscious of his image and his place in history, he had the intelligence to invent and encourage stories about himself that appealed simultaneously to those of radically opposed political and ideological positions. Bolívar is someone who can be interpreted in whatever way you want to.

The facts of Bolívar's life are often difficult to extricate from the fiction; but he almost certainly did not owe his name to some last-minute priestly intervention. He was probably named Simón after a sixteenth-century ancestor who was the first member of the family to settle in Caracas. Bolívar's family, one of the oldest in Venezuela, originated from the Basque town of Bolívar and included in one of its branches the mad and rebellious conquistador Lope de Aguirre, whose crazed confrontation of the Andes and other natural hurdles prefigured that of his descendant.

The most salient feature of Bolívar's background was its immense wealth and privilege, without which he would probably never have commanded the respect he did, however great his charisma. Detracting somewhat from his later image as a proto-communist man of the people was the fact that this fortune was derived from an early grant of indigenous labour, or *encomienda*. Slaves worked the family mines and plantations, several of which would be given to Bolívar as baptismal gifts. Inevitably, as was common to his class, one of his forebears seems to have had an affair with a black slave, which was said to account for Bolívar's thick lips and swarthy appearance. A genealogist, sent to ascertain the family's purity of blood with a view to granting them an aristocratic title, also discovered a female antecedent of Indian origin. This typically South American mixture of white, African and Indian blood deprived the family of aristocratic status, but was enormously useful for Bolívar's reputation as a man devoted to the cause of a united South America in which all races would be equal.

However noble Bolívar might have become in later life (and the evidence suggests that he never shook off the haughtiness and inherent racism of his upbringing), he was an obnoxious, arrogant and unruly child. After the early death of his dissipated father, Bolívar, aged three, was handed over to the care of the family lawyer by his desperate mother, who herself would die six years later. Andrés Bello, one of Venezuela's leading intellectuals behind the independence movement, was briefly Bolívar's tutor, and found him to be talented but lacking in application. More in tune with the wayward and distracted child was the eccentric Simón Rodríguez (known sometimes by the pseudonym Robinson), who took him to the family estate at San Mateo to instil in him Rousseau-inspired ideas about thinking for yourself and being true to your instincts. However, following a revolt against Spanish rule in 1795, Rodríguez was forced to flee to Europe.

The young Bolívar would soon go there himself. After being made to join an elite military corps founded by his grandfather, he sailed as a fifteen-year-old to Spain, and fell immediately in love there with a young woman, whom he married in April 1802, at the end of his first European stay. She died shortly after he brought her back to Venezuela. Bolívar returned distraught to Europe, finding consolation in the company of other women and immersing himself in intellectual studies. The man whose military exploits would be characterized by a blind impetuosity proved to be a highly sophisticated thinker who appreciated that the ideas of Rousseau and other Enlightenment figures had been formulated for the European middle classes and needed to be adapted to a continent as racially and socially complex as South America.

On this second stay in Europe he might or might not have refused to kiss the Pope's ring, as he related; but the story of his going with Simón Rodríguez to the top of Rome's Aventine Hill and falling on his knees to swear that he would never rest until Venezuela was independent is corroborated by letters he later exchanged with his former tutor.

Also true was his meeting in September 1804, probably in the Parisian salon of his lover Fanny du Villars, with Alexander von Humboldt, recently returned from his travels with Bonpland. The ensuing conversation, with Bolívar referring to the glittering destiny of a South America freed from its Spanish oppressors, and Humboldt replying that though the continent was ready for liberation, there was no one capable of leading such a movement, sounds like typically Bolivarian embellishment. What we do know, however, was that Bolívar was far more impressed by Humboldt than the latter was by him. Humboldt, recalling fifty years later his encounter with the man who would say of him that he had done more for the Americas than all the conquistadors put together, confessed that he had thought of Bolívar essentially as a lively and idealistic young dreamer. 'I never believed,' he wrote, 'that he was destined to be leader of the American crusade.'

Only a year after Bolívar's return to Venezuela in 1807 the prospect of a free South America seemed to be possible at last. The French had conquered Spain and ousted the Bourbon monarch Ferdinand VII; Spanish Liberals had taken refuge in Andalusia. The South Americans did not want to be ruled by Napoleon and did not trust the imperialistic Liberals. The immediate solution in Venezuela was to depose the Spanish captain-general and establish a junta, ostensibly to govern in the name of Ferdinand VII but in practice autonomous. Bolívar was sent to London in 1810 to try and enlist the support of the British. He failed in this task but managed to persuade back to Venezuela the former figurehead of the independence movement, the aristocratic voluptuary Francisco de Miranda. On 5 July 1811 an elected Venezuelan congress formally declared independence.

The first Venezuelan republic did not last long. Its end was presaged by a massive earthquake on 26 March 1812, which caused major destruction and loss of life all the way from La Guaira to the Andean town of Mérida. Caracas suffered especially, with nine-tenths of its buildings falling to the ground and up to ten thousand fatalities. A royalist chronicler, José Domingo Díaz, saw the city literally falling around him in the course of what had begun as a leisurely afternoon's stroll towards the cathedral. He climbed to the top of what was left of the church of San Jacinto to find Bolívar himself in his shirtsleeves clambering across the debris. On Bolívar's face was 'written the utmost horror or the utmost despair'. But Bolívar, with an eye to posterity, still had the presence of mind to declare: 'We will fight nature itself if it opposes us, and force it to obey.' With 'these impious and extravagant words', as Díaz called them, Bolívar staked his first claim to the superhuman status that he would later acquire while forcing his troops over the Andes. The tragic episode of this earthquake would be recalled in 1999, when destiny's chosen successor to Bolívar, Hugo Chávez, contemplated a Caracas devastated by a mudslide.

If Bolívar had appeared heroic amidst the ruins of San Jacinto, there was little that was admirable about his behaviour in the immediate aftermath of the earthquake. Entrusted with his first important military command, at the coastal town of Puerto Cabello, he lost out to counter-revolutionary forces in July 1812. Escaping from the ensuing massacre with only a few officers, he then handed over to the Spaniards the man whom he now repeatedly called the 'coward' Miranda – an act which his former tutor Andrés Bello would describe as 'perfidy'.

After the defeat of the First Republic, Bolívar took refuge in the Colombian port of Cartagena, which was then under revolutionary government. Given permission by this government to fight Spanish troops in present-day Colombia (then known as New Granada), Bolívar extended his new campaign into Venezuela. A vast amount of blood was shed in what he decreed a 'War to the Death', which culminated in the recapture of Caracas in August 1813. Crowned by laurels, Bolívar was driven around the streets of Caracas in a Roman-style triumphal chariot pulled by a dozen daughters of the city's patrician families. But Venezuela's Second Republic was even shorter-lived than the first, opposition coming this time from the lawless *llanos*, the vast tropical grasslands whose rough-and-ready inhabitants preferred being ruled by Spain rather than by a military dictator from the Venezuelan aristocracy.

A fugitive again in Cartagena, and then in Jamaica and Haiti, Bolívar succeeded in establishing a foothold in an eastern part of Venezuela heavily populated by blacks. Later that year he issued his first decree against slavery, though not for humanitarian reasons. Desperately in need of recruits, he offered slaves their freedom in return for fighting for him. Most of the slaves turned down his offer.

With the help of a brilliant black general whom he later executed (perhaps for racial reasons and from fear of a powerful rival), Bolívar embarked in 1817 on the campaign – whose route Hiram Bingham would trace ninety years later – which culminated in 1821 in the resounding victory over the Spaniards at the battle of Carabobo, just north of Caracas.

With the subsequent uniting of New Granada and Venezuela to form an independent Greater Colombia, Bolívar had begun to dream of a republic embracing the whole continent. This dream, later limited to the creation of a Federation of the Andes, would find little support among his contemporaries, but would fire the imagination of future leaders and ideologues who would talk about 'Bolivarian unity' while conveniently forgetting the contradictions of a man capable one moment of supporting a constitutional monarchy and the next of proposing South America as a protectorate of Great Britain. Those who have glamorized Bolívar have been unable to accept the idea, widely current even in his lifetime, that his ruthless driving of his army, along routes only the most madly determined would attempt, was motivated less by idealism than by personal ambition.

I remained looking at the painting in the Liberator's birthplace, riveted by the disturbed eyes of the young man astride Chimborazo's summit. Then the imminence of a tropical storm outside made Manolo hurry me back towards the car, which we reached just as the first heavy drops pounded against the windscreen. Walter left us safely back at the hotel, after which we realized, for the first time since arriving at Venezuela, that we were truly on our own.

# 6

# BOLÍVAR, MIRROR
# OF THE ANDES

We were approaching the Andes at last. We were doing so by plane. I had hoped to travel overland the entire length of South America, but the odd flight in the first weeks of the journey was perhaps going to be necessary if Manolo were to get back to Spain in time. We saved ourselves a long day's bus ride by flying directly from Caracas to Valera, a town in the foothills of the Andes. We were making for Venezuela's highest peaks, whose summits had been viewed by local poet Jean Aristeguieta as a reflection of the 'brilliance' and 'integrity' of the Liberator.

When our plane touched down at Valera my thoughts were less loftily engaged. I was thinking of the Liberator's dog. Of all the stories connected with Bolívar's crossing of the Venezuelan Andes, I had been particularly intrigued by the one about the dog he had been given there, a mastiff of a kind peculiar to the high mountain district of the Mucuchies. His fur was mainly black but with a white Andean-style crest that had given him his name of 'Nevado' or 'Snowy'. Then I daydreamed, as I so often did, about my own dog Chumberry. Was she still staring at the gate, waiting for my return?

As I grew older, I was giving in more and more to a sentimentality I had once despised. I had never believed that I would be travelling around South America showing a wallet photograph of my dog to those casually met on a plane. Or that when I thought of the pet I referred to in my weaker moments as 'my darling Chumbi' (whose breed was closely related to that of the Mucuchies mastiffs) I would find myself beginning to cry.

I rubbed my eyes, came to my senses and walked out into the hazy tropical sunlight. The high Andes were still some distance away, and the only mountains visible from Valera's small airport were some modest rounded peaks covered in trees and vegetation. Valera itself was an unremarkable modern town that had expanded enormously with the building in the 1920s of the Trans-Andean highway.

Our taxi seemed to us so cheap that we stayed in it to the nearby district capital of Trujillo, a far smaller and older place than Valera. Our driver was talking about petrol. 'If Chávez were to put up the price of petrol by a cent he would be out, just like his predecessor. Political popularity in this country is based almost entirely on petrol.' I remained glued to the side window, distractedly taking in a landscape with extensive fields of sugar cane and clumps of ragged banana palms disappearing into grassy slopes, humid forest, clouds and haze.

The ever denser sky restricted our first impressions of the Venezuelan Andes, whose higher peaks were still out of view, and whose lower slopes testified to an economy based principally on tropical produce – the sugar and cocoa that had been the main crops since the colonial period and the coffee that had been largely planted since Bolívar's time. We were climbing imperceptibly up a valley until a spreading mass of worn-looking buildings in plaster, adobe and concrete announced our arrival at Trujillo.

Still comparing European to Venezuelan prices, we felt flush with money and treated ourselves to what my guidebook called the best and most stylish hotel in the town, the grandly named Hotel Country Trujillo. This proved to be a small 1960s block in the town's upper outskirts, with a receptionist even less welcoming than the architecture. When Manolo asked her about the security situation in town, she replied with a characteristically Venezuelan expression, '*más o menos*', which literally means 'more or less', but we took to mean 'fairly bad'. Outside, in the car park, two soldiers patrolled with machine guns.

Trujillo was evoked by the British writer Lisa St Aubin de Terán in her fictionalized biography of her close friend code-named 'Otto', a well-known Andean-born revolutionary who was sent here after being expelled from his school in Valera. 'In Valera,' she wrote, adopting Otto's voice, 'if anyone thought anything of Trujillo (which wasn't very often), it was as a dismal fortress town lost in the hills on the old Royal Road through the Andes. It was where people went if they went to prison. It wasn't a place you would ever choose to go to. It had an old cathedral, and honourable mentions in all the history books, but it was a dump and cultural backwater.'

A handful of low white-walled buildings with wide eaves and wooden courtyards stood within the vicinity of the largely rebuilt cathedral around a humble main square named, like all main squares in Venezuela, after Bolívar. Bolívar had actually been to Trujillo, while leading the campaigns that had resulted in the recapture of Caracas in 1813 and the decisive victory at Carabobo in 1821. While staying in Trujillo in June 1813, he wrote the notorious decree that would besmirch for ever his reputation as a respecter of human rights and give the town a dramatically named tourist attraction.

The House of the War to the Death was a local history museum, laid out around a blandly modernized courtyard. Disappointingly, I found nothing in the museum about Bolívar's dog. There was instead the actual table on which Bolívar is said to have signed his 1813 decree, a facsimile of which was displayed alongside it, together with a modern transcription. It was a chilling and depressing read. After emphasizing the brutality of the Spaniards ('the monsters who have infested Colombian soil, covering it in blood'), it called for a similar brutality to make the monsters 'vanish for ever'. Any Spaniard who did not actively help Bolívar's cause would be eliminated, while any American would be forgiven. 'Spaniards and Canarians,' it concluded, 'even if you profess neutrality, know that you will die unless you work actively to bring about the freedom of America. Americans, know that you will live, even if you are guilty.' More than ever, after visiting the museum, I longed to be away from townships, to be high up in the mountains, freeing my mind however briefly of bloodshed and politics.

Everyone in Trujillo assumed we had come to the town for the outing to the statue of the Virgin of Peace, a massive monument crowning the highest of the surrounding mountains. The panorama on clear days was said to stretch as far as the snowy peaks above Mérida. Low-lying clouds had so far hidden the monument, making us abandon the idea of climbing up there for the views. However, by the time we left the House of the War to the Death the sky had cleared sufficiently for us to see the 47-metre-high statue, reputedly the largest statue of the Virgin in the world. We rushed back to the park in front of our hotel, from where jeeps carrying tourists officially set off to the monument along a rough forest track. We were told we would not have to wait more than half an hour or so.

After forty minutes of sitting on a bench, a man working in a refreshment kiosk told us that his brother would be arriving with his jeep any moment now. He chatted to us as we continued waiting. 'A few years ago,' he said, 'there were queues of tourists waiting to do the climb. Now hardly anyone comes except at weekends.' His brother never came.

With the first light of dawn I drew aside the curtains of our room to see the Virgin appearing and disappearing behind clouds. The sun was promising to come out, making me want to head off as soon as possible towards Mérida and the 'Balcony of Venezuela'. Manolo had struck a deal with our taxi driver from the day before, who had promised to stop wherever we wanted along the way. 'You'll be wanting to take photos all the time,' he added, reminding us that we would be travelling along Venezuela's highest paved road, along which Bolívar himself had marched.

We were already climbing sharply up to the Paso Pico del Águila, the road's summit, by the time the sun fully emerged, intensifying the colours of a landscape already very different from the surroundings of Valera and Trujillo. Luxuriant greenery and exotic cultivations had been succeeded by a sparser environment, with crude stone borders marking rough steep fields planted with potatoes and yams. The fields were still ploughed by oxen, a couple of whom, tied together by their yolk, stood outside the uninviting-looking village store and bar where we stopped in the hope of a coffee.

The interior of this establishment suggested a harsh Andean world populated by closed and suspicious people. Dark, concrete-walled and buzzing with flies, it was presided over by a surly, monosyllabic old woman who sat motionless behind the counter. Yet once she had stirred she became a completely different person, smiling, alert and interested to know where we were from and where we were going. Eventually she produced some coffee, brewed in a cracked enamel jug.

We chatted for so long that we left the store to find that the sun had gone and the landscape fast being obliterated by cloud. The driver assured us that we would probably be above the clouds at the top of the pass and that in any case the weather was so changeable that the sun would most likely be back again within a few minutes. He was wrong. We were soon overcome by thick fog. Visibility was reduced to a few yards once we had left behind the cultivated fields and entered the high moorland known in this part of South America by the old Spanish word *páramo*.

I had been looking forward to my first sighting of the *páramo*, with its low covering of the heather-like, russet-coloured 'Sheep's Sorrel' (so-called because sheep could graze on it impervious to its high content of oxalic acid), and, above all, its abundance of the strange, triffid-like plants called *frailejones*. K.G. Grubb, an English traveller to Venezuela in the 1920s, referred to the *páramo* as a 'desolate waste of coarse grasses, comparable with the surface of the

63

Altiplano (or high plateau) of Bolivia'. Through our driver I now learnt that altitude sickness in Venezuela was known as '*mal de páramo*' and the phrase '*pasar el páramo*' ('to cross the *páramo*') was a local Andean phrase for dying.

Unable to see what we were crossing thanks to the fog, I had to rely on Grubb's description of climbing up to the pass in spring, when the low vegetation was in flower. 'A low but brilliant yellow shrub persisted . . . with unconquerable optimism. A blue vetch still held up its head in irreducible confidence. The reign of stones then supervened and the hillsides were abandoned to primitive confusion. The people who live in this section were of markedly Indian types and were mostly modern representatives of the former Mucuchies. Their huts were low, exposed and misery-stricken. Finally we passed into a region where the soil was merely shale and bare earth, with some occasional tufts of coarse grass.'

By this stage in Grubb's climb, as he neared the summit, weather conditions were as poor as the ones we were experiencing. I had yet to read a single description of the Paso Pico del Águila when the weather was other than bleak, foggy and with the persistent drizzle that had now started once our driver had pulled to a halt. 'We're at the top,' he announced. Having been perspiring in T-shirts only half an hour earlier, we now climbed fully clothed out of the car to face temperatures approaching zero.

An old guidebook Federico had given me suggested what we might find at the summit: a 'warm refuge for a cup of coffee or hot chocolate by the glowing fire'. And if we were lucky, 'apple-cheeked youngsters, children of the *páramo*, might emerge from the mists, eager to be photographed or to receive a traveller's largesse'. 'Life,' the book added, 'is rugged on the *páramos* – the children look cold under their worn woollen *ruanas*.'

The refuge was closed and the only people around were some Venezuelan tourists jumping up and down to keep warm under their designer anoraks. When a burst of freezing wind temporarily revealed the surrounding landscape, I had a flashback to childhood holidays in the Scottish highlands. Turning around, I saw twenty yards higher up the mountain the bronze 'spread eagle' which gave the pass its official name. With chattering teeth I made my way towards it and was soon out of breath. The stone plinth supporting the bronze bird told us that we were at an altitude of nearly four thousand metres. The bird, oddly enough, proved not to be an eagle but a condor, which explained why the pass was popularly known as the Paso del Condor.

The monument was a commemoration of Bolívar and of his forced Andean march of 1813. The lofty mystical tone of the inscription, with its references to the 'immortal Liberator', could have been that of the poet Jean Aristeguieta, whose *Journey of Marvels* of 1958 is an account in verse and poetic prose of the author's Bolivarian journey all the way along the Venezuelan Andes. This range interested Aristeguieta in all its moods, from the euphoria conveyed by the sight of brilliant sunshine on virgin crests to the profound melancholy and mystery of the *páramos* in their bleakest moments.

During such moments Aristeguieta could imagine Bolívar as a figure risen almost from the mists of the supernatural, with the tragic expression of someone leading thousands of his soldiers to their deaths so as to 'bring freedom to those nations born out of the glow of his vision'. Bolívar, in Aristeguieta's words, was a 'mirror of the Andes'.

This noble image of Bolívar and his crossing of the *páramos* excluded a significant event that took place one bitterly cold and rainy evening, outside the nearby village of Mucuchies, when the Liberator first encountered the dog Nevado.

We passed the village shortly after beginning our descent towards Mérida, but the fog was so unremitting that we did not stop. In any case we had decided to come back to the area in a couple of days, to spend some time wandering around the *páramo*, in the hope of seeing it in clearer weather. We carried on driving, eventually coming out of the fog and finding ourselves in an idyllic valley just as Aristeguieta had described it, full of streams, brooks, torrents and cascades, and with a tropical, 'magically powerful' vegetation of palms, lianas, bananas and giant trees whose greens were 'as exuberant as those of Guyana'. The town of Mérida appeared languorous at the top of a tall cliff, surrounded by mountains whose upper slopes were hidden by darkening clouds.

If Caracas has the reputation of an urban hell, Mérida, capital of the Venezuelan Andes, is still widely considered a terrestrial Eden. Bolívar must have had particularly fond memories of the town. Whereas everyone in conservative Trujillo had gone in to hiding at his approach, the inhabitants of Mérida had rushed out to greet him and were the first people in South America to hail him as Liberator. Such a response was typical of Mérida, whose magnificent location, exposed to nature at its most sensationally varied, has been matched by a history of political and intellectual openness. A university town since the late eighteenth century, Mérida became from the 1960s onwards what Cambridge had been between the wars, a refuge to leftist intellectuals, including some of the seminal Marxist figures with whom the young Chávez was associated. The town had been variously described to me as Venezuela's major centre of learning and a popular holiday destination due to its equidistance between crisp mountain air and balmy tropical forest. My friend Elena had told me of childhood holidays with bracing mountain walks in the morning and leisurely afternoons bathing naked under tropical waterfalls that Gauguin might have painted.

I arrived at Mérida full of exotic images of the place, with the names of several artists and intellectuals whom I was assured were fascinating and extraordinary. These assurances admittedly all came from one person: the Spanish husband of Carolina, a Venezuelan woman I knew in Frailes. For him Mérida was like a corner of Paris's Left Bank and its presiding genius was a painter called Hilario, whom he thought would be particularly invaluable for my

Andean researches. Hilario was no ordinary painter. He was a luminary, knowledgeable about all subjects, a passionate archaeologist, a fellow collector and an amateur historian of Bolívar.

I lost enthusiasm for meeting Hilario and his circle on seeing the 'wonderful' hotel that Carolina's husband Manuel had recommended. It was called the Europa, and had been the venue of 'dazzling' intellectual encounters. The place was a worn survival of the 1940s, frequented by prostitutes, and with a grey hollow-cheeked receptionist whom I thought might keel over and die any moment. We would have moved on immediately had not a sudden torrential storm persuaded us to take a room.

When we got out into the streets of Mérida, the weather remained leaden and drizzly, influencing our first impressions of a town with little architectural charm. The same earthquake Bolívar had witnessed in Caracas in 1812 had left almost nothing standing from the colonial period other than some low-walled pastel-coloured houses similar to those of Trujillo. The rest of the town appeared to be an undistinguished sprawl of modern and nineteenth-century buildings spreading out from a square hemmed in by giant palms and a tall neoclassical cathedral.

Back at the hotel a call came through from Hilario. He had heard from Carolina's husband that we would be staying at the Europa, and he had been expecting us. I agreed we would meet him at his studio, which he said we could not miss. It was marked by a large canvas standing in the street.

A huge Andean scene, in an impressionist/expressionist style, projected out halfway across one of the town's busier streets, creating a nocturnal traffic hazard no one seemed to mind about. A hand-painted arrow next to it pointed to the Galeria de Arte 'Monet', which had as its motto the words 'My art as an instrument of peace.'

The studio was a crumbling hovel painted a dirty yellow on the outside. The scene inside was nightmarishly bright and strange. Two acolytes of the artist sat sullenly on stools on either side of the entrance. One was young, black and cherubic; the other swarthy, scarred and middle-aged. Scarcely registering our arrival, they seemed mildly irritated that we had interrupted their consultation with the master, who reclined in a deckchair at the other end of the tiny room, bathed in the light of a bare bulb. He was a tall, prematurely aged forty-year-old, with a sallow peaky complexion, dry lizard-like skin and a shabby pinstriped suit and tie. By his side was an ebony walking stick, a pile of books, catalogues and paint brushes, and a lowly placed easel supporting a canvas we could see only from the back. Manolo shot me a meaningful glance.

As the master welcomed us to his 'humble studio' and told us how friends of Manuel's were friends of his, I looked closely at his face, with its sunken eyes, barely moving lips and the hint of a black moustache. And then I studied the crowded contents of the room more carefully and my eye was caught by the three-dimensional, life-sized crib arranged against the back wall. It had grotesque papier-mâché figures lit up by coloured fairy lights.

'I can see you're interested by the crib,' observed Hilario. 'They're very popular in our country's Andean regions. We keep them up many weeks after Christmas.' Intrigued by this snippet of Andean ethnography, I immediately responded to Hilario's invitation to pull up a stool and sit down besides him. Manolo, I noticed, was more hesitant.

From my seated position, the studio and its occupants were more bizarre than ever. My back was no longer turned to Hilario's two acolytes, whose unsmiling stares followed me as I caught a sideways glimpse of a metal cube with circles cut out to reveal suspended geometrical shapes and dangling wires. I recognized what I thought in my excitement was a work by the leading Venezuelan kinetic artist Jesús del Soto. 'It's a homage to del Soto, an early work of mine,' Hilario explained, handing me over a bound collection of newspaper articles about himself. One of these, headed 'Local artist Hilario Brevas welcomes to Mérida leading representative artist of the avant-garde,' had a photograph of the young and gangly Hilario showing his metal cube to del Soto during the latter's visit to the town in 1982.

'I later changed my style,' he added, 'after my illness.' He talked about the artistic crisis he had suffered and how he had wanted to abandon abstraction and create paintings that reflected his enormous love for his country. While he was still able to walk he had started spending long periods painting the landscapes his great hero Bolívar had known, above all the 'wild and lonely Mucuchies'. Manolo shifted more and more in his seat, while I skimmed through reproductions of the paintings. Combining influences from Turner, German Expressionism and painted calendar images of Alpine scenes, they confirmed my theory that talent is usually in inverse proportion to the size of an artist's signature. The name HILARIO, written with a rococo flourish, appeared prominently in the left-hand corner of each canvas.

'Manuel told me that you're following Bolívar's route through the Andes,' remarked Hilario. 'I would be interested to know how our Liberator is regarded today in Europe.' I was about to say that most Europeans have probably never even heard of him, other than perhaps as a precursor of Chávez, but the tension of the situation made me mutter inarticulately. Hilario suddenly changed the subject to ask us if we wanted a cup of tea.

Before waiting for a reply he raised his voice and shouted out the words 'Mi amor!' Immediately the heavy green curtain at the back of the room drew apart. A short smiling woman appeared, like a puppet whose strings had suddenly been pulled. 'My wife,' said Hilario, presenting us to this woman, who responded with a swirl of her long floral dress, a jerky extension of her hand and the common Venezuelan phrase, 'A sus ordenes' ('At your command') – a liguistic legacy, perhaps, of Bolívar and his troops.

'Mi amor,' Hilario continued, in a sweetly plaintive tone, 'would you be so kind as to make tea for these two gentlemen?' 'Of course, mi amor,' she replied, swivelling around and disappearing. The two acolytes, unchanging in their expressions, turned their faces towards the curtain before resuming their stares at us. When the wife returned and then left again, after handing us our tea, I tried engaging them in conversation, asking if they too were painters. 'They're very talented,' Hilario intervened, 'but neither of them can speak.' Manolo had finally had enough. He got up from his chair, saying we really had to go.

Hilario, after failing to persuade us to leave the Europa and come and stay in his studio, insisted on us seeing the painting on which he was currently working.

The work was reminiscent of Turner's *Rain, Steam, and Speed*, except that instead of a train a huge animal was emerging out of the fog, white-crested, panting and determined. A thought occurred to me. I tried to dismiss it. I could not believe he might be painting the subject that had been so much on my mind over the past two days. The coincidence was too great, or perhaps the coincidence was not a coincidence, for the painting might not be a painting at all but rather the crystallization on canvas of some force that had entered the room. 'Bolívar's dog,' Hilario announced, 'a mastiff from the Mucuchíes.' Stunned and slightly clammy, I could react only by looking into Hilario's haunting eyes as he went on to tell me that I should read 'Nevado the Dog', a story by Tulio Febres Cordero. 'You'll find in it all that you need to know.'

As we left, Hilario's wife accompanied us out onto the street. '*A sus ordenes*,' she said after saying goodbye. 'Come back soon.'

'*Mi amor. A sus ordenes. Mi amor . . .*' Manolo and I repeated the phrases mockingly, at the same time moving quickly, looking round to see if we were being followed. It was early on a Friday night and we had no desire to return to our dismal room; but, while Manolo waited for me at an adjoining bar, I popped back into the hotel, to see if there was a message from a favourite cousin of Elena's, Alejo, whom I had tried to contact. There was. He insisted we ring him, no matter how late. 'I keep Spanish hours, you see,' he explained once I had managed at last to speak to him. We arranged to meet up in twenty minutes outside the main door of the cathedral. I sensed he would be our salvation.

Fog and persistent drizzle appeared to have set in for the night. In its midst I could see a man in a long overcoat walking towards us, instantly recognizing the two obvious gringos in the cathedral's vicinity. From close up he had a drooping moustache, a ponytail, and an elongated face like that of an El Greco knight. 'I would have met have you at your hotel,' he said with an amused smile, 'but after over thirty years of living in and around Mérida I have never heard anyone mention the Europa. Even after phoning the number you gave me I am still not convinced that the place exists.'

For many years Mérida's municipal architect and a part-time lecturer at the university, Alejo had taken early retirement so as to divide his time between an isolated house half an hour away from the town and a yacht moored at Puerto la Cruz. He had come into Mérida to attend the funeral of a colleague and had stayed on after hearing we were in town. He confessed that he was out of touch with the Mérida night scene, but he would take us to one of his favourite old haunts, the Bar Granada.

He reminded me of Elena not just physically, as Federico had done, but in his lively, observant and quick-witted manner, which I noticed even more when he reached the Bar Granada, a place satisfying a momentary pang of nostalgia of mine for Spain. I thought it ironic that this town which had done so much to help Bolívar liberate Venezuela from Spain seemed to have so many establishments catering to this nostalgia. The Bar Granada was authentically Spanish. After our recent experience in Hilario's studio, being with Alejo in this Triana-tiled bar and eating typical Andalusian tapas was wonderfully therapeutic. Alejo, who had not been there for ages, lamented the revamped decoration and the decline in the quality of the food, but was pleased to see many of its former clients, including some Spanish astronomers from a famous observatory in the Mucuchies.

Hearing we had not seen anything of that area because of the fog, Alejo offered to put us in touch with a cartographical company,

71

Los Andes Tropicales, which could organize an 'eco-tour' of the *páramos* for us. He would love to join us, he said, but he had got too used to his comforts, and had never been good with high altitudes. Despite having been born and spent much of his life in the Andes, he was, I was beginning to realize, an essentially Caribbean type, extrovert, sybaritic, in love with the sea.

Yet he had an instinctive understanding of what had drawn me to the Andes and what I was hoping to find here. The next day he became our guide to Mérida, taking us first of all to a pedestrian alley off the Plaza Bolívar, the Boulevard de los Pintores, where artists painted works to sell to tourists. Alejo went up to a worn and easily missed bronze plaque, in front of which was a painter engaged on a portrait of Bolívar riding through the Andes. 'When I was a student a friend of mine was pissing against this wall and looked up to find the name of Humboldt's companion Bonpland, whom he had always thought was one of history's great neglected geniuses. Someone later told him that Mérida was one of the few places in Latin America that commemorated him. Of course, as you know, neither Bonpland nor Humboldt ever came to the Venezuelan Andes.'

That virtually no one in Mérida knew of the existence of this tiny plaque was not really surprising. What did astound me was the neglect of the small, cliff-side garden to which Alejo drove us next. Along the balcony at its edge was a little pedimented tabernacle with crudely coloured blue columns and a lintel amateurishly hand-painted with the words BOLÍVAR Y HUMBOLDT. Within were bronze roundels of the two men, and an almost illegible marble inscription recording, with scant regard to historical fact, the 'noble friendship that grew under the shadow of these mountains'. The town's German community was apparently responsible for this. Humboldt would not have been pleased.

Nor would Bolívar have been happy with the fluted column in the middle of the garden's patch of sparse uncut grass. A bronze bust rested on its capital, while on its base was a rectangular hollow in which a bronze relief had obviously once been set. 'You wouldn't believe it,' said Alejo, 'but this was the first memorial erected anywhere in the world to Bolívar. I think it marks the actual spot where he was hailed as Liberator.' To check this, Alejo approached a soldier who stood outside a barracks at the top of the square. The soldier, looking hesitant, replied that it was. 'Are you sure?' persisted Alejo. No, the soldier was not. He suggested that Alejo ask his commander, who had been stationed at the barracks for twenty years. Alejo went inside the building and emerged about ten minutes later. 'Even after twenty years the man still does not know. Can you believe it? And I always thought soldiers had to study Bolívar's life as if it were the catechism.'

The thick clouds were rapidly lifting by now, exposing a brilliantly coloured panorama crowned high above us by the row of snowy peaks that made up the Balcony of Venezuela. Encouraged by this change of weather, we made plans for our trip into the *páramo*. Then we were driven by Alejo to his 'Andean retreat', a modern glass and wood construction overlooking a green and wooded valley broader but no less seductive than the one immediately below the town. 'You can understand now the hold the Andes still has on me,' said Alejo, as we walked around his flower-filled garden, pausing for a moment to admire a creature that symbolized the vitality of the tropics: the humming bird.

We could not leave Mérida without experiencing the town's most popular tourist attraction, its funicular railway, the longest and highest in the world. We booked our tickets early on our last morning in the town. Alejo declined to join us. The last time he had been on the funicular had been as a student, when he had fallen ill at the top and been brought back down wearing an oxygen mask. The ride, divided into four stages, is over twelve kilometres long and carries you up to a height of 4765 metres, nearly to the summit of Mount Bolívar. Many of those hundreds of tourists who daily undertake it suffer, unsurprisingly, from altitude sickness.

The very idea of such an ambitious construction dates back to the dictatorship of the Andean-born megalomaniac responsible for the Hotel Humboldt, Pérez Jímenez. The Mérida funicular railway is undoubtedly his most impressive legacy. Still one of the world's boldest feats of engineering, it must have seemed even more astonishing when completed in 1958.

Stalls selling sunglasses and warm clothing crowded the ticket office, as did notices warning people about the dramatic changes of temperature in the course of the ride and the potential dangers to those with asthmatic conditions and weak hearts. The morning was crystal clear and cloudless. The cabin swung off into space. Nearly an hour remained before we reached the highest of the funicular's four stations, in the course of which I would witness the full range of Venezuela's Andean scenery. Had this service existed in Humboldt's time, I thought as I peered down over fields of sugar cane and coffee, the German scientist would not have needed to climb Chimborazo to develop his grand theories of the cosmos.

The jolt on passing the first pylon, always one of the more worrying moments of any climb by funicular, brought us above the rainforest. A piped commentary in four languages kept us informed about the funicular's history and about each stage of the climb with their different flora and fauna. From the rainforest we leapt into the *páramo*, where we looked back towards a tilted relief map of infinite dark brown folds and minuscule grey peaks, glistening in the early-morning sun like gems under a microscope.

We had now reached the level of the *frailejones*, which seemed at first sight like giant pineapples, scattered across rocky slopes streaked by rushing streams. 'You will note also,' the voice continued, 'the path used since time immemorial by the inhabitants of the *páramo*, who can still be seen, with their mules and sheepskin jackets, making their way up to the hamlet of Los Nevados.' The ancient path could clearly be made out, but the only people negotiating it were a couple of backpackers nervously making their way past a herd of horned and hairy cattle.

In its last stage the funicular advanced near vertically towards a group of jagged peaks whose sheer rock faces were shiny with ice and patches of snow. We shot past a peak topped by a mannequin of a climber waving the Venezuelan flag, as if to ward away condors, though condors – as the voice reminded us – had disappeared from this part of the Andes. And then we reached the highest of the stations, the Pico Espejo, where one of the passengers, a middle-aged woman, got out and was violently sick.

We went for a short walk, past a concrete statue of the Virgin and up to a ridge-top viewing platform, where a faded map enabled us to identify Venezuela's three highest peaks, which, in descending order, were named after Bolívar, Humboldt and – I was pleased to discover – Bonpland. With the aid of a pair of binoculars I tried in vain to make out the bust of Bolívar that reputedly stood like a tor on top of the peak named after him. The view from the other side of the ridge disappeared into a mantle of cloud, above which rose the faraway peaks of Colombia's now terrorist-infested Sierra Nevada del Cocuy. In a gesture of Mediterranean bravado a couple of bronzed Italian men posed bare-chested for their girlfriends.

The clouds then advanced rapidly towards us, covering the top of Mount Bolívar within minutes, forcing the Italians to put their shirts back on and persuading Manolo and me to return to Mérida. The descending cabin appeared to be running away from the clouds, but they soon caught up with us, enveloping us in limbo. And then the cabin came to an abrupt halt, in mid-air, some fifty metres below the Pico Espejo.

The woman who had been sick at the top broke the silence by being sick again. One of her children burst into tears. Others started screaming. The wind was building up, and the sides of the cabin were becoming damp with condensation. The cabin rattled violently, a man fainted and a couple of women made the sign of the cross. Claustrophobia, agoraphobia and altitude sickness were spreading like an outbreak of hysteria.

I began studying the faces of our fellow passengers, mentally planning a work of fiction along the lines of Thornton Wilder's *The Bridge of San Luis Rey*, the story of the disparate lives of a group of unrelated people who happen to be on an Andean bridge at the moment it collapses, plunging them all into the abyss. Suddenly there was a loud noise from behind me, followed by shrieks. One of the bronzed Italians had stamped his foot as a joke, creating a surge of terror that gave way almost immediately to relief and laughter. The tense silence had finally been broken and we all began talking to each other, as we continued swinging in the clouds, discussing the power cuts that had become a regular feature of Venezuelan life.

Several hours after our safe return to Mérida we were in Alejo's car, talking to him about our funicular scare. 'I didn't want to frighten you beforehand,' he said, 'but stories such as these are always in the local papers. There are rumours that the funicular will soon be closed down indefinitely.'

Alejo had offered to drive us to the remote mountain farm which was our starting point for a three-day wander around the *páramo* of the Mucuchíes. We were back on the road on which we had first approached Mérida, but driving this time in late-afternoon sunlight. On the radio a reporter was giving a live account of the presidential inauguration of Chavez's Ecuadorian sympathizer Rafael Correa, who, in partial emulation of Bolivia's Evo Morales, had opted for a traditional ceremony in a Quechua-speaking Andean village. 'The Andes are in fashion,' commented Alejo wryly, as we continued climbing up into the mountains.

On the right of the road, just before coming to the village of Mucuchíes, Alejo pointed out the mountain track along which Bolívar had marched in 1812 and again in 1819. In that moment I was aware that we had just passed a monument of towering proportions. Alejo, who had not driven along the road for some time, dismissed this as 'some new Bolivarian monstrosity'. But he promised we would stop and have a closer look when he came back to collect us in three days' time.

After the village of Mucuchies, Alejo made a short detour to San Rafael de Mucuchies, the home village of a man whom he considered 'a true Andean hero', Juan Félix Sánchez. For Alejo, Félix Sánchez was the supreme example of the genius and ingenuity latent in this supposedly primitive region. The man had lived for most of his long life in a remote and isolated house right in the middle of the *páramos*, but he had gone back in his old age to live in the family home where Alejo now took us.

The house was a typical old Mucuchies home, with whitewashed walls, wooden-beam ceilings and a primitively arcaded central courtyard. Alejo had met Félix Sánchez here in the early 1990s, when the then nonagenarian and internationally famous master was bedridden, blind and living off charity. Umberto Eco had also come to the house at this time. Hanging near the entrance was a quote by Eco describing Félix Sánchez as 'a spiritual phenomenon who transcended the categories of the aesthetic and the ethnographic'.

Alejo had spoken about Félix Sánchez primarily as a self-taught sculptor, weaver and architect, but I soon learnt that this man had tried his hand at everything, including the installation as early as the 1940s of the village's first electrical generator. His tombstone, in a toy-like chapel he designed and built himself, had an inscription describing him as a 'sculptor, craftsman, tightrope walker, clown, architect, writer and philosopher'. A line from the great man himself was inscribed at the bottom of the slab: 'Wherever one passes, one should leave behind more than just a footprint.'

'It's a shame,' noted Alejo, as he continued driving us towards our night-time destination, 'that Félix Sánchez hadn't lived in Bolívar's day. There would have been no need to invent the story of that dog. Just imagine how the Bolívar legend would have been enhanced had the heroic general of noble birth met and made friends with his peasant counterpart.'

\*

77

Soon we were at the scattered hamlet of Mitibibó, where Alejo said goodbye to us at a house resembling a smaller and cruder version of Félix Sánchez's family home. A young woman from the *páramo*, María Romero, now studying architecture in Seville, had had the clever idea of putting up tourists in traditional Andean houses still used by the *páramo*'s inhabitants. Dubbing these places '*mucuposadas*', she saw them as boosting the local economy, helping to maintain the folk architecture of the area and giving tourists a unique opportunity of making contact with 'traditional Andean families'.

The agency, Los Andes Tropicales, had arranged for us to spend the first night of our *páramo* tour at the Mucuposada El Trigal ('The Wheatfield'). A ring of arid mountains enclosed an endearing small valley, with paths and rushing streams fringed by bands of grass, and stone-walled fields planted with potatoes and wheat. The agency leaflet referred to our surroundings as 'the most traditional *páramos* in the Mérida Cordillera', and ones 'which were considered sacred places by the Pre-Hispanic populations'.

Manolo, I noticed, was becoming ever more expansive as we settled into El Trigal and did our bit for 'responsible tourism' by getting to know the mucuposada's shy but friendly owners. Manolo had come to South America in search of worlds radically different to the one he had known all his life in rural Spain. And yet only now was he beginning to relax – in an environment which for him was not ethnographically exotic, but utterly familiar. Mitibibó, and its handful of interrelated families, immediately appealed to him. It reminded him of home.

I had always thought that close acquaintance with Frailes was an enormous help in understanding traditional rural communities the world over and Manolo was now confirming this. The similarities between life in Frailes and the *páramos* became even more striking once we had begun finding out about Mitibibó's rural calendar based on religious festivities, cattle fairs and such seasonal rituals as the annual pig slaughter. 'That's just what we do in our village,' an excited Manolo kept on saying – or more often, 'That's what we used to do, when I was a child.'

Manolo's nostalgia was reinforced by a visit to a flour mill, a modest blue-painted adobe structure with a commanding view of the valley. Manolo could hardly contain himself. 'That's just what the baker's was like in Frailes!' he exclaimed, as the owner milled some grains for us in a machine dating back to the 1950s.

Our sense of wonder persisted, as did the clear evening light. The miller's nine-year-old son was nagging us to come higher up the mountain, to a spot where another valley came into view. 'The observatory,' muttered the son. 'My teacher says it's the only place on the globe where you can see the southern and northern hemispheres.' Then the moon rose above the mountains and we walked back into the world of the past, under an expanding vault of stars.

# 7

# NEVADO THE DOG

I woke up after eight uninterrupted hours of sleep, untroubled by nightmares of Caracas, Hilario or the Colombian terrorists I might soon be facing. It was a freezing dawn, and María, the matriarch of El Trigal, was already up, kneading the daily supply of *arepas* – the corn pancakes that are one of Venezuela's main dietary staples. A tall man entered the room, wearing a white cowboy hat. He had a long narrow face, a drooping jaw and an inane grin that suggested inbreeding. María introduced him as Quique, and said that he would be guiding us over the mountains to our next night's stop, the Mucuposada Agüita Azul. It would be a short and easy day, she said, in case we suffered from '*mal de páramo*'. Quique had brought with him two horses, one to carry our luggage, the other to carry Manolo, an expert rider. I had said I preferred to walk.

The rising sun lit up the crest for which we were aiming, turning its tiny, puffy fringe of *frailejones* a luminous white. We left the valley and its cultivated fields, to ascend in zigzags up scorched, dark-brown slopes covered with a low shrub that traditionally provided the main source of fuel in the *páramos*. After only an hour the vista had widened and we could make out a growing number of other valleys converging like folds of crumpled paper towards the greater valley that led to Mérida. Quique, a man of few words, indicated with his forefinger the highest points in a saw-like silhouette of faraway peaks. He was pointing to the sacred trilogy comprising Bolívar, Humboldt and Bonpland.

We had reached the level of the *frailejones*, which, up close, were entirely different and much less impressive than I had imagined. Far from being the giant and malevolent creatures that could have inspired John Wyndham's apocalyptic novel *The Day of the Triffids*, they were small agave-like plants whose pale olive fronds sprouted from a tattered, yellowing base. Apparently we had just missed their period of brilliant yellow bloom. Quique told us that there were thirty-five different types of *frailejon* and these were the smallest, the *frailejones morrados*. These ones, he assured us, helped cure asthma and flu, but were very bad for the teeth of cows, which occasionally grazed on them. They were also used in the pressing of the local goat's cheese, which acquired a special flavour in the process. 'Very tasty,' he grinned, exposing a mouth that seemed to betray the plant's ill effects on human teeth as well.

Across the pass we descended sharply into a narrower and deeper valley, pressed in on both sides by precipitous mountain slopes and with a broad torrent flowing straight through the middle. The only sign of habitation was our next night's stop, a miniature white building standing at the top of a green field just above the river. Manolo managed to persuade me to take a turn at riding. I was anxious to learn some equestrian skills, to achieve a greater affinity with the Andean travellers I was interested in, not least with Bolívar himself. With Manolo's help I succeeded in mounting his short Andean horse, whose legs were barely longer than mine. However, I failed to persuade the creature to continue downhill. Manolo whacked the horse's flank, with predictable consequences. I was thrown headfirst on to a *frailejon*. Quique's grin was bigger than ever.

The *mucuposada* evoked for me neither Spain nor the dwellings of pre-Columbian man. Surrounded by simple stone walls prettily overgrown with flowers and ivy, it reminded me of a Welsh cottage tucked into one of the wild valleys above Abergavenny. A smiling woman with a woollen bonnet and ethnic cardigan was waiting for us on the doorstep. Unlike María and her family, she had no obvious trace of Latin or indigenous blood. Instead, with her pallid complexion, round gold-rimmed glasses and tufts of blonde hair peeking through the rim of her bonnet, she looked German perhaps or North American. Quique greeted her as Iris.

Iris said she had been observing our downhill progress for the past two hours. She took us inside the cottage, the interior of which, despite its Andean features such as a prominent crib, had something of a youth hostel about it. Iris's home was further down the valley, and she came to the *mucuposada* only to open it up and prepare food for 'the very occasional visitors'.

Her husband, a farmer with the quaintly Roman name of Eliseo, happened that day to be working in the fields behind the house. He dropped by to say hello. Serious, very formal and with the manner of someone who believed in the moral virtues of work, he spoke a stilted, ancient Spanish. 'You must forgive me,' he uttered after barely ten minutes in our company, 'I must withdraw. I have to return to my agricultural labours.'

The dog which had come with him stayed behind, to stretch himself out and fall asleep at my feet. 'He's very affectionate,' said Iris, 'he latches on to all newcomers. Often he prefers to stay here and spend the night with them rather than go back home.' He was a large dog, with thick orange-brown fur similar to that of Chumberry, but with white markings on his feet and face. I realized I was staring for the first time at a Mucuchies mastiff. 'He's called Nevado,' Iris continued, 'just like Bolívar's dog.'

Following directions given to me by Eliseo, I decided to go for a walk up the mountain facing the one from which we had come. He told me that after an hour or so I would find myself directly underneath 'Vulture's Peak', the summit of which was still streaked with snow. All I had to do was to keep close to 'the brook' and I would not get lost. And, if the worst came to the worst, I would be able to see the house for most of the walk.

After the unsettled weather we had had during our first days in Venezuela, the dry season seemed to have arrived. We could now expect, according to Eliseo, sunny mornings and clouds only by late afternoon, possibly accompanied by light rainfall. A few dark clouds had appeared by the time I went on my walk, and dusk was imminent. But I strode quickly and confidently up the mountain, unworried by terrain that was stonier and more overgrown than we had encountered earlier in the day.

The sky was completely overcast after forty-five minutes of walking, but I was enjoying the dramatic effects of the occasional tree silhouetted against lighter patches of cloud. Turning around to catch a last reassuring glimpse of the house, its lights now switched on, I scrambled over a ridge and tried to reach the view of Vulture's Peak before darkness made my return too difficult. I was just in time to catch a fleeting glimpse of snow in a world reduced to an ominous black and white.

I had reckoned I would make it back to the house just before night proper set in. But I had not imagined that the landscape would be so quickly enveloped by fog. I walked as quickly as I could back to where I thought I had last seen the house. But by now no lights were visible. The 'brook' was still beside me but, as I followed it downhill, it divided into other brooks, none of which I had noticed before. One of these ran through thick bracken, another disappeared among boulders, another led to a cliff, another trickled out altogether.

I became disoriented. I panicked. I envisaged breaking an ankle, succumbing to hypothermia. And as I tried rationalizing my fears, I became aware of a large animal advancing towards me in the fog – a wolf, a lynx, an Andean bear? Then I remembered the image on Hilario's easel. It was a Macuchies mastiff. Nevado had come to guide me home. He ran up to me, then ran back the way he had come, looking around every twenty metres or so to see if I was still behind.

I got back to the house to find that a power cut had occurred during my absence. Manolo was doing a Sudoku puzzle by candlelight, while Iris was using a torch as she put the final touches to a local dish of milk, eggs and potatoes called a Pisca Andina. She was not surprised by Nevado's behaviour. 'They're like that, those dogs. As it's now dark, he'll certainly be accompanying me back home later.'

Iris was back at the house early the next morning, her face as radiant as the dawn. She had been praying at the local chapel, as she did every morning at six o'clock. 'I have been praying for you both. The Andes are a dangerous place.' She laid out our breakfast of corn-cakes and homemade jam. 'And my prayers have brought you luck today. You're going to be accompanied by one of the best guides in the area.'

Edu, the guide, looked like a serious and sensitive student doing a holiday job. Bespectacled, lightly bearded and wearing a baseball cap, he appeared to have no obvious physical or mental defects. With Iris waving us goodbye with her smile of divinely induced contentment, we embarked on what Edu warned would be a 'long hard slog'.

Manolo was once again on horseback, while Edu and I were on foot, staying as best we could beside him. Without stopping, we gradually ascended the ever narrowing valley, with views only of the barren rocky slopes on either side of us. Manolo and Edu kept up a constant conversation about their lives.

Edu had indeed been an engineering student at Caracas University. But the pull of his native *páramos* had been stronger than his interest in engineering, so he returned to work on his family farm, which was when he met María Romero, founder of the *mucuposadas*. And María had told him that the future lay in eco-tourism.

So he became a guide for Los Andes Tropicales, which allowed him to do what he enjoyed best, wandering for hours in nature, studying plants and wildlife, supporting the environment, listening to foreigners talk about their own countries. If only there were more eco-tourists coming to the *páramos*, he sighed, before confiding that he had only about ten clients a month during the high season, and that the only way he could survive was by trying to pursue the self-sufficient lifestyle in the remote farm where he now lived with his wife and three young children, a good hour's uphill ride from their nearest neighbour.

Finally we climbed above the valley and into the domain of the *frailejones*. They were larger and more numerous than the ones we had seen the day before, and more like the science-fiction creatures I had expected. Growing straight out of the unforgiving rocky soil, they survived on the water that collected in giant hairy stems whose swollen upper extremities, with their crowning bursts of fronds, struggled to get nearer the sun. The higher and colder their surroundings, the taller the plants grew.

We had passed the 4000-metre mark when Manolo, the uprooted Frailero, insisted on having himself photographed next to a solitary *frailejon*, almost twice his height. Further up still, the plants multiplied as sinisterly as triffids, so that when we came to the freezing Lago de los Patos ('Duck Lake') serried ranks of them stood as if observing our every movement.

As we resumed our climb after lunch, the sun soon left us; views opened up of further bleak valleys and mountains. The path briefly became a gash in the cliff side until we reached a wide ridge littered with boulders and topped by a cairn. The wind was building up, carrying towards us distant rainclouds, so we did not linger at the summit, long enough only to take in the eerie frown of *frailejones*, whose grey-green fronds appeared frozen under the glacial sky. For the first time since reaching the Andes, I felt as if I were in a land that was not of this world.

The scene at the top of the pass was still haunting me late the next day, as Alejo drove us back to Mérida and on to the next stage of our journey. He had found me a leaflet published several years back by the Mérida Tourist Office. It was a reprint of the popular short story which Hilario had first mentioned. 'It's probably the only work people read today of Febres Cordero,' noted Alejo. The memory of boulders and *frailejones* touched by a preternatural stillness came back to me the moment I opened the touching tale of 'Nevado the Dog'.

Fog darkened a world that for Febres Cordero was like the ruins of a land once inhabited by giants and Cyclops. It was late afternoon in the winter of 1813, and Brigadier Simón Bolívar and a squadron of his cavalry were crossing the *páramos* on their way to recapture Caracas. In the middle of this desolate landscape they came across a house they assumed to be abandoned. But as they knocked on the door to make sure, a large black dog, with ears, tail and a spine as white as the snow of the Andes, rushed out to bar their way, barking furiously. The dog seemed prepared to take on the whole cavalry, a dozen of whose dragoons reacted by pointing their sabres at him. The commanding voice of Bolívar put a stop to their actions.

'Do not touch that animal!' he shouted. 'He's one of the most beautiful dogs I've ever seen!'

And at that moment the owner of the house, one Mr Pino, came out to scold the dog, who immediately stopped barking and went back inside the building, grumbling to himself. Mr Pino, a courteous man of strong republican sympathies, gave all the help he could to Bolívar and his officers, who wanted to know how to get to the village of Mucuchies, where they intended sleeping. Before leaving, Bolívar decided to take another look at the dog, who was called Nevado and was descended from mastiffs brought over by Spanish priests from the Pyrenees. Bolívar, unaware of the dog's Spanish pedigree, wondered whether he could obtain a puppy of the same type. Of course, said Mr Pino, who promised to send one to Mucuchies later that afternoon.

Mr Pino was true to his word. His twelve-year-old son Juan José arrived at Bolívar's lodgings carrying his father's gift. 'But that's Nevado himself,' protested the Liberator. 'He's only a puppy,' said Juan José, 'and he'll be of use to you for many years to come. My father wants you to have him as a souvenir of your visit to the *páramos*.' Bolívar started stroking Nevado, who soon learnt to respond in kind, occasionally jumping up with such force to embrace the Liberator that the diminutive man would lose his balance.

While still in the village Bolívar was told of an Indian cowherd, Tinjacá, who had known Nevado since the time he was born and was reputed to have complete control over the dog. Summoned into Bolívar's presence, Tinjacá impressed him by calling Nevado from a great distance with a whistling sound that Bolívar too would later learn. Nevado, together with Tinjacá, the dog's newly employed guardian, became henceforth integral to Bolívar's army, and was at the Liberator's side in the height of battle, and in Caracas at the time of the triumphant entry into the city in August 1813. The flowers thrown from balconies over Bolívar landed on Nevado as well. Nevado, commented Febres Cordero, was worthy of those flowers.

In the aftermath of this victory, with royalist troops recapturing Venezuela under the command of General Boves, the fortunes of Nevado and Tinjacá suffered a reversal comparable to that of their master. Boves, portrayed by Febres Cordero as a pantomime figure of evil, succeeded in capturing the dog and his guardian, but spared their lives in the hope that Nevado would in the end sniff out the Liberator's hiding place. Luckily the resourceful Nevado and Tinjacá managed to escape and then disappear, although avidly pursued both by Bolívar's and Boves's troops.

Several years later, when Bolívar was again passing through the *páramos*, this time on his way to Venezuela's final liberation, the Liberator had a hunch that Nevado might have returned to his former haunts. Hardly a day had passed without his thinking of his beloved dog. So it was in a deeply emotional state that he approached Mr Pino's isolated farm, only to find that the owner had died in the intervening years and the house was now deserted.

On the point of resigning himself to the dog's loss, he heard a distant voice shouting 'Long Live Bolívar! Long Live Bolívar!'

Out of the perpetual fog emerged Tinjacá to greet the Liberator with the words later perpetuated in everyday Venezuelan speech: 'Always at your command, my General.' 'And Nevado?' Bolívar anxiously asked. Tinjacá was about to call him when Bolívar decided himself to make the sound he had been taught years before. Pale with excitement, the Liberator scanned the horizon, until finally he saw Nevado running over a ridge. Within minutes the dog was rushing into the protection of the Liberator's cape.

From that time onwards, Bolívar, Nevado and Tinjacá were always together until the June day in 1821 when the Liberator was declared supreme victor at the battle of Carambobo. In the midst of his euphoria, Bolívar's main thought was for his dog. One of his men then nervously informed him that Tinjacá had been seriously wounded by a lance and that Nevado might also have suffered the same fate.

Hysterical with worry, he rushed to see Tinjacá, whom he found on the point of death. 'And Nevado?' he asked, as he had done in the *páramos*. But now no human sound was capable of calling the faithful Nevado to him. 'My general,' said the expiring Indian, 'they have killed our dog.' And in that moment a great tear welled up in the Liberator's eye.

'There used to be a charming small statue of Nevado in the centre of Mucuchies. And now they've built this,' said Alejo, stopping his car next to the roadside monument we had passed three days before. 'When I left you the other day I had to come and take a look. I could not believe at first that they could build such a huge monstrosity to commemorate Febres Cordero's slight little tale.'

We entered a massive stone enclosure, in the middle of which was a pile of projecting concrete slabs supporting a group of life-sized sculptures. It was the sort of absurd monument I had seen countless times in Russia and Eastern Europe during the communist period.

Except that instead of Lenin or some heroic steelworker, there was the spitting likeness of Chumberry, surrounded by the boy Juan José, the Indian Tinjacá and the caped Bolívar. In the background was a row of spikes I took to be the lances against which the valiant Nevado had thrown himself during his last battle.

'I now realize exactly why they've done this,' continued Alejo. 'They're probably about to begin a massive publicity campaign to market this breed of dog. It's the perfect pet for the Venezuelan patriot, a great souvenir of the *páramos*, a new symbol for the Bolivarian Republic. In the old days you'd see scores of Indian children selling off puppies by the roadside. Now, I imagine, they'll be sold through cheap deals on the internet.'

I went to take a closer look at the monument, and to say farewell to 'the beautiful dog who was worthy of the Liberator's tear'. This and other lines from Febres Cordero's tale were inscribed around the base, highlighting another side to the Liberator's personality, the side which showed that the great military leader, womanizer and magnanimous man of the people was also a human being capable of one of the most basic of emotions – a love of dogs.

However, as I thought more about the tale, I began to interpret it in a very different way to that intended by Febres Cordero. With the dog dying at the very moment of Bolívar's greatest triumph, the tale was perhaps really a bathetic commentary on the Liberator's life and on the ultimate shallowness of the glory he had so relentlessly pursued.

# 8

# DELIRIUM

The heavy, melancholy sky was turning bitumen black and a sudden wind began agitating the palms and the bushes. The last of the passengers rushed back into the bus, their leisurely conversations abruptly terminated by the changing weather and by the driver's repeated sounding of the horn. The dirty battered vehicle, so vulnerable in the face of the gathering storm, took off into the jungle to the accompaniment of mumbled talking, a sickly engine, the escalating drumming of rain and the piercing voice of a young American woman speaking on her mobile. The woman, freshly groomed and in neatly ironed cotton, was speaking to a man called Peter. 'We're trying to make it to the Colombian frontier,' she told him, 'the driver is hoping to get there before the road becomes impassable . . . Peter? . . . Peter? . . .' The line had gone dead, the track was getting rougher and the sky had become so dark that it could have been night. The bus struggled on for a few more kilometres and then skidded out of control, over ruts, stones and lianas, before finally getting stuck in a muddy hollow. Gasps, shrieks and the violent hurling of luggage to the ground gave way to an uneasy silence broken only by the odd wail, the fading patter of rain and a faint but growing rumbling. The American looked nervously around her, hoping perhaps for some explanation from her fellow passengers, but finding only the frozen faces of those who sensed the horror that was about to come.

We had been travelling since before dawn. The rain had been almost continuous from the time we had left Mérida's bus station. Instead of cutting through the mountains, our bus had descended at first into the *llanos* grasslands, to follow a dual carriageway past a featureless landscape shrouded in the distance by low-lying clouds. When eventually we returned to the Andes we could see even less, just fog, blinding rain, gaudily painted roadside bars, tin-roofed hamlets and blurred glimpses of a forest. There was little to distract me from morbid thoughts as we neared Colombia, and certainly not the Hollywood film being shown on the bus's video screen.

I was trying as hard as I could not to watch the film, which seemed intended to heighten my anxieties. Yet the piercing screams that now came from the screen forced my eyes again towards it, just in time to see it filled with a close-up of the American woman's face at the moment when the bus and all its passengers were dislodged from the mud and hurled over a precipice down to a river hundreds of metres below.

I had yet to become aware of the very real possibility of such catastrophes. I was still innocent enough to be far less concerned by natural dangers than by the desperation of human behaviour. All thoughts about the new environment I was about to enter had somehow come to be focused on the word 'delirium', which had recently been used as the title both of a show of unrestrained Colombian musical passion and of a powerful novel by the Colombian author Laura Restrepo, which, taking as its starting point a man's discovery that his beautiful young wife has gone suddenly mad, goes on to unravel a story not just of personal but also collective delirium, a story of a Colombia that fulfils general preconceptions of a country fractured by continual violence, guerrilla warfare, terrorism, drug-trafficking and a pervasive corruption.

91

Delirium . . . I kept on repeating the word to myself as my mind shifted restlessly between fears for my immediate future to my ever-present worries about my ailing 88-year-old mother, whose rapid decline into dementia had coincided with my last long stay in London, when I had been reading Restrepo's novel.

I went back to skimming a newspaper. Colombian guerrillas and paramilitaries were moving ever more freely into Táchira, unheeded by any government attempts to stop them. The older members of the Spanish family that had been captured by an unknown group in November were still being held in the jungle. A farm belonging to a family of hard-working and highly respected Colombian refugees had been attacked in the early hours of yesterday morning, leaving one of them killed and another missing. A bus, travelling by night to a remote mountain village near San Cristóbal de los Andes, had been held up by masked gunmen. Two of the passengers who had refused to hand over their money had been left seriously wounded by the roadside.

Over the past few days I had been pondering whether to travel from the Colombian border to Bogotá by plane, or to take the riskier but more attractive option and continue by bus. While Manolo was increasingly favouring the former, I had changed my mind six or seven times in the last twenty-four hours. Alejo had admitted that road travel in Colombia had become far easier and less dangerous in recent years, but said that he personally would not travel in this way. On the other hand, an elderly Colombian passenger who had been with us since Mérida was adamant that we would be completely safe if we stuck to the following rules: travel only by day and avoid at all costs the public bus station at the Colombian border town of Cúcuta.

The gloomy weather, the depressing Hollywood film and the unsettling local news were pushing me towards the plane option, until my mood lifted along with the clouds, less than half an hour from San Cristóbal. The emerging sun exposed a benign and friendly Andean panorama, gently rounded, intensely green, uninterrupted by snowy peaks or other elements of the sublime. San Cristóbal appeared from the distance to be a sparkling modern town unfolding amidst trees and extensive parkland, and crisscrossed by American-style highways. At closer quarters it revealed traces of its Spanish past such as a colonial-style nineteenth-century cathedral and a grand bullring whose whitewashed walls were plastered with posters promoting forthcoming fights. The town, as Alejo had told us, was in *fiesta* and its annual January fair was reputedly one of the liveliest in South America.

When our bus drove into the central station, my mind was full of the prospect of a night of Andalusian-style festivities. However, the person who came to meet us in the station had other plans for us, and further warnings. Gonzalo was a man in his late fifties, with thinning, brylcreemed black hair, an abundant moustache, an equally generous waist and an open, welcoming personality. I tried ineffectually to find any resemblance to his ethereally beautiful daughter Carolina, now living in Frailes.

'I've got good news for you,' he began. 'I've found an excellent place for you for tonight, clean, comfortable and, above all, safe. I was told that every room in town was taken because of the Feria. But the manager of the hotel where you will be staying is a good friend of mine and he did me a special favour.' The bad news came immediately afterwards.

'I've also asked around about the bus journey from Cúcuta. I strongly recommend you take the plane. This whole area is infested with guerrillas, paramilitaries and drug dealers. As soon as one of them spots a couple of foreigners like you, they'll be ringing up one of their colleagues further down the road.'

He said we would be all right up to Cúcuta, but he feared for our safety thereafter. The border areas of Colombia were among the principal remaining 'red zones' in the country. What was especially sad, in his opinion, was that we would be forced to miss the Sierra Nevada del Cocuy, which he had heard was one of the remotest and least-visited parts of the whole Andes, which unfortunately also made it a haven for 'undesirables'. The situation there had become tenser still recently, owing to the discovery of oil in land held sacred to the U'wa Indians. 'No,' he announced emphatically, 'I won't allow you to leave San Cristóbal without personally making sure you have bought your plane tickets. Carolina would never forgive me if anything happened to you.' Then his face assumed an expression of intense seriousness. 'We've now got to face a much more immediate problem. Where are we going to have lunch at this late hour?'

We were the last people to be served at a pleasant outdoor establishment set in leafy surroundings between the bullring and the grounds of the Feria. The owner, of course, was a friend of Gonzalo's. Gonzalo called the man over for confirmation of the dangers of the overland route through Colombia. The man smiled as if we were mad even to contemplate it. Later still, after a couple of whiskies on the rocks, we were listening to horror stories about San Cristóbal itself. It was no longer the safe, easy-going place it used to be. It had been infiltrated by Colombians and criminals. Kidnappings now regularly took place in broad daylight, and even the Feria had become notorious for muggings, pickpocketing and armed assault.

I recalled the pleasure-loving San Cristóbal that had been evoked for me by Alejo. He remembered in particular the days of the Feria, when life used to go on all night and the occasion attracted some of Spain's greatest bullfighters. 'But Cúcuta has changed even more,' Alejo had warned me. 'I used to love our monthly visits there. The main square, with its palms and elegant, turn-of-the-century cafés, was the ultimate in cosmopolitanism and sophistication.' Cúcuta today, I gathered, had turned into a tropical and threatening version of Andorra, an ugly tax haven buzzing with malarial mosquitoes and kidnappers.

Gonzalo succeeded in persuading us to limit our impressions of Cúcuta to its airport. He also weaned us away from San Cristóbal's Feria by ensuring that our first and only evening in his town was taken up almost entirely by visits to members of his large and delightful family. Manolo and I got to bed early, but were up again long before dawn. A trusted friend of Gonzalo's had come to drive us across into Colombia.

The driver was a serious young man who barely talked at first. Then we told him that Gonzalo had dissuaded us from taking the bus from Cúcuta. 'Two years ago,' said the driver, 'a favourite nephew of Gonzalo's had been travelling by bus into Colombia when his bus had been held up by paramilitaries. The next he heard about him the man had been killed. I too have a relative who disappeared in that way. Many people in this area have similar stories to tell.'

It was still pitch black when we arrived at the Venezuelan border town of San Antonio de Táchira. A solitary soldier directed our driver down dingy back streets to an equally unprepossessing Immigration Office, where we needed our passports stamped with a Venezuelan exit visa. A rough-voiced, unshaven soldier told us that the office was closed and that we should come back in two hours. We said we had a plane to catch before then. We proposed a bribe. The soldier yawned, took the money and stamped our passports.

As the sun rose over a tropical grey haze, we were already flying towards the Colombian capital of Bogotá. I was regretting not following at ground level the whole length of the green range that disappeared below us in and out of the greyness. Yet I knew that it was not just considerations of security and time that would prevent me from achieving anything other than the most partial vision of the Colombian Andes. It was the sheer complexity of this country's geography.

Had the weather conditions been clearer and the plane flying higher we would have seen that the Andes runs through Colombia in three separate cordilleras, which join together only at the southernmost tip of the country. The one continuing from Venezuela past

Cúcuta, down to the snowy Sierra Nevada del Cocuy and then to Bogotá and beyond is the eastern one and is divided from Medellín and the central cordillera by the enormous jungle-covered valley of the Magdalena. Another and more widely cultivated valley, that of the Cauca, lies between Medellín and the western cordillera, whose capital is Calí. Unconnected to any of these ranges, but often wrongly thought of as part of the Andes, is the Sierra Nevada de Santa Marta, whose steep, snowcapped slopes fall directly down to the sea through jungles populated by indigenous tribes and an expanding number of Colombia's illegal fighters.

High mountains and swampy and at times near-impenetrable jungle hindered the construction of a proper railway system in Colombia, so that overland travel in this country has nearly always been long and difficult. Colombia's traditionally poor communications and its fragmentary, often barely accessible terrain have in turn much to answer for this country's history of interminable internal conflict.

Laura Restrepo's novel *Delirium*, in seeking a reason for the protagonist's madness, delves ever deeper into her family's past, back to the time when her German-born grandfather moved to Colombia and thought he had found paradise. Similarly, in searching for the roots of the country's present-day problems, the historian has to unravel a history of violent rivalries stretching back to the 1530s, when Europeans first ventured into the Colombian interior.

The conquest of this interior proved far from straightforward. Whereas Pizarro's march into the Central Andes in 1532 brought about the almost immediate collapse of the Inca Empire with hardly any loss of life to the Spaniards, the establishment during these same years of what came to be called New Granada entailed costly, ill-conceived and often mutually antagonistic expeditions, during which the immense brutality displayed by the Europeans towards anyone who got in their way was more than matched by the scale of destruction within their own ranks, from disease, starvation, infighting and indigenous reprisals. The hope of finding an overland route to the South Seas, and even encountering the mythical 'land of cinnamon' (where the highly prized spice was said to grow in abundance), were major objectives for several of these adventurers. But as with Pizarro, the greatest incentive to those ragtag, multinational armies coming to brave the dangers lying beyond the Colombian coast was the prospect of discovering precious minerals, above all emeralds and gold.

That these minerals should be so difficult of access only added to their lure, and was also divinely ordained, according to a Jesuit naturalist of this time, José de Acosta, who believed that God had placed all this wealth with remote and primitive tribes to encourage Christians to come and show these people the true faith. However, the Christians would have made matters easier for themselves had they not also believed that gold was to be found the nearer you got to the equator and therefore the sun, and that their best course of action was to proceed inland by keeping as close as possible to rivers such as the Orinoco. They regarded the Andes at first simply as a formidable hazard impeding their true objectives, and they missed several opportunities to get to know the Andean tribe of the Muiscas, whose lavish adornments were a sign of the untold riches hidden in the mountains.

Contact was finally made with this tribe in the late 1530s and stories soon emerged of the gold-painted Muisca prince who threw offerings of gold into the sacred lake of Guatavita, a short distance to the north of the future Bogotá. The legend of El Dorado was born, and with this came a rush of explorers to Colombia's eastern cordillera. In the spring of 1539 three of the major figures associated with New Granada converged from different directions onto Muisca lands. One was the learned Jiménez de Quesada, who founded in that same year the town originally known as Santa Fe de Bogotá; another was the German Nicolaus Federmann, who was acting for the German banking family to whom the Spaniards had granted Venezuela, the Welsers; and the third was Pizarro's henchman Sebastian de Belalcázar, who, sent by Pizarro to chase Incas who had fled with their treasures into Ecuador, continued north into Colombia, founding in the process the cities of Cali and Popayán.

A wonderfully poetic vision of Colombian history appears in the Colombian novel that first popularized the notion of South America as a land of 'magical realism', Gabriel García Márquez's *One Hundred Years of Solitude*. Set in the imagined village of Macondo, in the far north of Colombia, it begins with the idyllic state of innocence of a village whose complete isolation from the outside world encourages a group of its men to make their way through the surrounding tropical swamps and mountains to find a route to the sea. In its description of the men's overwhelming awe at the silence and strangeness of the world, it captures the feelings of the first Spaniards, whose earlier presence is attested by the discovery in the middle of the jungle of a mysteriously stranded galleon.

The men give up in their attempt to reach the sea, but the outside world inevitably encroaches more and more on Macondo, and with this world comes death, a phenomenon hitherto unknown in the village. The greater part of the novel has as its background the ceaseless and senseless civil strife that took over Colombia after the ending of Spanish rule – a conflict to begin with essentially between Liberals and Conservatives, although those espousing these causes end up not knowing why they are doing so. One of them even concludes that all they are really fighting for is power.

The origins of the conflict in *One Hundred Years of Solitude* go back to the last years of Bolívar, when the Liberator had turned into one of those patriarchs so common to Márquez's fiction, 'lost in the immense solitude of his power', contemplating a labyrinth. At the root of Bolívar's and Colombia's tragedy was the Liberator's unwavering belief in centralist rule, which led to a major rift with his general Santander, who, like the Liberals who came after him, considered that such rule was impractical in a country so large and geographically diverse. Though the Greater Colombia that Bolívar had created did not survive even his lifetime, opposition between Centralists and Federalists continued long afterwards to be

Colombia's major political issue. The opposition was formalized in 1849 with the creation of the country's Conservative and Liberal parties, whose irreconcilable positions sparked a succession of wars culminating in 1899 in the so-called War of the Thousand Days, which left over 100,000 dead.

The Conservative victory at the end of this last war was followed by a period of relative tranquility, broken only by such incidents as the massacre in 1928 of three thousand workers at the American-owned United Fruit Company, an event also recorded in *One Hundred Years of Solitude*, though with more realism than magic. In 1948 Márquez himself was present in Bogotá when the charismatic and hugely popular Liberal leader Jorge Eliécer Gaitán was assassinated, an event that destroyed any chance of peace and which sparked off this city's equivalent of Caracas's Caracazo, the 'Bogotazo', the consequences of which was a civil war bloodier than any other, leading to well over 200,000 deaths and known with chilling simplicity as La Violencia.

A coup in 1953 brought briefly to power twentieth-century Colombia's only dictator, General Gustavo Rojas Pinilla, but in 1957 democracy returned in the form of a pact between Liberals and Conservatives, whereby each party would rule alternately for four years. However, ancestral hatreds could not be eradicated so easily. Tensions between the two parties increased as disillusioned Liberals veered increasingly towards Marxism, joining from the mid-1960s onwards outlawed groups such as the M-19 and the Fuerzas Armadas Revolucionarias de Colombia (FARC), which splintered into further groups such as the Ejército de Liberación Nacional (ELN) and the Ejército Popular de Liberación (EPL). To combat these groups, paramilitary organizations such as the Autodefensa Colombiana (AUC) were formed, which have generally been supported by the government. Guerrilla warfare has continued to this day, though, as with the fighting in *One Hundred Years of Solitude*, the idealistic aims have become blurred over the years, with guerrillas of all political persuasions now involving themselves in drug-trafficking, either as a way of raising money for their cause or as an end in itself.

The words 'brutal', 'violence' and above all 'labyrinth' seemed to have featured in every recent book I had read about Colombia. So I was surprised to find that my immediate impressions on arriving at Bogotá were of a strikingly modern world, ordered, efficient and completely lacking in menace. This agreed with what many people were saying about how Colombia had changed under the current presidency of Álvaro Urribe, a dry, unlovable and profoundly right-wing figure whose firm rule and fanatical anti-guerrilla and pro-American stance (his father had been killed by the FARC) had nonetheless helped remove much of the chaos and insecurity and won him the unlikely reputation of South America's most popular and successful president.

The bus station in particular seemed emblematic of the new Colombia, huge yet undaunting, and better organized and less seamy than any I had ever known. The heavy presence of soldiers armed with machine guns, a reminder of the grave problems still lurking beneath the surface, was, admittedly, needed to keep out unwanted elements from the main passenger area, such as pickpockets, lunatics, would-be porters, the homeless and representatives of rival bus companies desperate for clients. But at least this meant that you could choose a bus in a leisurely fashion from the huge selection of different companies and types of vehicles. With the aid of a friendly soldier, we opted for a large van, bought our tickets and were directed to one of the enclosed waiting areas assigned to each of the companies. We could have been in a VIP passenger lounge, as we reclined in our armchairs, drinking coffee.

The efficiency might have been Scandinavian, but the atmosphere was warmly Latin, with everyone striking up conversations with their neighbours and cracking jokes. The general amiability, punctuated by bursts of repartee, persisted once we had all crammed into the van, to be driven through the gently mountainous countryside.

We were off to see a couple of colonial towns just to the east of Bogotá, and were travelling through a short stretch of the eastern cordillera we had already glimpsed from the air. Sudden showers, alternating with ever larger breaks in the rising cover of clouds, revealed its emerald greenness. We were already in former Muisca territory and an appropriately golden light briefly illuminated the modern reservoir lying within a few miles of the perfect circle of Lake Guatavita, cradle of the El Dorado legend. A giant poster featuring the lake had welcomed us into the region of Boyacá, but visits to that hallowed place had been severely curtailed following centuries of ruinous attempts to dredge the waters in a largely futile search for gold.

Though the fabled lake could not be seen from the bus, we passed by another site of comparable status in the Colombian consciousness – the monument commemorating the battle of 25 July 1819 in which Bolívar had finally assured the liberation of the country from the Spaniards. Fought at Pantano de Vargas, but known generally as the battle of Boyacá, the battle had only narrowly been won by Bolívar, thanks less to a carefully worked out plan than to a near-psychopathic recklessness. The Liberator's strategy was to approach the Spaniards from a completely unexpected direction, which entailed marching hundreds of miles across the Orinoco plains during the flood season (the troops had to walk for long periods through waist-high water), and then climbing across the Andes by way of the desolate and freezing Páramo de Pisba. The surprise element worked, but at a tremendous cost: huge numbers of Bolívar's *llanero* troops, accustomed only to light clothing and sandals, died from exposure, while those who survived had to face a Spanish army that was well rested, much larger and better positioned. Only a desperate counter-attack led by an English legion whose colonel was killed, and the wild charge of some newly arrived *llanero* lancers, saved the day.

Our van climbed in a loop around this sprawling monument of gesticulating bronze figures. But my mind was not with Bolívar but with the Spaniards who had long preceded him here. The antiquated Spanish I was hearing all around me was taking me back to the area's earliest colonial times and also intensifying a curious sense of familiarity I had begun feeling at Bogotá's bus station, and which increased on reaching one of the first towns founded by the Spaniards in the Colombian interior – the district capital of Tunja. In being spirited back to the colonial past I was also returning to the 1960s, reliving my first, adolescent trips to a Spain I had romantically linked to its Golden Age.

Never before in my later travels through Hispanic lands had I been so vividly confronted as I was on this first day in Colombia with that Spain of my teens. To walk from Tunja's bus station through the narrow and grim residential streets and into a grand, formal seventeenth-century square on a massive scale, with palaces crowned with wooden galleries and churches with interiors encrusted from floor to ceiling with gilded ornamentation, was like stumbling across sleepy Castillian towns during the Franco period.

What reminded me of those years was the way in which the new and the old were casually intermingled, with little attempt to prettify the latter, as in the case of the place where we had lunch, a crowded, smoky establishment shiny with greasy formica and cheap tiles, lying behind one of the elegantly austere facades radiating from the main square. Even more evocative of the Spain I had once known was the friendliness and courtesy of the town's inhabitants, their relaxed attitude towards time and their fascination with foreigners. Entering a post office to buy some stamps involved long conversations about Europe, and being invited to share some exotic fruits; a trip to change money in a bank turned into a two-hour odyssey in which various charming employees were assigned to stay with us until the transaction was done; a visit to an empty local museum housed in a decayed palace replete with Talavera plates and other relics from the Old World led to our being escorted around the building by a gentle, elderly policeman with medals, braiding, a peaked hat and an immense curiosity about history.

I took a particular liking to this policeman. Referred to by everyone in the museum as Don Álvaro, he wanted to make clear to me that Colombia's colonial history was not just a story of atrocities against Indians, feats of empty heroism and a near-suicidal obsession with material wealth. He said we should always take into account the everyday reality of the past, which for him was contained in two photocopied pages he kept neatly folded in his jacket pocket. Sent to him by two visitors to the museum from Spain, they were taken from a book I too greatly treasured – a collection of sixteenth- and seventeenth-century letters written by ordinary Spanish emigrants to the New World and addressed to the families left behind in Europe. These letters told of the enormous pleasure of receiving news from loved ones, of the guilty consciences of men repeatedly claiming to their wives that they had not had dealings with other women, of the great fear of the sea-crossing from Europe and above all of the most acute homesickness. The photocopies were of letters specifically from Tunja, one of which – written by one Diego de Sandoval to his wife in Seville – poignantly conveyed an emotion common to them all: 'Since I have been in this land, my desire to have you by my side has been so acute as to take possession of me completely, and make any other happiness impossible.'

As Don Álvaro also noted, at least three of the more celebrated early personalities of Tunja were neither soldiers nor treasure seekers, but primarily intellectuals. The most successful of them materially was the royal scribe Juan Vargas, whose early-seventeenth-century house was covered, like the museum, with curious Renaissance-style frescoes with classical *putti*, griffons and cherubs mingling with exotic intrusions such as elephants, ostriches and jaguars. Better known outside Tunja was the older Juan Rodríguez Freyle, who popularized the El Dorado legend in his *Conquest and Discovery of the New Kingdom of Granada*, a highly readable mix of fact and fantasy with lengthy digressions on the awfulness of women. The third person mentioned by Don Álvaro was the Spanish-born vicar of Tunja, Juan de Castellanos, who had first come to the area as a member of Jímenez de Quesada's expedition of 1538. Don Álvaro appeared keen to expand my knowledge of Castellanos, but I had to stop him. Afternoon was turning into evening, and we wanted to arrive by nightfall at the nearby small township of Villa de Lleiva, by all accounts a place where I could immerse myself entirely in delusions about being back in distant colonial times.

A violent storm and the windiness of the mountain road slowed our bus down considerably and it was pitch black and moonless as we drew into Villa de Lleiva. Walking down a virtually deserted stone-paved street we could have been seventeenth-century travellers in search of an inn. Looking back over the past thirty-six hours, I realized that my fears of entering a world beset by delirium had developed into an ecstatic, dream-like state in which I myself appeared to be losing all touch with reality.

I was like an overwhelmed child, simultaneously elated and bewildered, as we pursued our quest for somewhere to stay in what seemed like a corner of seventeenth-century Spain, perfect in its preservation and detailing, with painted green balconies, simple arcading, sober plaster walls in whites and browns, and a massive square extending around a modest fountain to which a donkey was tied. It was the sort of town you might once have found in the Castillian region of La Mancha. It was a place where you could picture Don Quixote riding down the street.

Night-time, my susceptible mood and the recent end of the high tourist season disguised at first the reality of a town which had obviously become a summer and weekend retreat for the inhabitants of Bogotá, and whose picturesque buildings shielded craft shops, art galleries, rustic-style pizzerias and smart late-night bars. On closer inspection the place proved to be heading the way of the similarly intact Spanish town of Santillana del Mar, where intellectuals had once indulged in dreams of the Middle Ages and which had now become a bustling tourist trap.

Villa de Lleiva remained nonetheless a perfect place for a relaxing couple of nights, which we spent in a near-empty seventeenth-century mansion with a balconied courtyard lush with colourful trees and plants. Next to us was the family home of the town's most famous son, Antonio Ricaute, who fought with Bolívar and earned himself a place in Colombia's national anthem by supposedly blowing himself up rather than being captured by royalists (Bolívar later confessed that he made this story up 'to frighten the enemy').

The local monuments had little of the artistic or historical interest of those of Tunja, but the general pleasantness of the town, with its wooded and agricultural surroundings, idyllic nearby waterfall and lively Saturday market full of basketwork, weaving, and fruit and vegetables that neither I nor Manolo could identity, heightened our anticipation of what Colombia had in store for us. My greatest revelation in Villa de Lleiva was a purely cerebral one, experienced in our hotel shortly after Manolo had gone to bed. I was curious to know something about the history of the house we were in, and was told by the receptionist that it had belonged until his recent death to an American anthropologist called Richard Darmuton. Would I like to have a look at his large library of Colombian books, which the hotel management had acquired along with the building?

I settled down in an armchair with a volume that particularly caught my attention, partly because it was about Juan de Castellanos and partly because its author was a well-known contemporary Colombian poet called William Ospina. I had been invited in a few days' time to an international literary festival at the Caribbean town of Cartagena de Indias and Ospina was one of the authors whom I imagined I would meet there.

The book, *Dawns of Blood*, still had its flyer, which carried a quote by García Márquez calling it 'one of the finest works published in Colombia in the twentieth century'. I soon found myself wanting to heap even greater superlatives on it. I stayed reading for three hours, unable to let go of what was one of the most eloquent works of literary criticism I could remember, as well as an astonishingly successful piece of literary resuscitation. Except that the word 'resuscitation' was an inappropriate one to someone who had almost no previous literary reputation at all.

The persuasiveness of Ospina in convincing the reader that Castellanos was responsible for nothing less than the 'poetic discovery of America' owes much to the lucidity and hallucinatory beauty of a prose that captures the exceptional degree to which minds such as Castellanos's must have been stimulated by the revelation within such a short span of time of so many novel sights, experiences and sensations.

The facts of Castellanos's life, as outlined by Ospina, were not unusual for his time:

> The sixteenth century was like that. A man could have been the assistant to a scholar of oratory in Seville, and later an ocean traveller, a pearl fisher in Cubagua, and an adventurer in Curazao, a merchant in Margarita, a soldier in the army that conquered the deserts of Guajira, a searcher for gold in the Sierra Nevada de Santa Marta, and a military chaplain, and then afterwards a canon and treasurer to an Indian cathedral, the Parish priest of a war zone, and a convicted offender, and still not have found his true and irrefutable vocation. Castellanos had been exactly this man; and there still awaited him, at the age of forty, the great work to which he would dedicate half his life.

This work, taking him more than thirty years, was his monumental poem, *Elegies of the Illustrious Men of the Indies*, which in his lifetime fell into a literary void, being too historical for poets and too poetical for historians. It was remembered in later years mainly for the dubious distinction of being the longest poem in the Spanish language. A very different reception greeted Alonso Ercilla's near-contemporary epic *La Araucana*, which relates the author's experiences fighting the courageous Araucanian Indians in the far south of the continent, and was hailed from the start as the first great work of literature inspired by the New World. It succeeded where Castellanos's work did not because it wooed its Spanish public by evoking the faraway and unimaginable in a language this public would have understood – the rhetorical language of the classical epic.

Yet, as Ospina argues, the very fact that Castellanos does not cloak America in the expected classical apparel, but instead resorts to a rich and pioneering use of Indian names and terms, makes him the first authentic voice of the continent, which he conveys both in its immensity and its minutiae. Castellanos describes with encyclopaedic obsessiveness a dazzling multiplicity of phenomena – rains that never end, earthquakes, poisoned arrows, cauterization of wounds with red-hot metal, landslides, unpredictable seas, hurricanes, treasures guarded by Indian curses – and does so with the ability to marvel of a generation for whom America had yet to become 'the delirious prolongation of Europe', 'the final resting place of all Europe's dreams and lunacies'.

It was now three o'clock in the morning, and I could take in only odd phrases, images and ideas. Pulling myself at last from the armchair, I went off to bed, to lie for a few moments pondering the idea that the obscure Castellanos was more important than anyone could possibly have imagined, a key figure in that South American labyrinth linking magical realism with the world of another of that elite band of early travellers who came to this continent not just to plunder or evangelize but to engage in the far more important activity of learning – Alexander von Humboldt. I had not thought about the German scientist since he had disappeared with Bonpland down the Orinoco River, bewitched by the solitude of the Amazonian jungle. But I was about to catch up with him again, on his way finally towards a land of volcanoes, snows and hitherto unclimbed heights.

# 9

# THE CONSOLATION
# OF PLANTS

The sea was a different Caribbean from the calm translucent one that had greeted Humboldt on his arrival at Cumaná nearly two years before. An easterly gale was blowing, violently tossing the small vessel that was carrying him and Bonpland towards the port of Cartagena de Indias, 350 kilometres to the west. The coast was fast approaching, the sea was getting rougher and the pilot was trying to butt their way into harbour when a giant wave broke over them, leaving the boat lurching dangerously to one side, unable to right itself and on the point of turning over completely. 'I can't control the rudder!' shouted the pilot.

The sea had become a curse. In November 1800, soon after returning from the Orinoco, they had sailed from Cumaná to Cuba in a boat alternately delayed by calms and nearly destroyed by storms until finally catching fire. Then, after settling in to Havana, the Caribbean's busiest port, and still with virtually no news from Europe, they had to assume that much of what had been sent to them had been lost at sea, whether as a result of shipwrecks or pirate attacks. All this made Humboldt worry more than ever about the fate of the countless letters and geological, botanical and other natural-history specimens they were trusting to boats. His fears were confirmed when, a month after their arrival in Cuba, reports arrived of the wrecking off the coast of Africa of a ship carrying a large group of their plant collections (which had already been devastated by the tropical conditions) and all the insects that the ill-fated Bonpland had 'brought together under the most difficult circumstances'.

Humboldt, stoically, came to accept the strong possibility that either he, or Bonpland, or indeed both of them, would die in the course of their American adventures. So far luck had been on their side, aided by equal doses of optimism and – in Humboldt's case at least – an almost superhuman constitution. He must have been one of those infuriating travelling companions who never seem to suffer from anything. In his letters he emphasized how good the tropics had been for his health and how he had never felt better or stronger in his life. Whereas Bonpland had been laid low by fevers and malaria, Humboldt had suffered from little more than momentary discomfort caused by eating on one occasion too much bread too quickly. 'I work a lot,' Humboldt admitted to his botanist friend Karl Ludwig Wildenow, 'sleep little; and, while making my astronomical observations, am often exposed to the sun for up to five or six hours, without a hat.'

The ordeals they had gone through would certainly have defeated weaker individuals. For four months on their Orinoco voyage they had 'slept in the middle of the jungle, surrounded by crocodiles, boa constrictors and tigers (who attack canoes), eating nothing but rice, ants, yucca, bananas, and the odd monkey, and drinking straight from the river'. For one stretch of 'eight thousand square leagues', rowing continuously, their faces 'swollen from mosquito bites', they had not seen a single other human being.

Yet throughout all this Humboldt was sustained by his ability to marvel at everything. 'What a treasury of marvellous plants to be found between the Orinoco and the Amazon, a land covered in virgin forests, and inhabited by such a huge variety of different species of monkeys! . . . I repeat, I am now absolutely convinced that we are ignorant of three-fifths of the existing plant life on earth!'

Not only had Humboldt observed, recorded and collected innumerable botanical and zoological specimens and deepened his astronomical studies. He had also consolidated methods and ideas that were far ahead of his time. His life-long obsession with making scholarship accessible to everyone and his interdisciplinary approach to the sciences were now firmly allied to a belief that all natural phenomena needed to be understood in the context of their environment and that scientists should not just rely on books, herbariums and other secondary material. A pioneering ecologist, his experiences in the tropics made him perhaps the first scientist to recognize that deforestation (which he had witnessed in Venezuela) could potentially effect climate change and have a disastrous impact on the environment. He also developed in America his views on the equality of all peoples, the repressiveness of the colonial system, and the evils of slavery, his loathing of which became particularly strong during his three months in Cuba, where he dedicated much of his time to devising sugar-processing techniques that would greatly reduce the amount of slave labour needed.

Humboldt's passion for new experiences was such that he was reluctant to interrupt his wanderings and field researches to stay put long enough to publish the information and ideas he had gathered. He had reached that stage in travelling when it seemed impossible to imagine any other form of existence. With nothing published so far of his trip, with much of his collected material destroyed and the whereabouts of so much else he had dispatched unknown, Humboldt began planning the next stage of his journey with Bonpland. They would go to Mexico, then along the west coast of North America, up to the Canadian lakes, down to Ohio, along the still largely unexplored Mississippi and then back to Europe by way of the Philippines, Bombay, Aleppo and Constantinople.

They intended setting off on the next stage of their journey as soon as they had overseen the shipment of their material from

Cuba. But by the time they were ready to leave, an article in the local newspaper *La Gaceta* led to a complete change of itinerary. They read that Captain Baudin, with whom they had intended two years earlier to go round the world, was finally about to begin his journey. His idea was to sail first to Cape Horn and then to Peru. Humboldt, who had promised Baudin that he and Bonpland would do their best to join the expedition, determined now to head for Lima. The quickest route was by way of Cartagena de Indias.

This was why the two men were now trying to reach Cartagena's harbour, perhaps regretting their change of plan as they contemplated the strong possibility of their imminent deaths. But luck remained on their side. With the ship on the point of capsizing and the rudder not working, the sailors managed to right the vessel by cutting off a large section of trailing sail. Riding on the crest of another wave, the ship made its way around a promontory and into the safety of a protected bay, where the captain decided to spend the night. The night, however, was no ordinary one, as it coincided with an eclipse of the moon, which the ever excited Humboldt thought would be best observed from the shore. After being rowed there by a couple of helpers, he was alarmed by the sounds of shouting and the clanking of chains. A group of desperate black convicts, newly escaped from Cartagena's gaol, were rushing towards them brandishing axes. They clearly had every intention of killing them and stealing the rowing boat. Humboldt's group made a mad rush back towards the boat, their pursuers only seconds behind them. For the second time in little more than two hours, Humboldt's life hung in the balance.

Smiling black waiters dressed in loose, colourful cotton were strolling to and from the kitchen of Cartagena's yachting club, bringing food and drink to a long table shaded by palms and parasols. The humid heat of early afternoon was blurring the blues of a background bay flecked by yachts and surfers fading into a distant haze of apartment blocks. Seated at the table was a curious group made up mainly of European writers and journalists, but with a Colombian host, a couple connected with the British Embassy at Bogotá and the director of the British-organized literary festival that had brought us all together. I was one of four journalists invited to the festival as part of a press trip arranged by a Colombian export company. We stood out from the others by having been made to wear yellow T-shirts printed with the slogan with which Colombia hoped to woo foreign tourists: COLOMBIA IS PASSION.

A beautiful young Indian poetess was feigning polite interest as I told her what had happened to Humboldt in the bay below us. The festival director opposite me was staring periodically at his watch and wearing an ever thinner smile. A travel correspondent for the *Daily Telegraph* was asking her neighbour where Caracas was. The literary editor of the *Independent* was having an intense discussion about literature with the Norwegian authoress of *The Bookseller of Kabul*. The British Embassy couple was still wondering whether the empty seat next to them was going to be filled by celebrity guest Bob Geldof. Manolo, isolated at the far end of the table, gave me a wink and a wave.

This seemed a good moment to provoke an argument. I suggested to our Colombian host that the slogan 'Colombia is Passion' might be inappropriate for a country attempting to shake off its image of violence. The man smiled and talked about market research, while his neighbour, a respected British media personality, said that she 'rather liked the slogan'. Everyone agreed with her, including the glamorous editor of *Condé Nast Traveller*, who told me that I did not like the slogan because men could not appreciate passion in the same way women did. I protested that I liked passion as much as anyone, but the festival director was rising at this point from his seat and my words appeared instantly to vaporize into the hot, salty air.

It was already our third day in Cartagena, to where Manolo and I had flown immediately on our return from Villa de Lleiva, abruptly moving from an Andean to a Caribbean environment, from cold grey skies to sultry heat and a thriving enclave of international tourism that had been suddenly invaded by the motliest collection of writers and media types.

The festival's lectures, interviews, poetry readings and discussions (attended by a Colombian audience apparently desperate for literature) were less engaging for me than the pleasures of joining the crowds that thronged the old town's colourful grid of colonial streets. Distracted by this vibrant street life, I got to know most of the 'famous' writers merely as fleeting apparitions. Gabriel García Márquez proved elusive, while my only glimpse of William Ospina was as a bearded man in a panama hat striding past.

The one Colombian with whom I did become good friends was not a writer. Rafael Martínez, whom I had met through investigating Colombian food, was in charge of Cartagena's Cookery School. Silver-haired, and recently separated from his wife, he was a hedonist of enormous charm and energy. When I told him that everyone at the yachting club had loved the slogan 'Colombia is Passion', he said that most Colombians loathed it. In our subsequent search for an alternative, I toyed for a while with 'Colombia is Delirium.' But Rafael came out with an alliterative slogan that, he said, summed up his whole philosophy of life: 'Colombia is *Chévere.*'

'*Chévere?*' Manolo and I exclaimed simultaneously.

'Yes,' said Rafael. 'It's an expression often used today in Colombia and perhaps in some parts of Ecuador. Some say – horror of horrors – that it derives from a popular make of North American car, the Chevrolet.'

'But what does it mean?' I asked.

'I've heard some American tourists translate it as "cool", but that doesn't do it justice at all. *Chévere* . . . How should I put it? . . . *Chévere* implies a profound sense of well-being. I know what . . . Tomorrow is your last full day here, isn't it? Well, what would you say if we left the writers to their intellectual games and spent the whole day and night in pursuit of *chévere?*'

We agreed and met him the next day at a bar at eleven o'clock in the morning. The bar, a small smoky venue lurking behind an old arcade overlooking the Spanish fortifications, was a famous salsa venue. I was expecting live performances, but what we got instead was a large screen projecting salsa videos to a crowd of hardened drinkers.

Over the first of several bottles of freezing beer, Rafael outlined to me his theory of Caribbean culture and food: 'The Caribbean has always been what Cartagena is like today – a meeting place of different cultures, a refuge for adventurers from all over the world. The Spaniards, the English, the Africans, the French, the Dutch, all have left their imprint on the Caribbean, as you can see in the exotic richness of its food, literature, music . . . All these influences help explain the extraordinary creativity of the Caribbean people. I don't think there's any other part of the world as creative as this. No wonder that Humboldt, on passing through these lands, thought he was approaching the source of the life force . . .'

'Where else but the Caribbean,' he continued, pointing to the screen, and competing with the voice of Panamanian singer, song-writer and politician Rubén Blades, 'would you get a musician who's also his country's Minister of Culture?'

'Why bother with the Andes?' he teasingly asked after we had moved off to a friend's nearby restaurant, the Santísimo (the 'Holy of Holies'). 'Why not stay here? The coastal people are friendlier, more relaxed, more open . . . It's a different world that begins in Bogotá, less sensual, more conditioned by the hardness of the climate, the relentless greyness . . . Even the women there are less beautiful . . .'

By now I was beginning to understand what he meant by *chévere*. We were sitting in the cheerful colonial courtyard of the Santísimo, drinking a chilled Chilean wine and eating a succession of colourful and sensual Caribbean dishes, featuring curried prawns, mango-flavoured sauces, rice speckled with beans and spices, and the seductively named 'Temptation Plantains', which

Rafael joked were an excellent aphrodisiac. Rafael's quieter but equally sybaritic elder brother (the director of the local tourist board) had joined us, as had the restaurant's owner and chef, Fernando Moreno, who described his picaresque progress from washing dishes in a London pub to putting on dinner parties in his native Medellín for the likes of the drug baron Pablo Escobar. 'All that's lacking for the full *chévere* experience,' said Rafael, after asking Fernando to bring out a bottle of the best vintage rum, 'are some warm and sensuous Caribbean women.'

He tried remedying this by nightfall. Following a series of calls made on his office phone, he beamingly announced that he had spoken to a friend of his who was going to bring over to the Cookery School two 'sensational cousins of his'. Bob Geldof (a hitherto unknown musician in Colombia) was about to make his Colombian debut on the square outside and Rafael thought that the balcony of his school would be a civilized place to hear the concert. 'The security tonight in the square is ridiculous,' he commented, as police helicopters swirled above us, preparing for the arrival of Colombia's vice-president. 'The people in Bogotá forget that Cartagena is not like the capital. Terrorists and guerrillas have always had a pact never to touch the place.'

The worn Irish strains of Geldof's music made a surprising impact on Rafael and his circle of friends, aided perhaps by the copious quantities of rum and whisky, and, of course, the presence of the 'sensational cousins', who turned out to be not sensational at all but simply young, friendly and scantily dressed. When the concert had ended Rafael proposed that they should join us at a late-night bar appropriately named Carpe Diem, where a three-piece band was playing.

The mood of the night became progressively livelier and odder, with Rafael introducing me to a brother of García Márquez and the youngest daughter of Charlie Chaplin. Marquez's brother proved an excellent salsa dancer, while Chaplin's daughter could barely stand. Rafael himself, mouthing *chévere* to me over the loud music, walked up to the band and began playing the maracas with a perfect, infectious sense of rhythm.

Pushing out to sea moments before his pursuers could grasp his rowing boat, Humboldt was already being directed by fate towards Bogotá and the Andes. The fast way to Lima from Cartagena was to sail via the isthmus of Panama. But the delays in reaching Cartagena meant that the trade winds of the Pacific were over for the season and the voyage could take three months. Recent maritime experiences made this an unattractive prospect, and Humboldt and Bonpland were inclining towards the far more arduous land route to Lima. Travelling by land, furthermore, would enable them to study the Andes, with their extraordinary line of high volcanoes extending all the way down to Peru. More immediately, it would take them to Bogotá, where there lived the greatest botanist of the age, the Spaniard José Celestino Mutis. They had heard wonderful reports about Mutis's plant collections. On 19 April 1801, after less than three weeks in Cartagena, they headed off towards the mouth of the Magdalena River. They had embarked on a journey to Lima that would take them one and a half years.

The hardships and dangers of the Colombian stretch alone could have been relayed to them in great detail by Mutis himself, who had first travelled to Bogotá over forty years earlier, when he was twenty-eight. Mutis, a native of the ancient Andalusian port of Cádiz, was a man whose whole personality revolved around a lifelong obsession with plants. He had trained as a Jesuit priest and doctor but the pull of botany had made him accept the post of personal physician to the newly appointed Spanish Viceroy to New Granada, Pedro Messía de la Cerda. Setting off from Madrid for Bogotá in July 1760, Mutis would not reach the Colombian capital until late in the February of the following year.

The bulk of Mutis's overland journey had been through the jungles of the Magdalena Valley, whose plant life would provide him with material for a lifetime. More than twenty years later, when

116

Mutis had finally got permission from Spain to organize the Royal Botanical Expedition to the Kingdom of New Granada, this valley would become the focus of researches lasting thirty-two years and accumulating 20,000 types of plant and 7000 animal species. The valley's wonders were balanced by the difficulties of working there:

> A traveller must spend the greater part of the night ordering and laying out all that he has collected during the day, having suffered, of course, from the various changes of weather, which tend to be very extreme; the ruggedness and precipitous nature of the terrain he has traversed; and the scares and dangers of the many poisonous and fearful animals he is likely to come across. All these factors are a constant reminder of the austerity and harshness of a life in which the body is gradually worn down and destroyed.

Mutis did not have the robustness and cheerful disposition of Humboldt, who made little of his forty-five days canoeing up the Magdalena, a strong current against them, the river almost overflowing, and the rains and insects unceasing. Even Bonpland managed to stay fit while eight of their crew of twenty Indians had to be sent home in a state of exhaustion and the remaining twelve developed appalling tropical ulcers.

Colombia being a country where transport had gone straight from mules to airplanes, travellers from the coast to Bogotá had to continue taking the Magdalena route well into the twentieth century. Admittedly a steamboat replaced the canoes from the middle of the nineteenth century, but massive deforestation from the 1860s onwards was as devastating as Humboldt might have predicted. The deterioration of the Magdalena ecosystem did more than just irreparably damage the flora and fauna. It also made travel along the river increasingly unreliable, with the water level so low between December and April that stretches were often completely unnavigable.

Those setting out for Bogotá along the Magdalena generally hoped to make it as far along the river as the once-insignificant settlement of Honda, near to which, at Mariquita, Mutis planted Colombia's first botanical garden in 1761. The idea behind this garden was to propagate and study the plants and trees from which came some of Colombia's most important natural products, such as coffee, cinnamon and quinine. The last of these, derived from the bark of the cinchona tree and for many years the main defence against malaria, was discovered by the Quechua Indians of Peru, but Mutis controversially claimed to be the first person properly to examine its medical properties. Ironically, repeated malarial fevers eventually forced him to abandon his house and garden at Mariquita and settle permanently in Bogotá.

The road connecting the low-lying, tropically humid Honda to the invigorating heights of Bogotá's plateau was notoriously bad in Mutis's time, and would remain as such for the next hundred years. After 1900 an impressively engineered railway line came to the rescue of travellers ascending from the Magdalena up to Bogotá. The whole journey from the coast was undertaken in 1943 by the timid and impecunious fifteen-year-old García Márquez, who was going to Bogotá in the hope of obtaining a government scholarship to continue his education. He had never been away before from the tropical coast, and he did not realize what he had let himself in for until after leaving the steamboat and starting the climb by train. He felt mounting trepidation as, with each bend of the line, the atmosphere became colder and thinner, breathing became more difficult and his fellow *costeños* started to shiver and develop headaches.

The same journey from the coast was experienced four years later by Christopher Isherwood, who was at the start of a six-month journey through South America. The prospect of the continent continued to frighten him but he kept at bay the blackness of mood that would overtake him later in the trip. He had enjoyed Cartagena, was still getting on well with his irascible and alcoholic young partner Bill Caskey and – while slowly chugging down the

The Difficult Pass from Honda to Bogotá, from Alcide d'Orbigny,
*Voyage pittoresque dans les deux amériques*

Magdalena – 'never tired of watching the gradual unwinding of the river and the shores'. But something happened to him after getting onto the train. It was as if the thrills of the ascent up into the Andes had merged into a premonition of sadness and fear:

Above the woods are pale barren upland meadows, sloping steeply from ridges of naked rock. The gorges far below are choked with thick white cloud; now and then you get tremendous glimpses of precipice and valley. The terror of the great mountains stirs in you. Man ought not to live up here. It is far too high. The villages have a strangely mournful atmosphere of squalor, quite different from the squalor of the lowlands. Their huts look cold and wet and sad. Along the river, there was always laughter and shouting and the waving of hands. Here, the dark Indian faces are smiling and aloof. Wrapped in their small blanket-capes, people go silently about their business, or crouch in doorways, staring.

\*

119

The delayed plane from Cartagena was arriving at Bogotá in the middle of the night. I could clearly picture the city as I had first seen it flying in from Cúcuta nine days before – scattered toy-like over a giant green board wedged into the mountains, like a lost world. The picture vanished soon after landing at a now almost empty airport, where a passenger van was waiting to drive us to the centre of the city. We formed the press party. A travel journalist lay slouched and yawning on the back seat, while two literary editors were sitting exhausted in front of me, tall, hunched, grey and cadaverous. Manolo and I, the only ones smiling, remained glued to the windows, scanning the post-apocalyptic Bogotá for signs of human survival.

But there were none, and we drove towards the centre through a growing silence and darkness, eventually entering a grid of colonial streets that could have been the alleys of a cemetery. It was only then that we saw the soldiers. They stood in pairs at every street corner, their machine guns poised and ready to use. 'What's happening?' asked a nervous editor, as a soldier waved down our vehicle. 'It's a Sunday night,' explained the long-haired young woman assigned to look after us, 'people have to work tomorrow.' 'But the soldiers?' 'We're near the president's palace,' she said, leaning over to listen to the driver. 'It seems we might have to walk from here.' We followed her down a street and into the green mausoleum of the Hotel Opera.

I lay sleepless for ages, remembering the descriptions of Bogotá of earlier travellers, all of them critical. My childhood hero Aimé Tschiffely had thought the place of little interest, with 'streets in terrible condition, uneven and full of holes which were filled with water owing to the recent rains'. 'In the mornings,' wrote Isherwood after just a few days here, 'I feel tense, restless, and uneasy; in the afternoons lazy, exhausted and sad.' For García Márquez, accustomed to the sensuality and easy ways of the coast, the shock of Bogotá was so great that he would look back to the moment he first arrived there as the worst in his life. No one was waiting for him as, damp, freezing and breathing with difficulty, he dragged his heavy suitcase out into a world that seemed to him like the inside of a coffin. 'Bogotá in those days,' he recalled, 'was a remote and lugubrious city where an insomniac drizzle had been falling since the early sixteenth century. I was struck by the large number of men rushing around in the streets, dressed, as I had been then, in black cloth and unforgiving hats. In contrast, you could not see a single woman, their consoling presence being banned from the somber cafés of the business heart of the city.'

Unable to get back to sleep, I peered through the bedroom curtains onto a carless street frozen by the greyish-blue light of a cloudless dawn. Within half an hour I was down in a lobby already coming to life with businessmen trickling in and out of the breakfast room. I did not stop. I strolled out into the colonial district of the Candelaria.

Straight, narrow streets of low, whitewashed buildings with wide eaves and black-grilled windows ran uphill to forested mountain slopes streaked with cliffs. I walked in the opposite direction, down towards the enormous, adjacent squares named after Bolívar and his Colombian intellectual counterpart Nariño. Echoes of Spain in the baroque mass of the twin-towered cathedral were overridden by an overall French-style classicism, which confused me with memories of the royal palace district of Brussels. This was the civic and political heart of Bogotá, and quaintly uniformed palace guards with bayonets and pointed metal hats were supplemented by soldiers asking for identification, and a row of tanks. As they looked at my passport, retrieved from a hidden pocket next to my underwear, I looked across the square to the austerely modern Palacio de Justicia, whose recent history helped explain President Uribe's obsession with security. It had been rebuilt twice in the last sixty years, most recently in 1985 after it had been gutted by fire in a government attempt to oust M-19 guerrillas who had taken possession of the place. Before that it had been destroyed by rioters during the Bogatazo of 1948. On my roundabout way back to the hotel, I stumbled across the plaque marking the assassination that had sparked off the riots. Jorge Eliécer Gaitán had been killed on 9 April 1948, only six months after Isherwood's visit to the city.

The two literary editors were seated tensely in the hotel's breakfast room, one of them reading an abridged version of Humboldt's travels. Imogen, the travel correspondent, was telling us about an aspect of Colombia's floral life that Mutis could not possibly have foreseen: Colombia, together with Ecuador and Holland, was the world's greatest exporter of flowers. She was currently writing an article about this to be published on Valentine's Day. Such was the urgency of this piece that she sadly could not come on the official tour which we were waiting impatiently to begin.

Velkis, the long-haired young woman from the night before, apologized that she had been held up by traffic. Elegantly dressed, with a long black skirt embroidered with an ethnic swirl, she introduced us to our guide, a woman of Andean origins with straight black hair, a broad face and almost oriental eyes. Milena was shy, quietly spoken and projected none of Velkis's obviously privileged background. When Manolo and I got to know her better, she amused us by innocently referring to Velkis as 'a woman of advanced economic possibilities'. 'In Spain,' laughed Manolo, 'we just say spoilt brat.'

As Milena spoke in hesitant English about what we were going to see in Bogotá, Velkis handed out another T-shirt with the city's new tourist logo: 'And you, what do you know about Bogotá?' The press party tried pooling its knowledge of the city and had to admit that this did not amount to much. It was clear that the main purpose of the trip was to clear our minds of any negative prejudices we might have and see Bogotá as a vibrant city of the future.

We left the city centre, crossing bland US-style suburban developments to visit a park smelling of newly mown grass. The park, inevitably, was known as the Parque Simón Bolívar. The place, more surprisingly, was Bogotá's new public library. Bogotá has always prided itself on being a book-loving place, and even Isherwood said that he had never seen so many bookshops. We appreciated for an hour the building's pleasant exterior, and eventually found an open glass door that allowed us into a room containing a less-than-astonishing index catalogue. The Humboldt-reading editor politely suggested to Velkis that, as first-time visitors to Bogotá, we might perhaps find more instructive a museum or two, the odd colonial church, even an attractive viewpoint.

The hint was taken. Our tour of Bogotá assumed a more conventional character, revealing a city with the potential to become a major centre of international tourism, with art museums that made those of Caracas seem shameful and chaotic; an old-fashioned funicular railway spiriting you into a bucolic mountain paradise with woods of the brightest emerald green; and a nearby 'cathedral' quarried out of giant chambers of salt from deep inside the Muisca mines that had been visited by Humboldt.

Early on our last morning in Bogotá we were taken to the Gold Museum, a place so important that even Imogen, still engaged on her Valentine's Day article, was sternly told to stop playing truant and come with us. 'I'm so bo-red with gold,' she pronounced in a worn-out voice, as we gathered in a vault dominated by a one of South America's greatest pre-Incan treasures, a golden raft. 'This is the fourth Gold Museum I've seen in the last two months. They're all the effing same, excuse my French.'

We were driven soon afterwards to the airport, the two literary editors to fly back to England, the travel journalist to continue on to the carnival at Rio. Manolo and I were headed for Medellín and the central Cordillera.

Humboldt and Bonpland made it up to the plateau of Bogotá by 6 July 1801, with the Frenchman suffering from altitude sickness and a recurrence of malaria. The German, of course, was in the finest of spirits, though surprised perhaps at the reception that awaited them on the outskirts of the city. As guests of the distinguished Mutis, a cavalcade of costumed horsemen had been sent out to greet them, accompanied by sixty or more of the city's leading citizens. To Humboldt's amusement, he was invited to sit in the Archbishop's six-horse, London-built carriage. Arriving thus at Mutis's house, having picked up on the way a crowd of shouting schoolchildren and street urchins, they were, in Humboldt's words, 'warmly embraced' by the seventy-year-old botanist. Humboldt, in his habitual striped trousers, and clasping the barometer from which he was never parted, immediately and typically started talking of the plants he had seen during the day. Then they sat down to a marvellous banquet, at which 'I just couldn't believe my eyes when the famous Salvador Rizo, to whom Cavanilles had dedicated a plant, appeared as a waiter and served us at table.'

Mutis's widowed sister-in-law was moved out of her house so that Humboldt and Bonpland could stay next to the great botanist, whose plant collections were said by the German to be equalled only by those kept in London by Captain Cook's scientist Joseph Banks. With Bonpland laid low by malaria, Humboldt had plenty of time to study them. Not until 8 September of that year were the two men able to leave the city and head off south on their journey down the Andes. As for Mutis, he would die of a stroke in Bogotá seven years later. In 1816, with the long-term future of the Spaniards in New Granada increasingly in doubt, his collections would be transferred to Spain, to the Royal Botanical Garden in Madrid.

# 10

# TO THE ENCHANTED LAKE

And so we continued on south towards the land of volcanoes. Humboldt and Bonpland had done so the hard way, descending back into the upper Magdalena Valley, then up into the Cordillera Occidental over the notoriously dangerous and difficult Quindio Pass. The two of them, bringing with them provisions to last a month and refusing on principle to be carried up on chairs saddled to Indians, had climbed steeply up through uninhabited forest, emerged beyond onto vertiginous ledges blocked regularly by passing oxen, and then descended on the other side in continual torrential rain, across swampy ground and over bamboo shoots that ruined their boots and left their feet soaking and bleeding. Manolo and I did much of the journey by plane.

As Manolo's month away from home was fast running out, we decided to fly as far south as Cali, after a detour to Medellín and the Cordillera Central. From the moment of our arrival at Medellín, up to the end of our stay in Colombia, it was as if we were on a journey ever nearer to paradise. The physical sufferings of Humboldt and Bonpland seemed as far removed from our experiences of this part of the Andes as were the terrible histories of many of the places we passed through, beginning with Medellín itself.

'We call our city "The City of Eternal Spring",' said the young taxi driver as he drove us to the city from its distant airport. I thought at first he was being ironic. I knew that Medellín had changed radically since the shooting of Pablo Escobar in 1993, but I still thought of it as the city with the highest homicide level and worst drug cartel in the world.

'You've just come from Bogotá, haven't you?' persisted the taxi driver. 'Weren't you struck by the difference of temperature as soon as you got out of the plane? This is what it's like here, always warm, but never too hot, rarely cold. It's the best climate in the world.'

'And we have Colombia's most beautiful women,' he added, as we drove out of a forest to see Medellín leisurely spreading over the greenest of mountain valleys.

'In Europe we have a different image of Medellín,' interrupted Manolo, from the back of the taxi.

'Well, of course,' said the driver, 'we've had our problems in the past but, thank God, they're over now. Medellín is now one of the world's safest cities. Of course, like any city, there are parts you wouldn't visit by night, or for that matter by day. But on the whole . . .'

Then he quoted a local saying that perhaps every traveller should remember: 'We, the good, shall always outnumber the bad' (it sounded rather better in Spanish, '*Los buenos somos más*'). And with that he left us in an upmarket suburb, indistinguishable from somewhere in the United States, with little shaded gardens, trees and even a shopping mall with muzak and a branch of Dunkin' Donuts. One of the redbrick bungalows had been converted, incongruously, into the Australian-run backpacker's hostel where we went to stay.

Staying in the hostel made me feel that my life too had become one eternal spring. I barely slept for all the dormitory's sounds of sexual activity, rustling of backpacks, turning on of lights, pre-dawn departures and exchanges of travelling experiences. But I got up the next morning feeling forty years younger, with the sense of a whole life ahead of me and the thrill of a new city to visit.

Medellín did not disappoint. A stagnant and unimportant place in Humboldt's day, it had grown through coffee and textiles into a thriving late-nineteenth-century industrial town, full of towering neo-gothic edifices and other grand civic buildings in stone and brick. Seen from the long open sections of its impressive new Metro, it had something of the look of a Victorian boom town such as Manchester. But the greenness of the surroundings and the fresh-ness of the early-morning sun made it seem more like the vision of an early Utopian planner. Blair Niles, an indefatigable British trav-eller of the 1920s, was as unprepared as I was for this vision, writing of 'the pastoral peace' dominating Medellín's 'factories and mills' and of the way the place 'becomes for you a psalm of "green pastures and still waters"'.

The one complaint of earlier travellers was that it was a city of no culture whose inhabitants talked only about business. Today, it was difficult to look anywhere without seeing posters advertising a major cultural event or else some monumental work of art.

The next day we took a bus over Medellín's forested mountains and down to the region's former capital, Santa Fe de Antioquia. Only two and a half hours from Medellín, yet in a balmy, humid world of rare and exotic plant life, Santa Fe had grown up with the mining of gold in the sixteenth century, only to be stunted three hundred years later by the loss of its status as capital. A harmony of cobbled streets, blindingly white walls and coloured wooden grilles and balconies, it was like an intimate Andalusian village stranded in time and the tropics, and still dominated by the influ-ence of the Church. As in the old days of Spanish travelling, everyone referred us to the parish priest, regarded as the source of all wisdom and the holder of all keys. He was a friendly young man who showed us into a former Jesuit church quaintly resembling a

127

model in chocolate and marzipan of the Jesuiti in Rome. He also arranged for a seminarist to drive us to what the priest considered Santa Fe's greatest attraction after its nationally renowned Holy Week – a long and narrow late-nineteenth-century suspension bridge across the broad and fast-flowing Cauca.

That was when the vision recurred. The seminarist, shy and embarrassingly polite, was negotiating a steep, downward bend when a view opened up like a stage curtain being raised. The faint haziness of earlier had lifted. In its place was a shimmering clarity illuminating an idealized landscape painting from seventeenth-century Rome. The murky blue Cauca River, directly below us, made up the foreground, while the background was composed of a series of bands of diminishing intensity of colour, first the river's protecting ruff of trees, then scrubland, and then finally successive rows of arid mountains forming our first sighting of the Cordillera Occidental, whose furthest peaks, still in full sunlight, were becoming a timid purple. Instead of some classical temple, the artist of this perfectly balanced scene had placed a delicate and elegant bridge, whose black cables were suspended from elongated white pyramids that appeared from afar like the tombs of ancient heroes.

The plane from Medellín to Cali, the last I would take in the Andes, followed the bucolic Cauca Valley south, towards its source in the mountains near Popayán. Coffee plantations were to this valley what olives were to my adopted region of Jaén, but the crops of this potentially rich area had not always brought wealth, as was noted by an American traveller of the 1850s, Isaac Hutton. Hutton revealed his northern blood by claiming that the poverty then rife in the valley was caused by the laziness of the inhabitants. 'Their valley seems to be enriched with the greatest fertility and the finest climate in the world only to show the miraculous power of idleness and unthrift to keep a land poor.'

Cali itself was just beginning by Hutton's day to shake off three centuries of colonial stagnation, to become 'one of those old towns that I love to meet with, where most of the architecture is solid, and few indeed of the roofs are thatched'. Hutton was able to see two splendid colonial churches, a 'well-ordered primary girls' school', and a 'rude' loom which went some way to explaining why Colombia had yet to become a modern industrialized country. Had Hutton come to Cali forty-five years later, after the arrival here of the railway, he would have seen a place developing into a major centre of the sugar and other industries, with a vital strategic position both on the main route to Ecuador and at the head of the passage to Colombia's only important Pacific port, at Buenaventura. Had Hutton come here today he would have found Colombia's second-largest city, as well as a place whose huge black population has provided its principal fame for tourists: as the world's salsa capital.

Loud salsa hindered conversation in the taxi taking us from Cali's airport. The driver, tall, black and with dark glasses, was alternately listening to a cassette tape, answering his mobile and making comments neither Manolo nor I could properly hear. 'Sorry?' we both said in unison, for about the fifth time. 'The women of Cali,' repeated the driver, 'they're the most beautiful in the world.' 'And the women of Medellín?' ventured Manolo. 'No comparison.'

We were crossing dry, flat land like that of the African savannah and reaching the dusty outskirts of a chaotic-looking sprawl built at the foot of mountains daubed in green and ochres.

Cali struck me on arrival as the quintessential Colombian destination I had always imagined – humid, dirty, untidy and vibrant, with gaudily painted, fairground-style buses regularly hooting past, their wooden rows of seats crammed with loudly chatting passengers. Parts of downtown Cali were like a giant street market. On the quieter fringes of the centre, the odd white colonial building cowered beneath modern office blocks. The area where we stayed had restaurants and faded villas radiating upwards from a tree-lined river. The city's vitality had extended even to these more sedate, outer reaches, as had an infectious friendliness manifest in the number of passers-by who smiled at you, gave you the thumbs-up sign, helped you gracefully with directions, slapped you on the back and took an interest in where you were from.

'The place has always reminded me of Newcastle,' said Rod Wooden, an actor and playwright who had a small apartment just up the road from our hotel. I did not immediately spot the resemblance. But then Rod was from Newcastle, and had lived in Cali for years. The two cities had for him the same openness, the same raw edge. But he could never return to live in Newcastle. He loved Cali too much.

He appeared to be someone who did not quite belong anywhere. An actress friend in London had put me in touch with him. She did not know what he was doing out there. 'Must be some Colombian girl he's fallen in love with.' He was a couple of years older than me, but when I first saw him, walking towards our agreed meeting point, he seemed much younger, with long blond hair, a patterned cotton shirt and something about him of the eternal hippy. He took us to his house, almost a bed-sit, occupied mainly by books and a large computer screen, and with a ladder leading up to the roof terrace, where we sat. There was no sign of any woman.

Only when we were sitting did I notice his pallor and thinness. He was sensitive, quietly spoken and serious, an obsessive traveller, and happy to talk. Journalists came often to see him in Cali, to use his contacts and find out what was really happening in Colombia. 'But they always dramatize Colombia, make it far more dangerous than it actually is. That makes for better copy.' Martin Amis had recently written about a visit to one of the city's poorer districts. 'You'd have thought from his article that he spent his time in Cali under a constant hail of bullets.'

When he walked with us late at night back to our hotel, he asked us where we were heading next. I said to Popayán, and then to Pasto and the Ecuadorian border. 'The most dangerous road in Colombia,' he muttered. 'That's what it used to be known as. You never knew when your bus was going to be stopped, or by who. There were almost daily kidnappings and violent attacks. It's all right now, but you should still be careful, and don't travel by night. It still goes through what they call here "a hot zone". There's heavy fighting going on about forty kilometres away.'

He told me to keep in touch by e-mail. He had a great longing to spend more time in the Andes, though not in Ecuador, 'the convent of South America', but in Peru, or further south, in Patagonia or perhaps Tierra del Fuego. He had always been drawn to the end of the world.

At an internet café the next morning I found an e-mail from Rod, sending me some of his stories of Colombia, written under a pseudonym, sharp and atmospheric, poignant records of lives lived fully under the constant presence of death. There was also a message from Milena, telling me never to lose my smile, and one too from an old American friend, Dick Mahoney, whom I had not seen for ages.

Dick had a habit of reinventing himself two or three times a decade. The last time I had been with him he had been standing for the US Senate and fighting for the legal rights of Arizona's homeless Mexicans. Later I heard that he had moved to Buenos Aires to make a documentary chronicling the evils of North American intervention in South America. Now he was writing to me to say he was about to fly to Colombia. He knew about my Andean trip and was curious to know how far south I had reached. I stared disbelievingly at his next sentence. He said he would be arriving by nightfall at Cali.

He turned up at the lobby of the hotel by lunchtime the next day. I had been wondering about what had brought him to Colombia. I did not have to wonder for long. With him was a tall black Colombian woman, about thirty years his junior, with a broad smile and perfect figure. Dick removed his arms from her waist for the time it took to give me an embrace and shake Manolo's hand. His friend's name was Darlenys. They had met on the internet several months before, but last night was the first time they had been together.

Dick had not changed a bit. With his crew cut, muscular body, piggy blue eyes and slightly brutish, weather-worn features, he looked the archetypal brash Irish-American. Darlenys laughed as he talked about when we had first known each other, in a house full of 'sexually repressed Englishmen' to whom he had had to give constant advice about how to 'get women'. Yet there was another, completely contradictory side to Dick's personality, subtle, sharp, sophisticated and charismatic. As Darlenys led us to a place where we could have lunch and celebrate our reunion, Dick's mobile rang. It was Hugo Chávez's secretary. Dick had been granted an audience next week with 'Señor Presidente'. It appeared that he was keen to premiere Dick's documentary, *Creating Enemies*, which pointed to the CIA's role in Venezuela's recent coup.

Politics, sex and South America alternated as conversational topics over a lunch at which Dick smothered his food in a chili sauce most people would have found overwhelming. Darlenys was keen to discuss plans for the night, when we would all be meeting up again. As we were in the world's salsa capital, there was not so much to discuss. We would all go to a *salsateca* in the outlying nightclub district of Juanchito. Darlenys said she had the perfect woman for me, a cousin of hers. Weakly I said I was still the shy and inhibited Englishman of thirty years back. 'Give us a break, Michael,' exclaimed Dick, who later murmured to me in an aside: 'South America is the last resort for people like you and me.' He spelt this out. 'There's no stigma attached here to being an older man. We can have all the young women we want.'

Frances, my chosen partner, was introduced to me that night as we waited for a taxi outside the housing estate where Darlenys lived. She could have been little older that twenty, was more statuesque still than her supposed cousin, and was wearing a tightly fitting, shiny brown sequin outfit that left much of her body exposed. 'Michael's a very interesting man,' said Darlenys, trying to encourage her. 'And very interested,' added Dick. Frances's moon-like face, so unusual in this city of such expressive inhabitants, registered an off-putting blankness. Should I stand any chance of seducing her, I reckoned that this would not be because of a shared interest in Humboldt. I would have to make a dramatic improvement as a dancer.

We were driven into the savannah-like landscape surrounding the airport and on to a long wide road flanked by billboards and neon lights. 'Colombia, don't you just love the place?' commented Dick. 'Dance halls and hotels, sex and dancing, that's all there is.' Darlenys' favourite place was a 1960s *salsateca* with a massive oval dance floor like the ring of an art deco coliseum. There were plush crimson velvet walls, a couple of waitresses, numerous hefty bouncers and not a single client other than us. It was the sort of place where you could imagine a criminal confraternity gathered in a back room.

After an hour a few couples trickled in, some of whom started dancing, with a consummate professionalism but little sense of joy. Dick had disappeared somewhere with Darlenys and conversation with Frances had come to a stop. Dick finally reappeared to sweep Darlenys on to the dance floor and show himself as adept with salsa as he was with everything else. The pressure on me to do the same with Frances was growing. In the end she took the initiative herself and grabbed me by the hand. I tried warning her that I had no sense of rhythm or coordination, indeed I would be an embarrassment to her and a liability, and Manolo would be a much better choice of partner. But Manolo shook his head with a teasing smile and Frances advised me simply to listen carefully to the music.

I should have paid heed to my grandmother and learnt to dance when I was young. But bad dancing ran in my blood as surely as Irish genes ran in Dick's. My father had been an atrocious dancer, as had his own father before him, though both of them, like me, had always been willing to have a go. In the right mood, with a tolerant partner with the same sense of humour, I enjoyed nothing more than a burst of spontaneous, enthusiastic dancing. A *salsateca* where everyone was critically observing your movements was not the right place for this; nor was Frances the right person.

Her near-naked body was in close proximity to mine, and still I could not work out what if anything was on her mind. My dangerous and jerky dancing made her neither embarrassed, nor amused, nor even angry. She was dancing apparently merely out of obligation to her cousin, just as I was doing so largely because I was in Cali. My mind was elsewhere. I was nearing Humboldt's source of the life force, in a land where ageing men could enjoy an eternal youth, with a representative of the most beautiful womanhood on earth. And all I could think of was the condor I had seen that afternoon in Cali's zoo.

It was the first time in my life I had seen a condor. We had gone to the zoo after leaving Dick and Darlenys to their after-lunch siesta. The place was pleasant enough, located further up the wooded mountain slope from our hotel and with a river cascading through the middle of it. One of its more popular attractions was a butterfly enclosure where you could walk through thousands of multi-coloured, delicately flapping wings. Another, much-vaunted feature was the shy and retiring Spotted Andean Bear, South America's only bear and a creature – according to the information panel – who was 'considered a big brother to the Tuneo Indians'. The bear remained resolutely in hiding. Unlike the condor. The condor had nowhere to hide. Nor were there many people wanting to see him.

The condor was in a cage which Manolo calculated could be barely larger than his wingspan. We knew he was a 'he' because it said so on the plastic panel in front of him. Looking curiously unimpressive with his wings closed, like an unhappily over-sized turkey, he avoided our gaze as he prowled up and down a cage littered with the carcasses of what were said to be organically raised mice. For some reason he then decided to turn to us. Perhaps he had sensed we were travellers on our way to his true habitat, the high Andes. He encouraged us by staring straight into our eyes and spreading out his wings to their full extent, a good three metres. 'I'll do this for you,' he seemed to be saying, 'but you must get me out of here.'

True to Manolo's prediction, the wings of this sacred bird, ultimate symbol of the Andes, almost reached the sides of his cage. Humboldt had been amazed by the condor's remarkable adaptability, by how the bird's lungs and body temperature could cope with flying from heights of over three thousand metres down into tropical forests. But I could not imagine the bird being happy here, trapped in the sweltering heat of Cali. We looked at him pitifully as he violently flapped his wings for a few moments as if he were desperate to leave his prison, to come with us, to return to his homeland. Then he realized there was nothing we could do for him. He shrank back to his resigned, diminished state of before, picking at carcasses.

The cane fields of the Cauca Valley lay below us, as we drove in a minibus through fresh green foothills. The sky was completely clear, the greens were becoming greener and the blues more translucent. The outskirts of Colombia's 'white jewel', the colonial city of Popayán, appeared in the distance, sparkling in an early-morning landscape that Isherwood described as 'wonderfully peaceful . . . like New England with exotic vegetable touches – the sharp-leaved fibrous agave, the feathery bamboo, the palm'.

Popayán, the first settlement founded by Pizarro's henchman Belalcázar, was to Cali what Santa Fe de Antioquia was to Medellín, except that it was a long-established university town comparable in fame to Oxford or Cambridge. In terms of the survival of its colonial architecture, it had had the luck of Santa Fe of having lost in the nineteenth century its status as district capital. However, in other respects it had not been so fortunate.

On Maundy Thursday, 1983, it had been struck by an earthquake measuring 5.5 on the Richter scale. The English writer Charles Nicholl, hoping for a pleasant break from a dangerous assignment researching the Colombian cocaine trade, had arrived there the night before, still carrying in his memory an idyllic impression of the town from twelve years previously – 'the rinsed mountain air, the cobbled streets, the rococo colonial buildings, the seventeenth-century university, the chic restaurants, the leather shops, all bright white against the surrounding green hills, and all very much alive, no museum piece'. Luckily for him, as it turned out, there was no room available in the town's old colonial heart, so he had to settle for a place in 'a down-market, newish part of town'. Just after eight o'clock on the Thursday morning, he was woken up by 'an evil grumbling that swiftly became a roar'. Though his room had shaken so violently that he had taken refuge under his bed, he was not aware of the extent of the tragedy until walking later into the centre, which he found reduced to a cordoned-off bomb site. 'The churches, the cloistered university, the Hotel Monasterio were all in ruins.'

Since then Popayán had been reconstructed to appear exactly as it had been before . But for those who had known the town before the earthquake, the place had never really recovered. And it was not just nature that had intervened. Until only a few years ago the town had virtually been cut off from the rest of Colombia by intense fighting between guerrillas, paramilitaries and the army.

'Tourists simply stopped coming,' said the elderly waiter who served us our breakfast in the palatial green cloisters of the Hotel Monasterio, looking now as gloriously eighteenth century as if nothing had ever happened to it. The rest of the town, too, had a joyous if slightly over-restored aspect, with wide, uniformly white streets of baroque and rococo buildings converging onto a central square whose cathedral's original dome and roof had collapsed in 1983, killing the many people inside who had been attending early morning mass. If you could clear your mind of such apocalyptic visions you could still understand how Isherwood had found the town 'much the nicest place' he had seen so far on his journey south from Cartagena.

We did all the tourist things in a town where foreign tourists still remained a discreet presence. We followed a Way of the Cross up to a neoclassical sanctuary, for what seemed like an architect's panorama of the town, its sharply foreshortened grid of streets receding towards hazy mountains. We thought we could make out the first of the volcanoes we had so far seen on our trip, Mount Purancé. What we did see, as we returned down the hill and headed towards the town centre, was our first unmistakably indigenous Andean inhabitant – a woman dressed in her traditional costume, her baby in a sling, a coloured reed hat with tassels tied to her head. We were getting ever nearer to a more stereotypically Andean world, as we became aware on reaching the main square, where a thrilled Manolo had his first encounter with a llama, albeit a clean and prettified one, wearing a straw hat and woollen blanket so that tourists could photograph him.

While Manolo did exactly that, I went up to the statue in the centre of the square, the only main square we had come to in Colombia and Venezuela not named after Bolívar and lacking the usual pompous bronze of the Liberator. The statue, like the square itself, commemorated instead Humboldt's younger scientist contemporary Francisco José de Caldas, 'Caldas the Wise'. He was standing in a flowing cape next to a large globe. His face was long, pensive and lugubrious.

I felt I already knew Caldas personally from immersing myself in his diaries and letters, from which a vivid if difficult personality emerges. Superficially he had much in common with Humboldt, notably an encylopaedic interest in all natural phenomena: beginning his career as a member of Mutis's Royal Botanical Expedition to New Granada, and then going on to such achievements as determining altitude by variation in the boiling point of water, he had ended up in charge of Bogotá's newly founded observatory. Yet, unlike Humboldt, his passionate love of science and the recognition he received for his work did not prevent him from feeling often embittered, frustrated, jealous and under-appreciated.

'I am a poor man,' he wrote from Popayán in August 1801, 'living an obscure existence in this lost corner of America, without status or authority.' Most of his life was indeed spent working in isolation in his native town, where, at the time of this self-pitying letter, he was impatiently waiting the arrival of Humboldt and Bonpland. Even though he had yet to meet them, and was full of excitement at the prospect of doing so, he already had his reservations about them, believing their progress in South America to be too rapid for them to draw any serious conclusions. Later in life he would even be disappointed in his protégé Mutis. After not being appointed director of the Botanical Expedition in the latter's will, Caldas would criticize the man for his bad temper, poorly organized manuscripts, the gaps in his studies of Bogotá's flora and fauna, and the incomplete state of his investigations into quinine.

A family lawsuit in Quito obliged Caldas to leave Popayán shortly before the arrival of Humboldt and Bonpland. It was perhaps fortunate that he was not around to hear the German's patronizing opinion of the local intellectual circles, even though he would have certainly been in agreement. 'They have a much greater culture,' wrote Humboldt, 'than you could possibly have expected of them, but a much smaller one than they themselves imagine.'

Humboldt and Bonpland would spend a couple of weeks in Popayán before continuing towards present-day Ecuador, where they would finally catch up with Caldas. Their short stay in the town was said to be commemorated by a plaque, but Manolo and I never got to see it. Night was falling and we were distracted by the scratchy sounds of bolero coming from an enticing old bar called El Sotareño. We went inside for what we thought would be a quick beer.

The place was a legendary local establishment, run by a courteous old man and his wife, and much frequented by ageing associates of the university. The yellowing walls, thick with grease and smoke, were lined with improvised wooden shelves stacked to capacity with old vinyls. The music consisted almost entirely of popular Latin songs and dances from the 1950s and early sixties. It was an old student haunt that had got stuck in time, like some of its more badly scratched vinyls, which kept repeating the same snatches of music until finally the owner stopped serving drinks and lifted up the arm of the prehistoric gramophone.

We sat enthralled by all this at a dark wooden table, until suddenly the electricity failed, the lights went out and the music slurred to a halt. Given the state of the gramophone, we were not surprised that a fuse had blown. And clearly the owner was prepared for such emergencies. Within minutes each table had its own candle, which gave the place a more romantic aspect. Within ten minutes, however, it was clear that the entire street was also without electricity. Power cuts were a regular feature of Colombian life, just as they were in Venezuela. We ordered another drink.

Within half an hour a couple of moderately tippled old men at the table next to us invited us to come and join them. They were retired science lecturers from the university and persuaded us without much difficulty to share their bottle of rum. We asked them about the continuing power cut. They said cuts such as these were not uncommon and never lasted more than twenty minutes or so. By now a good fifty minutes had passed.

'Of course,' added one of them, 'we're quite used to cuts. They happened all the time during the troubles. They're a common terrorist tactic to seed panic.' The conversation, as so often in Colombia, turned to questions of security. Today's newspapers carried reports of the disintegrating situation at the Cauca port of Buenaventura and also confirmed what Rod Wooden had told us: fighting was going on very near to where we would be passing on our way to Pasto and the Ecuadorian border. Manolo asked about the safety of the once-notorious Pasto road. 'No problem,' said the slightly more drunken of our two new companions. 'I guarantee you'll be absolutely safe until you cross the border. That's when you have to be careful. You'll be besieged at Tulcán by Ecuadorians trying to get your money, passport and absolutely everything you possess.'

What did concern me was my plan to go the next day to San Agustín, Colombia's most important archaeological site. This would involve a good two-day round trip over the mountains and back on a rough side-road. All the guidebooks recommended that prospective tourists to the site should check the security situation beforehand. After less than three weeks in Colombia I was beginning to think such advice was the outdated scaremongering of bored travel writers. However, we had enquired at Popayán's tourist office and been told of increased guerrilla activity in the area over the past few weeks. Our best bet, the staff said, would be to ask tomorrow at the bus station. When we relayed all this to our drinking companions at El Sotareño, they just laughed. But they were already well into their second bottle of rum.

The electricity had still not returned and a distinct restlessness was affecting the other drinkers in the bar, some of whom were making calls on their mobiles. Rumours had begun to spread, some of them confirmed by the owner's calm and kindly wife, who was serving at the tables. It was not just our street that was in darkness, she said, it was the whole town centre. Later we heard that there was no electricity anywhere in Popayán. She had been phoning friends all over town. There had had not been a power cut of this magnitude since the troubles.

'There's no electricity in Cali either,' she said to me almost in a whisper, as she brought a third bottle of rum to our table. She had got her old battery radio to work and was listening to the news. No theories were being offered. No one knew what was happening. Even one of our companions was rising with difficulty from the table to 'make a call to the missus'. We could hear him telling her in a loud thick voice to lock all the doors and shutters at home. Then he slumped back on his chair and told Manolo and me that we were being slow with our drinks. 'There's nothing else to do,' he drawled. 'You can't leave this place. You're much safer here than outside.'

'It's got to have something to do with the guerrillas,' said the owner's wife, an hour later, 'the whole of Cauca province is in darkness, and Nariño as well.' Remembering Charles Nicholl's experiences of Popayán, I started foreseeing some imminent apocalypse. And then the electricity came back, and with it the continuation of a tango by Carlos Gardel. Everyone applauded. Manolo and I walked back soon afterwards to the Hotel Monasterio, through a completely silent town.

The uncertainty, the power cut, the copious amounts of rum and my still-desperate desire to see San Agustín influenced my dreams. I woke up in a panic. Guerrillas in camouflage gear were appearing from behind the grimacing pre-Columbian monoliths of San Agustín and were shouting out orders. What I had not dreamt was the commotion coming from below, with doors being knocked and boots resounding against floors. Hastily I dressed and walked out onto the upper cloister. Below me were about twenty soldiers with machine guns.

Again little help was forthcoming from reception. 'A routine manoeuvre,' said the man preparing our bill. It was another cloudless day and we went off to the bus station with a surprising sense of optimism. A few morosely resigned country folk were standing around the ticket window of the company serving San Agustín. There had been an 'incident' last night, again unspecified. The morning bus had been cancelled. The next bus would be leaving in the afternoon, perhaps tomorrow, no one could be sure. A friendly old woman advised us that it was not a good time to be visiting her village. 'Everything's been so quiet for the past few years ... and now this.' All that I could gather from her was that there had been some 'skirmishes'. I wasn't even sure if she knew herself who was fighting whom. There were buses to Pasto leaving every forty minutes or so. 'Any problems on the route?' The ticket salesman looked almost surprised by our question. 'None at all,' he replied, probably chuckling to himself at the cowardice and gullibility of tourists.

I sat contemplatively at a window seat, with Manolo in the row behind. I was thinking regretfully of San Agustín. There was a long tradition of travellers missing the site. The carved monoliths lay scattered in fields at the head of the Magdalena River, an obvious passing place for those travelling between Bogotá and Quito. Yet no one had mentioned these notable works until 1753, when a solitary Franciscan friar saw them on his way to Bogotá. The friar thought that the figures were grotesque parodies of monks and mitred bishops, but as they were clearly of ancient workmanship, and dated from a period when the natives were unlikely to have had any tools, there could be only one conclusion: they were the work of the devil. The next, more sensible, description dates from 1797, when they were seen by Caldas the Wise, who lived up to his nickname by finding these works indicative of the 'character and strength of a great people'.

A middle-aged man, introducing himself as Jorge, sat in the empty seat next to me, just as the bus was about to set off. He had matted curly white hair and gold-rimmed glasses. He said he had been travelling all night from Bogotá, and could not wait to get to his home in Pasto. 'By lunchtime,' he said, 'we'll all be eating guinea pig.'

I never knew that guinea pig was eaten so far north as this. Nowhere else along our route so far had offered this famous Andean speciality. This was another sign that we were approaching these mountains' heart. Jorge was dozing as we drove along what could have been the Vale of Paradise, a meandering river valley, as green and fresh as the West of Ireland under brilliant sunshine, with horses grazing under the spreading trees, oxen plowing the fertile earth, fields of thick grass and deciduous woods streaked incongruously with palms. Even as the road tightly hugged the valley's side to climb up into the bare summits of the *páramos*, the landscape of scrubland, heather and spongy grass was soft and gentle in character and bathed in a magical, translucent light. Were these the same *páramos* that Humboldt had crossed, the same bleak and freezing mountain plateau, with its mists and volcanic smoke and its horrible road paved with the bones of mules that had died from cold or exhaustion?

Descending back into the Eden of woods and ploughed fields, I realized how near we were to where the fighting we had heard about was reputedly taking place. As elsewhere throughout Colombia, there were frequent army checkpoints, as well as occasional army posters marked '*Por su seguridad*' ('For Your Safety'). Manolo tapped me every now and then on the shoulder to point out soldiers on motorcycles accompanying the bus in relays, across the emptier stretches of the journey.

Jorge, awake by now, and noticing the interest we were taking in such military details, began talking to me. He had a small construction company in Pasto, though there was a period when he had lived in Bogotá 'because of the troubles'. He was a cheerful person who had been lucky enough not to have had any immediate member of his family caught up in the 'tragedy'; but he had begun to receive threats and had thought it wise to leave his town for a while.

'My wife's family,' he added, 'is from a small village about sixty kilometres from Pasto. Everyone there has a terrible story to tell. It's always the isolated country communities that have suffered most in this country. The FARC comes along and gets some desperately poor farmer to pay protection money, and then the paramilitaries turn up and accuse the poor man and his family of being guerrilla sympathizers. And if the paramilitaries don't kill him, then the army will do the job. Worst of all, few of the villagers seem to know who's who, or who supports what. All they know is that they're always the victims.'

Half an hour before arriving at Pasto, we had our first glimpse of the notoriously dangerous volcano of Galeras. In January 1993 a small international team of geologists was standing on the lip of the summit crater, looking for signs of imminent eruption. A Russian member of the team had just finished taking a gas sample from a fumarole, while a leading British vulcanologist, Geoff Brown, had been making last-minute adjustments to an instrument detecting small changes in the acceleration of gravity. A deafening explosion caught them unprepared, and they were engulfed by a superheated cloud of gas and rock as they attempted to scramble to safety.

The volcano appeared now as a pleasantly innocent addition to the brilliant green scenery, a smooth mound towering above maize flecked by sunlight. 'Galeras tends to be active in November and Holy Week,' said Jorge. 'But no one here gets particularly worried by her. We think of her essentially as a good person.'

We did not have guinea pig for lunch. Pasto, an amorphous-looking agricultural centre regularly destroyed by earthquakes, was not an attractive prospect by day; and, after leaving our luggage at a Lebanese-owned hotel, we negotiated a taxi to take us to a lake twenty-five kilometres away, famed for its trout.

The Laguna de Cocha was the enchanted destination that had been beckoning us over the past weeks. There it was, visible below us through a gap in the woods, at the other side of cultivated fields fading out into reeds and sands, an enormous lake bordered on its other sides by forested hills, outlined against a far horizon of mountains.

We ate the trout in a wooden, Swiss-style lodge almost at the water's edge, surrounded by trees, vegetable gardens and an exuberance of flowers. The owner offered us what seemed like some magician's brew, a steaming hot cocktail made from aquavit, pineapple, passion fruit and what he called *lulo* ('an untranslatable local fruit'). He was a fat and elderly man, with a reddish complexion and a heavy, Central European accent. He said he was of Austrian-Polish extraction, but that everyone called him 'The German'. There were thousands of Germans, he explained, who

144

had emigrated, as he had done, to Cali, where he had run a factory for much of his life. He had purchased this restaurant and hotel thirteen years ago. He and his wife had always loved holidaying by the lake. Of course he would never have imagined the circumstances that would force him to leave the place only three years after buying the lodge. He had only just returned. He didn't seem keen to explain the reasons for his long absence.

Instead he wanted to talk about the forested island we could see from the wooden terrace where we were eating. He said that the Island of Corota was a place held sacred by the Indians, and that it was one of the 'great energetic centres of the world, together with Macchu Pichu'. A boatman who worked for him rowed us out there. The boatman told us that the whole place was covered in a rainforest. He walked with us along the nature trail that crossed it, at the entrance to which was a sign saying: 'The forest has its own music. The silence here is made up of a million sounds.' After ten minutes of penetrating the dark, dense forest, we reached the island's centre, which, another sign told us, had 'served for centuries as a place of ritual for the Quillacinga and Mocoa Indian cultures'. Our eyes took in the giant bromeliads and followed the lianas up to a tiny patch of softening blue sky.

We were rowed back towards evening, the sky streaked with thin purple clouds. Relaxed and renewed simply by the sheer beauty of the tranquil lake, I began thinking that I was probably as close as I would ever get to paradise. I then made the mistake of asking about the German. Why had he had to abandon for so long the lake of his dreams? The boatman's story took me by surprise.

It had been an evening like this, almost ten years to the day, towards the end of the summer season. A group of thirty-seven guerrillas lay hidden in the forest, waiting for the last of the season's visitors to be fast asleep in their beds. Shortly after eleven at night they ran down to the jetty and took all the boats they could find. Silently they rowed to the lake's distant shore, from where they continued on foot, hacking their way stealthily through the lianas up to the top of a hill where there was a small army camp. They knifed the two guards, machine-gunned forty soldiers, beheaded one whom they thought had been a traitor and kidnapped eight officers, including a general.

'The German was warned that the same would happen to him should he and his staff stay on in the area. Bravely he defied them for a while, but he left after a few months, together with almost everybody else. Nothing has been heard since of the officers. Presumably they are still held captive somewhere in the forest.' The tales of recently escaped kidnap victims in Colombia attested to the likely fate of these men, tied twenty-four hours a day to trees, their skin festering from the chains, their illnesses left untreated, their minds hovering at the point of madness.

The boatman pulled up his oars and let the boat glide towards the jetty. A faint Andean tune was playing on a distant radio, and a biting wind had come down suddenly from the mountains.

# PART THREE

# THE CENTRE

PIURA
Paita
Jaén
Chachapoyas
Kuélap
Celendín
CAJAMARCA

El Brujo
TRUJILLO

Cordillera de

BRAZIL

Yungay ▲ Nev. Huascarán
Huaraz ∴ Chavín de Huántar
La Unión  Huánuco

los Andes

Cerro de Pasco
L. de Junín
Junín  Tarma

PERU

HUANCAYO

LIMA

Vilcabamba Vieja
(Espíritu Pampa)
Machu Picchu
Ayacucho  CUSCO
Andahuaylas

BOLIVIA

Cordillera de

Cañon
de Colca
Chivay
Nev. Ampato

Lago Titicaca
Puno
Achacachi
Copacabana
Nev. Illimani

los Andes

AREQUIPA

LA PAZ

COCHABAMBA
ORURO  SANTA CRUZ
DE LA SIERRA

ALTIPLANO

L. Poopó

Cordillera de los Andes

SUCRE

POTOSÍ

Pacific Ocean

Salar de
Uyuni
Uyuni

Ollagüe
Tupiza  TARIJA
Villazón
La Quiaca
CHILE

# 11

# JOURNEYS TO THE MIDDLE
# OF THE WORLD

Bouncers with balaclavas guarded the Andean underworld. They searched our pockets and let us in, down into a crowded, noisy darkness full of swaying bodies and the breathy sounds of pipes and throaty voices. We found an empty table near the back. A young couple asked if they could join us. We were brought a plastic jug filled with a spicy alcoholic drink 'made from the bark of the *yusa*'. We were at Pasto's Discoteca Andina. A live band was playing. The smiling man at our table was giving us our first lesson in Quechua. You had to listen carefully. '*Achichay*' meant 'I am cold'. '*Achichuy*' meant 'I am hot'. The words conveyed a world reduced to elemental feelings and sensations. The music was beginning to drown them.

It was the typical music of the Andes, indistinguishable from one end of the range to the other, a fusion of the Indian and the Spanish, a plaintive cacophony of rattles, wails, panpipes, violins and the lute-like *charango*. It was a music I had once thought expressive of proverbial Andean melancholy, of a world of sacred ritual and of sullen resignation to an environment of unforgiving extremes. Now it was inciting to cheerful oblivion the customers of a Colombian disco.

'You can borrow my girlfriend,' shouted our neighbour, 'she'll show you the steps.' I followed her to the front of the concrete-walled basement. We pushed our way through the morass of agitated limbs. I tried copying her movements. The initial coldness of the room was fast wearing off. The *agua de yusa* was proving surprisingly strong. My hands were swaying above by head, my feet were wildly kicking. The music was accelerating. We were dancing what could have been a hysterical, anarchic version of a Scottish reel, a Spanish *jota*. We merged into a circle, dancing faster and faster, as if being pulled into the earth by some centrifugal force.

My head was still spinning the next morning, as our bus madly curved through a landscape that Isherwood likened to crumpled bedclothes. We were nearing the frontier with Ecuador, seeing the first snow-capped volcanoes, fast approaching the middle of the world. We had reached at last the northernmost outpost of the most famous Andean civilization, the Incas. We had caught up with Bolívar as he embarked on the last stages of his campaign to free South America from Spanish rule. We were on the heels once more of Humboldt and Bonpland.

Arrival in Ecuador was exactly as our drunken informant at Popayán had predicted. At the rundown bus station at Tulcán we were besieged on all sides by jostling men asking where we were going to, insisting that we travel with their particular bus company and trying to wrest our luggage from us. Inside the jam-packed bus, a market atmosphere prevailed, with vendors of all ages shouting out their wares as they strolled up and down the aisle selling everything from caramelized peanuts to hi-fi equipment.

Then the bus spluttered into action, shaking off all its vendors by the time we had left the outskirts of Tulcán, and entered a landscape progressively hazier and dustier. The passengers, unlike those on a typical Colombian bus, soon lapsed into silence, interrupted eventually by the loud music, shrieks and dubbed voices of yet another B-movie.

We had left New Granada and had reached the former Spanish possession known after 1563 as the Real Audiencia y Presidencia de

Quito. This territory, though stripped of its independent status in 1717, and incorporated into New Granada, was allowed after 1739 to retain its old name even while being governed from Bogotá. Nearly one hundred years later, when Bolívar's dream of a united Andean nation had failed, the former Audiencia became an independent small country that might have been called simply 'Quito' had not the inhabitants of Guayaquil, a rival, fast-expanding city on the coast understandably objected. The country, the smallest in South America after Paraguay, was named instead after its position on the equator. That Ecuador should lie at the very middle of the Earth greatly increased its attraction for travellers. It became a near-mythical destination for those who believed that gold originated from those places where the sun was strongest. It made it the focus of South America's first major scientific expedition, led by the so-called Geodesics. And it strengthened those feelings inspired by the country's unrivalled seismic and volcanic activity – that you were somehow nearing the origins of creation.

Volcanoes, non-existent in Venezuela, sporadically present in Colombia, are the salient characteristic of the Ecuadorian Andes, which run through the country in two parallel ranges forming what has been known since at least the eighteenth century as the 'Avenue of Volcanoes'. Volcanic eruptions and their frequent sequel, devastating earthquakes, have marked Ecuador's history with terrifying regularity. The ease with which Belalcázar routed the Incas on his path north to Quito was aided by the chaos after the eruption of Cotopaxi in 1533 and the earthquake that followed this. The earthquakes provoked by the repeated eruption of Pichincha from 1575 onwards focused the minds of Quito's inhabitants on God, and stimulated the construction in that city of some of the most exuberant churches in the whole of the Andes.

Humboldt and Bonpland came to Ecuador four years after an earthquake that had killed 42,000 people in a matter of seconds. Quito had suffered heavily and the once famously elegant town of Riobamba, to the south, had been obliterated. Humboldt needed only a short time in Ecuador to realize that his former status as a Neptunist was unsustainable and that fire more than water had moulded the Earth. He become an ardent Vulcanologist whose obsession with Ecuador's volcanoes would be inherited by his compatriot and fervent admirer Joseph Kohlberg, a Jesuit priest and scientist who came here in 1871, three years after an earthquake he described as the most destructive since that of Lisbon of 1755. Its epicentre was near Ibarra, the first town of importance you come to after entering Ecuador from the north.

Manolo and I were the only passengers to get off the bus at Ibarra. There was not even a taxi in sight. The bus pulled away, leaving us to walk through the hushed streets of an Ibarra taking an early Sunday afternoon rest.

The pages Kohlberg dedicated to the Ibarra earthquake in his *Towards the Equator* are so filled with memorable details that it was difficult not of think of the event as we walked down rows of squat buildings that seemed so flimsy under the looming presence of the Imbabura volcano.

Kohlberg's exceptionally vivid description of the earthquake was based to a large extent on his conversations with one of the survivors, the Italian Vicar General and Canon of Ibarra, Monsignor Pignatti, with whom he had shared a berth on the journey between Guayaquil and Southampton. Pignatti had felt beforehand that something terrible was about to happen. On 13 August 1868 a spectacular earthquake had struck the southern Peruvian coastal town of Arica, causing damage over an area stretching for hundreds of miles. Then, two days later, at eleven in the morning, when Catholics the world over were celebrating the Assumption of the Virgin, another earthquake took place barely fifty kilometres from Ibarra, at Tulcán. The great tremor that was sensed all over the region did not dampen the festive spirits of Ibarra's own inhabitants, who felt secure in the knowledge that their town had nearly always managed to avoid the calamitous events affecting the rest of their country. However, Pignatti was not so confident.

When night fell on the 15th, and the heat of a cloudless day gave way to the cold of a pellucid, starlit sky, most of the inhabitants of Ibarra went happily to bed, while some of the more drunken ones continued carousing and dancing in the streets. Pignatti remained restlessly awake in his room, disturbed as he was by the Ecuadorian belief that a large tremor is always followed by another one twelve hours later. He looked nervously at his watch and realized that it was already past eleven. He rushed out into the street, then returned to his house, after assuring himself that the only trembling was that of his heart. But he did the same at twelve o'clock, by which time only a few scattered sounds of guitars and inebriated shouts disturbed the tranquillity.

It must have been his guardian angel, he later told Kohlberg, who forced him out of his room again, just after one o'clock. He had scarcely time to register the noises of the last of the revellers before a deep and distant roar sounded from the Cotachi volcano, followed by another much louder one. Within seconds the whole earth seemed to be opening up, and a pitch-black cloud of dust had enveloped the town, bringing with it a cacophony of screams and pleas for mercy. Pignatti, thrown a metre into the air by the shock, realized in retrospect that in that very moment thousands had 'met their maker unprepared'.

Dawn rose that morning on what Kohlberg described as 'one of the most disturbing scenes in the whole history of humanity'. Wailing mothers wandering over the ruins in search of their lost ones competed in their misery with the shrieks and groans of the mutilated and the dying, and of those countless people who were still trapped alive beneath the collapsed walls, with nothing being done to rescue them. Everyone else was concerned simply with trying to stay alive.

Inevitably, some people of faith saw the earthquake as divine retribution for all the drunken pagan activities that had accompanied the holy rites of the 15th; but, as Kohlberg pointed out, for all the many blasphemers who were killed that day, there were far more who survived, and far more victims still who were innocent, God-respecting citizens. A more understandable response to the earthquake was that of the Indian population who lived scattered in the countryside, in straw-covered huts less likely to cause serious injury than a town dwelling. The Indians' high rate of survival was interpreted by some of them as ordained by fate. Rumours even spread that the disaster at Ibarra was part of a nationwide chain of events affecting Quito, Guayaquil and the country's other great colonial centres. As so often in Andean history, there was a widespread feeling among the mountains' original inhabitants that their moment of vengeance against the white invader had come.

Rebellious Indian groups confronted Ibarra's governor, making more difficult still the task of looking for the injured and bringing about some degree of order. Only the arrival from Quito of the ultra-conservative President García Moreno put an end to the looting and succeeded in getting the Indians back to their former peaceful lives, and working for the town's recovery.

Ibarra's present-day importance as the commercial and transport hub of northern Ecuador was not immediately evident to those, such as Manolo and me, coming from lively and prosperous-looking Pasto. As we searched for our chosen hotel, the Imbabura, we could not resist visiting an ice-cream parlour where fruit sorbets were being made the traditional way – in copper bowls manually rotated on beds of straw and salted ice. The young woman making them appeared as interested in hearing about us as we were in what she was doing. '*Chévere!*' she smiled, on discovering we had just arrived from Colombia.

The Imbabura, described in guidebooks as 'the best budget choice in town', was somewhere I had imagined echoing with the voices of backpackers. But all that greeted us on entering its large glazed courtyard were snatches of a Mozart sonata being played on a back-room piano. This did not seem like a hotel at all, but some genteel nineteenth-century residence inhabited by ghosts. We shouted to call attention to ourselves. The music ceased, replaced by footsteps. An elegantly dressed middle-aged woman led us upstairs so that we could choose from one of several padlocked rooms with heavy mahogany furnishings and religious images above grand bedsteads. She said that this was the oldest hotel in Ibarra and that if we were interested in its history we should speak to her father, Pepe Dávila.

Pepe, newly emerged from his afternoon nap, shuffled soon afterwards into the courtyard wearing a frayed chequered shirt and baggy cardigan. He was like some benign old man in a fairy story, elf-like in size, with a large, deeply lined head sprouting thick white hair and bushy eyebrows. He sat down with us at a table to outline the most famed attractions of his beloved Ecuador, then promised to talk to us at greater length later in the day.

A friend of his, also a keen historian, was a taxi driver. He was inveigled to take us for a special rate ('a scholar's rate') on an historical tour of Ibarra that would begin with a monument to another of Bolívar's victories. The battle had taken place a few kilometres outside the town, alongside what was now a riverside promenade named 'La Victoria'. If it had not been for our driver we would have missed the small plaque flatly recording that this was 'the spot where the Liberator triumphed over Royalist forces'. The victory of Ibarra in 1823 was more impressively commemorated on the steep slope in front of us, in the form of a commanding statue of Ibarra's patron saint, Saint Michael. But the easily missable plaque was a more diplomatic record of an episode in Bolívar's life whose exaggerated brutality even some of his most diehard supporters would prefer to forget.

It was July 1823 and, until recently, Bolívar had every cause for optimism and confidence. The Argentinean liberator San Martín had crossed the Andes and marched north up the continent's western coast, taking Lima in the process. Bolívar himself, after sweeping south through Popayán and Pasto, had already subdued the

Audiencia de Quito, to where he had dispatched an army led by his best general, the 26-year-old Antonio José de Sucre. Sucre, victorious at Guayaquil, but temporarily thwarted at the inland town of Ambato, was – with the aid of reinforcements sent by San Martín – finally able to capture Quito in May 1822. Bolívar entered the city three weeks later, and immediately found a soulmate in Manuela Saenz, *'la libertadora del libertador'*. In July of that year he moved on to Guayaquil, to have inconclusive discussions with San Martín about both the future political order of South America and how they would proceed in their campaign. The main outcome was that San Martín, exhausted by Bolívar's intransigence and Machiavellianism, withdrew so as to allow his rival sole responsibility for defeating the continent's last bastion of Spanish rule – the Peruvian interior.

But in June 1823, when Bolívar was hoping any moment to leave Quito for Peru, news came to him of a rebellion masterminded in Pasto by a wise, brave and charismatic Indian leader called Agualongo. The rebellion was a predictable response to the tyrannical behaviour of the man whom Bolívar had left in charge of the town, General Salom. Nonetheless it provoked in the Liberator the unmeasured reaction of a near psychopath: 'The infamous Pasto has again raised her hateful seditious head, but this head shall be cut off for ever . . . This shall be the last time in the life of Pasto; she will disappear from the catalogue of peoples, unless her vile inhabitants surrender their arms to Colombia without a shot . . .' He would almost be true to his word. At the beginning of July he went off with an army of two thousand men to meet the rebels at Ibarra. The rebels, far fewer in number, were armed with sticks, spears and whatever weapons they could get hold of. On 15 July, according to an eyewitness, 'eight hundred bodies of Partusians were left on the field, for no quarter was given'. Afterwards Bolívar left instructions with Salom that virtually amounted to an order to exterminate Pasto's population.

We were driven up to the victory monument for a panorama whose peacefulness removed all thoughts of the events that had taken place here. The undulating green valley below us, with its

outer ring of mountains and volcanoes, contained not only the battlefield and its scattering of suburban houses and gardens. There
was also the lake whose surrounding villages had borne the brunt
of the 1868 earthquake, the Lago de San Pablo. Kohlberg had
described how its few survivors had 'wandered hungry, naked, and
inconsolably lonely through the upturned landscape'. Now its
crowded shores helped explain the earlier emptiness of Ibarra itself.
Everyone from the town appeared to be here, enjoying what was
left of the dry season.

We drove back into the town, and further back into its history. In
the centre of a quiet intersection stood a disproportionately tall white
obelisk, honouring Ibarra's early-seventeenth-century founders. Then,
in a suburb indistinguishable from the rest of the town, came a truncated pyramid made of roughly hewn stones. We were told this was
a memorial to Atahualpa, who was born here. 'Atahualpa?' I
repeated, unable at first to accept that this was the same person
whose ignominious capture by Pizarro had brought about the
destruction of the Inca empire. I knew that Atahualpa's father had
granted his son the leadership of the newly conquered Inca lands to
the north of present-day Peru. It was also sometimes said that
Atahualpa had been born in Quito, where his father had wanted to
establish a second Inca seat of power. But nothing I had read mentioned Ibarra as his birthplace.

The association between Ibarra and Atahualpa probably went
back no further than the 1960s. I suspected that this had been a
ploy to attract foreign visitors, who, from the time of the Geodesics,
had taken more of an interest in Ecuador's short-lived Incan past
than the Ecuadorians themselves. When the pioneering Victorian
alpinist Edward Whymper came to the Ibarra region in 1880 in the
hope of purchasing Inca antiquities, he made a very surprising discovery: none of the country people whom he talked to had actually
heard of the Incas.

'There was a time when you could pick up priceless Inca objects
for almost nothing,' said Pepe Dávila, once we had returned to his

hotel and he had taken us up to see the antiques he had been amassing since his student days. Pepe had limited his collecting activities
to a combination of miniature bottles and 'Pre-Columbian antiquities'. Smiling like a child he daintily picked up from one of the
shelves what he said was a rare Inca necklace. 'Can you guess what
these are made of?' We shook our heads. 'Scorpion eggs,' he
beamed. Then he went over to a nearby axe blade which, when held
to the light, revealed a faint red discolouration. 'This is one of the
rarest pieces of all. It's an Inca weapon, of course, but what makes
it special is that you can still see the blood stains. I know, from
where it was found, that it was used in the decisive battle at
Ambato between Atahualpa and his brother Huascar.'

I was developing a deep fondness for Pepe. He had a gentle, sensitive manner and a touching innocence. In his presence I began to
feel as if I were a blasé cynic. After he had started clasping lovingly
to his chest his many realistic ceramic figures of the pre-Inca period,
I made a great effort to look serious. I tried emulating Manolo, who
appeared as convinced as Pepe was that these were antiques of the
Mochica civilzation rather than late-twentieth-century copies.

I simulated wonder as Pepe produced an oriental-looking figure
that, for him, conclusively proved that the Chinese had reached the
Andes long before the Spaniards. I did the same after he had
brought out from a cupboard a jug representing a copulating
couple. By the time he had begun playing on an 'ancient Andean
horn', I felt ashamed for wanting to laugh. I looked down at the
ground and hoped that the old man's bathetic, conch-like sounds
would free my imagination from the hold of academic logic. But
soon something else distracted me. I was staring at a dusty pile of
offprints lying on the floor.

'The Proceedings of the Bolívar Society of Ibarra,' said Pepe,
wiping his lips with a handkerchief and laying down the horn. 'I've
been a member for years. What a shame it's a Sunday, I would have
introduced you to the president, you could have given a talk. But
we're affiliated to the Bolívar Society of Quito. You should look

them up when you're there.' I confessed that my interests lay more in Humboldt than in Bolívar. 'Then I've got something for you, if I can find it.'

He suggested we should have a beer together, and asked us if we could go and buy some. We returned from the nearest shop carrying two giant bottles of an 'Andean beer' called Conquer. He was waiting for us at one of the tables in his now darkly lit courtyard. No other guests had turned up, but we could hear his daughter playing Mozart once again on the piano. Pepe carefully extracted from one of his cardigan's capacious pockets a dog-eared offprint. 'I knew I would lay my hands on it in the end,' he murmured, passing it over to me. It was a talk given at the local Bolívar Society on 19 May 1963. It was entitled 'Humboldt in Ibarra'.

It was Humboldt's third Christmas away from his relatives. He and Bonpland had spent it struggling with deep mud, fallen trees and freezing night-time temperatures. They had been in Pasto since late November 1821, but had left the town on 22 December to avoid having to spend Christmas there. Someone had warned them about the 'exaggerated expenses' they would be obliged to pay if they were to join in the local festivities. Their journey from Pasto to Quito was partly related by Humboldt in detailed diary entries, in which he recorded with characteristic matter-of-factness such features of the roads as the high number of crosses marking the spots where travellers had frozen to death. But such typical Andean hazards did not deter their appreciation of the scenery, and their ever greater superlatives as they followed the river that runs into present-day Ecuador, the Guáitara. Humboldt counted the Guáitara Valley, with its abundant fast-flowing waters, dense motley vegetation, steep narrow gorges and views of sublime volcanoes, as one of the grandest and most beautiful he and Bonpland had ever seen. In fact he was now able to say of the Andes that 'everything here is grander and more majestic than in the Swiss Alps, the Pyrenees, the Carpathians, the Apennines, and all the other mountains I have known'.

159

As they neared Ibarra and entered the Avenue of Volcanoes, their excitement almost reached fever pitch. They seem to have come to the same conclusion that Kohlberg would seventy years later: that the unique beauty of the Andes was due to the predominance of their volcanoes – the most perfectly shaped of all mountains, the most genuinely sublime, and the ones that seemed to hold more than all others the secrets of the Earth. For Kohlberg the Andes were quite simply the 'grandest mountain range in the world'. How could the volcano-less Himalayas possibly compete?

Dreaming of higher volcanoes still, Humboldt and Bonpland continued southwards, reluctant to break their journey for more than a night. Ibarra was just another brief respite. But another man, as excited as they were, had got there beforehand and was waiting for them. José de Caldas might have made an odd first impression. Awkward and diffident in manner, and lacking by his own later admission Humboldt's outer fire, he was an introvert whose various complexes were probably immediately noticeable to the perceptive.

Caldas's anxiety about his meeting with Humboldt and Bonpland had reached the stage when he could wait no longer. He had been based in Quito since leaving Popayán in the autumn. The three men were now due soon in Quito. He could easily have waited for them there a few more days. But the news of their impending arrival in Ibarra inspired him to bring forward their long-delayed meeting. He was desperate to see if they were as remarkable as their reputation had led him to believe and, if they really were such great men, he was hoping more than anything to accompany them on their journey south to Lima.

Humboldt's later doubts about Caldas's reserved personality might well have stemmed from this first meeting; but nonetheless he would soon glimpse the man's brilliance and learning. Mutis had been right to speak so highly of his pupil's achievements. Indeed, not since being with Mutis in Bogotá had Humboldt and Bonpland met someone of such obvious talents, and they would not meet anyone quite like him for the rest of their time in South America.

Caldas himself came away more enthralled still from this encounter. Outwardly he might have appeared stiff and emotionally withdrawn, but inwardly he was alight with a passion he would pour into effusive, unrestrained letters peppered with exclamation marks. The one he wrote to Mutis on his return to Quito is like that of an adolescent in love. His first contact with Humboldt and Bonpland, on 31 December, was one he sensed to be of such consequence that he recorded its exact time: eleven in the morning.

It was with enormous pride, born perhaps of a deep insecurity, that he told Mutis how Humboldt had been the one to make the first move, and had instantly recognized him as the renowned José de Caldas of whom he had heard such estimable reports, and whose outstanding astronomical and geographical studies he already knew, having been shown them by Caldas's father in Popayán. Humboldt, what is more, the great Humboldt, had gone on to praise Caldas before Ibarra's intellectual community, and to assure him that his exceptional talents deserved to be recognized well beyond his own country. From the moment they had met, Humboldt had taken Caldas unhesitatingly into his confidence, as had the no less 'wise and profound Bonpland'. The former, like a child showing off his toys, unwrapped for Caldas's benefit each one of his marvellous scientific instruments, the hydrometer, the antracometer, the euridometer, the aerometer, the legendary hair hygrometer (which measured humidity according to how much a strand of hair expanded); and, as the most special of privileges, revealed to him what few others had seen before – a detailed map he had prepared of the Magdalena River. Bonpland, meanwhile, gave him free use of his notebooks, and allowed him to copy from his immense herbarium. What so exhilarated Caldas was how much more he was able to learn from the briefest contact with these two men than from a thousand visits to a library.

I opened our bedroom curtains for a view of the Imbabura volcano rising above television aerials, inner courtyards roofed with corrugated iron and the distant obelisk of the Foundation Monument, glinting like a white rocket with the first rays of the sun. It was Manolo's last day. He had a plane to catch early the next morning from Quito. He had one great wish before leaving the Andes. He wanted to visit the Middle of the World, the Equator. He thought it was his duty as a mathematician to go there.

Soon after continuing our journey, we saw Ecuador's third-highest volcano, Cayambe, through our bus window. The shimmering whiteness at its summit seemed at first like an optical illusion. I was still pondering the volcano's reality when another apparition loomed up in the blurry blue distance, and then another, until finally the horizon looked like a childhood doodle of an imaginary land. One of the volcanoes was surely Cotopaxi, and the almost imperceptible white speck far beyond could have been Chimborazo. Any moment now we would be in Quito.

Some travellers, coming to Quito by land, have sensed something threatening about the city's unreality. Such a person was the Belgian Surrealist poet Henri Michaux, one of Ecuador's most fervent foreign enthusiasts. 'The first impression is terrifying and close to despair,' he wrote.

The tetchy, world-weary Isherwood could be counted on for a more down-to-earth response to Quito. The Andean gloom he had picked up on approaching Bogotá had overcome him yet more forcibly as he neared the Ecuadorean border at Tulcán. The same landscape that had driven Humboldt and Bonpland to ecstasy had appeared to Isherwood under a low rainy sky to be 'the saddest place I've ever been in'. His photographer companion Caskey had compared it to purgatory. Even when the sun emerged, Isherwood had still felt depressed: 'This titanic landscape seems to have overpowered and degraded its inhabitants. Such places are only suitable for seer and giant; ordinary mankind is too small for them. The terrible cold mountains tower into the clouds while wretched villages huddle at their feet – miserable crowds of huts, with smoke-blackened interiors and crumbling adobe walls.'

The Pan-American Highway, which Manolo and I had been following from Popayán, seemed to Isherwood too grand a title for the sad little road it had become after entering Ecuador, a rough cart-track, swept away in places by the rains and blocked in others by fallen earth. And whereas in Colombia he had often passed road-gangs at work repairing the damage, here there was nobody. The last stage of his approach to Quito, far from being the enthralling moment he had once dreamt of, had been marked by his and Caskey's relief at managing to hail down the rail bus that covered the journey's final kilometres: 'That is the irony of travel. You spend your boyhood dreaming of a magic, impossibly distant day when you will cross the Equator, when your eyes will behold Quito. And then, in the slow prosaic process of life, that day undramatically dawns – and finds you sleepy, hungry and dull. The Equator is just another valley; you aren't sure which and you don't much care. Quito is just another railroad station, with fuss about baggage and taxis and tips.'

What looked like a dirty accumulation of heat and pollution provided a disappointing accompaniment to our own entry into Quito. This sky, apparently unusual for Ecuador at any time of year, deadened the impact of the city's setting, which in any case could not have lived up to the drama of the approach. Unable to focus on the volcanoes, arrival at Quito was like arriving at any other city, a slow progression through ugly, little-planned outskirts, then on to an upper ring road with a panorama down to long lines of office blocks. The bus station, famously chaotic and a renowned magnet for pickpockets, muggers, vagrants and swindlers, appeared little more menacing or unnerving than crowded, uncared-for bus stations the world over. And we were immediately out of it, transferred by taxi to a hotel in the modern district of the Mariscal, where most of today's visitors to Quito are lodged.

We were put up at a hotel whose dull cube-like design was like that of the district in general, a district with little else other than hotels, hostels, restaurants, bars, cafés, 'cybers' and travellers' laundries. We had reached the starting point and ending place of so many cross-continental journeys through South America, and it all seemed dispiritingly banal.

We went as quickly as we could to the Middle of the World. The bus took us to the end of a string of interconnected outer townships, and there it was – a squat and sturdy obelisk made from andesite, a volcanic rock named after the Andes. Supposedly straddling exactly the northern and southern hemispheres, it was the unimpressive centrepiece of a tourist complex of whitewashed neo-colonial buildings selling craft souvenirs.

The complex obviously relied heavily on weekend trippers, for on the Monday of our visit the only other tourists were a small party of retired Swedes. Their tour guide got them to try and balance an egg on the equatorial line. Manolo wanted instead to be photographed with a foot in either hemisphere. Neither he nor anybody else seemed to mind that recent calculations had indicated the line to be about 250 metres off. The monument itself was only constructed in 1979, as a grander replacement of another one erected in 1836 seven kilometres to the east, on a site where the remains were discovered of one of two pyramids recording the equatorial investigations of the Geodesics.

Over lunch at the complex's restaurant, Manolo the maths teacher came into his own, and gave me the most concise account he could of the Equator's history. He said he had been honing it for years on his pupils.

It had all started with Pythagoras, who proposed in the sixth century BC that the Earth might be a sphere freely floating in space. Three centuries later another Greek scholar, Eratosthenes, came up with a sound theoretical method for determining its size, namely by calculating the distance between two points on what was called a 'meridian' (a north-south line) and then measuring the angle to the sun from each of the two points. Not long afterwards yet another Greek, the astronomer Hipparchus, worked out that the globe could be divided into 360 degrees along its breadth and length, thereby creating a grid of latitude and longitude lines. Latitude (the lines running parallel to the Equator) could be calculated from the height of the sun above the horizon at a specific time and date. Longitude was more complex to ascertain, involving as it did comparing time in two places at once. Ptolemy, using sundials and hourglasses, expanded on Hipparchus's idea to create the first crude atlas.

Then Christianity appeared, and with it came fanciful notions about the flatness of the Earth, and places inhabited by dragons and one-footed giants. The invention of the compass in the twelfth century did much to dispel these: it initiated the great age of maritime exploration and made Europeans turn again to Ptolemy's atlas. However, when Columbus accidentally came across an entirely New World, the Earth was found to be bigger than originally anticipated. Just how big became of vital concern to navigators.

Up till now I had managed, as a scientific and mathematical ignoramus, more or less to take in Manolo's more technical explanations. Now matters became more confusing, as theories and counter-theories accumulated to try and solve a problem which had been virtually abandoned for nearly one and a half thousand years.

There was also the brief distraction caused by the arrival of our main course – roast guinea pig. Manolo, knowing that after today he would probably never be in the Andes again, felt he should try it. My previous encounter with this quintessential Andean dish had been in a remote Bolivian village, when it had tasted like gelatinous chicken riddled with bones. But this was much fleshier, more like turkey in flavour. The waiter told us that his mother raised them in a nearby village. The light-brown ones, he said, were best for cooking, and with a good diet could grow up to two kilos. The dark ones, he smiled, tended to be used for medical diagnoses. 'The shaman,' he explained, 'rubs the animal all over the patient, and then cuts it open to see what part is inflamed. This is still very common in Ecuador.'

It was incongruous hearing about this practice as we sat eating next to a monument celebrating the achievements of western science and reason. For a moment I had an image of the sweet and furry creature whose bones and wrinkled skin lay on my plate. Then I devoted my full attention again to Manolo's account of geodesy, the study of the Earth's exact size and shape.

He was talking now about trigonometry, a subject I thought had been devised purely to torture schoolchildren. Apparently an early-sixteenth-century Dutch mathematician had proposed 'triangulation' as the basis of a more scientific method of measuring land distances. Instead of measuring distances directly to a given point, he suggested determining the location of this point by measuring angles to it from different points at either end of a fixed base line of several miles. The point could then be fixed as the third point of a triangle with one known side and two known angles.

Manolo then listed some of the later discoveries that advanced the discipline of geodesy, for instance Huygens's invention of a totally reliable way of telling the time – the pendulum clock. Or Galileo's tables charting meticulously over six years the orbits of Jupiter's four moons – a considerable improvement on Eratosthenes's measurements based on the position of the sun.

By the early eighteenth century the whole issue of geodesy had focused on the conflict between Cartesian and Newtonian physics. The disciples of Descartes believed that streams of particles swirled around the sun like water in a whirlpool, carrying along with them the planets. Newton and his followers advocated instead the importance of gravitational pull. The Cartesians concluded that fluid dynamics had made the Earth elongated at its poles, and slightly pinched at its centre, rather like a 'pot-bellied man wearing a tight belt'. The Newtonians, on the other hand, argued that the rotation of the Earth's axis created a centrifugal force greater at the equator than at the poles. Thus they were convinced that the Earth bulged at its centre like a squashed orange.

Belonging as I did to a generation in which heated debates tended to revolve around such issues as whether Elvis was a better performer than Sinatra, I found it touching to think of an age in which the precise shape of the Earth could be the subject of passionate dinner-table discussion. But this was a topic that had literally divided eighteenth-century society. French and British pride was naturally at stake and Voltaire was exiled from Paris for the unpatriotic gesture of coming out on the side of Newton.

By the 1730s the French Academy of Sciences decided conclusively to resolve matters by organizing two expeditions to extreme corners of the globe, to measure a degree of meridian arc. One would be sent to Lapland, the nearest feasible point to the North Pole; the other would go to the Audiencia of Quito, the only mountainous region on the equator. The mountain peaks came in handy for the purpose of establishing triangulation points. But for bureaucratic and other practical reasons it would have been easier had the South American party gone to flat French Guyana, which was near enough to the equator for their purposes. This was suggested by one of the team's members, La Condamine, who had failed to grasp a major ulterior motive behind the expedition: to find out more about a part of the world which the Spaniards had kept so much to themselves.

After lunch we took a final stroll around the site, approaching the monument this time along a sloping cobbled path lined with monolithic concrete busts of the Geodesic expedition's eleven identically wigged members. The man who had proposed the voyage was Louis Godin. Hugely ambitious, vivacious and bitingly witty, he showed his enormous promise as a mathematician and astronomer by getting into the Academy at the age of twenty-one. As the longest-standing academician of the group, he was appointed official leader. But in reality the leadership was shared between him and two others, Pierre Bouguer and Charles-Marie de La Condamine.

Bouguer, in many ways the most brilliant member of the party, and at thirty-seven the oldest, had been a child prodigy at maths and a professor of hydrography at fifteen, but he was a grumbling perfectionist who had firmly resisted going to South America until being flattered by the offer of being called 'resident astronomer'. La Condamine, in contrast, had instantly seized the opportunity. Scarred with smallpox, and consequently timid with women, he sought his thrills elsewhere – in quarrels, reckless exploits and exotic travels that had already taken him to the Middle East and around Africa. Though initially the least prepared of the three as a scientist, he would become the most famous. He was also the only one to have consistently supported the ideas of Newton.

When, in May 1735, after over a year and a half of preparations, the expedition was finally ready to set sail, seven other Frenchmen had joined up, including a hyper-sensitive botanist prone to melancholy, Joseph Jussieu, and Godin's soon-to-be-lovesick nephew, Jean Godin. As one of the conditions of carrying out research in South America, the Spanish Crown had arranged for two young Spanish marine officers to accompany them, Jorge Juan y Santacilla and Antonio Ulloa. As well as assisting and keeping watch on the expedition, the two men were asked to carry out their own investigations on the state of the countries they were to visit.

The two Spaniards met up with the rest of the group at Cartagena de Indias, where there was talk of going from there to Quito by the overland route later taken by Humboldt. The forceful La Condamine persuaded them that this would take too long. However, he would not get his way in the next major argument, which took place in March 1736, on sailing into the Ecuadorian bay of Manta, already within sight of the high Andes. Tensions had been slowly mounting between him and Godin. And these exploded into a violent quarrel after La Condamine and Bouguer proposed staying put by the coast, rather than heading up to Quito, as had been agreed with the Spanish Crown. A compromise was finally reached, with Godin and the others continuing on to Quito by way of Guayaquil, and La Condamine and Bouguer remaining for the moment near Manta. Bouguer eventually tried to catch up with the main party, while the individualistic La Condamine forged ahead with his own route up to Quito.

The journey to the Ecuadorian capital from the coast proved a dangerous ordeal for everyone. Ulloa and Juan described the sheer terror their party had felt as they travelled on mules across swinging bridges and along muddy ledges above deep abysses. Bouguer suffered the frustration of missing them at Guayaquil by three days and then having to make the climb on his own and in ill health. The person who fared worst was La Condamine, who after being abandoned by his porters in the middle of the jungle, had to subsist for eight days on bananas and exotic fruits. Low on gunpowder and provisions, and without any money at all, he finally made it to the top of the pass, where he was rewarded by the lifting of the clouds and a first view of Quito that induced in him a reaction contrary to most people's – of having been 'transported to the most beautiful of provinces in France'.

Their adventures on getting to Quito were nothing to what they had to face next. Personal antagonisms and lack of coordination had exacerbated a range of other problems: struggling to create a baseline in mountainous terrain; working at altitudes higher than any westerners had ever reached; searching for means to raise money; and being harassed continually by bureaucracy, the suspiciousness of the locals and prejudices against the French.

Not even the eventual erection of two commemorative pyramids at either end of the baseline was without its difficulties. Juan and Ulloa's indignation at being listed merely as 'Spanish assistants' rather than 'Spanish academicians' led to La Condamine's omission of their names entirely, and the prominent placing of a fleur-de-lys. This in turn resulted in a protracted lawsuit, at the end of which the Spanish authorities had the monuments pulled down. It was with considerable understatement that Ulloa would write on returning to Spain that theirs had been a mission marked by 'a series of labours and hardships, by which the health and vigour of all were in some measure impaired'. The mission's goals would not be fully completed until early 1744, and only five members of the original nine would make it back to Europe.

A Field Camp in the Andes, from Charles-Marie de la Condamine, *Mésure des trios premiers degrés du meridian dans l'hémisphere austral*, 1751

At the end of all this Newton had been proved right, and much more than geodesy had benefited. Major work had been carried out in the fields of geography, topography, astronomy, physics, ethnography, archaeology, linguistics, zoology, botany, mineralogy and vulcanology. Cork, quinine and platinum had been made known in the West. La Condamine's proposal for a universal unit of measure for longitude would lead indirectly to the adoption of the metre; his memoir *Journal of a Voyage to the Equator* would give Ecuador its name. South America had been popularized as never before. The idea for Humboldt's voyage had been born. The Age of Wonder had been launched. 'Anything else?' I teased Manolo.

I accompanied Manolo early the next morning to the airport. I was sorry to see him go. We quickly embraced at the entrance to the check-in area, where only those with air tickets were allowed to enter. 'See you in five months,' he said. There were scenes of departure rather more emotional than ours: lovers being parted, crying grandparents waving goodbye to emigrating families, emigrants trying to look confident as they set off to the Spain their ancestors had rejected. After I had returned to the city centre I was struck by a sense of emptiness and panic. I felt all alone in the middle of a huge continent. I shuddered at the thought of the vast Andean distances to come.

# 12

# ANDEAN BAROQUE

I soon began to settle into Quito. Exactly the same had happened to Isherwood. For the first and almost last time in the Andes he actually felt happy. 'This is a charming city,' he wrote. 'I wouldn't mind spending six months here, or even a year. Not that I should ever care to live permanently in the high mountains. But here the Andean sadness is no more than a faint shadow in the mind. And on clear days, when part of the great dazzling avenue of snow-peaks is visible, your heart really rejoices.'

Humboldt could find happiness anywhere. What he found so special about Quito was how the cheerfulness of its inhabitants had survived the precariousness of their environment and the dramatic after-effects of the 1797 earthquake. The place had become subject to continual earth tremors, and the average daytime temperature had fallen from the 19°C or 20°C recorded by Bouguer to between 5°C and 12°C, rarely getting higher than 8°C to 10°C. Nonetheless, 'in spite of the horrors and dangers with which Nature surrounds them, the inhabitants of Quito are cheerful, lively and amiable. Their city breathes only voluptuousness and luxury, and no other place is governed by such a strong and widespread taste for enjoyment. In this manner humans learn to sleep peacefully on the edge of a precipice.'

With Manolo gone, I found myself being gradually taken under the wing of Quito's friendly inhabitants. Some of them, I soon discovered, even frequented the bars and cafés of the Mariscal district's main square, a bland cosmopolitan enclave that could have been anywhere in the world. The night I had spent there with Manolo the two of us had felt very much outsiders in a square full of foreign backpackers who all seemed to know each other from the backpacker circuit. But now I was on my own, I became conscious of the presence of Quiteños, with whom I often ended up talking. They invited me to their tables, gave me their phone numbers and displayed the same openness and helpfulness I had found in Colombia. But the hedonism and vitality Humboldt had seen was not so apparent. Young Quiteños told me they went at night to the Mariscal because there was not much happening elsewhere. If I were looking for excitement, I needed to go to Guayaquil and the coast. Quito was proverbially the quietest of capitals.

I contented myself with the architectural thrills of Quito's old town, often staying there until dusk, when the crowds left, as if a bell had announced closing time. I was seeing as many as I could of its colonial churches and convents. There were eighty-six of them. Nowhere else in South America had so many. Perhaps, as some historians suggested, their predominance reflected an isolated conservative city turned in on itself. The earliest was San Francisco, with its massive porch where Indians were obliged to convert if they wanted to enter (today you were asked simply to switch off your mobile). Interiors, comparatively plain to begin with, became progressively more luxurious, to strengthen the faith of believers, to woo the hesitant, to convince converts they had made the right choice. The true style of Quito was the baroque. Its decorative zenith was the newly restored Jesuit church of the Compañía.

After a while I realized I couldn't look at these buildings in the way I used to as an art history student. Conventional stylistic analysis had come to seem petty in the sublime and volatile context of the

Andes. I assimilated the mixture of Castilian, Italian, Flemish, Moorish and indigenous influences. I stared dazed at all the acanthus, tendrils, angels, oversize volutes, wings, spirals, Corinthian capitals, twisted columns, projecting entablatures, strap-work coffering and soaring retables. And I ended up seeing all this as a crazed, hysterical, vainglorious response to a seismic world capable of destroying it all in seconds.

Hoping for a more academic assessment of Quito's monuments, I rang up Carlos Burneo, an architect who was collaborating with Spanish friends of mine in an Andalusian government scheme to help restore and catalogue these. He had already supervised a two-volume architectural guide to the city. Carlos had the ponderous, reflective manner of other architects I had known. He had a greying beard tucked under his chin, and the look of someone who enjoyed smoking a pipe. There was also something typically Ecuadorian or at least Quiteño about him: he was quiet, gentle and kind. The first time we met he proposed supper at a panoramic restaurant on top of the Panecillo, a hill directly above the old town, crowned by the enormous white Virgin of Quito. We went there in his car around nine o'clock, driving along deserted colonial streets. Did fear of muggings drive everyone indoors? 'Oh, no,' he said without a smile, 'people in Quito like to go to bed early. We're not late-nighters.'

We sat next to the window, eating roasted and salted maize kernels. 'Did you know that Quito was UNESCO's first urban world heritage site, along with Cracow? That was twenty-five years ago. The old town was in a terrible state then, far worse than it is now. When everyone with any money moved out to places like the Mariscal, the old town was just left to fall into ruins.'

He paused, as if taking a puff at his imaginary pipe. 'It's the largest colonial area of any American town. And the one with the largest number of baroque buildings.' He paused again. We were looking almost straight down at San Francisco and the enormous square in front of it. 'That's where it all began, in 1534.' That was the year when Pizarro's captain Sebastian del Belalcázar moved north from Peru to capture the famously prosperous northern lands annexed to the Inca empire after 1495 by Atahualpa's father, Huayna Cápac. There were reports that a rival Spanish party, heading from Central America under the command of one Pedro de Alvarado, had its sights on the same territory. Belalcázar, urged by the conquistador Diego de Almagro, pre-empted Alvarado by founding the town of San Francisco de Quito on 15 August 1534.

'As you can see,' Carlos said, gesturing with his hand towards the window, 'the site he chose to build on was completely uneven, and flanked on one side by this hill, on another by the Pichincha volcano and elsewhere by ravines. The ravines were obviously useful for defensive purposes, though one of them was later ingeniously blocked up when the town started rapidly to expand.'

There was another long pause. I munched some kernels. 'It's so typically Spanish to do what Belalcázar did. To go ahead and blindly impose a regular grid on such unpromising terrain. Of course, we don't know what the original Indian settlement of Quito was like. There's a lot of speculation.'

The person, he said, who could talk to me about ancient Quito was his art historian colleague Inés del Pino. She had co-authored the pioneering book about the subject. I met her the next day. A lover of all aspects of Quito, she too had a personality that lived up to my perceived, soft-edged Quiteño stereotype. Bespectacled, warm-hearted and with mouse-like features and colouring, she could well have ended up in one of the convents she would soon offer to take me to. She lived on her own, and seemed to have devoted much of her fifty years singlemindedly to research. With her immense knowledge and scholarly objectivity, she was able to correct many of the fanciful ideas I had picked up from guidebooks and travel accounts. I realized that almost everything I had read about pre-colonial Quito was probably wrong. There might never have been anything here of great importance.

'What is suspicious,' she said, taking me on a tour of the Church of San Francisco, 'is not just the lack of any archaeological evidence testifying to a great city. It's the fact that no one bothered to record even schematically what was on this site when the conquistadors arrived. In contrast, when the Spaniards got to Cuzco, they described in detail the buildings they encountered.'

The Spanish chroniclers, finding at Quito possibly little more than a few stone huts roofed with straw, went on to relate and perhaps even invent legends about the existence of some major Inca centre. Diego de Cieza was the one responsible for writing that Huayna Cápac transformed Quito into the second capital of the Inca empire and brought here 'more than five hundred cartloads of gold and over a thousand of silver, and vast amounts of stone and fine garments'. These gold-lined palaces and temples then had to be taken apart on Atahualpa's orders after he had been captured by Pizarro at Cajamarca: the gold was needed to pay off the ransom. Afterwards, when Belalcázar began his march northwards, an Indian chief loyal to the Incas, Rumiñahui, supposedly burnt down all that was left so as not to leave the Spaniards with anything. Another account has Belalcázar himself destroying the buildings in a desperate search for gold. Yet another story has a Spanish soldier systematically dismantling the town stone by stone with the aid of ten thousand vengeful, Inca-hating Indians.

'Some sort of Inca settlement did of course exist here,' continued Inés, 'and foundations of Inca workmanship have been discovered directly under the floor of this church. It is also possible that Atahualpa intended this settlement to rival Cuzco at some future date. But there is absolutely no evidence of any fire. The most likely reason for the disappearance of the walls that were here is an entirely prosaic one. They were probably taken down gradually as the colonial town expanded.'

I quoted to her a line from Paul Theroux's Latin American travelogue, *The Old Patagonian Express*, in which he stated that the Church of San Francisco had been built 'on the site of Atahualpa's summer residence'. 'That's what the guides still tell tourists,' she smiled. I also told her about Theroux's referring to the 'Inca touches' evident in the artistry of this and other Quito churches.

This clearly amused her. 'There are probably fewer indigenous, let alone Inca touches, in Quito's churches than in those of any other colonial school of architecture. In fact, there is even a debate as to whether there actually exists a specifically Quito School. Most of the churches here are indistinguishable from ones in Spain.'

Inés's persuasive comments dovetailed with my own thoughts. The role of the Incas in Ecuadorian history had clearly been relatively small, and not especially glorious. But travellers have rarely been objective about the Incas. Foreigners are bewitched by the Incas the moment they enter former Inca territory, long before reaching the mythical Inca heartland of Peru.

The period of Inca rule in Ecuador lasted barely forty years and was as tyrannical as what came after it, but this has not stopped foreigners from seeing it as a 'Golden Age'. This attitude was already evident in the eighteenth century, when travellers such as Jorge Juan and Antonio de Ulloa became highly critical of their fellow Spaniards for neglecting Ecuador's Inca remains. Humboldt, too, developed in Ecuador a passionate admiration for the Incas and even considered their road-building skills to be 'greater than the Romans'. But it was with later travellers such as Kohlberg that fascination with the Incas turned into an Inca-centric view of history. Ecuador, in Kohlberg's view, had enjoyed a magnificent flowering under Huayna Cápac, who had ruled in Quito from a 'new and immense palace', embellished the city with 'resplendent palaces and temples shining with gold' and won the love of his subjects by the imposition of a single language, Quechua.

By glorifying the achievements of the Incas, Kohlberg and others were perhaps unconsciously trying to redress the wrongs that had been done to that civilization by the West. On one of my meetings

Frontispiece to Humboldt, *Atlas géographique et physique du Nouveau Continent,*
Paris, 1814–34

with Inés, she brought with her a reproduction of a curious 1865 painting based on the frontispiece to Humboldt's *Geographical and Physical Atlas of the New Continent*. The frontispiece, illustrating 'America lifted out of its ruin by commerce and industry', had shown the classical gods Mercury and Minerva giving a helping hand to a cowed and vaguely Aztec-looking chieftain. In the painted version of this the background of Chimborazo had been kept, but the other elements had been reinterpreted as a representation of Wisdom and Eloquence pulling Atahualpa out of the grave. Thus the unwise decision of the semi-literate Spaniards to kill Atahualpa had been revoked and history rewritten.

Romantic notions about the Incas and anger with the Spaniards for having destroyed their civilization intensified as travellers compared the glories of Ecuador's Inca past with the piteous modern reality of the country's indigenous inhabitants, impoverished and discriminated against.

The plight of South America's Indians in general, and the injustices perpetrated on them by the Spaniards, had famously been publicized in the early sixteenth century by two Dominicans, Padre Antonio de Montesinos and Fray Bartolomé de las Casas. The writings of Casas in particular had served to foster Spain's legendary reputation as a country of extreme cruelty. But the Indians themselves had hardly benefited, as Juan and Ulloa observed. The two Spaniards, in their report about the present state of South America, listed numerous examples of continuing Spanish ill-treatment of the Indians. 'The tyranny to which the Indians are subjected,' they wrote, 'derives from the insatiable appetite for wealth motivating those who go to America to govern them.'

Humboldt took an even stronger line on Spain's treatment of the Indians in the diary notes of his journey from Pasto to Quito. The numerous ruins and traces he came across of old indigenous dwellings, 'like those from Inca times', were proof that the Indian population of places such as Tulcán had once been infinitely greater. The reason he was usually given for this was measles and smallpox.

But he reckoned that the sharp decline was the result of a deliberate policy of extermination, for there were far fewer Indians in those communities that had a heavy presence of whites. Indians, according to him, were being pushed towards places that were colder and less fertile; and, once few of them remained in a village, these few were forced by 'a cruel and irrational old law' to abandon their homes and lands. Priests, to whom the Indians were unable to pay baptism fees, had no interest in keeping them, and the white authorities were keen to get rid of them altogether.

My walks through Quito's old town had brought me into close contact with South America's indigenous past and present. I was in a country where half the population was said to be Indian. If the old centre of Bogotá had appeared to be an enclave of Europe, that of Quito was unmistakably Andean, still with many of those features that had caught the attention of past travellers, still the same Indian underclass, selling humble goods on the street, trawling through dustbins, wearing ponchos, carrying babies in their shawls.

The streets of Quito had once served almost as a laboratory for travellers wishing to study the customs, appearance and habitat of the Andean Indian. Some of these travellers fancifully imagined the Indian as a direct link to the ancient Incas; others considered him a 'debased Mongolian type'. Harry Franck, a young American 'vagabonding down the Andes' before the First World War, summarized the Indian as 'stocky and short, very muscular, with the strength of a mule for carrying loads on his back'.

Not every traveller was reduced to compassion by the scenes of poverty in the once notoriously insanitary old town. Franck wrote that 'the newcomer's sympathy for the Indian of Quito gradually evaporates with the discovery that he is utterly devoid of ambition, as completely indifferent to his own betterment as any four-footed animal'. Kohlberg, an altogether more enlightened observer, disputed such stereotypes, and found the Indians to be kind, intelligent, devout, hard-working and prone to drunkenness only when plied with drink by their masters. But even he saw a future of limitless subservience for them, despite the resentments lurking behind their tranquil, resigned facades.

The next time I met Carlos, at a mall blandly converted out of a colonial palace next to the old town's main square, he assessed Ecuador's current political and social situation. The irony of Ecuador was that as a country 'blessed', in Carlos's words, 'with a pleasant climate, peace-loving inhabitants, and petrol resources', its contemporary history should also have been one of South America's most politically and economically turbulent. The recent violent disturbances had all involved the still-marginalized indigenous population.

Perhaps the most alarming moment had come during the presidency of a former mayor of Quito, Jamil Mahuad, who had been elected in 1998, when the economic crisis had been one the worst of the century. Carlos had known him since their schooldays together in the south of Ecuador. 'He was a terrible mayor, and an even worse president.' After drastic austerity measures, followed by the predictable wave of strikes, Mahuad made a desperate bid in January 2000 to stay in power by changing the Ecuadorian peso to today's currency, the dollar. 'The main benefit from this,' noted Carlos, 'has been all the millions of dollars being sent into the country from Ecuadorians living abroad.' However, this benefit was not immediately appreciated by the indigenous electorate, who saw the introduction of the dollar as favouring banks and private interests at the expense of the poor. CONAIE, an umbrella organization of the country's indigenous peoples, sprung into action. There were violent riots culminating in the storming of the Congress on 21 January.

A new president, the sixth in four years, was brought in, followed by another two years later. This last president, Colonel Lucio Gutiérrez, came to power in an alliance that included the main indigenous party, Pachacutik. But, encouraged by the rising price of petrol, Gutiérrez changed political direction, supported George Bush and American neo-liberalism, and allied himself to the centre-right

Social Christian Party. Abandoned by Pachacutik and his indigenous supporters, he too was ousted by a popular uprising, in April 2005. The vice-president took over until a General Election was held in January 2007.

For the past few weeks Ecuador had been ruled by Rafael Correa, an economist with a doctorate from Illinois University, who was now the great hope of Ecuador's underprivileged and of liberal intellectuals everywhere. An ally of Chávez and Morales, he had learnt Quechua while working on agrarian projects in the Andean village of Zumbahua. He promised to put an end to years of political corruption in Ecuador, reform the country's declining health and educational systems and give thirty dollars a month to the poorest members of society. Already he had taken the novel step of having a government featuring eight woman ministers and representatives of all the country's ethnic minorities.

I asked Carlos what he thought of Correa. As with many in his profession, Carlos had the look of a socialist intellectual. But he took more time than usual to answer. He talked about the need for change and about Correa's heart being in the right place, but he was also worried about the man's lack of political experience. Then he took a long sip from his glass of lemonade, put it down and shrugged. 'We'll see,' he smiled.

Inés took me to a rundown part of the city, where the Andalusian government was helping to restore the old town's oldest cemetery, that of San Diego. Overlooked by a modernist concrete block whose construction had been stopped by the Town Hall, the place was ringed by dingy houses and warehouses spreading up onto the Panecillo hill. There were the grand and bombastic mausoleums of important Quiteño families, lots of histrionic angels and the tombs of a few nineteenth-century presidents.

I was more interested in the superimposed rows of modern concrete niches dating from the time when the rich moved out of the old town and the poorer families multiplied. To keep some level of order and taste in the cemetery the Town Hall had prohibited the use of colour and plastic flowers, but the will of the people had eventually triumphed. Some of the niches had carvings of footballs, guitars and other attributes of the deceased. Many had vitrines protecting photos, devotional images and other offerings from family and friends.

Conversation with Inés moved rapidly and soon we were back to the subject I had been talking about with Carlos – Ecuador's indigenous peoples. I mentioned a recent article I had read by the Peruvian writer Mario Vargas Llosa. He wrote that one of the more popular misconceptions about the Andes is that its social make-up is essentially Indian. Inés nodded. 'After five centuries of constant interbreeding,' she interjected, 'you're obviously going to get a predominantly mestizo society. But no one of course makes a point of stressing their mestizo roots. In contrast, there have been a number of our distinguished nationalists who have made much capital out of their pure Indian blood. Usually their claim is an exaggeration. Sometimes it's a downright lie.'

Inés spoke about some recent research on one of Ecuador's greatest indigenous heroes, Eugenio Espejo, a late-eighteenth-century doctor who got caught up in the independence movement and became a pioneering spokesman on indigenous rights. 'The accepted story is that his father was a Quechua Indian from Peru and his mother a Quito mulata. But a recent historian has found that he was registered at birth as white, and that his father's family was Spanish.'

Then she brought up the name of Oswaldo Guayasamin, Ecuador's leading twentieth-century artist, someone whose museum I intended seeing the following day. 'Well, his father was definitely Indian and he was brought up in the poor Quito district of San Roque, but he rarely mentioned that his mother was mestiza. I don't think it matters what your background is. But he spent his life promoting himself as a man of the people, as an Indian who had risen from the direst poverty and had a unique insight into human misery and the indigenous condition.'

*

I was full only of the most positive thoughts the next morning as I walked to the suburban museum that had once been Guayasamin's house and studio. The polluted haze was still there, but a brilliant sun was trying to burn its way through it. The sloping suburb where the artist had lived and worked during his years of international fame was green and prosperous, with pleasant modern buildings and views down to the sprawling city. As I neared the wooded summit an inviting mountainous landscape towards Cotopaxi came into view.

The museum was spread over three buildings whose cheerfully decorated white interiors reminded me of the Chilean homes of his great poet friend Pablo Neruda, another socialist with a taste for the good life and for amassing beautiful objects. Some of the rooms housed collections of pre-Columbian and colonial art, which Guayasamin insisted were the two greatest influences on his work. As for his own paintings, I tended to prefer his portraits, which were bold in scale and execution and conveyed great empathy for their subjects. His numerous canvases depicting the 'struggle of the Indian' appeared cruder and less heart-felt. Full of Picasso-like clenched fists and despairing hands, they seemed, as Isherwood had noted of Guayasamin's murals, 'too conscious of their social significance'.

I continued up the hill, to the hugely ambitious monument he hoped would be his greatest legacy but which he never saw completed. This was a chapel built directly in front of his last residence. Whereas the house was like a modernist Swiss chalet with colonial touches, the chapel was a futurist Inca temple formed out of a truncated cone rising out of an austere block in prison-wall brick. It was claimed as the only chapel in the world dedicated not to God but to Mankind. The interior was full of giant paintings recording human suffering and oppression. The horrendous mines at Potosí were depicted in the dome, while another painting, symbolizing the conflict between the Incas and the Spaniards, portrayed the Indian ritual of tying a condor to the horns of a bull. Everywhere there were inscriptions by the artist, including an account of his years in the 1940s travelling around the Andes by bus: 'From village to village, from city to city, we were witnesses to the most immense misery: villages of black mud, on black earth, with children muddied black; men and women with faces scarred by the cold, and with tears that had congealed to the point that they seemed made of salt.'

The unease the whole place left me with was not of the kind the artist had intended. I did not want to express these misgivings openly. Had I done so, even Inés, I imagined, would have rushed to the defence of her country's great hero. However, later on in Ecuador I would meet a woman who, without prompting, put into words what I had sensed. She had known Guayasamin well when she was young and had sat for him several times. 'He managed to take everyone in. He was the worst and most tedious of alcoholics. He was also an appalling macho who never stopped beating his wife. The Chapel to Mankind? What a joke! It's a chapel to the massive ego that was Guayasamin.'

It was not Guayasamin himself who reminded me of Bolívar; it was a quote in his chapel calling for a South America without borders. I had not thought much about Bolívar since Ibarra and there was not that much in Quito to remind you of him. The cult to Bolívar, as Inés pointed out, was far greater in Venezuela and Colombia than in Ecuador. This was not surprising. The man to whom the Ecuadorians directly owed their independence was not Bolívar but his general, Sucre, the victor of the battle of Pichincha.

Eventually I got round to paying my homage to Sucre. A taxi took me part of the way up the Pichincha volcano to see the monument to his victory. A modest cenotaph had now been encased in a grim concrete complex. Chávez had recently donated a plaque as a gesture from the Venezuelan people and there was also a Guayasamin-inspired mural with lots of hands breaking chains.

Before I left Quito, there was an institution I had been meaning to contact ever since my arrival. The owner of the Hotel Imbabura in

Ibarra, Pepe Dávila, had told me about it, but baroque churches and other distractions had got in the way. I was reminded of it while visiting the house where Sucre had stayed in the city centre. I asked the man at the ticket desk if he could lend me his telephone directory. I thumbed through its pages and checked every variation on its name. But I could not find the Sociedad Bolívariana de Quito anywhere.

The man at the desk offered to call a member of the staff. A deceptively gentle woman in army uniform said she would take me personally to the information booth on the old town's main square. The man at the booth had never heard of any Bolívar Society in Quito, nor did it feature in his list of the city's institutions. She persuaded him with a smile to extend his searches. He rang a friend at the National Museum, who put him in touch with a former history professor with a great interest in Bolívar. An address and telephone number were finally revealed. I would have given up long before, but the woman was now demanding that he called the number there and then. The man did as he was told. There was no answer. The woman now addressed me: 'You should keep on trying.' I promised I would, and she saluted me goodbye, her duty fulfilled to the best of her ability.

Just as I was about to leave the information booth, it occurred to me that there might be in Quito some commemoration of Bolívar's Quiteña mistress, Manuela Saenz. The man told me that there was now a whole museum dedicated to her, but that few people had heard of it. It was on the very edge of the old town. I did not hold out much hope for a place that made so little attempt to publicize itself, but I made my way there all the same, hoping that it might shed light on a figure even more legendary than Bolívar's dog. The story of Manuela and Bolívar was one of the great love stories of the Andes, though in its day it had struck most people as squalid. Manuela was a married woman and Bolívar a notorious womanizer famous for his many conquests.

Manuela's reputation in conservative Quito society had been doomed from birth. She was the illegitimate offspring of a high-ranking Spanish official and a wealthy Quiteña who had died soon after her birth. Entrusted to the care of a convent, and then taken in by her father's liberal-minded wife, she was finally married off to a English merchant resident in Lima, James Thorne. The problem of what to do with an illegitimate and increasingly rebellious daughter, with some of her stepmother's silly notions about the emancipation of women and South American independence, appeared to have been solved. Unfortunately, she did not love her husband and preferred the company of those patriot conspirators waiting in Lima for the liberation army of San Martín. She was in Lima long enough to share in some of the glory of San Martín's victory, after which she returned alone to Quito in time for the battle of Pichincha. She had been in love with Bolívar for ages, long before the day they actually met – the day of his triumphant entry into her native city.

She was able to brief Bolívar before his fateful meeting with San Martín at Guayaquil. Allowed to accompany his forces into Peru to battle with the royalists at Ayacucho, she thwarted a plot on his life in Bogotá. She shared his vision, his intelligence, his sense of humour and his eventual fall from grace. Her last years were spent in exile, obscurity and poverty in the Peruvian coastal town of Paita. She was posthumously rehabilitated at the same time as Bolívar, and turned by Bolivarians into a model of female devotion, bravery and idealism. The subject of various historical novels, she achieved world-wide notoriety after 1988 as the bisexual heroine of a Colombian erotic novel called *Mrs Thorne*, an international bestseller.

I realized, as I approached the Museo Manuela Saenz, that my knowledge of this much-maligned Bolivarian heroine was based heavily on fiction, in particular on the most recent novel about her, *Our Lives Are the Rivers*, by a Colombian-American author, Jaime Manrique. I could sense the author's emotional devastation as he finished writing the novel's culminating scene, when all the letters, diaries and other contents of Manuela's treasure-chest of Bolívar mementoes are burnt, in fulfilment of her dying wish.

I did not expect to be moved by her museum in Quito. I expected even less of the place once I got to it. The building in which it was housed had no association with her whatsoever, but was instead a neo-gothic late-nineteenth-century residence, with a grimly institutional interior like that of a Victorian hospital. The museum was divided between three floors, one of which seemed to be reserved for leisure activities for the elderly. The caretaker who took me round showed me at first some rooms full of coins, guns, swords, photos of old Quito, carved crucifixions and a large group of Chinese and African ivories. I failed to see the connection with Manuela. There was none, he said.

About halfway through the second floor, the whole tone of the museum started slowly to change, as if the world of the prosaic had been infiltrated by spirits. I was guided through a collection of Bolivariana, progressively more interesting, intimate, moving and surprising. There was a signed portrait by Sucre, followed by a Napoleonic portrait by David with Napoleon's face replaced with Bolívar's. Then came some of Bolívar's personal belongings: his stirrups, a pen-holder, a spittoon, a porcelain bowl presented to him by another of his lovers, Fanny du Villars. There was even the cross that was placed on his body at the time of his death.

All this was soon drawing me in like the pages of a good novel, so that when I reached the mementoes of Manuela herself, she could have been standing before me with her fan, her perfume flask, the prayer book that was presented to her on her marriage, the black shawl with pink flowers she always wore towards the end of her life. My eyes watered on seeing the objects testifying to her and Bolívar's love. There were the many gifts Bolívar had given to her, such as a set of silver combs and brushes, and a copy he had found of one of her favourite childhood books, Lope de Vega's *Shepherds of Bethlehem*, into which he had pressed a tulip. There was his last gift of all, a portrait of Manuela dressed to attend a bullfight, inscribed for the benefit of officialdom with the words, 'For Doña Manuela, whose loyalty does so much honour to the Fatherland.'

188

A different, more likeable Bolívar emerged in his letters addressed to '*mi adorada Manuelita*', framed copies of which hung on the walls, alongside her own letters to him and pages from her diary. I read the page in which she described her mixture of nerves and elation on the day when Bolívar had entered Quito, and the embarrassment she had felt when she had thrown a bouquet at him from the balcony and hit him in the face. The caretaker told me the true version of Manuela's death, and why, contrary to fiction, her letters, diaries and other treasured belongings had survived. Manuela had fallen victim to the outbreak of diphtheria that was drastically reducing Paita's population. The authorities had ruled that all personal items of the deceased should be incinerated, in an attempt to stop the disease from spreading. Everything of hers had been thrown on to the fire, when someone, no one knows who, decided on impulse to save some of the objects. 'You can still see some of the burn marks,' he added.

Like a magician coming to the climax of a trick, he then took me into another room to show me the most important of all the objects that had been saved. In an act of near-miraculous resuscitation he had placed before my eyes the very chest that Manrique had described. 'It was absolutely stuffed with Manuela's personal papers, and most of the mementoes that you see in this museum.'

I was almost beginning to like Bolívar. So much so that on taking leave of Manuela Saenz, I gave the Bolívar Society another ring. Still no answer. Then I looked at the address, and realized that the institution could be only a short walk from the main square.

The words 'Sociedad Bolívariana de Quito' were inscribed in worn bronze letters next to the portal of a lugubrious building in a neo-Renaissance style. The caretaker suggested I return the following evening, at around 6.30. There would be a meeting of the Society at seven and I might be able to have a word with its president before it began.

The next evening, at exactly 6.30, I arrived at the Society. The caretaker told me to go to the top floor, where the 'General' was waiting for me. I began wondering whether I was appropriately dressed. I was wearing deck shoes, black jeans, a grey T-shirt and my North Face fleece. I wasn't sure what to expect of the Bolivarians of Quito. Would they be informal Chavistas, benign and scruffy eccentrics or a group of right-wing, sartorially correct fanatics? As I climbed up the marble stairway with its heavy bronze chandelier and imitation classical torches, I feared I knew the answer.

General Germán Moraneda Bosch, president of the Bolivarian Society of Quito, was pacing up and down in his study, wearing a dark three-piece suit of a kind that might have been tailored between the wars. He had a narrow bald head as shiny as his black shoes, and lacked only a monocle to resemble one of the Ruritanian-style villains in *Tintin*. He shook my hand, and presented me with his gold-embossed visiting card. 'You're the English Bolivarian I've been told about,' he said, with a welcoming smile. 'You're very lucky to have found me here today. Our premises have been closed for the past year for refurbishment. This evening is our re-opening.' His manner contradicted his appearance. He seemed as open and friendly as everybody else I had met in Quito.

He wanted to know how he could help me. I said I was interested in the specific aims of his Society. 'It's quite simple,' he answered, 'our aims are to keep the memory of the Liberator alive and to ensure that the views of our members are reflected in the political sphere.'

I wondered how these aims were put into practice.

'We have lectures on aspects of the Liberator's life and ideas, and we invite as members leading politicians, businessmen, academics, educationalists, military officers and so on. This evening we shall be appointing a new member, who will be obliged to make a short speech. It would be an honour if you could join us.'

I mumbled a hesitant acceptance, and pointed out that I wasn't properly dressed for the occasion.

'Everyone will understand. People know what it's like to travel. Perhaps, at the end of the meeting, when I formally introduce you to the Society, you might explain to everyone what you're doing in Ecuador, perhaps you can even say a few words about the Liberator himself, and what you've discovered about him during your time in South America. If you'll excuse me for a moment . . .'

I could glimpse through the open door a trickle of Bolivarians gathering outside, all men, mostly elderly, and uniformly dressed in dark suits and ties. Two of them came into the office to greet the president. I was introduced to them. They handed me their visiting cards. They too were generals.

The president encouraged us all to move into the adjacent lecture hall, where he would be joining us later. We entered a long and narrow room hung with portraits of Sucre and other Bolivarian heroes. A massive canvas of the Liberator in a gilded baroque frame stood directly behind the desk reserved for the president, secretary and treasurer of the Society. I tried hiding at the opposite, back end of the room, hoping that I would pass relatively unnoticed. If the worst came to the worst, I could always make a discreet getaway.

Bolivarians kept arriving, until there were about sixty altogether, all of them identifiable as part of the same sect. There were just four women, of a type recognizable from my student years of evening lectures at London's Courtauld Institute of Art – genteel socializers, slightly batty, with blue-rinse hair, high heels and much jewellery.

The president and his two co-officials arrived, followed at a discreet distance by the man who was presumably the Society's new nominee. Everyone rose to their feet. They remained standing while the president made a short speech of welcome, referring to the Society's 'long recess', expressing the hope for a successful new season of activities, and saying how pleased he was that the Society was to be joined today by a leading member of Quito's academic community. He rounded off his opening words by welcoming this evening a 'Bolivarian visitor from England, which, as you all know, was a refuge to some of our leading patriots, and has always been a byword for Liberty and Independence'. I was beginning to get nervous.

Then the president extended his hand into the air, making what I would have sworn was the fascist salute. Everyone did the same. Half-heartedly I followed suit. I didn't seem to have much choice.

'*Viva la Sociedad Bolívariana de Quito!*' boomed the President.

'*Viva!*' came the unanimous response.

'*Viva La República de Ecuador!*'

'*Viva!*'

'*VIVA EL LIBERTADOR!*'

'*VIVA! VIVA! VIVA!*'

We all sat down, after which the president listed the achievements of the new member, an economics professor at Quito University. Liberation from Spain in the nineteenth century had clearly not entailed liberation from the Spanish love of pompous ceremonies.

A gong signalled it was time for the new member's speech to begin. The professor moved over to the lectern, placed on it a worryingly large wad of pages and took out his reading glasses. After a formal preamble, he soon veered off into a speech of flowery abstraction, of which I caught only such occasional snippets as 'the loneliness the Liberator must have felt as he stood atop the lofty peak of Chimborazo'. There seemed to be no unifying thread. But then I was not completely focused on what he was saying. I was anxiously trying to compose some words of my own, should the president really call me up to speak.

The professor appeared finally to be nearing some conclusion, with an overall assessment of a Bolívar who was obviously not the same person that Chávez had in mind. 'From the Liberator's later writings,' he was saying, 'it is clear that he saw as the only solution to South America's problems a government modelled on the enlightened constitutional monarchy that England is still fortunate enough to have.' A few heads turned towards me. I was looking towards the door, about five metres away. My nerves could not stand much more of this. What on earth was I going to tell these people?

There was a round of applause. The professor's speech was definitively over. The president got up to thank him, and then announced that 'our Bolivarian visitor from England now has something to say to you all'. I walked down the aisle, feeling as you do in one of those dreams in which you have gone shopping without your clothes on.

I had planned a short speech expressing British admiration for a general able in battle to shed a tear for his dog. But in the end I opted for a few sentences thanking the president and the Society for the privileged opportunity – for which I had been completely unprepared – to be with them all on this special occasion. I also announced that I was halfway through an Andean journey inspired by such exemplary visionaries as Bolívar. Afterwards, when the official part of the meeting was over and I was invited to stay behind for a glass of wine, I found myself surrounded by eager Bolivarians full of enthusiasm for my project and asking me specific questions about my route. Would I be climbing Chimborazo? Would I be visiting the battlefields at Junín and Ayacucho? Would I be ending the journey in Bolivia? They only wished they could be as young as I was. In their youths they would not have hesitated to come with me.

I could no longer delay my departure southwards from Quito. I had reached only the middle of the world and had just a few months to be at its end. But there were places north of Quito I felt unhappy about missing. Also my body and mind were in need of rest. From my guidebook I settled on what appeared to be the perfect weekend retreat – a cheap hotel occupying one of Ecuador's oldest haciendas. I rang to see if there were any rooms available. There were. The only problem was that a wedding was taking place there that weekend. The woman who took my call hoped that I would not be put off by all the noise. I said not at all. I added as a joke that I would mind even less if the happy couple invited me to a drink or two. 'Of course,' she replied seriously.

Travel writers are often asked how they chose their itineraries. The Irish writer Dervla Murphy says she thoroughly researches the country beforehand and then goes to those places no one ever mentions. Instead, I often feel I am guided by some irrational, intuitive force. A guidebook might have been the initial cause of my wanting to go to the Hacienda Guachalá, but it was with a sense of having little choice in the matter that I set off there from Quito at dawn one Saturday morning.

A local bus left me within a couple of kilometres of the hacienda, a rambling one-storied complex dwarfed by a grove of tall eucalyptus trees and the odd palm. Beyond its humble main door was a large courtyard whose simple arcading consisted of plain wooden pillars supporting the broad eaves of the roofs. The wedding guests, over a hundred or so, sat at long tables laid out under the arcades. There was no obvious sign of this being a hotel, no reception area, no receptionist. I felt like an intruder who had wandered into a slightly decayed country house. A young woman, the daughter of the owner, spotted me and my confusion, and asked if I was the Englishman who had spoken to her on the phone. She led me across the courtyard and into another, larger one, without people and open on its further side, behind which rose the twin belfries of a chapel. My assigned bedroom, white, with a small chimney and rough plastered walls, had a damp musty smell suggesting months of disuse. If I wanted lunch, the woman told me, I should come and look for her. 'We'll find you somewhere to sit.'

Shyly I stayed at first in my room, thinking perhaps that I would go afterwards for a long walk, then sit by the chimney, light a fire, and let the distant sounds of the wedding lull me at dusk into dreaminess. There was something profoundly poignant about the hacienda's empty courtyard, about the place in general. The atmosphere reminded me of somewhere I had visited in the distant past. Underlying the faded Spanish colonial look was a mood I had encountered in the rundown homes of the Anglo-Irish aristocracy. The sounds of enjoyment from the first courtyard brought me back to my present dilemma. I could not hold out much longer in my room. And I was hungry. I was not sure whether the offer of lunch also meant an invitation to the wedding. But I took out of my rucksack my main concession to smartness – an ironed shirt. I also brought with me my notebook, in case I was put at a table on my own, like a solitary newcomer at a restaurant packed with regulars.

I was. I started writing some notes, while taking furtive glances around me. Later I would realize that people had been looking with similar interest at me, the foreigner on his own, the only foreigner in the building, the only non-guest. Or was he a guest? Or was he a journalist reporting on the event? Or was he the strange Englishman who had made such a brilliant intervention at the Bolivarian Society?

I was not on my own for long. The guests on the long table next to me asked a waiter to squeeze in another place so I could sit next to them. I explained that I knew neither the bride nor the groom and just happened to be staying in the hotel. They offered to point out who everyone was. They themselves formed a mixed group, mainly middle-aged, most of them not obviously dressed for a wedding, some in jeans and corduroys and casual shirts. The man directly opposite me, the only one in a traditional smart wedding outfit, was stiff and reticent, slightly annoyed perhaps at the unexpected presence at the table of a scruffy foreigner. The others, in contrast, were all shouting to me across the table, asking questions, trying to get me involved in the conversation.

Lunch had yet to be served, but much Chilean wine had already been drunk. Ecuadorean inhibitions had been discarded, and the whole occasion was turning into one of those gregarious, repartee-fuelled social events that can be hell at first to the shy. However, years of living in Spain had accustomed me to occasions such as this. The odd joke was certainly being made at my expense. I was used to this. I was feeling quite at home.

I knew also that I had seen the man at my side somewhere before. Then I remembered an event I had attended at the Spanish Embassy in London. He nodded when I asked him if he had lived in London. His wife joined in to say that they had been living there for four years, when her husband, Francisco, was serving as Ecuadorean Ambassador. A woman on the other side of the table said that Francisco had almost been president of his country. The man next to her commented jokingly that the wedding guests were 'not your typical hoi-polloi'. Apparently I was surrounded by some of Ecuador's leading families. They seemed heavily inbred. Many of those present were connected to past presidents. Most of them were linked in some way to the hacienda's owner, Diego Bonifaz, whose ex-wife had married the father of the groom. Soon I was discovering that I too had links to several of these people. We had friends in common in Europe and elsewhere in South America. The world was fast becoming smaller.

Lunch was finally ready. We formed a queue that stretched across the courtyard. Two whole pigs had been roasted on a spit and giant slabs of beef were being served straight from charcoal grills. Everyone returned with laden plates to their tables and conversation became more fragmented as we began attacking the food with gusto. Bottles of wine kept appearing, particularly during the long pause before the dessert. Some of the guests started rising from their chairs, to move from table to table. We were joined by some of the groom's family, including the stepmother, Marisa, who pulled up a chair next to mine.

She was a youthfully beautiful woman in her late fifties, with only a few streaks of grey in her long dark hair. Her ankle-length ochre-velvet dress, like something from a theatrical costumier's, enhanced her motherly bohemian look. She had heard already that I was studying Andean history. She said that her years of living at Guachalá with Diego had provided her with abundant material for a book and she had already begun writing a novel based on those who had once lived and stayed here. 'So many important names in

Ecuador's history have been associated with this place.' I was excited but somehow not surprised when she mentioned such names as Humboldt, the Geodesics and the Victorian alpinist Edward Whymper. I had come to Guachalá with an intuition that it might bring together various strands in my research. I was coming to think of my Andean journey as the fitting together of pieces in a giant jigsaw puzzle.

Another piece of the puzzle was supplied by Marisa's present husband, the father of the groom. He was standing greeting friends at the top end of our table. Everyone was calling him by his nickname of 'El Pájaro', or 'the Bird'. Marisa said he was an actor turned satirical journalist who signed his articles '"El Pájaro" Febres Cordero'. When I told Marisa that his name sounded familiar, she said that he was one of Ecuador's most popular writers. She also thought I might be confusing him with his cousin León, a onetime President, and long-term leader of Ecuador's Thatcherite Social Democrat Party. I said I was thinking of somebody else.

She called her husband over. He was tall and angular, with a small, amused face, a trimmed beard and long, nervously agitated limbs. She told him I had been travelling all the way from Venezuela. He said that was where his family was originally from. They had been stalwarts of the Andean town of Mérida. The penny finally dropped. He was a descendant of Tulio Febres Cordero, the local author and historian who had popularized the legend of Bolívar's dog.

A local brass band entered the courtyard and soon started playing Andean dance tunes. The hippy-like bride and groom timidly led the way, followed by the more confident 'El Pájaro' and his wife. A woman who was now at my side was wondering if I had witnessed the marriage ceremony. They didn't want to marry in church, she said, they wanted an unusual, informal ceremony. The occasion was slightly odd, she confessed, but beautiful all the same and quite moving. They had opted for some Inca-style rite, you know, praising the harvest gods, and that sort of thing. Well, they're all a bit funny around here, starting with Diego Bonifaz. Have you met him yet? I'll have to introduce you.

Diego had moved over to our side of the courtyard and was laughing loudly with Francisco and a couple of others, who were teasingly addressing him as Pachacutik. That's his party, the woman explained, the indigenous party. According to her, he was about the only white person in it, certainly the only prominent white, the only one from one of Ecuador's grandest families.

He came towards us. Close to, he bore an uncanny resemblance to most people's image of Don Quixote. Emaciated, with a pointed white beard, a mad shock of hair and wildly staring eyes, he wore an ancient dark waistcoat and a crumpled white shirt eaten away at the collar. He was the archetypal Spanish gentleman fallen on hard times. The Ecuadorians I was meeting at Guachalá were unlike the elites I had known in any other South American country. They were warm, open, informal, badly dressed and eccentric.

Diego made me promise that I would meet him the next day at breakfast. He would talk to me then, he said, about the hacienda's history, which had always obsessed him. Right now, he added, whisky and wine were having their effect on him. My confidence and elation were surging accordingly. I found I barely had to move from the spot which I had been keeping since lunch. More and more people were coming up to me. Beautiful women were asking if I was 'the Englishman' everyone was talking about. The owner of Ecuador's major newspaper, *El Universo*, enquired about the possibility of doing an interview. The charming Peruvian wife of another diplomat was telling me to get in touch in Lima with her brother, Gaston Acurio, rising star of South American cuisine. I was getting invitations to stay in country estates all over Ecuador; I was being told of people who would be prepared to help me everywhere from there to Patagonia.

'Quick!' shouted a young voice from inside the house. 'Fireworks!' It was past midnight. The young had crowded into an inner room to dance *techno cumbia*; and then suddenly everyone was back under the arcades, the women with shawls and blankets, the men with cigars and big tumblers of whisky, the young with their arms entwined around their partners. There was a great noise as a large anthropomorphic structure in wooden slats, like a ritual offering, was pushed into the centre of the courtyard, then ignited. Rockets shot off from its sides, Catherine wheels revolved, there were sparks and flashes at every joint, until, with one last explosion, giant flames leapt up into the sky and lit up the staring faces.

An Andean festival would be incomplete without such a pyrotechnic gesture, observed a bearded young man next to me, watching the final flames die down. He turned out to be the person who had designed it. He introduced himself as Cristóbal, the husband of Marisa's daughter with Diego, the young woman who had taken my reservation. He was a scientist, and had been working the past few years on a project I could not leave the area without seeing. He imagined I had already been to the Middle of the World Monument outside Quito. That, he told me, was just a vulgar tourist trap. Tomorrow he would show me the real thing. The place whose location had been almost exactly established long before the Geodesics had arrived, long before westerners had come to claim the continent and to ruin it. The real middle of the world. The Indian middle of the world.

I lay in bed for a while, staring at the embers of the fire I must have lit around three in the morning. It was now almost nine and a bright light was shining through the thin curtains. My head was surprisingly clear. I remembered the promise to have breakfast with Diego Bonifaz, but I doubted if he had.

Once out of the cold room and into the pleasantly warm air outside, the return to reality proved unexpectedly gentle. The remains of the party had already been cleared up and the hacienda, for all its signs of decay, looked cheery under a blue if hazy sky. I sat down at one of the tables of the arcade, happily sipping an exotic fruit juice brought to me by a maid. No one else seemed to be up, except for the woman who looked after the hotel, Cristóbal's wife. She told me that Cristóbal would be waiting for me at midday at what she called the 'Quitsaco Monument', about a quarter of an hour away by car. Friends of the groom wanted to go there themselves and had offered to give me a lift. They would then be driving back to Quito. 'My father, by the way, will be with you shortly. He's getting dressed.'

The young children who had been staying overnight were soon up and screaming. The next to appear was the bride's father, Oswaldo Hayo, with whom I had talked only briefly yesterday. Balding, with rounded features and a timid smile, there was something about his quiet sensitivity that made you want to hug him and reassure him about the state of the world. Within a few minutes of sitting down in front of me, he was back to his two pet topics: the destruction of the Andean environment and the importance of trees.

'A journalist once asked me about the greatest love of my life, and I surprised him by mentioning not my wife nor my children but trees. For without trees, I argued, I would have no wife or children.'

Diego rushed by and mumbled a quick good morning. He said he would be back in a moment. He looked as if he hadn't got dressed at all, but had woken up in yesterday's clothes. His shirt tail flew like a crumpled handkerchief behind him. Oswaldo returned to what he was saying.

'Humboldt, as always, was right. He was years ahead of his time. He said that if you destroyed trees, you destroyed everything. Without the moisture that attaches itself to trees the earth dries up. You only have to see what's happened to the Andes. Without their protective mantle of trees, mountains such as Cotopaxi and Chimborazo are losing all their snow, all their beauty.'

He was getting quite emotional. 'And we're doing nothing about this in Ecuador. The country that inspired Humboldt has no proper ecological conscience. We allow barbarities.'

'And what about Peru?' I asked.

'Even worse! I never want to go back there. They're going to turn the whole country into a desert. There's so much corruption. The politicians let foreign companies do anything they want to. There's no control over anything. Nothing's being done to halt pollution. They're pulling up all the trees.'

Bolivia, 'poor Bolivia', had too many other problems to worry about ecological ones. The only Andean countries that inspired him with any confidence were Chile and Argentina. If you had to be an Andean tree, one of the few places where you stood any chance of survival was Patagonia. He adored Patagonia.

'But before leaving Ecuador, you must come and see my property, at Bombolí. I've spent the past twenty-five years trying to restore its ecology. I think the place will give you an idea of what the Andes used to be like. When Humboldt saw them.'

Diego was now back. During his absence animated shouting had been heard outside the main door. He apologized for having had to rush off, but 'a delegation of Indians' had come to see him, as they did every Sunday. 'It's one of my duties as mayor of Cayambé,' he explained. There seemed something inappropriately feudal about a supporter of indigenous rights addressing the Indians from the door of his ancestral estate rather than at the Town Hall.

Diego laughed as I mentioned this. 'The estate has only been in my family's possession since 1924. Feudal rights, technically speaking, were only granted to the first Spaniards in this country. From about the 1580s the descendants of the conquistadors were rewarded not with fiefdoms but with large plots of land. Of course the owners of these estates ended up becoming extremely important, especially after the mid-eighteenth century, when all these little bits of land started being amalgamated. Land ownership came to reside into the hands of the very few.'

I could see this was going to be a long breakfast. But a combination of Diego's appearance, fiery manner of speaking and general idiosyncrasies promised an account of Guachalá that might illuminate the whole history of Ecuador.

His skills as an actor were already apparent as he evoked the arrival here of the Incas. The Incas built fortresses around Guachalá and crushingly defeated the Cayambis and their allies the Carangues, who had peacefully ruled this area for centuries. The Gauchalá garrison was ordered to cut off the heads of every Indian opponent over the age of twelve and throw the bodies into the nearby lake, still known as 'The Lake of Blood'. The Incas in turn fled at the approach of Belalcázar and destroyed everything that was here. 'The Spaniards were greeted at Guachalá just by a herd of grazing llamas.'

The estate dated back to 1580. Diego pointed across the courtyard to where there had stood the oldest surviving part of the complex, the original chapel. 'It fell down last December, making a terrible noise. I'd been warning the government's architectural inspectors to do something about it for years. But they ignored me. I had no money to restore it myself.'

Oswaldo was shaking his head. 'That's so typical of this country. We leave everything to fall into ruin.'

Diego continued his account of Guachalá with the stay here of the Geodesics. Antonio Ulloa, he said gleefully, was quite shocked at finding that the estate's priest was an eighty-year-old who lived openly with his concubine and used his illegitimate children as altar boys. The Geodesics had also an insight into the Spanish treatment of the local Indians. All the markers the scientists placed on top of a neighbouring hill were repeatedly removed by the Indians, who were convinced this was another Spanish ploy to rid them of their lands.

We came to the nineteenth century. After the liberation of Ecuador the property had come into the hands of a German general, Adolfo Klinger, who had fought with Napoleon and then Bolívar, only to be impaled outside Guachalá by irate locals who wrongly suspected he was going to impose a government tax on them. 'Towards the end of his life,' Diego continued, 'Klinger had a daughter called Rosa, who ended up as a secret lover to our most famous nineteenth-century president, García Moreno. García Moreno often stayed in Guachalá in the 1870s. He planted Ecuador's first eucalyptus trees here in 1875. He was assassinated a few months later.'

Oswaldo, whose love of trees clearly did not extend to the eucalyptus, seemed to think that the last event was a fitting
consequence of the former. 'The planting of eucalyptus trees was
our country's first great ecological tragedy.' While he elaborated on
the eucalyptus's properties as 'a selfish impostor that merely takes
and never gives', Diego went off to fetch something he thought
would really interest me. He returned shortly carrying the white
shirt of someone who looked as if he had had a horrendous nose-
bleed. This was the very shirt, he claimed, that García Moreno
was wearing when he was shot outside Quito's Parliament
building.

The rest of his account of Guachalá was less dramatic. It focused
instead on those aspects of the estate's history that prefigured his
own socialist tendencies. He talked about the founder of Ecuador's
socialist party, Juan Manuel Lasso, who had been a governor of
Guachalá up to 1924 and had created a revolutionary army formed
from the estate's indigenous workers. He also spoke of the Agrarian
Reform Acts of 1964 and 1973 which had broken up the estate and
encouraged his family to give away the lands to the Indians who
had worked on them. When his daughter came to interrupt him, he
had got on to the subject of his involvement with Pachacutik, and
of how his party was fighting so 'that Indians could take a full part
in the democratic process'.

The friends who had offered to drive me to Quitsaco, 'the Indian
middle of the world', were ready to leave. Oswaldo wrote down the
address of what he called the Reserva Ecológica Bombolí, and told
me he and his wife would be expecting me there soon. I got into a
car occupied by two couples who were studying with the groom at
Quito University.

Cristóbal, in peaked cap and sunglasses, was striding impatiently
near the centre of a gigantic sundial laid out in stones at the flattened summit of a wooded mountain. Specifically he was striding
along a light band of stones representing the equatorial line. He had

a speech already prepared. He delivered it with the eloquence and passion of a preacher.

'If only western science had been less conventional,' he began, 'if only we had paid more attention to the example of the Indians, travellers from the West would have been drawn to this spot centuries ago. The Indians recognized the importance of the area long before even the Incas came. We are surrounded by ancient sites.'

His right arm roamed over a horizon of faraway volcanoes and mountains largely obscured by the growing haze.

'Over there is Pambamarca, the largest archaeological site in South America. Over there is Catequilla and, further away still, is Cochasquí, the only important pre-Inca site in Ecuador to have been commercially exploited in recent years. Pambamarca and Catequilla are accessible only by Land Rover, and almost never visited. As with many other smaller sites in this area, the Ecuadorian government and conventional archaeologists have never shown much interest in them. Worse still, the government seems actively to have condoned their destruction. Mining with explosives still goes on at Catequilla. Pambamarca is still used for military exercises.

'What have all these sites got in common? They are all connected in some way with the cult of the middle of the world. The equatorial line has always defined the culture of our country. The Indians worked the line out through calculations based on the stars and on the sun. The truncated mounds you see at Cochasquí can only be explained in terms of an observatory. No other place in the world is like this because there are no other mountains situated anywhere else on the equatorial line. The mountains have been landmarks of fundamental importance in making the calculations.

'But the middle of the world is much more than just the equatorial line, it's a state of being. The Indians of this area understood this, which is why they defended this area with such passion. Why did the Incas come to Ecuador? Because they envied us, they envied our unique geographical situation. Being situated in the middle of the world has always made us a defensive nation. Not having it has made the Peruvians traditionally aggressive. Why do we have here a Ministry of Defence, and the Peruvians a Ministry of War?

'When we created Quitsaco – which, by the way, means "middle of the world" in the ancient language of Tsafiqui – we had two main intentions. One was to save the ancient cultural heritage of this area from further deterioration. The other was to reaffirm South America's cultural identity after all the damage that had been done to it by the West. We believe that the European conquest disturbed the balanced, harmonious relationship the American people once had with their environment and cosmogony. We believe that our whole future depends on understanding the Indian system.'

The five of us listening to Cristóbal clapped, asked him a few questions, took some photos and then got back into the car. We were all quiet to begin with, as if trying to assimilate everything we had just heard. We had been sufficiently taken by Cristóbal's words to stop off on our way back to Quito at Cochasquí, whose overgrown, man-made mounds required considerable imagination to make any sense of them. The site would have been more memorable had the distant volcanoes towards which the mounds seemed to be directing you been more clearly visible. As we continued towards Quito, with the radio playing Andean music, I thought again about what Cristóbal had said. I remained sceptical about the special, spiritual relationship man had enjoyed with the middle of the world. I could nonetheless understand how the seismic Andean landscape could have had a great mystical impact on its inhabitants. I could accept, too, that Cochasquí and other nearby sites could have served as giant observatories: given the proximity to the sun and the fact that in this part of the world stars from the two hemispheres could be seen simultaneously, the idea was not so far-fetched. And if these had been observatories, I was prepared to believe that the ancient Indians had developed complex mathematical skills in advance of their western contemporaries.

My thoughts then took wing. I began thinking of recent coincidences and strange encounters, of the way disparate themes had starting coming together, and of how Humboldt himself, during his time at the middle of the world, had felt himself getting significantly nearer the ultimate, indefinable goal to which his journey seemed to be leading him.

# 13

# CLIMBING THE VOLCANOES

Humboldt had waited several weeks in Quito before making his first attempt to climb the Pichincha volcano. When not covered in clouds, it was the dominant feature of the city's skyline. It had two peaks of seemingly identical height, one with an active crater, the other with a long-extinct one that had collapsed. The irascible Whymper, making the climb nearly eighty years later, was irritated that no one in Quito seemed sure even then where the respective craters were situated or which of the two peaks was the higher. The higher of the two turned out to be the rockier Guagua Pichincha, whose crater, seemingly dormant in Whymper's day, was nonetheless the active one. The lower peak was the gently rounded Rucu Pichincha, now bristling with aerials and transmitters.

Muggers and rapists allegedly lie in wait for today's tourists tempted to ascend the green and easy-looking Rucu peak. Tourists, understandably, opt for the Guagua, which, though the more difficult of the two, reputedly requires no special mountain gear or skills. Danger is only likely to befall you if you decide to follow the precipitous path down into the crater, or are overcome by clouds of ash or poisonous gas. You would be extremely unlucky to be caught out by a full-scale eruption. The last one took place in 1660.

The Guagua was issuing occasional dainty puffs of smoke as Humboldt stared impatiently at it from Quito. With a height of nearly 5000 metres, it was higher than any other mountain the German had previously scaled. He wanted to get to the top to observe the effects of altitude on the human body and for further proof of his evolving Vulcanist position. He was attracted, too, by the challenge and was probably motivated by something baser: he did not want to be outdone by the Geodesics.

The Geodesics had used the Pichincha as their first triangulation point. Their experiences on the ascent were an indication of what Humboldt might expect. Everyone, as Bouguer reported, was 'considerably incommoded by the rarefaction of the air'. Several started vomiting and Ulloa fainted. The entire summit, unlike that of today, was permanently covered in snow, making their working and living conditions unbearable. Establishing a hut on top of the Rucu peak as their base, they spent many nights listening to blizzards severe enough to trap them on one occasion inside their shelter by an unbreakable wall of ice. During daylight hours they often diverted themselves by throwing stones over the precipice; but most of their time on the mountain was not amusing at all. After twenty-three days they had finally had enough and were forced to continue their meticulous calculations at a lower altitude. Before leaving, La Condamine went to take a hurried look inside the Guagua crater, which was then buried under snow.

Humboldt headed directly for this crater, followed of course by Bonpland. Whymper would dismiss the climb up to the Guagua peak as a mere 'excursion', but he belonged to a generation which had already devised special mountaineering techniques and equipment. Humboldt just threw a poncho over his everyday clothes and started slogging his way up the Pichincha. After a while he became dizzy and then passed out. He made two more failed attempts on the mountain with Bonpland.

Near the end of their six-month stay in Quito, Humboldt had another try at the mountain, this time in the company of an Indian called Aldas. There were some hairy moments, such as when Aldas sunk up to his chest in a crevasse, and when a tremor shook the projecting rock which the two of them were edging their way across. But they made it to the crater. Humboldt described this as 'the most imposing, melancholic and terrifying spectacle you could ever possibly imagine'.

Amazingly, he returned to the summit the next day, carrying electrometers, barometers and of course the hair hygrometer. He was able to record fifteen quite pronounced tremors in the course of thirty-six minutes, which convinced Quito's terrified inhabitants that he was causing these by throwing gunpowder into the crater. He was thrilled by what he had been able to achieve, which he compared favourably with the 'few minutes without instruments' that La Condamine had spent at the top. He finally had an advantage over the Geodesics and could now set his sights on higher mountains. He had plans for Cotopaxi and Chimborazo.

These plans included bringing along a new companion to complement Bonpland. This person would remain with them for the rest of their stay in South America. He was not Francisco José de Caldas but rather someone whom Caldas detested: Carlos Montúfar, son of the Quito aristocrat who had been Humboldt's main host in the city, the Marquis of Selva Alegre. Caldas acknowledged Carlos as an 'Adonis', but an Adonis who was 'ignorant, unprincipled and dissolute'.

The shadowiness surrounding Humboldt's personal life becomes murkier than ever during his stay in Quito. The friendship between him and Carlos Montúfar has been depicted by Humboldt's early biographers as purely platonic. Montúfar is remembered in Ecuador less for his connection with Humboldt than for having ended up as one of the country's main martyrs in the cause of independence.

Historians have traditionally found it more acceptable that Humboldt should have been flirting not with Montúfar but with his beautiful sister Rosita; but if this were the case, Rosita herself does not seem to have noticed. 'The baron,' she noted, 'was always

amiable and polite. At table he never remained longer than was necessary to satisfy the claims of hunger and pay courteous attention
to the ladies. He seemed always glad to be out of doors again,
examining every stone and collecting plants. At night, long after we
were all asleep, he would be gazing at the stars. To us young ladies,
this mode of life was even more incomprehensible than to my father
the marquis.'

Humboldt is popularly depicted as Rosita had seen him, the
dreamy scientist so absorbed in his work and lofty thoughts that he
had little time for more human activities. But another Humboldt
seems to have emerged at Quito, a persona already glimpsed during
the evenings of passionate dancing at Cumaná. He was rumoured
to have enjoyed here an illicit affair with a local woman with whom
he had a child. Whether or not there was any truth to this, or to the
idea of his having now turned into an insatiably active bisexual,
there is little doubt that he had become someone able happily to
indulge in the wild social activities referred to by the shocked and
prudish Caldas.

Caldas's opinion of Humboldt changed radically in Quito. The
trigger was a visit Caldas made to Humboldt's house early in April.
He wanted to know the baron's response to a letter of Mutis's
urging Caldas to be taken on as a travelling companion. Caldas was
confident that Humboldt would accept him, having already proved
himself to be talented and helpful. Yet Humboldt treated him now
with considerable coldness. At first he strenuously denied all knowledge of the letter. On repeated questioning, however, he confessed
that he had lied to avoid telling Caldas that he and Bonpland had
decided to head south on their own.

The devastated Caldas later found out through a friend that
Humboldt did not want Caldas to come along because he thought
there were irresolvable personality differences between them.
Humboldt, according to this friend's account, saw himself as someone who was talkative, highly sociable, fun-loving and burning with
energy and vitality. Caldas, in contrast, was 'somewhat slow, taciturn,

rather austere in life-style, and a lover of solitude . . . a person who rarely smiles, doesn't jump, doesn't sing, doesn't run, doesn't fight.' In short, Caldas was 'inflexible, severe and sad'.

Caldas's reaction on hearing later in April that Montúfar had been preferred was predictably extreme. In the letters he wrote to Mutis, he revealed a degree of anger that makes you realize how wise Humboldt had been in wanting not to have too much to do with him. Caldas, searching for a rational explanation, concluded that Quito itself was ultimately to blame for Humboldt's transformed personality. Long before meeting the baron or having anything to do with Montúfar, he seems to have detected in the city the very voluptuousness and frivolity which for him totally spoilt the baroque facade of the church of the Compañía. Now he was convinced that these same pernicious qualities had corrupted Humboldt himself.

'How different was Humboldt's behaviour in Bogotá and Popayán than it has been here! In the first two cities it had been worthy of a wise man; here it has been unworthy of an ordinary man. The air of Quito is poisoned; all that you breathe here is depravity; traps await to ensnare virtue at every turn.'

With a mixture of sarcasm, relief and insane jealousy, Caldas noted on 21 June that Humboldt at last had set off south, taking with him Bonpland and his Adonis, 'whose company clearly does not disturb him as Caldas's would have done'. Humboldt was probably relieved to have got going. He had stayed longer than he had intended in the city. For the past few months he had been waiting to hear news about Captain Baudin, whose expedition he was still intending to join in Lima. Finally he received a letter from Paris saying that Baudin had had a change of itinerary and was nearing the Cape of Good Hope in Africa. Life was once again teaching Humboldt not to put too much faith in others.

Humboldt never wrote the Andean sequel to his first book of South American travels, partly perhaps because he would have had to include Montúfar in it. This might have raised awkward questions among scurrilous-minded readers. It might also have stirred memories in Humboldt of a relationship that had come to embarrass him.

Unconquered peaks lay ahead. La Condamine and Bouguer had already climbed the heart-shaped summit of the Corazón, which was two hundred metres higher than the Pichincha, and had been claimed by the two Geodesics as the highest point ever reached by human beings. The Corazón rose to Humboldt's right, as he and his party headed south along the corridor of volcanoes. Perhaps he could picture the Geodesics waving to him from its summit. He would no longer have minded their taunts. He was aiming for loftier heights, more immediately for a mountain a thousand metres higher, on the opposite side of the road. The mountain was Cotopaxi. It was the highest active volcano in the world and, in Humboldt's eyes, the most beautiful and perfectly formed of all the Andean peaks.

I was on the road again. The haze was still there, bluish-grey and merging almost imperceptibly into cloud. The white summit of Chimborazo was vaguely visible, as the bus passed a landscape of heather and scrub scattered with occasional trees, and then was covered by clouds as we descended into a flatter, more agricultural countryside. I got off at the village of Lasso, a straggling, feature-less little community on either side of the straight main road. At the end of this was a lane marked 'Hacienda La Ciénaga'. I walked along it, towards a distant grove of trees bursting up from the ploughed fields.

Since Guachalá I had developed a taste for Ecuador's historic haciendas. The Hacienda la Ciénaga was also one of the country's oldest, with a history dating back to 1580 and a distinguished guestlist beginning with the Geodesics. Cotopaxi, dormant since 1534, had erupted in 1742, with La Condamine and Bouguer watching amazed from the summit of the Corazón. The two men, fascinated by the spectacle of their first volcanic eruption, moved down into La Ciénaga to be closer to Cotopaxi, which erupted several more times over the following years. In June 1801 this is where Humboldt and his party were put up while planning their ascent of the volcano. It was now a hotel where I was hoping to stay myself.

The approach to La Ciénaga, with a faint sunlight through the trees, an empty dirt lane dusted with fallen leaves and the sound only of birds, raised expectations of a place as evocative as Guachalá. The architecture was grander, however, on three floors and painted white. As the mansion became clearly visible, behind a pair of bronze gates and a centrally placed fountain, it seemed to be an eighteenth-century chateau lost in the French provinces. The plasterwork, at close quarters, looked as if it had been shaken by another eruption; and the paint had flaked so much as to make the central dome seem blistered as if by some great heat.

The interior contradicted these first impressions of romantic decay. The place had been brashly converted into a four-star hotel. The young, uniformed woman at the reception said I was in luck, as there was one room still available. She made me pay in advance. Only then did I notice a board welcoming to the hotel Crotchley Travel's 'Magic of Ecuador' tour. Soon afterwards, as a member of the staff was taking me to see the 'historic parts' of the hotel, I could hear the noisy arrival of a large tour party. But I had paid for my room. There was no escape.

The garden at the back remained for the moment pleasantly peaceful. With my guide filling me in with complex genealogical details about Ecuador's ruling families, I took in a garden of palms, narrow rows of privet hedges and beds of aloe and flowering shrubs. I looked also towards the blurry distance, where, on clearer days, the faraway Cotopaxi would have intruded incongruously into this sophisticated world. Then the peace was broken. A medley of British voices and guffaws had caught up with us, interrupting my guide after he had begun speaking about Humboldt. We moved back into the main building, where I was asked if I wanted to see 'Humboldt's room'. It was naturally the best room in the building, on the third floor and directly under the dome, decorated in an

Empire style, with a grand mahogany bed worthy of a pampered neoclassical courtesan.

Did I intend to climb Cotopaxi myself? I said I wanted to get as far as I could without the use of ropes or crampons. The hotel guide proposed to accompany me early the next day up to the refuge, which, at a height of 4800 metres, was as high as it would be reasonable to go if I had not yet acclimatized to high altitudes. He advised me to go to bed early and to drink no alcohol.

I did not envisage too wild a time at La Ciénaga. In fact, after putting my head into the dining-room, with its mass of elderly British tourists, I could not imagine how I would manage to stay awake until nightfall. So I walked back the three kilometres to Lasso. I was searching for somewhere congenial to collect my thoughts. The only place open looked like a cross between an American diner and an English 'greasy spoon'.

I ordered a bottle of Conquer beer and mentally calculated if I could afford to move on the next day to the nearby and far more expensive hacienda hotel of San Agustín de Callo. This sounded like one of Ecuador's most intriguing monuments – a hacienda built over a colonial monastery which had in turn incorporated some of the most celebrated Inca ruins in the northern Andes. According to Kohlberg, this was also the best place to appreciate the full beauty of Cotopaxi.

I paid for my beer and went off in search of Lasso's only public phone. I rang the hotel and was told that most of its six rooms would be free the next day. Then I was quoted a daily price equivalent to an annual Ecuadorean salary. I asked if it would be possible just to come and see the place and perhaps talk to the owner, Mignon Plaza, another name full of resonance in Ecuadorean history. The man at the other end of the line put me on hold. A woman's voice took over. 'This is Mignon Plaza speaking.' She had two questions: was I a writer, and had I had lunch? I was a writer, I said, and I hadn't eaten yet. She said she would wait for me. I could also stay the night, she added. Unfortunately, I replied, I had already booked in at La Ciénaga. 'Well come and have lunch now, and come and stay tomorrow.'

A shaggy black sheepdog rushed out to bark at me as I neared a group of stone buildings evocative of farmhouse holidays in Britain. The dog soon calmed down, pressed his head gently against my trousers and made me follow him into a yard guarded by a St Bernard. It took me a few more minutes before I found someone who worked here, a nervously talkative young woman who immediately identified me as the 'writer guest'. She led me straight to what she called 'the informal dining room', where a solid wooden table had been elegantly laid for two. Mignon, she said, would be with me shortly. In the meantime I might be interested in the press dossier she had prepared for me. It contained a brief history of the estate and facsimiles of two early descriptions of the place. One was from Juan and Ulloa's *Historical Account of a Journey to South America*; the other was from Humboldt's *Monuments of the Indigenous People of Peru*.

I learnt that the Geodesics had stayed at the hacienda when it was a recently founded Augustinian monastery, and that it was here that Juan and Ulloa had developed their enormous admiration for Inca culture. Humboldt, too, had enthused at length about the Inca parts of the monastery and in a more scholarly manner than the two Spaniards, whom he accused of producing a reconstruction of the original Inca structure that was 'purely imaginary'. For Humboldt, the ruins at San Agustín de Callo were a superlative example of one of the fortress palaces that lined the Incas' 'magnificent roads through the Andes'.

Elsewhere in the dossier I discovered that the property had been turned into a hacienda in 1921 by General Leonidas Plaza, grandfather of Mignon and 'leader of the Liberal Revolution'. Both Leonidas and Mignon's uncle Galo Plaza had been among Ecuador's most successful and longest-serving presidents. Mignon's father, meanwhile, José María Plaza, was a 'distinguished congressman and legendary amateur bull-fighter'.

I looked up to see Mignon standing before me. In her fifties, with long reddish-brown hair, light skin and casual sports clothes, she looked commanding and feisty, but also endearingly vulnerable – a sophisticated, emotionally complex American heiress, perhaps, and when she opened her mouth she actually spoke like one. She addressed me in perfect English with a slight American accent. Her mother, she explained, had been Californian. Her parents had met at a Californian tennis school and she had been born and brought up in California.

The food was served by an Indian maid in a long blue pinafore, with a white blouse and headdress, like someone from a nineteenth-century painting. Mignon had prepared the *sopa de locro* herself, a corn soup that was sweetish, thick and soothing. Its delicious taste lingered on into the rest of the lunch, which was blurred by glasses of Chilean Chardonnay. With the maid's opening and closing of the door, I caught occasional glimpses of some unmistakably Inca stones.

Mignon, speaking initially in a slightly distant manner, mainly about the hacienda, became noticeably warmer and more open on switching from English to Spanish. She saw herself as a Latin countrywoman at heart and had a passion for Spain. After her short-lived marriage ended, she had had a long and unconventional affair with the Andalucían bullfighter Luis Miguel Dominguín. She had always remained friends with him, but she could not imagine living with a man again. She valued her independence too much.

Then she got up from the table and briskly changed her tone. The tour began. We finally walked through the door I had been eyeing and into the 'formal dining-room', a strange and extraordinary sight. This was the first Inca ruin of my trip and also the first and only time I would see a major archaeological monument adapted for elegant domestic purposes. It was if someone had been allowed to roof Stonehenge and turn the place into a smart country house.

The room was dark and narrow, and centred on a polished mahogany table with silver candelabra. The ceiling had been added by Mignon's father, on top of walls made of smooth, regularly shaped stones whose carefully bevelled edges left not a single gap. I was seeing a perfect example of the imperial Cuzco style. Juan and Ulloa had marvelled at the way the stones fitted so tightly that 'not even a sheet of paper could be slipped between them'. Humboldt wrote of their having been carved from rock ejected from Cotopaxi's crater. Mignon said that the stones were indeed volcanic, but their blackness was due to a kitchen fire. Had it been a clearer day, she added, I would have seen the Fuji-like silhouette of Cotopaxi perfectly framed by the dining-room's single tapering window.

We moved on into the adjoining drawing-room, a lighter and cosier area, with big picture windows and a floor of ceramic tiles whose shiny redness had been achieved by staining them with pig's blood and then waxing with plantain skins. Most of the floor was covered by a colourful woollen carpet, on top of which were writing desks, comfortable old sofas and chairs, and coffee tables laden with books and magazines. What space was left was occupied by a striking portrait of the young Mignon by Guayasamin and an array of family photos and mementoes.

The centrepiece was the cloister of the eighteenth-century monastery, a secretive space with an uneven stone floor. Hammocks swung in the arcades, flowerpots were attached to capitals and a couple of bulls' heads were suspended on one of the sides. One of the maids was already inside the 'Inca chapel', placing candles in the niches of a windowless space as evocative of an Inca interior as anywhere else I was likely to see. The dark stone floor was seventeenth-century Spanish, as was the blackened shallow vault, but the slightly inclined walls were intact Inca constructions. Behind a modest altar flanked by candlesticks was a small crucifix, but alongside it was a crude statue of a bull 'used in Indian festivities'.

'Some archaeologists believe it to have been an astrological centre in Inca times,' said Mignon, before adding that the Ecuadorean government had offered not a penny to carry out the restoration work that was still urgently needed. She then looked at her watch. She said, apologetically, that she was going to have to leave me, as she was expected in Quito. But before the remaining daylight had all gone, she announced, she would take me quickly around the grounds.

We were walking for a good half-hour, through English-style gardens with duck ponds and geese, and up to a hill where the view of Cotapaxi was meant to be as memorably beautiful as Humboldt had described. But the weather, Mignon admitted, had been strange recently. The rainy season should have begun some time ago, but it hadn't rained yet. It was after a storm that Cotapaxi usually chose to reveal herself at her very best. For the past days her summit had been hidden by an unseasonal haze of heat and dust.

An hour later we were in the large and beautiful kitchen of the hacienda. She said she probably wouldn't be going to Quito until the next day now, and there'd always be someone to drive me back to La Cienága whenever I wanted. If the worst came to the worst, I could even stay the night; she would make sure that I was driven there at the crack of dawn, to collect my luggage and to keep my early appointment with the Cotapaxi guide who had warned me against alcohol. She opened a bottle of wine. Would I like a glass?

The bed was so comfortable and warm that I could not imagine ever getting out of it. Yet someone was continuing to knock at the door. It was six in the morning. I slowly realized where I was, and where I should be. I sat up, placed my feet on the ground and found myself staring at some Inca foundations.

I made it back to La Ciénaga within an hour. I had forgotten to phone to say I wasn't coming back last night. I had last been seen walking at lunchtime to Lasso and the staff seemed anxious. They had heard of tourists who had wandered off on solitary climbs and never returned.

I just had time to get to my room, pick up my luggage and be back in the hall to greet my guide, Diego. He hoped I was fully rested. I replied I had rarely felt better, and I wasn't being completely sarcastic. The thought of being up in the mountains was such an exciting one that it was already renewing my energy. Only the weather was disappointing.

I had set off from San Agustín under a clear sky, but the clouds were now so low that barely the base of Cotopaxi could be seen. As Diego drove me towards it, he said that we might be all right and that when it was cloudy on one side of the mountain it was often clear on the other.

The clouds had engulfed us completely shortly before we reached the Cotopaxi Natural Park. The road turned into a track of volcanic pebbles, increasingly obscured by the worsening visibility. Then a tiny little break appeared in the clouds. Within seconds the break had grown into a sizeable patch of blue. In a further few seconds a fragment of Cotopaxi's brilliantly white summit had appeared in sunlight. I realized in that moment how much I was still the child overcome with wonder at the sight of snowy mountains.

I was in a different world. The clouds had been shattered into tiny cumuli and a limitless vault of vivid blue extended before us. The sun had now left Cotopaxi almost completely exposed and had also uncovered the long, craggy profile of the neighbouring Rumiñahui, each fissure of which was now razor sharp. We were driving between the two mountains, across flat, volcanic terrain, along a monumental curve stretching towards further arid and more distant mountains and volcanoes. No trace was left of the lush greens around La Ciénaga and San Agustín. It was as if the vanishing clouds had lifted them all away.

The repeated explosions of Cotapaxi, culminating in a succession of devastating ones after 1877, provided a more scientific explanation of a landscape described by Blair Niles in 1923 as 'rugged, volcanic, barren, desolate and parched'. Among the only signs of vegetation in this wasteland were some widely scattered clumps of a lupin known as *chocho del páramo*. Higher up still was the occasional thistle-like *chuquiragua*, whose orange flower has become as much of a symbol of the Ecuadorian Andes as edelweiss has of the Alps.

The road eventually doubled back on itself and headed towards Cotopaxi's northern face. 'The neck of the sun,' said Diego, giving his version of the mountain's Indian name. Others had interpreted it as 'the throat of the fire', while La Condamine was insistent that Cotopaxi meant 'the resplendent mountain'.

We pulled up at the road's end in a near-empty car park. My first mountaineering feat in the Ecuadorean Andes did not seem as if it would pose any challenge at all. Our destination was a mountain refuge just below the snow level, separated from us by scree. I thought we would get there in about ten or fifteen minutes, but Diego said that the distance was misleading and most people took at least an hour. He said he would time me.

Whymper obviously reckoned the climb up Cotoplaxi was going to be so easy that he planned to do it several times, in order to test variations in his body's reaction to the altitude. At a time when people were attempting to climb higher and higher, the ability of the body to cope at great heights was a subject of paramount importance. Whymper, a proponent of the 'stuff-and-nonsense' school of medical thought, had believed altitude sickness was a largely psychological condition, until he first climbed Chimborazo. By the time he got around to Cotopaxi, he was thoroughly aware of the need for acclimatization before exertion above a certain altitude.

I had never suffered before from high altitudes, but I had never climbed as high as I was going to do today, especially not after barely three hours' sleep and enough alcohol to give anyone a serious hangover. So when I strode up to the refuge without much of a struggle I was feeling quite relieved. 'Thirty-five minutes,' said Diego, who had got to the top a good five minutes before me. 'That's not bad.'

We decided we would continue up to the first glacier, but not before having a brief pause in the refuge. Inside was a monument to Humboldt, 'the true discoverer of America, who climbed up Cotopaxi so as to unravel its secrets'. La Condamine had wanted to do the climb, but could not find anyone mad enough to come with him. The knowledge that the Geodesics had limited their studies of Cotopaxi purely to the lower slopes must have been a spur to Humboldt, as was the mountain's newly acquired reputation as 'the most dreadful volcano of the kingdom of Quito', whose explosions were 'the most frequent and disastrous'. However, Humboldt never made it to the summit – a fact unmentioned on the refuge's plaque to him. He tried to mitigate his failure by saying that no one else would be able to reach the top.

For a while it seemed that Humboldt was right. A Frenchman tried unsuccessfully in 1831 and a German naturalist, Moritz Wagner, made two further attempts in 1858, both of which were thwarted by bad weather. Not until 1872 did another German, a celebrated naturalist called Dr Wilhelm Reiss, finally succeed in conquering Cotopaxi, which he achieved by following the unstable trail of rocks left by a lava flow. Three more successful climbs had been made by February 1880, when Whymper was able to ascend the mountain effortlessly and spend a night by the crater.

Diego and I continued climbing for an hour so. I wanted to go on longer, but we had no crampons and, as Diego reminded me, those who now daily get to the summit, set off from the refuge at about one in the morning, so as to be back there by noon at the latest, which was when the weather can suddenly change. I was able to admire the view from close by the first glacier before Diego insisted we turn round. When we looked back at the sweeping view across to the Pichincha and beyond, the sky had changed. Bands of dark clouds were rushing towards us at a rate I would have barely thought possible. These made for some dramatic photographs, but Diego interrupted me before I could take any more. The summit had now disappeared and the sky had become menacing. We almost ran towards the refuge, where, instead of pausing, Diego proposed a hurried scramble down the scree.

'We could have been trapped in the refuge for hours,' he said, after I had almost slid all the way down to the car park. We got into the car moments before the arrival of the bus carrying Crotchley

Travel's Magic of Ecuador group. The only remaining band of light was shining from behind Rumiñahui and creating a ghostly silver strip across the lake in front of it. Then the world went black, and with this came a downpour so strong that the car could barely makes its way through it. The rainy season had arrived.

# 14

# LOST TREASURES

The next day was Valentine's Day. I remembered only as I woke up, back at San Agustín and alone in a huge bed, with the sunlight dappling the carpeted ceramic floor, the Inca stones, the remains of the fire which the maid had lit for me in the evening, the blue sofa identical to one my grandmother had had, the dark wooden door leading into my own private sitting-room crammed with old books. I bathed in an antique enamel tub, ate breakfast in the Inca dining-room and walked outside into a glowing landscape extending from Cotopaxi to the distant white speck of Chimborazo. I wondered what it would have been like to have shared all this with someone you loved.

Instead I joined a horse-riding party planning to set off by mid-morning. My fellow riders were a Dutch journalist called Annemique, who was writing a piece on the hacienda, and her photographer, Jimmy Nelson, who had insisted on sleeping up on Cotopaxi. He was a lean and completely bald Englishman, who told me that he had lost all his hair overnight as a teenager. His resulting crisis of confidence, he said, would later serve him in good stead as a photographer. After emerging from his teens he had never felt self-conscious again and had no inhibitions about using his camera anywhere.

He was wearing a sleeveless green T-shirt that exposed muscular arms. He seemed a born rider. Annemique had rather less experience with horses, but had the graceful bearing of an Amazon when seated on one. My riding abilities were comparable to my dancing skills, though considerably less practised. The longest I had ever ridden was on a donkey at Whipsnade Zoo. I was pleased that the calm-looking young man in charge of the horses was going to come with us. He had reassured me that we would go no faster than a trot and that Ecuadorean horses were as gentle as his country's inhabitants.

We crossed fields with views of Cotapaxi and the Corazón, and then entered a hilly wood. Once I had got the hang of starting and stopping the horse and persuading him to go roughly in the right direction, I began to relax. I needed to learn to ride. I knew of no Andean traveller who had been unable to, and there were stretches of my route ahead where I might have no other transport.

The young man stayed close to me. We spent much of the ride talking. He had been brought up in one of the several wooden shacks on the outskirts of San Agustín de Callo. He had lived for a while in Quito, but could never get used to being away from the countryside. He loved its traditions and legends.

He told me some of the stories he had heard from his grandmother. He said that in the old days men had to prove themselves as good workers before they were allowed to get married. His grandmother and another woman had been betrothed to one of two brothers whose test was to cultivate a barren piece of land in the *páramo*. The parents of the two prospective brides went after a year to inspect what they had done. The men had been turned into wolves.

And then there was the story about the condors. Condors, said the young man, were much bigger then than they are today. They were able to carry away sheep, and seduce young girls. The girls enjoyed being seduced. They used to put on white scarves to make themselves more attractive to condors. One girl, the daughter of one of the hacienda's farmhands, was taken by a condor all the way to his canyon. When his parents found her she had begun to grow feathers. They took her back to one of those round straw-roofed houses you still see occasionally in the area, and kept her in a large, earthenware jar, so that the condor wouldn't steal her again. But the girl sprouted wings and flew back to her avian lover.

That evening back at the hacienda, I picked up from a coffee table a book about the nineteenth-century American painter Frederick Edwin Church. Annemique was with me. She was learning about the history of the area. I wanted to show her the works of someone who had done more almost than Humboldt to excite western interest in Cotopaxi and Chimborazo.

Church was a landscape painter with a grand and visionary style that made him naturally drawn to the Andes. He belonged to a generation of American artists whose search for a national identity in painting had led them to their country's wild and empty spaces. These artists travelled to the most remote areas to gather memories and sketches which would later serve as the basis for finished canvases. From the 1830s onwards they began visiting South America. The impetus for these journeys was not just the prospect of new, unusual and little-explored landscapes. There were other motives, such as legends of El Dorado, the idea of a last frontier, the still-to-be discovered remains of great civilizations and the draw of a lost paradise. By the 1850s, there was another aspect of the continent's appeal to artists: scientific curiosity. Geology was then at the height of fashion and with it came a fascination with volcanoes, which perhaps held the answer to what Darwin would turn in 1859 into the major issue of the century: the mystery of creation.

Interest in South America also had its less noble side. The origins of America's political and commercial designs on the continent can be traced back to this period. Church's paintings could even be interpreted, by a Marxist Bolivarian, as presaging America's rampant and sinister interventionism in Latin American affairs. Church, on his first visit to the continent, between April and October 1853, was accompanied and sponsored by a supreme representative of American capitalism, Cyrus Field. Field, the future financier of the world's first transatlantic cable, was hoping that the paintings from the trip would help promote some of his South American enterprises.

Church himself would certainly have seen the huge commercial potential of South America for his own career. Yet he was also motivated by a genuine fascination with Humboldt and by a desire to see the places of extreme nature so intriguingly described by the baron in such works as *Cosmos*. There were many artists, beginning with the German painter Ferdinand Bellerman, who had responded to Humboldt's plea for a visual representation of phenomena that words could not adequately describe. But Church was by far the most successful in conveying Humboldt's vision of nature.

Church's first journey through South America followed almost exactly Humboldt's itinerary from Cartagena to Ecuador. The climax of Church's Andean trip was, as for Humboldt, Ecuador's Avenue of Volcanoes. A contemporary compatriot of Church's, James Orton, a science professor at Vassar College, probably spoke for all Americans of this generation when trying to convey the impact on him of this extraordinary landscape: 'Imagine fifty mountains as high as Etna, three of them with smoking craters, standing along the road between New York and Washington, and you will have some idea of the ride down the gigantic colonnade from Quito to Riobamba.'

Already, after his first stay in Ecuador, Church had produced in his New York studio the first of several paintings of Cotopaxi. One of these was a work of 1855 now in the Smithsonian Institute in Washington. Praised especially by those critics who had had 'a surfeit of volcanoes spitting fire and fury', it confounded popular conceptions by showing Cotopaxi in a calm and pastoral light, despite the gentle puff of smoke issuing from its crater. Cotopaxi had shown signs of activity in 1853, but the smoke in Church's painting was perhaps merely a nod to Humboldt, who had advised painters to distinguish between a volcano that was active and one that was dead. In any case, the work would certainly have delighted the baron, for it illustrated his perception of Cotapaxi as a mountain with a unique geometrical beauty and harmony.

Ironically, it was as a volcano 'spitting fire and fury' that Church would represent Cotapaxi in the most famous of his later paintings of the mountain. After his return from his second South American journey, he had initially concentrated his efforts on the giant, Chimborazo-inspired *Heart of the Andes* of 1859. This work attained heights of popularity hitherto unprecedented for an American artist and also conveyed an idyllic impression of the Andes that would have been hard to surpass. A follow-up was going to be difficult. The solution was to produce a blockbuster of radically different character. He went on to exhibit in 1862 the *Cotopaxi* now in the Detroit Institute of Art. One critic of the time said of it that it was 'the *Heart of the Andes*, throbbing with fire, and tremulous with life. It is a revelation of the volcanic agencies which made the landscape of Alpine South America what it is.'

Church himself had never witnessed a volcanic eruption and he might have got the idea for Cotopaxi from reading Humboldt's vividly detailed description of one in *Cosmos*. But it is also possible that in choosing a subject so suggestive of the beginnings of Creation, Church intended this canvas as a response to Darwin's theory of evolution. Church, as a deeply religious man, was likely to have been a supporter of one of Darwin's greatest scientific opponents, Louis Agassiz. The apocalyptic character of his exploding Cotopaxi, which brought together billowing black smoke, an eerie low-lying sun and a large foreground expanse of water, seems to confirm the idea that this painting refuted Darwin by showing a world created by a great natural cataclysm.

Church's contemporaries were unanimous in praising the veracity of the geological detail and realism in the portrayal of the eruption. Nonetheless, the overall look of the canvas is utterly fantastical and brings to mind the megalomaniac delusions of the

William Forest, 'The Heart of the Andes' (engraving after F. E. Church)

British romantic artist 'Mad' Martín. Unlike Church's 1855 representation of Cotopaxi, his painting of 1862 seemed to bear no resemblance whatsoever to the real volcano.

Annemique wondered if there was in fact a spot where Cotopaxi could be seen rising from behind what looked like a water-filled crater. I explained that Church, following the example of the great American landscapists of the time, brought together in a single Andean scene elements observed in a variety of different places, including along Colombia's Magdalena River.

But Annemique was convinced that the lake in the Detroit painting must be a nearby beauty spot, for she had seen photos of such a place. Later, I showed the painting to Mignon. She took one look at it, and came out with the name of my next destination – 'Quillotoa'.

Many of the backpacker conversations I had overheard in Quito revolved around whether or not someone intended doing the 'Quillotoa loop'. To do the loop involved leaving the corridor of volcanoes for a couple of days and touring a district barely visited until very recent times. I found it difficult to believe that Church had been to Quillotoa; I had never come across a mention of the place in any of the early travel literature on Ecuador. Yet the possibility, however remote, of finding the viewpoint that had inspired Church's great painting seemed a good enough excuse to go off into a steeply mountainous area with an almost exclusively indigenous population.

The young man in charge of Mignon's horses was able to give me a lift to the village of Saquisili, at the start of the slow way round the loop. He asked me where I intended staying that night. I said I had heard good reports about an American-run hostel outside the village of Chugchilán called the Black Sheep Inn. The man shook his head as I mentioned it. 'You don't want to go there,' he said. 'It's very expensive, and you'll only meet foreigners.' He confessed he had never been there but he was convinced I'd be better off going directly to Quillotoa. However, the weekly bus from Saquisili was going no further than Chugchilán and there would be no way of getting to the lake by nightfall. In any case I liked the sound of the Black Sheep Inn, which was 'committed to sustainable eco-friendly agriculture'. As I had planned afterwards to take up Oswaldo Hayo's invitation to visit the Reserva Ecológica Bombolí, I thought this might help me prepare for the experience.

There were four other foreigners on the peeling brown bus, all of whom were going to the Black Sheep Inn. The other passengers were all Indians returning from Saquisili's weekly market laden with goods. It was the most battered and crowded bus I had been on so far, and the most uncomfortable. My knees were almost pressed up to my chin, and a giant bag of potatoes wedged me against the window. Yet I could not have been happier. The people around me were friendly and inquisitive, there was no B-Movie, and the weather was as joyfully sunny as the day before.

Within half an hour the clouds had obscured most of the views, rain had started and drops of freezing water were falling down my neck from some hole in the ceiling. I wasn't worried. I felt confident the weather would soon clear, as it had done on my outing to Cotopaxi. It didn't. I arrived at Chugchilán five hours later, having had little impression of the journey other than that the bus had gone steeply up and down almost continuously, and that there were a number of swollen torrents.

Chugchilán, notoriously the poorest village in the area, lived up to its notoriety. It was a dripping, muddy huddle of blackened, unfaced concrete. I got to know most of its inhabitants in the course of trying to make a phone call to Spain. The one phone was in the office of the telephone company Andinatel. No one was sure when this office would be open. One person said I was going to have to come back the next day; someone else thought it was on the point of opening; a third person suggested I should go and see the man who had they key. He had just been seen standing outside the village store.

I proceeded without much optimism to the store and found the man exactly where he was said to be. But he hadn't got the key. His wife had it. He helped me track her down. She had the key, but had no idea how much she had to charge me for a European call. One of the many bystanders said that the schoolteacher would know. We went to the school and interrupted the teacher in the middle of a class. She had a long talk with me about Spain. She, too, didn't know what the call would cost. A discussion ensued, in which some of the schoolchildren joined in. The outcome was that I was going to be charged sixty cents a minute. We moved on triumphantly to the office. The phone was not working.

I was growing to like this village more and more. It was like a poorer version of Frailes. The slightest undertaking involved the opinion of almost everyone and took at least an hour. I walked on to the outlying Black Sheep Inn feeling the warmth of the Ecuadorean people more than ever.

The establishment comprised a group of thatched adobe huts spreading up a green wooded slope. It looked promising, but the American woman in charge had a bossy manner, a harassed look and a slightly phoney smile. She designated a young English volunteer with no smile at all to show me around and explain the 'house rules'. The most impressive feature of the complex was the glass-fronted composting toilets designed so you could shit organically while enjoying the best views of the landscape. The most irritating feature was the smug, self-satisfied signs, telling you which activities were less organically wasteful than others and emphasizing how the Black Sheep Inn was making a major contribution both to the environment and to the local community. The place turned out to be more expensive than anywhere else I had to pay for in Ecuador. Obviously it benefited some members of the local community, but the people benefiting infinitely more were the owners. For all their wonderful ideals, they were just another foreign enterprise exploiting underdevelopment in the name of progress.

When the rain stopped and the clouds lifted slightly I walked up to the high ridge behind the Inn. I could see some of the landscape at last: meagre ploughed fields, enclosed by hedges and stone walls, held tightly to wind-swept slopes dotted by occasional trees. The fields fell below into what seemed a bottomless canyon, on the other side of which were bare wrinkled mountains stretching out of sight towards the hidden Quillotoa lake.

I encountered several aggressive sheepdogs, and a friendly shepherd who pointed across the valley to the spot where his cousin and her three children had been killed last year by a landslide. He identified various plants for me, all of which were apparently good for curing cancer. 'There's a lot of cancer around here,' he added, in an almost matter-of-fact tone. 'There are a lot of people who die around here. That's life.' He shook my hand and went back to his four sheep.

Further along the ridge path I met a fresh-faced, long-haired blonde recently settled in Hawaii. She was making tutting sounds while trying to photograph a newly born lamb. 'Isn't he just cute,' she sighed, introducing herself as Megan. There was no need to ask where she was staying.

She wondered if I was thinking of going tomorrow to Quillatoa. I said I was. She told me there was a bus going there at four in the morning, and that she was hoping to return by foot. The Black Sheep Inn had given us both a crudely drawn map indicating the footpath back from the lake. 'It's meant to be a great hike,' she said. She persuaded me to accompany her. I hoped there wouldn't be any landslides.

Supper that night at the Black Sheep Inn was around another long candlelit table. There was no carnivore option. We ate a lot of pulses and discussed our respective itineraries around South America. A couple of elderly Canadian ornithologists recited a list of all the strange and wonderful birds they had seen over the past three weeks. Another younger Canadian offered to fetch his guitar. The unsmiling English volunteer briefly disturbed all the fun by coming in to ask us about our eating requirements and transport arrangements for the next day.

Drink was not included in the obligatory dinner and the atmosphere of enforced communal bonhomie was somewhat marred by everyone keeping their bottles of organic wine to themselves. I upset the house tradition by buying three bottles to be shared around the table. By this stage of the meal I would have happily taken up smoking and thrown all the empty bottles and tins into the garden.

I was a rather more sober person six hours later. It was nearly five in the morning, and Megan and I had been standing freezing and damp for nearly an hour, waiting on the roadside for a bus that might not exist. A few shadowy figures passed by in the darkness on their way to work. They all shook their heads, as if united by an unspoken local rule never to say anything to anyone from the Black Sheep Inn.

The bus finally came, as a grey, rainy dawn was breaking. We saw snatches of a beautiful valley, but then were immersed in thick fog as we climbed up to Quillotoa. The bus driver had to tell us where to get off, the only ones to do so. The bus drove away and we could see no lake. We could see no further than ourselves. We were colder than ever. We thought we saw some lights in the distance.

The lights belonged to some Indian shacks. One of them had a hand-painted sign offering breakfast and coffee. We went inside. An elderly woman was sitting squatting above the cold concrete floor stirring a murky liquid heated over a camper's gas canister. She called for her daughter, as she poured out the liquid into two used plastic cups. Megan took out her sterilization tablets. The daughter produced a couple of stale rolls for us. She spoke to her mother in Quechua.

A young boy, the daughter's son, came into the room to ask if we needed a guide. His mother said that we would certainly get lost if we returned alone to Chugchilán in this weather. We might even fall off a cliff. We believed her.

233

Outside the sky seemed misleadingly to be getting lighter. We went on our way, guided by the boy. A path climbed up from his house to the rim of the crater, where we stood for a while looking down into nothing. But then a sudden gust of wind brushed away a patch of fog for a few moments, just enough time to see the steely blue waters of the primeval lake. I could not decide whether I was seeing the beginning of the world or its end.

'What a shame the weather's like this,' said the boy, looking towards the lake's further shores, now disappearing again into fog. 'When it's clear you can see Cotapaxi over there. It looks as if it's rising out of the water.' Then he gave me a smile and a wink. I wondered if he was having me on.

A truck took me the next morning on the first stage of my journey to the Reserva Ecológica Bombolí. I had been thinking the past few days about what its owner, Oswaldo Hayo, had told me over breakfast at Guachalá. That the Andes were no longer the same, that they had been ruined by the modern world. The most obvious change since Humboldt's time had been the rapidly diminishing snow level on the high peaks, some of which, like the Pichincha, were now completely bare. The cause of this, according to Oswaldo, was not just global warning, but deforestation, whose terrible consequences had been predicted by Humboldt.

Then I thought again about the Ecuadorean paintings of Church, the foregrounds of which were often idyllically forested. I had told Annemique that this was just poetic licence, the result of channelling disparate observations of nature into a single picturesque scene. But I wondered now if Church's scenes were a more realistic picture than I had assumed of what the Andes had once been like.

I was completing the Quillotoa loop, returning anti-clockwise to the corridor of volcanoes. The truck driver was dropping me off at the small village of Zumbahua on market day. Llamas, stalls and a great mass of ponchos and hats were spread over a large expanse of earth. The weather was clearing and there were views over a tree-less horizon towards the half-hidden Chimborazo, now seeming deceptively close.

'You should have been here a few weeks ago,' said my indigenous driver, 'for the inauguration of our president. Fifty thousand people were crammed into the square, mostly Indians. Correa addressed us in our language, which he had picked up while living in the village many years ago. He called himself our *mashi cuna*, our companion. Evo Morales was there, and so was Chávez. I got a glimpse of them from about twenty metres away.'

I had arranged to meet Oswaldo at midday, at a famous stopping-off place, the Café de la Vaca. Surrounded by cows and horses, it looked like a cross between a recreational ranch and a thriving motorway service station. I was early and walked up to the counter to order a coffee. A middle-aged blonde woman standing nearby said she recognized me from somewhere. Then she remembered. 'Of course, you were at the wedding, weren't you, at Guachalá?' She said that the bride, Oswaldo's daughter, had worked for several years at the Café de la Vaca, looking after the horses.

We sat down to continue talking. She introduced herself as Carolina, the owner of the place. She wanted to know if my inter-est in South America had ever led me to Seville's Archive of the Indies. I said I often used to go there. Did I ever meet the archivist there whom everyone knows as 'the Ecuadorean'? Many times, I replied. 'He's my ex,' she said.

I was treated to a digression on Ecuador's threatened environ-ment and those crusaders, such as Oswaldo, who had bravely come to its defence. Oswaldo was a great friend of Carolina's ex, with whom he shared the same ecological obsessions. The ex's major publication to date was a work which dealt with the old forests of Ecuador and how Cotopaxi, Chimborazo and all the great peaks of Ecuador used to be completely surrounded by forests.

The wooden swing doors separating the bar area from the dining-room of the Café de la Vaca swung open and in walked

235

Oswaldo the crusader. He said we should be getting going. I got into his ancient truck, with its half-dead battery, which finally spluttered into action. We soon left the corridor of volcanoes and took a road headed towards the coast.

Outside the town of Machachi we passed one of Oswaldo's proudest local achievements, 'a biodegradable bullring', where spectators could watch the bulls being massacred while seated on benches of turf. 'Why destroy the environment by building another concrete structure?' demanded Oswaldo, in his gentle, slightly pained manner. '"Do not kill life to build death", that's what I'm always telling people.'

Further along the road I asked him about Carolina's ex and the book he had written. 'It's a wonderful book,' Oswaldo answered. 'He managed to collect all these documents proving that the destruction of Ecuador had begun with the arrival of the Spaniards. In 1534 all the land from Machachi to Cotopaxi was covered in forest. Only seventy years later all the trees had been cut down.' My theory that Church had recorded the Andes in their former, barely touched state was already looking thin. The Ecuador he had painted was already a devastated place.

Within half an hour we were at the property to which Oswaldo had dedicated the last twenty-seven years of his life. It came down to the road in a jumble of trees, bushes and tall cascades. Before entering the grounds he drew the truck up on the opposite side of the road next to a huge rubbish tip, about which he was always complaining to the authorities. We walked over crushed pans and kitchen units to a viewpoint over a deep, narrow valley carpeted in the patchy jungle where La Condamine had got lost coming up from the nearby Pacific. The mountain opposite had already been largely denuded and a couple of bulldozers were getting rid of some of the surviving trees to create another tract of arable land. Oswaldo looked towards me and then back again towards the bulldozers. There was no need for him to say anything. He merely sighed.

236

What seemed like the stone gatehouse to an English country house marked the entrance to Bombolí, which Oswaldo had purchased after the break-up of his first marriage, after many years of working as an agricultural adviser in the Argentinean pampas. He had been brought up in Quito and had become tired of a city increasingly buried in concrete. The land he had acquired had been mainly turned into fields for dairy herds. But he had also replanted a huge area with typical Andean trees and plants.

The winding lane up to the house appeared as English as the gatehouse and I thought of the Dorset hills as I caught glimpses of healthy cattle peeking over the stone walls and hedgerows that enclosed us on either side. However, a close look at the hedgerows destroyed this illusion. They were bejewelled with orchids of every conceivable type and colour, some like paper streamers in yellow and brown, others like delicate purple lanterns, others still like Lilliputian bunches of grapes. 'We have 587 different kinds of orchid at Bombolí,' said Oswaldo, as we walked the final fifty metres to the house, stopping every few seconds for him to admire the beauty of each orchid and for me to photograph them.

Inside the cosy and welcoming house I felt as if I had been taken in under the protection of friendly forest spirits. The sensitive and dreamy Oswaldo had found the perfect match in his second wife Mariana, a perceptive, witty and practical woman, white-haired and slight in figure but full of energy. The house itself, dominated by wooden surfaces and old furnishings, and lit at night only by candles, was again quite English, like a Victorian cottage lost up a wild hillside, surrounded by trees and cows and with a family of sleeping dogs.

The next day Oswaldo embarked on my botanical education. We spent hours walking through woods that were a lesson in biodiversity and the delicate balance that held together this lush dense world of orchids, ferns, lianas, bromeliads, mosses, liverworts, avocado trees and untranslatable but apparently emblematic Andean exotics.

I learnt how orchids were nature's way of controlling the destructive effects of other epiphytes such as fungi and lichen, and I registered for the first time such obvious facts as the way that rivers and streams are dependent for their existence on woods, which attract all the moisture from the clouds. Oswaldo explained the difference between trees that were 'atropical' and those that were 'heterotropical'. The former were the forces of good: they captured all the nitrogen from the air and brought it down to their roots, enriching all the earth around them. The bad trees were the pines and the eucalyptuses, the heterotropicals, who took away all the water and richness from the surrounding earth and allowed nothing else to grow in their shadow. The only conifer native to the Andes was the *Podocarpus*, but if I had understood correctly, that was an atypical heterotropical and did no harm whatsoever. Confusingly the *Podocarpus* was known in Ecuador as an *olivo*, or 'olive tree'.

The next morning Oswaldo introduced me to a woman called Betty Andrade. He teasingly referred to her as a former girlfriend of George Bush's. She responded that the Bush she had known when they had been students together at Yale was a different person to the abstemious moralizer he became after his marriage. Then she changed the subject to the reason why she had joined us on an outing that Oswaldo saw as a major step in letting the world know of the environmental barbarities taking place in Ecuador. We had all got together at the gatehouse of Bombolí. Betty, who had driven from Quito, wanted to know when and where we were going to meet the journalists from *El Universo*. Oswaldo said that they were coming from Guayaquil, and we would be meeting them further down the road, at a restaurant verging on the tropical lowlands.

I went in Betty's car. Formidable in her stature and directness, with a shock of unruly blonde hair, she was another strong-willed, independent-minded woman in her fifties. She, too, was from one of those Ecuadorean families that had probably produced several presidents, or would-be presidents; but the only member of the family I had actually been told about was her father, Rafael Andrade Ochoa, Ecuador's first air force commander.

We drove speedily down through what became a tropical jungle brimming with palms. As Betty impressively negotiated the many dangerous curves, I learnt in quick succession that she edited a series of travel reprints for a Quito publishing house, that she was a passionate hiker and lover of the outdoors and that she had been to almost every corner of the Andes. With all the new places and people she was recommending, I doubted now if I would ever reach Peru. Perhaps the more you travelled, and the older you got, the more you appreciated Pascal's dilemma of man trapped between two infinities. In terms of discovering that everybody everywhere seemed to be linked in some way to almost everybody else, the world was coming to seem infinitely smaller; but in terms of what you still wanted to see and discover, it was becoming infinitely larger.

When we reached the restaurant, I was struck with a momentary yearning to get to know the tropical, coastal areas of Ecuador. We sat waiting in the garden for the journalists, whom Oswaldo was going to take slowly back to Bombolí, showing them on the way evidence of illegal burning of trees and other examples of wilful destruction of nature, beginning with what was happening just outside the restaurant's grounds. We were in the municipality of San Domingo de los Colorados, a town so rapidly expanding with Colombian refugees that it had been nicknamed San Domingo de los Colombianos. The town council here, according to Oswaldo, was so corrupt that it had allowed the 'savage vandalism' that was clearly visible on the other side of the valley below us. A large swathe of forest had been removed to create an unauthorized dumping ground.

Oswaldo was expecting the journalists who had been sent from *El Universo* to have a similar sensibility to his own. He was disappointed. The photographer, a chubby man in his mid-fifties, was courteous and easy-going, and happy with the idea of a leisurely day in the country; but the writer, Carlos, was brusque and irritable, obviously wishing to get the assignment over and done with as fast as possible.

Carlos took in the rubbish dump from a distance, scrawled down a couple of notes and asked, 'Where next?' He rolled his eyes when Oswaldo mentioned a place that had nothing directly to do with the piece commissioned by *El Universo*, but was instead somewhere that would show the kind of botanical uniqueness currently under threat – the nearby country estate that had been bought by Betty's father. Grudgingly he agreed to go there, but reminded Oswaldo that he had to be back in Guayaquil that night at the very latest.

His face registered nothing but boredom after we had parked next to a white Bauhaus-style building of the 1950s and the enthusiastic, knowledgeable and sophisticated Betty had taken us through the thick grass to a tranquil river bordered by arched rows of giant bamboo. The river narrowed into a stream and then into cataracts as we walked alongside it. Climbing up a dark jungle path whose surrounding plant-life provoked shrieks of delight in Oswaldo, we came out into a brilliantly sunlit clearing where a waterfall, gushing out from underneath the mass of overhead palms, cascaded down into an enticing natural pool. Betty had intended suggesting a swim but Carlos was already looking at his watch. All he needed for his article was one further example of ecological damage in the area and then he could go home. Oswaldo proposed two examples. Betty had had enough and went off back to Quito, while Oswaldo, with me now in the passenger seat, veered off the main road and followed a rough mountain track which soon got us lost. Three hours later we were on the top of a mountain ridge, staring with the aid of binoculars at a faraway patch of burnt ochre. As we did so, an elderly man rode past us on a donkey. Carlos saw a way of redeeming his increasingly unpromising-looking article.

He hailed down the old man and said he wanted to ask him a few questions. Carlos's approach as a journalist was that of the bullying interrogator. 'What's that over there?' he demanded, pointing to the patch we were looking at. The cowed old man was so terrified by

240

Carlos that he told him the truth. 'It's a parcel of land owned by an Evangelical mission. They're getting rid of the trees so they can plant sugar cane.' As Carlos continued firing questions, the slightly embarrassed Oswaldo explained to me that the sugar cane was used to make a popular alcohol similar to the Brazilian cachaca. The photographer took some shots of the old man, while Carlos rounded off his interview: 'Name?', 'Address?', 'Date of birth?'

For the first time in the day, Carlos seemed almost to smile. We continued back to the main road, pausing to study a ravine that had once been densely carpeted with *olivos* and some silver-fringed trees I had first admired from the cable car at Mérida, *guarumos*. The cutting-down of many of these trees, and their lush accretion of epiphytes, had already resulted in a large area of erosion.

Carlos, far more relaxed than he had been at the beginning of the day, was happy now to let Oswaldo take us wherever he wanted, and he recognized that spending the night at Bombolí would be the sensible option, given how late it was and the imminent threat of fog. Oswaldo interpreted Carlos's change of mood as indicative of nature's beneficial effect on him.

We drove up into the clouds to stop off at one more site, another rubbish tip, but the worsening weather brought an end to our working day. Oswaldo would have willingly continued, even though he was clearly suffering from exhaustion. The emotions of the day, and his concern that the article should alert people to what he called 'these crimes against humanity', had worn him out. He was also a weaker man than I had realized. He had problems with his heart and liver.

'It truly pains me,' he said, 'to think I might die before I can put a stop to all these crimes.'

We arrived at last at Bombolí as night was falling. The dogs rushed out to meet us and Mariana could be seen in the distance, carrying a large pail of milk.

'There's something else I want to do before dying,' he said, turning off the engine and looking towards me. 'I want to see the Sierra

241

de Tandil again, in Argentina. It's a paradise, a magical place. It's the oldest range in South America, one of the oldest in the world. It's the kernel of the Andes.'

We got out of the truck.

'To think,' he reflected, 'that a tiny range in the pampas could be the source of all this surrounding beauty. And all this tragedy.'

Leaving the cocoon of Bombolí was like being a child sent out to face the world on his own. Mariana drove me back to the corridor of the volcanoes, to wait by the main road for the first bus heading south. The bus, when it came, was so crowded that I had to stand for the whole journey. Most of the passengers were going to the same place as I was, Ambato. It was the last day of Ambato's carnival.

Ambato rose timidly over a landscape of agricultural fields and must once have been a pleasant colonial hill-town, but it had been almost razed to the ground by an earthquake in 1949. Its main attraction was its carnival, but as every hotel and hostel in the town was full, I experienced little of this festivity other than the sounds of a few bands rehearsing. In the main square visitors were lining up to have a look at some new decorations inside the town's white and fussy modern cathedral. A young painter from Ambato had decorated the dome with a celestial vision that featured no angels or saints or any noticeable religious element, but instead consisted of a pantheistic landscape of volcanoes.

The only other monument open was the family home of Ecuador's most celebrated writer, Juan Montalvo, who had been born here in 1832. This whitewashed building was the oldest structure in the main square and the only one in the whole town to have survived from the colonial period. The adjoining mausoleum had a marbled art deco interior that could have been designed for a Cecil B. DeMille epic.

Montalvo was essentially an essayist who had also written a rather wordy and worthy sequel to *Don Quixote*, set in America. His life appeared to me more exciting than his works. A life-long liberal and anti-clerical, whose views had cost him exile, death threats and the banning of his works, he had a virulent hatred of dictatorships and of that of García Moreno in particular. In his book *Perpetual Dictatorship* (1874) he predicted García Moreno's death, which did indeed occur the following year, inspiring him to declare, 'I have killed him with my pen!'

On his mausoleum he was described as a writer 'Between Glory and the Storms', which I took to refer not just to the violent ups and downs of his career, but also to his deeply romantic approach towards nature. The major influence on his writings were the works of the French Romantics, with whom he had direct contact from the time of his first visit to Paris in 1857. In Paris in that year he made a point of visiting the ageing, neglected and increasingly impoverished poet Alphonse de Lamartine, whom he believed would find a visit to the Ecuadorean Andes immensely beneficial to his spiritual well-being. 'Together,' he optimistically wrote, 'we shall climb up Chimborazo; and from its summit cast our glances over a giant panorama at the heart of that immense land of America.' Montalvo believed that America, for all its failings, had the advantage over Europe in that nature showed herself here at her most sublime and transcendental. The Andes, in his view, were able, more than any landscape in Europe, to lift the spirit and renew the energy of those who came into contact with them.

Lamartine's reaction to all this was to invite Montalvo to come hunting with him in France. Victor Hugo, another of the Romantics with whom Montalvo corresponded, seems to have been more stirred by the thought of the Andes than Lamartine was. At least he responded memorably to Montalvo's plea that he shed a tear for Ecuador in the wake of the Imbabura earthquake of 1877. Hugo wrote to say that he had always denounced the tyranny of dictators, but there was another type of tyranny: that of the elements.

There was a growing possibility that I would witness such tyranny as I neared Chimborazo by way of a volcano currently considered Ecuador's most dangerous, Tunguruhua. Dramatically renewed volcanic activity in October 1999 had led to the volcano's being declared on orange alert, indicating that a full-scale eruption was likely within days or weeks. The army was sent in to evacuate the town of Baños, directly underneath the volcano; but, after an eruption failed to take place, some five thousand inhabitants of the area fought their way through a military blockade to return to their homes. The volcano was upgraded again to orange alert in July 2006 and in August the mountain exploded, causing rocks and ashes to cover most of the province, including Ambato, whose terrified population started to flee. After remaining since then on the less serious yellow alert, Tunguruhua had begun ominously belching and shooting rocks ever since my arrival in Ecuador in early February. Over the past few days there had been renewed talk of evacuating Baños.

Clouds had obscured Tunguruhua during my afternoon at Ambato, but they were rising by early evening, after I had managed to find a place to stay in an up-market resort hotel spread out along the bottom of a cultivated green river valley. The valley had a lushness and micro-climate that had given it the nickname of the 'Valley of Eternal Spring'. The hotel itself, an eerily silent complex of swimming pools, tennis courts, bungalows and wooden lodges, had an old-fashioned, out-of-season feel. Towards dusk, as I walked through the hotel's shady, riverside gardens, the cone of Tunguruhua was at last fully revealed, blocking off the southern end of the valley. It was murkily green, and unexpectedly tall. But there were none of the sparks of flame that had been issuing nightly from its crater over the past weeks. The solitary waiter at the hotel's restaurant told me afterwards that he found this sudden stillness more alarming than the regular nightly pyrotechnics. 'It's as if the volcano is waiting to surprise us.'

I was directly underneath the volcano at dawn the next day, visiting the small spa town of Baños, a backpackers' destination whose relaxed subtropical atmosphere made it a venue for ageing hippies. Humboldt might have been surprised, as he had been at Quito, by

244

how people could be so easy-going while living with the daily possibility of catastrophe.

The mood was particularly sybaritic on a Sunday, with many of
the carnival weekend's visitors heading off by bicycle or bus down
to the nearby village of Río Verde, a renowned beauty spot where
I too was going.

Baños was the first place I had reached on the Andes' tropical
eastern slopes, whose jungles extended all the way into Amazonia.
The twenty kilometres from here to Río Verde were along a steeply
descending road that went through many tunnels and kept closely
to the side of a deep jungle-covered gorge. Colourful Colombian-
style open buses or *chivas* went up and down the road, carrying
loads of tourists. There were roadside signs advertising such attractions as bunjee-jumping and 'the longest cable car in Ecuador',
apparently a perilous box with sides that barely reached your waist.

Río Verde itself was like a tropical, third-world Butlin's, with
cheap restaurants, food stalls, fairground booths and hundreds of
day-trippers lying around a huge shallow pool. The weather was
balmy and cloudy, though occasional bursts of sunshine penetrated
through the jungle as I followed the more energetic of the tourists
down to the 'Devil's Cauldron', where you can see a waterfall, eat
under a thatched hut and complete the jungle experience by walking out onto an unnervingly swaying footbridge made from lianas.

Only after returning sweaty from the gorge did I finally come
across at Río Verde what I had been hoping to find – a monument
to one of the most famous of the Victorian botanist explorers,
Richard Spruce. Spruce, the son of a Yorkshire schoolteacher, was
a serious and anti-social man. 'My delicate health and retiring disposition,' he once wrote, 'have combined with my love of botanical
pursuits to render me fond of solitary study, and I must confess that
I feel a sort of shrinking at the idea of engaging in the turmoil of
active life.'

His passion for botany dated back to his Yorkshire childhood,
when his idea of fun had been to list in alphabetical order the names

of all the three hundred or so plants surrounding his village. He had continued such activities after going off in 1849 to South America, where he lived for fourteen years, concentrating initially on the Amazon. After seven years he moved on towards the Ecuadorean Andes. He was in Río Verde for six months in 1857 'discovering', according to the monument to him here, 'an extraordinary biodiversity unequalled anywhere in the world'. He was in fact on his way to the western slopes of Chimborazo, where he had been entrusted by the British government with gathering seeds and plants of the cinchona tree, the source of quinine, the only cure for the malaria then raging in India. But Spruce was waylaid in the Baños area by a discovery that a true man of science would have done best to ignore.

Spruce, approaching the Andes from the Amazonian forest, had been making his way upstream towards Baños when a storm forced him to take refuge in a small village. After a couple of days here, when the sky had cleared, he walked up to the plateau above the village and was able to see the Andes for the first time. On the western side of the gorge into which I had just descended, he could make out four volcanoes, including Chimborazo and Tunguruhua. On the other side of the gorge, directly north of him, he was offered a rare, unclouded view of an isolated spur of the Andes he identified only later as the dreaded and legendary Llanganates.

Afterwards, on reaching the Baños region, villagers had told him a tale as implausible as that of El Dorado: the tale of Atahualpa's ransom. After the Spaniards had captured Atahualpa in Cajamarca in 1533, the Incas had tried to buy his release by offering them a massive treasure. Pizarro agreed to this, and then reneged on his promise. On hearing of Atahualpa's execution, his loyal general and half-brother Rumiñahui, already on his way south with the ransom, detoured into the inaccessible Llanganates to bury what he and his men were carrying and prevent the Spaniards getting hold of it. The hoard amounted to 70,000 llama-loads of gold and silver, weighing some 2500 tons. Rumiñahui swore his men to secrecy, and set an example by refusing to reveal the treasure's location after being captured by Belalcázar. The incensed Belalcázar had Rumiñahui burnt at the stake.

Spruce was then told about the Spanish soldier known simply as Valverde, who, perhaps fifty or sixty years after Rumiñahui's death, went to the obscure village of Píllaro at the western edge of the Llanganates. There he fell in love with and married the daughter of the local chieftain, who at last broke the Inca vow and told him of the existence and whereabouts of the buried treasure. Valverde and his wife took enough of the gold and silver to make them wealthy for the rest of their lives, but left by far the greater part of this treasure in its original burial place. On his deathbed in Spain, Valverde appears to have suffered a crisis of civic conscience and produced a guide or *derrotero* explaining to the Spanish king exactly how to get there.

The *derrotero*, with its accompanying map, found its way into Seville's Archive of the Indies, where it disappeared. Another version was deposited in an archive at the Ecuadorean monastery of Latacunga, where it was frequently consulted and copied until the 1840s, when it too vanished.

At some indeterminate date while the *derrotero* was still in Latacunga, a priest called Padre Longo, together with the governor of the region, made the first known attempt after Valverde to locate the hidden gold and silver. They would have found out straight away that the Llanganates was one of the most inhospitable regions in the whole of the Andes. Constantly rainy, even in the so-called dry season, it has lower slopes of impenetrable pathless forest and upper ones of cloud-covered *páramo*, full of half-hidden ravines and treacherous bogs. Padre Longo went missing one day, never to be seen again. His companion the governor, after organizing a search party, concluded that he must have fallen into one of the *páramo*'s natural traps.

The fate of Padre Longo would be suffered by many of the numerous treasure-hunters who have been drawn to these mountains right up to the present day. The idea of an Inca curse hanging over anyone brave enough to come to this daunting and mysterious land would of course make the whole story of hidden gold more alluring still. Even by Spruce's time, the tale of the Llanganates' treasure had acquired such a hold on people's imaginations that each week a new search party was setting off from Baños into the mountains.

Spruce himself wrote that he found 'the legend so improbable that I paid little attention to it'. He devoted himself instead to the more sensible activity of collecting flora from the slopes of Tungurahua. But, one cloudless September night in 1858, after another privileged sighting of the Llanganates, bathed this time in moonlight, he seems to have realized how much the mountains and their tale of treasure had affected him.

Whether or not he then went off in search of the treasure himself will never be known, for his Ecuadorean journals, alone of all his extensive papers kept in London's Kew Gardens, were lost. However, perhaps because he was getting bored with his tranquil botanical existence, he began to investigate the story and sent a paper on the Llanganates to London's Royal Geographical Society. Among his hypotheses was that Padre Longo had been murdered by his companion.

But Spruce's real breakthrough at Baños came about after hearing the story of a Spanish botanist called Atanasio Guzmán. Guzmán had lived at around the turn of the eighteenth century in the same village as the Spanish soldier Valverde had done, Píllaro, and had gained an extensive knowledge of the Llanganates in the course of looking not just for Atahualpa's treasure, but also for Inca goldmines. He was said to have produced a map of the area that was still in existence. Spruce managed to track down its owner, an Ambato 'gentleman' who kept it in Quito. Amiably this man had the map brought to Spruce at Baños so that it could be studied and copied.

Battered and barely legible, it was like a treasure map drawn up by a child, with a representation of the smoking Cotopaxi, lots of fantastical-seeming peaks and lakes, and numerous haunting inscriptions, such as a cross marked with the words 'Death of Padre Longo'. Guzmán's name was also regularly featured, in relation to such events as the 'Revolt of the Indians – Guzmán's Leap' and the 'Quarrel and Reconciliation with Guzmán'.

From the evidence of the inscriptions, and from his exhaustive local enquiries, Spruce pieced together a convincing story about his Spanish colleague, who, though failing to find gold, had clearly uncovered silver and copper mines that had been worked in the time of the Incas. With a team of Indian workers, Guzmán had begun mining these; but the Indians, 'disgusted with that slow method of acquiring wealth when there was molten gold supposed to be hidden close by', rebelled, forcing Guzmán to make a quick getaway by jumping over a river. Though apparently there was later a reconciliation with him, the mines were abandoned.

When Humboldt and his party passed through Baños on their way to Chimborazo in July 1802, they were reported to have met Guzmán. Guzmán, in Spruce's words, was said 'to have shown his drawings of plants and animals to that prince of travellers'. The only other thing Spruce managed to find out about Guzmán was the manner of his bizarre death, which took place 'about 1806 or 1808' in a small farmhouse very near the summer camp to where I had gone after Ambato. 'He was a somnambulist, and having one night walked out of the house while asleep, he fell down a steep place, and so perished.'

In 1884, twenty-one years after Spruce's return to Yorkshire, an English sea-captain called Barth Blake and his second-in-command Lieutenant Chapman found themselves having to wait three months in Guayaquil while their ship was repaired. This allowed them time to go and visit the Llanganates, whose buried treasure they had heard about from Spruce's nephew, a colleague of theirs in the Royal Navy. From Spruce himself they got Guzmán's map. Spruce was now ageing and hard-up, and may have agreed to give them this in exchange for a share in whatever riches the two sailors stumbled upon.

Blake and Chapman proceeded from Guayaquil to Ambato, and from there travelled down the Valley of Eternal Spring to Píllaro and the Llanganates. With the aid of their map they eventually located a cave brimming with Incan and pre-Incan artefacts in silver and gold. They took as much as they could carry, but were caught out by freezing fog and wandered around lost for days, during which time Chapman suspiciously died suddenly of a tropical fever. Blake returned to England and had some of the pieces appraised by the British Museum. After telling Spruce of his findings, he set sail for North America with the aim of selling some of the precious objects and raising money for a better-equipped expedition to the Llanganates. He never made it across the Atlantic. Somewhere off the east coast of Canada, near Halifax, he got drunk, lost his bearings and fell overboard.

On the crowded bus journey from Río Verde back to Baños I wondered if Humboldt and his party had got to hear of the Llanganate's mysteries, perhaps even from Guzmán himself. The risk-taking Montúfar, soon to appreciate the commercial possibilities of quinine, might have jumped at the opportunity of a treasure hunt. Humboldt, in contrast, would probably have been interested only in the legend itself and what this revealed of human greed and delusions. From Baños he was only a short ride away from Riobamba, where he would be almost at the foot of Chimborazo. The climb up this mountain, still thought to be the highest in the world, was all that was now on his mind. The idea of conquering such a peak was far more thrilling for him than the discovery of any treasure. He almost believed that everything he had been searching for throughout his whole journey would be found at Chimborazo's summit. The challenge of getting there held all the appeal of an impossible love. 'Everything that seems unattainable,' he wrote, 'has a mysterious power of attraction; you want to get to know, or at least try to get to know, everything that cannot be attained.'

# 15

# HEART OF THE ANDES

Late the following afternoon, I walked through the smarter suburbs of Riobamba looking for the house of Marco Cruz, Ecuador's most celebrated mountaineer. He had been up every major peak in his country, most of the highest ones in South America and nearly all the famous mountains of the Alps. He had scaled Kilimanjaro and Mount McKinley and had been on the first successful Spanish expedition to climb Everest. He had made more than six hundred ascents of Chimborazo and knew the mountain better than any other living person. He seemed a good person to talk to before attempting it myself.

On one side of the large entrance courtyard to Marco's Spanish colonial-style home was the office of his successful mountaineering and trekking company, Expediciones Andinas. A man from the office led me into the main house, left me in a book-lined study and told me Marco would shortly be with me.

The hundreds of old much-thumbed books about the Andes were a welcome sign of life in a house that seemed cold and unlived-in. Despite its colonial detailing, there was also something Germanic in its character, perhaps because of the extensive use of dark wood and blocks of coarse grey stone. Someone, perhaps Betty Andrade, had told me that he had lived for a while in Germany, spoke fluent German and had been married to a German woman. I doubted if he was now married to anyone. The house had a feel of grandeur, wealth and solitude, as if it were the residence of some Ecuadorean Citizen Kane.

Marco's appearance and initial manner were daunting. His clothes were in keeping with the house – Bavarian-style cords, with a neatly ironed checked shirt and a stiff, sleeveless woollen cardigan buttoned almost to his neck. But his face was a cross between that of a Spanish conquistador and some figure from Andean mythology. For someone whom I knew to be in his sixties he looked strong and youthful, with greying shoulder-length black hair, weather-worn skin the colour of dark leather and a beard that was white at its edges. He shook my hand brusquely and asked what I wanted.

His apparent wariness soon wore off, especially after realizing I was someone who had been drawn to Chimborazo by Humboldt, Bolívar, Church and Whymper. He became impassioned and charismatic. Within half an hour he had brought out from his study a cardboard box stuffed with objects wrapped in yellowing newspaper. Seven years earlier, while reconstructing Whymper's two ascents of the mountain, he had found the remains of one of his camps. Among the rusty buckles and empty tins were a few items you would not normally expect on an Andean climbing expedition – some empty bottles of muscatel wine. Marco reminded me that Whymper's faithful French companion Jean-Antoine Carrel had refused to treat altitude sickness with chlorate of potash, but had favoured instead red wine. Wine for Carrel was the cure 'for all human ills . . . from dysentery to want of air'.

Seeing these relics, while listening to one of today's great Andean mountaineers, enhanced the reality of a mountain I had come to think of as existing in some purely spiritual dimension. I responded enthusiastically to Marco's offer to be my guide the next day. As I didn't have any climbing experience, he didn't think it wise or practical that I should attempt the summit. He asked me if I had ever

252

suffered from high altitudes. I assured him I hadn't. 'We'll go, then,' he said, 'as high as the Whymper refuge.'

The Whymper refuge was just over five thousand metres high. That was five hundred metres less than Humboldt had reached on the mountain, but four hundred more than La Condamine and Bouguer. I decided I'd settle for that.

A faint sun was still shining as I left Marco's house, but Chimborazo was hidden. The chances of having a complete view of it the next day were slim: Spruce's first unclouded sighting of the mountain on approaching the Andes had also been his last. I stopped looking in its direction, and took a bus back to the centre of Riobamba, to see what the town had to offer. I found the last of the year's carnival processions, with women in colourful long dresses, and masked men in black, but not much else.

After the disastrous earthquake of 1797 the once famously elegant town of Riobamba had to be completely rebuilt, on a site eighteen kilometres north-east of the original one. The result was like so many other provincial Ecuadorean towns, a grid of streets with occasional stuccowork facades in an Empire style alternating with the shabbily modern. However, with a bit of imagination, and the aid of the procession, I could just about picture its centre as a frontier town from America's Wild West, with some of the older bars and hotels standing in as gun-slinging saloons and the asphalt and cars replaced with parading horses and carriages.

The town Humboldt saw was barely in embryo. Looked after here by Montúfar's brother, the district magistrate, he made use of his time by talking to survivors of the 1797 earthquake and getting to know an indigenous leader called Leandro Sepla, a man 'with a peculiarly cultured spirit', who showed him some sixteenth-century Quechua chronicles written by his ancestors. Someone had fortunately attached a Spanish translation to these documents, allowing Humboldt to read about the fate of a nearby mountain known to the Spaniards as the Nevado del Altar, and to the Indians as

Caparcurcu, 'the chief of mountains'. Once far higher than Chimborazo, it had erupted with such force that its whole top had blown away, creating clouds of ashes that had enveloped the country in a seven-year darkness. Humboldt did not find the story too far-fetched.

The story was probably more plausible than Bolívar's supposed climb up Chimborazo, which I had forgotten to ask Marco about. I would have plenty of time to do so the next day, I reminded myself, as I entered the charming little courtyard of a restaurant named El Delirio after Bolívar's bizarre essay 'My Delirium on Chimborazo'. The whitewashed house with its blue-painted pilasters was said to have been where Bolívar stayed in Riobamba.

Bolívar had his revenge on me that night for being so sceptical about his climbing achievements. I spent the night suffering from nausea and stomach cramps, and I was feeling little better the next morning. Perhaps my great mistake had been not to drink any red wine. When Marco drew up outside my hotel as arranged at six in the morning, I was shaky and clammy, and hardly able to walk the two metres to his Land Rover.

I was almost delirious before even reaching Chimborazo, but was reluctant to admit this to a mountaineering super-hero. So I pretended to be in the finest form as we drove off towards the Indian hamlet where Humboldt and his party had spent their last night before their climb. It was still dark when Marco picked me up but already a most beautiful dawn was forming, with just a few wispy clouds in the sky. 'Look!' commanded Marco, as the broad summit of Chimborazo appeared directly in front of us, already touched by sunlight. 'The gods must be smiling on you today.'

Our first stop was to see the *hieleros*, the men who climb four or five times a week up to the snow level of Chimborazo to collect ice to sell at Riobamba and on the coast. In Ecuador today, Marco said, people largely bought the ice from Chimborazo for mystical reasons.

The earnings of the *hieleros* must have been pitiful. We stopped in the ramshackle outskirts of their hamlet. Across an abandoned railway track was an eroded hillside shaded by two eucalyptuses looking like worn pipe-cleaners. Near the top were a couple of shacks made from adobe, plastic and bark, next to which were some mules tied by chains to a field. As we climbed up to them I pretended to make adjustments to my camera, so as to disguise the fact that I was having to stop every few steps to regain my breath and my balance.

Over the years Marco had gradually won the trust and friendship of the *hieleros* and was now bringing them some pastries as an excuse for my interviewing them. Two snarling dogs tried to prevent us getting any closer to the shacks. A girl emerged to throw a stone in their direction, but they still eyed us angrily as we continued climbing. The girl's skin was blackened by grime, as was the interior of her dark and precarious-looking home. She told Marco in Quechua that the *hieleros* and their wives had already gone off to the market. I had to make do with the sight of the pits where the ice was kept. The ice was hidden under straw held down by a large trunk. The straw was covered with used cartons and a couple of crushed Coca Cola tins.

The road from here turned into a sandy track running between fields that had been cultivated since pre-Columbian times. The view of Chimborazo was now as clear as I could possibly have hoped for.

Chimborazo, a long-extinct volcano, as Humboldt had suspected, had a summit of three distinct peaks, which, from where we were standing, looking northwards, decreased in size from left to right. The middle peak, only slightly lower than the highest of the three, was named after the man who was Ecuador's president at the time of Whymper's visit, Veintimilla. The highest peak was named after Whymper himself. Calculations of its actual height had fluctuated considerably since the time of the first attempted ascent, by La Condamine and Bouguer. Humboldt's estimate had been the highest by over two hundred metres, while Whymper's was the lowest. The Geodesics' had been the nearest to the actual figure of 6268 metres. Everest, continued Marco, was 8848 metres high, but,

Chimborazo – 'An illustration of the differing types of vegetation at different altitudes'

given the squashed shape of the earth at the equator, it was only 6382 kilometres from the centre of the Earth, two kilometres nearer than Chimborazo.

Marco had once tried to follow Humboldt's route up and down the mountain: it had taken him under ten hours. He drew me a map showing where Humboldt had given up, some way below the present snow line. Parallel to the right, and coming to an end below the gully between the two main peaks, was the route taken by the *hieleros*, and presumably by La Condamine and Bouguer. Had Bolívar ever been on the mountain, added Marco, he would certainly have chosen this latter route, which he could be done up to the snows almost entirely on mule.

I realized how much the snow line had receded even in the past three or four years. The regular fall of ash from Tungaruhua was partly responsible for this; but most of the melting had been caused by recent changes in Ecuador's ecology. Deforestation was obviously one of these factors, but no less important in Marco's opinion was the destruction of the country's *páramos*, which have always played a vital role in containing moisture. Despite their apparent barrenness the *páramos* were the home to 3600 types of plant.

In Marco's childhood, the arable land had taken up much less of the foreground and had been separated from the *páramos* by a band of forest. The Agrarian Reform Act of 1964, while being wonderful for democratic progress, had been ecologically disastrous. The new landowners had cultivated vast new areas of land, which had entailed not only the destruction of large areas of forest, but also an uncontrolled expansion into the *páramos*.

We continued driving west around the mountain, past a stone hostel built on what were probably Inca foundations, and along an overgrown track that was like a serrated scar in a geometrical, ochre landscape of ploughed, stony fields and esparto grass. We had reached the famous Camino Real which, long before the Incas, had been the route of a once-thriving trade in gold from the Andes and much-prized conches from the coast. The bulk of the Geodesic expedition had entered the Ecuadorean interior along this road and the single-minded Whymper, making his way almost directly from London to Chimborazo, had used it as he approached the mountain from Guayaquil and Guaranda.

Every ten minutes or so I had to step outside the car to take photos and be sick. Marco was soon aware that I was not as well as I had claimed. He thought I might be suffering from altitude sickness. I said I merely had a mild stomach disorder. We left the car and began a long uphill walk to see the last remaining woods around Chimborazo. I had more camera adjustments to make than ever. I was continually out of breath and feeling feverish.

But I made it to the woods. To ascend a barren ridge and to find on the other side a group of delicately twisted, softly coloured trees like those in a Japanese print was briefly reviving. Marco told me to touch the bark, which came off like wafer-thin strips of papyrus. The Latin name for the tree was *Polylepis incana*. It was perhaps one of the very cinchonas that Spruce had harvested. It might also have been one of the trees in the lush foreground of Church's *Heart of the Andes*, in which case I would have to revive my earlier theory about his work capturing the spirit of a now vanishing Andes. 'One hundred years ago,' commented Marco, 'dense woods of these trees encircled Chimborazo.'

We sat down so that I could gather what little energy I had for the afternoon's climb up to the Whymper refuge. Marco took out a picnic he had prepared, but I was unable to eat any of it. Instead I listened to him reflect on his past. He had made his first climb up Chimborazo when he was thirteen, with a couple of Italian priests. Italian priests, I was beginning to discover, had played a major role in the history of Andean mountaineering. The ones whom Marco had known as a child had changed his life. 'I would have liked to have been a bullfighter, like my nephew,' said Marco, 'but the priests showed me my true vocation.' Earlier we had been talking about Betty Andrade and Ecuadorean high society. 'Without mountaineering,' he added, 'no one in that world would have paid any attention to me. I would have been just a poor boy from Riobamba, without hopes or prospects.'

Large white clouds, appearing as if from nowhere, were starting to shroud Chimborazo, leaving only a tiny tip of snow above them. It was apparently almost unheard of to have a cloudless sky that lasted all day. This was not a mountain where you could stay still in one spot for any length of time. The sudden cold compelled us to move on.

We drove into the Chimborazo National Park and up to its highest point reachable by car, only two hundred metres below the Whymper refuge. There was a pyramid commemorating Bolívar, near which were the tombs of some of the hundred or so climbers who had been killed on Chimborazo over the past thirty years. Clouds encased us on all sides and all that we could see ahead was a dark, rocky slope leading up to cliffs of dirty snow, in front of which was the refuge.

The act of extricating myself from the car had left me exhausted and nauseous. After painfully walking the few metres around the pyramid, I had to admit to Marco that I didn't think I would make it to the top. 'Of course you will,' he said sympathetically. He led the way, with me a good thirty metres behind him and pausing every minute to try and recover. He waited for me to catch up, and then strode on ahead again. 'You'll make it,' he assured me. 'You'll never forgive yourself if you don't.'

I didn't think I would ever get to that point. I was expecting to drop dead at any moment. I had never before felt so close to collapse. I wondered who would look after my dog. I thought how awful it would be to die in this limbo, without even a beautiful panorama to distract my soul as it rose from my body. I tried thinking of something else. I thought of Bolívar's troops climbing the Andes only to march directly into battle. Then I thought of Humboldt and Whymper.

Of all the thoughts that came to Humboldt on 23 June 1802, the day of his ascent of Chimborazo, the most persistent one was probably how much the human body could endure and how much longer his luck would last.

He did not do the climb on his own. He would later get the credit, but the glory of the achievement should have been shared equally between him, Bonpland, Montúfar and an unnamed mestizo from the nearby village of San Juan. This last person, 'a man of colour', would stay with them almost to the very end, doing so, according to Humboldt, 'out of pure affection, and without any ulterior motive'. All four of them 'suffered horribly', as Humboldt confessed to his brother, but the mestizo, 'a simple, and very robust countryman, suffered more than any of us'.

The mestizo had been one of the Indian party who had started off with them at dawn, after a night of heavy snow up on the mountain. As the climb proper began, fog soon enveloped them, rendering Humboldt's instruments useless for calculating the triangulation point. The path became narrower and steeper as they advanced towards cliffs of rock, rising up from the snow and broken up in parts into tree-like pillars. One by one the Indians turned around and went back to where they had left their mules, oblivious to all attempts to make them change their minds. They claimed they were having greater difficulties in breathing than Humboldt and his two friends. Only the mestizo remained.

The fog did not lift, but they managed to reach the crest, which turned out to be like a rocky blade eight to ten inches wide. To their left was 'a precipice of snow whose frozen crust glistened like glass'. To their right lay 'a terrifying abyss', 250–300 metres deep, with rocks thrusting above the snow. They chose to lean more to the right, as at least there was something there to break a fall. Their progress became ever slower, especially as they were sometimes forced to crawl on their hands and knees. The rocks were crumbly and sharp, and cut into their hands. Humboldt himself, as he later apologetically admitted, thinking such 'insignificant detail' unworthy of mention for an explorer, was further impeded by having ulcerated feet caused by recent insect bites.

F.G. Witsch, 'Humboldt and Bonpland High in the Andes of Ecuador' (detail)

The breathlessness they experienced was accompanied, more distressingly, by a regular sensation of nausea and giddiness. Then their eyes became bloodshot, and blood began exuding from their lips and gums. 'These symptoms,' commented Humboldt, 'were not particularly alarming, for we had become used to them from our previous climbs.'

Unable to see the summit because of the continuing fog, they decided to make a barometric reading at a point where the ridge was just about wide enough for two people to stand on. They calculated to their dismay that they were only at a height of 5500 metres. In fact they were probably much lower. Their spirits were fortunately revived soon afterwards by the fog's brief disappearance, revealing the 'grandiose spectacle' of the exposed summit, which seemed easily within their grasp. The slope became easier and safer and they climbed it at greater speed only to reach an insurmountable obstacle: a ravine about a hundred metres deep and twenty metres wide. They contemplated descending to the bottom of it and coming up the other side, but the steepness of the slopes and the looseness of the newly fallen snow made them give up the idea. The weather moreover had turned threatening and their boots were full with snow.

Going down proved more dangerous and difficult than going up. A violent hailstorm was followed twenty minutes later by a snowfall so heavy that the ridge was soon several inches deep. But they were able to collect some rock specimens, so as to have something of Chimborazo to show back in Europe. When they reached the spot where their mules were being guarded, they found everyone seriously concerned about them. 'They were worrying a little too much,' said Humboldt.

Even though he had failed to conquer Chimborazo, Humboldt must already have had an inkling of the extraordinary importance of the day. He had done something of far greater significance than merely beating the altitude record set by La Condamine and Bouguer. He had had the satisfaction of getting nearer than he ever physically would to the heavens, while having now reached a literal and symbolic peak in his studies of the Earth. It was the proudest of his life's achievements, the day for which he would be most popularly remembered and the moment when his ideas on the make-up of the cosmos had finally begun to crystallize. Many years later, he would write: 'Chimborazo has been the repeated object of every question to which I have set my mind on my return to Europe.' On Chimborazo he focused his developing ideas on the alignment of mountains along geological faults, 'on the general laws of nature, on the geography of plants, on the climates determining different cultivations, on the superimposition of climatic zones'.

The actual conquest of Chimborazo seventy-eight years later by Edward Whymper was an almost mundane achievement. Whymper spent over a fortnight on the mountain with Jean-Antoine Carrel, a celebrated Alpine guide, and his cousin Louis, himself a professional mountaineer. They began their ascent on 26 December 1879, and established that day the first of three camps. Their provisions included tins of ox cheek, mutton, beef, potted ham, preserved soup, Leibig's extract, cocoa, condensed milk and lemonade powder, blackcurrant and cayenne lozenges, and of course the bottles of muscatel wine.

The ox cheek went off and had to be thrown away, and all three of them were 'feverish, had intense headaches, and were unable to satisfy our desire for air, except by breathing with open mouths', which left them with parched throats (thank goodness for the lozenges). Jean-Antoine Carrel, having rejected any 'doctor's stuff' for the altitude, was obliged to take a 'solution of sulphate of zinc' after being virtually blinded by inflammation of the eyes.

The blindness did not seem to matter very much. The visibility was so poor that at first they climbed the wrong peak, the future Veintimilla. Then they rectified the mistake and reached the right summit on 4 January, after a day of disgracefully slow progress. Whymper's thoughts had been largely occupied with the effects of altitude and why he and the Carrels had taken so long. On getting back down to the third camp, he had decided that it would be 'desirable to ascend Chimborazo again, to see whether we could improve our route, to learn whether our deplorable rate at the upper part was due to the softness of the snow or was to be attributed to diminution in atmospheric pressure'.

The weather had now seriously worsened and Jean-Antoine Carrel, though having pledged earlier to do whatever Whymper wanted, had had enough. He claimed that too much time at so great a height was doing his health no good, and that he had aches and pains all over, and was afflicted with dysentery. 'To tell the truth,' commented Whymper, 'I did not think much of the ailments he mentioned, for he appeared to be in very good preservation.'

Generously Whymper did not judge the Carrels 'too harshly' and agreed to descend the mountain. But he would return to Chimborazo five months later, having discovered that few people believed he and the Carrels had actually got to the top. With the additional company of two Ecuadorean mountaineers, he was lucky enough this time to do much of the climb in sunlight and to have a panorama whose impact on the ever receptive Humboldt might have inspired further reflections on the cosmos. 'Between us and the sea,' wrote the less easily impressed Whymper, 'the whole expanse from north to south was filled by the Pacific Range of Ecuador, with countless peaks and ramifications – valleys, vallons, dells and dales, backed by the Ocean, rising above the haze which obscured the flat coastal land.'

Yet an event happened to make Whymper express, for almost the only time in his mountaineering life, a feeling of overwhelming wonder in the face of nature. Cotopaxi erupted. An immense column of blackness shot up into the sky, after which the clouds from the volcano descended upon Chimborazo, creating 'truly amazing' effects of light and colour as the sun's rays tried to penetrate them:

We saw *a green sun*, and smears of colour something like verdigris green high up in the sky, which changed to equally extreme blood-reds, or to coarse brick-reds, and then passed in an instant to the colour of tarnished copper, or shining brass. No words can convey the faintest idea of the impressive appearance of these strange colours in the sky – seen one moment and gone the next – resembling nothing to which they can properly be compared, and surpassing in vivid intensity the wildest effects of the most gorgeous sunsets.

Then the habitual fog came and Whymper was back to his normal, phlegmatic self, pondering barometric pressure and the weight of the particles of dust from Cotopaxi. The summit was attained again without difficulty or excitement.

As I panted in a cold sweat towards the refuge bearing Whymper's name, I realized how my irritation with the man was growing. He was a smug and friendless misogynist whose interest in the Andes seemed mainly limited to barometric readings. He could stay in such a magical place as the Hacienda Guachalá and remark afterwards only that he had found there 'fourteen types of insect . . . of which eleven were new to science'. He was the complete antithesis of Humboldt.

But even had I been feeling better, there was something about Chimborazo's heights conducive to negative and morbid thoughts. It was a monochrome, oppressive landscape made greyer and blacker still by the recent ash from Tunguruhua. Humboldt's immediate impressions of these heights had also been far bleaker than you would have thought from the exhilarating account of the climb he published thirty-five years later. In a letter to his brother Wilhelm sent from Lima only three months after descending from Chimborazo, Humboldt referred to his few moments near the summit as 'incomparably sad and gloomy': 'We were enveloped by a fog that allowed us only the occasional glimpse of the terrifying abysses surrounding us. Not a single live creature, not even a condor . . . brought any life to the scene. Some small lichens were the only reminder that we were still in a land that was inhabited.'

Marco, standing talking to another man, turned to look at me as I hobbled the last few metres to the refuge. 'Congratulations,' he said, 'you have reached a height of 5030 metres.' He took a photo of me next to a plaque in which Edward Whymper's name was carved in large letters and introduced me to the person next to him, the refuge's keeper. We had been the only visitors of the day. There were some weeks when the keeper would be on his own for days on end.

I sat for a while on a rock, shaking with a slight fever. I failed to see how anyone could have a spiritual or mystical experience here. I remembered Bolívar's description of his delirium on Chimborazo, and his words seemed now more unbelievable than ever.

I sought the tracks of La Condamine and Humboldt, following them boldly. Nothing could stop me. I reached the glacial heights, and the atmosphere took my breath away. No human foot had ever blemished the diamond crown placed by Eternity's hands on the sublime temples of this lofty Andean peak . . . I left Humboldt's tracks behind and began to leave my own marks on the eternal crystals girding Chimborazo. I climb as if driven by this frenzy, faltering only when my head grazes the summit of the firmament. At my feet the threshold of the abyss beckons.

No sooner had Bolívar completed his pioneering solo ascent of the mountain than he fell into a delirious fever, in which Father Time appeared to reveal to him his destiny. Though, amazingly, there have been historians who have taken Bolívar's essay as a true account of an actual experience, it must surely be interpreted as an allegorical justification of the next phase in Bolívar's megalomania: the meeting with San Martín at Guayaquil and Bolívar's emergence as the supreme leader of South America's fight for liberation.

I remained seated on the rock, with my heart racing and sweat dampening my shivering body. I closed my eyes, hoping perhaps for a visitation from Father Time, but all I saw was Church's enormous painting of *The Heart of the Andes*, the picture that had made me first interested in Chimborazo, the image with which I hoped always to remember the mountain.

Church had portrayed Chimborazo as a component of paradise. He painted it as a single peak, draped entirely in snow, luminous under a large patch of pale blue sky. He made the mountain the eye's final resting place in a composition alive with rich reddish browns, olive greens, silvers and golden ochres. He placed it in the top left-hand corner of a three-metre-long canvas whose foreground is taken up by a glistening cascade and rock pool, hidden within a wood. He had planned to put some palms on the right-hand side. They were his favourite trees, the ones he included in almost every one of his South American works. But in the end he substituted fern trees. The fern tree, according to Agassiz, the creationist, was a more ancient kind of tree than the palm. It was a tree more likely to have been found in Eden.

There might have been hints in the painting of Chimborazo's former woods, but the work is clearly an idealized composite, reflecting Humboldt's vision of the cosmos in its telescoping of different climatic zones, while being infused with romantic pathos through the addition of a tiny roadside shrine – a reminder of death's presence even in arcadia.

Praised by one critic as the 'complete condensation of South America', *The Heart of the Andes* was also regarded by Church's contemporaries as a scientifically impressive exposition of botany and geology. The artist himself was keen that the work be viewed as a mirror of nature. He exhibited it in an illusionistic frame resembling a window casement; and he arranged alongside it plant and rock specimens brought back from his travels. Many people came to see the work armed with opera glasses. The public was wooed. The exhibition, held in 1859 in Church's New York studio, was the most successful single-work exhibition in the history of American art. On its closing day alone, six thousand paying visitors formed a queue that seemed to stretch from Broadway to Sixth Avenue.

*The Heart of the Andes* was the painting that Humboldt had always dreamt of – a work to instil in the non-travelling westerner a sense of the Andes' grandeur and magic. Its appearance in 1859 must have seemed part of a grand scheme of destiny. 1859 was a year in which events conspired to focus western attention on South America, on the make-up of the cosmos and on the whole question of Creation. It was the year of Humboldt's death. It was the year when Darwin published his *Origin of the Species*.

Marco tapped me on my shoulder. I woke from my delirium and rose shakily to my feet. He wondered how I was feeling. I said I was much better. We went back to the car, down to the bottom of the mountain and out of the clouds. The landscape became comfortingly green and rolling and touched by a late-afternoon sun. I was not returning to Riobamba. I was continuing south with Humboldt, aiming towards a long stretch of Inca road.

Marco left me by the roadside. I took a bus going to the small town of Alausí. The countryside seemed to be turning into that of the west of Ireland. We arrived at Alausí at nightfall, a town at the bottom of a deep valley. It was shrouded in fog.

# 16

# ANCIENT ROADS

The fog had lifted by dawn. I saw the clouds rising from a pinewood lodge at the very top of the town, alongside a single-track railway line at the edge of a large wood. I was the only guest at a guest house run by the sort of elderly couple you would want to meet if the world was coming to an end. They were called Violeta and Achilles. They still seemed deeply in love after fifty years of marriage.

Violeta, plump and motherly, had busied herself after my arrival making a warming soup she thought would help cure me of my remaining fever. Achilles, meanwhile, a retired civil servant, shared with me his love of history. He was a tall man with a quizzical smile, a small moustache and a slightly military manner. He wore a cloth cap and spoke with a measured old-fashioned precision.

Early in the morning he showed me around Alausí, an endearing small town. Ringed by smoothly rounded mountains carpeted in what seemed like faded green felt, it had an ironwork bandstand, a promenade with cafés and bars, and an overall atmosphere of the days when the place was an important stop on the Guayaquil–Quito railway.

Achilles wanted to introduce me to some of the local dignitaries, notably his good friend Don Bolívar Silva, a newspaper proprietor who knew just the right person to guide me along the Inca trail to Cuenca. Don Bolívar, the local boy made good, seemed the least likely person to merit being referred to as 'Don'. Years of working in New York in the music business ('I represented all the great Latino stars') had given him a direct, North American manner, complete with Hawaiian shirt and Rolex. He had retired to his home town to revive its defunct local newspaper, the second oldest in Ecuador, *La Voz de los Andes* ('The Voice of the Andes'). Achilles politely asked about the guide he knew. Don Bolívar lay back on his swivel chair, placed his feet on the desk and made a quick call. A man whom he called Señor Sea was going to come into the office towards the end of the morning.

We returned to Don Bolívar's office by noon. The obsequious Señor Sea was already there, together with his sad but determined-looking wife and a sulky mustachioed young man with long curly black hair and white reversed baseball cap. Señor Sea was unable to come with me on the Inca road, so he proposed instead the services of the young man, his son Genaro. Don Bolívar acted as intermediary as we discussed the cost of the trip. Genaro, eyeing me suspiciously, was continually trying to up the price, but eventually bowed to his father's more reasonable demands. It was agreed that Genaro would pick me up that night to drive me to the village of Achapullas, where the Seas lived. The next day he and I would set off by horse towards the Inca ruins at Ingapirca. Most people took two days over the ride, but if we were quick we could just about do it in one. I shook hands with Genaro, who remained sullen. One day with him, I thought, would probably be enough.

Afterwards I voiced my doubts about Genaro. Achilles reassured me. 'You must remember, Don Michael, that the Seas are simple, country people. That is their manner.'

Violeta had heard that I was leaving that evening and had prepared me a large lunch at her family house in the centre of the town. When I got there, she tried persuading me to postpone my journey, 'just for a few more days'. She was worried that I wasn't well enough yet to travel. She said that it was going to be pouring with rain and freezing at night. She was concerned about my lack of riding experience.

The tranquil domestic world she and Achilles inhabited, with their many pets, their well-tended cottage garden, and their established routines made me pause and consider. Why indeed did I want to move on so quickly?

I was asking myself this again a few hours later. It was dark, the fog had returned and a few drops of rain were beginning to fall. By the time Genaro turned up half an hour late, the rain was beginning to pour.

Genaro had been delayed by the fog. Very apologetic, he was a different person from before, talkative and friendly and laughing with a cousin of his, an engineering student from Quito, whom he had brought along for the ride. I squeezed in next to the two of them at the front of his old van. We collected my luggage at the guest house, by which time visibility was so poor and the downpour so heavy that we found ourselves for a time driving along the railway line. There was no place to turn around, so we had to keep on following it. Genaro wasn't sure when the next train was due.

Eventually we rammed our way through bushes back onto the main road, where we could see even less than before. Later, after turning off it and taking the dirt track that climbed up to Achapullas, Genaro claimed we would soon be out of the clouds. But we weren't. The track was hugging a cliff, which could just about be made out. On the outer side, however, the hairpin bends vanished into a dark void. We were like the victims in a horror film, awaiting the appearance of evil at every turn.

But the evil that Genaro went on to relate as my body tautened at each curve of the road had nothing to do with the supernatural. His story explained his earlier, suspicious behaviour. It was a story that made you ashamed to be a westerner.

271

Genaro, one of eight children, had reached a critical stage in his life. He saw no way out of his poverty other than to emigrate to Europe. He hoped at least to earn enough money to pay for the university education of one of his sisters, who was desperate to study. He had been told of a Spanish agency which ensured a work permit and visa for Spain on payment of a deposit of $4500, an inconceivably large sum for someone from his background. The agency seemed a reputable one: its director said he was a friend of the Spanish ambassador in Quito. Genaro's family had pooled their resources, including money that had already been put aside for his sister. The outcome hardly needs telling. The papers never materialized, the deposit was never returned. There was nothing Genaro could do. The family was now heavily in debt. The mother was ill with nerves and depression, the father was receiving treatment for prostate cancer.

Perhaps unwisely I promised to try and help. I would do all that I could to expose the Spaniards who had been so shamefully involved in this. Genaro was smiling as we finally emerged into the moonlight, at the top of the climb, within sight of his village. I realized I might have made a terrible mistake and had raised hopes that could never be fulfilled. Yet I was fuelled with such indignation that I was convinced that something would come out of this. I was as naïve as he was.

The family owned the village shop on the main square in front of the disproportionately grand parish church. The mother, statuesque in her long dark dress, and looking in the half-light like some classical representation of tragedy, had waited up for us. I was welcomed with a huge bowl of boiled potatoes and given the use of Genaro's bedroom, above an unlit, partly collapsing courtyard with two horses and an outside toilet. I slept fully clothed and freezing in a room where the light of a full moon penetrated a threadbare curtain.

'God has sent you here to help us,' the mother said to me at seven in the morning, over a breakfast of more potatoes. Genaro had told her about my offer to let the world know about the great injustice that had been done to them. I could see him outside the main door saddling the horses, watched by an old man. 'Please don't forget us,' she repeated as the time came for me to mount the horse. 'We're counting on you.'

The elderly spectator had now been joined by several other bystanders. They looked more intrigued than amused as I tried lifting my foot over the saddle. Genaro was carrying my rucksack in his hands, while my horse, Golondrina, or 'Swallow', was weighed down by food and camping equipment. Spurs had been attached with rope to my boots.

Golondrina seemed a tame enough horse, but, just as we had left the village, an inadvertent movement of my spurs prompted her to make a mad gallop down a side-track. Genaro caught up with us in time to stop me being thrown headfirst into mud.

She calmed down slightly as we got back to the right path, which narrowed and became rougher as it continued climbing. In between ducking to avoid the many overhead branches, I timidly looked back down to the small plateau on which the village was situated, and across to faraway terraced mountains crisply lit by snatches of early-morning sunlight. Further up, all colour and brightness disappeared as we entered the *páramo* of Azuay, and the path became a long straight line ascending slowly though moorland towards a grey horizon. This being the 'Inca Trail', I had imagined meeting numerous groups of hikers along the way, but we saw only a surprised English couple, who shouted out 'That's cheating!' as I rode past.

Before leaving this gentle gradient and climbing sharply up to a tall ridge, Genaro stopped to put on an anorak, tie up its strings and cover his hands and head. We were in a *páramo* that Humboldt had described as notorious for its freezing temperatures.

A few drops of rain were falling and the wind had begun to bite. At the top of the ridge the wind was so strong that Golondrina suddenly started to neigh and move erratically. Without a second thought, Genaro took us off the path and down the slope in a series of near-vertical zigzags that had me clinging terrified to Golondrina's neck. Had we stayed on the ridge, Genaro explained, our horses would have been blown over. We crossed the mountain at a lower point and rejoined the path just as it descended down to a long bleak valley, where a stream could be seen snaking its way towards a distant lake.

We fought our way across the valley's boggy ground, which had also impeded the progress of Humboldt and his party. Through widely scattered gaps in the soaking earth we saw at last some of the stones of what Genaro said was the original Inca road. Humboldt's encounter in this valley with what he called 'the grandiose Inca road' had been more memorable. The exposed stretch he had recorded here was well over a mile long, 'about seven metres wide', built over deep foundations and paved with 'slabs of dullish black porphyry'.

To come across this road in its complete original state must have been extraordinary. The first Spaniards in the Andes must surely have thought it the work of some superior race. 'Not since the beginning of history,' wrote the chronicler Diego de Cieza, 'has there been anything as grand as this highway. It runs through deep valleys and over mountains, through miles of snow, quagmires and living rock, along turbulent rivers; in some places . . . it is smooth, paved and carefully laid out; at other times, when crossing over sierras, it cuts through the rock, with walls skirting the rivers, and steps traversing the snow; everywhere it is clean and swept free of rubbish, with lodgings, stone houses, temples to the sun, and posts along the way.' With the road in this condition it had been possible for Inca relay-runners to deliver messages the thousand kilometres or so between Quito and Cuzco in little more than a week.

As Golondrina slipped and struggled on the sodden path, I tried calculating how long the inland journey from here to Cuzco was likely to take me simply by bus. Given the famously difficult, dangerous and slow Andean roads I would mainly be following, I reckoned I would be lucky if I managed to reach the former Inca capital in less than a month. Then I thought of the frustratingly brief glimpses of Inca stone beneath the bog, and I wondered why no one had bothered to clear this particular stretch of the road, which was reputed to be perfectly preserved underneath the accumulated soil.

There are still people who believe optimistically that it is possible to follow the great thoroughfare described by Cieza all the way from Colombia down to Bolivia and beyond. The first foreigner to try and re-establish part of this long-abandoned trail was the early twentieth-century German archaeologist and explorer Victor von Hagen. Von Hagen attempted to recreate only the route followed by Pizarro between Cajamarca and Cuzco, but even this proved an impossible task. Not only is the so-called 'Inca Road' actually composed of numerous roads, but the fragments of these roads regularly give out in the middle of nowhere, with little indication of where the traveller should be aiming next.

Beyond the lake at the end of the valley, the path climbed to the ruins of the Inca fortress of Culebrillas, where Genaro usually spent a night with those whom he accompanied along the Inca road. It was now two o'clock, and we thought we would just stop here for lunch, and get going soon for the more important Inca site of Ingapirca. We hadn't had a break for the entire day and my legs were so stiff that I could hardly dismount.

The ruins had a largely romantic interest. The structure itself might have been little more than a barn, and indeed the Inca walls could easily have been those of a sheep pen. But the sky cleared just long enough for us to take in the full wildness and isolation of the valley we had ridden through.

The storm arrived after our last climb of the day, when we were in the middle of a landscape that could have served as the blasted heath in *Macbeth*. Through steamed-up glasses I glimpsed for the first time in ten hours a huddle of distant farms. To the left was a field of what I mistook for bulls. 'They're cows,' Genaro corrected me. 'The bulls are straight ahead.' As we passed them, I calmed myself by looking ahead at the strip of sunlight shining above the valley into which we were about to descend.

The scene was as reassuring as Brueghel's *Return of the Hunters*. We were out of the clouds and away from the bleakness, climbing down towards a village glowing in the warm light of a late-afternoon sun. On the outskirts of the village, surrounded by ploughed fields and groves of trees, was Ingapirca, which from above looked like a complex geometrical puzzle. Genaro announced that this was where we were going to sleep. He said he was friendly with the keeper, who wouldn't mind if we put up our tent in the middle of a national monument. We tethered the horses to a tree, and assembled the tent in the middle of a stone circle.

I hobbled out of the tent at dawn to take a proper look at a site which had first been seriously studied by La Condamine, Juan and Ulloa. All three of them believed it had served a purely military purpose, as did Humboldt, who, along with his Geodesic predecessors, would have had little other contact with Inca architecture on such a scale as this. Their scholarly enthusiasm for the monument would be shared by Francisco José de Caldas, who came here in 1804. He called it the 'the most sumptuous and complete work of the Inca rulers to have come down to us', but he criticized the Geodesics for discussing the monument as they would some work of European military architecture.

Caldas was right. Recent archaeologists have argued that the military aspect of the complex was subsidiary to its ritual purpose, and that the massive oval platform to which I was now heading had originally served as a temple. The platform was the main part of the site still standing, and the only structure with the smooth and bevelled masonry typical of the imperial Cuzco style.

I stood in front of the platform reading a panel that described it as an Inca Temple of the Sun. According to Humboldt this was a valley that the sun hardly visited; but the sun was doing so now, its glow faintly present in a pale sky streaked with thinning clouds.

Genaro was up by now and taking down the tent. We had break-fast together in the village and I reiterated my offer to help. We embraced as he put me on a local bus whose woman passengers, young and old, wore the traditional costume of purple jackets and white bowler hats. It was like finding yourself in the middle of some folk-dancing ensemble. I would experience the same feeling several more times over the next ten days. Every village between here and the Peruvian border still seemed to wear its own distinctive and beautiful costume.

I broke my journey for a few days in Cuenca, which was like a smaller and even quieter Quito, and with greener and less dramatic mountain surroundings. Laid out on a typical Renaissance grid, it had several baroque churches, many colonial cobbled streets and a large number of North American language students, who treated the place like some exotic, Andean Oxford. It was currently cele-brating 450 years since its foundation by the Spaniards. But the town's actual origins long predated even the Incas. In fact Cuenca claimed to be South America's oldest town after Cuzco.

Fresh from the Inca trail, and with the prospect of an imminent rush of archaeological sites in Peru, I was keen to immerse myself as soon as I could in Cuenca's pre-colonial past. However, the town's post-colonial present prevented me at first from doing so. I had a long list of people to contact here, though I hardly needed to use it. Either my social confidence was growing, or else some bogus prior reputation had already filtered through to southern Ecuador. Within twenty-four hours I could already see myself becoming a regular fixture of the Cuenca social scene, attending all the private views, addressing the local literary society, being constantly dragged away from the solitary world of scholarship.

Easing my entry into Cuenca society was the statutory single woman of presidential stock, the tall and blonde Rosa Vintimilla, who happened also to be a cookery writer with two sisters and who ran the town's most elegant and traditional restaurant, La Villa.

Under Rosa's energetic guidance I acquired such culinary skills as tearing up live crabs and learning how to make a multi-ingredient bean stew known as *fenesta*, a local Lenten speciality.

Hovering all the time on my conscience was my promise to Genaro. Eventually I had what I thought was the brilliant idea of getting in touch with a famous Spanish priest, Padre Sánchez Aguilera, who had worked for years in Cuenca with an organization called the Messengers of Peace. The priest was from a neighbouring village to mine in Spain and I knew his family well.

Padre Sánchez Aguilera had a reputation for charisma and saintliness, and this showed in the adoring reaction to his name of the middle-aged female staff who worked at his organization's headquarters. Unfortunately he was staying in his house in the country, said one of these sweetly smiling women, who thought I was also a priest, perhaps because I was dressed in black, or perhaps because I had reached a stage in my journey when I radiated wisdom and inner serenity. In the end I had to make do with a telephone conversation. After outlining Genaro's case to him, he responded more frankly than I had expected. 'There's absolutely nothing that can be done. Every day hundreds of Ecuadoreans are gullible enough to act as your friend has. These deals are actually quite legal.' Others I talked to in Cuenca said exactly the same.

I returned at last to the Incas. A municipal architect gave me a preview of the newly restored Old Cathedral, which had been built after 1700 on top of an Inca temple and where a couple of the original Inca stones had recently come to light. He said I would find many more Inca and other stones if I walked to the edge of the old town, to a long street overlooking the Tomebamba River.

A local poetess was the directress of a little-funded ancient site running steeply down from this street to the river's banks, where there were the ruins of mills built originally by a tribe that had dominated this part of Ecuador for centuries before the arrival of the Incas. The Cañaris, unlike the Incas, made their walls with diagonally laid stones, and worshipped the moon instead of the sun.

'Most foreigners who come here,' said the poetess, 'think this is an Inca site. They think that anything ancient in the Andes must be by the Incas.' She was hoping one day to have the funds for laminated information panels explaining who the Cañaris were.

The person to talk to about the Cañaris, she added, was an archaeologist called Raul Marca, who worked at the Museo del Banco Central, a museum situated next to the ruins of the settlement, Tomebamba, on which Cuenca's fame as South America's second-oldest city rested. Tomebamba, the birthplace of the Inca ruler Huayna Cápac, had also been the centre of Cañari civilization.

The museum was a bold glass and concrete affair that, like its counterpart in Quito, could easily have been mistaken as the headquarters of the bank whose name it bore. Ecuador's national bank was the only Ecuadorean institution able to fund archaeological work and to build museums on this scale.

From the building's vestibule I was directed to the archaeological site outside, where a group of men in workers' overalls were digging a large hole. Supervising them was a man who looked like an artist's impression of an ancient hunter, tall, young, swarthy and strong, with a black beard and flowing dark hair. As he interrupted his work to turn towards me, we realized we knew each other from before. We had coincided in a secondhand bookshop in Seville specializing in books on Latin America. We had both been looking for exactly the same books.

Raul Marca was someone whose strong physical presence was complemented by a serious reflective manner. As he showed me around the site, he talked about the Cañaris having a far greater importance in Ecuador's history than the Incas. They were also the one Andean tribe whom the Incas never conquered in battle. They were skilled warriors who, after managing at first to hold back the advance of the overconfident Incas, wisely decided to capitulate to the enemy in return for a relatively autonomous coexistence. Thus the cult of the moon was allowed at Ingapirca to be practised alongside that of the sun, and the Cañari capital of Tomebamba became

279

for a while the administrative centre for the whole northern half of the Inca Empire. The Cañaris fought side by side with the Incas as this empire continued spreading northwards, but then, in the civil war between Huayna Cápac's appointed successors, Húascar and Atahualpa, the Cañaris supported the former, which led the irate Atahualpa to raze Tomebamba. The negative view of the treacherous Cañaris that was current at the time of Pizarro's arrival was inherited by the Spaniards, who characterized them as dirty and ignorant.

'The Incas aren't very popular in Ecuador,' said Raul as we walked back to the museum from the recently excavated site. 'They were here for only forty years, and they ended up successfully defaming and almost erasing from memory a centuries-old civilization that was in many ways no less remarkable than theirs.'

We talked about how unfair it was that the Incas had come so much to dominate the popular image of South America's pre-colonial past. 'For some reason,' said Raul, 'people today don't think of the Incas as bloodthirsty conquerors who did to their predecessors what the Spaniards did to them. They are thought of as an intensely sophisticated and spiritual people with a unique understanding of the world's mysteries.' We went on to discuss the growing fashion for 'spiritual tourism' in the Andes and how the Incas were somehow central to this; a visit to the Cuzco area was frequently complemented by a consultation with a shaman.

We were still talking about this when we got back to a lawn of neatly mown grass directly in front of the museum. A middle-aged man and a woman were trying to arrange some red and white petals in a circle, but the wind was continually ruining their efforts. They could have been a pair of ageing hippies. The man had a ponytail and a loose, patterned cotton shirt, while the woman was completely dressed in diaphanous white. The sounds of pipes and chanting were becoming louder in the background. A group of costumed Indian men and women emerged from behind a concrete outbuilding.

Raul and I, together with some of the museum staff, were the only witnesses to a ceremony involving much bowing, touching of the earth and recitation of Quechua. Raul explained not without irony that the man was a shaman who had come to bless the new section of the museum dedicated exclusively to the history of Tomebamba. This section was to be officially opened that very night. He invited me to the inauguration party.

The Indians were from the village of Saraguro, which I would have to pass the next day on my way south towards Peru. They seemed that night as out of place as I was at the party, which brought together a mass of suits and evening dresses and the occasional indigenous equivalent of the ceremonial kilt. There were numerous interminable speeches, profusely thanking the authorities.

Raul had warned me that he hated occasions such as these, but he eventually turned up when drinks had begun to be served and the atmosphere was beginning to loosen. I discovered through him that every important archaeologist in the country was present in the room. He introduced me to one of them, his uncle Emilio Marca, the 'foremost authority on the Inca Road'. Emilio told me that every book on this subject had been romantic and unscholarly until the publication of his own.

I spotted Rosa Vintimilla, who came up to me to say that there was a photographer whom I really must meet. No one else, she insisted, had captured the spirit of the Andes as well as he had. This person turned out to be the Cuenca-born Pablo Corral Vega, whose book of photographs of the Andes (with an introduction by Mario Vargas Llosa) was indeed one of the most memorable visual records of the mountains I had ever seen. A timid and self-effacing man, he said to me with a smile that the Andes had taught him the virtues of humility. His bespectacled face was open and friendly.

He spoke to me about the magic and beauty of all the magnificent empty places he had photographed. But he said that what he most treasured from all his Andean journeys were his memories of the people he had encountered. The people who lived dwarfed by

281

this massively scaled and dangerous landscape had sustained his belief that the rich man was not the person who had the most money but the simplest needs. They were noble survivors, he said, of the 'violent racial mix' of the Spanish and Indian worlds. They were the product of extreme adversities that had encouraged a quality I would soon find in ever greater measure, as I continued south along perilous roads that brought home the fragility of life – a spirit of solidarity and cooperation.

17

# OMENS

South from Cuenca the buses became less frequent, the roads narrower and the journeys much longer. The bus to Loja slowly
negotiated an olive-green and wooded landscape struck by alternative bursts of rain and sunshine. Two hours into our five-hour
journey I realized we must be nearing Saraguro, as many of the
women who now got on to the bus were dressed identically to
the ones in yesterday's blessing ceremony, with white linen shirts
and black capes held in place by silver brooches. The young
woman who came to sit next to me said she preferred the ride
when the visibility was very poor. She suffered from vertigo if she
could see what was below her. Hers was a fear I had never had
before. I had no inkling of how real this fear would soon become
for me.

Humboldt's route south from Loja into the former Viceroyalty of
Peru involved a huge loop into the tropics and a boat journey along
the Amazonian tributary of the Marañón. In the woods below Loja,
Humboldt and Bonpland were able to extend their studies of the
cinchona tree. Montúfar noted in his diary that the quinines
extracted from this area were 'among the best that are known' and
it was probably at this stage of his journey that he conceived an

ultimately disastrous plan to obtain the exclusive rights for the commercialization of this Andean product.

From Loja I had hoped to reach Peru by way of Vilcabamba, a town whose high percentage of aged inhabitants had made it a magnet for alternative and not-so-alternative westerners searching for the secret of eternal youth. But the obscure frontier post I would have had to cross while trying to catch up with Humboldt at the Peruvian town of Jaén de Bracamoros had been described to me as problematical. Transport would have been erratic, and there would probably have been no Peruvian guards to put the necessary stamp on my passport.

My last night in Ecuador, a Sunday, was spent in a fast-food joint poring over maps and the *South American Handbook*, contemplating the labyrinthine problems of following the spine of the Andes from here all the way down to Bolivia. The survival of the Inca Road would have made life much simpler. Present-day roads through the Peruvian interior, though reputedly much improved in recent years, were still largely unpaved and very circuitous. Bus transport, away from the coast, was erratic. Several of the bus services I planned to use ran on a very occasional basis, sometimes only once or twice a week: if you were thinking of using a combination of these services you needed a computer to work out your itinerary.

A powerfully built man with a shaved head and a Hummer parked outside had noted my perplexity. He sat down next to me with his food and asked if he could help. He was from Lima, and was driving back towards Peru early the next morning. He said I could go with him if I didn't mind a week's detour into the Amazonian jungle, where he had some business to attend to. I asked him about his line of work and he told me he was a debt collector. I needn't worry about safety, he added. He always carried a gun.

I thought it better to trust my luck to Peruvian buses than to a probable drug runner. I imagined I would find some form of transport to Jaén from the Peruvian lowland town of Piura, which was now linked to Loja by a direct bus.

The journey to Piura took me through a long-disputed border-land which had led to three military conflicts between Ecuador and Peru, the last one in 1997. As we drove through a rainy mountainous landscape, I thought of these and all the other border disputes – between Peru and Chile, Bolivia and Chile, Chile and Argentina – that proved the impossibility of the Bolivarian dream of a united Andean nation. As I neared Peru I recalled all the negative comments about its countrymen that I had heard from Ecuadoreans, Bolivians and Chileans. The Peruvians, they all said, were aggressive, boorish, devious and criminally minded.

We began descending towards Piura, passing the first of the fantastical, baobab-like trees known as *palo borrachos*, with their swollen 'drunken poles'. The border crossing took less than half an hour. The Peruvian guards seemed as friendly as the Ecuadorean ones.

We left the clouds and the rainy season, and entered the haze of heat and dust that hung over the Sechura desert, where men wore wide-brimmed straw sombreros, and shreds of black rubbish bags blew around over the dry flat expanses. Near the entrance to Piura was a sign pointing to the coastal town of Paita. I remembered that Manuela Saenz had died there of dysentery, after years of exile.

Arrival at Piura was brutal and disorientating. It was difficult to tell where the countryside ended and the city began. There was no main bus station or any immediate sign of a proper city centre. There was just a gathering chaos of warehouses, shacks, people and vehicles. The traffic seemed entirely composed of lorries, vans, ancient taxis and the motorized rickshaws so mysteriously popular only in Peru. I could have been in India.

Each of the numerous bus companies had its own little garages, some of them of completely improvised appearance, with corrugated-iron roofs precariously attached to walls of unfaced breeze blocks. Vulnerably loaded with my luggage and sweating profusely, I repeatedly crossed the two broad and traffic-congested avenues along which most of these garages were situated. I was tracking

285

down the three companies that reputedly served Jaén. Opinions differed as to which of the companies was the safest, quickest and most reliable. Ultimately, however, I did not have much choice. There was only one bus leaving for Jaén within the next twenty-four hours. It was setting off next day at noon and was scheduled to arrive at its destination eight hours later.

I found for the night an old-fashioned hotel from the 1950s, situated between a dried-up river popularly referred to as the 'crazy river' and a quiet palm-lined promenade that would have been relatively pleasant had it not been in the process of being dug up. My bedroom overlooked one of Peru's few remaining statues of Pizarro, a figure as politically incorrect in this country as Franco is in Spain. It was from Piura that Pizarro had set off in 1532 to his confrontation with Atahualpa in Cajamarca. Two years later Piura had a population of two hundred Spaniards, including the first Spanish women to come to Peru. This made the place Peru's first colonial town, though there was little evidence of this today.

The next morning I went in plenty of time to the garage from which the Jaén bus was due to leave. The waiting area was already crammed with people. One of the irritating idiosyncrasies I now discovered of Peruvian bus travel was that you had to leave your luggage at a special office within the station. The Jaén bus was half an hour late in arriving and a further half an hour was wasted waiting for the luggage office to open. Passengers queued up carrying such varied items as a wardrobe, a table, a canister of gas and several cages of live chickens. I did not know how the rickety old bus was going to fit all this in, let alone the passengers. The scrappy stencilled ticket I had been given, with its seat number scrawled in biro, did not fill me with confidence either.

But the bus managed to accommodate everyone and everything, even if some of the passengers had to stand with their belongings in the aisle, and a formidable, swaying load of luggage was strapped to the roof. We set off only an hour and a half behind schedule. The bus's ultimate destination was a place in the middle of the jungle about fifteen hours away. My neighbour doubted if the chickens would make it there alive. I doubted if the bus would even reach Jaén. The only part of the vehicle in perfect working order was the video.

We emerged from the desert after four hours and began climbing up an arid canyon. The oppressively hazy sky turned dark and thundery, and the bus had its first of several breakdowns. I had long conversations with the driver while his assistant set about repairing what I was told was a faulty fan belt, 'nothing serious'. We would probably be arriving at Jaén 'slightly late', possibly around midnight, a proverbially dangerous hour when the guidebooks suggested only muggers would be there to greet passing tourists. However, the driver said he would not drive on from Jaén until he had found someone reliable to take me to a hotel.

The storm came as the bus got moving again along a barrier-less cliff-side stretch of road that would have been frightening had it not been recently broadened and asphalted. The good state of the road, so surprising for one that was so little used and out of the way, was due to a foreign company's having purchased some nearby mines. This was the case with several of the better roads in the Peruvian interior, my neighbour told me. 'We seem to value foreign commercial interests more than the safety of ordinary people.'

We were at Jaén shortly after midnight. Repeated flashes of lightning over the past hour had lit up a landscape that had become tropically wooded in patches. The storm had now passed and a congestion of rickshaws surrounded the bus. As the only foreigner to get off, I was the focus of much of the attention, but the bus driver did not leave my side until he had found me a rickshaw whose owner he knew to be 'trustworthy'. I was driven off to the centre of a town far larger than I had imagined.

Humboldt had passed through Jaén without comment while travelling between the Marañón and Cajamarca. I too was aiming for Cajamarca, but by a roundabout route that would enable me to see one of the most famous pre-Incan sites in the Andes: Kuélap.

The only visual similarity between present-day Jaén and its Spanish namesake was its predominantly ugly architecture of the late twentieth century, the town having been destroyed by a recent earthquake. However, there was an unexpected Spanishness about the place that had nothing to do with appearance. The large main square, at nearly half-past twelve on a Tuesday night, was still full of strolling families, just as you might have found during an Andalusian summer. Typical, too, of traditional Andalusia was the amicable curiosity shown towards the solitary *forastero* or outsider. I moved on from Jaén before its pleasant familiarity sidetracked me from my goal of reaching Kuélap. To get to Kuélap I had somehow to make it to Chachapoyas, one of the smallest, most isolated and distant of Peru's regional capitals. The quickest way of getting there from Jaén was by a combination of *colectivos* or shared taxis, which had set routes and waited around until there were enough passengers to make their journey worthwhile. The first one took me across the Marañón, from where La Condamine and the Spanish conquistadors before him had set off on the exploration of the Amazon. The river's exciting history was not apparent from the stretch we crossed, which ran through an intensely agricultural valley obscured by the day's unending rains. Two agricultural engineers with whom I shared the second taxi lamented the area's unchecked forestation and the blight of eucalyptus trees scarring the landscape. Only twenty years or so earlier we would have been driving through uninterrupted rainforest.

The road was unpaved as it skirted the gorge of the Marañón's tributary, the Tingo, where low dense vegetation entangled mossy cliffs and rock. We ascended in a torrential downpour up to the green mountain-encircled plateau where Chachapoyas was situated. The place was more like a large village than a town, with streets ending in muddy tracks lined by adobe houses. The centre was like a transposed corner of sixteenth-century Spain, with whitewashed stone buildings converging onto a picturesquely irregular main square. I had not seen places like this since Colombia.

The rain was so unceasing that I had to wait until evening for a proper look around. A handful of sad-faced young tourists in bright plastic rainwear appeared the only other foreigners in town. In between repeated downpours they wandered around a main square which consisted of a peculiarly South American combination of pharmacies and internet cafés. I searched in vain for any commemoration of the most interesting historical figure associated with this remote outpost of colonial Spain, the Jesuit priest Blas Valera.

Valera was the son of one of the first colonizers of Chachapoyas, the Andalusian-born Luis Valera, who came with Pizarro's henchman Alonso de Alvarado to claim the area for the Spanish Crown. Luis had a wife back in Spain, but as they were apart for twenty-five years he had no qualms about living openly with an indigenous mistress, who was baptized Francisca Pérez. No one would have guessed from this common name (the equivalent of Smith or Jones) that Francisca was possibly a princess at Atahualpa's court.

Francisca's fate is unknown, for she disappeared from history at some time before Luis's wife was finally reunited in Peru with her husband. But before this happened, she had two sons with Luis, one of whom was Blas. Blas became a passionate defender of Indian rights, but he was marginalized in his lifetime and is little remembered today. His writings glorified the Incas and fuelled the idea of an Incan golden age brought to an end by the arrival of the Christians. His unpublished manuscripts were given to and copied by the far more famous mestizo Garcilaso de la Vega, who portrayed Atalhualpa's empire in an idyllic light as a way of validating his own Incan ancestry. Garcilaso's vision of Inca history would in turn influence later travellers such as Humboldt, Kohlberg and the majority of tourists visiting Peru today.

Of all the early Christian writers on South America, Valera took the most extreme position on the Incas. He appeared to advocate the belief that their culture, religion and language were equal to their Christian counterparts. The Church, unsurprisingly, did not like this. In 1580 the Jesuits decided to accept no more mestizos into the order and in 1583 they threw Valera into their underground prison in Lima, on the probably trumped-up grounds that he was a fornicator. He spent the rest of his life in captivity.

Or did he? Part of the fascination of Valera, and also part of the reason why he is not as well known as he deserves to be, is connected with the continuing controversy surrounding his last years. The official story is that, for health reasons, Valera asked to be transferred to prison in Europe, to where he was finally well enough to travel in 1596. He was locked up in Cádiz, where, in 1597, he died from wounds resulting from the raid on the city by 'the pirate Drake'.

This version of events was contradicted by the discovery in the mid-1990s of some sensational if disputed documents in a private Neapolitan collection. According to these, Valera's journey to Europe was prompted by a desire to tell the Pope the real story of Pizarro's conquest of the Incas at Cajamarca: Pizarro, as Valera's father had witnessed, had poisoned the Incas with a combination of arsenic and wine.

The Captain General of the Jesuits was deeply opposed to Valera's informing the Pope of this, so he decided to declare Valera dead and to invent the story of his being killed by the English. Valera then secretly returned to Peru under the pseudonym of Felipe Guaman Poma de Ayala, who later became famous as the Indian author of the illustrated *Nueva corónica y buen gobierno* ('New Chronicle and Good Government'), one of the most important written sources about Inca culture and a testament to indigenous resistance to Spanish hegemony.

While back in Peru under this assumed identity, Valera attracted a large number of followers in sympathy with his ideas. Among the many things he taught them was that, contrary to what is always said about pre-Columbian civilizations, the Incas did in fact have their written language and used a secret, phonetic 'quipu' to record history. What is more, Valera claimed to have sent some of these quipus to Garcilaso de la Vega, who then lied about them.

Whether because Valera's life dissolved into an inseparable blend of fact and fiction, or whether because the Church was still trying to repress his memory, there was not even a mention of Valera in the small history museum on Chachapoyas' main square. As I thought about this (and the rain gave me plenty of time to think), I wondered whether another factor in Valera's neglect here was his exaggerated pro-Inca bias. This bias would surely not have gone down so well in an area whose historical loyalties were to the people who had ruled here for centuries before the Incas had arrived – the people after whom the town was named.

'The Incas could be much crueller than the Spaniards,' said Julio Soto Valle, the man whom several people had recommended as the best guide to take me the next day to Kuélap. He was a fresh-faced enthusiastic man in his mid-thirties who had studied history and archaeology and worked variously as a taxi driver and tour guide. I located him in a dark restaurant whose only other client was an old man slurping his soup.

Julio, assuming rightly I was a relative novice in ancient Peruvian history, summarized the various pre-Inca civilizations that made Peru one of the most archaeologically complex areas of the world. The first Peruvians, according to him, were descendants of the migrants who crossed over to the Americas from Siberia during the last Ice Age. Though evidence of human occupation in Peru dated back to around 20,000 BC, the first great Peruvian civilization was the one responsible for the pyramids at Caral, on a stretch of coastal desert just north of Lima.

Then came the Chavín cult, a religious movement which developed at the same time as agriculture and village life were established, between 1200 BC and AD 200. The most important known site related to this cult was in the Cordillera Blanca, about three hundred kilometres further south down the Andes; but jaguar and other jungle motifs incorporated in Chavín art could imply that the cult began in the Amazon and then spread to the Andes along the upper Marañón River.

Julio paused. The slurping noise in the background seemed to be getting louder.

'Possibly other Andean civilizations had their origins in the Amazon, the Incas for instance, or even the Chachapoyas, who also appear to have worshipped the jaguar. There is a new theory that the whole of the Amazon was densely populated in pre-Columbian times, before western illnesses took their toll.'

He briefly went back to where he had left off in his rapid exposition of Peru's early cultures, continuing with the coastal ones of the Mochica and the Nazca, famed respectively for their realistic pottery and mysterious lines in the desert. Over this same so-called 'Classical Era', between AD 200 and AD 1100, there evolved in the Andes the agriculturally highly sophisticated Tiawanako civilization, which began around the shores of Lake Titicaca, extended south into present-day Chile and most of Bolivia, and then, in their later more military phase, allied itself to the Huaris in the north to reach well into Ecuador. The decline of the Tiawanako–Huari civilization at the beginning of the twelfth century coincided with the emergence of the Incas, whose main rivals by the time their empire had begun expanding dramatically, from the 1440s onwards, were the Mochica's successors, the Chimus.

'The Chachapoyas were nonetheless a force to be reckoned with,' added Julio. 'They had dominated this area since at least the eighth century, and put up fierce resistance when the Incas seized their territory in 1470.' Cieza de León wrote about them as a tall fair-skinned race, whose warriors were famously ferocious and whose women were prized for their beauty. They also had a reputation for constantly fighting with each other. But, as with other Andean peoples under Inca rule, they were united at first by a common hatred of the Incas, under whom they considered themselves worse off than they would be under the Spaniards. 'Well, they got that wrong,' smiled Julio, pouring himself out a glass of Inka Cola.

'To judge by the six hundred or so Chachapoya ruins that have come to light in the area,' he continued, 'there must have been between 300,00 and 530,000 Chachapoyas living here in the 1530s. Two hundred years later this population had been reduced by ninety per cent.'

I was almost glad when Julio changed the subject to ask me if I wanted to visit anywhere else in the area apart from Kuélap. Had I thought, for instance, of going to see the area's latest tourist attraction, the Gocta waterfall?

This turned out to be the same waterfall whose 'discovery' I had read about in the Spanish newspaper *El País* several months earlier. I was incredulous that it was already being commercialized. The Spanish article had caught my attention by announcing that the third-tallest free-leaping waterfall in the world had come to light in the middle of the Peruvian jungle. A German explorer called Stefan Ziemendorff had apparently stumbled upon this marvel, which had been jealously guarded by a local tribe who had threatened to put a curse on anyone who revealed its whereabouts.

Julio laughed when I told him what I had read. 'Everyone in Chachapoyas has known about the place all their lives. It's only about a two-hour walk from the nearest road. The "tribe" are just locals from an ordinary modern community called Gocta. The story about the curse was the invention of a Peruvian journalist, who also made up something about a beautiful mermaid living in the waters.'

All Ziemendorff had apparently done was to bother to measure the waterfall's height and even then he seems to have gone it wrong. Some people now listed the waterfall as only the fourteenth tallest in the world. 'It's impressive all the same,' said Julio, 'but probably not worth a visit in the rainy season.'

Julio was still talking ceaselessly the next morning as we headed off to Kuélap along the Tingo gorge. The rains had finally stopped and the sky was clear enough to appreciate this landscape of low forest, moss, ferns and cliff-scarred mountains that Julio referred to as the 'Amazonian Andes'.

We passed the spot where, only a few years earlier, the village of Tingo had stood. The place had been entirely destroyed by a landslide. On the other side of the murky fast-flowing river was the village of Magdalena, whose inhabitants had always had a great enmity towards those of Tingo, but who had rushed over to help at the time of the disaster. 'Their action,' said Julio, 'exemplified the whole history of this area. We have always forgotten our differences in times of a crisis, such as a landslide or the Inca and Spanish invasions.'

Julio stopped the car near the beginning of the gorge. 'The ruins of Macro,' he observed, pointing to a sheer mountainside rising up from the river, a slope seemingly no different to others nearby, with its rich carpet of palms, bromeliads and other tropical plants and trees clinging to a rocky cliff. But, as you studied the cliff more carefully, you noticed that much of it was made up of parallel rows of stone walls. The word 'macro' in Quechua meant 'twisted', which has led some scholars to suggest that the site was a sanctuary for the curing of sprained and broken legs, rheumatism and other muscular problems.

Above the gorge large areas of the cloud forest had been cleared to make way for steep and rolling fields, beyond which the views were of ever broadening, craggy mountains. The road was looping towards Kuélap, which lay surrounded by trees at the very top of the mountain across from us, high above the cultivated fields, looking like a diminutive and forgotten medieval hill-town fast being reclaimed by forest. The last forty minutes of the journey were on foot, and took us up to a height of three thousand metres. Though the vegetation was lushly tropical, the temperature dropped dramatically at night, which was why the site was known as *Kuélap*, 'the cold place'.

The first view of Kuélap's long line of nineteen-metre-high walls was a sight I imagined few of Peru's other archaeological monuments could equal. There were no other tourists to distract from the sensation of being an explorer encountering a lost civilization in the middle of nowhere. The narrow, immensely tall, parabolic arches through which you penetrated these walls had themselves all the enticement and mystery of a children's adventure story.

Through one of the arches was a dark and slippery stone ramp leading up to a partially excavated site extending over an enormous oval-shaped area, largely hidden by rampant vegetation. Some archaeologists think the place was once a military fortress; others have more elaborately explained it as a sanctuary where supernatural powers were called upon to ensure the right atmospheric conditions for the cultivation of crops. The most likely theory was that the place was exactly as it seems from both afar and nearby – a walled township, which in the manner of a Roman citadel had its separate residential, military and religious areas.

It dated back to AD 1000, with parts possibly two centuries older, announced Julio, as he confidently identified every feature of the site, from its round domestic dwellings to some holes in the ground once thought to be granaries, but now considered as hiding-places for those called up by the Spaniards as part of the notorious mita system. This Inca-inspired system – introduced in the late sixteenth century by the Viceroy of Peru, Francisco de Toledo – entailed a regular quota of villagers from all over the Andes being sent to work far from their homes, for example in the mines of Potosí. To be separated from the land of your ancestors was the worst fate that could befall a Chachapoya. Those who did not try and hide from the Spaniards often committed suicide. So many tried to resist the mita in Kuélap that Francisco de Toledo eventually had the whole place burnt down.

Julio showed me stones that had been blackened by this fire, as well as walls in which the remains of skeletons had been found – a way of burial reserved for those who had been bad in life and which was intended to prevent the soul from rising to heaven.

I found it difficult to know what to believe about South America's pre-Columbian sites. In the absence of inscriptions or documentation other than the unreliable chronicles of the Spaniards, most of what you read or were told about them was pure speculation. Julio seemed at first as reliable and down-to-earth an informant as any but, as with every guide I would meet in Peru, he dwelt heavily on those esoteric aspects that tourists loved.

Our ascent into what he called the 'ritual' area of Kuélap was pre-ceded by a long pause outside 'the shaman's house', identified by its stone relief of diamond shapes that could clearly be interpreted as serpent's eyes, which in turn substantiated the theory that the whole layout of the site was serpent-shaped and indicative of a serpent cult. Up in the ritual area the constructions were rectangular rather than circular, and there was a 'ceremonial table' where only animal sac-rifices were carried out. Human sacrifices might have been practised instead within a flimsy structure in the form of an inverted cone, on whose exterior was carved a worn head which appeared to be facing a mountain worshipped by the Chachapoyas. This, said Julio, was an example of 'sacred geography'. I knew the concept well. It turned up in almost every recent book on Andean archaeology.

A white cloud rose from the valley to blot out the view. Julio advised me to stare fixedly at the cloud as a way of focusing my mind and clearing it of negative thoughts. As I meekly obeyed him, he told me of a dream he had had shortly after saying goodbye to me last night. In this dream a spirit had appeared to him to say that his plans to continue his studies and give up taxi-driving were going to be realized. He also said that the spirit had said something about me.

'What did he say?' I asked, slightly startled.

'He said that your life was in imminent danger.'

The serene effects of staring at the cloud suddenly disappeared.

'I'm only joking,' he laughed.

I wasn't entirely sure that he was.

# 18

# EXTREME ADVERSITIES

At four in the morning I was walking hurriedly in the rain through the sleeping and dimly lit streets of Chachapoyas. Away from the main square and down the hill towards the town's outer districts, I tramped through squelching mud as I aimed for an open door with light coming from beneath it. A small bus marked 'Virgen del Carmen' was already parked in front of it. Beyond the door was a dingy waiting room with a long wooden bench occupied by an elderly couple and their two grandchildren. Other people leaned against the bare walls or sat on the concrete floor, wrapped in blankets and ponchos, their belongings tied together in cloth bundles or kept in chequered plastic hold-alls. They looked like shocked refugees.

After the rain had stopped I went outside to join a group of men pacing around next to the bus to keep warm. I talked to two of them, a smiling middle-aged man with a woolly hat and his younger companion. They were transitory labourers who had been working the past year on a couple of building sites in Chachapoyas. Every two months they went back to see their families near the small town of Celendín, the bus's final destination. I said I was going to spend the night there before continuing the next day to Cajamarca. They assured me that the transport between those two towns was far better and more regular than it was between here and Celendín. The bus we were now taking only did this route once a week in the rainy season. Under dry conditions the journey could take as little as ten hours. The rains of the past few days had apparently caused problems with the road. Our bus had set off from Celendín at five in the morning the day before and had got to Chachapoyas only about three hours ago. They had taken over twenty hours to cover 226 kilometres.

The driver, a man in his fifties with thinning black hair, was rubbing his eyes as he opened the bus door from the inside shortly before five. He and his young assistant had been sleeping on mats rolled out along the bus's aisle. They could have slept for little more than two and a half hours. They now had to do the same journey again, under conditions likely to have got worse.

The assistant loaded the luggage on to the roof with the help of the passengers. The bus had several broken seats, three windows whose cracked glass was held together by tape and other windows so dirty that you could barely see through them. On the credit side, there was no video and no radio. I was seated at the front, next to a shy young mother with a sleeping baby. I was happy and relaxed, full of a sense of oneness with the world and excited by the prospect of potentially one of the most sensational drives in the Central Andes. We would be climbing up to a height of nearly four thousand metres, descending down again to the Marañón and then negotiating another formidable pass before reaching Celendín.

We had first of all to go back to the Tingo gorge and follow the river almost to its source, above the first of only two villages along the whole route, Leymebamba. I was asleep until it was light enough to see anything, about half an hour after leaving Chachapoyas. We had still to reach the Kuélap turning, but the stretch of road we were on seemed more dangerous than it had been before. The loose suspension of the bus, in combination with the roughness of the road's surface, made the vehicle lurch disconcertingly from side to side on the slightest bend. At moments I felt as if we were going to tip over into the river. I wondered what chance there would be of surviving should we fall the thirty metres or so into the water.

But no one else seemed bothered by this, so I gradually got used to the bus's movements and was lulled by them briefly back to sleep. We were in the attractive village of Leymebamba in time for a 9.30 breakfast. From the map it looked as if we had already covered well over half the distance to Celendín.

Many more passengers got on at Leymebamba, over-filling the bus. The young mother next to me had been succeeded by an elderly woman with a giant bag of potatoes under her legs.

The ascent so far, through a damp and cultivated green landscape, was relatively gentle and anticlimactic, but the visibility was patchy and getting worse. I was no longer so worried by safety. I was more concerned about not seeing anything on the other side of the pass. Then suddenly a new silhouette of mountains appeared in the distance. My heartbeat accelerated. The patch of blue sky was becoming enormous, the clouds below fast dissolving. The panorama was promising to turn into one of the most sublime of the whole journey. A few more metres and we were over the top and there was nothing to impede the view. Soon afterwards I remembered what the woman had told me on the bus to Loja. Sometimes it was better not to see.

The road became like a horizontal slit following into the far distance the contours of a slope dropping hundreds of metres. The bus fitted on to the ledge with less than half a metre to spare. The surface was pitted with holes and regularly blocked by stones that the driver's assistant had to get out and remove. The lurching of the bus became ever more pronounced, particularly on bends where the surface had been pitched at an angle by recent landslides. Parts of the road had crumbled away in the rains, leaving only a few centimetres to spare between us and the void. There was no place for other vehicles to pass.

Passengers who had hitherto been relaxed began gripping the sides of their seats; everyone who had been talking became silent.

The physical sensation was like being on a rollercoaster. The emotion was like playing an interminable game of Russian roulette. There seemed no escape from a mountainous landscape that stretched in the clear light for what could have been up to a hundred kilometres. I breathed with relief only when passing isolated clumps of trees clinging to the outer edge of the road. They gave me the illusion of having something to hold on to in case we fell.

We rounded a bend and the road began at last to descend. A few hundred metres further on we came to a cluster of buildings whose inhabitants must have felt like bivouacking mountaineers. One of the buildings was a humble restaurant, where the driver and others went off to have a quick lunch. I got down, shaking, from the bus, not hungry at all, but glad for the momentary sense of being on solid ground. I had a look over the edge and saw the Marañón running like a silver thread through a desert-like canyon dotted with palms. I could not see any way the road could possibly get down there.

The road did no more descending for the time being. It continued as a horizontal line hugging the ever more parched mountain. Some of the passengers who had eaten began to nod off under the bright glare of the sun. I tried to rationalize my fears, and then to distance my mind from the body. For a short while I could almost picture myself as a bird swooping over this panorama of cosmic proportions.

I was almost feeling calm when there was a loud bang. There were a few screams behind me, as the bus swerved to the edge and came to an abrupt halt, at a noticeable angle. Some of the passengers shouted at the driver to let us off. It took me a few moments to realize that the front tyre nearest to the precipice had exploded and its wheel was half hanging in the air. The moment of greatest fear came after streaming out of the bus and seeing how the vehicle was positioned. There were several mutterings of how lucky we were to be alive.

The men immediately went to work. We pushed the bus until it had righted itself on the road. We then stood back to watch the driver and his assistant crank up the vehicle and remove the wheel. He went to the back of the vehicle to take out what I assumed would be a spare one. I had clearly not spent enough time in Peru.

The driver returned carrying the remains of an inner tube, out of which he then cut a broad strip that he applied with glue to the tube of the broken tyre. Afterwards he pumped up the tyre, which exploded again. He repeated the process several more times, until finally the repaired tube seemed to hold.

My friend with the woolly hat shook his head as he saw this. 'What the man is doing,' he said, 'is extremely dangerous. The tyre could easily explode again, and the next time we probably won't be so lucky.' He gestured with his head towards the precipice. An engineer from Celendín nodded in agreement. I had little under-standing of vehicles or technical matters, but I had sufficient to appreciate that the driver's repair would not have met AA stan-dards. My face must have been furrowed with worry, for the engineer calmly told me that of course nothing would happen to us. The basis of this confidence could only have been a belief that we were being protected by some supernatural power. In any case, when he thought I was out of earshot he began criticizing the bus company. 'With the lives of so many people at stake I can't under-stand why they allow their drivers to take such risks. It's utterly irresponsible.'

Andean fatalism appeared to have taken over the other passen-gers as we continued our slow descent. Danger was so ingrained into the lives of Andean peoples that ultimately perhaps this was the only attitude you could adopt. Most of the people on the bus prob-ably did this journey on a regular basis; at least four of those I talked to were returning to Chachapoyas on next week's bus. To me the thought of getting through the rest of the day was bad enough. The remaining descent would probably take at least another two hours and then we had to climb again almost to the same height as the first pass. The knowledge that the tyre was likely to explode again at any moment made me feel as if I were in a re-creation of the film *Wages of Fear*, the story of a group of men forced to drive two trucks three hundred kilometres across the rugged South American terrain carrying dangerously unstable nitroglycerine. Luckily, I was still unaware of the statistical likelihood of being involved in a fatal bus accident during the Peruvian rainy season.

We made it down at last to the Marañón, and to the tropically hot and dismally poor riverside village of Balsas, with its adobe, plaster and corrugated-iron huts scattered over caked mud. The Marañón was a different river from the one that flowed through the fertile valley near Jaén. Here it was like a flash flood in the middle of eroded badlands. Parcels of bright tropical vegetation, the main greenery in the valley, were desperately trying to hold on to its banks, but it shook them off as it entered the barren gorge we had to cross immediately on leaving the village. The brilliance of the late-afternoon sunlight exaggerated the blackness of the clouds that were gathering over the mountains behind us. We began our second climb of the day. I opened my wallet to see if I still had my photo of the Santo Custodio, the guardian angel of Frailes.

While standing outside the bus at Balsas, there had been much debate among the passengers as to which was the harder of the day's two passes. I found it impossible to tell. My nerves were so shot that I could not be objective. I had resorted to closing my eyes at every turn of the road.

The bus halted suddenly again about an hour after leaving Balsas, when the landscape had become greener and partially wooded. We were in the middle of nowhere and I had no idea what was happening, until I saw a small farm hidden among trees. The driver had stopped to buy some firewood from a farmer he knew. The passengers stepped outside to watch him cramming the logs onto the already overloaded bus. I started to help him in this task. Others joined in. Experiencing the Andean spirit of solidarity and cooperation made me feel better.

We reached the hamlet where the man with the woolly hat lived. His last words to me were that I would be in Celendín very soon.

I assumed that the climbing was almost over. It was now almost night, and a few drops of rain were falling. I strained my eyes to see where the road would be aiming next. A surly mother at my side nudged me in the arm and pointed to a slope that the clouds had kept entirely hidden until now. High above us, through a brief gap in the clouds, was a tall, zigzagging line that seemed like a Masonic symbol violently scrawled on to the sky.

I was thinking an hour later of the elderly couple at Alausí, Achilles and Violeta. They would probably have finished their supper by now and would be sitting happily by the fire. I had reached a stage in the journey when I could barely believe such peaceful scenes were possible.

The driver's young assistant had taken over. He lacked the experience of his colleague. Only a miracle seemed now to be keeping us on a road whose hairpin bends gave the bus hardly any space to manoeuvre. Torrential rain, the darkness of the night and a thick fog made it almost impossible to see anything. The front window had begun to steam up. The new driver was forced to keep just one hand on the wheel and to use the other repeatedly to clear the glass with a dirty rag. His colleague had gone to have a sleep at the back of the bus. Perhaps he knew that there was no more he could do.

I closed my eyes, and when I opened them again I thought I saw the lights of a town.

Once again I was in another world. The Hostal Celendín was like an old-fashioned Spanish inn, with a central flower-filled patio, lined with wooden balconies. On the ground floor was a popular bar whose main entrance opened out onto a colonial square still full of people late into the night. I had a few beers with the owner to celebrate being alive.

The memories of the day already seemed distant. The more I got into the momentum of Andean travelling, the more dream-like the whole experience was becoming. Radically varied climates and terrains fractured the Andean lands into hundreds of separate

303

self-contained worlds so different from each other that, after you had moved on into the next, you began to doubt the reality of the one you had just left behind.

The parched harshness of Balsas and the terrors of the two passes seemed inconceivable in tranquil Celendín, which, by daylight, was revealed as lying in rolling agricultural country bordered by smooth green slopes. A road in the process of being paved led without unpleasant surprises from here to the seductively situated town of Cajamarca, which lay in a flat oval valley whose 'marvellous fertility' had enraptured Humboldt. He described the valley as being 'covered with cultivated fields and gardens striped by rows of willows, different varieties of datura, large red, white and yellow flowers, mimosas and cinchonas, and beautiful trees like rose bushes.'

Humboldt's enchantment with the valley echoed that of the first conquistadors to have penetrated the Andes. Led by Pizarro, and numbering a mere 150 soldiers, they had set off from Piura on 24 September 1532, after having optimistically set their sights on conquering the Incas. Pizarro had had his first contact with this civilization four years earlier at the Ecuadorean coastal town of Tumbes. Deeply impressed by their wealth and orderliness, he saw them as worthy objects of Spain's imperial ambitions and wanted now to confront them in their Andean homeland.

Most of Pizarro's party would have been happy to have gone straight to the Inca capital of Cuzco, which, from Piura, would have entailed travelling for much of the way along the flat and easy coastal route. However, Atahualpa, fresh from his victory over his brother Húascar, was currently stationed with his army outside Cajamarca and, as the Spaniards had already proclaimed their intention of visiting him in his camp, Pizarro thought the Inca leader would be contemptuous of them were they not to do so.

Pizarro's march across the Andes from Piura, and his momentous confrontation with Atahualpa, were recorded in some detail by the contemporary Spanish chroniclers. But in terms of sheer narrative and descriptive power, no account of these events has equalled that of the American nineteenth-century historian W.H. Prescott. Prescott, partially blinded as a student when a piece of bread was thrown at his eyes, wrote and researched *The Conquest of Peru* towards the end of his life (he died in the same eventful year as Humboldt, 1859), when he was confined to Boston and reliant on Braille and assistants who read to him. For decades Prescott's remained the book on which popular knowledge of Peru and Inca civilization was based. It was the book which made my Eurocentric grandfather appreciate the greatness of the Incas. It was one of the volumes in his library that helped form my childhood image of the Andes.

'Before him,' wrote Prescott of Pizarro's first sighting of these mountains, 'rose the stupendous Andes, rock piled upon rock, their skirts below dark with evergreen forests, varied here and there by terraced patches of cultivated garden, with the peasant's cottage clinging to their shaggy sides, and their crests of snow glittering high in the heavens, – presenting altogether such a wild chaos of magnificence and beauty as no other mountain-scenery in the world can show.'

Though Prescott had himself never seen the Andes, he wrote about them as if he had. In the aftermath of my journey from Chachapoyas, Prescott's description of the mountain track followed by Pizarro and his men (a 'narrow ledge of rock, scarcely wide enough for his single steed, where a single mishap would precipitate him hundreds, nay thousands of feet into the dreadful abyss!') seemed more believable than ever, as was the sense of relief felt afterwards by the Spaniards on beholding the Cajamarca valley, 'which, enamelled with all the beauties of cultivation, lay unrolled like a rich and variegated carpet of verdure'.

I began thinking of Prescott as soon as I entered this valley. His version might have been outdated and unfashionable, but it was the one that had been with me since my mid-teens. As the bus from Celendín approached Cajamarca itself, I remembered Prescott's description: 'Along the slope of the hills a white cloud of pavilions was seen covering the ground, as thick as snow-flakes, for the space, apparently, of several miles.' Pizarro's tiny army was confronting one over fifty times larger.

Atahualpa himself, at the time of Pizarro's arrival, was staying at the thermal springs known as Baños del Inca, which my bus passed on the outskirts of Cajamarca. This leafy place, with its modern chalets, was still a spa resort. In Humboldt's day the spa was still excellently preserved, if lacking the gold couches and other extravagant furnishings from Inca times. He was even able to see the actual pool, 'large and deep', where Atahualpa had bathed. He calculated the temperature of the waters at their source to be a remarkable 70°C.

Before making approaches to the emperor, Pizarro and his troops went straight to the town of Cajamarca, which they found largely deserted. They gathered in the main square, 'larger than any square in Spain'. Surprised there by a hailstorm, they took refuge in the long, barracks-like buildings surrounding it. Pizarro, aware of the vulnerability of his army, so outnumbered, so isolated and so deep in the heart of Inca territory, was anxious to respect protocol and to avoid doing anything at this stage that might offend Atahualpa. He sent envoys to the Baños del Inca to receive official blessing for their stay in the town and to ask the emperor to come and visit him the next day. He realized, on the basis of what had happened to the Aztecs in Mexico, that the only chance they stood of conquering the Incas was to capture their leader.

The envoys found Atahualpa surrounded by his nobles. They concluded that 'his countenance exhibited neither the fierce passions nor the sagacity which had been ascribed to him and, though in his bearing he showed a gravity and a consciousness of authority well becoming a king, he seemed to discharge all expression from his features, and to discover only the apathy so characteristic of the American races'. They had, in other words, absolutely no idea of what was going on in his mind. Even to this day it is difficult to understand why such a seasoned warrior as Atahualpa was not more suspicious of the Spaniards' intentions and why he was so gullible as to fall into Pizarro's trap. Perhaps he was convinced of his own invincibility, or perhaps he believed in historical destiny and knew there was nothing he could do. Or perhaps it was nothing more than mere curiosity that made him agree to meet Pizarro the next day, 16 November, in the main square at Cajamarca.

As with all main squares in Peru, it is not named after Bolívar, but is called instead the Plaza de Armas. I found a spacious landscaped area, with topiary llamas in the centre, and sides lined with low colonial buildings and the town's two dominant churches. One of them was the cathedral, with its magnificent towerless facade whose wealth of classical detailing included examples of distinctively Indian workmanship. The other was San Francisco, in whose sanctuary the bones of Atahualpa were said to lie.

Among the tensest moments in the whole conquest of Peru had been the interminable wait on this square for Atahualpa's visit. On the night the envoys returned to Pizarro to tell him of the emperor's acceptance of his invitation, the Spaniards were understandably unable to sleep. There was now no turning back.

They had to capture the emperor at all costs, and Pizarro for the time being would not reveal to his troops how they would do so. The Spaniards had no way of knowing how the Incas would behave, let alone fight. They knew only that they could not take on the Incas in battle without making Atahualpa a prisoner beforehand. They might have the advantage of firearms and horses, but they were seriously outnumbered. Retreat was not an option. This would betray human weakness and rid the Incas of any notion they might have had about the divine status of the mysterious white men from overseas. And Atahualpa would almost certainly respond to cowardice by killing them all.

'The clouds of the evening had passed away,' began Prescott's account of the next day, 'and the sun rose bright on the following morning, the most memorable epoch in the annals of Peru. It was

307

Saturday, the sixteenth of November, 1532. The loud cry of the trumpet called the Spaniards to arms with the first streak of dawn.'

But nothing happened at first, and the Spaniards spent the morning vainly scanning the horizon for some sign of movement from Atahualpa. Atahualpa was in no hurry; and when he and his accompanying party finally got going, around noon, they stopped to set up camp for the night 'half a league' from Cajamarca. This unexpected change of plan was too much for the Spaniards to bear, and Pizarro had to tell Atahualpa through the latter's messenger how disappointed he was by this, as 'he had provided everything for his entertainment, and expected him that night to sup with him'.

Incomprehensibly, Atahualpa not only fell this for this ploy and resumed his march, but also told his general that he would enter the square with only a few of his soldiers, that these should be unarmed and that he would be spending the night in Cajamarca. Now that the emperor seemed to be doing exactly what Pizarro had intended, the Spaniards might well have thought that everything was going too easily for them and that some Inca plot was afoot. They remained tense and frightened, and could only have been overawed when, shortly before sunset, Atahualpa finally entered the gates of the city, borne on an open litter, seated on a massive golden throne and preceded by a huge cortege of servants, noblemen and guards forming a swaying mass of reds, whites, silvers, coppers and azures. Prescott omitted one telling observation made by Pizarro's brother Hernando: some of the Spanish soldiers were literally pissing themselves with fear.

According to the Spanish version of events, Atahualpa, after entering the square with his six thousand followers, was surprised to find not a single Spaniard to greet him. In the end a Dominican friar called Fray Vicente de Valverde (to whom there was now a statue in the Plaza de Armas), appeared, carrying a bible and a crucifix. The friar explained at great length about such matters of the faith as the mysterious doctrine of the trinity, the creation of man, his fall, his redemption by Jesus Christ and the appointment of popes as God's representatives on Earth. This was perhaps not the sort of entertainment that Atahualpa had had in mind. In a fit of anger he threw the Bible to the ground.

The shocked friar called to the Spaniards to come out of hiding and avenge the Lord. The Spaniards duly obliged. Invoking the name of St James, wielding their swords, firing their guns and attaching bells to their horses for terrifying effect, the Spaniards quickly captured Atahualpa and managed to kill every other Inca in the square within half an hour. As for the Spaniards, all they sustained was a slight hand injury when Pizarro used his sword to stop one of his men from killing Atahualpa. Pizarro still seemed at this point to have retained a modicum of nobility and respect for military convention. Either that or he did not want Atahualpa to die before revealing the secret source of his gold. He also owed him a supper.

The two men had supper served to them in a hall still littered with corpses. Atahualpa, looking gloomy, said that he had not expected so small a group of soldiers to be capable of doing so much damage. Pizarro tried cheering him up. He told him 'not to be cast down by his reverses, for his lot had only been that of every prince who had resisted the white men'.

I too stayed in the square to have supper in a building I liked to think of as having replaced the hall where Pizarro and Atahualpa had eaten. The restaurant, called Salas, had obviously not changed much since it first opened in 1947. Large and packed, it had the atmosphere of one of those traditional establishments in Madrid where families went to have Sunday lunch. As the waiters at Salas questioned me about the possibility of getting jobs in Spain, I found myself distracted by thoughts of the ignominious sudden collapse of one of the world's great empires. I was still puzzled by the implausibility of many of the details of the story, not least the sheer numbers of people killed so quickly and the far greater number of Inca soldiers who, on hearing of Atahualpa's capture, merely ran away. The Spanish chroniclers obviously made massive exaggerations so as to stress the valour of their small band of isolated men. But such patriotic propaganda would later backfire on them.

Growing western fascination with the Incas coincided with a disillusionment with Spain comparable to present-day hostility towards the United States. Even Prescott, whose interest in the conflict between Pizarro and Atahualpa was essentially as a gripping story, labelled Pizarro a 'vile malefactor'. Almost everybody else to have commented on the conflict, apart from diehard Spanish patriots, has polarized it as a clash not just between civilizations but also between good and evil.

The romantic simplifications of the nineteenth century have been echoed in the politically correct attitudes of today, with such results as the recent removal in Lima of an equestrian statue of Pizarro to make way for an Inca flag (the Incas never had a flag). I put much of the blame for Spain's image as a land of cruel fanatics on St James, or rather on his repellent reincarnation as St James the Moor-Slayer, who had apparently helped the Christians to victory at the legendary but bogus battle of Clavijo of 844. After Pizarro's victory at Cajamarca, St James the Moor-Slayer became in South America St James the Indian-Slayer, in which guise he can be seen in churches and museums throughout the Andes. In the National Museum at Quito I had even seen St James portrayed as St James the Republican-Slayer. But by then the saint's powers had clearly begun to fade.

The undeniable atrocities committed by the Spaniards and the Catholic Church in South America did not make me any more sympathetic towards the Incas. Now that I was in Peru, I kept recalling the opinions of the great national novelist and would-be president Mario Vargas Llosa, who has claimed never to have had much of a liking for them. Vargas Llosa thought they might be responsible for the streak of sadness which he identified as one of his country's most pronounced traits. For him Inca society was 'a regimented and bureaucratic one composed of ant-like people in whom all individualism was flattened out by a giant steamroller'. Only perhaps a society such as that could have collapsed so rapidly as a result of the gullible actions of their leader.

Vargas Llosa was on less controversial ground when he talked about Inca art, whose coldness and austerity he compared to the delicacy and fantasy of that of earlier Peruvian civilizations. There was almost none in Cajamarca itself, where the conquistadors had pulled down almost every old wall in a search for Inca treasures.

The morning after my arrival there, I hunted down what remained of Inca Cajamarca. From near the Plaza de Armas I walked up the neo-baroque stairway that climbed the hill of Santa Apolonia. A few stones of what might have been an Inca palace or temple were arranged around a formal modern garden.

A number of children on the hill persistently offered their services as guides. Humboldt had been lucky enough to be accompanied around the town's Inca remains by a friendly seventeen-year-old whose father, a local Indian chieftain called Astorpilco, claimed descent from Atahualpa. The boy's family lived 'in great poverty' within 'some sad ruins testifying to Cajamarca's vanished past'. Though desperately poor, the family was 'happy with the little they had and, far from complaining about their fate, was movingly resigned to it'.

From Humboldt's vague description of Astorpilco's ancestral residence, it stood alongside Atahualpa's supposed burial place, the sanctuary of San Francisco. The young Astorpilco led the baron through its rubble, evoking as he did so the gilded magnificence of former days. The baron was also taken to the nearby so-called 'Ransom Room', Cajamarca's only standing Inca structure of today.

This might have been the room which Atahualpa offered in 1532 to fill with gold in return for his release; or it could have been the cell where he was imprisoned and then killed by Pizarro nine months later, despite having assembled much of the promised treasure. Visitors in Humboldt's day were told that the reddish marks on the stone on which Atahualpa was said by legend to have been decapitated were blood stains. The crafty baron would have none of this. He knew that Atahualpa was originally going to be burnt alive, but was then garrotted as a reward for a last-minute conversion to Christianity. Enclosed today by a much later building, and surrounded by a ramp of steel and concrete, the Ransom Room appeared to me disappointingly small and dull.

The pathos I should have felt in Cajamarca for the destruction of the Inca civilization came instead in the most unexpected of places – a late-night music bar called Usha Usha. It was a small bar lit by candles and lanterns, its white walls scrawled with the comments, signatures and doodles of its hundreds of customers over the years. I got there early, shortly after ten on a Saturday night, and the only person there was its owner, Jaime Valera, whom the Peruvian National Institute of Culture had recently nominated part of the Cultural Heritage of Cajamarca.

He was sitting on a bench propped up against the back wall of his bar, a guitar in his hand. He was perhaps in his early sixties, broad-faced, largely bald except for a few wispy strands of white hair at the back. The customers took their time arriving, allowing the two of us to have a long talk about his life, his bar and his beliefs. His father had been a local farmer with a passion for music and a huge collection of records, to which the infant Jaime had listened whenever his father was out in the fields tending the livestock. He learnt by heart the tunes and lyrics of hundreds of songs, Peruvian, Andean, international. He knew he was destined to be a musician from the age of five. Even when he had become the manager of the bar and restaurant of the Hotel Cajamarca, he had taken every opportunity to sing to the clients. He had been persuaded by them to take on his own bar. For the past thirty years he had been singing every night without fail at Usha Usha.

He loved the cheerful musical traditions of his native region, but he had also been keen to popularize in Cajamarca what he called the *trova*, from the word 'troubadour', a type of plaintive and often

312

improvised folk song, reflecting the soul of the people, and which was sometimes a cry of protest.

His great hero was Che Guevara, a large photo of whom was on the wall behind him. He had always been a socialist, cursing in his music the injustices of Peru and the treatment of the country's indigenous population. His father had been friendly with an enlightened mayor of Cajamarca, who in the 1930s had taken the bold step of decorating the Plaza de Armas with statues of famous Indians. The man had then been ordered to take them down.

I asked him what Usha Usha meant. He said it was a Quechua expression used to get cattle moving, but which also implied liberation, freedom, the rising up of the oppressed. He said it was the title of his most famous song, which he'd sing me later when the bar was full.

The three members of Jaime's band turned up, including a tall and handsome black percussionist with his hair tied up in a ponytail. Four slightly tipsy middle-aged American tourists made their noisy arrival and embraced Jaime. As Jaime introduced them to the 'English wanderer', a couple of hardened male drunks came in and slumped down at one of the darker tables. Again Jaime made his courteous introductions, after which somebody else appeared, an enthusiastic, smiling man in his early thirties, who told Jaime he had met him ten years earlier. 'Of course, I remember,' said Jaime unconvincingly, as the man sat down next to me. He was a Limeño architect on a business trip to Trujillo. He had come to Cajamarca simply to hear Jaime sing. He had been to the bar just that one time years ago but had never forgotten the experience.

By midnight Jaime decided it was time for the music to begin. In a powerful, throaty voice, he started off with what he called some 'lively *carnavalitos*', which got the Americans laughing and clinking glasses at their table. With his voice becoming ever rougher and more expressive, he launched into a rendition in Spanish of Frank Sinatra's 'My Way'. The stirring conclusion to this, with the words '*A mi man-eeeee-raaaaaa*', had the Americans wildly clapping. A few songs later and they were dancing in the middle of the bar, almost knocking over my table.

Jaime's voice was at times so hoarse and guttural as to make me feel a pain in my own throat. He confessed that he had had laryngitis since the beginning of January and had been advised by his doctor neither to sing nor to talk. 'But singing is my whole livelihood, my soul.'

Before the Americans left Jaime wanted to sing for them his signature tune, '*Usha Usha*'. His eyes closed, his face contorted into a Goya grotesque, he began. Within a few moments he stopped. The two male drunks were giggling to themselves. Jaime, as politely as he could, but clearly angry with them, told the two men that you don't talk and joke when '*Usha Usha*' is being sung, 'you go to other bars to do that'. He prepared to start again. The young architect whispered excitedly to me that the bar hadn't changed at all in ten years, Jaime was exactly the same as ever.

When Jaime returned to the song with increased and surprising volume, I remembered the Spanish poet García Lorca's description of the concept of *duende*, a feeling that everyone recognizes but which no one can define. As an example Lorca had quoted the time he had heard a famous flamenco singer sing with great skill and power but without at first moving the audience. Only later, at around three in the morning, after this *cantaor*'s voice had become almost raw with aquavit, had the *duende* emerged.

'*Oooooooshaaaaa! Oooooooshaaaaa!*', sang Jaime, showing how close the ridiculous was to the profoundly moving. Here was *duende* as Lorca had known it, indefinable yet unmistakable. My skin had become goose-pimpled and my eyes watery.

'*Oooooooshaaaaa! Oooooooshaaaaa!*' Jaime continued, bursting into a stream of Quechua words whose meaning I could only guess at. They seemed too sad to be about liberation and freedom. They suggested monumental aspirations and yet greater setbacks.

'The song is about tragedy,' Jaime explained to me afterwards, when the Americans had left, 'the tragedy of life, the tragedy of

South America, the tragedy of the Andes, the tragedy not just of the Incas, the Indians and the Andean poor, but also the tragedy that ultimately engulfed Pizarro, Bolívar, Che Guevara, and almost all the other great adventurers and idealists who have been ensnared by this wonderful and terrible continent.'

The remaining three customers filed out, followed finally by the musicians. Jaime and I were once again alone. 'Do you know what García Márquez has recently called South America?' he asked me. He smiled, cleared his throat, and took a long glass of water before telling me. '"The laboratory of failed illusions."'

Cajamarca would be the last important Andean stop on Humboldt's South American tour. When he and his party left the town in November 1802 it was with the intention of moving on to the lowland city of Trujillo and from there to travel mainly by boat to Lima. Nothing he had done in his recent travels could have had the same significance for him as his climb up Chimborazo. However, on crossing the Andes for the final time, he began anticipating with growing impatience a moment he had dreamt of since childhood: his first sighting of the Pacific.

'Our desire to contemplate certain things,' he wrote, 'does not always depend on their magnitude, beauty or importance, but is linked to the accidental emotions of our youth.' As a child he had always been taken by the tale of Vasco Nuñez de Balboa's discovery of the Pacific from the Quarequa heights of Panama, and his desire for distant travel had been stimulated by accounts of the Pacific journeys of Cook and Bougainville.

The guides that had led Humboldt, Bonpland and Montúfar from Cajamarca had promised them that they would be able to see the Pacific after crossing the pass of Hunagamarca. Thick clouds hung over them as they approached the pass, but then suddenly and miraculously disappeared as they got to the top. They were so elated that they forgot to take their usual barometric reading to ascertain the pass's height. 'The entire western slope of the cordillera, and the

315

plains of Chala and Molinos as far as the coast near Trujillo, lay stretched out before our eyes. Thus we were able to see for the first time the Southern Sea, under a dazzlingly clear light that radiated from its shores right out to a limitless horizon.'

In their imaginations their eyes wandered even beyond the horizon, to the islands of Tahiti. 'From the spine of the Andes, surrounded by the ruins of a wise and industrious people, our eyes searched for those happy islands where there still existed that innocence of customs and energy of personality which the Europeans have all but destroyed here.'

A few days later, when Humboldt was able to put his hands into the Southern Sea, three kilometres to the south of Trujillo, he found out that the water's temperature was only 6°C, lower than could be expected for this latitude. He presumed the existence of a current running parallel to the shoreline. In a matter of minutes he had made the discovery that ensured his name would be remembered long after most people had forgotten the man himself. He had discovered the Humboldt Current.

I followed Humboldt to Trujillo, catching my first glimpse this trip of the Pacific while sitting on a fully reclining leather seat. I was enjoying my first luxury bus in Peru, as well my first asphalted and well-graded road in the Peruvian Andes. I too was leaving the Andes, though only for a fortnight or so. I was heading slowly towards Lima.

Back again near the coast I returned to the Peruvian summer and to days of hazy sunshine, spent at first in Trujillo, the capital of northern Peru. 'You have to be used to Peruvian cities to find Trujillo beautiful,' wrote Humboldt, who admired its attractive church and broad straight streets but who found that, instead of houses, there were white walls five metres high. Great changes must have happened in the years immediately following his visit. The predominant whiteness of the town, blinding under the brilliant light, had been broken up by palace facades in exuberant primary colours. If Cajamarca had the austerity of Castile, Trujillo, with its balmy lively atmosphere, had all the exotic sensuality of Seville.

I stayed in a hostel run by an Anglo-Peruvian couple, Clara and Michael White, who introduced me to the extraordinary achievements of the Mochica and Chumí civilizations. The passion and feistiness of Clara was complemented by the restrained Englishness and encyclopaedic knowledge of Michael, a former high-powered accountant who reeled off facts and statistics about the Peruvian past as if they were the latest fluctuations on the stock market.

Prepared beforehand by a lecture from Michael on Mochica ceramics, I visited what turned out to be one of Peru's most memorable museums, the Casselli Museum. Its situation wasn't promising, in the basement of a former car salesroom attached to a Mobil filling station. But inside was an eye-opening collection of what Isherwood caustically described as 'remote ancestors of the Toby Jug'. The faces, animals and erotic and other scenes carved on these Mochica vessels were at times as uncannily life-like as Roman-Egyptian funeral portraits.

These works brought the area's ancient past alive even before Michael himself, wearing one of the giant straw hats of the area, guided me around the Mochica and Chumí sites that lay scattered around the outskirts of the town, over a flat rubbish-strewn waste-land lying between barren mountains and the coast. The size and sophistication of these civilizations were brought home by the extent of the remains, featuring a complex of canals, fortifications and aqueducts, temple-tombs in the form of giant pyramids or *huacas*, and the immense labyrinth of wind-shaped earthen walls that once formed the Chumí capital of Chan Chan.

As Michael explained the esoteric symbolism of the one of the *huaca*'s magnificent carved friezes, I realized we were being watched by a grey hairless dog, a strange beast who had assumed the role of guardian of the site. Michael, briefly distracted from his speech, told me that this uniquely Peruvian breed was sometimes known as an Inca dog. They were much treasured by the Incas, though not by the

317

conquistadors, who nearly killed them off and tried populating South America with mastiffs like Chumberry. The Inca dogs survived in isolated rural communities, where they were valued for their mystical qualities. The glare of the one looking at us was extremely off-putting.

Humboldt would have certainly commented on this ugly creature had he seen one. Chan Chan, however, lacking its recently discovered detailing, was too bare to be of interest to him other than for its size. Isherwood – who had made his way here directly from the Ecuadorean coast – found the emptiness of Chan Chan utterly gloomy. For him the place was a 'vast desolate maze', which graverobbers had left 'littered with bones, skulls still tufted with hair, rags of burial garments'.

What made Chan Chan even more sinister for Isherwood were its recent associations as an execution ground. In 1932 the American Popular Revolutionary Movement (APRA) had led a violent uprising in Trujillo against the local sugar barons, which resulted in an estimated five thousand deaths. A brutal sergeant major from Arequipa, Sánchez Cerro, was responsible for taking hundreds of *apristas* or suspected *apristas* to Chan Chan to be shot. Dogs, vultures and rodents came to strip the bodies clean and for weeks a pestilential odour could be smelt for miles around. Carleton Beals, a globe-trotting American journalist, investigated the site a few months later and encountered – among such objects as a chauffeur's cap, a tennis shoe and a rusted buckle – 'a skull, cleft open by a machete blow, hair still clinging to it'.

I found nothing of that kind in Chan Chan but I did feel that I had wandered through the land of the dead after being taken by Michael's wife Clara to one of the far less visited Mochica sites, fifty kilometres north of the city, beyond some sugar plantations, at the end of a dust track that petered out into a flat expanse of grey sands and pebbles stretching out to the sea.

Shamans had often visited El Brujo ('The Witch') for years, to draw on its enormous reserves of energy. *Huaqueros* or graverobbers had come to the area more regularly still, to brave the curse on their profession of dying slowly by asphyxiation. At La Prieta archaeologists were now exposing some of the finest of all surviving Mochica decorations, including a relief of a warrior with feet made of real human bones, and rows of prisoners on the point of being sacrificed, some with their genitals amputated 'so that their blood could be collected for sacred rites'.

Near the apex of the *huaca* a mummy of a Mochica princess had come to light in 2006. *National Geographic* had called this the most important archaeological find since Tutankhamen. The body, shrouded by thirty-six twists of drapery, had hands and feet tattooed with snakes and spiders and was completely naked, save for a gold face mask, gilded copper earrings, nose jewellery and a gold neck collar studded with lapis lazuli.

The sea was red from the evening sun as we climbed down from the *huaca* and walked to the neighbouring shell of a colonial church – the only remaining relic of a village that had been destroyed by an earthquake in 1619. Clara pointed out that we were walking over a buried cemetery used by the Spaniards, the Incas, the Chimús and the Mochicas. What I thought were scraps of paper and plastic were the tatters of cotton shrouds disturbed by *huaqueros*. Sifting through the earth with our hands we found fragments of candles, human hair, a few teeth, and shards of bones and skulls. I began imagining that the whole of Peru was like this. A country built on a foundation of corpses. A gigantic cemetery guarded by hairless dogs.

## 19

# AND THE MOUNTAINS
# CAME TO THE CITY

I woke up in Lima. I had never known such a comfortable bus. The seat turned into a bed. A steward brought food, a bottle of wine, blankets and a pillow. We had left Trujillo around eleven o'clock at night, and for a couple of hours or so I had remained in an indeterminate state in between thinking and dreaming.

I thought for a while about Isherwood, who had made the same bus journey by day, and had spent much of it calculating the possibility of dying. Wondering if South American drivers 'accept homicidal speeding as a necessary condition of travel', he developed a theory that the Peruvian love of bullfighting had something to do with it: 'Just as the *torero* is expected to work as close to the bull as possible, so the chauffeur feels in honour bound to graze the side of every passing vehicle.'

We were not speeding. We were floating, in a luxurious vacuum sealed off from the outside world by tinted windows. When I closed my eyes I could picture a monotony of desert, scorched mountain slopes, occasional glimpses of sea, haphazard communities in concrete and adobe, untold fragments of the ancient past, pyramids as old as those of Egypt and a subsoil of corpses stretching as far as the sands. The ruins near Trujillo had affected me. They testified to the vast archaeological wealth still waiting in Peru to be discovered and understood. They were suggestive of a land where violence was barely hidden below the surface.

Nothing so far in my personal experience of Peru had borne out the negative stereotypes of this country. Warmth, friendliness, openness and a body clock similar to that of the Spaniards had seemed to me far more common Peruvian characteristics than their reputed aggressiveness. However, I had rarely turned to the local newspapers or to the television news without seeing some report of a demonstration that had turned violent or of a savage community action taken to check the rising crime rate. Once I had switched on the television to see an entire village stripping and tying up a terrified young delinquent and condemning him to be burnt alive.

Images such as these were in my mind as the bus headed towards the Peruvian capital. They merged with the story my brother Francis had told me about his own brush with death, outside a remote village between Cuzco and Lake Titicaca. He was travelling with the journalist Matthew Parris and an Italian woman friend. Shouts, chanting and a barrage of stones had surprised them in the middle of the night in their improvised camp. The Italian rushed off to the village in search of help but all doors were barred to her. The villagers were in collusion with the attackers, one of whom ran into her as she made her way back and would have raped her had she not disoriented him with an anguished cry of help to the Virgin. The attacker returned with reinforcements, who began to set fire to the land around the tents. My brother and his two friends survived by scrambling up the mountain behind.

They were lucky. The history of tourism in the Peruvian Andes is full of stories of westerners and city-dwellers straying into isolated lawless regions and being killed. The whole history of Peru is full of senseless atrocities that in the 1980s and early nineties had culminated in the emergence of the Andean-born Sendero Luminoso, once described as the 'world's most dangerous terrorist movement'.

Only Colombia has had a greater reputation for violence than Peru, but the violence in Colombia, largely linked today with drugs, is rooted in the post-republican conflict between Liberals and Conservatives. The violence in Peru is more nebulous in its origins. Archaeologists have tried to establish links between the Peruvian present and a past as remote as that of the Chavín cult. Ecuadoreans might tell you of the connection between Peruvian aggressiveness and the age-old desire to possess the middle of the world. Others might blame the Incas for Peruvian violence, just like Vargas Llosa had blamed them for Peruvian sadness. The early-nineteenth-century Swiss traveller Johann von Tschudi was more specific still. He believed that Peru's indigenous population was happy and smiling until turned by the Spaniards into a race of the lost, the angry and the depressed. There is a popular perception that the violence of modern Peru is a result of Pizarro's having disturbed the balance of nature at Cajamarca.

Much of the violence since Pizarro's time has of course involved Indian resistance to Spanish rule. For over two centuries before the Americans of Spanish descent – the Creoles – resisted Spanish rule, Peru had regularly been disturbed by indigenous uprisings followed by vindictive Spanish reprisals, the worst of which was sparked off by the rebellion in 1780 of Túpac Amaru II, who claimed royal Inca descent. When caught by the Spaniards a year later, he was taken to Cuzco's main square, forced to watch the execution of his wife and children, had his tongue cut out and was finally torn apart by four horses. His head was sent to the Andean village of Tilca, where his revolution had broken out.

The story of Túpac Amaru II later merged in Andean folk memory with that of Atahualpa and was then grafted onto a local millenarian tradition probably long predating the conquest. Out of this arose the mythical figure of the quartered and decapitated Inkarri, whose remains were distributed between the four corners of the former Inca empire, and whose head is said to be growing onto another body, which will one day exact a devastating revenge on the white man and bring the world to an end. In the meantime the spectre of Túpac Amaru II has been continually invoked, most recently in the name of a still-active terrorist movement which came into being at the same time as the Sendero Luminoso, the Movimiento Revolucionario Túpac Amaru.

If Colombia has traditionally been polarized between Liberals and Conservatives, the divisions in Peruvian society have been epitomized in the clash between Spanish-founded Lima and the indigenous world of the Peruvian Andes. I would shortly be visiting places in the Andes whose names were resonant with both native resistance and the desperate last stand of the Spaniards in South America. But first I wanted to view the Andes from a city whose inhabitants have variously contemplated the mountains with fear, indifference, disdain and the longing of separated lovers.

When I opened my eyes in Lima I expected the worst. Lima, once the largest and most imposing South American city, has always inspired extreme reactions, usually negative. Melville described Lima in *Moby Dick* as 'the saddest and strangest place imaginable'. The climate has not helped. During the months of the year when the Peruvian Andes are bathed in continual sunshine, Lima is covered by a grey mist and a slight drizzle but rarely proper rainfall. The culprit for this is the Humboldt Current, which produces cold air that evaporates on contact with the equatorial heat.

Humboldt hated Lima. He and his party spent two months here, during which he became the first scientist to draw attention to the fertilizing properties of compacted bird shit or guano, shortly to become a mainstay of the Peruvian economy. However, this major discovery, for which Humboldt is today rarely acknowledged, was incidental to a stay largely intended to pack up their plant and rock collections for shipment to Mexico and thence to Europe.

As with many travellers who have fallen for the charms of Quito, Lima seemed to Humboldt a squalid city, unworthy of its mysteriously acquired sixteenth-century title as the 'City of the Kings'. He claimed to have seen 'neither magnificent houses nor expensively dressed women', and stated that most of the city's good families were 'utterly ruined'. Entertainment was limited to a 'showy' bull ring and a 'mediocre and poorly attended' theatre. At night, the dirtiness and unevenness of streets littered with dead donkeys and dogs made driving around by coach singularly disagreeable. What confirmed Humboldt's opinion of Lima as the last place in South America where anyone could possibly want to live were the city's 'sterile and desert-like' surroundings, extending infinitely to both north and south. He was already missing the Andes, which he would never see again, except from the sea.

Other Europeans, visiting Lima in the early nineteenth century, had similar feelings. Robert Proctor, an English financier who came here in 1824 to broker a loan for the new republican government, found it an 'immoral' place where everyone went to bed very late, slept naked in bed and had the 'truly disgusting' habit of depositing dead bodies wrapped in bundles outside church doors. His compatriot Charles Brand was scathing about almost every aspect of Lima, from its 'disgusting' drunken priests to the 'depravity of morals' of its brazenly smoking women. He was also struck by the dangers of the city. During his two-month stay Brand witnessed three murders and experienced 'several temblors and earthquakes, one of which was very severe'.

Brand's account of Lima in 1828 is indicative of the chaos that set in after Peru was finally liberated from the Spaniards. 'Business,' he wrote, 'was at a stall, government in suspense, one party scarce knowing how to trust the other, armed bodies of banditti were fearlessly infesting the public roads, committing murders with impunity.' By 1835 the situation had become even worse, with four armed factions vying for power. The Peruvian president threatened to shoot anyone who disobeyed his orders and much of the frustration of the city's inhabitants was vented on foreigners, particularly the British. Inauspiciously, that was the year when Lima was visited by Humboldt's great successor in South America and the man whose footsteps I would shadow during the last stages of my Andean journey – Charles Darwin.

Darwin had fallen for Humboldt as a student at Cambridge in 1831, after making his way through the full seven-volume, 3754-page *Personal Narrative of a Journey to the Equinoctial Regions of the New Continent*. He had given up on the book on his first attempt, but had been almost unable to put it down on his second. Thrilled by the German's ability to mix poetry with science, he had been fired by a passion to undertake an ambitious, exotic journey himself. Later in 1831 he accepted the unpaid post of naturalist on the HMS *Beagle*. After sailing from Buenos Aires down to Tierra del Fuego and then up the Chilean coast, the *Beagle* landed at Lima on 6 July 1835.

Darwin's impressions of Lima were similar to those of most travellers. He noted the 'wretched state of decay', the huge population of mongrels and the sheer number of churches rising above the 'heaps of filth'. As with everybody else, he made no mention of the men of Lima, but was obviously taken with the city's women. Their most exotic feature was a black veil or *saya* which they used to cover their faces, leaving one eye exposed. For Brand this 'disgusting' item of clothing allowed them to go out anonymously into the streets and flirt with impunity with anyone they wanted to. For the pioneering French-born feminist and grandmother of Gauguin, Flora Tristán, the *saya* was one of the reasons why the women here were freer than in any other place in the world. Darwin, sex-starved after so much time on the *Beagle*, wrote that the one eye left uncovered by the *saya* was 'so black and brilliant and has such powers of motion and expression, that its effect is very powerful'. So powerful as to make him conclude that Lima's women were more 'worth looking at than all the churches and buildings'.

The *saya* remained a feature of Lima well into the twentieth century and for many proud Limeños contributed to the city's exotic, mysterious and Andalusian-style allure. However, the women of Lima seemed generally to have disappeared from the consciousness

325

of later travellers, whose perceptions of the city were otherwise unchanged from those of their predecessors. Lima for them was still as dirty and depressing as ever, still the place the Peruvian poet César Moro would define as 'Lima, the Horrible'. The ten-year-old Vargas Llosa moved with his newly reunited parents to Lima in 1946. He formed an instant loathing for the city, but later, as an adolescent in prosperous middle-class Miraflores, learnt how close hatred was to love. The Lima which he first began to appreciate and to use as a setting for his novels was for him a 'small, safe, tranquil and deceitful city', rigidly divided into wealthy, middle-class and poor districts. The great change to the city occurred from the 1960s onwards, brought about, in Vargas Llosa's opinion, by the introduction of agrarian reform acts intended to share Peru's land more evenly but ultimately making the rural poor worse off than ever. Thousands of Andean villagers started moving to Lima, creating huge shanty towns on its outskirts and overstretching the city's sanitary, housing, transport and security resources. The once-strict divisions between the various districts broke down and the better-off were forced to witness the reality of crime, overcrowding and a massive street population of beggars, vagrants and ambulatory salesmen.

Matthew Parris, a devoted Andean hiker, expressed the typical reaction of his kind when he devoted a whole chapter of his popular book *Inka-Cola* to 'Atrocious Lima'. 'Lima,' he wrote, 'is an atrocity. Ankle-deep in urine and political graffiti, the old Lima rises from the middle of the largest expanse of wet corrugated iron in the southern hemisphere: the new Lima.'

I loved Lima from the beginning, perhaps because my first view of the city was of empty streets touched by the bluish light of a cloudless dawn. Unlike most Andean travellers to Peru, I was visiting the city during its dry season, which corresponded to the rainy one of the interior. The sun did wonders for Lima.

Spaniards were the only people I knew who had regularly praised Lima, and the more I got to know the place the more I realized why.

Miraflores, where I stayed, was like one of those districts of Madrid (another not immediately seductive city) where grand, single-family residences and alleys of trees still held their ground against the invasion of high-rise modernity.

I rented a room in one of the coastal promenade's few remaining early-twentieth-century houses. Directly facing a luxury tennis club and a hazy sea, it had a small front garden protected by railings and a little conservatory at the back where breakfast was served by a maid. The place was the family home of a retired businessman called Hernán, who always joined me in the conservatory for leisurely over-polite conversations. He belonged to a local writing and reading group, and spoke often about a wife whom I never saw (and whom I began to suspect was like the mother in *Psycho*). His only obvious oddness was probably a cultivated eccentricity: every nook of the house was crammed with tiny sculpted representations of owls, including a Mochican relief of one being buggered by a man.

Hernán's home had something about it of the quiet ghetto-like Lima of Vargas Llosa's adolescence. Leaving it to travel to the city centre was a brutal wresting. The taxi and *colectivo* drivers on the multi-lane Avenida Arequipa sped and swerved across a monotonous urban landscape of warehouses and dirt-stained housing blocks set against a dusty sky crisscrossed with cables and aerials.

The adrenalin of the ride would still be pumping through my body as I reached the old town. Dismissed by Parris as a 'great colonial shipwreck . . . waiting for the next earthquake to do the decent thing', this was now an exhilarating, anarchic mixture of the run-down and the newly restored, with drab and flaking streets full of old-fashioned stores, alternating with massive baroque churches, brightly repainted colonial palaces and haughtily swollen buildings of the belle époque. Some of the detailing, such as the wooden grilles covering colonial balconies, had a touch of southern Spain, but much else was uncannily reminiscent of the first years of post-Franco Madrid, particularly the sudden transitions between the brilliant, the grand, the dark and the decadent.

My time in Lima was spent mainly away from the centre, in museums distributed around its suburbs. The oldest and most welcoming of these was the National Museum, on the quiet leafy main square of Pueblo Nuevo, in a former country estate where Bolívar had stayed.

In this museum I learnt how to distinguish the various phases in Peru's pre-colonial art and about the two father figures of Peruvian archaeology, Max Uhle and Julio Tello, both closely associated with the museum's foundation early in the twentieth century. They had had radically contrasting approaches towards their discipline.

The German-born Uhle, often referred to as the discoverer of the Mochica and Nazca civilizations, was the archetypal blinkered scholar, working from his study, obsessed largely with questions of chronology, completely uninterested in the Peruvian present and – like many foreign archaeologists who have worked in Peru – indifferent to problems of conservation. Julio Tello, in contrast, was someone whose pioneering work in the early Andean civilizations was intimately tied up with his ideological beliefs. The Lima-born son of Peruvian peasants, he saw the Peruvian past as integral to an understanding of its present, and as a reflection of the greatness and sophistication of an undervalued indigenous culture. In 1919 he uncovered the major site of Chavín de Huantar, from whose sunken temple he removed what is one of the National Museum's most fascinating treasures – the elaborately carved granite obelisk now called the Tello Obelisk.

Learning about Tello introduced me to the controversial issue of Peruvian national identity and to the related phenomenon of *indigenismo*. *Indigenismo* was a cultural and political phenomenon in which Tello had been heavily involved; it appeared indeed to be the major preoccupation of most modern Peruvian intellectuals not side-tracked by the national obsession with Paris.

In the bookshop of the National Museum I found out that Vargas Llosa had written about the subject in *The Archaic Utopia*.

Vargas Llosa was full of surprises. His political views and espousal of Thatcherism had lost him many former admirers and probably his chances of winning the Nobel Prize. But few intellectuals wrote as well, as persuasively and as widely as he did. His energy was prodigious. He could produce some of the best novels of modern times, lead an international existence, run for the Peruvian presidency, have a regular column in *El País* and still have time to make such an academic-seeming subject as *indigenismo* as vital and exciting as a work of fiction.

Lima, as the proverbial antithesis of the Andean world, had produced some of the most virulent detractors of *indigenismo*, such as the philosopher Alejandro Deustua, who wrote in 1937 that 'Peru owes its misfortunes to the indigenous race, whose psychic degeneration has taken on the biological rigidity of a being that has definitively stopped evolving, and which has failed to contribute to the mestizo the virtues of a progressive race . . . The Indian is not, and cannot be, anything but a machine.' However, it was also in Lima that *indigenismo* essentially took root, almost entirely promoted by Creoles and mestizos with patronizing attitudes towards 'the Indian'.

*Indigenismo* was initially a literary movement whose preoccupations were similar to those that made European writers and artists of the late nineteenth century find inspiration in the harsh lives of traditional farming, fishing and mining communities. French naturalism was an important force behind one of Peru's earlier and more notorious *indigenista* novels, Clorinda Matto de Turner's *Birds Without a Nest*, which deals with a Creole couple's move to an Andean village, where they invest in a mine and become aware of the sufferings of the Indians, and their cruel treatment at the hands of the *caciques*, or local political bosses. A concerted campaign on the part of the Church resulted in the storming of Matto de Turner's house and the burning of every copy of the book. This invested the work with an importance which, in strictly literary terms, it probably did not deserve.

329

When *indigenismo* began to inspire Peruvian painters, in the first and second decades of the twentieth century, the results were scarcely more original. Andean Indians were painted by artists such as José Sabogal with the same sentimentality and love of the picturesque which European painters had once applied to Breton peasants, Cornish fishermen and Andalusian gypsies. The art museums I saw in Lima were filled with sad-faced Indian peasants and glowing Andean festival scenes.

However, with the Mexican Revolution of 1910–20 the concept of *indigenismo* in Peru acquired a much more radical character. The activities and beliefs of Tello were mirrored in the writings of figures such as Raúl Haya de la Torre, the founder of the APRA party, whose crest included a symbol taken from Chavín de Hunatar. When in exile in 1927 Haya de la Torre brought out a series of polemical essays under the title *Towards the Emancipation of Latin America*, which was a diatribe against Pizarro, the conquest and Spanish colonialism, as well as a glorification of the downtrodden Indian. In that same eventful year for Peruvian *indigenismo*, Tello's Cuzco-born colleague Luis E. Valcarcel, another Creole, published the far more extreme *Tempest in the Andes*, which featured a prologue by the leading Peruvian Marxist of his generation, José Carlos Mariátegui.

Mariátegui saw *indigenismo* as inseparable from socialism and thought that only the replacement of Peru's feudal and capitalist society with a Marxist one would do justice to the memory of the country's Inca past. Though Peru had turned into a vibrant multi-racial society, he believed that the Indian alone represented the true spirit of the nation. Such views were taken by Valcarcel to their racist conclusion in a book that is a bizarre and disturbing mixture of sociological essay and messianic proclamation.

Culture [wrote Valcarcel] will radiate once again from the Andes . . . From the Andes will flow, like rivers, the currents of renovation that will reform Peru . . . For ten thousand years, the

Indian has been the only worker in Peru . . . The Indian did it all, while the mestizo idled and the white gave himself over to his pleasures . . . The Andes are an inexhaustible fountain of vitality for Peruvian culture. Neither the Incas nor the Indians of today have lost their telluric balance. They live with the mountains and rivers, linking their society to nature and mixing themselves with it, in a nebulous pantheism with the world around them . . . The tremendous tragic silence of which Peru has been the theatre for four hundred years is the denial of a cardinal truth: this is a nation of Indians.

Vargas Llosa reduced Valcarcel's romantic and unhistorical rant to three basic premises: that the Inca race was superior to the European one; that the 'masculine' sierra was superior to the 'feminine' coast (lazy, sensual and despised by the Incas); and that autochthonous Cuzco was superior to Lima, 'a denationalized and frivolous city'.

The views of Valcarcel and his *indigenista* generation did not prevent Peru's being ruled until 1956 by a succession of right-wing dictatorships that continued discriminating against the country's indigenous population and upholding a Creole view of Peruvian nationhood. The fourth centenary of the Spanish conquest was celebrated by the dictators and their allies with the fervent enthusiasm with which they greeted in 1939 Franco's victory in the Spanish Civil War.

In the unstable years following the APRA uprising in Trujillo, there emerged the most interesting of Peru's *indigenista* writers, José María Arguedas, the main subject of Vargas Llosa's *The Archaic Utopia*. Arguedas, born in 1911 to a middle-class provincial family in the small Andean town of Andahuayllas, became a fluent Quechua speaker from an early age. After the death of his mother, when Arguedas was only three, his father, a local magistrate, remarried and his childhood became traumatic. During his father's long absences in Lima, his stepmother relegated him to the servants' quarters, where he encountered his true friends and family among the Indians. The sadism and violence of his much older stepbrother forced him to take refuge on a relative's remote Andean farmstead, where his love of Quechua language and culture was consolidated. His profound knowledge of the Andean world intensified after 1923, when for the next three years he accompanied his father on his frequent trips to Andean communities usually accessible only on foot or by mule.

Based for much of the rest of his life in Lima, where he worked latterly as a university teacher and in the National Museum, Arguedas made his debut as an *indigenista* novelist with *Blood Fiesta* (1937). Written in a Spanish considerably influenced by Quechua, this novel revolves around the attempts of the Lima authorities to tame and civilize a typically bloody and anarchic Andean village bullfight, involving much drunkenness and the throwing of dynamite. Yet the Indian bullfight, though derived from a custom introduced by the Spaniards, is the one event of the year that lifts the impoverished villagers out of the reality of their existence and one of the few aspects of their lives that the omnivorous white man has not been able to take away from them.

As Vargas Llosa pointed out, the *indigenismo* displayed in *Blood Fiesta* and in Arguedas's later novels is a deeply conservative one, revealing an attitude towards the Indians that would prefer them to remain isolated in their magical, irrational, animistic, collectivist and anti-liberal world than to embrace modernity. The tragedy of Arguedas was that he himself was stuck between two worlds, between the traditional Andes of his childhood and modern, westernized Lima. Though imprisoned for a year in the 1930s for taking part in an anti-Franco, pro-republican demonstration, he was a shy, retiring man who otherwise involved himself little in politics; but this did not stop the Peruvian left from hailing him as one of their leading intellectuals. And yet, towards the end of his life, there were also Indians who criticized his view of indigenous culture as antiquated. The accumulated tensions of his life, unresolved issues from childhood and perhaps a growing awareness of his contradictory intellectual position proved too much for him. In April 1966 he made his first attempt at suicide in his office in the National Museum. Three and half years later, on 28 November 1969, he tried again. This time he was successful.

Arguedas's widow allied herself after his death with a revolutionary group originally calling itself El Sendero Luminoso de Mariátegui ('The Shining Path of Mariátegui'), which had been formed in the Andean town of Ayacucho. Over ten years later this group would initiate an all-out war on the Peruvian state, the beginnings of which were announced by dead dogs hanging from the lamp posts of Lima. The fighting was at first largely limited to rural Andean areas, but by the late 1980s the lighting of beacons on the slopes behind Lima proclaimed that Andean terrorism was about to reach the capital. The mountains were at last at the gates of the city.

*Indigenistas* such as Arguedas would have derived little joy from this. Nothing in the tedious theoretical writings of the Sendero Luminoso suggested that they had specifically indigenous interests at heart. Their Creole founder, Abimael Guzmán, was a Maoist fanatic who exploited indigenous resentments and Andean messianism to perpetuate a bloodthirsty vision that had as little room for the archaic utopia of Arguedas's Andes as it did for decadent and frivolous Lima.

Before I left for the Peruvian heartland, I tried to make the most of Lima's decadence and frivolity. Every morning at Miraflores, over breakfast with my landlord, I was asked what I intended doing over the day. After the first few days of intensive museum visits and sightseeing, I realized that my plans involved an increasing amount of eating. Hernán, a man who prided himself as much on his gastronomic sensibility as his literary one, plied me with restaurant suggestions and even passed on to me the suggestions of his invisible wife. One morning he looked at me with an expression of envy mixed with disbelief when I told him I was going to spend the day with Gastón Acurio, Peru's most famous chef, one of the few South American chefs with an international reputation. Nervously he asked me if I could take along with me a book for the great man to sign. His wife, he explained, was an enormous fan of Acurio's.

'Lima,' Flora Tristán had written in 1834, 'is distinguished by the great advances it has made in cooking.' Lima is widely regarded today as South America's gastronomic capital and the food of Peru as unequalled by that of any other Andean country. But most travellers' accounts of Peru failed to discuss food other than as an anthropological curiosity. Andean travellers in particular seem to have been affected by a culinary puritanism, as if it were somehow obscene to enjoy food in a land where the people were so poor and the scenery so sublime.

I had been promised lunch at Acurio's La Mar as part of a gastronomic day that would begin with an interview with Gastón at his office in Barranco, the quiet coastal suburb adjoining Miraflores. Barranco had become at the end of the nineteenth century a coastal resort for the wealthier inhabitants of Lima, and many of the more elegant buildings of that time had recently been renovated by young artists, intellectuals and media types, earning it a reputation as Lima's Left Bank.

Gastón was typical of these new residents. A youthful forty-year-old, he slid in sandals down the corridor to greet me. His eyes were as baggy as his trousers, over which he wore a crumpled, capacious T-shirt. He had the look of a misbehaving angel, with a round face and a mass of curly black locks. He said with a smile that he had had a late night.

The son of a leading politician, Gastón had trained in Paris and married a French chef called Astrid. Family backing and influence had helped him open his first restaurant in Lima, Astrid y Gastón, which now had three branches in South America and was about to open in Madrid and London. Celebrity had burgeoned with his own television programme and a series of cookery books available to readers of Peru's leading newspaper, *El Comercio*.

He believed that Peruvian cooking was on the point of being recognized as one of the great cuisines of the world. In the past people would have laughed at the idea. His parents' generation had been brought up to think good food could be only French. A French traveller of 1815, Julien Mellet, had written that Peruvians felt they were at fault if they were unable to offer such food to their European visitors. The sophisticated dishes that had so surprised Flora Tristán had actually been French ones.

There were many reasons why Peruvian food was beginning to conquer the West. It used fashionably nutritious ingredients such as the grain quinoa. It pleased modern European chefs such as Ferrán Adriá by introducing the western palate to a whole range of exotic unfamiliar flavours, such as the Andean tuber called *la oca* ('the goose') or the fruit from the *sauco* tree or *Sambucus peruviana*. Above all, it was what Gastón defined as 'the original fusion food'. Not only did it reflect Peru's extraordinary biodiversity. It also brought together the remarkable range of influences that made Peru such a culturally rich and historically complex country.

Gastón's success was already making it difficult to get his undivided attention for any length of time. He was still only half awake, but already he was talking to me, awaiting the editor from *El Comercio* and on the point of giving a television interview. After fifteen minutes, he was called away from the room, saying he would be back shortly. In the meantime his assistant presented me with the complete ten volumes of an encyclopaedia he had edited on Peruvian food.

I flicked through these, thinking what a shame it was that the old debate on national identity had not included Peruvian food, which seemed to exemplify more than any other aspect of Peru the richness of cultural fusion. I decided that *indigenistas* such as Valcarcel had had little potential as foodies. Had their vision of a Peru dominated by Andean Indians become a reality, the country's chances of enjoying a gastronomic triumph in the West would have been slim.

I glanced at the volume on the Andes. The great Andean staples had been maize (originally from Mexico), potatoes (of which there over a thousand varieties in Peru) and such autochthonous grains as quinoa, tarwi and kiwicha. The Spaniards took a liking to the maize and potatoes, but found the grains tiresome to clean, too much associated with pagan religious rites and unsuitable for all-year-round consumption. They were also unaware of their high protein value. As replacements they brought in beans, barley and wheat, and greatly expanded the Andean meat diet of guinea pigs, llamas and chicken by introducing cows, sheep and goats.

I moved on to the volume about fish. The Mochicas, the Chimús and the Nazcas were all great fishermen and might have evolved a primitive version of Peru's most famous dish, *ceviche*, a mixture of fish and seafood, spiced with hot chili and cooked by marinating in citrus juices. However, the Spaniards gave *ceviche* its present-day form by the introduction to Peru of lemons and onions.

Before Gastón's return, I had time to read about the enormous contribution made to Peruvian cuisine by black slaves from Africa and by the Chinese and Japanese immigrants who originally came over to Peru to work, respectively harvesting guano and sugar cane. From these last two cultures came '*la cocina de los chifas*' and '*la cocina Nikkei*'.

Gastón was back in time to talk about '*la cocina novoandina*' or 'the new Andean cuisine', which had been gathering pace since the early 1980s, and involved the lightening of traditional Creole and other dishes, the revival of the grains and other local produce rejected by the Spaniards, and the bringing together of chefs and culinary ideas from all the Andean countries. As a concept it seemed to have more of a future than Bolívar's vision of a united Andes.

Before lunch with Gastón at La Mar, one of his young assistants prepared me for the experience by driving me to markets and gastronomic establishments all over the city and its outskirts, finishing off at a delightful old-fashioned *cevichería*, where I learnt that the texture and flavour of roast maize kernels were an essential complement to a *ceviche*. By midday I had already been fortified by several Pisco sours (a delicious cocktail featuring egg whites, sugar, lemon juice and the Peruvian equivalent of Italy's grappa) and had even tried a New Andean variant made from coca leaves. By two o'clock I was sitting under the bamboo awning of the lively and chicly informal La Mar, trying out a selection of Gastón's exquisitely light *ceviches* and his miniature, artistic version of the Peruvian potato pie known as a *causa*. By nine in the evening I was sitting down for supper in the more formally elegant Astrid y Gaston. By midnight I had long given up wondering how anyone could think of Lima as being in any way atrocious.

My last breakfasts with Hernán became increasingly strained. I was getting up later and later, and with a diminishing desire to talk when I did so, especially not about literature, *indigenismo* or the New Andean cuisine.

One morning there was a knock on the door. 'Your friend has arrived,' Hernán shouted out. For a few moments I was as astonished as if he had told me that his wife had finally appeared and was waiting for me downstairs. And then I remembered. I recalled last night's vain efforts to get to bed at a reasonable hour. An English friend was arriving this morning from Spain. I needed to be in a fit state to greet him. He was going to spend a whole month with me in Peru.

Chris Stewart was another author, a best-selling one. He had led a varied life until settling fifteen years ago in a remote Andalusian farm and then writing a book about it, *Driving Over Lemons*. He had two great advantages as a writer. He had been a founder member of the rock group Genesis and he was an optimist of boundless enthusiasms. I had featured in his last book as an amiable polymath who spoke like Bertie Wooster. He also wrote that I was a man of formidable metabolism who could spend all night drinking and get up fully rested after only one or two hours' sleep. I didn't want to disappoint him.

'Michael!' he screamed excitedly, rushing into the room before I had even had a chance to get dressed. He had never been to South America before. He had come in an enviable state of ignorance. He confused Uruguay with Paraguay. He had read only Paul Theroux and was now raring to take in the wonders of the New World.

We left Lima the next day, to head north to the town of Huaráz in the Cordillera Blanca. Bolívar's troops had got there before us.

20

# BLOOD FIESTA

The last years of Spanish rule in South America were chaotic and confused. The conquest of Peru by the Liberators proved far more difficult than the conquest of the Incas by Pizarro. The patriots faced not just the resistance of the Spaniards, but also internal conflicts and national opposition that augured badly for the future of the continent. Bolívar himself, before embarking on his final campaign, was aware of the huge and perhaps insurmountable problems that lay ahead. 'I have reached the point in life,' he had written as early as August 1821, 'when I could either lose my way or follow the path of glory.' Peru and its complexities would bring him as close as he had ever been to admitting defeat.

Everything had begun promisingly. The Liberator San Martín, at the head of an army of Chileans and Argentineans, had met with no resistance on entering Lima on 28 July 1821. As Manuela Saenz had witnessed, cheering crowds had greeted San Martín and his proclamation of Peruvian independence. However, the royalists still held power in the Andes and the enthusiasm that had greeted San Martín on the coast was tempered by growing Peruvian resentment that their future was being determined by outsiders. Furthermore the Peruvian ruling class was angered by the hard line now being taken against Spaniards with whom they had enjoyed amicable relations, while the Peruvian Liberals took against San Martín's monarchist views.

In addition there was a fear common to all Creoles: that a liberated Peru would not be strong enough to resist another Túpac Amaru II, a threat which could plunge South America into a bloodbath of unimaginable proportions. Even the liberal and humanitarian Humboldt had thought so. In Lima he had claimed to have got hold of documents signed by Túpac Amaru II that convinced him that the values of western civilization were being threatened by the forces of 'barbarism'.

San Martín, foreseeing that his days as protector of Peru were limited and that he stood little chance of conquering the rest of the country on his own, sailed in July 1822 to Guayaquil for his momentous meeting with Bolívar, from whom he had already pleaded for assistance. The two men were publicly cordial with each other, while privately having reservations. Bolívar did not think San Martín's ideas 'subtle enough to rise to the sublime', while San Martín thought that Bolívar was vain, superficial and too much in love with power. But San Martín also realized how much he needed Bolívar's help and that there was 'not enough room in Peru' for the two of them. Soon after his return to Lima, where he found his power further weakened, San Martín set sail for Chile, and from there to Europe and to exile and death. The man whose feat in leading his army across the southern Andes in 1819 had been as monumental as anything Bolívar would achieve, had become the first of the Liberators to lose his way.

The situation in Peru deteriorated further, particularly after February 1823, with the appointment as president and grand marshal of a man who – as Bolívar bitterly noted – had not 'fought in a single campaign or a single battle', José de la Riva Agüero. Bolívar's subsequent offer to come to Peru's aid was rejected by the Peruvians, but Bolívar believed it was his duty to intervene in the interests of the American revolution. In April he sent Colombian forces into Peru under the command of his most faithful supporter, Antonio José de Sucre, the conqueror of Quito. Within three months the isolated Sucre would be cursing the moment he came to Lima. By then royalist forces had retaken the city and the government had had to flee to the port of Callao. Riva Agüero, deposed by congress but refusing to stand down, went off to Trujillo to raise an army and dissolve congress. Congress reconstituted itself in Lima after the city had been evacuated by the royalists, and nominated as rival president the monarchist sympathizer and Sucre ally, Torre Tagle.

The growing anarchy into which Peru was falling, with half the country ruled by the Spaniards and the other half disintegrating into civil war, gave the Peruvians little alternative but to accept Bolívar's earlier offer of help and even to greet his arrival in Lima in September 1823 with considerable enthusiasm. The English financier Robert Proctor, who had settled in Lima shortly after Sucre, witnessed the Liberator's entry into the city. 'The streets of Lima were one continual display of flags and ornaments from the windows and balconies: . . . Lima seemed to give herself up to the most enthusiastic expression of admiration for this successful American warrior.'

Proctor also described the general excitement at Bolívar's visit to the city's bullring and theatre. Bullfighting had been banned by congress as 'unfit for the present enlightened and civilized age', but the city authorities, hearing of Bolívar's love of the activity, and seeing an opportunity to make money, temporarily lifted the ban.

As for the theatre, there was a general scramble to procure boxes as soon as it was known that Bolívar was going to attend a performance. The interior was 'ornamented with the Colombian colours in every part, and over the president's box, immediately in the centre of the lowest tier, were the united banners of Peru and Colombia'. The house was full long before Bolívar's arrival, which was announced by rockets being fired off outside. When finally he took his seat in the box, there was rapturous applause. Proctor noted:

341

He is a very small thin man, with the appearance of great personal activity; his face is well formed, but furrowed with fatigue and anxiety. The fire of his quick black eye is very remarkable. He wears large mustachios, and his hair is dark and curling . . . I may say that I never met a man with a face which gave a more exact idea of the man. Boldness, enterprise, activity, intrigue, proud impatience, and a persevering spirit, are plainly marked upon his countenance, and expressed by every motion of his body.

Bolívar appears at first to have liked Lima as much as its inhabitants were initially taken by him. 'Lima,' he wrote, 'is a large pleasant city which was once rich. It seems very patriotic. The men appear to be loyal to me and say they are ready to make sacrifices.' He even found the food excellent. However, as with most male travellers of this time, he was struck more than anything by the women, whom he described as 'very pleasant and very pretty' and with 'beautiful eyes and attractive figures'. Altogether, he summarized, 'the men respect me and the women love me'. He was probably right about the latter, though this was not the moment in his life to act upon it. His new love Manuela Sáenz was in town, albeit still living with her tolerant and pliant English husband James Thorne, to whom she would shortly write, 'You are boring, like your nation.'

Bolívar's love for Manuela would last the rest of his life, although punctuated by ever longer absences and numerous infidelities on his part. But his liking for Lima barely survived his first week there, by which time Peruvian suspicion of foreigners had returned more strongly than before. 'This is not Colombia, and I am not Peruvian,' observed a frustrated Bolívar as early as 11 September. 'I shall always be a foreigner to Peruvian people and I shall always arouse the jealousy and distrust of these people.' He was already regretting having come.

The Colombians had become almost a greater enemy to the Peruvians than the Spaniards, with whom Riva Agüero would begin seeking an alliance before being finally forced to flee to Europe. Torre Tagle, seeing his role as president invalidated by Bolívar's presence, was also tempted to follow his rival's treacherous example. Bolívar summed up Peru as being now 'divided into three parties: first, anti-Colombian patriots; second, Spanish loyalists; third, loyalists of Torre Tagle and Riva Agüero'. He added: 'The rest of the unarmed masses has no commitment at all.'

The liberation of this country was beginning to seem less and less likely. Bolívar no longer had any faith in the Peruvians. The Peruvian army, unsure as to whose orders they should obey, was in a shambles and greatly depleted after the Bolivian-born Marshal Andrés Santa Cruz had been sent by Sucre on a disastrous mission to fight the Spaniards near Lake Titicaca. In the meantime little help seemed forthcoming from Chile and Argentina, both of whose governments were threatening to recall the troops San Martín had left in Peru. Bolívar's main hope lay in being sent large reinforcements from Colombia, but Colombia's congress was already wary of the Liberator's ambitions. 'Discord, misery, discontent and egoism reigned everywhere,' concluded Bolívar, shortly after falling seriously ill while sailing back to Lima following a visit to Trujillo.

The illness, possibly the first symptoms of the tuberculosis that would eventually kill him, brought him close to death and entailed a two-month stay in the small port of Pativilca, 150 kilometres north of Lima. While he was recuperating there, the Chilean and Argentinean soldiers stationed in Lima mutinied for back pay. Not receiving any satisfaction from the Peruvian government they handed over their fortress to loyalists. At the end of February 1824, Lima, through the connivance of Riva Agüero and other turncoats, was again occupied by an army of Spaniards, Creoles, blacks and Indians.

'Peru is a chamber of horrors,' moaned Bolívar in despair in Pativilca. Unvisited by Manuela Sáenz (obliged to remain with her husband in Lima) and with almost everything conspiring against him, he began turning into what he would become at the end of his life – a figure from a Shakespearean tragedy. In one of his many revealingly personal letters to his soon-to-be-treacherous Colombian deputy Santander, he exhibited all the requisite attributes of such a figure – world-weariness, self-insight, disillusion, solitude and a realization of life's pointlessness. For all his actorly hyperbole, the now-weakened Bolívar was at last becoming a figure capable of arousing our sympathies:

> Until now I have fought for liberty: in future I will fight for my glory, no matter what it costs. My glory now consists in ruling no more and in thinking of nothing but myself . . . My years, my ill health, and my disillusion with all the dreams of youth prevent me from taking any other way. The revulsion I feel is such that I do not wish to see or to eat with anyone. The presence of another person kills me: I live among the trees of this miserable place on the coast of Peru and I have become a misanthrope overnight . . . Ambition, says Rousseau, guides men when they have reached the age of forty, and I have reached that age. But my ambition has died. I have nothing to hope for and everything to fear . . . On all sides I hear the sounds of disaster. My era is one of catastrophes. Everything comes to life and dies before my eyes as though struck by lightning. Everything passes, and I would be a fool to flatter myself that I can stand firm in the midst of so many upheavals, in the midst of so much destruction, in the midst of the moral subversion of the world.

But beneath this self-pity, ill health and apparent loss of ambition Bolívar still retained the superhuman willpower of old. The Colombian envoy to Peru, visiting the Liberator at Pativilca, found him skinny, decrepit and unable to raise himself from his chair, but still insisting that he would have an army ready within three months 'to climb the cordilleras and defeat the Spanish'. Bolívar would remain true to his word.

On recovering at the beginning of March 1824 he established his headquarters first in Trujillo and then in the nearby Andean town of Huamachuco. Aided by Sucre he devoted much of his renewed energy to building up a substantial and regularly paid army. He acquired money by confiscating royalist property, imposing taxes and badgering the Church. The Colombians sent more reinforcements than Bolívar had expected and the Peruvians finally decided it was time to lend a hand. By April he had formed a patriot army numbering some eight thousand men. Though this was half the size of the Spanish army, it had exceptional cavalry made up of Argentinean gauchos and their equivalent in Venezuela and Chile, respectively the *llaneros* and the *huasos*. The Spaniards were also suffering now from divided loyalties, following King Ferdinand VII's abolition of the Spanish constitution in October 1823 and the restoration of absolutism.

By mid-May Bolívar's army was advancing down the Andes towards the Cordillera Blanca. The Englishman General Miller, a veteran both of the Peninsular War and of San Martín's Chilean campaign, set off from Lima to meet them there, at the head of a large Peruvian legion. A man of renowned bravery, he had lost the use of one hand after being shot with a musket-ball and, according to Proctor, had been blown up in Chile 'while mixing combustibles'. Miller, a 'tall and gentlemanly' person, was also 'well acquainted with Peru, and much liked by the natives'.

Miller's first meeting with Bolívar took place in Huaraz in June. Miller's memoirs would later provide an invaluable account of the nature-defying march of Bolívar's army across the Andes, through country near Huaraz described by Miller as being 'of inconceivable boldness and magnificence'.

The bus to Huaraz from Lima left from somewhere in the middle of the urban no-man's-land between Miraflores and the city centre. My guidebook advised being particularly alert in this area for pickpockets, muggers and armed robbers. Like the streetwise Manolo before him, Chris had offered to take charge of our combined finances but he was not so streetwise. He was still getting the hang of Peruvian currency. He stood outside the insalubrious bus station counting out the notes from a wallet stuffed with dollars, Euros and soles. A small crowd collected to watch and giggle. I realized that his literary image as an innocent abroad was utterly genuine. I reckoned – and hoped – this innocence would protect him.

The bus, an aged double-decker, headed north along the coast for a couple of hours before stopping for lunch at a low concrete block with a bamboo awning and an exhausted palm tree. A hazy Pacific was visible over a field of sugar cane and the strip of dirty sand into which it merged. This was where Bolívar had almost died, on the outskirts of Pativilca.

Shortly after leaving this desolate place, the bus turned off into a valley that became refreshingly lush as it approached the cloud-covered Andes. We were following the now paved route which General Miller had taken on his march to join Bolívar at Huaraz. Chris engaged me in a conversation about altitude sickness. He was convinced that he was going to suffer from it. I said that if that was his attitude he probably would. It was, I elaborated, a purely psychological condition.

Within half an hour of starting to climb, Chris was clutching his head in his hands. I was not sure if this was in response to the altitude sickness or to the Bollywood musical being shown on the screen. He had closed his eyes. His anticipated elation at first entering the Andes had been dissipated by an intense headache, and now heavy cloud and torrential rain. Sleep seemed the best solution.

It was night-time and still raining when we reached Huaraz, a town which Bolívar had designated 'very loyal and very generous'. It was also extremely ugly. In 1970 this once-thriving colonial town, at the head of the prosperous Huaylas valley, had been subject to the one of the worst earthquakes in recent South American history. Almost the entire town, dating back to Pizarro's day, was flattened, with the loss of ten thousand lives. The place now had an improvised ephemeral look, as if its inhabitants had been temporarily rehoused while awaiting something better.

Chris, though still with his headache, would not hear of taking a taxi to the cheap hostel that had been recommended. For the next half-hour we wandered in the rain and darkness amidst a mass of tin-roofed, single-storey dwellings. We could have been looking for a gravestone amidst thousands. Chris made a show of enjoying the fresh air.

At first light the next morning he was standing on the roof terrace of our hostel trying to get a glimpse of the Cordillera Blanca through the unbroken grey sky. The arrival of the rainy season in earnest was beginning to worry me. There was a reason why so few tourists came at this time of year to the normally popular Huaraz. You could stay here for a few days and fail to see the one feature which redeemed the town visually – the backcloth of snowy mountains that had brought so much cheer to the war-scarred General Miller. The Cordillera Blanca was not just the highest range in Peru. It was the highest tropical range in the world.

While hoping for the rain to stop we walked to the outskirts of the town to see a friend of a friend who worked for the Instituto de la Montaña, an organization dedicated to the protection of the Peruvian Andes. Karen Price was a young Peruvian ecologist of distant British ancestry. She said that several of Huaraz's richer families in the past were descended from former British and Irish soldiers of a similar background to General Miller's. They had settled in the area after the Wars of Independence and seem to have treated the town like a Himalayan hill station.

Prompted by Chris, a passionate ecologist, Karen then outlined the Institute's current project for trying to save the local environment. Chris had already been inveigled in the street into signing a petition against the construction of a Japanese-sponsored dam. But Karen spoke about a plan to reintroduce Alpaca llamas. The Spaniards, by persuading the Andean farmers to breed non-indigenous animals such as cows and sheep, had done untold ecological damage. The cows produced little milk at high altitudes, and trampled around clumsily. The sheep similarly lacked the agility of the llamas, whose feet had evolved to do minimal damage to the ecosystem. The llamas also produced shit that had an especially regenerative effect on the soil and they could graze at a height of 4800 metres.

It was still raining. We were just in time to catch a guided tour headed for Chavín de Huantar, an hour and a half's drive away. The only other takers were a young Swiss backpacker still desperate about the loss of his camera and a young English woman who had had her nose pierced in Thailand. She had a heavy cold and mucus came out of the hole when she blew into a handkerchief.

To reach Chavín we had to cross one of the lower passes of the Cordillera Blanca, whose snowy southernmost crests became briefly visible during a momentary clearing of the clouds once we had climbed above the ubiquitous eucalyptuses and reached the bare *páramos*, known in Peru by the Inca word '*puna*'. The road, newly asphalted to begin with, went through a tunnel before plummeting down on the other side of the pass into a steep valley whose hundreds of tiny stone-bordered fields made the rainy grey-green landscape look as if it had been covered in a fishing-net. We were nearing the kernel of Andean civilization.

The village of Chavín de Huantar, a huddle of adobe and stone houses around a small plaza, seemed unaware of the area's importance in history. A couple of women sat weaving, while a group of drunken shouting men shared what was left of a large beer bottle. Outside the rainy season the place would have had rather more visitors than the four there were today, but there were few signs of commercialization. When Julio Tello came here in 1919 the village was just another forgotten and impoverished Andean community.

Tello had come here to investigate what a Spanish traveller had recorded in 1616 as 'a large building of impressively sized stones'. The Spaniards must have assumed that this was an Inca structure. But a colleague of Tello's had suggested that the site – much depleted over the years by the villagers' house-building – probably pre-dated the recently 'discovered' Machu Picchu. No one could have imagined that the place probably did so by at least two thousand years.

After beginning to excavate, Tello soon became aware not just of the place's remarkable antiquity, but of the possibility that he was in the presence of Peru's oldest civilization. His uncovering of jaguar heads and reliefs of caimans and snakes led him to formulate a theory profoundly satisfying to his *indigenista* beliefs: that the origins of Andean culture were not in the decadent Peruvian coast but in the jungle interior. He did not live long enough to witness the discovery of Peruvian coastal civilizations earlier than that of Chavín, but he was able to glory in his jungle theory over the next twenty-five years of intermittent investigations of the monument.

By 1945 Tello had built a small museum on the site to house the jaguar heads and other finds and was satisfied that the whole place was ready to become one of his country's major attractions. In the January of that year, at the height of the rainy season, the prefect of Huaraz, accompanied by some officials and his eighteen-year-old daughter, an archaeology student, visited Chavín to see how this barely accessible area could be opened up for tourism.

I found out the rest of the story only after a guided tour of the site which left even the normally enthusiastic Chris unimpressed. My own response was probably influenced by my having been so recently to Kuélap, whose monumental walls rising out of jungle made those of the riverside Chavín seem like sheep pens peering above grassland.

Inside the temple, with its dark and narrow hidden passageways, I had expected a world of magic and mystery. Our guide had excited us beforehand with a comparison of the public ceremonials and human sacrifices of later Andean civilizations with the strange private rituals that had taken place in this underground world centred on what became known as the Tello obelisk. Within the darkness, and to the accompaniment of trumpet-like wails from above, the officiating priests had apparently worked themselves into a trance by taking a hallucinogenic drug made from the San Pedro cactus.

349

No such out-of-body experience awaited us. Instead Chris and I patiently queued behind the Swiss backpacker as – armed with a far inferior replacement for his stolen Leica – he took photos of the difficult-to-see copy of the obelisk. The main sounds were of the English woman blowing her nose. We could have been inspecting an empty wine cellar.

What did catch my imagination was hearing afterwards the full story of what happened on the prefect's visit to Chavín in January 1945. A huge block of ice from the mountains had fallen into an upper lake. The lake had overflowed, creating a flood of water and mud which had rushed down towards the site. The prefect and his party, emerging from the temple, had been killed instantly. Much of the village had been wiped out as well. Soldiers had to shoot dogs to prevent them from eating the corpses.

Tello's museum was swept into the river. A huge layer of mud and earth destroyed twenty-five years of painstaking excavation. Tello himself had stayed behind in Lima that day but he died two years later, heartbroken by the destruction of much of his life's work. It took decades to repair the damage that was done.

Tales of natural catastrophe were common to every part of the Andes but they seemed to magnify in the Cordillera Blanca, perhaps because images of apocalypse became almost overwhelming the deeper you steeped yourself in the Andean past.

Before following Bolívar's troops towards the Inca heartland, we spent a few more days travelling around the Cordillera Blanca, discovering both the beauty of nature and its tyranny. A change in the weather encouraged us. The morning after our return from Chavín I could hear Chris almost screaming with excitement from the roof terrace. I rushed up to join him. A giant patch of calendar-blue sky was exposing a larger expanse of snow than I had come across so far in the Andes. In the middle of the long white range stood the rounded twin peaks of the Huascarán, looking like an ermine throne.

Below these mountains, and separating them from the lower Cordillera Negra, was the valley known as the Callejón de Huaylas, which we decided to follow. We drove along the valley in a bus run by the Ancash Company. We wanted to see the site of old Yungay, a town which had had the reputation as the cleanest and most elegant in the whole valley. Everyone had referred to the place as 'Yungay Hermosura' – 'Yungay the Beautiful'.

The Callejón de Huaylas has had a history of disasters. In January 1725 a violent earthquake produced an avalanche that destroyed the whole town of Ancash, with its population of fifteen hundred. In 1941 a landslide destroyed part of Huaraz and several nearby villages, killing eight thousand people. In 1962 four thousand people spread out over several villages were crushed by an avalanche from the Huascarán.

But none of these events was comparable to those of 31 May 1970. At 15.23 on a Sunday afternoon, when football fans everywhere were absorbed in the World Cup, an earthquake measuring 7.8 on the Richter scale struck the northern half of Peru, causing panic and destruction over a huge area, emptying the cinemas and theatres of Lima and creating chaos on the streets. After a few minutes the tremors stopped. The epicentre had been on the coast, about fifty kilometres north of Pitivilca, but the Callejón de Huaylas had been by far the worst-affected part of Peru. For the survivors of Huaraz, surveying the rubble that had once been their town, the scene of desolation could not have seemed greater. But as they began their desperate search for lost friends and relatives, the inhabitants of Yungay were contemplating a spectacle as horrific as anything in Dante's *Inferno*.

A beautiful park now marks the site of Yungay Hermosura. Several boys were waiting around at the entrance, asking us if we needed a guide. I thanked them, smiled and moved on. But Chris proved an easier target. One of the boys had engaged his sympathies by claiming to be an orphan from the 1970 tragedy. He could have been little older than fifteen. The discrepancy in date did not seem to matter to Chris, who had a habit of dispensing charity to anyone who asked him. The boy came with us. He did little more than recite by heart the inscriptions dotted around the park. But his mumbled, shyly delivered account of the Yungay disaster somehow made the facts all the sadder.

At the centre of his story was the Huascarán, whose snows gleamed benignly at us as we walked in between flowers, trees and memorials. At an altitude of 6768 metres, it was the highest mountain in Peru. It was protected by UNESCO. On the afternoon of the tragedy those watching it had seen what they thought was the world coming to an end.

The silence following the tremor at 15.23 had been immediately interrupted by what someone likened to the sound of a hundred low-flying jets. The tremor had dislodged 9 million square metres of snow from the summit of Huascarán, which in turn had taken with them 5 million square metres of rock face, 6 million square metres of glacier and 33 million square metres of earth and mud. The combined avalanche and landslide had formed a wall between eighty and a hundred metres high. Moving at a speed of up to four hundred kilometres an hour this had covered the fourteen kilometres between the summit and Yungay in three minutes. By 15.26 there was nothing left of the town except its hill-top cemetery.

We stopped in front of the rusted, compressed shell of a bus. It projected from the memorial park's lawn like a piece of 1960s Pop Art. The bus belonged to the same company which had brought us here; it had been heading to where we were now going – the small town of Caraz, at the northern end of the valley. The boy said we had to see Yungay's main square, which had been the pride of the area. When we got there, he took out a photo of the square as it had once been, full of people in their Sunday best, with palms and flowerbeds radiating from a white columned church. The stump of one of the church's piers was still standing, as were four of the palms. The rest now was grass.

Turning to go back to the road we faced the cemetery hill, where a statue of Christ with outstretched arms stood in the wind like the sail of a gigantic boat. The town had had a population of 25,000. Only a few hundred survived the tragedy.

The two of us remained haunted by the Yungay story for some time. That evening, after we had settled for the night in the pleasant small town of Caraz, I found a booklet in our hotel entitled *The Day When Yungay Disappeared*. I made the mistake of reading it before I went to sleep. It contained eyewitness accounts of the day, one by a woman who had been sitting after Sunday lunch with her husband, son and mother. Their house began to shake violently. They had to break down the front door with a hammer. Outside they heard screams that the Huascarán was collapsing. The husband tried to rally everyone up to the cemetery, the town's highest point. The woman could not go without her mother; but the mother, with tears in her eyes, told them to leave her. The landslide was upon them in seconds. They all were killed, except for the woman, who found herself on top of a black sea of mud churning with corpses.

# 21

# SHINING PATHS

On the other side of the mountains from Yungay, in a high isolated valley in one of the remoter parts of the Cordillera Blanca, lived a community of Italian priests under the protection of the saintly Padre Ugo de Censi. Padre Ugo was reputed to have saved hundreds of lives from poverty and initiated a woodcarving renascence in the middle of nowhere. The missionary order to which he belonged, the Salesians, seemed to have a special spiritual link with the Andes. The relationship between mountains and spirituality was occupying more and more of my thoughts. My months of travelling in the Andes had filled my mind with images of the sublime and made me aware of the precariousness of life. Chris was unconvinced of my latent spirituality. He still saw me as a hedonistic urbanite with a rather cynical attitude towards New Age travellers who came to the Andes in search of spiritual transformation. But the idea of visiting Padre Ugo's community in the village of Chacas appealed to him for the journey alone. The road there from the Callejón de Huaylas had to negotiate a pass almost five thousand metres high, one of the highest in South America.

Chris had yet to experience the terrors of travelling by bus along rough, narrow Andean roads. At first he behaved calmly.

He himself was an excellent driver and was able to give me reassuring technical information about suspension as the bus swung
from side to side in stomach-churning fashion. But as the climb
proper began, his confidence in the bus began to wane. The sky
had darkened and we were nearing a monumental wall of snow,
ice and rock whose craggy crest was periodically hidden by
clouds. There seemed no way either of bypassing or climbing over
this. Only when the slope was barely a few metres in front of us
did we notice how the road turned suddenly into a vertical jagged
line.

Chris talked about automatic steering and the wonders of
modern brakes, and he also praised the driver's skill in taking curves
that left just a few centimetres to spare. But he was keeping up this
technical commentary as much for his own sake as for mine. When
we went above the snow level and the road became icy and slippery,
Chris's words of reassurance became especially unconvincing.
He talked about how the weight of a vehicle such as this made the
grip on the road that much stronger. After we had got to the top
of the pass only to discover that the way down was as steep as the
way up, he started praising the excellence of the bus's tyres, and
then stopped.

The skidding of the bus had become quite noticeable. Worse still,
we could see far below us the rusting wrecks of a van, a lorry and
an overturned digger. The digger was blocking the road. A group of
men were trying to right it with aid of a truck and some chains.
They rapidly dispersed after our bus had dislodged a large stone
which fell fifty metres and went straight through the digger's roof.
Our driver did not notice this. Everyone else on the bus was fast
asleep.

The digger had been engaged in road improvements. It took a
couple of hours to remove it from the road. We made it into Chacas
shortly after nightfall. The passengers on the bus, as well as the
handful of people waiting on one of Chacas's dark streets for its
arrival, were convinced we were priests. I said we were not, but that

we were hoping to see Padre Ugo. A woman took us to the house where he and the Italians lived. Even though we weren't priests she was sure that the Italians would take care of us for the night. They always offered hospitality to those passing through the village from afar.

A boss-eyed Italian woman opened the door and looked at us warily. She told us that Padre Ugo was currently staying in a village four hours away and was in any case not in a state to receive visitors. They currently had no beds to offer us. There was no other priest who could see us until morning. She closed the door.

We walked down into the main square and were amazed. It was an enormous space, with a neatly cut central lawn, Victorian lamp posts, stone-paved streets, a stone-towered modern church atop a monumental flight of steps, and rows of clean white houses with wooden doors and balconies exquisitely carved with Renaissance motifs. There was no evidence of concrete, dirt, corrugated iron, exposed brick, neon lighting or any other of the usual attributes of a Peruvian village. Even the signposting was tastefully in wood. One of the signs, attached to a house with a particularly grand balcony on the upper floor, read 'Alojamiento' ('Lodging'). We thanked our luck that the Italian woman had been so unpleasant. This looked much more appealing.

The facade was deceptive. Behind was a courtyard looking like a filthy scrapyard hung with rags and old rope and balconies hastily put together with odd planks of wood. Chris and I looked hesitant about staying, but the woman who owned the place insisted there was no other accommodation in the village. Upstairs were three bedrooms, divided by low concrete partitions, with doors that did not close. The room I chose had an arched opening leading out onto the facade's grand balcony. The opening was unglazed, allowing bats and freezing air to enter. The floor was littered with screwed-up balls of dirty toilet paper. 'So the Italians wouldn't take you?' said our proprietress with a sneer. 'They're a strange, arrogant lot. They think they own this village.'

We delayed going to bed as long as possible. We were pleased to see lights and activity from the building adjoining ours, which turned out to be the Town Hall. The young and friendly mayor was inside and greeted us with great warmth. The village had just been given an old computer from Italy. Communications with the outside world had always been a problem, the mayor admitted. There was a time when there had been almost weekly fatalities on the road we had taken. It was now better maintained than before, but today's loss of the digger would put back repairs for some time. The regional authorities had already dropped a project to build a tunnel that would save having to drive to the top of the pass. 'With better access,' added the mayor, 'Chacas could become an important tourist centre.'

I told him of our surprise at such a majestic main square. He said that Padre Ugo was entirely responsible. Padre Ugo had taught the villagers to appreciate the value of natural materials such as stone and wood. He showed us photos of Chacas around the time of Padre Ugo's arrival in 1976. The buildings were humble structures in adobe bricks, including the church, which had an endearing simplicity.

I thought of those old photos as I rose at dawn to survey the square from my balcony. The serrated and snowy silhouette of mountains provided a thrilling setting. But in daylight the square could have been part of some pretentious housing scheme in a neo-colonial style. The difference between it and the old square was highlighted in the way the church had been remodelled. Whereas the original building looked as if it had grown organically from the setting, the new one resembled a fussy hybrid.

Inside the church one of the walls was covered with an enormous modern mural showing Christ carrying the cross below Chacas's dramatic ring of mountains. The hundred or so onlookers were in anachronistic modern dress, with mainly European faces, presumably because they were all portraits of the village's Italian community. At the foot of the cross, and helping to bear its weight, was a kneeling young man in jeans whom I was later able to recognize as Padre Daniele. Padre Ugo, standing up and in flowing church robes, was supporting one of the arms of Christ, who seemed, in comparison to him, a small figure lacking in charisma.

In the background, directly below the Andean snows, was a portrait of the founder of the Salesians, Saint Giovanni Bosco. Saint Bosco was a nineteenth-century priest from the Italian district of Piedmont. When training for the priesthood as a young man, he entertained people as a juggler, magician and acrobat. Later he became a miracle worker. He founded the Salesians for the education of the young and poor, whom he taught on the principles of 'reason, reasoning and kindness', to the accompaniment of much music and games. He also placed a lot of importance on his dreams, in one of which he found himself in a world inhabited by primitive peoples who spent their time fighting against soldiers in European uniforms. A first group of missionaries came to try and reform them and were horribly massacred. A second and more cheerful group turned up preceded by children. This group succeeded in taming the fierce savages. St Bosco recognized them as Salesians. After much library research he identified the land in which the dream was set as Patagonia. Thanks to his dream the Salesians became a missionary order, active initially in South America.

In a corner of the painting was the Salesian coat of arms, with its ragged range of mountains similar to that above Chacas. The mountains, I was later told, signify Perfection and Aspiration. I learnt more about the Salesians after returning with Chris to Padre Ugo's house. This time the door was opened by a young woman with long dark hair, large brown eyes and a most engaging smile. She was called Antonella and came from my Italian birthplace, Genoa. She let us inside a building that was spotlessly clean, with shiny stone floors and wooden beam ceilings, reminiscent of some Alpine house done up for tourists. Antonella said she would find Padre Ugo's deputy, Padre Lorenzo. Chris told Antonella that her smile had already made his morning.

By lunchtime, a large and mainly elderly crowd of villagers was queuing up in a vestibule to take away bowls of soup. We were led to an intimate country-style kitchen-cum-dining-room beyond. I had persuaded Chris with difficulty to come along. The thought of lunching with a group of priests did not appeal to him. But my fantasies of being served delectable Italian cuisine finally got to him. Also Antonella was doing the cooking. We spoke to Antonella as she stirred a tempting bowl of polenta. She herself did not think highly of the local cooking: for a few months she had been living in a nearby village where the main diet was a 'truly disgusting dish called *kotush*', which consisted of potatoes that had been left to rot for several months under a stone.

Padre Lorenzo said grace after we sat down at a long wooden table. I noticed that there were twelve of us. There were bottles of Italian red wine, a large slab of parmesan cheese in the centre, Tuscan olive oil and large plates of salami and other Italian charcuterie. Local farmers had been taught to produce the mozzarella that was served as a first course, but the rest of the produce came in monthly shipments directly from Italy. I had thought this particular group of Salesians encouraged its priests and volunteers to embrace the poverty of the local population, but I let that pass. However, I could not refrain from commenting on how the wine and charcuterie were from my ancestral homeland of Sondrio in the Italian Alps.

Padre Ugo, I now discovered, was from a village outside Sondrio called Poleggia. Padre Lorenzo was from there as well, as were two of the volunteers seated at the table. Several of the others came from nearby, including a visiting priest called Padre Leonardo, who invited Chris and me to come and stay with him near Lake Titicaca. Chris had expected conversation at the table to be stiff and solemn, but the mention of Sondrio sparked off a stream of nostalgic, mainly gastronomic memories.

Padre Lorenzo finally turned the conversation away from food by talking to me about the Poleggia which Padre Ugo had known as a child. The village had then been a place of almost primitive simplicity, without cars, electricity or crime. But then gradually, as sophistication and the modern world began to reach the village, Poleggia started losing for Padre Ugo its wonderful innocence.

'He found this same innocence again in Chacas,' said Padre Lorenzo. Padre Ugo had come across this village almost by chance and immediately fallen in love. 'First of all it was the landscape that seduced him. It reminded him of his beloved Alps. And then it was the way of life, so reminiscent of the Poleggia of his childhood.' The attraction of the Andes to the Salesians was as much sentimental as spiritual. The romanticism underlying Padre Ugo's Peruvian mission suddenly struck me: he wanted to improve the quality of people's lives but in a way that largely resisted the modern world. 'Padre Ugo,' continued Padre Lorenzo, 'is always saying that he has been lucky enough to have had two lives. The first was centred on his childhood in Poleggia. The second began after moving to Chacas in 1971. He has relived here his early years in an unchanged Alpine village.'

Padre Lorenzo then asked us about ourselves. Chris, in typically modest fashion, said he was just my acolyte, obliging me to tell everyone that he was a celebrated author and former drummer for Genesis. Mention of the Genesis connection made an immediate impact on the assembled company. The band had been the idols of both Padre Lorenzo's and Padre Leonardo's youths. Chris was adamant about not wanting to give the community a demonstration of his musical talents.

He was let off the hook by Padre Lorenzo playing us a recording of a song called 'Dove sei?' ('Where are you?') The song, a Dylan-like number sung to the backing of the Chacas choir, had been written and composed by one Padre Daniele. The singing left our table rather pensive. I was told many of the photos around the community were of this musical priest with a warm open face. I asked what had happened to him. Padre Lorenzo said that God had 'called him back'.

In March 1997 the 35-year-old Padre Daniele had been kidnapped from a neighbouring village and brutally killed, possibly for political reasons, probably for money, no one knew for sure. Less than five years earlier he had given a memorial speech in Chacas in memory of an Italian friend and contemporary of his, Padre Giulio Rocca, murdered by the Sendero Luminoso. 'The blood of martyrs,' Padre Daniele had said on that occasion, 'has always been regarded by the Church as a precious gift; martyrs are the saints closest to God. And Jesus has rewarded Giulio with a violent death, just like his own.'

I was wondering later that day if God also reserved a special place in Heaven for the victims of earthquakes, landslides and buses that fall off cliffs. We were returning to the Callejón de Huyalas the same way we had come. There was no alternative. The bus left late, and storms overnight had muddied the road and blocked it with stones. One stretch was now so rutted that we all had to get out and walk for a couple of kilometres, to lighten the bus's load. It was dark and sleety as we neared the top of the pass, and foggy and rainy as we descended the other side. The woman across the aisle from me, a Marxist school inspector highly critical of Padre Ugo, noticed my fear. She accused me of being a closet bourgeois egoist, and said I would be a more relaxed person if I thought less about my own safety and more of the horrendous sufferings of all those revolutionaries prepared to sacrifice their own blood in the Andes just to make the world a tiny bit better.

I tried thinking of Bolívar and of the impulsiveness that made him lead his army on one of the most daunting marches of history. The dilemma that faced him early in 1824 was whether to go on the offensive or to hold back for a while. Delays in getting information from one end of the Andes to the other meant that he had insufficient knowledge of the enemy's movements to consider tactics too carefully. His instinct was to attack. From Huaraz he wrote to Sucre in June to say that he was 'consumed by the demon of war, determined to finish this struggle one way or the other'.

The greatness of Bolívar resulted from these impulsive fits, and his refusal to retract once his mind was set. In July 1824, after a few weeks in Huaraz, Bolívar led his troops over what General Miller called 'the most rugged districts, of the most mountainous country in the world, presenting at every step difficulties which in Europe would be considered perfectly insurmountable'.

The cavalry led the way, each soldier riding a mule and dragging behind him a horse that was 'to be mounted only in sight of the enemy'. They were continually going up and down passes of a kind known only too well even to today's Andean traveller. 'The shelving ledges,' continued Miller, 'which afforded the only foot-hold on the rugged sides of the Andes, are so narrow, as to render the passage indescribably harassing.' Advancing single file along these tracks, they regularly found their way ahead interrupted by deep gullies or obstructed by numerous projecting rocks and waterfalls, 'all of which required great caution, and much time to pass in safety'.

Thanks to these hazards, the day's march was often not completed until nightfall, which led to further potential dangers, notably 'going astray', and 'tumbling headlong down frightful precipices'. The riders tried to improve their safety at night-time by dismounting from their mules and proceeding on foot.

The infantry, unimpeded by mules and horses, ran less of risk of falling over cliffs or getting lost. But the greater energy expended by walking must have made them more susceptible to the sometimes fatal effects of altitude sickness. Additionally, many had attacks of snow blindness; and almost everyone suffered from the freezing night-time temperatures.

Bolívar's army took six days to travel from Huaraz to the town of Huánuco. Chris and I did the journey in two. The landscape and sky kept changing. Shortly beyond Huaraz came a long stretch of flat featureless moorland surrounding Lake Conoconcha. Dark clouds made it seem even greyer. Then we reached the moorland's edge and the landscape dramatically opened up, though not at first the sky.

Clouds over the deep valley below us hid on the other side the higher, snowy slopes of the Cordillera Huayhuash where in 1985 the British climber Joe Simpson had hung for hours at the end of a rope, 'touching the void'. Simpson's companion Simon Yates had been forced in the end to make the controversial decision to cut the rope, so that at least he could survive. Simpson fell into a crevasse and miraculously survived as well. For three days he had crawled between life and death, before eventually reaching safety.

I felt almost guilty at the ease with which we were travelling. The road that clung to the valley was broad, well graded and newly asphalted. Inevitably, it was a private road, built for the lorry traffic transporting minerals from a foreign-owned mine. The valley was rich in minerals. Miller thought their metallic properties were responsible for his troops' respiratory problems. The sky finally cleared. There were dark rocky peaks on one side of the valley and snow-crested ones on the other. In between was bare, ochre-coloured *puna* fading into patchy green. We descended the valley to Huallanca, a large village where silver mines had been discovered in the late eighteenth century. These had long been exhausted. The asphalt had given up and the village, without a Padre Ugo to educate its inhabitants, had remained a long pleasant street of whitewashed adobe houses, some with the thatched roofs common to the poorest rural dwellings.

As the sun sunk towards the horizon, the bus continued along the snaking banks of a river to the town of La Unión. We found a small filthy hotel with a vestibule like that of a decayed brothel. The obsequious mustachioed owner recommended we try and get to Huánuco the next day before nightfall. There had been a spate of attacks on those travelling on the road after dark. Drug traffickers from the jungle north of Huánuco regularly went along it, holding up traffic at gunpoint. All the buses now left La Unión early in the morning, though we might find a *colectivo* going later if we wanted to visit the nearby Inca ruins of Huánuco Viejo ('Old Huánuco').

He got a driver to take us to the ruins at the crack of dawn. A starlit night was sadly followed by a cloudy, damp morning, and the weather got even worse on climbing up to the top of one of the valley's slopes to a broad soggy plateau. When we could see more clearly, we made out some scattered specks of grey in the middle of a huge unguarded site. Dinosaurs rather than Incas seemed more likely to emerge from the mists. We trod through mud and water to reach the former stronghold of Illa Túpac, one of the last Incas to hold out against the Spaniards. The larger of the specks proved to be the platform of a temple. Some distance away were the walls of a barracks and a palace. The scale was impressive, the empty bleakness atmospheric. But Chris, seeing an Inca site for the first time, was unmoved. 'So all this was contemporary with the works of Michelangelo in Rome?'

We returned to La Unión to wait for a *colectivo*. Two hours later we were still waiting. We were told that there had been problems with the road due to the rains. None of the *colectivos* that had set off yesterday to Huánuco had returned. We would soon be faced with a dreadful choice: staying another night at La Unión or risking night-time assault should a *colectivo* turn up and be prepared to take us.

When a *colectivo* fortuitously appeared, its driver thought we might just make it to Huánuco before dark. He had set off at five in the morning and had taken eight hours to get back to La Unión. He agreed to return now to Huánuco on being offered double his normal fare. All he needed was a half-hour rest before setting off again. He made the sign of the cross as he did so.

The descent was tortuous and only the excellence of the driving prevented us from getting stuck in the mud. At regular intervals the road was blocked by boys demanding the payment of tolls for having cleared away a few stones. More often still, there were roadside crosses marking the sites of fatal accidents. A great cluster of crosses commemorated the curve where a crowded bus had collided with a lorry and been sent down the mountainside.

We got to the end of one valley and then had to descend an even steeper one. But we made such unexpectedly good progress that we had time to stop at an improvised corrugated-roofed shelter standing on the edge of a tropically wooded slope. Wisps of smoke were escaping from a mound made of layers of newspaper and plastic. Underneath was a hole in the ground where apparently a pig was cooking on top of stones heated by burning wood.

The driver was surprised that we had never eaten what he called a *pachamanca*. The dish, which could be made from any meat, was apparently of Incan origin and still had associations with offerings to the most universal of Andean deities, the earth mother, or *pachamama*. The man who ran this simple roadside eatery removed the various layers from the mound. The leaves of banana trees had once been used as layers, but these trees were now being pushed out by the eucalyptuses. Our fears of trichinosis were soon forgotten as we tucked into the delicious meat, which was flavoured with garlic and accompanied by yams and potatoes. At last, in Chris's view, the Incas had got something right.

We made it to Huánuco by early evening. A sign on the outskirts welcomed the visitor to 'the town with the most pleasant climate in the world'. Full of trees, and with parkland bordering the tropical river Huallaga, it was 'a pleasant town' similar to the one Miller had enjoyed. 'The streets,' wrote Miller, 'are rectilinear, and each house has a garden in which are grown pine apples and other tropical fruits in abundance. The climate is agreeable.' Miller's troops rested here three days, gathering their strength for the coming battle. Chris prepared himself for future Peruvian bus journeys by buying some earplugs.

There was no immediate need for these. The next stage of our route – and Bolívar's – was to the nearby mining town of Cerro de Pasco, to which *colectivos* set off from Huánuco at fifteen-minute intervals. Chris and I were squeezed into a small car with three other passengers. A road like the one from La Unión would have been unbearable under these conditions but the one to Cerro de Pasco was said to be excellent.

After some problems closing a back door, the driver took off. Within a minute we were driving uphill at over a hundred kilometres an hour. Our impatient young driver appeared to be engaged in a race with his colleagues. He drove right up to the vehicles in front, and overtook them without hesitation, even on blind curves. After ten minutes Chris noted that the speedometer had risen to 110. The driver barely slowed down even on hairpin bends. Chris buried his head in his hands.

I tried to appreciate the landscape. Driving at this speed made you more aware than ever of the sudden changes in Andean scenery. The tropical vegetation around Cerro de Pasco had been succeeded by no vegetation at all. We had climbed within a quarter of an hour into a world of bare slopes with rocky crests glistening with ice. There were no houses, just the stones from a few ruined huts.

We had our first sighting of Cerro de Pasco just over an hour after leaving Huánuco. My expectations of the place had not been high. Proctor had described it as 'a large straggling place, composed principally of inferior dwellings'. It was the same today. We had emerged from our climb to a daunting high plateau that we would be following all the way to the battleground of Junín and beyond. In the foreground was a monotonous expanse of corrugated-iron roofs around a forbidding lake. High dark clouds streamed hurriedly past, running parallel to a distant horizon of black snow-capped mountains.

We alighted at the bus station, shaky, stiff and suddenly cold. We had exchanged the best climate in the world for a land of perpetual bitterness. We found a *colectivo* headed for the town of Tarma, where we planned to stay. The driver, a tall man in his early thirties, was happy to leave straight away, without other passengers. He promised to drive slowly and to stop off on the way at Junín. He seemed excited by the prospect.

Luis was a likeable man with a passion for history and books. And he drove as carefully as he said he would. The road to Junín had one of the worst reputations for accidents in the Peruvian interior. The surface was smooth and there was not a single curve, which was precisely why it was dangerous. Drivers such as the one we had just had went wild on it. There were no speed limits. The weather was usually foggy, the rain incessant.

Today we were lucky, said Luis. The violence of the winds was beginning to clear away most of the clouds. The horizon kept on expanding. The distant mountains were reduced to a thin, ragged ribbon. There was little else but stones and pebbles. And a faraway strip of water that could have been a mirage. And a light olive stubble of grass extending indefinitely over this land as flat as water.

The strip of water turned out to be the vast lake known to the Spaniards as El Lago de Reyes, the Lake of Kings. This landscape, said Luis, had been inhabited since prehistory. For thousands of years people had lived off the raising of alpacas, the hunting of vicuñas (wild relatives of the llama) and the cultivation of potatoes, the only crop that could grow at this altitude of over four thousand metres. Potatoes had the vitamins necessary to survive this desolation. There was one particular kind of tuber that had more vitamins than any other. It was the secret of the Incas' energy and was called the *maca*. The *maca* absorbed so many minerals from the earth that a field planted with it was useless for any other crop for the next five years. We were nearing its heartland – the village of Huaray.

Luis hoped we wouldn't mind if we stopped at a shop on the outskirts of the village. He had been asked by a friend to buy some *maca* in its powdered form, which, added to tea or coffee, was better than any vitamin pill. We pulled up next to a billboard on the pavement marked 'The Bethel Fruit Bar, Specialists in Maca'.

While Luis studied the prices of the various types of '*maca* flour', Chris and I debated whether we should have a special '*maca* cocktail'. Luis urged us on. We had to wait for the owner's daughter to come and make it. We looked on as she mixed together raw eggs, pollen, honey, papaya, carob beans, dried yeast, hot water, milk, cinnamon, beer and a huge helping of *maca* flour.

'What do you think?' asked Luis, after we had each managed to down a milkshake-sized glass of it. I quite liked it, which Chris thought perverse. 'You won't be able to sleep tonight,' observed Luis. 'You'll be filled with energy for the next twenty-four hours.' He smiled timidly. 'We call a *maca* cocktail the "Andean viagra".'

In the neighbouring village of Junín, a place associated with one of the most famous battles in South American history, a memorable example of Andean kitsch awaited us. Junín was typical of the grim modern-looking communities of the plateau, and we would have driven straight through it had we not known about its history. Luis pointed out that every street was named after one of the generals in the battle. We left the main road to drive down the Calle Miller, to visit a neglected square. The square was taken up by a memorial commemorating the battle.

There were three bronze equestrian statues, one of which was of Bolívar in the guise of Marcus Aurelius. The other statue should by rights have been of General Miller, but was instead of the Argentinean-born commander of the hussars, Manuel Isidoro Suárez – the Argentinean government had stumped up the money for this. The third work, on top of a domed pavilion, was of an unknown rearing cavalryman with his sabre raised high in the air. Behind the statues was a fifty-metre-high sword shooting out from a blue pavilion to spear on the tip of its blade a hussar's red helmet.

The pavillion was a museum and the helmet was a viewing platform. To reach the latter you had to climb inside the blade, which took the form of a cement cylinder not much wider than my body. There were rungs to do so, but two or three were missing and others were bent. Chris went first. I weakly decided not to risk a combination of vertigo, claustrophobia and real physical danger, but Luis egged me on. I looked up again inside the unlit cylinder. At the end of the dark tunnel there was a bright light into which Chris disappeared. As he pulled himself out onto the open platform, a piece of caked mud from his boots hurtled towards me, grazing my forehead. 'Go on! Go on!' shouted Luis behind me. I began the climb. I felt as if I were potholing in space. I cut my ankle against a protruding nail. I could sense the blood pouring out from the wound. My forehead was hurting. I kept going. I hoisted myself above the large gaps left by the missing rungs. A rung became loose after I had put my whole weight on it and my sock was damp with blood. I was over halfway up now, there was no turning back. I was panting from my efforts. I made it to the light.

Out on the platform I surveyed the ugly village, which had been burnt down by royalist troops in 1821. Single-storey, block-like buildings petered out into the immensity of the plateau. Though blue sky and clouds alternated as rapidly as in a fast-forwarded film, the light remained preternaturally clear, allowing the eye to roam for limitless kilometres. Looking south I focused my attention on a faraway obelisk marking the site of the battlefield. A long bare ridge surged up behind it, interrupting the surrounding flatness. Bolívar had assembled his troops here by 2 August 1824.

Miller's memories of the landscape below me seemed from my present height distorted by emotion. However good the visibility had been then, it could not have been greater than it was now. The panorama could not possibly have been as all-encompassing as Miller's description suggests. The ridge would have blocked it. Yet Miller's exaggerations, like his errors of geography, served to underline the universal consequences of the battle about to take place:

The view from the table-land, upon which the troops were reviewed, and which is at an elevation of more than twelve thousand feet above the level of the sea, is one of the most magnificent in the world. On the west arose the Andes, which had just been surmounted with so much toil. On the east were enormous ramifications of the Cordillera stretching towards the Brazils. North and South, the view was bounded by mountains whose tops were hidden in the clouds. On that plain, surrounded by such sublime scenery, and on the margin of the magnificent lake of Reyes, the principal source of the Amazon, the mightiest of rivers, were now assembled men from Caracas, Panama, Quito, Lima, Chile, and Buenos Ayres; men who had fought at Maypo in Chile; at San Lorenzo on the banks of the Parana; at Carabobo in Venezuela; and at Pinchincha at the foot of the Chimborazo. Amidst those devoted Americans were a few foreigners, still firm and faithful to the cause, in support of which so many of their countrymen had fallen. Amongst those few survivors were men who had fought on the banks of the Guadiana, and of the Rhine; who had witnessed the conflagration of Moscow, and the capitulation of Paris. Such were the men assembled at, what might be considered, a fresh starting point in the career of glory. American or European, they were all animated by one sole spirit, that of assuring the political existence of a vast continent, and to ascertain whether or not the period had arrived when the influence of South America upon the rest of the world, should be rendered commensurate with its extent, its riches, and its situation.

Luis found a piece of bandage to staunch my battle-memorial wound. Then he drove us off to the obelisk, hoping to get there before the monument closed for the day. Bolívar had approached Junín from the opposite side of the plateau to the one we had driven down. The Spanish General de Canterac, astonished by reports of the appearance of an army of nine thousand patriots, had set out to meet them from his headquarters to the south in the valley of Jauja. As the confrontation neared, Bolívar addressed the patriots with the words, 'Soldiers! You are about to finish the greatest undertaking Heaven has confided to men – that of saving an entire world from slavery.' His army, according to Miller, had responded with 'exhilarating *vivas*'.

We advanced towards the battlefield down a long straight track leading off from the main road. Vicuñas, surprised by our car, ran away terrified as we made for the obelisk, now repeatedly cast in dark shadow by the fast-moving clouds. A barrier blocked the track soon afterwards. The guard who looked after the monument's enormous enclosure had already gone home. A vicuña's skull looked at us menacingly from the top of one of the posts of a formidable barbed-wire fence. Luis was undeterred. He walked up to the barrier, picked its lock and opened it. We drove all the way to the obelisk, a late-nineteenth-century granite memorial topped by a bronze globe representing the sun.

The battle took place on 6 August, and was fought entirely with swords, lances and horses. General Miller, employing a useful trick he had picked up in South America, ordered the *llaneros* to retreat towards the line of patriot infantry and then got them abruptly to turn around to take the charging royalist cavalry by surprise. 'The charges of the *llaneros*,' wrote an Irish officer, 'made the earth tremble.' The whole battle was over in less than an hour. The patriots had won, thanks to longer lances and superior cavalry. Forty-five of their men had been killed, as opposed to 259 of the enemy. The royalists, shaken but with their army still largely intact, moved south.

General Canterac retreated swiftly all the way to Cuzco, worried that his troops, mainly Peruvian recruits, would desert him if he delayed. Bolívar had similar worries about his own Peruvian infantry, whom he defined as 'more royalist than the Spaniards themselves'. He did not trust them to go off in pursuit of Canterac. Neither did he appear immediately interested in doing so. It was as if the burst of extraordinary energy that had stirred him out of his illness and into marching into what the Spaniards had thought to be an impregnable Andean stronghold had been dissipated.

Bolívar's situation after Junín became more complex than ever. At Huaraz he had begun a passionate affair with the eighteen-year-old Manuela Madroño. He could not have been too pleased when the other Manuela threatened to come to Huaraz and join the army. He tried dissuading her. He emphasized the 'suffering and anguish' of the soldier's life. But Manuela Saénz was nothing if not persistent. She caught up with him by the time of the battle of Junín and later became a captain of the hussars. He carried on meanwhile with Manuela Madroño and made several later attempts in the Peruvian campaign to break with his former love. Manuela Saénz remained oblivious. She was so taken by now with soldiering that she went on to fight against the Spaniards at the decisive battle at Ayacucho. Bolívar would not be there with her.

The battle of Junín had obviously shaken him. The Spaniards could easily have defeated the patriots had they set off earlier from Jauja, and not wasted valuable time. And the Spaniards, though humiliated, were still in a far stronger position. With their greatly superior numbers, the untrustworthiness of the Peruvians and Colombia's continuing support of the patriots still in doubt, Bolívar must have wondered how much longer his luck would last. The fear of failure and ignominy still hung over him. Two days after the battle he invited his officers to a supper at the town of Tarma to make a startling announcement. He was standing down as commander of the patriots' army. He proposed as his replacement the most senior general present, the Colombian General José de La Mar. But La Mar rejected the offer. Sucre took over.

Though the shadows were lengthening by the time we drove away from the battlefield, Luis appeared to be in no hurry to get back home to Tarma. He was a gentle and sensitive man who had clearly no vocation to be the driver of a *colectivo*. He was so pleased to be deviating from his normal route that he offered to take us to Tarma the slow way. We descended from the plateau on to rough side-roads regularly blocked by sheep. The roads curved in the growing darkness through bare mountain valleys.

Throughout the drive from Junín, I had the feeling that Luis wanted to tell us something. His life's true ambition had always been to be a footballer. He had almost become one. He had been singled out as a potential star when he was thirteen. He had been part of the national youth team when he was eighteen. His face had appeared frequently in local newspapers, children had often asked for his autograph. But then his father had run away from Luis's mother and Luis, as the oldest of five children, had no other choice but to stay behind to look after his family. He could not go to Lima. He had to find a job locally. 'Life never turns out the way you want it to,' he said with a sad smile.

He seemed reluctant to leave us as he dropped us off at a country house on the outskirts of Tarma and was delighted when we asked him to drive us in two days' time to Huancayo, the next stage on our route to Bolivia. He'd already started thinking about places we could see on the way.

A young woman in a pink-striped maid's pinafore came out to greet us as Luis took the luggage from the boot. We had arrived at an ancestral estate that had fallen on hard times and now took in guests. The Hacienda Santa María was like a colonial dwelling in the tropics, an assembly of whitewashed, slightly askew walls, with a long wooden balcony rambling its way around the exterior, and overgrown gardens giving out onto cultivated fields that had been divided up in the agricultural reforms of the 1970s. Residues of grandeur were to be found inside, including a dining-room decorated with faded early-nineteenth-century murals of European-style hunting scenes and *fêtes champêtres*.

The sitting-room, with its neoclassical paintings and Empire wallpaper and furniture, could have served as an informal meeting place for Bolívar and his generals. When the maid showed us inside, half a dozen people were indeed seated around the fire, engaged in serious discussion.

We were introduced to the kind and relaxed owner, Delia Velarde, and her bearded, intellectual-looking husband, Ernesto Bustamante. Both of them had ancestors familiar to Bolívar: Delia, a close friend of a former pot-smoking left-wing journalist whom I had met in Lima, was distantly connected with Torre Tagle; Ernesto was from a family of Cantabrian origin who had settled in

Arequipa, in southern Peru. They had come up for a few days with an enigmatic Japanese entrepreneur and television director who spoke perfect Spanish and Californian English. With them was the dashing middle-aged mayor of Tarma and his beautiful young wife.

They had been discussing a potential Japanese-backed scheme for Tarma's economic revival. But when I told them about Chris's Genesis connection, we found ourselves being almost offered the keys to Tarma, as well as the possibility of starring roles on Japanese television. What we really wanted was to go for a walk the next day along a nearby stretch of the Inca road. Delia immediately offered us the services of a neighbour who worked as a guide. She said we would find him a fascinating man. He was an Indian sage and faith healer whose real name was José Luis but everyone referred to him as 'El Caminante' ('the Wanderer').

We were having a leisurely breakfast the next morning when the Wanderer arrived. He was an unmarried man in his late thirties with a smug smile and obsequious manner. He took us first to his house, where he had placed offerings of coca to a stone that had apparent curative properties. He said he had cured his mother's hernia by rubbing this stone on her.

Tarma is at the confluence of two small valleys overshadowed by mountains. The town is famous for its trade in flowers, and its nearby rivers and streams form part of the Amazonian watershed. But above the level of the Hacienda Santa María the mountain slopes were rocky and arid. The Inca trail was easily visible from afar. It climbed up one of the slopes in a straight line. According to the Wanderer, the Incas improved earlier trails by broadening them and laying out stones, but they never liked hairpin bends.

The main plants we passed during our gradual ascent were magay cactuses, which were said to ward off evil spirits. The Wanderer also said that the Incas tended to place bushes of magay alongside stretches of the road where treasure was buried, which was why several of these bushes still showed evidence of scorching by robbers. He added that the presence of llama bones along the trail was also evidence of nearby treasure. Whenever a gold-carrying llama died the animal was buried with its gold.

I was beginning to doubt the Wanderer's wisdom. Chris was more generous towards him, but even he looked slightly sceptical after the Wanderer proposed reciting an Inca prayer. We had reached the highest point of our walk, with panoramic views over Tarma's two valleys and the unending rows of mountains beyond. The ridge was wide enough for the three of us to kneel in a circle holding hands. In the middle was a tiny mound of milled and roasted maize which the Wanderer had laid out as an offering. We were instructed to hold our breath in for several seconds and then breathe out while making the sound '*Trooooooooollaaaaaaay*'. The Wanderer said a few words in Quechua in praise of the 'great god Wiracocha, protector of the Incas and now of the Peruvians'. He then thanked Wiracocha in Spanish for making us healthy enough to do today's walk and for having ensured the right weather conditions for it.

Amazingly, a distant rainbow appeared at that very moment. The Wanderer interpreted this as a sign. 'Of what?' Chris and I asked in unison. He carefully considered his answer. 'It's a sign,' he said, 'that the rainy season is now over, and that the rest of your journey through the Andes will be blessed by good fortune.'

Wearily we kept to the trail as it descended to the village of Tarma Tambo, around which were lushly cultivated terraced fields scattered everywhere with fragments of Inca structures. Bolívar had passed through the village, as had Pizarro, who, on leaving Cajamarca, had marched towards Cuzco on the same trail we were now walking on. Pizarro's brother Hernando had turned a small Inca temple into today's parish church, and had created on top of the village what the Wanderer claimed was Peru's earliest cemetery.

The present cemetery, built in 1787, was a ruinous small plot of land surrounded by the crumbling remains of fortifications. The headstones and inscriptions had all gone; but many of the corpses were meant to be of Chileans and others who had participated in a battle that had taken place outside the village on 15 July 1882. The battle testified to yet another period in Peruvian history when Wiracocha's protective powers had been ineffective.

The guano deposits that had done so much to improve Peru's finances in the wake of the Wars of Independence had been exhausted by 1874, when the government went bankrupt. Hope was then placed on nitrate deposits, which were concentrated in the Atacama Desert. In 1879 Peru persuaded its then ally Bolivia to impose an export tax on nitrates mined by the Anglo-Chilean Corporation. Chile, backed by Britain, went to war with the two countries and immediately seized Bolivia's entire coast and part of Peru's. By 1881, Chilean troops had occupied Lima and the Peruvian president fled to Europe. The war, which lasted until 1883, brought chaos to the country and deflated national pride. It also underlined the fractured nature of Peruvian society, as Chinese-Peruvians helped the invaders attack their masters in the northern plantations and black Peruvians rebelled against both Chinese and whites. After 1881, the situation became more confusing still as prominent Lima families began to believe that their interests would be better served by the Chileans than by their own countrymen.

In response the future president General Andres Avelino Cáceres rallied a resistance movement in the highlands of Junín province. He was supported by peasant guerrillas, who went on to establish a breakaway peasant republic between Tarma and Huancayo that would last twenty years. The Chileans went off into the highlands to quell Avelino Cáceres's rebellion, but were defeated at Tarma Tambo and elsewhere.

'Avelino Cáceres was a very astute man,' said the Wanderer. 'He wore a metal sheet beneath his jacket, and deceived the enemy by dressing up llamas as soldiers.'

The day we left Tarma was Chris's birthday. Luis, our driver of the day before, turned up as promised to take us on to Huancayo. We descended slowly with him down into the broad and famously fertile Jauja valley, whose capture by the patriots after Junín was regarded as the greatest immediate reward of their victory. As Luis stopped by the shores of the large Laguna de Paca, to tell us the legend of a Peruvian Sodom and Gomorrah that lay buried beneath its waters, Chris conceived a scheme to have him accompany us right up to the Bolivian border.

The idea thrilled Luis, and was briefly exciting to us as we thought about the many dangerous bus journeys likely to be ahead. Later that afternoon Luis went off to phone his wife. But he came back to report that his wife would not let him go for such a long time.

A rather deflated Luis continued driving us in the rain to Huancayo. On the outskirts of the town was a large sign, 'Welcome to the Wanka Nation'. We explained to Luis that the name of the local Indian race sounded like an English word appropriate to the Wanderer. Luis informed us that the Peruvian expression 'You are a Wanka' is used of people who are stubborn and determined. 'My wife,' he said, 'is a Wanka.'

He left us in the centre of Huancayo, a large and vibrant but visually dull district capital. Our hotel, next to the Cyber Wanka, was a place where Luis had stayed with the other potential young stars of Peruvian football. Whether as a result of memories of those days, or because he was leaving us, or because he was returning to the staid life of a *colectivo* driver, Luis became quite emotional as he said goodbye.

In Huancayo, three months after the victory in Junín, Bolívar received distressing news from Bogotá. A law had been passed in congress revoking his extraordinary powers and transferring them to Santander. The grounds for this were that he had accepted the dictatorship of Peru. Bolívar was hugely insulted, especially as he was also requested to do what he had already done – hand over the command of the army to Sucre. He nonetheless responded to the news with magnanimous politeness, replying to congress that he had already appointed Sucre and thanking them for the troops that had been sent. Perhaps, more than anything, his behaviour was another indication that he was becoming the tragic figure already glimpsed at Patavilca – a person resigned both to his own fate and to South America's.

Bolívar travelled from Huancayo to Lima, leaving Sucre to continue towards Ayacucho and Cuzco. Chris and I went with Sucre, traversing a long stretch of Peru where transport is still notoriously slow. Thanks to an extraordinary example of late-nineteenth-century engineering, Huancayo has been linked by train to Lima since 1908. Cuzco was also accessible by train from the 1870s, though only from Lake Titicaca, Arequipa and the port of Mollendo. There was talk for many years of building a line between Huancayo and Cuzco, but nothing came of it. The only way of travelling today between the two highland towns is by a road which Luis said had improved little since the time Sucre and his troops had marched along it.

The traditional isolation of the area into which we were heading had once made it a base for the Sendero Luminoso, who, for much of the 1980s, had succeeded in dissuading tourists from visiting Ayacucho and its district. Earlier in the twentieth century this very remoteness had made the area romantically appealing to travellers such as the historian José de la Riva Agüero, the great-grandson of the identically named first president of Peru.

Riva Agüero was typical of the conservative nationalists who had dominated Peruvian politics from the 1930s to the 1950s. As with most Peruvians of his generation, and most foreign commentators on Peru up to the present day, he was brought up believing that the Spaniards' main contribution to his country was the purely negative one of having destroyed the great Inca civilization in its infancy. But his views (which went on to embrace the ideology of Mussolini) changed considerably in the course of a journey on mule-back made in 1912 from Cuzco to Huancayo and beyond. He learnt to

378

appreciate the importance of the Spanish legacy to Peru, and to see the three centuries of Spanish rule of his country as a golden age comparable to that of the Incas.

Chris and I barely registered Huancayo's once famously bucolic utskirts. It had not stopped raining since nightfall and the view, on leaving the town on the early-morning Ayacucho bus, was of a landscape that was grey, sodden and ordinary. As the city's fertile surroundings faded out, the surface of the road suddenly became rough. We were entering a narrowing mountain valley with precipitous and rocky slopes. Much of the route to Ayacucho would be following the fast and furious Mataro River. There were no high passes to cross, but the road, continually ascending and descending one of the sides of what was soon a gorge, was littered by stones and partly washed away by the rains. There were times when the road was so impassable that replacement tracks appeared to have been hastily carved into the slope above.

After five hours of this, we saw a bus from the same company as ours heading towards us. There was just enough room for the two buses to pass. The drivers stopped to pull down their windows and have a chat. The wheels of our bus were on the crumbling edge of a sheer slope of scree. Some passengers, led by a nervous fifty-year-old taking her teenage daughter to Ayacucho's Holy Week, pleaded with our driver to move away from this dangerous spot. After he had moved on, voices began muttering all around us. The bus we had seen was the night bus from Ayacucho. It was hours behind schedule. A major obstacle was rumoured to be ahead.

At a point where the road curved around a cliff, a mountain torrent gushing across it had reduced it to a watery ledge of deep mud and loose stones. The nervous mother insisted that the driver let her off. Everyone keenly followed her example. 'There's no way that the driver is going to get round that,' commented Chris, as we all stared at how the bus was positioned, its back wheels stuck in the mud. But after an hour of trying, the driver extricated the vehicle, to a big round of applause. The large lorry behind us was not so successful.

We would find out several days later that the main road to Ayacucho was still blocked because of it.

The sun was out as we emerged at the end of the afternoon into the broad valley of Ayacucho, yet another Andean location where spring was said to be eternal. Riva Agüero's overwhelming impression had been of an aristocratic Spanish town fallen into decadence, where on moonlit nights you could see old men, 'wrapped in old Castilian capes', strumming lutes and humming plaintive Andean tunes below window grilles and wrought-iron balconies fragrant with flowers. Ayacucho, he concluded, was a place with an 'intensely Creole atmosphere' that still maintained 'the beliefs and customs taught to its inhabitants by the Conquistadors'.

Childhood memories of Spain came back to me forcibly when we arrived at dusk in the colonial centre. We put up at an old-fashioned Castilian-style hotel with wooden-beam ceilings. We walked into a main square as big apparently as that of Cuzco and bordered by colonial arcading. We were drawn by the strolling evening crowds into pedestrian streets whose long rows of shabby white and ochre houses were dignified by tomb-like stone lintels, wall-mounted iron lanterns and by churches that were alternately austere or exuberantly Renaissance, in brick and in stone.

But it was the atmosphere more than the architecture that recalled the Spain I had perceived as a teenager. Though an asphalted road had at last been built between Ayacucho and Lima, the place still seemed as remote and uncommercialized as Spain in the 1960s. As in the traditional Spain portrayed by romantic travellers, the town exuded the influence of the Church and was impregnated by a religiosity full of pomp, drama and mystical resonance. Its Holy Week was the most famous in Peru. And it was about to begin. Bells were ringing continuously and priests and monks scurried through the streets. An infectious excitement reminded me of how I had once felt waiting for the start of Spain's Holy Week processions.

And as if to counter the town's religious conservatism, there was a sense of something clandestine in the air, a lingering whiff of violent rebelliousness. Ayacucho's university, one of the oldest in South America, had always been a centre of left-wing politics. The ideology behind the Sendero Luminoso had been formulated there.

We had arrived at Ayacucho in time for the inauguration of a Spanish cultural centre in one of the arcaded houses of the main square. A Spanish friend from Lima, Ricardo Ramón, had turned up for this, together with a large group of Lima-based Spaniards, including journalists, cultural bureaucrats and the Spanish ambassador to Peru.

Ricardo invited us to lunch the next day with the ambassador, who soon got talking about the battle of Ayacucho. As with almost every Spanish ambassador I had ever met, he was a tall and aristocratic-looking intellectual who spoke a nearly accent-less English. He had greying hair and a military-style moustache, and had written extensively on military history. He told me how the Spaniards would easily have won at Ayacucho had they not arrived so tired. After lunch Ricardo lent us his car and chauffeur so that Chris and I could visit the site ourselves.

The driver, elderly, calm and wise, had the strange name of Odonacro. He was from a village near Ayacucho, but had moved with his family first to Lima and then to Brussels in the mid-1980s, after the Sendero Luminoso had initiated in his native province the worst decade of violence in recent South American history. Like so many other refugees from this region, he had no desire to return to his village when the violence was over. His memories of the period were too painful.

The battlefield was some distance from the town and we went there at a leisurely pace, making a detour to walk around the ancient ruins of Huari, the capital of the civilization that had allied itself to that of Tiawanako to form an empire almost as large as that of the Incas.

None of this particularly interested Chris, who was fascinated instead by Odonacro's memories of the Sendero Luminoso years. As we strolled among the tuna cactuses so abundant in this area, Odonoacro went on to tell us how his father, the village school-teacher, was exactly the sort of person whom the terrorists had originally targeted. 'Teachers, mayors, government workers – anyone who was associated in some way with the state was in danger. Of course, the people who ended up suffering most from the whole conflict were the desperately poor peasants.' He said they formed the vast majority of the 69,000 people killed in Peru between 1982 and 2000.

The Sendero Luminoso had moved from political theory to political action in 1980, at the time of the democratic elections that had succeeded the twelve-year leftist dictatorship of General Velasco Alvaredo. On May 17 a group of students burnt the ballot boxes in the village of Chuschi near Ayacucho. Then came the dead dogs, with notices around their necks accusing Mao's successor Deng Xiaoping of being a 'son of a bitch'. But no one as yet, other than dog lovers, thought the Sendero Luminoso were anything more than a group of harmless crackpots perverse enough to support the Albanian communist leader Enver Hoxha.

The village executions and massacres that followed caught the country unprepared. The president who had won the 1980 elections, the centre-right Fernando Beláunde, answered brutality with brutality, executing any peasant suspected of being a sympathizer with the guerrillas. Extreme retaliatory measures, and rapidly increasing recruitment to the Sendero Luminoso, continued under Beláunde's successor, the APRA member Alan García, who came to power in 1985 and completed his first term of presidency in 1990, when he was succeeded by Alberto Fujimori. Fujimori crippled the Sendero Luminoso after capturing its founder Abimael Guzmán in 1992, but his popularity was followed by the exposure of his own appalling record of corruption and human rights abuse. He is now behind bars, as are most of the former leaders of the Sendero Luminoso. In July 2006 a supposedly reformed Alan García was re-elected president.

'No wonder there are some Peruvians who say we were better off under the Spaniards,' concluded Odonacro, as we continued our discussion of politics and bloodshed back in the car. On top of the hill in front of us was a white monument. We were finally nearing the Pampa de Quinoa, the scene of the last Spanish battle in South America. When we made it to the top we found what looked like a golf course with mountains on one side, and, on the other, an exhilarating panorama of the richly variegated plain of Ayacucho.

The combined Spanish forces, including Canterac's troops, had gathered on this field on 8 December 1824. There were 9300 of them, as opposed to only 5800 patriots, who were camped in the village of Quinoa, further down the hillside. For the previous few weeks the Spanish and patriot forces had been playing a game of cat and mouse. As Sucre advanced towards Cuzco, the Spaniards had attempted to march across his rear, to prevent him from retreating to the north. Sucre pulled back just in time to escape this flanking movement. He then had to make frantic efforts to stop the Spaniards from bringing him to battle in unfavourable mountain territory. The Spanish forces were more accustomed to the altitude and were able to march quicker. By 8 December Sucre had had enough. He had been instructed by Bolívar to try and avoid a fight with the Spaniards at all costs. But he was now keen to risk everything on a final decisive battle. Bolívar was convinced he would lose.

Each account I had read of the battle contradicted every other in almost every detail. I thought it best simply to trust what Odonacro told me as we got out of the car and approached a monument resembling a tapering futuristic wedding cake.

'One of the great questions you have to ask about Ayacucho,' said Odonacro, 'is why the Spaniards lost. They not only had far more men, but also far greater resources. For every patriot cannon that was fired, the Spaniards fired ten.'

The usual reason given for the patriot victory is the exceptional bravery, skill and indefatigability of Sucre, who as a strategist always grasped the bigger picture while being famously good on detail. On our way to the monument, we stopped to look at a modern equestrian statue of him that made him look like an enraged monkey.

'But there was something highly suspicious about the battle. The official reports by both Canterac and Sucre were far too cursory. Some people even think that the generous terms of surrender offered by Sucre were agreed beforehand. In which case the battle was a complete charade in which the Spaniards made a token display of fighting so as not to lose face completely.'

A few drops of rain began to fall. We quickened our steps and reached the monument before the downpour began, and took shelter within the sparse museum at the monument's base. An inscription told us that the whole structure had been completed in time for the battle's 150th anniversary celebrations – the ones that the young Hugo Chávez and his fellow cadets had excitedly attended.

'The Spaniards,' continued Odonacro, 'seem in any case not to have had any heart for the battle. They may have realized that history was against them. They could not expect reinforcements from Spain. They knew in their heart of hearts that the fight for independence in South America had gained so much momentum as to be unstoppable.' Or they might simply have been tired. In rushing to try and outflank Sucre they had probably over-exerted themselves. They had also approached the battlefield from a more demanding direction than Sucre had done – over the mountains known as Condorkunka, 'the Condor's Neck'.

Whatever the reasons for the Spanish defeat, the battle itself was an anticlimactic ending to the struggle for liberation. It was over in two hours, with the loss of only sixty-four patriots on the field. More patriot lives had been lost elsewhere defending the baggage train.

That evening Ricardo introduced me to a young and earnest assistant of his, Santi, who had come up from Lima to help with the opening of the Spanish cultural centre. Santi was a native of Ayacucho and his family still lived here. 'He knows all the good bars,' whispered Ricardo, slipping me a leaflet he thought might amuse me. The leaflet was a series of warnings for tourists coming to Ayacucho for its Holy Week. It listed the areas of the town best avoided by night, unless you wanted to experience the new Peruvian fashion for 'strangle mugging', whereby you were strangled to the point of losing consciousness and then had everything stolen from you. Among its other pieces of advice was: 'Never perform your bodily functions in places that are dark or out-of-the way.'

'So we'll perform them in brightly lit public spaces,' quipped the Spanish ambassador, who was keen to join us in the early part of our nocturnal tour of Ayacucho. The first of the Holy Week processions was beginning that night. The ambassador's bodyguard accompanied him as we wove our way through lively streets towards the church from which the devotional image of Christ was about to be carried out. Periodically I could hear the bodyguard murmur that this was not a safe street, or that he did not like the look of the people around us. But the ambassador carried on regardless. A head taller than almost everybody else and dressed like Ricardo in an immaculate black suit, he walked with a confident stride, commenting knowledgeably on some of the colonial buildings we passed. I felt I was on a tour of inspection with the Spanish Viceroy.

We arrived in time to see a small but brilliantly illuminated white float swaying from side to side, as bearers solemnly marched through the open west portal of the church. In the middle was a modest statue of Christ shrouded in blue. All around him were candles. Behind came a band playing drums, saxophones and trumpets at a funereal pace. The fervent faces, the general humility of the whole occasion, the lack of other tourists and the tragic Andean-tinged tone of the music mesmerized me – just as I had been as a teenager in Seville watching long lines of candle-bearing penitents crawling to the slow beat of drums.

The moments in Ayacucho trailing behind the procession were the last conventionally beautiful ones of a night that would end up as a descent into the seediness that Ricardo and I both loved. Gamely the ambassador joined us at a bar owned by a friend of Santi's who organized a weekly seventies-themed musical night. A few Genesis numbers were put on for the benefit of Chris, who was given a hero's welcome. He went off soon afterwards to bed. The ambassador stayed on for a karaoke bar and then left us. The bars became smaller, dirtier and noisier as we moved further away from the historic centre. The background music became too loud for me to hear what Santi was telling us. During occasional lulls I could hear snatches of Santi's childhood memories of Ayacucho in the eighties and several mentions of the Sendero Luminoso.

At three in the morning, Ricardo asked Santi to take us on to the town's transvestite bars. I was surprised that a town this size had more than one. The first one we went to was closed. The second one looked too ordinary for Ricardo. We went further down Ayacucho's hill, into the dangerous deserted streets where the strangle-muggers lurked. The third bar was an illegal establishment. No one but a local would have known it was a bar at all. Santi knocked on the closed metal shutters of what seemed to be a garage. A man with a balaclava pulled the shutters up and looked aggressive. Santi said a few words and we were let inside. The shutters were pulled down. We walked down steps into a space so dark that we stumbled in search of somewhere to sit. There were a handful of wooden boxes serving as stools, and some seating that had been ripped out of a car. As far as we could make out there were only four other customers, including a man holding hands with someone who could have been a transvestite. The man with the balaclava doubled up as the barman.

At least we could speak. The darkness of the bar prompted Santi to talk about his childhood again. He said that between the ages of four and seven he had spent his nights hidden under the floor-boards.

'That's when Sendero Luminoso gangs used to come knocking at the doors,' he explained. 'They used to kidnap children at night and take them off to be brainwashed. They would knock at a door and ask if there were any children inside. Everyone of course said no, so they would come in anyway and search every corner of the building. My mother remembers the screams and cries as neighbours' children were carried away. Sometimes you would hear gunshots. Three times they came into our house. My elder brother used to put his hand over my mouth to stop me making a noise.'

Santi's parents believed that people capable of abducting children and training children to kill could have been sent only by the Devil. They found it difficult to accept that this Devil, Abimael Guzmán, had been a colleague of Santi's father's at Ayacucho University. The father never had any personal contact with Guzmán, but he knew plenty of people who had. The devil, to those who had met him in Ayacucho, was a polite man remembered by some as a charismatic lecturer and by others as ordinary and dull. He was the most unlikely of devils, just as he was the most unlikely of cult figures.

'I don't think my father and Guzmán would have hit it off,' observed Santi. 'My father likes people with whom he can go drinking and have a laugh. Humour wasn't Guzmán's strong point. He had a reputation in Ayacucho for being puritanical and abstemious. But who knows what he was really like. Or is like. I keep forgetting he's still alive.'

One of the most memorable pieces of journalism I read in the 1980s was an attempt by the English writer Nicholas Shakespeare to uncover the man behind the legend. His quest made for a thrilling tale of travel in a Peru on the verge of complete anarchy. However, he discovered no telling personal details about this evil bogeyman other than his hatred for the American film *Porgy and Bess* and his love of the popular tune '*Pepito mi corazón*'. When Guzmán was finally caught, four years after the appearance of Shakespeare's article, he had been hiding all the time in a prosperous Lima suburb. He used to amuse himself by watching cookery programmes on television.

Ricardo, stifling a yawn, thought Guzmán had been wise not to have given away much about his personal life. 'Secrecy always makes people more exciting than they actually are.'

'There are still people at the university who refer to him as a brilliant thinker,' added Santi, 'but they tend to be people of the same generation, desperately clinging to outmoded ideas.'

I had always believed that Guzmán's ideology was an intriguing blend of Maoism and mystical notions of Inca revenge, until I came across an account of the Sendero Luminoso by the Peruvian journalist Gustavo Gorriti. I learnt then that Guzmán's philosophy of armed rebellion owed nothing to the Incas but a great deal to *Macbeth* and – more bizarrely – to a biography of the prophet Muhammad by the romantic author of the *Tales of the Alhambra*, Washington Irving. Hadn't Ayacucho University got anything more up to date and scholarly about the prophet?

'Probably not,' said Ricardo, rising abruptly to his feet. 'Remember, it was closed for a hundred years and only reopened in 1958.'

We left the bar to find it lighter outside than it was indoors. Ayacucho's muggers and transvestites were now probably all sleeping, but Chris was likely to be on the point of getting up. The two of us had a bus to catch in less than three hours. I felt exhausted at the thought of it. I was also shivering.

Random thoughts, images and memories were churning around in my mind as we dragged ourselves up the hill under the cold dawn sky. All day I had been trying to remember a prophetic line about Ayacucho by Carleton Beals, the American journalist who had been at Trujillo in the wake of the APRA massacres. It finally came to me at the threshold of our hotel: 'Ayacucho seems more closely tied to death than life . . . It has always been a place of battle and death.'

## 22

# RESURRECTION

Sucre and his forces headed on towards Cuzco to consolidate their victory and quell any remaining opposition from the Spaniards. Chris and I faced a two-day bus journey to get there, if the rainy season allowed.

The road was unpaved for most of the journey. The buses were double-deckers. We bought front window seats at the top. This gave us the full benefit of the additional swaying caused by the movement of a tall bus on a rough road. The bus from Ayacucho had been subject to such violent jerks that one of the upper sides had become detached slightly from the front window. Rain and cold air blew in through an inch-wide gap directly in front of me. Leaving the town, I was tempted to say a prayer.

The journey was the usual rollercoaster of dramatically changing landscapes, weather conditions and emotions. We ascended from the plain of Ayacucho up into gloomy and rain-covered pampa, and then descended into the sporadically sunlit sublime, on yet another heart-stopping road and with further heart-lifting panoramas of a mountainous infinity. We spent the night in the welcoming valley town of Andahuaylas. The next day was similar, except that the rain kept up all morning. Nearing the top of a bare and fogbound pass, our bus slithered in the mud to a halt.

A massive truck coming in our direction was trapped in the mud ahead of us, blocking the road completely. The truck driver, aided by a couple of boys, was digging frantically in the rain trying to extricate the vehicle. Forty minutes later he gave up. There seemed no way his truck would budge.

When the rain became less heavy, Chris and I and several of the other passengers got out of the bus to find out what was going to happen next and to see if we could help. Our driver told us that he had managed to use his radio to contact Andahuaylas. A tow-rope was being sent out in a taxi. It would take about three hours to reach us.

One of the passengers became furious and demanded to know why we did not have such a rope in the first place. The other passengers proposed giving the truck a push. Our driver was not optimistic, but ten of us tried pushing all the same. We were unable to move it at all. Chris came up with the suggestion of making the truck lighter by removing all of its hundreds of fifty-kilo sacks of potatoes. No one offered to do so.

We all stood outside chattering in the drizzle. I got talking with a middle-aged woman whom I recognized from the restaurant where we had eaten the night before. She said that there was always something blocking the road at this time of year; you had to be philosophical. She also giggled as the only other foreigner on the bus, a tall thin man wearing a pair of minimal shorts, passed in front of us. 'Do you think he's lost his trousers?' she asked.

The foreigner came up to talk to me. He was a Scotsman who could not speak a word of Spanish. He seemed desperate to speak to somebody. He had an infected sty, a gash in his leg and a haunted look. His manner was awkward and depressing.

He told me he was halfway through a world tour. His liking of places seemed to be entirely dependent on how cheap they were and what bargains he had made there. He was now saving time and money by travelling to Cuzco non-stop from Lima. Last night, his second night in a row sleeping on a bus, there had been a similar hold-up. He had been one of the many travellers affected by the lorry which had got stuck halfway between Huancayo and Ayacucho. In the middle of the night, when he had been fast asleep, everyone in his bus had been told to get out and walk with their luggage to a replacement bus. The occupants of a large van which had been travelling behind them were also forced to abandon their vehicle. The Scotsman had been 'slightly disconcerted' when these men climbed onto the second bus carrying boxes and rifles. They were drug-smuggling terrorists. 'They were awfully polite,' he added. 'One of them even asked if he could sit next to me. His rifle was almost resting on my lap.' About two hours before dawn the men got off.

I relayed the Scotsman's story to the woman with whom I had been talking. She now became serious and sad. The story had triggered memories of travelling around Andahuaylas during the 'years of terror'. Every time a bus had to stop she had feared the worst. She had been held up five times by the Sendero Luminoso. The fifth time she would never forget. She had been sitting across the aisle from a friendly young German couple. 'They couldn't speak much Spanish, but we were able to communicate. They were full of enthusiasm for Peru.'

I already knew the story she was going to tell me. In the mid-1980s, when horrors from Peru were filtering through to the British newspapers, one report in particular had haunted me. It was about a bus that had been travelling from Andahuaylas to Cuzco when it was stopped by the Sendero Luminoso. A young German couple had been taken out and executed by the roadside. No other information was given. The very lack of specific information had made me want to fill in the details, to recreate the last moments of this couple.

The story had obviously affected Vargas Llosa as well. In his Senderoso Luminoso novel *Death in the Andes*, the couple are French. They are travelling to Cuzco by bus, having rejected the advice of the French consul in Lima. The man is particularly reluctant to miss out on the spectacular journey. Once in the mountains near Andahuaylas, his girlfriend begins to suffer from the altitude, but the beauty of the scenery, in the sparkling weather of the dry season, convinces them they have made the right choice. Even after the bus has been stopped by a group of desperately poor Sendero Luminoso *campesinos*, the Frenchman still thinks of all the stories he will be able to tell his friends on returning to Paris. He believes that by virtue of being foreigners he and his girlfriend will be saved. He does not realize that it is their foreign status which will kill them. When the bus is finally allowed to leave, the French couple are forced to stay behind. They are stoned to death.

It was strange that a woman met by chance on a bus should now be telling me the real version of a story that had first caught my attention twenty years earlier. These events had not taken place in daylight during the dry season. Everything had happened at night, 'at around this time of year, on a bus owned like this one by the Molina Unión'.

It had also been raining. 'A group of Sendero Luminoso terrorists, some little more than young boys, had blocked the road with boulders. We all had to get out of the bus. They took everything we had, even though most of us were as poor as they were. What we minded more than anything at the time was having to stand shivering and soaking in the rain. The Germans of course did not really know what was going on. I told them that there was nothing to worry about. But they weren't stupid. Many people around them were sobbing and moaning.

'Eventually we were all told we could get back on the bus. The Germans were on the point of stepping in through the door. A young man, the leader of the terrorists, held them back. "Not you!" he shouted. I pleaded with him to let the Germans go. I said they had done nothing. They were innocent tourists who loved Peru, and were sympathetic to the cause of the *campesino*. "They are traitors," he replied. "All foreigners are traitors."

'The Germans asked me to repeat what had been said. Strangely, they did not seem frightened any more. It was as if they suddenly knew they were going to die, and that there was nothing that they could do about it. I just told them everything was going to be all right. They held hands tightly and looked into each other's watery eyes. They obviously were very much in love. I was shoved back onto the bus. I could hear the gun shots as we pulled away. I can still picture them beside me.'

We were able to get going again before the tow-rope arrived. All the men on our bus got out to make a concerted attempt at pushing the truck. This time we succeeded, to everyone's surprise. By mid-afternoon we had reached the town of Abancay and the asphalted road from the coast.

The asphalt changed everything. I had seen little of it in Peru. I realized after an hour of this new road how much I missed the dangers and inconveniences of the unpaved. The greater the difficulties in getting somewhere, and the greater the fears, the more exotic your destination came to seem. I was falling victim to an elitist romanticism all too common among travel writers – a romanticism that wanted the world to remain unchanged so that a few hardy members of the middle classes could enjoy places out of reach of the great majority.

I was thinking of all this as we approached Cuzco and Machu Picchu. I was coming to a world whose existence I had almost forgotten about – the world of mass tourism.

We came into Cuzco just as its lights were being turned on. A taxi, charging almost triple the official rate, drove us into the centre along an avenue named after the sun. The driver tried to justify the extra expense by taking on the role of blasé and laconic tour guide. He said the city's foundation was linked to the sun and that Manco Cápac, the original Inca, was sent from the Island of the Sun armed with a golden staff, which was swallowed up by the earth on the site of the future Cuzco. He pointed to the floodlit walls of the former Temple of the Sun. The walls dated from the time of Pachakutic, the 'Shaker of the Earth', the man who in the 1430s repelled an invasion from the tribe of the Chacas, turned the Incas from a peaceful into a warmongering nation, and created Machu Picchu and most of the great Inca remains that survived Cuzco's transformation into a Spanish colonial town replete with churches, palaces and the leading Andean school of painting.

Fortunately the driver did not have any more time to continue his historical exposition. We had arrived at our destination – an old colonial house with a picturesquely askew courtyard and a couple of tastefully furnished rooms for rent. The centre of Cuzco was unexpectedly compact if predictably attractive, even in the rain.

Within moments of settling in to our colonial digs, we were outside again, trying to see as much as we could of the town between downpours. Water continued to drip from the mass of brown roofs as we kept to the narrow stone pavements, brushing past white walls, taking in the blue-balconied house of the Inca Garcilaso de la Vega, admiring all the ornamental granite facades, repeatedly crossing the arcaded Plaza de Armas, climbing up an alley lined on one side by the slanting wall of an Inca palace, encountering a maze of vegetarian and alternative cafés, having a pint at the legendary Cross Keys, noticing the Gucci, Armani and Benetton stores, and eating a 'quinoa risotto' in one of the numerous restaurants serving *novandina* cuisine in designer settings. I began to realize why Cuzco was known in Inca mythology as 'the navel of the world'.

Most of the travellers, dreamers, soldiers, adventurers and others whose paths I had been crossing over the past months seem to have come to Cuzco. Humboldt was the one great exception. Later in life, after reading Prescott, he must have regretted this. The Inca structures in and around Cuzco, even in their demolished state, were far more evocative of past grandeur than all the other Inca remains that had so impressed him on his travels. 'The capital of the Incas,'

Prescott had written, 'though falling short of the *El Dorado* which had engaged their credulous fancies, astonished the Spaniards by the beauty of its edifices, the length and regularity of its streets, and the good order and appearance of comfort, even luxury, visible in its numerous population.'

Pizarro's forces, after having successfully fought off an army loyal to Atahualpa, entered Cuzco on 15 November 1533. At first sight the Inca capital, with its stone and adobe houses protected by wide eaves and high-pitched thatched roofs, seemed little different from other Inca settlements. However, on reaching the centre, they became aware of how special the place was. Water rushing along gutters in the centre of the streets contributed to its impressive cleanliness and, above the main square, there was an area of monumental buildings constructed of the finest Inca masonry and filled with treasures. 'This city,' wrote one of the chroniclers to the Holy Roman Emperor Charles V, 'is the greatest and finest ever seen in this country or anywhere in the Indies. We can assure Your Majesty that it is so beautiful and has such fine buildings that it would be remarkable even in Spain.'

The Spaniards soon did their best to remedy this. They allowed the sanitation to decline, pilfered everything of value they could find and melted down all the gold and silver. They had particularly rich pickings in the Temple of the Sun and had no scruples about their brusque, sacrilegious manner of entering it. At least one Spaniard of the time, the priest Cristóbal de Molina, was shocked at the behaviour of his compatriots in Cuzco. 'Their only concern,' he wrote, 'was to collect gold and silver to make themselves all rich . . . without thinking that they were doing wrong and were wrecking and destroying.'

But it was the Incas themselves who initiated the destruction of the actual fabric of the city. The Spaniards, shortly after arriving at Cuzco, allowed the coronation as puppet emperor of an Inca prince hostile to Atahualpa, Manco Cápac II. Soon tiring of being subjugated by the Spaniards, Manco Cápac II left the city and gathered a huge army of supporters. On 6 May 1536 he returned to Cuzco to embark on a six-month siege of the city, which he almost captured thanks to the use of red-hot stones wrapped in cotton and fired with slings. These missiles succeeded in burning down most of the town.

After finally being chased away by Spanish cavalry, Manco Cápac II took refuge in the jungle city of Vilcabamba. The Spaniards meanwhile set about dismantling most of the ruined structures that remained. Unlike in Quito, Cuenca or Cajamarca, they incorporated magnificent segments of Inca masonry into their own buildings, to particularly spectacular effect in the transformation of the Temple of the Sun into a Dominican monastery. However, as far their future reputation was concerned, it might have been better had they pulled down the city's Inca walls entirely: the presence of Spanish structures alongside Inca ones in Cuzco would have a provocative effect in later years. It would highlight the conflict of the two civilizations and act as a permanent reminder of how much the Spaniards had destroyed.

Bolívar, passing through Cuzco on his way to meet Sucre six months after the battle of Ayacucho, did not have much opportunity to reflect on the town's history of injustice: he found himself being as lavishly fêted here as he had been in Lima, and was also caught up in a brief but probably demanding affair with the formidable wife of his former general, Agustín Gamarra. Nonetheless, during his short stay in Cuzco, he made a gesture towards trying to redress the wrongs perpetrated by the Spaniard: he instituted soon-to-be-abandoned land reforms that had the local Indians briefly thinking of him as an Inca deity.

Bolívar's example in winning Indian support was emulated by the Quechua-speaking Gamarra, a one-time Peruvian hero who likewise extolled the Inca past and promised a return to that era of grandeur. The ultimate shallowness of such attitudes was captured in a phrase recently coined by a Peruvian historian: 'Incas Yes, Indians No.'

Every foreign traveller to Cuzco in the wake of the Liberation gave a big 'Yes' to the Incas and a big 'No' to the Spaniards. The kindly General Miller was one of the first to do so. Miller's memoirs of his military campaigns contain a lengthy paean to the Incas, influenced admittedly by the silly legend that the original Inca was not Manco Cápac but a shipwrecked Englishman known to the Quechuas as 'Ingasman Cápac'. Miller was also flattered on his arrival at Cuzco on Christmas Day 1824 by being quoted an Inca prophesy, recorded by Garcilaso de la Vega, that the Inca emperors would one day 'be restored to their throne by a certain people from a country called Inglaterra'.

Miller's praise of the Incas would be repeated by later travellers to the city: 'The monuments which in Cuzco still survive the destructive barbarity of its conquerors attest, more strongly than the concurring accounts of early Spanish authors, to the power, the splendour, and the civilization of the people by whom they were erected.'

Cuzco clearly had the potential to be one of the world's great tourist destinations, as well as a leading centre of *indigenismo*. But when the American explorer Hiram Bingham came here in 1911, it was still a week's journey from Lima and visited solely by the more adventurous. His discovery that year of the nearby Machu Picchu was the catalyst that paved the way for the city's future tourist boom and enhanced the place's appeal to the burgeoning *indigenista* movement.

By 1925, when the aviator Alejandro Velasco Astete made the first flight to the city from Lima, Cuzco had an important group of *indigenista* intellectuals based at its university, including the authors respectively of *Storm in the Andes* and the rather more temperate *The New Indian*, Luis E. Valcarcel and José García Uriel. Also living in Cuzco at this time was one of the greatest indigenous artists the Andes have produced, the photographer Martín Chambi. Chambi, brought up in dire poverty near Puno, in southern Peru, was introduced to photography by two local British mining engineers. He first practised his trade in the predominantly white and mestizo Arequipa, but later found a more receptive response to his work in indigenous Cuzco. The first great photographer of the Andean landscape, he obsessively recorded every aspect of Cuzqueño life, from society outings to popular pilgrimages. His photos enshrined the popular image of the Andean world as solemn and tragic. Even when shown at play, the subjects of his works are never smiling. In the case of his photograph of Velasco Astete drinking a glass of wine at a banquet, this element of foreboding was prophetic: the aviator died a few hours later in a plane crash.

When Isherwood arrived at Cuzco in January 1948 by train, the town already had a regular plane service from Lima, and was 'right on the Trans-Andean tourist trail'. He called Cuzco 'one of the most beautiful monuments to bigotry and sheer stupid brutality in the whole world'. But the view he formed of the Incas was more realistic than that of many of his fellow travellers. He recognized that they, too, were 'imperialists' and that 'one can't think of them simply as a harmless peaceful nation overrun and butchered by bloodthirsty adventurers'. He seems also to have got their true measure: 'Much ritual, little spirituality. Much gold, little elegance. Much feasting, little fun.'

On our first full day in Cuzco I thought also about the young Che Guevara. He had followed a similar itinerary to mine, but in reverse. He had started off in Buenos Aires on a motorcycle, accompanied by a young doctor called Alberto Granado. He himself was a medical student. By the time he and Alberto got to Cuzco, in April 1952, over three months after setting out from Argentina, they had abandoned the motorcycle and were looking as scruffy as backpackers.

In between their visit to Cuzco and Isherwood's, the city had in 1950 suffered a serious earthquake whose consequences would still be noticeable thirty years later. Church towers had fallen and many other colonial structures had been damaged, exposing unsuspected Inca walls beneath and even the main chamber of the Temple of the Sun. Inevitably the catastrophe was interpreted by some people in terms of Inca justice. Martín Chambi was not one of them. Much of his life's collection of glass negatives had been destroyed. Astonishingly, he still had the heart to go out and record the destroyed city. He did so with tears in his eyes.

I thought of Che because his visit to the city had also coincided with the most famous of its Easter processions, that of the Christ of the Earthquakes. We saw the procession in its opening moments, when, with the cathedral's bells ringing above, the float carrying the most venerated of the city's devotional images had emerged from the west portal to greet a sea of umbrellas. The Christ was black and stylized. At his feet and hanging from the cross were decorations made from red *nucchu* flowers. When the Christ was being paraded around the square, thousands of *nucchu* petals were thrown at him from the balconies, creating a storm of red confetti that scattered over a swaying mass of ponchos, coloured headdresses, plastic raincoats and cameras.

On the day when Che had watched the procession the city's bells had been rung for the first time since the earthquake. The restoration of the bell towers had been paid for by the Franco government in Spain and, as an expression of the town's gratitude, the band had been ordered to play the Spanish national anthem. Whether wilfully or not, the band had mistakenly begun by playing the Spanish republican anthem, much to Che and Alberto's amusement.

The procession itself impressed Che as an almost pagan festival, what with the float's clash of silver, violent red and intense bronze, and the 'many-coloured clothes of the Indians, who wear for the occasion their best traditional costumes'. Che contrasted these Indians with the banner-carrying ones dressed in European costume, whose 'tired, affected faces resemble an image of those Quechuas who refused to heed Manco II's call, pledging themselves to Pizarro'. As he observed the crowd, Che also singled out the odd North American tourist. He referred to them as the 'blonde, camera-toting, sportshirted correspondents from another world, lost in the isolation of the Inca Empire'.

Che had yet to become the revolutionary of later years, but his meandering, picaresque journey from Buenos Aires had heightened his awareness of the social and economic injustices of South America and fostered an antipathy towards North America. Yet, unlike other travellers who have come to feel an empathy with South America's indigenous 'conquered races', Che was no less fascinated by the continent's Spanish heritage, which, after all, was partly his own. Indeed what made Che and the more down-to-earth Alberto so appealing as travellers was their openness towards what they saw and experienced, and their limitless curiosity, desire to learn and capacity for wonder. In the absence of Humboldt and Bonpland, they would have made the perfect companions on a journey to Machu Picchu.

Long before the moment of visiting Machu Picchu finally loomed, Chris had told me on various occasions that he had no desire to go there. As a travelling companion, he had been up for anything, apart from the transvestite bars of Ayacucho. However, his mass appeal as a writer did not make him any more tolerant of large crowds, blatant commercialism or the stereotypical American tourist featured in the pages of Isherwood. He also had moral qualms about visiting the place. He had heard that an Anglo-Chilean consortium now ran the site and made from it vast sums of money that belonged by rights to the Peruvian people.

Though I sympathized with him, and was half expecting to be disappointed by Machu Picchu, I reminded Chris of all those visitors whose lives had been enhanced by the place, even Che Guevara, who had later decried its exploitation by the Americans.

Chris eventually realized that there was no way he could come to Peru without visiting Machu Picchu, if only to confirm his misgivings. He was more inclined to go after we had climbed from the centre of Cuzco up to the ruins of what some of the more waggish local guides persisted in calling 'Saxy Woman', Sachsahuamán. The indented walls of this Inca fortress, with their blocks of stone praised by General Miller for their 'extraordinary magnitude', had more of an impact on Chris than the other ancient sites we had seen. But there were other non-archaeological factors that influenced Chris's conversion to the Inca past.

I realized at Sachsahuamán how much Chris had in common with Che's companion Alberto Granado, who had developed at Cuzco an interest in ancient Peruvian ceramics after having taken a fancy to a woman who worked in the ceramics department of the city's main archaeological museum. Chris did not fall in love with anyone at Sachsahuamán, but he became better disposed to mass tourism after an attractive American backpacker came up to him there to say that *Driving Over Lemons* was the best book she had ever read. Then a trio of her swooning female friends turned up to shake hands with its author. These would be the first of Chris's readers to recognize him over the next few days.

As I continued wandering around the site armed with Peter Frost's authoritative *Exploring Cusco*, I noticed that Chris had disappeared. I was worried he had been abducted by one of his admirers. However, something worse had happened. When he emerged again, I discovered he had engaged the services of a local guide. 'He had such an interesting face,' Chris enthused.

The guide seemed warm and open, but the props he had brought with him made me suspect that we were in for another Tarma Inca trail experience. He had some offerings to accompany the recital of an Inca prayer; a photograph in which a picture of a puma was superimposed on the view of Cuzco from Sachsahuamán; an illustration of the Inca cross containing the names of all the deities it represented; and a diagram in which the words '*llamkha*', '*whachha*' and '*mhumba*' featured alongside drawings of a snake, a puma and a condor. The words and the animals, the guide explained, corresponded to the three realms of the Inca universe: the world of the here and now, the world of the dead and the world of the gods.

The guide was an engaging and persuasive man, and though I remained unconvinced that I would achieve a spiritual brotherhood with the Incas, I was happy for him to take us on a long after-noon's walk that included an Inca *huaca* and a place that had been described to the disbelieving Che Guevara as an Inca bathing-place. Chris himself was now in a mood to believe anything. He claimed he had been re-energized by the coca leaves the guide had offered us.

Long after I had discreetly spat out my own masticated bundle of leaves (which had left me with a numb tongue and a bitter after-taste), Chris had continued enthusiastically to chew on his. At the end of the afternoon, as we were led through fields and a wood back towards Cuzco, an overexcited Chris began bombarding the guide with questions about Machu Picchu, which he now could not wait to visit. The guide had convinced him that the experience of going there would justify the whole trip to Peru.

The only way of approaching Machu Picchu other than on foot is by the railway that was built in the 1930s. Che Guevara and Alberto Granado were unable to afford it. Fortunately, by this stage in their journey, they had become adept scroungers: a Cuzco doctor whom Alberto had met at a conference in Argentina arranged for them to have free train tickets.

We went to Cuzco's railway station to buy ours, only to be told that no tickets were available for the next week. Earlier we had had to discount the possibility of getting to Machu Picchu on the Inca trail that clings precipitously to the upper slopes of the Urubamba Valley. Chris did not have the time to spare and, in any case, the daily quota of visitors allowed on the trail was filled for this period.

The bureaucratic problems and expense of getting to Machu Picchu proved greater than anything I had so far experienced in the Andes. In the end we managed to acquire some black-market tickets at one of the travel agencies in Cuzco's main square. Then we decided to make the journey even costlier by hiring a car to take us meanderingly to the village of Ollantaytambo, halfway along the train line.

But the beauty of the morning on which we set off from Cuzco soon made us forget our frustrations. For the first time in a while the sun was shining uninterruptedly as we drove down into the Sacred Valley, with its fields of corn, vegetables and fruit trees, and its enclosing green mountain walls scarred by rocks, ravines, red cliffs and Inca terraces.

The village of Pisac, with its popular tourist market, had been crowded with tour buses even in 1948, when Isherwood described it as 'too tourist-conscious to be truly attractive'. But we managed to beat the buses to the Inca ruins high above the village, where the only person around was a bearded man dressed completely in white, who was squatting with arms outstretched facing the rising sun.

We detoured up into a bare and rolling high plateau, which had views of the snowy, craggy heights of the Vilcabamba range and some concentric terraces built into a natural depression, interpreted by some as an Inca laboratory for experimenting with the cultivation of maize. A family of four lay flat out at the centre of the innermost circle, imbibing the energy.

The Sacred Valley began to narrow as we neared the village of Ollantaytambo, towards the end of the day. Serried rows of tourists, occupying the same vantage-point where Manco II's troops had made a desperate last stand against the Spaniards, were spread over the terraced fortress built into the steep rocky outcrop at the back of the village. But the crowds had all been spirited away by their buses as evening set in, leaving us to wander peacefully down into a haunting village, still laid out as it was in Inca times, with a grid of narrow stone-walled, stone-paved alleys. We took the night train to Aguas Calientes, the village nearest to Machu Picchu. The Urubamba River had become a noisy mountain torrent within a tropical world. We were conscious even in the dark of being hemmed in by steep jungle slopes, whose sounds and humidity could be felt as we walked up the single street of a village that had grown up only over the last decade or so, to become a random brick-and-concrete accumulation of bars, restaurants, shops and cheap hotels.

The journey to Machu Picchu is usually completed by one of the fleet of buses that ascend to the site shortly after dawn. But we took the advice of our guide at Sachsahuamán. We rose at four thirty in the morning to do the ascent on foot, avoiding the road and taking the same steep jungle track that had been followed by such an unlikely assortment of people as Che Guevara, Christopher Isherwood, Pablo Neruda, Martín Chambi and Hiram Bingham.

I had not thought much about Bingham since standing in front of Bolívar's tomb in Caracas. I had left him as a man whose journey retracing Bolívar's march to Boyacá had made him restless for fame and adventure. In 1908, a year after his return to Yale, he had managed to wangle his way back to South America, this time as an American delegate to the first Pan-American Scientific Congress at

'Hiram Bingham at Pampaconas with Mule', photograph
from the Yale Peruvian Exhibition, 1911

Santiago de Chile. As a result of this conference Bingham would write a book highlighting the great business opportunities America was missing by not investing more in the continent.

When the conference was over, Bingham exploited his credentials as '*Delegado oficial de los Estados Unidos*' to pursue a plan to follow on mule-back the old Spanish trade route between Lima and Buenos Aires. Still considering himself a scholar of post-Columbian history with a specialist interest in Bolívar, he made a detour to see the battlefield of Ayacucho. On his way there the prefect of Abancay persuaded him to come on a treasure hunt to the remote and little-known Inca site of Choqquequirau.

Despite travelling there in the middle of one of the worst rainy seasons in living memory, Bingham fell in love with the Central Andean scenery. As they neared their destination, he found himself at the top of a valley, 'held . . . as though by a spell' by a panorama embracing the white torrent of the Apurimac thousands of feet below, sheer precipices, slopes 'covered with green foliage and luxuriant flowers', and a distant 'maze of hills, valleys, tropical jungle and snow peaks'.

Choqquequirau turned Bingham's impressionable and romantic mind away from Bolívar and towards the Incas. Some writers thought that Choqquequirau was in fact Vilcabamba, the final stronghold of the last Inca emperor Manco II. Bingham did not. Looking from the ruins of Choqquequirau up to the snowy Vilcabamba range, he seems to have conceived his future project of looking for Manco II's last capital on the other side of those mountains, along the Urubamba Valley: 'Those snow-capped peaks in an unknown and unexplored part of Peru fascinated me greatly. They tempted me to go to see what lay beyond. In the ever famous words of Rudyard Kipling there was "Something hidden! Go and find it! Go and look behind the ranges – Something lost behind the Ranges. Lost and waiting for you. Go!"'

Back again in Yale in 1909, Bingham dreamed up other schemes, including one to find a new way across Amazonia from La Paz to

Manaus in Brazil. He failed to get backing for any of them. Nor was he successful at first in getting funding for exploration of the Urubamba, which he included in a project whose principal aim was the climbing of a mountain thought by him and a few others to be the highest in South America, Mount Coropuna. Eventually, after giving a speech to the Yale Club at New York, he managed to get some of his wealthier former classmates to provide money for a Peruvian trip. Others were persuaded to join in for adventure. The Yale Peruvian Expedition of 1911 was formed. It left New York in June.

The idea of ascending Coropuna was soon abandoned and the expedition headed directly to Cuzco. In July Hiram and his team began their descent of the Urubamba Valley, whose access after Ollantaytambo had been greatly facilitated by the recent blasting out of a mule trail to assist the transportation of rubber from the jungle. Much further down the valley from Machu Picchu, they came across the ruins of Manco II's settlement of Vitcos and further on they encountered overgrown Inca ruins at a place known as Espiritú Pampa, which he romantically translated as 'the Field of Ghosts'. More than fifty years later a ruthless and heavily financed adventurer called Gene Savoy undertook further excavations at Espiritú Pampa that almost conclusively proved it to be the strong-hold which Bingham had been looking for.

Bingham did not lend much importance to this last site. Nor to begin with did he realize the significance of Machu Picchu, which had first been mentioned to him by a local farmer called Melchor Arteaga. On 24 July he paid Arteaga to guide him to the place, and he remained there just a few hours, after matter-of-factly jotting down some of the details and dimensions of the buildings. The other members of the expedition had stayed behind. Bingham, arriving back at their camp, appears to have spoken little of his discovery.

Machu Picchu, for reasons we can only speculate about, was not mentioned in any of the chronicles, but the reputation Bingham later gave it as the 'lost city' was not strictly accurate. Quite apart from the many locals such as Arteaga who knew of its existence, evidence suggests that other westerners had got there a long time before him, including a British missionary, a German engineer and a German speculator who, as early as 1860, appears to have received the permission of the Peruvian government to plunder the ruins. Bingham was merely the first to embark on the scientific study and excavation of Machu Picchu, and he did so only after mounting further expeditions to Peru from 1912 onwards, after which he twisted historical evidence to prove that the site was really Manco II's capital of Vilcabamba.

Machu Picchu was the place which brought Bingham the fame he so desperately sought. It turned him into an American hero comparable to the astronaut John Glenn, and was likewise responsible for his eventually becoming an American senator. However, his political career would bring him far less satisfaction and respect than his youthful adventuring. In 1948, the same year that Isherwood went to Machu Picchu, Bingham paid a sentimental return visit to the place of his earlier glory. He was inspired afterwards to refine and compress all his various writings on Machu Picchu into his gloriously exaggerated and deeply nostalgic *Lost City of the Incas*.

I had read the book two years before coming here, but its pages were still fresh in my mind, as Chris and I walked down the only street of Aguas Calientes two hours before dawn. Guided by the roar of rushing water, we came almost immediately to the Urubamba and followed the white foam of its rapids down into the jungle blackness beyond the village. The road we were on, in the words of Bingham:

> runs through a land of matchless charm . . . In the variety of its charms and the power of its spell, I know of no place in the world which can compare with it. Not only has it great snow peaks

looming above the clouds more than two miles overhead and gigantic precipices of many-coloured granite rising sheer for thousands of feet above the foaming, glistening, roaring rapids, it has also, in striking contrast, orchids and tree ferns, the delectable beauty of luxurious vegetation, and the mysterious witchery of the jungle. One is drawn irresistibly onward by ever-recurring surprises through a deep, winding gorge, turning and twisting past overhanging cliffs of incredible height.

There were no stars in the sky and the clouds were low above us, spraying a light drizzle as they had done on the morning of 24 July 1911, when Bingham had managed only after much persuasion to rouse Arteaga from his hut. After half an hour we came to the ironwork bridge that had replaced the more primitive structure that existed in Bingham's time. 'The "bridge",' wrote Bingham, 'was made of half a dozen very slender logs, some of which were not long enough to span the distance between the boulders, but had been spliced and lashed together with vines!'

Perhaps flimsy bridges were necessary for the protection of lost worlds, which was how Bingham ended up imagining Machu Picchu, his discovery of which coincided with the publication of Conan Doyle's *The Lost World*. When Bingham came to write *Lost City of the Incas*, the dangers of getting there in 1911 had considerably increased in the telling. The waters had now become so swollen from the recent rains that Bingham feared there would be no bridge at all for him to return on, and that he would be stuck forever on jungle slopes crawling with deadly fer de lance vipers.

Chris and I strode boldly towards these slopes across the modern bridge. Tiny patches of light could be seen appearing through the thick layer of night and clouds. I thought I could make out a crag.

On the other side of the river was a road which ascended up to Machu Picchu in giant loops. The quick way up was along a near-vertical mule track, the only route available to travellers before 1950. 'There was no highway then,' wrote the Chilean poet Pablo

Neruda of his life-changing visit to Machu Picchu in October 1943, 'and we rode up on mules.' Isherwood did the same five years later. Some suffering American women whom he had met in his hotel at Cuzco were the limping survivors of a visit to Machu Picchu, which for them was the 'great via dolorosa' of their South American adventures. They had returned to the hotel's lounge to 'boast of their hardships' and 'scare us newcomers': '"*Well* – I wouldn't do that again for ten thousand dollars!" "I couldn't stop the brute, but the guide just laughed and told me to hang on tight". "Muriel's mule was the meanest of the lot. It ate grass, *right* on the *edge*, and wouldn't budge." "When mine started to *skid*, I just shut my eyes. I thought, oh boy, this is the *end*!"'

Che and Alberto, walking to the summit from the railway station, were able to choose between the road and the mule track. They chose the latter, as did Chris and I. Chris was so excited that he burst ahead, soon to vanish into the jungle shrubbery. I was puffing some way behind him, but was spurred on by the fast-rising clouds. As dawn broke they became whiter and wispier, until finally a definite silhouette of crags came momentarily into view on the other side of the valley. We made it to the top in just over an hour. We were now wandering in a light mist.

The first bus-loads had arrived but the mist absorbed the tourists who poured out of them. We rushed up to the top of some terrace and got there before the clouds dissolved to reveal the view I had seen reproduced so many times that I thought I would be indifferent to it. First to appear was a labyrinth of tidy walls hugging a smooth green ridge and then, from behind, emerged the soaring rocky outcrop of Huayna Picchu, Japanese-like in the way it began peeping from the clouds, and finally came the curving background of cloud-capped green mountains that held the whole site in a protective embrace.

When Bingham first saw this view, most of the ruins had already been cleared by the Indians farmers living on the site. But in his *Lost City of the Incas*, Bingham distorted reality for the sake of narrative effect. He described his amazement at the beauty of the landscape, but also wrote how the only signs of a former Inca settlement were the agricultural terraces. Only when an Indian boy guided him through the jungle that had spread all over Machu Picchu's ridge were the extraordinary Inca structures gradually exposed to him, like the opening of a treasure chest. The photographs that Bingham himself took on this first visit contradict this description, but then these photos, along with those that appeared in his *National Geographic* account of 1913, are primarily of archaeological interest, and fail to capture what Bingham might have called the place's romance and mystery.

Had Humboldt discovered Machu Picchu, he would have urged one of his artist followers such as Bellerman or Rugendas to paint the site. Frederick Church might have succeeded in providing a visual image with a sufficient balance of realism, grandeur and poetry. However, Machu Picchu's discovery came at a time when the role of the artist-traveller had been succeeded by that of the photographer. The problem was that few of the good early photographers could be bothered to carry their heavy equipment and delicate glass plates up to the top of mountains.

The first outstanding photographer to do so in the Andes was Martín Chambi, who escaped to Machu Picchu whenever he could during the 1920s, sometimes alone, sometimes with friends and clients. The solemnity of his style memorably conveyed the silent eeriness of a site replete with all the proverbial spirituality of the Andean world. He was helped by the absence of other tourists. He also had the advantage of being an Indian.

That Machu Picchu should have come to light at a time of intensifying *indigenismo* must have seemed a blessing ordained by the supreme Inca deity Viracocha. For *indigenistas* such as Luis E. Valcarcel (one of the archaeologists working on the site in the wake of Bingham), Machu Picchu became not just the ultimate expression of indigenous aspirations, but also an example of how the Inca spirit had triumphantly survived all the Spanish attempts to suppress it.

Just as there are people today who still believe that only someone born in Granada can fully understand the Alhambra, so too have there been *indigenistas* convinced that the true significance of Machu Picchu can be grasped only by someone such as Chambi. Because most of the *indigenistas* were either white or mestizo, this belief was amplified so that all South Americans could form part of an exclusive circle of Machu Picchu admirers from which the likes of Bingham would be permanently excluded.

Che Guevara, for all his early tolerance, also supported this view. After pondering the irresolvable problem of the site's original function, he concluded that all that mattered was that the place was 'the pure expression of the most powerful indigenous race in the Americas – still clean of contact with a conquering civilization'. There were also subtleties about the site to be appreciated only by 'the semi-indigenous spirit of the South American', and which 'North American tourists, bound down by their practical world view', would never be able to see.

The way in which Machu Picchu gave South Americans a sense of identity received its most eloquent expression in the writings of Neruda. Though some claim his initial reaction to the site was to comment on 'what a wonderful place it would make for a roast', he would later respond with high-flown sentiments worthy of Bolívar's supposed delirium on top of Chimborazo: 'I felt infinitely small in the centre of that navel of rocks, the navel of a deserted world, proud, towering high, to which I somehow belonged. I felt that my own hands had labored there at some remote point in time, digging furrows, polishing the rocks. I felt Chilean, Peruvian, American. On those difficult heights, among those glorious, scattered ruins, I had found the principles of faith I needed to continue my poetry.'

Later still, after writing one of his most famous poems, *The Heights of Macchu Picchu* (he spelt the name with an additional 'c', 'perhaps to imprint his own stamp on the miraculous site', as one of his biographers has suggested), he expounded more fully on the feelings that the place had inspired in him:

After seeing the ruins of Macchu Picchu, the fabulous cultures of antiquity seemed to be made of cardboard, papier mâché. India itself seemed minuscule, daubed, banal, a popular god-fest, compared with the haughty solemnity of those abandoned Inca towers. I could no longer separate myself from those constructions ... Our aristocratic cosmopolitanism had led us to revere the past of the most remote peoples and had blinded us to discovering our own treasures ... I thought about ancient American man. I saw his ancient struggles intermeshed with present-day struggles ... Now I saw the whole of America from the heights of Macchu Picchu. That was the title of the first poem of my new conception.

What distinguishes Neruda's *The Heights of Macchu Picchu* from the parochialism and indeed racism of so much *indigenismo* is its obsession with the transitoriness of the human condition seen against the vastness of time, an obsession that can be developed by anyone who spends any length of time in the Andes. It had come to my grandfather. It was coming to me.

However, during my day with Chris at Machu Picchu there was little time to give serious thought to anything. Chris, even without the aid of coca leaves, had been manically affected by the energetic Andean forces. And I had become just like him.

From the time of our pre-dawn rush right up to the moment we left the site, we barely stopped, neither to regain our breath, nor to eat anything, nor to top up the recommended daily water intake, nor to consult the seminal writings of Peter Frost. We were like speeded-up versions of the dreamers mentioned by Che Guevara, wandering Machu Picchu's ruins 'for the sake of it', oblivious to what each structure might once have been, and not really caring much anyway, because most of what was currently said was probably wrong and, in any case, we would never really understand the site.

Victims of the 'spell' to which Bingham had so often referred, we were childishly overexcited by the place, and eager not to miss out on anything. We saw almost everything there was to be seen, from

412

the cliff-hanging Inca bridge at its southernmost extremity, up to the summit of Huayna Picchu and then down the other side of that needle-like pinnacle into vertical jungle, losing sight of all other tourists for about two hours, as we descended on rope and rotting wooden ladders, ducking under lianas and slipping on exposed roots. We were worried we would end up back at the river, but we came out finally at a small clearing with an Inca ruin all to ourselves, a Bingham-like moment, at which point it was all uphill again, until we rejoined the crowds.

A desire to sit down finally overcame us after nearly eleven hours on the move. Immediately beyond the site's main entrance was Machu Picchu's only hotel and restaurant, crowded, luxurious and unappealing. It was where Che Guevara had stayed.

Che and Alberto had been lucky enough to turn up when no one else was around. The man in charge was a writer in whom Alberto immediately identified left-wing tendencies. He was playing football with some of his employees. Che and Alberto surprised them all by asking if they could join in. Afterwards they introduced themselves. The man in charge, in Alberto's words, 'got the measure of us at once and, seeing we weren't as short of intelligence or knowledge as we were of clothes and money, he offered us free board and lodging'.

They stayed there two days and nights, during which time Che borrowed from the hotel's library Bingham's recently published *Lost City of the Incas*. Alberto began reading instead a book that one of the guides had lent him. It was a collection of letters written by Bolívar. He turned to it every night before going to sleep. 'Profound and topical, they fired my imagination. I thought I was right to follow the imperious voice of my blood, which called me to wander through America until I found something new, where I could develop my full physical, scientific and intellectual potential.'

One afternoon, after making maté tea in the ruins, Alberto lay down dreamily on a sacrificial stone, while Che sat on a rock reading Bingham. Alberto interrupted him by saying he had decided

413

to marry the woman at the ceramics department at Cuzco museum: 'Since she's a descendent of Manco Cápac II, I'll become Manco Cápac III. Then I'll form a pro-Indian party, I'll take all these people to the coast to vote, and that'll be the start of the new Túpac Amaru revolution, the American Indian revolution!' Che took him seriously. 'Revolution without firing a shot? You're crazy, Alberto.'

Their brief idyll at Machu Picchu was interrupted when they were asked to move out of the hotel to make way for paying North American guests. This pushed Che over the edge. On the train journey back to Cuzco he vented his spleen on 'American tourists' and the cattle-like travel conditions faced by the Indians. 'Naturally the tourists who travel in their comfortable buses would know nothing of the condition of these Indians . . . The majority of the Americans . . . fly directly from Lima to Cuzco, visit the ruins and then return, without giving any importance to anything else.'

His anti-Americanism was developed in an article he published the following year entitled 'Machu Picchu, Enigma of Stone in America': 'All the ruins were cleared of overgrowth, perfectly studied and described . . . and totally robbed of every object that fell into the hands of the researchers, who triumphantly took back to their country more than two hundred boxes containing priceless archaeological treasures . . . Where can one go to admire or study the treasures of the indigenous city? The answer is obvious: in the museums of North America.'

We did not eat at the Machu Picchu Sanctuary Lodge. A waitress whom we had approached about the possibility of a table took a liking to us. She recommended we walk a kilometre down the road to the canteen reserved for Machu Picchu's employees. All we had to say was that Silvia sent us.

The name Silvia had a magical effect. The canteen had a quiet shaded terrace with seductive views over the Urubamba Valley. We were served with simple Peruvian food and drank a couple of litres of Pilsen Callao. We were charged one dollar each. We almost missed our train.

We ran down the mule track in a record thirty minutes and just made it before the train left and a tropical rainstorm began. Chris declared that our day in Machu Picchu had been one of the best in his life. His boundless enthusiasms were now completely in step with my own feelings.

The day after Machu Picchu we were crossing a scorched landscape out of the Wild West or Mexico, full of dunes, stony wastelands, cross-sections of yellow-and-red-striped earth, and bare ochre mountains with gleaming white summits. By mid-afternoon the emptiness of this world was broken by tin-roofed, ochre-walled shanty developments spilling over into a hazy-edged plateau of agricultural fields. A cluster of snowy mountains was getting closer. They were all volcanoes. One of them, far apart from the others, had a hood of snow that seemed to have an ethereal existence independent of the pale golden cone below it. We were reaching Arequipa. The volcano that dominated the city was the sacred Misti.

I already knew this view from an exultant description by Gauguin's grandmother, Flora Tristán. Her moment of approaching Arequipa had been a brief lull in a life of increasing hardship and misery. She had been waiting for this moment since childhood. Her father, Don Mariano, had been a member of one of Arequipa's wealthiest families. He became a colonel in the Peruvian army and had known Bolívar when the two of them were young officers in Spain. He had also fallen in love in Spain with a young French woman escaping from the French Revolution. The two of them had a Spanish wedding and then went to live in Paris, where Flora was born in 1803. Bolívar and his tutor Simón Rodíguez had gone to visit them there.

Don Mariano died young, when Flora was only three. No inheritance came from Peru and Flora's mother was forced to move to a squalid tenement building off the Place Maubert, then one of the poorest areas in Paris. Flora was raised on tales of Bolívar, exotic

Arequipa and the vast amount of money to which she was entitled should she go to Peru to collect it. Her adolescence was also marked by the discovery that she was a bastard: the only marriages allowed under new French law were civil ones.

She was barely seventeen when she went to work at a lithographer's workshop. She married its owner and had three children by him, one of whom, Aline, became the mother of Gauguin. Flora came to hate her husband so much that she ran away to London, where she discovered that the 'condition of slaves is no worse than that of the British working classes'. On her return to Paris, she was pursued and beaten up by her husband. She became a leading workers' activist and fighter for female emancipation. News of her parents' friend Bolívar and his success in freeing South America might have inspired her much-quoted comment that 'the level of civilization . . . is in proportion to the freedom that women enjoy'.

To assure her own independence she needed to get her inheritance from Don Pío, Don Mariano's brother in Arequipa. In April 1833 she set sail from Bordeaux to Peru. Vargas Llosa, whose early childhood was spent in Arequipa, would write a novel in which Flora's tale, with all its idealism and dreams of faraway shores, was intercut with Gauguin's life and squalid death in the South Seas. The novel was called *Paradise is Elsewhere*.

Flora herself wrote up her Peruvian adventures in her controversial and vividly detailed book, *Peregrinations of a Pariah*. She was ill for much of the sea crossing and the heat, dust, dangers and discomforts of the desert climb up to Arequipa proved a further burden on her self-confessed 'nervous temperament'. She was also worried about the outcome of her quest. Rightly as it turned out. She would find that Peru since independence was fundamentally the same as before, with class and social barriers as rigid as ever, with the old ruling families still in place and still holding tightly onto their money.

Yet, after the hardships of her journey, she was filled with what she described as an ecstatic, divinely induced happiness on first setting eyes on Arequipa. For someone brought up in the slums of Paris, Arequipa's setting was as exotically beautiful and powerful as she had been led as a child to believe:

> Suddenly, in front of us, were an immense plain, a chain of moun-tains, and Arequipa's three gigantic volcanoes. On seeing that magnificent spectacle I forgot all my troubles. I was living now with no other aim than to admire . . . I was in ecstasy . . . Never before had I seen a spectacle that had moved me so much. Neither the fury of waves on a vast ocean . . . nor the brilliant sunsets below the equator, nor the majesty of a sky pulsating with stars, had produced in me so much admiration as did this sublime manifestation of God.

Arequipa, Peru's second-largest city, with a population of almost a million, still has a colonial centre which Flora Tristán would easily recognize. Its straight raw streets of bleached low dwellings seem always to be leading the eye towards the outlying volcanoes. The colonial architecture is distinguished by its white and pinkish vol-canic stone which Isherwood likened to sugar-candy.

Isherwood loved Arequipa. 'There is something delightful in the atmosphere,' he wrote, 'something soft and lucid, soothing yet stim-ulating, which immediately invites you to remain, settle down and work.' Chris and I felt exactly the same on settling into a delight-fully rambling hotel whose arched vaulted ceilings were apparently typical of Arequipa's grand interiors of old. On one of the walls of our enormously tall room was a photograph of a nineteenth-century bishop of Arequipa who had lived in this house. The photo, taken exactly a hundred years earlier, showed the bishop celebrat-ing the first mass on the summit of the Misti volcano.

It was Maundy Thursday and the holiday atmosphere soon enticed us into a nearby street blocked off to traffic and laid out with food stalls and tables. We went back there at night to eat, and found two places at the end of a crowded bench. One of our neighbours recommended that we should drink as many beers and piscos that night as we could manage. From Good Friday until the end of Easter Sunday, he said, the drinking of alcohol was strictly prohibited in Peru. It was a ruling of the Church.

Another shock, a literal one, woke us up early on Good Friday. I was lying half asleep when there was a sudden loud noise that lasted for over a minute. I thought I saw the ceiling tremble, but there was sleep in my eyes and I hadn't got my glasses on, so I wasn't quite sure. Chris, already up when the bang occurred, was out of the room in a second. He had a strong instinct for self-preservation.

Most of the hotel's clients were out in the garden before I got there myself. Later, over breakfast, the owner told us that this had been the worst tremor in many years. It had measured 5.8 on the Richter scale and several buildings near its epicentre twenty miles away had apparently collapsed.

People were still talking about the earthquake when we went out for a morning's sightseeing. A local shopkeeper told me that tremors at this time of year usually signalled nothing more sinister than the end of the rainy season. We continued down into the double-arcaded Plaza de Armas, one of the grandest colonial squares in the Andes. That night the square would be the focus of a long procession featuring several bands, hundreds of drummers and great crowds. But now the place was so empty that you would have thought that the city's inhabitants had fled in a panic from the tremor.

We passed by the ancestral home of Flora Tristán's father. Its austere volcanic walls must have heightened her mounting anxieties about her reception by his family, but its portal must have seemed as fantastical as anything in her early dreams of Arequipa. Its ornament was typical of the baroque flourishes that enlivened the simplicity of the city's traditional architecture. The mestizo craftsmen had responded to the hardness of volcanic stone with a style that was stiff, heavily stylized and overblown. The portal could have been the entrance to a Mayan temple.

I peered though a crack in the door into a courtyard painted the same reddish ochre of much of the city's surrounding landscape. Flora had arrived here by night to find 'a multitude of black slaves' crowded around the door, and a mass of torches and candelabra illuminating the courtyard and salon. The theatrical nature of her initial reception, however, had been followed by long solitary hours in her bedroom, wondering if this had been the room in which her father had been brought up.

I walked on with Chris to the nearby Convent of Santa Catalina, which Flora visited at a time when her mood was darkening and the chances of her receiving any money from her avaricious uncle dwindling. I did not expect to get into the convent on a Good Friday, but a commercially minded nun took pity on a party of pleading tourists, to which we attached ourselves. The interior was a revelation. It was like a miniature seventeenth-century township, with a maze of stone alleys, gardens, squares, and deep-ochre-painted walls, over which all you could see of the outside world were the faraway volcanoes.

Flora had imagined that such a place would lighten her 'oppressed heart', but instead she wept at the thought of all the women who were 'buried alive' behind its stones. Her sadness was heightened by the way the nuns all rushed out of their cells the moment they heard that the by now famous young Frenchwoman had come to pay them a visit. She found pathetic their eager questions about what Paris and France were like and whether she had heard the music of Rossini. I felt a similar pathos on noticing that all the alleys and little squares had names of Spanish towns such as Seville, Toledo and Granada. The names spoke of an incurable longing for a world that would never be known.

We spent the rest of the morning hearing of the fate of a young Inca girl dubbed 'Juanita'. The only museum in the city officially open that day was the Museum of the Andean Sanctuaries. Its star exhibit, the mummy of the sacrificed Juanita, was away for yet more of the many tests to which she has been subjected since her discovery in 1995. But her llama-hide shoes were there, as well as her red and white blood-spattered vestments. There was also a highly informative student guide who told us Juanita's tale and set our minds thinking about the worship of high mountains.

No one knows where Juanita came from, but it was certainly from a place far lower than where she ended up. Her life had probably been an ordinary one until the age of about twelve, when she had been singled out by the Inca priests to enter the realm of the gods. She and her parents would have been thrilled by the honour.

Her selection also meant an exciting trip to Cuzco to witness the ritual dancing and drinking accompanying the important ceremony in honour of the sun god, Inti. When that was over she would have been led in procession all the way to the Colca Canyon near Arequipa. Her final destination was the top of a 6310-metre-high volcano where the mountain god Ampato lived.

The pilgrims who had followed the procession stopped at a *tambo*, or group of buildings, that had been constructed at the foot of Mount Ampato. Only priests and their assistants could accompany Juanita from this point upwards. In the course of the climb the girl would almost certainly have suffered from nausea, headache and extreme cold; but these were the least of her worries.

The sacrificial party spent two nights on a hillock on the crater's rim, sleeping in tents and protected from the cold earth by grass matting. On the morning before making the final climb to the end of the summit ridge, she was given a light vegetarian meal. She was then led up to a low stone structure, next to which the priests laid out the mass of offerings they had brought with them, including gold and silver figurines, bags of coca leaves, incense and maize beer.

The group chewed coca leaves in honour of the gods and burnt the incense. The smoke from the incense told the pilgrims below in the *tambo* that the ceremony was reaching its climax, and that they could start singing and dancing.

The priest raised to the sun a wooden cup full of maize beer, which, to the playing of music, was poured afterwards into the ground. Some more beer was then given to Juanita. With any luck, the alcohol went straight to her head and rendered her half insensible for the next and final stage of the procedure, when she was placed in the middle of the stone structure, covered with a cloth and struck on the head with a five-pointed granite mace.

Around five hundred years later, in 1995, the neighbouring volcano of Sabancaya exploded, shrouding Mount Ampato with ash. The weight of the melting snow was such as to drag away a tiny section of Ampato's crater ridge, which, on falling, carried with it the bundle containing the frozen and mummified Juanita. The bundle was torn as it fell, scattering the Inca artefacts that were also inside; but Juanita herself landed safely fifty metres further down the mountain.

Exposure to the strong sun would have led to her disintegration within a very short time. However, help would soon be on hand in the form of American high-altitude archaeologist Johan Reinhard, the Hiram Bingham of the modern age.

High-altitude archaeology was a new discipline and Reinhard was the ideal person to practise it. A lover of mountains and mountaineering from childhood, and an avid reader of tales of exploration, he had had three near-death experiences before reaching his middle years. Twice he had been almost killed by lightning and once he had started falling down a snowy slope in the Swiss Alps, stopping only moments before a precipice.

A passionate world traveller, much to his father's disapproval, he had developed a great knowledge of anthropology and archaeology in the course of his far-flung travels. Eight years in Nepal in the 1960s and seventies had honed his mountaineering skills and awakened the spiritual side of his nature. He became fascinated by shamanism. He also took an interest in the way that the Sherpa climbers placed offerings of juniper berries at the top of the Himalayan peaks. In 1980 he turned his attention to the Andes.

The study of the Andes promised to unite his various loves and interests. By 1980 climbers had reported more than forty Inca sites at heights of over 5000 metres. Reinhard began scaling Andean peaks all the way from Ecuador to Chile. In the mid-1980s he had one of the great spiritual experiences of his life while attending the annual Christian pilgrimage up to the snows of Qoyllur Rit'i near Cuzco. Later he was able to prove what had always been suspected: that the Catholic Church had appropriated and turned to their own ritual ends the Inca practice of worshipping the peak at Ausengate.

In 1995, searching for further Andean peaks to investigate, he enlisted in Arequipa the help of a local climber, Miki Zárate. Miki had an intuitive feeling that something would be found at the top of Ampato. Their subsequent encounter with the four-foot-ten Juanita, the best-preserved mummy yet discovered in South America, was like finding themselves suddenly back in the time of the Incas.

They were then faced with the huge problem of how to get her safely to the nearest reliable freezer. Thanks to a combination of Reinhard's near-superhuman strength, and the overnight bus service from the Colca village of Cabanaconde to Arequipa, the two men managed to do so in the nick of time.

Juanita became an overnight sensation and went on a world tour. Vargas Llosa, a lover of women though not generally of mummies, was overwhelmed by her: 'Her exotic, lengthened face, with high cheekbones and large, somewhat slanted eyes, suggest a remote oriental influence. She has her mouth open, as if challenging the world with the whiteness of her perfect teeth that purse her upper lip in a coquettish expression . . . I was moved, captivated by Juanita's beauty, and, if it were not for what people would say, I would have stolen her and installed her in my home as the woman of my life.'

With a team of investigators and the support of the *National Geographic*, Reinhard returned to Ampato and made further important discoveries, both there and elsewhere in the Andes. He concluded that sacrifices were probably made at times when drought and volcanic activity coincided. The hot ash from eruptions made possible the burial of sacrificial victims on the frozen summits, while also polluting the already depleted water supplies. The only solution to the water problem was to try and please the gods.

Reinhard still harboured a final ambition. The face of Juanita, during its brief exposure to the sun, had acquired a leathery look. Though Reinhard had gone on to uncover mummies in their original positions, these had been destroyed by lightning. He now dreamt of finding a mummy whose features had been perfectly preserved by ice. He was finally to realize this dream on an expedition in 2002 to one of the highest and remotest peaks in the Andes, Llullaillhaco in northern Argentina.

To get to the top of Llullaillhaco meant an arduous desert trek of many days before climbing to a height of 6739 metres. That Reinhard and his team were able to show that the Incas did indeed achieve this was extraordinary enough: few more persuasive examples have come to light of the Incas' exceptional mountaineering skills and the strength of their faith in the mountain gods.

But that the finds at the summit should include a mummy so uncannily life-like was almost supernatural. Perhaps there was some truth in that most persistent of Andean beliefs: that the Incas are still in hiding in the mountains, waiting to return.

Around lunchtime on Good Friday, in a village on the outskirts of Arequipa, Christ was getting ready to be sacrificed for the future good of humanity. The passion play at Paucarpata is one of the best known in Peru and explained the absence of people in the centre of the city. Everyone was streaming out of Arequipa for a leisurely country outing climaxing with a crucifixion.

Paucarpata is now more a suburb of Arequipa than a village but there were still a few fields testifying to its bucolic past before the Agricultural Reform Act of 1968, which the villagers seemed to regard as a watershed in the history of Arequipa's surroundings. 'Arequipa was once entirely surrounded by fields,' a local police-man told us, 'but then came the reform act, and everyone started building houses and shacks wherever they felt like.'

The policeman was trying to find out for us where and when the passion play began. Reports were contradictory and no one seemed particularly bothered. Everyone was packed into the restaurants around the main square, or else wandering up and down between the various stalls and fairground booths that had been set up on the main road leading into the village.

The passion play turned out to be an ambulatory spectacle taking place throughout the village. We caught up with it in the midst of some modern chalets. We could not tell from a distance whether anything had begun. A group of about thirty people in white robes and garish nylon drapes were standing arguing in the middle of the street, watched by considerably fewer spectators. Christ had a wig and false beard. One of the actors, looking like a Bedouin, con-sulted his watch. Instantly they all started moving. After a few moments a woman threw himself on her knees in front of Christ. I could not hear clearly what she was saying, but Christ seemed better disposed towards her than were his apostles. I guessed she was the repentant Magdalene.

After half an hour of moving hardly more than fifty metres, St Peter had still not brought up the subject of where they were going to celebrate the Pascal supper. Chris and I were getting hungry. One of the spectators suggested we would have plenty of time to have lunch before the Last Supper began.

We ate in the main square in a large and crowded restaurant with a back terrace overlooking what was left of the countryside. Every-one was eating a spicy vegetable stew accompanied by Inka Cola. The owner promised to let us know when anything significantly dramatic began happening outside.

We were paying the bill when the owner announced that Christ and his apostles were on the point of entering the square. Already we could hear a lot of music and shouting. Outside we had to push our way through a large crowd infiltrated with police and Roman centurions. A long table with bowls, bread and jugs of water had been arranged in front of the church.

The actors had become more concentrated, and the atmosphere was becoming more vibrant, as spectators and costumed performers kept on arriving. The pace was no quicker, but the drama was beginning to draw me in.

With the slow, ominous ringing of the church bells, the emotion of the occasion intensified further, as everyone left the square to walk up the hill behind it. I had thought that the only spectators watching the Passion were the five hundred or so walking with us behind Christ and his growing entourage. But, visible only after several minutes of climbing, were a good two thousand people packed into the large sloping field towards which we were heading.

On the way up we passed a large tree from which Judas was about to be hanged. The noose was already around his neck. Centurions pushed us aside as we tried to find space to stand within the crowded field. Vendors passed by, selling roast maize and candy floss. The mood was a curious blend of celebration, solemnity and tense expectation, which was more or less how I imagined the mood at a public execution.

One of the spectators started talking to me as the magnified sound of nails being hammered into wood became audible. He said he had gone the year before to see the passion play at Lima and the actor playing Christ had taken his role so seriously that he had died of heart failure on the cross. The Christ at Paucarpata was not physically being nailed to the cross as he would have been in one or two other villages in South America, but his simulated screams, rising above the cries of the vendors, sounded realistic enough.

The three crosses were finally lifted up to reveal Christ's naked, blood-stained body framed against the now darkening cone of the Misti volcano. Numerous men with baseball caps took photos on their mobile phones. The lance was plunged into Christ, and the bodies were taken down from the crosses. The crowd went silent for a moment, and then began talking noisily again as an ambulance with a blaring siren made its way towards where Christ was lying, mourned by his mother and family. His corpse and those of the two thieves were lifted up on stretchers and driven away. The sun was lowering and the crowd dispersing. I looked back at the three empty crosses as they faded into obscurity, watched by the Misti, with its reddish-white crown.

Chris had only a few days left with me in South America and he still had one unfulfilled desire: to see a condor.

Late on the Saturday morning we took the bus to Cabanaconde, the reverse of the journey that the mummified Juanita had made. We climbed from desert up to stony plateau, and then looked down on a stretch of green fields enclosed by further mountains on its northern side, with a snowy range in the distant background. Shining among the sunlit fields below was the village of Chivay, at the head of the Colca Canyon.

Had Juanita travelled in the same bus that we did, the history of archaeology would have been the poorer. Our bus never made it to Cabanaconde. At the bus station at Chivay it stopped for what we were told was going to be twenty minutes. The driver disappeared completely. The later bus, the last one of the day, never turned up. The light and colours were becoming sharper and deeper, but it now looked as if we were not going to be able to enjoy driving along the canyon under these ideal conditions. The next scheduled bus to Cabanaconde was not due until the next day, Easter Sunday.

Once again, we were rescued by a taxi driver, an hour and a half before the sun set. The driver was the only one prepared to take us to our destination, a rough two-hour ride away. The fields became terraced and then petered out into stonier, rockier ground as the road ascended the southern slopes of what soon became a sublime canyon deeper than most others in the Americas. Through a gap on the southern side we could see the snowy heights of Ampato, while across the canyon was the Nevado Mismi, the official source of the Amazon.

At the canyon's highest and rockiest point was a lookout point known as the Mirador Cruz del Condor. This was the place where the guidebooks said you could 'almost guarantee' seeing condors circling above you. Chris had spoken to a foreign student at Arequipa and she had told him that she had been there five times and hadn't seen a single one.

We did not expect to see any towards sunset, as apparently condors were early birds who usually do not deign to entertain tourists later than midday. But we stopped for the view and were immediately surrounded by smiling women trying to sell us the beautiful embroidered black hats that most of the village women wear in the western half of the canyon. We bought a couple of the hats, but Chris insisted he did not want to come back to this spot the following morning. We agreed that the sighting of condors should be a special and private moment. 'The condors will search you out wherever you are, if they want you to see them,' said the driver enigmatically.

We drove the remaining half-hour to Cabanaconde in darkness. Our eyes and imaginations settled on some widely scattered lights on the other side of the canyon. They were the lights of three tiny villages accessible only on foot or muleback. The driver said they had hardly changed since the time that Pizarro's brother Gonzalo was the feudal lord of the area. We made them our goal for Easter Sunday.

We were up at first light, almost subliminally conscious of a perfect dawn outside. The sky was cloudless, and the rising sun was just touching the snowy crags high above the villages at which we were aiming. Slowly the sun penetrated the deep chasm that lay in between. In the dry season the world that was opening up below us would have been dusty and yellowing but, after the recent months of rain, it was buoyantly green, sprinkled with agaves and cactuses, and terraced and lush on the lower slopes opposite.

427

The day would turn out another of the best in Chris's life. The energy that had driven us in Macho Picchu returned, enabling us to carry out in one day a trek supposed to take three. We descended on foot over 1200 metres to the bottom of the canyon. Then we climbed the same distance on the other side, walking at first through orchards and shaded fields before gradually making our way to each of the three half-deserted villages, with their crumbling colonial churches and views looking back to Ampato and its snowy neighbours. Back down again at the river, we delayed the arduous uphill return by relaxing and swimming in a tiny and unexpected oasis of hot springs and green lawns.

It was a day in which all the thoughts of bloodshed and catastrophes that had been accumulating on my way down the Peruvian Andes were blown away by uplifting images of a kind that are permanently stored in the mind. It was the day the condors found us.

The day had barely begun. An hour into our descent, exhilarated by the expanding sunlight, observing our narrow ledge of a path as it dropped to the winding silver line of the Colca River, I heard a sudden shout from behind me. 'There!' screamed Chris, pointing to the sky, as a condor soared towards us. Its huge wings were scarcely moving, and came so near to us that we could the feathers profiled against the radiant sky. 'There!' he called again, as a second condor came to join the first, followed by a third and a fourth, their eyes glinting in the sun. For five minutes we stared disbelievingly as the condors repeatedly swooped down, hovered above us, glided away and then returned. They were giving us their Easter blessing. We felt reborn.

# 23

# VILLAGES OF THE
# RUNAWAY SLAVES

The tiny silhouette of an ancient steamship stood out against a vast blue sea. Our bus was pulling in to the town of Puno. The sea was Lake Titicaca. The steamship was the *Yavari*, built in Britain in 1861, shipped in pieces to the Peruvian port of Arica and carried across the Andes to the highest navigable lake in the world. In 1913 my grandfather Bethel had travelled to the lake from La Paz carrying a piece of equipment for the ship's repair.

The fleeting glimpse of the *Yavari* from the Arequipa bus made me feel as if I were coming home. Puno was the furthest place I had reached on my first trip to the Andes, when I had retraced my grandfather's footsteps. Puno was the northernmost boundary of Bethel's world for a critical period of his life. For four years he had gone backwards and forwards across the enormous high plateau that opens up near Puno, at the point where the Andes divide into two.

This world, the *altiplano*, had regularly featured in the bound copies Bethel had collected of the *National Geographic Magazine*. As a child I had pored over black-and-white photos of weather-beaten people fishing in reed boats unchanged since prehistoric times. I also read how the *altiplano* had drawn some of the earliest settlers to the Andes. The extent of its arable land and its great scope for grazing had once made it more attractive than lower areas with better soil, more rain and generally easier and less harsh conditions. Its minerals had made it more alluring still.

The minerals were indirectly the reason why my grandfather had come here. He was working for the British-owned railway company which transported them. Though he thought of himself as contributing to South America's glorious economic future, he was ultimately assisting the massive foreign exploitation of what the Uruguayan writer Eduardo Galeano has called the continent's 'open veins'. Pablo Neruda, on his journey to Peru in 1943, had not just discovered the wonders of Machu Picchu. He had also found out that the United States controlled eighty per cent of Peru's oil production and nearly all of its mineral output. The natural resources that should have been benefiting some of the poorest countries of the world were being siphoned off by the capitalist West.

The foreign companies which began moving into the *altiplano* from the late nineteenth century had merely been following the example of the Spaniards, whose expansion southwards from Cuzco had been hastened by the prospect of the minerals they might find there. In 1535 Diego de Almagro became the first person to lead an expedition through the *altiplano*, but he had moved on quickly to Chile and then returned to Cuzco to fight against the Pizarros. The Pizarros, after beheading Almagro early in 1538, were left with the colonization of the *altiplano*, which they made the original nucleus of what later became the Audiencia de Charcas or Upper Peru and, later still, Bolivia. In 1538 in a temperate valley on the south-eastern edge of the *altiplano*, the Spaniards founded the regional capital of La Plata. Seven years later, in the bleak highlands just to the west of this town, they discovered at Potosí silver deposits which – when mined by forced Indian labour – would provide much of the wealth of the Spanish empire.

Potosí became a synonym for fabled riches and Spanish cruelty. Many centuries earlier the minerals of the area had been integral to the prosperity of the Tiawanako civilization, whose empire came into being around AD 500, off the southern, Bolivian side of Lake Titicaca. Its capital of Tiawanako was lavishly encrusted in gold and silver, and within sight of the two most sacred places to this civilization – the lake itself and Mount Illimani. The people who lived there managed the difficult conditions of the *altiplano* by an elaborate irrigation system that recent agriculturalists have been trying to reproduce. However, a series of droughts in the twelfth century seems to have defeated them, and the Tiawanako civilization died out.

The tough and resilient Aymara people moved in from the east. The Aymara language was one of the few Andean languages to resist attempts by the Incas and the Spaniards to suppress it. The Aymara are still the dominant race of the *altiplano*. Bolivian president Evo Morales is an Aymara. Morales has raised hopes of an end to centuries of discrimination against the indigenous people of

'Quaint Picture of the Toilers in the Mines of Potosi', from Gottfried's
*Historia Antipodum*, 1655

the Andes and has tried to ensure that foreign companies will no longer be allowed to exploit his country. His inauguration ceremony in the ruins of Tiawanako played on visions of a return to the greatest and purest period in Bolivia's Andean past.

I had not been back to Bolivia since Morales's election. I was impatient to see what had happened to the country, and to the friends I had made there. Chris had a plane to catch from La Paz in a few days' time. Neither of us was keen to stay any longer than necessary in Puno, which looked, under bright sunlight, even uglier than I had remembered it. The sun accentuated its resemblance to a waste tip of dirty brown boxes washed up by the lake.

In the old days we could have travelled on into Bolivia by the combination of steamer and train. The stretch of railway between the tiny Bolivian port of Guaqui and La Paz passes right through Tiawanako. Few people, perhaps not even Evo Morales, seem to be aware that the construction of the line led to considerable damage and alterations to the site, with some of its stones even being pounded into gravel. The ancient Gate of the Sun, under which Morales's ceremony took place, does not owe its present location to ancient esoteric calculations relating to the summer solstice, but to the whims of my grandfather's colleagues.

We continued towards Bolivia on the first available bus. The arrival of the dry season had greatly increased the number of tourists. The bus to the lakeside town of Copacabana was full of backpackers whom we recognized from Machu Picchu, including two avid British readers of *Driving Over Lemons* and a bearded young Argentinean of more serious literary tastes.

The Argentinean, in whom I saw something of the young Che Guevara, was someone whom I would continually meet again, as I aimed south towards Patagonia. He too had been travelling from the northern Andes, coinciding with the same like-minded spirits at different stages of his route, finding sometimes that they had the same friends in common. Buses had become his permanent home and he could not imagine what life would be like when his journey ended. I was beginning to feel the same.

I remained gazing at Lake Titicaca, which our bus was following into Bolivia. Even under a clear late-afternoon sky, the lake's unnaturally blue waters seemed to extend indefinitely. Only as we neared the Bolivian border did I realize that some faint clouds above the distant watery horizon were in fact the snows of the Illimani range, the Cordillera Real. I was still looking at them an hour later as the bus arrived at Copacabana, where Chris and I were going to spend the night. Before reaching La Paz, the least peaceful of cities, we were hoping to have a couple of restful days by the shores of the lake. I still had an ambition to visit the Island of the Sun, one of the most famous ancient Andean sanctuaries.

I had stayed for a few hours at Copacabana during my first, rainy visit to Titicaca, the weather so stormy that all boats to the island had been cancelled. After returning to Bolivia in 2005 to lead a small tour group around the country, I had included the island as a major feature on the programme, but then the volatile political situation in Bolivia had intervened.

We had been caught up in the near-revolution that would eventually bring Morales to power. Bolivia's history had always been unstable, with few of its presidents lasting more than a few years before being ousted by coups or mass protests. But tensions had worsened considerably since the discovery in the 1990s of large reserves of natural gas, which the Bolivians feared would be sold off by their leaders. Bolivia's indigenous majority had little reason to trust its presidents, who tended to belong to an elite group of interrelated families of European origin, some of whom were linked to drug traffickers and even to war criminals such as the Nazi Klaus Barbie.

In October 2005, a few months before my first stay in Bolivia, riots in La Paz against President Gonzalo Sánchez de Lozada had resulted in the deaths of sixty-five protesters. 'Goni' had fled the country. He was replaced by his popular vice-president Carlos

Mesa, a second-generation Bolivian. Though his family half-owned the Bolivian media, he was honest and uncorrupt. His main problems were that he was too weak and too much of an intellectual.

When I arrived with my tour group in 2005, Mesa was facing the same situation as Goni. La Paz had been cut off from the rest of the country by roadblocks. Fortunately we had flown directly from Europe to the lowland city of Santa Cruz and would not be reaching La Paz until near the end of our trip. But the troubles rapidly spread to the rest of the country. Our bus was attacked by stick-waving *campesinos* shortly after leaving Santa Cruz. We finally left Santa Cruz after a pre-dawn rush to the airport.

We managed to fly to Sucre, and then we were stuck. The whole country was paralysed. I knew that Mesa had no other choice than to resign, after which the country would soon be back to normal. After some extremely tense moments, that was more or less what happened.

When we were finally able to move on from Sucre, we were almost the only tourists left in Bolivia. Unfortunately we then had to speed around the country to make up for lost time. I promised everyone in compensation a relaxing last day on the Island of the Sun. But we never even made it to Copacabana. The direct road there from La Paz involves a short ferry crossing. The people operating the service had gone on strike.

I was telling all this to Chris as we strolled towards sunset on Copacabana's beach, whose background of terraced fields and a volcanic hill had been invisible on my first visit. I could now almost recognize the town as the place with the 'sunny, Italian charm' described by Isherwood. I could not imagine politics disturbing its peacefulness.

And nothing prevented us from sailing off the next morning to the Island of the Sun, with its widely dispersed ruins of the sanctuary which the Incas had built to celebrate their origins on Lake Titicaca, while usurping much earlier cults. The Spaniards had in turn exploited the area's pilgrimage associations by founding on the mainland a shrine to the Virgin of Copacabana, which would become so venerated that the Virgin's name would later be given to Brazil's most famous beach. The island, without its Inca pilgrims, had declined into a place of poor farming communities living today off tourists and the cultivation of its once-sacred and highly sought-after maize.

We spent a day and a night on the island, walking from one end to the other. The Inca structures, after nearly half a millennium of being despoiled by villagers and grave robbers, were more atmospheric than impressive. But the ridge-top walk to the island's tapering and more sacred northern point made you fully conscious of the area's strange beauty. People often talk about the island's Mediterranean character, but the bare green slopes falling down to rocky bays of the deepest blue reminded me strongly of the Cornish coast. Then I looked eastwards across the lake, and was back again in the Andes. There lay the snowy range of the Cordillera Real, floating in the far distance above the ultramarine waters. It was indicating the direction of our next destination.

Off the eastern shores of the lake lived one of the Italian priests whom we had met at Chacas, Padre Leonardo. He was a tall smiling man whose portliness and auburn hair gave him an appropriately leonine appearance.

Padre Leonardo intrigued me. A keen traveller, a lover of mountains and an intimate of Bolivia, he had been based for the past ten years in a part of the country which tourists have tended to avoid. The eastern side of Lake Titicaca is no less beautiful than the western one, but it has an off-putting reputation as the heartland of Aymara extremism and the place where most of Bolivia's recent disturbances have begun.

The bus from Copacabana to La Paz left Chris and me on the outskirts of the village of Huarina, where Padre Leonardo gave catechism classes once week at a school run by Belgian nuns. As he drove us to his home village of Santiago de Huata, he told us of the pleasures and frustrations of working in the *altiplano*. The Bolivians in general, he said, were exceptionally kind, hard-working and respectful, yet he was always battling with stubbornness and resistance to new ideas.

He talked about the area's history of outbursts of intense anarchy and violence and had got on to some of the more disturbing stories by the time we reached the town of Achacachi, the most notoriously rebellious of all the *altiplano*'s communities. The name came back to me from the newspapers I had pored over during my last stay in Bolivia. This was the very town whose protests in 2005 had sparked off Mesa's downfall. Like so many places in the *altiplano*, it was an ugly chaos of redbrick cubes, mainly unfinished, some painted in fluorescent colours, others daubed with political slogans and the tattered shreds of posters. It was near evening and everyone was out on the streets, the men with their baseball caps, the women with their many-layered skirts and miraculously balanced bowler hats.

This was a town without a police force, said Padre Leonardo, a town completely under the control of its councillors, who meted out all justice. Achacachi was Padre Leonardo's nearest large town. I wondered if he had ever felt threatened as a European Catholic priest in a highly militant Aymara area. He said that up until now he had generally been regarded as a force of good. The small religious centre he ran at Santiago de Huata provided the best medical service in the area, helped the very poor and looked after orphans. Many people came to him when they were in need of help.

At the time when every major road in the country was closed off by protestors, he had managed to cross the blockades to bring back necessary medical and other supplies to the village. These emergency missions had not always been successful. Once he had volunteered to carry a dangerously ill and pregnant young woman to hospital but the two of them had been dragged out of the car and threatened with violence. Padre Leonardo had urged the attackers to direct their anger onto him. 'Kill me if you like,' he had pleaded, 'but spare this poor woman, and take her to hospital. Otherwise she might die, and you will have on your consciences the death of one of your own, an Aymara sister.' But he and the woman were forced to drive back to Santiago de Huata. The woman died. His village was situated on a hilly peninsula. Instead of going straight there across the hill, he took us on the 'scenic route' along the lake's shores. 'Whenever I get depressed,' said Padre Leonardo, 'there's always the landscape to turn to.'

Padre Leonardo seemed a cheerful person, particularly on arrival at his village, which was set back slightly from the lake between fields and a steep green hill. The Salesian community he ran was like a miniature version of the one at Chacas, homely, spotlessly clean and manned by adoring parishioners, grateful orphans and friendly young Italian volunteers. With his circle of admirers at Santiago de Huata, as with the nuns and pupils at Huarina, I noticed how Padre Leonardo had adopted a priestly, paternalistic manner full of bonhomie; but alone again with Chris and me, he revealed a more human and vulnerable side. He spoke of an Italian woman with whom he had a 'deep friendship'. He referred ambiguously to events in Italy that had almost made him leave the priesthood. But Bolivia had saved him and given a sense of purpose to his life. He insisted he would never be able to return to Italy. He needed the rural simplicity of Santiago de Huata. He needed to feel wanted. He was another escapist, another Andean dreamer.

The moment he rose from his chair and led us into the dining-room he became once more the admired priest. His acolytes were sitting waiting for us around a sturdy table. He stood to say grace at its head. I prayed that we were about to receive mozzarella and pasta and copious quantities of good Italian wine. Instead we were given glasses of water, bread that almost broke your teeth and broth with a few bones in it. Padre Leonardo repeatedly teased a bearded young Italian called Paolo, and got him later to go and fetch a guitar. We took it in turn to sing some songs. The only one I could think of was the Italian communist anthem '*Bandiera Rossa*'. Padre Leonardo rewarded the six of us who had stayed on to the end with a thimbleful of marsala from a long-opened bottle.

The next day, after Padre Leonardo had given us a lift to Achacuchi, we found ourselves competing for seats on *colectivos* in a square heaving with students returning home on a Friday afternoon to La Paz and its former satellite district of El Alto. We joined forces with four of them, who proved more successful than we were at pushing and bartering.

We moved on into the chaos of El Alto, an hour's drive away, a place that was like Achacuchi but a hundred times bigger. It had grown in twenty years from a satellite district into a city of nearly a million inhabitants. It was a completely unplanned sprawl; its population was almost exclusively Aymara; it was the site of La Paz's airport; and it controlled the main road into La Paz. The traffic congestion in El Alto was always so bad that you needed a full hour to get through it. On a couple of occasions it had taken me six hours.

A Bavarian priest who was also an architect had recently had the brilliant idea of constructing a series of tall belfries of fantastical appearance throughout El Alto. They provided employment, raised the spirit and gave you something to look at while stuck in traffic. They also lightened the transition between the prosaic ugliness of El Alto and the first astonishing sight of La Paz, when the flat *altiplano* is brusquely wrested apart as if by Moses's rod and a sublime valley is revealed below you, fantastically fissured and cragged, guarded by the snowy god of Illimani, and descending towards eroded peaks resembling gnarled and colossal fingers. The view made Isherwood gasp. To my grandfather it was a glimpse into a world of fairy tales.

The sense of exhilaration I had felt on my first visit to La Paz in 2004 came back to me now, as we plunged from El Alto into the snowballing chaos of a city whose main unifying feature was a central thoroughfare leading from the indigenous upper slums into the more temperate lower depths where the wealthy live. Somewhere in the middle was the colonial town founded by the Spaniards as a staging post between Potosí and the coast, but the little that was left of this was engulfed by a blight of high-rise structures in competing styles from twenties neo-baroque to fifties functionalism, the whole clashing mix enlivened by the atmosphere of a giant marketplace. From streets clogged with a solid flow of buses, taxis and Japanese-made *micros* came the shouts of drivers' assistants precariously leaning out of doors and screaming out their destinations. Along the pavements were armies of sinisterly hooded shoeshine boys, salesmen of every kind, stalls of pirated films and music, squatting country women with maize kernels and potatoes, and men with mobile phones strapped to their wrists with chains.

My impressions of La Paz had always been imbued with the strangeness of its fairy-tale setting. It had satinwood-panelled coffee houses straight from Central Europe, with white-jacketed waiters and elderly men who looked variously like Jewish refugees or Nazi fugitives (post-war La Paz had welcomed all-comers). I had become a regular at a gloomy late-night bar whose owner had psychic powers and a love of Hitler. I had spent time with the impoverished son of a Scottish mining engineer, who had known Che Guevara when he lived incognito in La Paz prior to his execution in the Bolivian jungle. I had wandered, like all tourists, through the city's central 'Witch's Market', where I had stared at llama foetuses and acquired numerous talismans to protect me on my travels.

After Chris and I finally alighted in the very heart of La Paz, I could see that he was as absorbed as I had once been by the city's surreal and hectic blend of western and Aymara, urban and rural elements. My main reason now for spending any time in the city was to meet some old friends and perhaps persuade them to come for a few days to the nearby tropical district of the Yungas. I hoped also to glean something of the changes Bolivia had undergone under Morales.

*

The friend I wanted to see more than anyone was Marbel Garrón, a woman I had got to know in 2005. I had met her and her Chilean husband on the weekly passenger train that ran between Calama in Chile and the *altiplano* junction town of Uyuni. After a disturbed night in a crowded and unheated carriage, I had woken at dawn in a still and translucent world of bare volcanoes tipped with snow, one of them emitting gentle puffs of smoke. We were approaching the Bolivian border and I had got talking with Marbel and her husband. Marbel, with her long black hair, dark make-up and large dark-brown eyes, resembled a benign witch. Her impassive expression belied an animated personality. She was full of life and enthusiasm. She and her husband invited me to her home town of Sucre, where she was finishing her law studies. The last time I had seen them there was in June 2005, when the town had virtually been under siege.

Marbel was now separated from her husband and working in a tiny law firm in La Paz. Her two small children were with her parents in Sucre. She was living with her law partner Pablo. She would not hear of Chris and me staying anywhere in La Paz but with them. She arranged to meet us at her office in a huge 1950s complex.

The Marbel who greeted us was different from the Marbel I had known. Slimmer and smartly dressed, with a sleek new hairstyle, she was with a man who looked fifteen years younger than her. Pablo, her current boyfriend, was short, with Brylcreemed black hair and a three-piece pinstriped suit. He was friendly and sincere, but like a hyperactive teenager, constantly playing with his mobile and listening to an i-pod. Within ten minutes he had taught me the new vogue Bolivian term, '*full*'. Based presumably on a misunderstanding of English, it had the same meaning as the Colombian word '*chévere*'. The closest English equivalent was 'cool'.

Marbel and Pablo lived in a quiet residential district of modest villas halfway between the city centre and the luxurious American-style district of the Zona Sur. No sooner had we got there than

Pablo was proposing a *full* night on the town. Marbel knew me as a lover of bars. She had retained her taste for karaoke, mysteriously one of the most popular of Bolivian entertainments. We were also going to be joined later by another friend from that period, Silvia. Chris was not so excited by the prospect, and decided to stay behind. It was his last night in South America and he wanted to spend it quietly assimilating a journey he was already describing as one of the most memorable he had ever undertaken.

Silvia turned up late at the first bar. The background music was still quiet enough to allow us to have a proper talk. A proper talk revealed everyone's recent crises and tragedies. The break-up of Marbel's marriage had brought on a period of deep depression, which had coincided with her father's falling seriously ill. Silvia's father, meanwhile, had been robbed and murdered in his home in El Alto. Even Pablo was still in shock from a recent terrible event. 'A cousin of his was travelling on a bus in the Yungas,' said Marbel. 'It went over a cliff.'

We finished the night at a genuinely *full* club in the Zona Sur where I was certainly the oldest person. Pablo introduced me to a giggling and nerdy friend of his from his schooldays. The friend and I had to scream to make ourselves understood over the deafening music. He told me he worked in the Bolivian Parliament as assistant to Morales's new 'Master of Ceremonies' and that he would be happy to set up an interview with him.

My interview with the Embajador Cancio Mamani López, the Master of Ceremonies, was scheduled for the day after Chris's departure for Europe. I arrived with two hours to spare at the green and pleasant Plaza Murillo, at the heart of the city's peaceful old town. I wanted to revisit a former colonial palace on the opposite side of the square to the Parliament building which now housed Bolivia's National Museum of Art.

I went straight to the works of the greatest artist in its collection, the eighteenth-century Potosí artist Melchor Pérez Holguín. Holguín was a more powerful painter than any of the artists I had seen of the Cuzco and Quito schools. His style was the opposite of El Greco's: his mystics and saints were small squat figures with over-sized heads. He was said to have been a dwarf himself. He was certainly a mestizo. The few facts that are known about him had been brought together in a book by the parents of former president Carlos Mesa, a couple who had once virtually monopolized art history in Bolivia.

The paintings of one of Carlos Mesa's daughters had under-standably been removed since my last visit, to make way for a ragbag collection of nineteenth- and twentieth-century paintings and sculptures of predominantly Andean, *indigenista* and anti-colonial subject-matter. What particularly struck me were the numerous references to nature and the earth mother, Pachamama. Of all the Andean countries, Bolivia was the one most obsessed with the Pachamama.

The Spaniards themselves had recognized this. One of the new didactic panels in the museum reproduced a famous painting from seventeenth-century Potosí in which the Virgin Mary undergoes a pagan transformation: the artist did this by turning the Virgin's pro-tective cape into the silver mountain from which Potosí's wealth was derived, the Cerro Rico.

An English anthropologist working in La Paz's Aymara Institute had taught me in 2004 a new word for the current mania for the Pachamama – *pachamamismo*. She told me that the indigenous worship of the Pachamama had been taken up by increasing num-bers of western sociologists, anthropologists and tourists. *Pachamamismo*, according to her, had diverted many intellectuals away from serious indigenous issues such as discrimination and lack of access to education.

The National Museum of Art was more enjoyable now than it had been in Mesa's time, but perhaps for the wrong reasons. *Indigenismo* and *pachamamismo* had led to the salvaging from the museum's storeroom of numerous examples of high kitsch, such as a 1928 painting called *The Triumph of Nature*. The painter, Cecilio Guzmán de Rojas, was described as one of a group of pioneering artists who had 'rewritten national history to include the country's indigenous legacy'. He had achieved this by portraying the earth mother as a seductive young nude resting against one of the statues of Tiawanako. Behind her was a naked Michelangelo-inspired male in a desperate pose, as if he had failed her in some unforgivable way.

By now two hours had pleasantly passed by. I left the museum and walked towards my meeting with Morales's Master of Ceremonies. The Plaza Murillo looked deceptively peaceful, like a corner of old Paris. Yet some of the most violent incidents in recent Bolivian history had taken place here. A few years before Isherwood's arrival in the city, President Gualberto Villaroel had been dragged by an irate mob out of his palace and hanged from one of the square's belle époque lamp posts. A few months before my 2005 visit, President Gonzalez Sánchez de Lozada had made his narrow escape by helicopter from the palace's rooftop.

The Master of Ceremonies' assistant was waiting for me. He made me promise to keep a straight face on entering his boss's office. He wouldn't explain why. The Embajador Cancio Mamani López was wearing a striped red-and-blue indigenous jacket that clashed delightfully with the formality of the grey neoclassical setting. Unfortunately he was not a man of many words. I was also under the erroneous impression that he had had been responsible for devising Morales's inauguration ceremony in Tiawanako, which was the main reason I had wanted to speak to him.

'No,' he said, 'the inauguration took place before I was appointed.' He gave a faint smile and lapsed into silence.

Pablo's friend was looking at me fixedly, waiting for my next move. I asked Mamani López what his job entailed. He began talking about the Arch of the Temple of the Sun in Cuzco. I was not quite sure why, until I realized that a reproduction of this arch was now used to receive visiting dignitaries to La Paz.

While he spoke, I noticed out of the corner of my eye a strange altar with offerings laid out on a marble Empire-style table. Pablo's friend caught me doing this and flashed me a grin.

Mamani López had now broadened the conversation to discuss indigenous aspirations in general and to outline his theory that Andean history had been characterized by three periods in which the indigenous peoples of the continent had all come together. The 'first unification' happened 30,000 years ago, during the time of an Andean civilization I had never even heard of, the Tunupa civilization. All I knew about Tunupa was that he was the Aymara god of creation and was embodied by a volcano near Oruro. The 'second unification' was the Tiawanako civilization, and the third was under the Incas. He was about to elaborate on this theory when a delegation from Sucre came into the room. They were organizing a cultural event that required Mamani López's advice.

Mamani López suggested we all gather for a moment in front of the altar, where he took out from his pocket a bag of coca leaves. After placing a few of them on the table, he distributed some more among us. We started chewing them as he pointed out to me the various offerings from all over the world, including some North American tobacco. He explained the symbolism of a carving of a frog and a snake. They had something to do with energy. The altar itself of course was in honour of the Pachamama, whom he described as not just the mother of the earth but also 'the mother of the Andes'. Pablo's friend, seeing the serious look on my face, bit his lip to control himself.

Before turning his full attention to the delegation, Mamani López completed his theory of Andean history: a fourth unification was imminent and this time the indigenous peoples of the Andes needed to take the interests of nature more to heart. Nature needed to be saved from all the harm to which humankind was subjecting it: 'Without nature we are nothing.'

I was very much in agreement with him. He said that he was now devoting much of his days to preparing for the fourth unification.

He added with a smile that he was taking things easy since he had until 2032. I was puzzled at first, until I realized that 2032 would be the fifth centenary of Pizarro's arrival in the Andes.

I had been to the Yungas once before, at the end of my ill-fated tour around Bolivia the year the country fell apart. After announcing to my group that a ferry strike made it impossible to continue on to Copacabana and the Island of the Sun, I had to come up with an enticing alternative. Our Bolivian guide suggested the idyllic Yungas town of Coroico. He assured me that it was just a short drive from La Paz, now that a new and safe road there had finally been opened.

The new road had been completed, but it had also just been closed. In darkness and rain we took the old unpaved road that had been hastily built in 1931 to transport Bolivian troops to a disastrous war with Paraguay. It was dubbed 'the most dangerous road in the world'. It had sheer drops of over a thousand metres and had to go under a waterfall, but it was probably no more dangerous as a piece of engineering than many others in the Andes. The dangers were the result of its having once been the main route between the *altiplano* and the Amazon, and between the Pacific and Brazil. Overloaded lorries continually had to back up to let others pass. Nearly a thousand vehicles went over the edge between 1999 and 2005.

My group had behaved with remarkable calm over the past fortnight, but the so-called 'Road of Death' proved too much for almost all of them. When we reached our hotel at ten o'clock at night, faces were ashen and irate. I was accused of being utterly irresponsible. The Bolivian guide told me not to worry. When our clients saw the view the next morning, he said, they would have no regrets.

He was right about the view. I felt as if I had woken up in a painting by Frederick Church. Lush jungle vegetation formed a dark carpet of green rising up all the way up to the pink-white peaks we had come from. This was the paradise view that Andean travellers after Humboldt had searched for.

Memories of that view had influenced my desire to return to the Yungas. It would be my last glimpse of a tropical Eden before heading south first into desert and then into the increasingly Nordic landscapes that extended to the tip of Patagonia. But there was a more specific reason for wanting to come here. During my one morning in Coroico I had been sitting in the palm-shaded main square when a group of women had passed by, carrying clothes and other goods presumably bound for the local market. They were wearing the typical costume of Bolivian *cholas* or mestizas: the long pleated skirt or *pollera* that the Spaniards had forcibly introduced (and which now had become a symbol of indigenous pride), the four or five obligatory under-skirts, and the bowler hat whose origins are said to derive from a cheap job-lot sold off by a British merchant in La Paz. They were already walking away from me when I saw them. But one of them turned round to greet a friend. She was completely African in appearance.

Seeing her confirmed what I had been told but did not quite believe: that the Yungas still harboured descendents of African slaves who had run away from the mines of Potosí. Potosí was not a place I intended going back to on my current journey through the Andes. I had spent enough time there in 2005, visiting its magnificent colonial buildings, descending into its horrific mines and confronting one of the most notorious chapters in the history of western exploitation of South America's indigenous peoples. This time in Bolivia I was more interested in a subject often treated as a footnote in Potosí's appalling history: the story of the thousands of black slaves who were sent to work there and who were now almost entirely forgotten. Their fate seemed to me even more terrible than that of the thousands of indigenous Andeans forced by the mita system to leave their homelands. I wondered how much of their culture and memory survived in the Yungas today.

*

To get from La Paz to Coroico by public transport was easy; to get to some of the small villages and hamlets known for their black populations was going to be more difficult, but at the very last moment Pablo got hold of an unemployed friend to drive me there. This friend, a smiling young man with a round shaved head, was called Nelson. He was the perfect person to accompany me to 'the villages of the runaway slaves'. The son of a leading feminist and anthropologist, he had a bookish background and a taste for adventure. He had a particular love of the Yungas, from where four of his past girlfriends had come. All four were of African origin.

We headed straight for Coroico. We climbed in sunshine up to the bare snowy peaks above La Paz and then began our descent into the jungle. The new road had now been open for some time, but we passed a large group of tourists on the point of indulging in the adventure sport of cycling down the old one. Landslides had been a major problem with the new road requiring a hugely costly solution whereby the less stable slopes had been held to the mountain by giant pins. The views were far less spectacular than those on the Road of Death but I was glad to reach paradise quickly and alive.

Coroico and its setting were as astonishingly sensual as I had remembered, but my eyes and imagination kept turning this time towards the east and the mountainous jungle that stretched into Amazonia. Across the deep river valley below us, between gaps in vegetation splashed with agapanthus, jasmine, amaryllis, dalias, banana palms and yellow lilies, we could make out the tiny scattered community of Tocaña, where we aimed to spend the night. It was one of the better known of the Yungas' African villages. It had also played an important part in the revival of the Afro-Bolivian music known as *Saya*.

Before leaving Coroico, Nelson wanted to get in touch with friends and acquaintances, for contacts and information about Tocaña and other places we intended to see. We managed to track down one of Nelson's exes when her school classes were over for the day. She could not have been much older than seventeen. She said that we should speak to her uncle Vicente in Tocaña. He was the president of the local Saya Asociation.

Nelson played me Saya music as we drove off through the jungle towards Tocaña. He said it was essentially dance music incorporating African, Aymara and Spanish influences. Though the harsh chanting accompanying the hysterical pounding of drums was in Spanish, the music itself sounded completely African. Nelson explained that with growing Afro-Bolivian pride, ever purer forms of Saya were being performed. The music, shorn of its more sentimental and harmonious elements, was becoming very fashionable in the alternative clubs of La Paz.

Tocaña was a straggling community of about fifteen humble houses sheltering among trees near the top of a mountain. The track running through it was so rutted and muddy that we had to abandon our car and walk. At the far end of the village was a house slightly grander than the others, with a weather-worn balustrade overlooking the view towards Coroico. We had been told that this house put up visitors, but the building, like the rest of the village, seemed deserted. We eventually found a woman who showed us to a room that had been occupied for several years by an Italian priest.

By dusk the villagers had begun returning from the fields. Vicente's house of wooden planks and corrugated iron lay just below the track. Nelson shouted out his name from where we were. A tall black man appeared. Nelson introduced himself as a friend of Vicente's niece and said that he was with someone who had come all the way from Spain to interview him. Vicente saw a good opportunity for a night of drinking. He arranged to meet us at the village's only store.

The store sold little else but bottles of beer kept cool in a barrel of water. We sat on wooden crates under a collapsing portico. Vicente was funny and friendly, and continually punctuated the conversation by slapping his hands against ours. He thought his family might originally have been from the Congo. To ensure the beer would continue to flow he tried supplying me with tidbits about his African background, but there was nothing very much he could tell me. He told me about funeral and marriage rites that might have some connection with the traditions of his ancestors. However, the only certain legacy of his roots was Saya. Giving Nelson a wink, he said this was 'very popular with young people and anthropologists'.

He still enjoyed playing the drums, but he had just resigned as local president of what he called the '*Movimiento cultural Saya Afroboliviano*'. A few minutes later the society's new president, David, walked past us along the darkened track. Vicente called him over. David, a man whose Africans roots were not apparent, had a suspicious and taciturn look. He nodded his head as Vicente explained that most of the young Afro-Bolivians from the Yungas had moved to La Paz in the past few years. Some of them supplemented their earnings or helped finance their studies by playing Saya in the city's clubs. David broke his silence by offering to sell me the CD of dance music I had listened to in Nelson's car. On my paying him a fee, he said he would be happy to show us the new headquarters of the local Saya Association in the morning.

We met up with him just after dawn, to walk down a jungle path to a field planted with coca, the main crop of the Yungas. The Centro Cultural Afroboliviano stood at the edge of this, a modern brick building. David took out some photos of young smiling black women dancing with bowler hats and white *polleras*. There was also a locked cupboard with a dozen or so articles relating to Afro-Bolivian history.

I skimmed through a long document of 1596 in which the city authorities of Potosí explained to the new Peruvian viceroy, Luis de Velasco, that the quota of indigenous labour provided by the mita system was now insufficient to extract the minerals from the mines. They urgently requested the purchase of four thousand black slaves from Brazil.

Having spent just a few hours in the Potosí mines as a tourist, I could imagine their fate: they would have suffered from violent changes of temperature, crawling along muddy passages, breathing fetid and dusty air, wondering when they would be struck by a falling rock or overcome by poisonous gases. A Spanish historian of 1701 had written about people who had entered out of curiosity 'that horrible labyrinth' and had come out 'totally robbed of colour, grinding their teeth and unable to pronounce a word'.

David told me of a local woman directly descended from one of the few who had escaped. Her name was Angelina Pereiro Pedrero and she was eighty-seven years old. David thought our only chance of speaking to her would be if we offered her money. He himself had to get back to his work in the fields, but he showed us the path leading to her isolated home among the trees. We found her standing in a garden full of discarded tins and bones.

We sat on a log listening to her as she talked incessantly, sitting on a precarious stool. Her only child still left in the Yungas, an unmarried son whom she thought to be in his fifties or sixties, was out in the fields and she had to prepare some food for him. Her other six children had all left, four had gone to Canada, the others were in La Paz, but they were too busy to come and see her. She had twenty grandchildren and five great-grandchildren. She had seen none of the latter and hardly any of the former. 'That's life,' she said. 'You spend your best years raising and caring for others, and then they all abandon you, and you end up on your own.'

She had a taut mat of white hair, a slight limp and ankles that were gnarled, bluish and veined. I asked about her ancestors. She said that her grandfather used to tell her as a child that her family had been 'stolen' many centuries ago from a country in Africa whose name she could not remember. I tried prompting her. Guinea? Angola? Senegal? 'Yes, that's it, Senegal. Or was it Guinea? But does it really matter? It was all so long ago. They were stolen, that's what's important. They were taken to Brazil. They were taken to the Andes. They were taken to a place that was so high that they couldn't breathe and were always ill and shivering. And one of them decided he would rather run away and be punished and killed than die slowly in this place that wasn't meant for humans. So they came here, and worked on the coca plantations.'

She said that her family had cultivated coca leaves for as long as anyone could remember. When they had been given their own land in the 1950s they had tried to grow bananas, oranges and coffee, but now everyone in the village grew only coca. I tried to get her back to the subject of her ancestors, but she said she had too many stories and didn't have the time to tell me them. I asked her instead about surviving ancestral traditions in the village. There weren't any, she said, except for music. 'But Saya,' she added, 'is not the same as it used to be. When I was young there were other instruments, not just drums. There were bells and maracas. Today it's all loud beating, and little else.'

Antonia was the oldest person we would meet in the Yungas and the one with the closest link to her ancestral past. As we meandered south through the region, we learnt little more about the Afro-Bolivians other than that most of them had now emigrated. The most eloquent of our informants was Don Ricardo Casto, an elderly man of Spanish descent who lived in a world straight out of a Márquez novel. We had reached his village of Pacha after a long day's drive from Tocaña. Sloping fields of coca, glowing in the sun, had added to the intense green of foregrounds now backed by mountains of increasing aridity; thousands of leaves of coca had been spread out to dry on quiet village streets, forming a beautiful barrier that cars crawled pass. I had taken many photos of the fields and the leaves, and once I had been spotted doing so by two blond bearded men in khaki trousers. I was sure they were drug traffickers and I soon became convinced they were following us, perhaps taking me for an undercover CIA agent.

Their car was far behind us as we climbed up the high ridge which Pacha straddled. Nelson remembered that a friend of his had been living there for the past few months, looking after Don Ricardo, who had a large estate on the outskirts of the village. We shook off our pursuers as we left the road and drove through the gates of Don Ricardo's property. Nelson's friend, delighted by our unexpected arrival, closed the gates behind us and said there would be no problem with our staying.

The first thing that struck me about the estate was its panoramic view over banana palms and orchards of oranges towards faraway mountains now slowly being hidden by red wispy clouds. The second was of its appalling state of decay. Its fields and orchards were barely tended, and the main building overpowered you with smells of putrefaction and animal urine and the sight of a lifetime of accumulated rubbish. The room where we were going to sleep had stained damp mattresses, numerous birds' nests (some still being used) and a surreal collection of straw hats adorned with feathers, shells and other objects.

Turkeys ranged the interior, as did a baby deer, adopted by Don Ricardo after its mother was shot by hunters. Don Ricardo told me this and many other stories as we sat talking by candlelight in the company of two women schoolteachers from a neighbouring village. Don Ricardo enjoyed the company of women. He still had a sparkle in his eye even though he could hardly walk and his elongated face had the appearance of bleached parchment. He was not originally from the Yungas, he told me. He had spent his childhood and youth in Potosí, where his father had worked as a mining engineer. There he had known the family of a once-celebrated but now largely forgotten French-born engineer and entrepreneur, Louis Soux, a friend of my grandfather's. He had uncovered at Potosí one of the supposedly lost herbariums of the French botanist Joseph de Jussieu, a member of the Geodesic Expedition who had stayed on in South America for a further thirty-six years.

History and natural history were his life-long interests, although after 1947, when he had moved to Pacha, he had made a living as the owner and founder of what had once been the only radio station in the Yungas. In those days the Yungas seemed completely cut off from the rest of the world. The jungle extended everywhere; the rains never stopped; and the road to La Paz, a two-day ride away, was regularly blocked by falling snow at the top of the pass. People lived in the Yungas beyond the control of the law, including the notoriously cruel governor of the province, a man known by the nickname of 'Mucho Gallo' – 'Much Cock' (in other words, 'very cocky'). Mucho Gallo kept a jaguar which was often fed on the disobedient prisoners employed in road building. Those who saw the prisoners being slowly torn apart by the jaguar shat themselves in fear. Mucho Gallo was eventually thrown to the jaguar himself.

Don Ricardo paused to ask Nelson's friend to pass around a bottle of aquavit, which he described as his necessary '*combustible*'. Then he started talking about the people to whom he referred by the politically incorrect term '*negritos*'.

In his time, he said, the *negritos* of the Yungas barely mixed with the whites. However, he became fascinated by their history and customs, then so little known to the world at large. As someone brought up in the cruel environment of Potosí, he could fully understand the plight of those wrested from Africa and forced immediately to work in freezing temperatures and at an altitude of nearly four thousand metres. Thousands of blacks died within months of arriving at Potosí. The only way of surviving was to try and leave. According to Don Ricardo, very few slaves from Potosí actually managed to flee. The majority of those who made it to the Yungas did so by exchanging slavery in the mines for slavery in the coca plantations. Slavery in Bolivia had lasted well into the late nineteenth century and only after the Agricultural Reform Act of 1954 did the blacks get their own lands.

Don Ricardo claimed to be one of the first Bolivians to have taken an interest in Saya and seen its commercial possibilities. In 1974 he had led a group of Saya musicians from the Yungas to the carnival at Oruro, where they had won first prize and been invited to La Paz. He had had to finance their first journey himself, but now he began to receive offers of sponsorship from the once utterly uninterested Yungas government. He told the authorities to go to hell. The blacks, he stressed, needed to promote their own music and win the recognition they deserved. But he feared he would not be around much longer to help them.

I left La Paz almost as soon as I got back there, to travel south to Oruro, the present starting point of what Paul Theroux has described as 'one of South America's great trains'. Marbel and Pablo insisted on accompanying me to the Argentinean border. Pablo wanted to bring along his mother. Marbel's friend Silvia offered to drive us to Oruro, together with her new husband and six-month-old baby. Only the mother was eventually dropped from this plan. We left La Paz predictably late and had to speed across a typically featureless stretch of *altiplano*. There were odd clusters of adobe houses, the occasional cultivated field and a flat, sharply lit void. There was nothing to break the view towards the first of the long row of snowy volcanoes separating Bolivia from the Atacama Desert.

The mining town of Oruro, beneath the greyish slopes on the opposite side of the *altiplano*, finally appeared before us in all its dusty ugliness. We were just in time to have lunch at a favourite restaurant of mine near the outlying railway station, but it was not a relaxing experience. Marbel and Pablo disappeared before sitting down, only to re-emerge a few minutes before we had to catch the train. Silvia profited from their absence by asking me to be a godfather to her son. I said I had no idea when I would be next in Bolivia and that I would be the most irresponsible of godfathers. She interpreted this as a yes. 'Goodbye, godfather!' she shouted as she and her husband stood on the railway platform waving us off, holding up their baby son, my new link to the Andean world.

The train glided past the shores of the Lake Poopó. As the light outside faded, and Marbel and Pablo fell asleep against each other, my mind wandered. The train journey ignited memories of my two earlier trips to Bolivia, which in turn made me think of my grandfather and of how this part of the Andes had so profoundly affected him. In his long and solitary months between the Atacama Desert and Oruro he lost the confidence and optimism with which he had embarked for South America in 1910. He began to question the values of his high-achieving, intellectually minded, Eurocentric ancestors, and was close to mental collapse. He was saved by being transferred to the green and spectacular Andean valley that descends from the *altiplano* towards the agricultural centre of Cochabamba. He had never known beauty on this scale. He was taught humility. As Europe headed rapidly to war, he began even to conceive a future married life in some simple Andean retreat far from the disintegrating world.

The railway line he had built between Oruro and Cochabamba had been abandoned by the time I visited Bolivia in 2004. I tried following its course with a cheerful Bolivian engineer. We crossed half-collapsing bridges, negotiated near-vertical slopes and found long stretches of track that had been mangled by falling boulders or swept into the river. We managed to escape by seconds from being caught up in a landslide that killed a few villagers who had been running behind us.

I had recovered afterwards in Bolivia's quiet official capital of Sucre (the former La Plata), a place with a temperate climate, a relaxing atmosphere and the character of an old university town, with colonial quadrangles, a park with a miniature version of the Eiffel Tower and grand buildings in a belle époque style.

I had known a different Sucre on my return the following year. The events of that year were vivid in my memory. I thought of them again near midnight, as our train stopped at Río Mulatto, the start of the branch line that had once led to Sucre by way of Potosí. I now found it difficult to dissociate those events from the signing in Sucre in August 1825 of one of the last major documents in the history of South America's battle for independence.

Soldiers had been assembling water cannons on Sucre's main square when I had taken my small group of tourists to the House of Liberty. We had made our nail-biting escape from Santa Cruz two days earlier. I had been relieved to arrive safely at a place of which

I had such pleasant memories and where there would be plenty to distract the group while the country's political situation stabilised. Our Bolivian guide Tito reckoned that this would take two or three days at the most. I reassured the group that Sucre was not like La Paz – it had no history of political extremism. We could be guaranteed, I said, a peaceful and enjoyable few days.

Carlos Mesa resigned on the evening of our arrival and everything would have gone smoothly had not his unpopular vice-president, Hormando Vaca Diez, chosen to stay on. An emergency meeting of Parliament was scheduled to be held in La Paz but was cancelled after Vaca Diez (suspected to be under orders from former president 'Goni') refused to make major political decisions while the city was under siege and fast running out of food supplies, medicines and petrol. The meeting was rescheduled for Sucre. Several politicians were expected to be put up at our hotel. Journalists dressed in khaki took over the computer room. Reports came of ten thousand miners marching towards us from Potosí bearing sticks of dynamite.

The House of Liberty was the only monument still open in Sucre on the day when the first politicians and miners were due to arrive. The building, originally a seventeenth-century Jesuit college, was the place where an independent Bolivia had officially come into being. The dignitaries had all gathered in the deconsecrated Jesuit church, a simple white structure. I succeeded in getting my group into the church, where they sat down in the nave. I stood in front of them, below a portrait of Bolívar which the Liberator himself had declared the best likeness ever done of him. I took the opportunity to talk about Bolívar's life. I concentrated on what had happened to him in the wake of Ayacucho.

Bolívar, I told my group, had not fought at Ayacucho, nor even believed that Sucre could win, but after the victory of December 1824 he had the world at his feet. For a while even those who had been opposed to him were united in his praise. He had sent his resignation as president to the congress of Colombia, but this had been turned down. He had attempted to resign from the presidency of Peru, but this too had been rejected by congress. Everyone still wanted him.

In the first months of 1825 he had stayed in Lima to engage in civil administration. General Sucre had been left with the task of claiming Upper Peru for the patriots. In February Sucre had angered the Liberator by issuing a decree at La Paz proclaiming the virtual independence of this region, which was then linked administratively both to Peru and Argentina. Bolívar would probably have done the same, if only to have stopped endless disputes about which country had a right over it. But Bolívar was annoyed that Sucre had taken a decision that only he had the right to make. He would later be placated by having the new country named after him.

On April Fool's Day 1825, patriot forces under Sucre had defeated at Tumusla the last of the rebellious Spanish troops. Later that month Bolívar set off towards Upper Peru by way of Arequipa and Cuzco, taking with him a library of books that included works by Montesquieu, Bentham and Napoleon. He did not reach the region until ten days after the August meeting that had resulted in the creation of what was originally known as the República Bolívar. General Sucre went to meet him at a point halfway between Puno and La Paz. On alighting from his horse to greet the Liberator, his sword fell from its sheath, which he regarded as a bad omen. The next day, after punishing a servant by hitting him with the back of his sword, it broke in two.

That was the point when my talk was interrupted by the arrival of soldiers and a crew from Bolivia's national television channel. We were forced out of the hall, so that 'the room could be got ready'. It was only then that I realized the next day's meeting was going to be held within this historic monument. For a few minutes we were allowed to walk around an adjoining space containing portraits of every Bolivian president since the time of General Sucre, who was left in charge of the country after Bolívar's departure; the number of portraits indicated the brevity of their presidencies and the political confusion Bolivia has known since its inception. Security forces then obliged us to leave the building. We had no other option but to return to our hotel. We were among the few foreigners left in the town. A German tour guide who had remained in the hotel told my group that I was a madman, and that we should all be leaving Bolivia before a bloodbath ensued. I called everyone together for a military-style briefing. I urged calm. I insisted that no one listen to the German, who had no idea what he was talking about. I had hardly slept for a week but I spent another night trawling Sucre's karaoke bars with Marbel and her friends. I had no idea when I would be seeing them next. The town's authorities had urged everyone to stay off the streets the next day.

The first sounds of dynamite came shortly after breakfast. They were indistinguishable from the firecrackers at the beginning of every fiesta. Tito drove me around town to investigate. Not much was happening as yet. The explosions were sporadic and the streets were as deserted as on a Sunday morning. We heard that the meeting was not going to start until the afternoon. The full contingent of Potosí miners reached Sucre by midday. By lunchtime the roar of protesters could clearly be heard from our hotel. The explosions were multiplying and large clouds of smoke were visible from the rooftop. Tito had ideas as to how I could keep our group entertained – he knew some fashion models who would be prepared to give us a show of traditional Bolivian costumes.

His suggestion was not in keeping with the serious historical aims of the Cambridge tour company for whom I worked. Two members of the group asked if I would continue my interrupted talk on Bolívar. We all met up in the hotel's conference room on the ground floor. The shouts of protesters were getting closer. We could hear the sounds of running footsteps. I evoked the excitement of Bolívar's triumphant entry into La Paz on 18 August, when he had been presented with a diamond-studded gold crown. I described how the scenery of the southern Andes had raised his spirits and how he had often thought of Napoleon's glorious crossing of the Alps.

A loud explosion almost immediately outside the window briefly disturbed my train of thought. I continued with an account of how Bolívar and Sucre had travelled on 20 September from La Paz to Oruro and from there had begun climbing towards Potosí.

At Potosí, Bolívar was received by his former general William Miller, now the district prefect. Miller had staged festivities of exceptional exuberance and colour for his arrival. Bolívar was touched more than anything by the welcome he was given by the local Indians, who, in the aftermath of his reforms at Cuzco, thought of him as their saviour. Indians danced around him in circles and arranged for their children to be lowered from a triumphal arch and shower flowers on him to the accompaniment of fireworks. He was briefly tempted to proclaim himself 'Inca' in emulation of the rebel leader Túpac Amaru II.

Instead, together with Sucre and his staff, he made the supreme symbolic gesture of climbing to the top of the great silver mountain of the Cerro Rico. Once there the flags of independence were unfurled and Bolívar gave an emotive speech, recalling his epic journey from the Orinoco all the way down to Potosí: 'Standing as I do now on this great mountain of silver called Potosí, whose enormously rich veins were for three hundred years the treasury of Spain, I can only regard all this opulence as nothing when compared with the glory of having carried the standard of freedom victoriously from the burning shores of the Orinoco to fix it here, on the peak of this mountain, whose breast is the wonder and envy of the universe.'

As I finished reading out the extract, there were three more explosions, followed by the sounds of shattering glass and of a large crowd rushing past. My assistant from the Cambridge company came into the room with her mouth covered by a handkerchief. She indicated with a gesture that she needed to talk to me. I went to the back of the room, while the group anxiously muttered among themselves. 'I don't want to be alarmist,' she said, 'but you've got to try and keep people in this room for as long as you can. There's tear gas in the lobby.'

An ambulance could be heard in the far distance, but the sounds immediately outside had died down. Members of the group wondered if I had had any news about what was happening at the meeting in the House of Liberty. I pretended that my assistant had just given me an update, and that it seemed that the talks were progressing well. No one believed me.

I had difficulties in getting back to the subject of Bolívar. I told everyone that my grandfather had become fascinated by Bolívar while staying in Potosí, where there was a curious arcaded monument to the Liberator in the middle of the main square. My grandfather had pronounced Bolívar a truly great man. I wondered if he was aware of the link between the Liberator and the western companies responsible for South America's 'open veins': Bolívar, having wrested South America's major source of wealth from the Spaniards, now proposed selling this to the West to pay off the national debt.

My talk about Bolívar regained momentum. I said that his moments on the top of the Cerro Rico had represented the pinnacle of his Andean career. Afterwards everything began to turn against him. He was physically unwell and was also expressing ideas that must have seemed symptomatic of madness and deluded grandeur. While at Potosí he even considered helping out the Argentineans in a plan to wage war against Brazil.

On his return to Lima he produced his highly controversial constitution for the newly created Bolivia. The document exemplified the ambivalence of Bolívar's political position. It was full of liberal talk of civil rights, equality and freedom for slaves, while enshrining Bolívar's growing conviction in the need for a president for life (an unpopular conviction later to be shared by Chávez and Morales). Bolívar confessed to the British consul at Lima 'that his heart always beats in favour of liberty, but that his head leans towards aristocracy . . . if the principles of liberty are too rapidly introduced anarchy and the destruction of the white inhabitants will be the inevitable consequences'. In the actual constitution Bolívar dismissed elections as 'the greatest scourge of republics', and referred to the president as 'the sun which, fixed in its orbit, imparts life to the universe'.

There was still a smell of tear gas when we emerged into the lobby and the news from the receptionist was not good. The meeting at the House of Liberty had ended inconclusively and Vaca Diez had gone into hiding. While I had been talking about Bolívar, a miner had been killed a few hundred metres from the hotel. An escalation of violence seemed unavoidable.

At one in the morning I was sitting in the hotel's empty dining-room with two of the politicians who had taken part in the meeting. They confessed they had no real idea of what was going on. But an hour later, after a long conversation with them about Bolivia and its recent history, their mobile phones rang. Another meeting had just been convened.

At three in the morning, I watched in the lobby a live broadcast of Vaca Diez's resignation speech. Tito was with me. Isolated sounds of cheerful animation punctuated the silence outside. One or two of the bars were still open. We went for a long stroll. A drunk shouted out 'Fucking gringo!' as I walked past. A couple of others invited us to come and celebrate. History had been made. The way had been paved for South America's first indigenous president. The speed with everything had happened had left me slightly incredulous. The great journey that Bolívar had undertaken from the Orinoco had ended up here, early in the morning, on the near-empty streets of Sucre, to the jeers and laughs of drunks.

After one in the morning the train approached the ghostly small town of Uyuni. On both sides of the tracks were the wrecks of carriages and engines from an earlier age, relics of another dream. I could see the first of the town's enormously wide streets, laid out at a time when Uyuni had been envisaged as an Andean metropolis of the future. The train disgorged most of its backpackers here. They were off to see the surreal expanse of the Salar de Uyuni, an enormous salt flat that cast a whitish glow in the distant darkness. This time I would not be joining them. I stayed on the train, as it headed southwards into a part of Bolivia neither I nor my grandfather had visited. The lights in the carriages were turned off as soon as we were moving again. The night sky was so clear I could make out every star of the Southern Cross.

# PART FOUR

# THE SOUTH

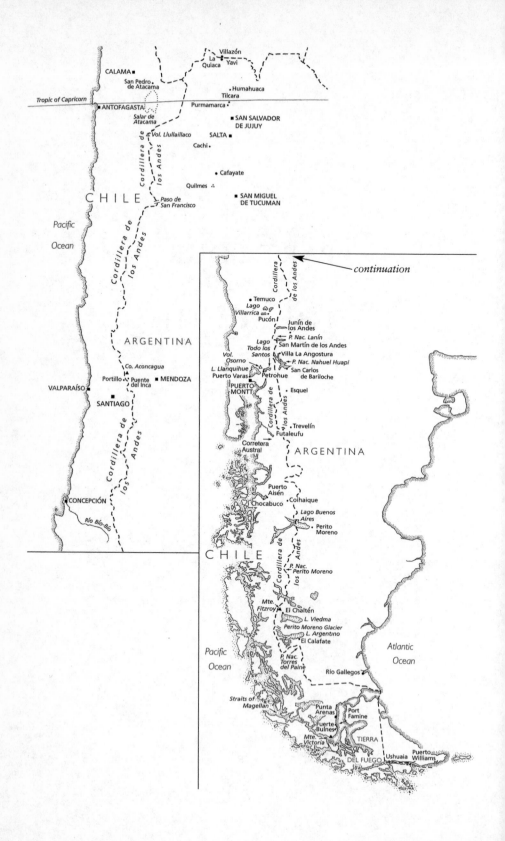

# LENGTHENING
# SHADOWS

Sitting up half asleep on the night train from Oruro, I remembered an incident that had happened in Peru's Colca Canyon. An old tramp had come up to me on a dark street in Cabanaconde. I thought he was going to ask for some money, but instead he had asked which way was south. I told him that my sense of direction was poor but I pointed to where I thought the south lay. He seemed pleased by my reply. He said he was heading in that direction. 'Death,' he mumbled, 'lies to the south.'

The train I was on was going only as far south as the Argentinean border. In the old days I could have got on the train at La Paz, slept lying down in a luxurious carriage and stayed there until Buenos Aires two days later. Isherwood and Caskey had done precisely that, and found entering the train at La Paz to be like 'starting for an exciting cocktail party'. They were thrilled to be leaving the Andes. 'We had grown weary, weary to the bone, of those inhumanly gigantic mountains, that somber plateau haunted by its Incaic ghosts, that weird rarefied manic-depressive atmosphere.'

Theroux, travelling on the same train down towards the Argentinean pampas, felt the same. He was depressed by the mere sight from his window of Andean communities such as Tupiza, the last stop in Bolivia before the frontier town of Villazón: 'Just the thought of standing on the platform in such a place, and watching the train depart as silence sifted down on the village, was enough to make me shudder.'

The train shunted away into the night, leaving the three of us on the platform at Tupiza. It was four in the morning. Butch Cassidy and the Sundance Kid had alighted here exactly a century earlier. After fleeing America's Wild West in 1901 they settled in remote Patagonia, where their past as notorious bank robbers eventually caught up with them. They escaped to Bolivia but did not get much further than Tupiza. They were reputedly killed in a shoot-out at a remote mining village a hundred kilometres north of the town. No one knows for sure.

When the sun finally appeared over sun-bleached streets backed by red eroded cliffs, we could just about picture ourselves in a frontier town from a western. We were now too alert to want to sleep but not alert enough to want to spend the next six hours on a Butch Cassidy and the Sundance Kid Tour. I was keen to move on.

I was at an ever more restless stage in my journey south, anxious always to see what lay beyond the next horizon of mountains, increasingly attracted by the notion of travel as escape. Though I had no specific interest in the two famous outlaws who had taken refuge in Tupiza, I was beginning to like the idea of finding some faraway place where I could cast off my previous life and reinvent myself. My imagination had become fixed on a valley 230 kilometres to the east of Tupiza. This valley had the attraction of remoteness and also appealed to me sentimentally. It was regarded as a Bolivian Andalusia. It had been heavily settled by Andalusians. It was a wine-growing area with what was said to be a relaxed Andalusian atmosphere. The river running through it was known after the Guadalquivir, the 'Great River of Spain'.

Tarija, the valley's capital, was perhaps the most inaccessible of Bolivia's major towns. All the roads leading to it at present are unpaved. It is the nearest community of any size to the east of Tupiza. At Tupiza's bus station we were told that it would take a good six to eight hours to get to Tarija.

Typically for Bolivia, the three buses to Tarija went only at night, when bus travel was not recommended in the Andean districts of Colombia, Ecuador and Peru. However, Bolivia was different: its criminals appeared to enjoy a good night's sleep and preferred to attack buses by day. And in any case, on narrow and dangerous roads, the lights of oncoming traffic gave drivers more warning of approaching vehicles. The road to Tarija was clearly of the 'narrow and dangerous' kind. The man we spoke to at the station said that he had once counted 478 crosses along it.

We went to Tarija by taxi. We could not face another sleepless night and I wanted to see the scenery. We left Tupiza shortly after breakfast, with the sun touching the tips of its valley's rocky sides. We followed the river into a canyon, where there were fields of sugar cane, a profusion of cactuses, and pinnacles of sandstone twisted into monsters. Butch Cassidy and the Sundance Kid would have felt at home in this landscape of progressive erosion whose scale seemed greater every time we climbed one canyon to descend into a yet deeper and more perilous one. The scenery was like that in a geology textbook. A large herd of goats slowed us down as we climbed up a pass whose views were of a lunar-like infinity. The final ascent came after a high stony plateau, where the road became an endless straight line, across scrubland and past an eerie blue lake. We reached a viewpoint whose panorama was like an elongated aerial photograph. Between two crumpled ranges ran a long wide valley marked by the undulating Guadalquivir, whose tree-lined banks faded into vineyards. After our hours of crossing the Wild West, we could have been arriving at the Promised Land.

Tarija itself, founded by an offshoot of Diego de Almagro's Chilean expedition of 1535, was the typical Bolivian jumble of colours and brickwork dotted by the faded colonial and the French-style eclectic. But the place had a Seville-like liveliness and sensuality, with pedestrian-crowded streets radiating from squares bursting with palms and greenery. The town and its surroundings might have rid Isherwood of some of his *altiplano* gloom, especially if he had gone on a Sunday to the outlying wine-growing villages of Tomatitas and San Lorenzo.

These were villages where the area's proverbial similarities with Andalusia were most apparent, places where people came to relax on a Sunday, enjoy family barbecues by the Guadalquivir, have long lunches in the bars and restaurants, drink wine under pergolas, sing and play music. Even the whitewashed balconied houses resembled those from the rural Andalusia of old. I could happily have stayed much longer in this valley that was like an oasis in the middle of the moon; I could almost imagine living there. But the south was calling.

Travelling in Bolivia always has its last-minute uncertainties. I discovered at Tarija that the nearest frontier with Argentina had been closed by protesters. Antagonism towards Morales was growing, especially in the regions of Tarija and Santa Cruz, whose desire for autonomy presented his government with its first major challenge.

I had to go back most of the way to Tupiza and hope that the protests would not spread. Marbel and Pablo came with me to Villazón, where I left them waiting for the Oruro train. Pablo looked forward to seeing me soon, at the baptism of my 'godson'. Marbel and I both had an intuition we would never see each other again.

The emotions of the train-station parting were cut short by fears that the frontier post even here was about to be blocked by lorries. I rushed to the border and crossed into the Argentinean town of Quiaca. Once more I was on my own, and in a country I barely knew.

My only previous visit to Argentina had been to its capital, Buenos Aires, where I had spent an exhilarating and sleepless few weeks several years earlier, researching its night life for an American magazine, while satisfying my own curiosity in a city I had almost conceived as an imaginary construct devised by Borges and other writers. It had seemed to me the urbanite's dream city, as well as a glorified version of Europe, existing in the limbo of the pampas and from which all traces of its indigenous past had been erased.

I had wondered then what the rest of Argentina was like. An elderly and charming composer whom I had interviewed there, Ariel Ramírez, had helped me to gain some understanding. He spoke to me of his 'world-famous' *Creole Mass*, which incorporated folkloric elements from all over the country, in particular from the Argentinean Andes. He impressed on me above all the importance and beauty of the Argentinean region bordering on Bolivia. He talked about its colonial towns, the oldest in Argentina. He also said how necessary it was to be reminded every now and then of his country's indigenous roots. Argentina's indigenous peoples today formed three per cent of the country's total population, the majority of them Quechua speakers from the north-west.

Quiaca itself was not the most prepossessing introduction to the region. As with Villazón, this was a town travellers have generally thought of as bleak, unwelcoming and even desperate. I had now several hours to spare in Quiaca and took a taxi to a nearby village church described in my guidebook as 'one of the finest in north-west Argentina'.

The church stood in a tiny silent village of adobe houses sheltering in an oasis of cultivated gardens. From the outside this seventeenth-century building looked as humble as its surroundings, but behind its simple white facade was an astonishing interior dominated by colonial altarpieces whose gilded mass of ornament soared up to a wooden ceiling of distant Moorish inspiration. The old woman who had opened the church for me wondered if I wanted to see the palace next door, whose main entrance lurked under the shadow of trees. She showed me an enormously long suite of near-empty rooms and a large and much-neglected courtyard. She explained that I was in the residence of the former Marquises of Yavi, Argentina's only marquisate, and that caravans laden with gold and silver had regularly rested here on their way from Potosí to the Río de la Plata. Nowhere I saw in the Andes was more eloquent of powerful empires and their collapse.

I remained in a dreamy mood on returning to Quica to take up my seat on a late-afternoon bus heading southwards. I listened to the conversations around me, adjusting my ears again to Argentinean Spanish, with its Italian intonation. I studied some of the faces of my fellow passengers, trying to work out their ancestral origins. Among the few with unmistakably indigenous blood was a tall and very striking woman with dark eyes and long dark hair. She got on the bus at the last moment and sat down next to me.

We found out that we were both going to the village of Tilcara in the heart of the Canyon of Huamamarca. Tilcara was where her parents lived and where she had been born and brought up. She had spent the last fortnight in Bolivia, where she often went to collect craft objects to be sold in a shop she owned in the village of Purmamarca. Her name was Patricia. Shy but talkative, she was soon telling me all about herself. She spoke Quechua with her parents. They were now looking after her four-year-old son, who meant everything to her. She was a single mother. Her boyfriend had left her the moment she had become pregnant. She spoke of love and relationships as night fell and the road descended into a canyon whose craggy sides were soon outlined against the clear starry sky.

I helped her with her many bags after the bus had left us by the roadside. We walked for half an hour in the darkness to her parents' adobe house. On saying goodbye, she made me promise I would go and see her the next day at Purmamarca.

Once I had left Patricia to go and look for somewhere to stay, I began to notice the smart commercialization of Tilcara's dimly lit warren of adobe buildings and dirt streets. The small hotel I found had a desert-style chic, as did the only restaurant I found open late on a Monday night – a place where glamorous young waitresses in black aprons served the first New Andean cuisine I had seen since

Cuzco. I also encountered an off-season tourism unimaginable in most of the other Andean places I had visited. The few tourists I met were all Argentinean pensioners leisurely driving around the country in their cars. I had the depressing thought that I was nearing the age of many of them.

I was also assimilating the cultural shock of moving from Bolivia to Argentina. At Tilcara I sensed I had returned to a world that was normal and predictable, efficient in its tourism, lacking in dangerous roads, not subject to regular roadblocks and bandit attacks, and full of well-maintained buses that respected speed limits and drinking laws.

Even the archaeological site I went to the next morning on the outskirts of Tilcara was as tame as if it had been managed by the National Trust. The site, a fortified medieval settlement or *pucará* built by the Tilcara Indians, was one of the first places visited in the Andes by my childhood hero Tschiffely, who had found the whole area and its inhabitants 'full of mystery and superstition'. He also thought the hill-top ruins to be prehistoric and had excavated its tombs in the hope of pilfering treasures. He had been punished by getting serious blood poisoning after being pricked by a thorn. He almost had to curtail his journey and return to Buenos Aires.

The sanitized and orderly adobe foundations of today's *pucará* contrasted with a setting of scorched mountains whose fissures were as sharp under the desert sun as the cracks in a smashed pane of glass. I walked afterwards for hours along a cactus-strewn path that led to a rock poised over a narrow gorge of a kind that the indomitable Tschiffely might have leapt over on his horse. The pleasure of being on my own in such a wild landscape was such that I resolved to spend much of my remaining time in the Andes escaping from civilization.

At the end of the afternoon I went on a gentler walk around a rocky outcrop famed for having eroded into candy stripes of purples, greens, blues and oranges. The rock, known as that of the

Seven Colours, rose above the small museum-like village of Purmamarca. The colours seemed as artificial as the village itself, but they affected me like some persistent romantic tune as I wandered down to the huddle of crafts shops that lay at their foot. A few pensioners were browsing in one of them as I made my way past them to say hello to Patricia.

She was with her four-year-old child. The three of us went off to have supper at a restaurant where a famous old folksinger sang mournfully late into the night. Patricia told me how much she adored travelling and that her great ambition was to go one day to Patagonia. Patagonia seemed a place where everyone wanted to go to one day. If I waited for a few more weeks in Purmamarca she would come with me. I enthused about how lovely that would be, not thinking at first of practical or other considerations, or about whether her wailing and kicking child would be coming as well. However, I eventually added with a sad and resigned smile that I was unable to wait any longer, as the winter was about to set in and the roads would be closing.

We went together on the morning bus as far as the district capital of San Salvador de Jujuy. She was going to the market. We sat at the very front of the bus, where her son fell asleep against my arm. Halfway to Jujuy, the bright sky disappeared as if someone had turned off a switch. We were enveloped in fog and it started to drizzle. Apparently the weather often changed like this on approaching Jujuy, where the scorched Canyon of Huamamarca metamorphosed into a richly agricultural valley.

Nearer Jujuy, the bus stopped to pick up a drenched backpacker, who turned out to be the Argentinean Che Guevara lookalike I had first seen at Machu Picchu. He hung around next to me at the grey and crowded bus station of Jujuy, where I took my final leave of Patricia, promising her that I would write and tell her what Patagonia was like. She slipped me a small sandstone carving of the Pachamama, so that I would always remember her and her people. When she and her child had turned to give me a final wave, the

Argentinean, whose name was Martín, confessed he had thought I had picked up a family since we had last met. I told him I had only acquired a Bolivian godson.

Salta appeared under a fleeting patch of blue sky, surrounded by tobacco fields and low green mountains. I had been led to think to think of Salta as some Wild West town full of men with cowboy hats and handlebar moustaches. But its centre had an indeterminately European feel, with echoes of bygone corners of Italy, Central Europe, France and Spain. Instead of a main square with horses tied to wooden posts, there were outdoor cafés spreading over rain-washed pavements and arcaded eclectic structures whose grey-stone pomposity clashed with the few whitewashed buildings left from frontier days.

From Salta I took a bus heading westwards, across a high pass whose famous views were hidden at first by heavy rainclouds that made the moorland scenery look like the Scottish Highlands. The views appeared towards sunset, after the sky had miraculously cleared and we had begun our descent into the desiccated Valley of the Cachalqui. The distant reddish mountains on the other side had streaks of snow. Using my imagination to picture what lay beyond them I could see salt flats and deserts and the snowy mountains and volcanoes that guarded the great emptiness of the Atacama. One of the peaks was Llullaillaco, which I had known from the Chilean side, wandering through the Atacama while chasing my grandfather's shadow. In my mind's eye I could also make out one of the more notorious passes leading from Argentina into Chile, that of San Francisco, scene of the first of the great European crossings of the Andes.

Diego de Almagro, the 'discoverer' of Chile, had approached the country by way of Tupiza and Salta in 1535, having gathered on his march from Cuzco an army of five hundred Spaniards, lured to the south by the promise of gold. With them were ten thousand Indian bearers and over two hundred black slaves. Many of the Indian porters had rebelled before Tupiza and run away. New ones had to be press-ganged. One of them almost succeeded in murdering Almagro by shooting an arrow which killed his horse.

The worst part of their journey had come after Salta. They lost many of their llamas in a flash flood and, long before reaching the pass into Chile, had had their food supplies severely rationed and known the harshness of a desert landscape with some of the greatest climatic extremes in the world. As they began their climb up to a height of nearly five thousand metres, they were already half dead from cold, heat, exhaustion and hunger.

Almagro had known hardship almost since birth. Handed over at the age of four to the care of a cruel uncle, he had run away from home in his early teens and made his way in tears to his mother in Seville; she gave him a few coins and a piece of bread, and told him never to bother her again. He had been in the New World since 1515, having escaped from Spain after seriously wounding a man in a fight. However, nothing he had experienced so far had prepared him for the crossing of the San Francisco Pass.

The winds were constant and the temperatures fell to well below freezing. There was no food and nothing with which to make a fire. Everyone suffered from frostbite. One of the Spaniards, on taking off his boots, removed all his toes as well. Seventy horses died in a single night. The worst losses were among the Indians and the slaves. The Indians wore no shoes and were protected only by light textiles. The track became littered with their corpses. Condors swept down to tear apart the flesh.

Almagro's hugely depleted expedition got almost as far south as present-day Santiago de Chile, before turning back to Peru. They found no gold. Their losses on the return journey were almost as great as on the outward one, but they stayed clear of the San Francisco Pass, preferring instead the coastal desert up to Arequipa. The few who managed to make it back to Cuzco were known as 'the defeated of Chile'.

*

A full moon was lighting up the snow on a faraway peak named after the Liberator San Martín. In a week's time I would be following San Martín's own epic crossing of the Andes, three hundred kilometres to the south. For the moment I was heading towards a diminutive scattering of lights above a dried-up riverbed. The bus from Salta was nearing its final destination, the village of Cachi.

We pulled up at a dark and mysterious square. I walked down empty cobbled streets, between moonlit rows of white-painted adobe. Cachi was how I had once imagined Salta, but in miniature. It looked like a small Mexican village from a western, where the presence of a stranger is immediately registered from behind barred windows. A man in riding boots offered me a bare white room for the night. Later he told me of a place to have supper that was in stark contrast to a typical New Andean establishment. It was a rough bar full of beer-drinking unshaven men, some of whom were eating slabs of roast goat.

For a few hours the next day, I was able to maintain the illusion of being off the beaten track, as I set off south down the Cachalqui Valley. The solitary bus leaving Cachi that morning was going only a short way down the valley, after which no one was quite sure how I could continue south to the next important town, Cafayate. For the last time on my trip I was in a bus whose passengers were almost entirely indigenous.

The road was narrow and virtually unused and I did not realize for some time that this was the legendary Route 40, which, beginning in Quiaca, goes all the way to Argentina's southernmost tip. The road was now running parallel to the Cachalqui, skirting the oasis-like patches that clung to its banks, passing between giant cactuses, swerving occasionally away from the valley's orange sides to offer views of far-off snows.

The bus's final stop was at a village less than an hour away from Cachi. It had a pleasingly simple colonial church and a long white house that had belonged to the last Spanish governor of Salta, but little else. There was a bus that was travelling south to the next village in two days' time. There was a truck driver who could not be found. I started walking.

The only car I had seen all day, a smart Mercedes, pulled up beside me shortly. The occupants were a couple of genteel pensioners. They told me to jump in. They were originally from Buenos Aires but had recently retired to a farm in the pampas. Every year they took a driving holiday around different parts of their country. Their favourite region was the north-west.

After a dramatic stretch of badlands, the exotic Route 40 joined up with a main road and entered a smart-looking town that could have been in France or California. We had reached the wine-growing town of Cafayate. The elderly couple drove off. At the tourist office in the middle of the neatly mown main square, I heard a familiar voice. It was Martín, the Argentinean backpacker. He had just arrived and was just about to leave. The blandness of Cafayate had already got to him. 'I'm not sure when we'll next see each other,' he said. 'Perhaps in Patagonia.'

To try and escape the blandness I walked beyond Cafayate's vine-yards and into a poor suburb that petered out into a rocky wilderness backed by bleached gaunt peaks. At the far end of the path from the village, I found myself walking alongside a painfully thin woman with a pinched face and jet-black hair. She said hello and asked where I was from. I told her I had been born in Italy. 'That's where my father was from!' she exclaimed in delight. Her father had immigrated to Argentina from Calabria. She had an Italian name, Liliana. She was married to a potter whom she knew would be fascinated to meet me. She referred to him simply as 'the Indian'.

Liliana and the Indian lived in a shack made from grey adobe bricks, surrounded by pots, cactuses and home-made furniture. Theirs was the most remote and isolated house in the village. The Indian, a portly man with a dusty leather hat, was holding a little snake when I turned up with his wife. They had a baby and two small children smothered in dirt. With them was a friend,

476

Marcelino, an elderly serenely faced man with long white hair tied in a ponytail.

Both he and the Indian introduced themselves to me as descendants of the Diaguitas, an indigenous tribe that officially died out in the eighteenth century. The great settlement of the Diaguitas people was nearby Quilmes, whose ruins Marcelino hoped would eventually be managed by the Indians themselves.

He also told me that he was about to take part in a meeting with Indians from all over South America. He said that I should make the effort to come along. He explained to me that not just Indians but people of every race and nationality from all over the world would be present. It was an international gathering of what he called the Humanist Movement. Its inspiration was an Argentinean sage who lived near Mendoza and was known to his followers as Silos. The meeting was to be held near Silos's home, high up in the Andes, on the very route taken by San Martín while marching from Mendoza to liberate Chile.

I started off late the next day towards Mendoza, by way of Quilmes. I got as far as the nearest village to the ruins, Amaicha del Valle, whose dominant indigenous population shared their tranquil oasis community with a handful of artists, hippies and laid-back weekenders.

It was a place where the pseudo-indigenous and the neo-indigenous thrived. I was still mulling over the mysterious link between indigenous beliefs and Marcelino's 'humanism' when I came across, on the outskirts of the village, a 'Humanist Chapel' built by a former German resident who called his work 'a message of peace and love' – it was an open organic structure sheltering a carved swooning woman who could be interpreted both as the Virgin and the Pachamama. Near to this a self-taught indigenous artist had created a massive Pachamama Museum, which looked like the work of a deranged amateurish Gaudí.

I was glad and moved to be confronted afterwards with the genuinely indigenous at Quilmes, to where I was driven at sunrise, before any other visitors had appeared. Its ruins, spreading among thousands of tall cactuses, across a flat stretch of desert and up a steep rocky slope, were on a far larger scale and far more haunting than the near-contemporary ones I had seen at Tilcara. In its small museum was a revealing quote by an Arequipa bishop who had passed through this part of the Andes in 1768: 'I have wandered on foot and on horseback through this region which, according to the historian Herrera, was populated by Diaguitas; and though I have spoken about these people with many who now live in the area, no one has taken me to see them. What, dear Lord, has happened to all those Indians? I ask around, I read, I research; but I end up merely speaking with shadows.'

My vivid image of the desert kingdom of the Diaguitas was soon overlayed by other impressions as I continued rapidly south. The landscape became green and Alpine on reaching Tafi del Valle, a luxury summer and weekend resort whose wooden chalets and pine-shaded gardens faded out into fields dotted wit crudely carved Celtic-like menhirs from prehistoric times. By late afternoon I was descending through tropical jungle into the great plains of sugar cane surrounding the regional capital of San Miguel de Tucumán. In this city of neo-baroque civic splendour, Argentina had declared its independence from the Viceroyalty of La Plata as early as 1816. Everything was becoming too much to take in. I fell into a profound sleep almost the moment I sat down on the night bus to Mendoza. When I woke up at dawn, I felt I was seeing the Andes as if for the first time.

Across the last fields of the pampas, beyond groves of elms and poplars yellowing in the autumn, a ragged band of dark-brown mountains glistening with snow extended the length of the horizon. This same view, so suggestive to me of my earliest memories of Spain's northern mountains from the plateau of Castile, had been a much-needed stimulant to Robert Proctor in April 1823, in the course of his arduous journey from Britain to Lima. It was his first view of the Andes: 'Nobody can imagine the effect the view of this stupendous barrier of mountains produces on the traveller . . . The enormous mountains were entirely covered with snow, and rose to such a height that we were obliged to strain our necks back to look at them: they seemed to belong to a different world.'

The Tucumán bus approached Mendoza through autumnal parkland. An hour later I would be circling the city centre in a taxi, in an ever more desperate search for somewhere to stay, while the driver broadcast to me his enthusiasm for the city.

Its women were the most beautiful in the world (a comment I had not heard since Colombia) and its wines put French ones to shame. He praised its leisurely lifestyle, the extent of its parkland and the elegance of the architecture. I reserved my judgment on the wines and the women, but what I could see from the taxi supported everything that I had heard about the city. Rebuilt after a major earthquake in the late nineteenth century, it had the unified look of a light and radiant Paris, with lots of outdoor cafés and broad pavements shaded by bushy sycamores and plane trees.

But I had arrived at a bad moment. A long holiday weekend was about to begin; most of the city's monuments were on the point of closing and nearly all the available hotel space had been taken up by participants at a major congress. I ended up in an old hotel which recalled my student days in Paris. I stayed there as little as I could. Much of my time in Mendoza was spent instead with the Liberator José de San Martín.

In the northern Andes I had begun thinking of San Martín primarily as the man who had capitulated to Bolívar. In Mendoza I came to see him as Bolívar's equal. Mendoza is the South American city most closely associated with him, though he was not born here. He was from a Jesuit mission in the tropical north-east of the country. His features were so dark that it was rumoured his mother had had an affair with a Guaraní Indian.

He had a career in the army and was sent to Spain. He mixed with South American exiles in London but returned to Argentina in

1812 in time to celebrate General Belgrano's victory against the Spanish at Tucumán. He was put in charge of the Army of the North. He planned to liberate Peru by marching across the Central Andes to Cuzco, but the royalists' mountain stronghold was still impregnable.

Then he had an idea that was bolder still. He was a soldier known for rational thinking and fanatical discipline. But what he now proposed suggested that the contemplation of the Andes had pushed him into lunacy: to lead an army across the southern and highest part of the whole range, capture the Chilean capital of Santiago and then sail north to Lima.

He managed eventually to get backing for his scheme and be appointed governor of the remote province of Cuyo, from where he intended beginning his march. Cuyo's capital was Mendoza. At Mendoza, San Martín's meticulousness reasserted itself in the obsessive way he planned his campaign and in the rigid, almost manic routine he imposed upon himself. He always rose at the crack of dawn. He worked while continually smoking big black cigarettes. He supervised every detail of his projected march, from the food provisions to the number of ponchos and blankets needed. He had a break for a lunch that usually consisted of stew and cakes, accompanied by two glasses of wine and coffee. He returned to his work in the late afternoon. His main relaxation was chess.

By January 1817, when the snows had melted from the high passes, the Army of the Andes was ready to leave. It was divided into three main divisions, taking separate routes. It included 5200 men, and 12,900 animals. Among the provisions were large quantities of the easily transportable beef jerky, made from powdered dried beef, chilies and fat. There were also large quantities of garlic and onions, which were thought to ward off the effects of the cold and the altitude.

San Martín's crossing of the Andes would take him a month. His army marched for 200 kilometres and negotiated five passes, the highest of which was 4000 metres. The hard conditions killed off

a fair number of his men and decimated and weakened the animals. But his achievement was a remarkable one and it was
characteristic of San Martín that he should later describe it in a
completely matter-of-fact way. He lacked not only Bolívar's risk-
taking impulsiveness, but also the latter's love of hyperbole and
self-propaganda. He did not record any mystical experiences
amidst the lofty peaks.

Proctor carried letters of introduction to San Martín and saw
much of him while staying in Mendoza. San Martín had recently
come back from Peru and was 'leading a very retiring time' in this
city to which he 'seemed as much attached . . . as the inhabitants
were to him'. Proctor was especially taken by the man's 'strongly
expressive countenance': 'I certainly never beheld more animated
features, particularly when conversing on the events of past times:
and though he praised the retirement of Mendoza, I fancied I saw
a restlessness of spirit in his eye which only waited a proper opportunity for being again called forth with its wonted energy.' This
opportunity never came. Estranged by now from the government in
Buenos Aires, which accused him of being a conspirator, he was
forced to sail to France only a few months after Proctor's visit.

The Museo de San Martín looked like a dull municipal library from
the 1950s, but it was full of evocative memorabilia. The earliest was
a lock of hair from the fourteen-year-old girl whom he married in
1812 when he was thirty-four (her parents did not object to the age
gap but to his doubtful racial origins). From the period when he
was planning his Andean expedition, there were his sofa and writing desk. From the actual crossing, there were some woollen gloves,
a helmet, a moth-eaten red jacket, a three-cornered hat and a first-
aid kit that included homeopathic medicines for his severe stomach
ulcers. There were slippers, a comb and other personal items dating
from his last years in Boulogne-sur-Mer.

I then spent what remained of the afternoon crossing one of
the largest municipal parks I had ever known. I was aiming for the

481

densely wooded 'Hill of Glory'. A park-keeper warned me of muggers hiding behind the trees. He did not warn me that the monument I wanted to see at the top of the hill was largely encased in scaffolding.

Even though I had only a partial view of this 1914 monument to the Army of the Andes, I saw enough of it to prove my theory that the Argentineans were unrivalled in South America in the creation of bombastic commemorative sculpture. They might have treated their great hero shoddily in his lifetime, but they had done his memory proud in this giant outcrop of rock covered in life-like bronze statuary of him and his army, above which soared a triumphant representation of Glory and her retinue.

The monument was an outstanding work of art of its kind, but its lofty spirit seemed alien to the personality of San Martín himself. An old man sitting on a bench seemed to read my thoughts. He said he'd been watching me and asked if I'd seen the 'San Martín Cycle' by an artist called Fidel Roig Matons. The prospect of some paintings of San Martín's campaign by a local early-twentieth-century artist did not seemed wildly exciting, but the old man was persuasive.

I reached the municipal council chamber where the paintings were hung moments before closing time. The receptionist delayed going home so as to show me what turned out to be detailed impressionist-style canvases. She said that Roig Matons' works were much loved in Mendoza. They were certainly more impressive than I had imagined, even if in need of a good clean. Layers of dirt and discoloured varnish had tempered what must have been their original luminosity. Then the receptionist produced a leaflet about the artist. The works became more interesting still on knowing something of their gestation. The story of Roig Matons was a typical Andean tale of ill-fated obsession.

In 1908 a 21-year-old man arrived at Mendoza from Spain, carrying a violin and a set of oils. He was undecided as to whether he wanted a career as a musician or as a painter. Mendoza and its surrounding countryside soon made up his mind; he knew then that his destiny was to record it.

He began by portraying the life of the city, the long strolls in its park, the days spent in its vineyards and the evenings in its cafés. Later he transferred his attention to those aspects of the province in danger of disappearing: landscapes threatened with development, traditional rural lifestyles, the province's few remaining Indians.

His passion for Mendoza found a final outlet in the life of San Martín. From 1930s to the time he stopped painting in 1952 he devoted his entire artistic energies to the depiction of San Martín's crossing of the Andes. He set about his task in a methodical minutely researched way very much in keeping with San Martín himself. First of all he needed to establish a convincing likeness of his hero. He did not want to do what other history painters would have done and directly copy contemporary portraits. Instead he took as his point of departure what he called the only 'true physiognomic likenesses' of San Martín – the daguerreotypes taken of him in Paris in 1845. Then he fleshed these out with 'a physical-psychological study' based on the faces of San Martín's brother and sister from portraits in Mendoza's history museum, and on the writings of those who had known him, such as Miller and Proctor. His primary aim was to convey what he considered San Martín's essential 'modesty and simplicity'.

The next and most important phase of his project was to go out into the Andes, and paint *in situ* every Andean landscape through which San Martín's army had passed. Once again he did not embark on this haphazardly; he set aside eight years for each of the three main routes followed by the army, beginning with the one through Uspallata. The artists whom Humbolt had inspired to come to the Andes, such as Church, had done only quick sketches from nature, which were afterwards worked up into finished paint-ings in the comfort of the studio. Roig Matons, by painting whole canvases outdoors in the Andes, had to endure more than just violently fluctuating weather conditions and long periods in the wilderness. He also had to put up with lengthy exposure to the sun's ultraviolet light.

More than twenty years of painting under ultraviolet rays eventually took its toll. He developed an incurable eye condition and his sight began to fail rapidly. But he was determined to finish his project and continued to paint high up in the mountains, despite his doctor's advice. He painted until the very last moment. He was already seven years into the last of the three routes when he finally had to give up. He could no longer appreciate the hallucinatory brilliance of the Andes. He could see only shadows.

At the start of Argentina's public holiday, I took a bus to Uspallata. I was on my way to Chile, following today's main route between Mendoza and Santiago. I would be seeing many of the landscapes painted by Roig Matons. I would also be making a journey that profoundly influenced several British travellers who came to this part of the Andes shortly after San Martín's epic crossing.

The earliest of these travellers was the anonymous author of a work entitled *Narrative of a Journey from Santiago de Chile to Buenos Ayres in July and August, 1821*. A pencilled annotation on the flyleaf of the copy kept by his publishers, John Murray, indicated that the author was 'the son of Mr G. Hibbert', and that he 'died on his travels'. His parents brought out his manuscript in an edition of fifty copies, for family and friends. The preface stated that the work 'has no pretensions to merit, either from its style or from the information it conveys'.

Hibbert Jr wrote that he undertook the journey 'to carry dispatches across the continent of South America, with the view of embarking in the River Plate for England'. As well as making money, and trying to further his career, Hibbert was clearly attracted by the adventure and undertook the route in the middle of winter, when the only other travellers around were the odd desperate courier, such as the one who accompanied him. The dangers of a winter crossing were considerable, as the author gleefully stressed: 'If a high wind were to overtake the traveller at any distance from a refuge he must perish, as the drift snow would overwhelm him.'

Hibbert's manuscript, as its author admitted, was 'a catalogue of vexations', hastily written down, at the end of days in which he was so fatigued and distressed by his most recent feats of endurance that he would collapse asleep. His style was one of youthful bravado in which he played down the beauty of such famed spots as El Puente del Inca and even emphasized the monotony of the Andean scenery. He also made fun of the contemporary fashion for including in a travel account lengthy mineralogical observations. Mineralogy, 'with its constant accompaniment of the utmost enthusiasm', was, in his view, no help at all in sustaining a man's strength while 'groping' through mountains; and in any case the turbulence of Andean nature was such as to have destroyed a geologist's labour 'ere he could have paused to apply his hammer'.

Proctor was an altogether more mature and sensible traveller. He did the journey to Santiago before the winter set in and was overawed by much of the scenery, though generally unimpressed by the dangers. Some of the more famously dangerous stretches of the route were referred to by him as 'so much exaggerated by those who have passed them, and so much dreaded by those who have not'. He paid no heed to all the warnings he had been given in Mendoza. He took all the sensible precautions of the day such as eating many onions and drinking a lot of wine before ascending the route's main pass, and then crossed it 'in the highest spirits'.

Charles Brand, journeying from Britain to Lima five years after Proctor, did so at the end of a winter in which so much snow had fallen that much of his descent had to be done sliding down on his back. He was so undaunted by the experience that he returned to Britain by the same route two years later.

For Charles Darwin, the journey from Santiago to Mendoza and back in 1835 introduced him to the most memorable scenery he encountered during his five years with the *Beagle*. At the end of the twenty-four days it took him to travel from Santiago along the southern Portillo route, and then return along the Uspallata one, he concluded that never did he 'more deeply enjoy an equal space of time'.

This interior excursion came at the best possible time for Darwin. The *Beagle*'s captain, Robert Fitzroy, was becoming ever more erratic, difficult and unbalanced, and Darwin himself had begun to suffer from cabin fever and pangs of homesickness. At the same time he had recently been a witness to two natural catastrophes that had set his mind thinking more feverishly than ever on geological evolution. While anchored in the Chilean archipelago of Chiloé on 19 January he had seen a spectacular eruption of Mount Osorio. Exactly a month later he experienced at Valdivia what was described at the time as the 'worst quake' in Chile's history.

The quake had lasted only two minutes, during which time he had had the disorienting sensation of the earth's moving 'like a crust over a fluid'. The destruction and horror in the town were mild in comparison to what he would later find on reaching the quake's epicentre at Concepción, two hundred miles north. Once he had regained his scientific composure, he made an exciting discovery: some fresh mussel beds had been raised by a few feet.

This appeared to provide proof of one of the theoretical speculations in Charles Lyell's *Principles of Geology*: that mountains are not thrown up in one colossal upheaval, but are the product of thousands of rises such as this, over an unimaginable span of time. Darwin was now also convinced that 'the earth is a mere crust over a fluid melted mass of rock'. And he became more aware than ever of the puniness and vulnerability of man in relation to the terrifying power of nature.

With ten mules, a mare and two guides he set off on 18 March towards what he would call 'the forlorn and stupid town of Mendoza'. Nothing created by man was comparable to the scenery he saw on the three-day ascent up to the 4000-metre Portillo Pass. His attention was absorbed by every detail – the intensity of the colours, the profundity of the sky, the extreme clarity of the air, the 'magical' effect of a full moon on frosty heights, the emergence of the rising sun as a giant orange disk sliced in half by a level horizon. On attaining the summit he felt as if he were in another world:

> When we reached the crest and looked backwards, a glorious view was presented. The atmosphere so resplendently clear, the sky an intense blue, the profound valleys, the wild broken forms, the heaps of ruins piled up during the lapse of ages, the bright coloured rocks, contrasted with the quiet mountains of snow, together produced a scene I never could have imagined. Neither plant nor bird, excepting a few condors wheeling around the higher pinnacles, distracted the attention from the inanimate mass. – I felt glad I was by myself, it was like watching a thunderstorm, or hearing in the full orchestra a chorus of the Messiah. This one view stands distinct in my memory from all others.

He was troubled only mildly by the altitude, which was remarkable given that he had ascended almost directly from sea level. He felt 'a slight tightness over the head and chest', and found the exertion from walking to be extreme and that 'respiration became deep and laborious'. He was also incapable of comprehending 'how Humboldt and others were able to ascend to the elevation of 19,000 feet'. Nonetheless all his minor discomforts disappeared upon 'finding fossil shells on the highest ridge'. This was further proof of Lyell's theory of geological evolution.

On his return journey through Uspallata, Darwin continued to have geological surprises, such as evidence of strata that had been 'tossed about like the crust of a broken pie' and a grove of fossilized trees that must have come from the coast. His mind was now going from one bold hypothesis to another, as he dwelt on thoughts of heaving continents and crustal oscillation. He became so addicted to geology on this journey that he could hardly sleep at night. He

487

was also discovering what would be the hub of all his later biological thinking: that the whole magnificent story of nature could be explained by the accumulation of little things.

When, in 1838, Darwin finally published an account of his journey on the *Beagle*, with its enthralled description of the Andean crossing, he timidly sent a copy, with accompanying letter, to the man whose spirit runs through the whole book, Alexander von Humboldt. Humboldt's approbation was the greatest praise he could hope to get. 'You told me in your kind letter,' wrote the great German, 'that, when you were young, the manner in which I studied and depicted nature in the torrid zones contributed towards exciting in you the ardour and desire to travel in distant lands. Considering the importance of your work, Sir, this may be the greatest success that my humble work could bring.'

The sky was still clear and there were glimpses of snow behind the arid foreground range to which the Uspallata bus was heading. Around us was a stretch of flat desert-like scenery, as we neared the smart thermal resort that had replaced what Darwin had called 'the solitary hovel which bears the imposing name of Villa Vicencio'. The holiday traffic was slow and came to a complete halt once we had started climbing into the barren mountains where Darwin had found his petrified forest. A lorry about a kilometre ahead of us had broken down and the road was too narrow for large vehicles to pass it.

I had thought the passengers on our bus were a random group of day-trippers and weekenders from Mendoza. But many seemed to know each other. Now that the bus was stuck, people stood up to shake hands with friends and introduce themselves to others. I felt baffled until the middle-aged woman next to me asked if I too was part of the 'Silos crowd'.

I had quite forgotten that the great Humanist Movement reunion which Marcelino had told me about in Cafayate was about to begin. This was the reason why all the hotels in Mendoza had been full. It was why most of the accommodation between here and the Chilean frontier was going to be occupied over the coming days. People really were coming to the reunion from all over the world. On our bus alone, according to my informant, were Germans, Italians, Colombians and people from every part of Argentina.

She told me how the 'Message of Silos' had changed her life. She was Chilean by birth but had always loathed her country, which she characterized as 'dull and reactionary'. She had moved to Buenos Aires just after Pinochet came to power and married an Argentinean with whom she had had a daughter. With the collapse of her marriage, her life had lost direction. It was then that she discovered the Message of Silos. Silos himself, she said, was a charismatic speaker and his philosophy was direct and straightforward. It appealed to someone like her who disliked organized religions and was sceptical about mystical cults. She appeared reasonable, intelligent and down-to-earth.

I asked the Chilean woman about the humanist element in Silos's thinking. She talked about the need to 'establish the centrality of human values', to 'affirm the equality of all human beings and all beliefs', to 'recognize personal and cultural diversity' and 'to repudiate all forms of violence'. This was all very unobjectionable if scarcely original, but later, as I browsed through the pamphlet she gave me, there were ideas that contradicted this rationalism: there was much talk of energy, spiritual revelations, a coming apocalypse and the mystical power of the Andean mountains.

The obstruction on the road now finally cleared, I was able to concentrate again on the landscape. After a couple of hours of slowly ascending through bare mountain scenery, we descended into the flat valley in which the village of Uspallata was situated. Thick groves of elms and poplars and lines of pollarded plane trees on both sides of the road lent a slightly French character to the landscape. The beauty came from the vividness of the colours, with the autumnal yellows and browns outlined against the intense blues of the sky and the white peaks of the main range of the Andes, now directly in front of us. The whitest peak was that of Aconcagua, the highest mountain in the whole of South America.

In earlier times, when the snows of the Andes were so much more extensive than they are today, the sight of the mountains on the other side of the valley was one that provoked fear and rapture among the travellers who were about to cross them.

'The mighty cordillera,' wrote Brand, 'broke upon our view in all its awful magnificence, covered with snow down to its very base. This was the first full view we had of it, for while on the eastern side of the mountains we had just crossed, the summits only were visible; but now, the whole mass broke upon our sight like a world of snow. I was struck with amazement . . . and thought it almost presumption to attempt such an undertaking as crossing them.'

Most of the passengers got off the bus. The Chilean woman stayed on. She was part of an advance team that had volunteered to help with last-minute preparations at Punta de Vacas, where Silos's followers were due to assemble the next day.

As we climbed into the mountains, the sky acquired a grey glaze and the environment became bleaker, until finally it was reduced to slopes of dark-brown earth scattered with stones and rocks and progressively streaked above with snow. A huge white dome standing on a wide projecting ledge was the meeting place where Silos would deliver his annual message. The Chilean woman tried to persuade me to get off, so that I could achieve enlightenment, but I preferred to continue on the bus to its final stop, El Puente del Inca.

The road past Punta de Vacas, once so narrow and vertiginous that even the phlegmatic Proctor considered it dangerous for women travellers, climbed until reaching the entrance to a grim valley, along the bottom of which were the dark concrete blocks of the summer resort of Los Penitentes, now closed for the season. El Puente del Inca, a huddle of bars, souvenir shops and chalets, lay a short distance beyond.

The cold hit me as soon as I left the bus to look for a bed for the night. I found a former industrial building that had been turned into a cheap hostel. The young owner, a blond bearded film buff called César, had just completed a degree in environmental studies in his native Mendoza. His brother had come to stay with him for the weekend, and César was about to take him on a short tour of the area. He invited me along.

We began with the Puente del Inca itself, a natural bridge over a rushing stream whose mineral-coated sides looked like the erosion on a copper pipe. The place, as disappointing as Hibbert had said it was, now supported the ugly concrete foundations of a vanished thermal hotel, once one of the most important in the southern Andes.

The hotel had been built at the time of the now similarly abandoned Transandine Railway, a masterpiece of late-nineteenth-century engineering that had linked Santiago with Mendoza, from where you could continue by train to Buenos Aires and La Paz. César led us along rusting tracks to some ghostly sidings and collapsing sheds, inside one of which was a turntable resembling the skeleton of a fairground carousel. The railway had been a symbol of South America's future.

We went on to the ruins of another grand scheme – one of several brick structures built in the late eighteenth century as shelters for travellers crossing the mountains. The idea had been that of the Irish viceroy in Peru, Ambrosio O'Higgins, whose neglected son Bernardo had become a general in the Army of the Andes. The domed observatory-like structures must have seemed boldly neoclassical when first erected, but travellers such as Darwin, Brand, Proctor and San Martín's soldiers had described them as dark, squalid and infested with the deadly Chagas beetle. Eventually, passing travellers had preferred to sleep outside and the buildings were left to crumble.

We walked up a side valley for what César had promised to be the finest view of Aconcagua, but we saw only a tiny fragment of snow disappearing beneath a grey blanket of clouds. We then rushed back to César's truck to try and reach in the remaining daylight the 4000-metre summit of La Cumbre Pass, which marks the border between Argentina and Chile.

Turning off the main road into Chile before it entered a long tunnel, we took the rough track used by Darwin and his predecessors. We climbed above the snow level until we came to the ridge dividing the Atlantic and Pacific watersheds, where we parked underneath a monumental statue of Christ made in 1904 from melted-down cannons of San Martín's army. We looked towards Chile. The old road zigzagged steeply below us into a white oblivion. In front of us were rows of jagged peaks forming a depressing composition of blacks, greys, whites and browns. This did not seem a view capable of inspiring the 'intense delight' that Darwin had felt on top of the Portillo Pass. Instead this was a view that Proctor had observed with feelings of gloom and anti-climax:

> I certainly thought from what I had read in the accounts of other travellers that I should be able to stretch my sight to Chili, described as the richest country of the globe, spread out at our feet like a map, and repaying our toil by the boundlessness and luxuriance of its prospects. I was much disappointed to find quite the contrary ... above us, on each side, were the craggy peaks and snow-crowned tops of mountains, which towered still higher into the skies: before us the view was still more dreary and unpromising. Enormous black mountains were piled together, without order, and seemed much more barren and savage than those we had already passed.

*

The sun and brilliant blue sky had returned the next morning at El Puente del Inca when I caught a luxury double-decker bus going to Santiago. Seated beside me on the front row at the top was a young family of three. The husband was a handsome Italian, the wife a tall blonde Chilean with a strong and independent spirit. We got into conversation during our protracted crossing of the Chilean frontier. This was the longest and most bureaucratically tiresome crossing I experienced during my whole journey down the Andes and it provoked in the Chilean woman I had just met a sarcastic diatribe against her country.

Rosa, my new travelling companion, said she had wanted to run away from Chile from the moment she was old enough to have a passport. When she was eighteen she had gone to live in France and from there had moved on to Italy. After her marriage she and her husband had become fixated on the idea of travelling around the world in search of a remote and unspoilt corner where they could establish new roots. They had spent the last few years on a Polynesian island. Now they were looking for somewhere else. They had come back to Chile so that her family could get to know their four-year-old daughter. But they wouldn't be staying long in Santiago, 'South America's most depressing city'.

After an hour and a half at the frontier, our bus was finally allowed to continue. The road curved sharply down, before emerging after an hour into a rolling green countryside carpeted with autumnal vineyards. A modern metal cut-out of a giant soldier holding a sword in the air marked the site of the battle of Chacabuco, where the Army of the Andes had liberated from Spain a land that the conquistador Pedro de Valdivia had described to Charles V as a terrestrial paradise.

Rosa was still talking to me about places in the world to escape to when we entered the cloud of dust and pollution that hangs almost permanently over Chile's capital of Santiago. I had a feeling that my path and Rosa's would cross again one day.

I knew Santiago well enough from my first journey to the Andes. It was the least loved of the Andean capitals, an American-style city where everyone seemed in a hurry. The sky was never clear enough to see the Andes other than in hazy profile, if you were lucky. The city was the main reason why the prosperous and politically stable Chile of today was reputedly the least happy of South America's countries.

This time I was only passing through, before taking a night bus the next day to Patagonia. I was here mainly to see friends, one of whom was Gonzalo Donoso, someone with whom I had first visited the Andes. He was the tall, eccentric and Anglophile brother of the late José Donoso, one of Chile's most famous novelists. The last time I had seen him was in his beautiful isolated property in the Andean foothills. Since his retirement as a doctor for the World Health Organization, he had mainly lived there on his own. He loved walking and botany and had introduced me to many of the exotic plants and insects on his estate.

Gonzalo had recently been forced for health reasons to move back to Santiago, which he hated. We met up in a bookshop as I wanted to look for books on Patagonia. He picked out in the travel section two works that had been written by a friend, with whom he had once walked much of the way along the coast of Central Chile. One of the books was about Darwin in South America. The other one was about Humboldt's travels through the Andes. He and his friend had always wanted to retrace Humboldt's route from Cartagena to Lima but they had never got round to it. He insisted on buying me the books as a present.

This would be my last meeting with Gonzalo. I heard several months later that he had died. His body, as he had wished, had been taken to his beloved property looking towards the Andes. Villagers had placed candles around him and stayed with the body all night, drinking coffee and aquavit. He was buried in a cotton sheet, to the accompaniment of an Indian prayer.

25

# SPAIN WAS HERE

I was accumulating books. In earlier days I would have been collecting plants, rocks and insects; but instead I was periodically sending home large packages of books, hoping that these would reach their destination, unlike most of Humboldt's shipments.

The unsent books were now weighing down the rucksack I had put in the hold of the overnight bus from Santiago to Temuco. They were mainly about Patagonia. The travel shelves of the bookshops of Santiago and Mendoza had been crammed with travelogues and memoirs by the first Patagonian explorers and settlers, with studies of every conceivable aspect of Patagonian history and wildlife, and with accounts of journeys by the many writers who have continued coming to the region in the wake of Bruce Chatwin's highly influential *In Patagonia* (1977). I had put aside one of the latter for reading on the bus, even though I never really read on journeys, but just skim through a book in the hope of coming across passages that dovetail with the rapid and random succession of thoughts that come to me when travelling.

The book I was now glancing at was a recent work by an Argentinean novelist, Mempo Giardinelli. His *Ending of the Novel in Patagonia* was the sort of travel book that rarely gets published in

England, a travel book of ideas, replete with literary and philosophical digressions, in one of which, near the beginning, the hugely well-read author disingenuously claims that in finally fulfilling in his fifties a life-long ambition to drive down in a Ford Fiesta to Patagonia, he did not want to read or reread beforehand the travels of other writers and in particular not the 'famous book by Bruce Chatwin', which would 'corrupt' his own view of the place and curtail the sense of freedom he felt in fleeing to the south.

Giardinelli, in other words, was aiming in his travels to get away as far as possible from the mythical region conjured up by Chatwin, who had convinced millions of readers that Patagonia was a place few people visited or wrote about, a bizarre and mysterious region, once roamed by mastodons, inhabited later by the desperate, the mad and the Welsh, a place existing in a largely imaginary dimension. I was already asleep.

I must have entered Patagonia at around four in the morning. I pushed aside a curtain to see a sign marked Los Angeles, beyond which we crossed a river I was sure was the Bíobío. Patagonia is a region without official boundaries, but its symbolic frontier in Chile is this river that for centuries had been the dividing line between what the Spaniards considered the civilized and savage worlds. Pedro de Valdivia, the Spaniard who had colonized Chile after Diego de Almagro's ill-fated attempt, would never get further than the Bíobío, near whose banks he met a dreadful end in 1557, tortured slowly to death by Indians, who cut off his limbs, roasted them in front of him and then cut out his heart. Some claim that they even poured molten gold down his throat.

The Indians who did this were the Mapuche, who ruled the forested mountains of Patagonia, while the Telhueche controlled the plains to the east. The former were known to the Spaniards as the *Araucanos*, after the name of the *Araucaria araucana* or monkey-puzzle trees so abundant in the area. They were famed for their bravery and skill as fighters and for their refusal to be subjugated.

Alonso de Ercilla, the poet-soldier who accompanied Valdivia in his campaigns to the south, wrote about them in a fittingly heroic way in his classically inspired epic poem *La Araucana*. Ercilla stressed a feature of their fighting from which the Incas could have benefitted: as soon as one of their leaders was killed, four more rose up in his stead.

Legends inevitably came to accrue about the apparently unconquerable territory that extended south both of the Bíobío and its Argentinean equivalent, the Río Colorado. Antonio Pigafetta, the Italian whose record of Magellan's round-the-world voyage would be claimed by García Márquez as the continent's first work of magical realism, was responsible in 1520 for the earliest of these: he called the inhabitants of the region's eastern shore 'giant-footed' ('*patagones*') probably on the basis of footprints left by shoes made from vicuña hides.

But the legend that spurred on the Spaniards in their efforts to penetrate Patagonia was that of the *Ciudad de los Césares*, a city of fabled wealth but shifting geographical location, originating perhaps in the story of some finds made west of the Río de la Plata by Francisco César, a Spanish soldier later involved in the search for El Dorado in Colombia. This place, known sometimes as *Trapalanda*, was also rumoured variously to have been founded in southern Argentina by escaping Incas carrying part of Atahualpa's ransom, and even by Spaniards who came across Inca treasures after being shipwrecked off Patagonia's coast.

The legend persisted for three centuries, during which time the Spaniards made thirty-five attempts to invade Mapuche territory. Following the collapse of Spanish rule in South America, the patriots thought they would have no trouble in controlling the Patagonian Indians, whose numbers had been greatly depleted by smallpox. Despite valuing independence so highly themselves, they saw no contradiction in wanting to impose on the Indians the 'civilized' values of the West. The process euphemistically referred to by the Chileans as 'the pacification of Araucania' began in the early 1860s.

Chilean troops, under the command of Colonel Cornelio Saavedra, moved south into Patagonia on hearing reports in 1862 that a crazed and impoverished French nobleman, Orélie-Antonie, had declared himself King of Patagonia after forging an alliance with a Mapuche leader. Seventeen years later, the Argentinean General Julio A. Roca embarked in Patagonia on the War of the Desert, incited by the marauding bands of Mapuche who frequently crossed over the Andes to raid the cattle on the eastern plains. By 1881 most pockets of indigenous resistance had been eliminated.

The Telhueches, described in 1879 by the Patagonian explorer Ramón Lista as 'a vanishing race', have died out completely. The Mapuche, persecuted and driven out of their natural habitat by the logging of forests, were forced to move into newly founded urban centres such as Temuco, the childhood home of Pablo Neruda. An estimated 930,000 Chileans of Mapuche blood have managed to survive into the twenty-first century, but the humiliating fate of their race in post-colonial times was well evoked by Neruda, who was brought up surrounded by its poor and illiterate members:

> Every kind of weapon was used against the Indians, unsparingly: carbine blasts, the burning of villages, and later, a more fatherly method, alcohol and the law. The lawyer became a specialist at stripping them of their fields, the judge sentenced them when they protested, the priest threatened them with eternal fire. And hard spirits finally consummated the annihilation of a superb race whose deeds, valor and beauty Don Alonso de Ercilla carved in stanzas of jade and iron in his *Araucana*.

*

My first stop in Patagonia was the small lakeside town of Pucón, a popular summer resort under the snow-capped cone of the Villarrica volcano. My friend Gonzalo had characterized the place as a metropolitan tourist trap full of dainty boutiques and summer apartments. I was expecting somewhere as artificial as the tourist resorts I had seen in Argentina, but the simple B&B where I stayed was in a part of town like a modest North American suburb surrounded by forest. The houses were mainly of weathered timbers.

The woman who ran the B&B treated me as if she had known me all her life. She started telling me about her town and its remaining Mapuche population. The town, she said, was far poorer than people imagined. 'People think we must be rich from all the tourism. But the season lasts only two months, from December to February. There's massive unemployment throughout the province.' The worst-off people were of course the Mapuche. She told me how many of them were now 'in arms against other Chileans'. They wanted to reclaim lands their ancestors had sold to Germans 'for nothing, for drink money'.

She changed the subject. She said how lucky I was with the weather. Everyone was telling me the same. I had anticipated spending much of the rest of my travels journeying through rain, mist, perhaps even snow. In Pucón, she said, it normally rained for seven months of the year. During the autumn and winter months you could go for weeks without seeing the sun.

I wanted to make the most of the brilliant late-autumn sunshine. I was hoping to stick to my recent resolution of escaping on my own into the wilds. 'Look out for the pumas,' warned the woman at the B&B, as I went off on an afternoon's outing to a small lake called Caburgua. A local bus left me halfway there, near a couple of small waterfalls, from where I intended walking to the lake through the woods. In the summer months the area would have been packed with hikers and picnickers but when the bus drove away, I was all alone.

A few sheep were grazing in a small clearing, where I had an uninterrupted view back towards the Villarrica volcano, with its cream-like cone of snow, resting in the deep blue of the sky, floating above the autumnal trees. Then I walked into the forest, thinking of

Neruda. The opening pages of Neruda's memoirs are a famous prose poem conjuring up the Chilean forest of his Temuco years:

> Under the volcanoes, beside the snow-capped mountains, among the huge lakes, the fragrant, the silent, the tangled Chilean forest . . . My feet sink down into the dead leaves, a fragile twig crackles, the giant rauli trees rise in all their bristling height, a bird from the cold jungle passes over, flaps its wings, and stops in the sunless branches. And then, from its hideaway, it sings like an oboe . . . Anyone who hasn't been in the Chilean forest doesn't know this planet.

I wish I had known what a rauli tree was. I wish I had had Humboldt's knowledge to be able to identify all the other natural marvels featured in Neruda's pages, the 'golden carabus beetle' with its 'mephitic breath', the 'red parasite plants', the 'ramulose, lanceolate' foliage, the 'innumerable calceolarias', the red and white 'copihues'. I recognized only the firs, the monkey puzzles, the beeches and the larches. But I was enjoying the fact simply of walking over fallen leaves, alongside a stream full of pools and cataracts, through a dark and vertical world penetrated by violent shafts of light, splashed with all the yellows, reds and russet browns of the autumn. I was loving the solitude.

'Never did I think so much,' wrote Rousseau, 'exist so vividly, and experience so much, never have I been so much myself . . . as in the journeys I have taken alone and on foot. There is something about walking which stimulates and enlivens my thoughts. When I stay in one place I can hardly think at all; my body has to be on the move to set my mind going.'

I was immersed less in thoughts than in memories. The further I went down the Andes the further my memories seemed to stretch back. I was now dwelling on the time when I was an eight-year-old in New England, discovering the deep colours of the fall amidst the lakes and forests of Maine.

When I came out of the forest in front of Lago Caburgua, with its long jetty projecting into the still blue water, I stood transfixed for a few moments, remembering a place in Maine called Latty Cove where we used to have barbecues on a jetty, looking out onto forested mountains. I continued walking, down to a strip of rocky beach. There was a smell of wood smoke, though I could not work out from where it was coming. Some log cabins were set back among the trees, but they were closed down for the season. The only person around was a morose middle-aged man collecting leaves into a barrow. I sat down on a stone to stare for a while longer at the lake, with its fading memory of summer in the trio of pedalos moored a long way from its shores.

To follow the Andes southwards down towards Patagonia's tip, I was going to have to weave my way between Chile and Argentina, staying as close as possible to the controversial line between the two countries and relying on increasingly irregular transport. At Pucón I caught a twice-weekly bus that drove for hours through a narrow forested valley, where cows and a handful of tumbledown wooden farmsteads were hiding among the trees. Then we slowly climbed up to a pass on the Argentinean border. An expanse of monkey puzzles formed a green ruff around the snowy crested Licán volcano.

The road was barely used, but the frontier still took over two and a half hours to cross. At the Chilean frontier post, and then at the Argentinean one a few kilometres further along, a border guard came on to the bus to read out the passenger list in alphabetical order, after which we had to take our respective places in a queue. It was like being back in school, or in the army.

The only town we passed had been founded as a military post during General Roca's War of the Desert, as had the town we were aiming for. You could tell by their names. The former was called Junín de los Andes, the latter was San Martín de los Andes, at the corner of an elongated lake.

San Martín de los Andes was a glorified leisure centre, with hotels and *pensions* in a smart Tyrolean style and almost every shop a boutique, restaurant, bar, tearoom or tourist agency. Most of the establishments were shut down until the summer. Most of the current residents and visitors seemed to be dog-owning pensioners.

A small group of Mapuches formed an incongruous presence in the main square. They were handing out leaflets protesting at the way tourism was taking away their water supply. I slipped into the local history museum, just behind where they were standing. It had two tiny rooms, with some old photos of traditional Mapuche life. There was little to detain you for more than five minutes and I wanted to walk down to the lake shore before sunset. But the enthusiastic young woman in charge, an anthropology student from Buenos Aires, did not want to let me go before giving me an hour-long lecture on Mapuche folklore and customs. Just as I finally managed to get away, she told me of a long walk I could do the next morning. It would give me the best view of the lake. The site was within the Mapuche reservation.

I headed off there early in the morning, under another cloudless sky. The student had drawn me a detailed map, which I was able to follow as far as the reservation's entrance, a crudely made gate of logs, with a sign telling the visitor to respect nature and the Mapuche people and to leave a donation. Beyond the gate there was a series of unsignposted forest paths thinning out into nowhere. I ended up scrambling up a slope slippery with pine needles, hoping to reach the top of the mountain in the quickest way possible. I found another path, down which two Mapuche girls were skipping. They giggled and said I was going in the right direction. The path forked. I kept climbing towards a clearing and passed what could have been either a dog kennel or a shrine. It was in fact a shrine to an adolescent called Ceferino Namuncura, who had been one of the first Salesian pupils in Argentina and had died aged nineteen after performing several miracles. Next to him was a prayer that began with the words, 'Ceferino Namuncura, you who are of Mapuche blood, help us from your heavenly throne to find our way.'

Walking a bit further I came to a place where I could see all the way down to the far end of the lake. Whether or not this was the view I had been told about did not matter. The sight of a receding mass of deep-blue water snaking through the mountains was wonderful enough. The town of San Martín was completely out of sight and the only signs of human habitation were some widely scattered timber homes in the wood below, the nucleus of the Mapuche community.

I walked down into the Mapuche village, where I coincided with the mid-morning break at the small primary school. The teacher had a pointed grey beard and looked like an elf. He showed me a computer installed with a version of Microsoft Word in Mapundungun, the Mapuche language.

I was reassured to discover that this language was still widely spoken and, as I tried finding my way back to San Martín through the maze of paths through the forest, I was amused by the idea of a people almost wilfully confusing potential visitors, making an anarchic stand in a world of clearly laid out trails and uniform tourism.

From San Martín I took a near-empty bus to a smaller resort to the south, Villa Angostura. The road, one of the most famously beautiful in Patagonia, wound its way from one forested lake to the next, ending in territory barely penetrated by white men until 1876.

The first person to popularize the area was someone whose name today is linked to many of Patagonia's best-known tourist spots, Francisco Moreno, better known as 'Perito' Moreno, 'Moreno the Expert'. The Buenos Aires-born Perito Moreno was a passionate naturalist whose first trip to Patagonia in 1873 had led him to search out sites described by Darwin off the eastern coast of the region. Yet, unlike Darwin or Humboldt, his love of the natural world was not an entirely disinterested one.

503

He was one of a group of Patagonia-obsessed scientists whose activities coincided with Roca's War of the Desert. He was a staunch patriot whose explorations – specifically his researches into the continental divide – played a key role in establishing the Argentinean-Chilean frontier. He was also someone with a firm belief in Patagonia's potential for development.

Part of his success as an explorer depended on his good relations with the Telhueches and the Mapuche, but his attitude towards them was ambivalent. He was a humane person utterly opposed to attempts to exterminate the Indian population. However, he believed that western values were innately superior to 'savage' Indian ones, and that if you treated the Indians as human beings, they would eventually accept this and do whatever you wanted them to.

Perhaps it is best to think of Moreno essentially as someone who championed Patagonia's areas of outstanding beauty. One of his most significant 'discoveries' was the lake to which I walked from Villa Angostura, the Lago Nahuel Huapi. It was a lake that made me lose what little sense of direction I had. My first proper view of it was from the top of a wooded promontory, from where it appeared not as an uninterrupted expanse of water, but as a blob of blue mercury, magically contracting and expanding as it slithered through the forests and mountains. To one side the view was towards slopes whose rocky summits were dabbed with snow. To another the view was of further wooded headlands, successive patches of water, rising mists, superimposed silhouettes of mountains, the whole composition progressively lighter, until the eye finally came to a jagged faraway horizon.

'The splendour of nature becomes prodigiously greater as you advance towards the south,' wrote Moreno of the day in January 1876 when he first set eyes on the Lago Nahuel Huapi. 'Arriving exhausted at the lake I drank with pleasure from its crystalline waters, in which I saw reflected the colours of the fatherland. In that moment of pure joy, I began to consider my physical and mental state. What was left of all those terrible hardships I had endured in getting to this place? Absolutely nothing! My spirit, as calm that day as the blue waters of the lake, was free from all its earlier storms.'

Another person to enjoy the lake in the days before tourism was Moreno's collaborator, Clemente Onelli, an Italian-born zoologist and palaeontologist. In his eloquent book of Andean memories, *Treading the Andes*, Onelli reflected on how lucky it was that the lake had not been discovered at the height of the Romantic period, when writers would have praised its idyllic bucolic charms with poetic excess. 'This lake, this king of world lakes,' in Onelli's opinion, 'is not one you can describe. You should admire it instead in silence, and then later, during the long winter nights, surrounded by children and grandchildren, talk of its wonders as you would relate a fairy tale.'

In 1902, three years before Onelli's book was published, Perito Moreno revisited the Lago Nahuel Huapi in the company of a wealthy young socialite and adventurer from Buenos Aires, Aarón Anchorena. Aarón was accompanied by a group of like-minded friends. They spent the summer at a place on the lake whose name, Bariloche, was derived from the Mapuche for 'people behind the mountains', *vuriloche*. Their visit there is often described as the first package tour. It would encourage Bariloche's eventual transformation into one of South America's most popular inland resorts. Bariloche was little more than twenty kilometres along the lake from Villa Angostura. The direct bus there would have taken me half an hour, but I spent three days getting there.

I went back into Chile, to travel to the town by a now-popular tourist route that had been pioneered in 1672 by an Italian Jesuit missionary called Nicolás Mascardi. Mascardi had discovered a way of crossing the Andes largely by boat, along a series of near-interconnected lakes. He and his companions were probably more interested in finding the Ciudad de los Césares than in evangelizing, but they founded a mission on Lake Nahuel Huapi, which lasted until 1717, when everyone was killed by Indians.

To follow Mascardi's route I signed up for a very expensive tour involving three bus and boat rides, and a stay in the Chilean hamlet of Peulla at the edge of Lago Todos Los Santos. The boats and buses along the entire route, as well as the only two hotels at Peulla, were owned by a single company, the Cruce Andino.

This situation had remained unchanged since the time when Che Guevara had travelled this route with his friend Alberto Granado. The two men had been near the start of their epic life-changing journey across South America, when their shared motorcycle had still been functioning, more or less. They did the lakes' journey in the opposite direction from me. Alberto weighed up its pros and cons:

Once more we see two sides of the coin – heads, the beauty of the landscape and kindness of the people; tails, the fact that all this beauty is exploited by the company that owns the hotel, the coaches that bring in the tourists, and the yachts that cruise the lake. A company, in short, that owns the whole place and every-one living here, since it is the only source of jobs. Nobody passes this way without leaving a few pesos in the company's pockets. Naturally, we broke with tradition and, instead of heading for the hotel, went straight to the quay. There, after chatting with the caretaker, we slept in a shed among torn yacht sails and tar-covered ropes.

I stayed with a dissolute architect friend at the very Germanic Chilean town of Puerto Varas. We had been up talking for most of the night and I arrived at the tour's starting point after only a few hours' sleep. A fresh-faced guide was greeting a predominantly smart and elderly group of tourists from different parts of South America, mainly Brazil. Bariloche was so popular now with Brazilians that it was sometimes known as 'Brasiloche'.

The day had dawned grey and misty, but the low clouds that had hung over the Lago Todos Los Santos like the froth on a cappuccino were now rapidly dissolving and the sunlit snowy cone of the Osorno volcano rose free from a lake whose colour had once given it the name Emerald Lake. The two large luxury hotels at Peulla appeared diminutive beneath sheer slopes of dark forest and snow-crowned rock. There was no possibility of sleeping in the boat shed or protesting at the Cruce Andino's monopoly of the lakes' crossing. However, I was given a special dispensation as an impoverished writer: I was allowed to stay at a greatly reduced rate at a private bed-and-breakfast reserved for the bus drivers on the tour.

We reached Peulla at midday. Once again I struck out on my own. I headed up a steep forest path which soon became overgrown and difficult to follow. I had not paid much attention to the puma warnings at Pucón but the far greater isolation of Peulla made me take them more seriously. I remembered the advice given to trekkers in the States in the unlikely event of being faced with the animal: you tried to appear much larger than you were and made frightening growling noises.

After more than three hours of uphill walking, with occasional glimpses through the forest of the lake below, I had the sensation of being observed. In Perito Moreno's day, there was the strong likelihood of Mapuches spying on outsiders in their world. Today the most likely creature to take an interest in the activities of intruders was the puma. I stood for a few moments in complete silence, conscious of vague rustlings in the undergrowth, followed by a sinister stillness. I saw nothing. I was hoping to emerge from the forest soon and come to a tiny mountain lake marked on the map, but I turned round. The sun was already beginning to lower on the horizon.

We arrived at Bariloche late the following afternoon. Bariloche was like San Martín on an much greater scale, with hundreds of Germanic villas lining the shores of a Nahuel Huapi that looked just as Perito Moreno had perceived it, the Andean equivalent of

Switzerland's Lac Leman. The place, even off-season, brought together people of all nationalities. Bariloche had been cosmopolitan well before Che's day. He had dreamt here of sailing away to distant seas. I had a renewed longing for wilderness.

After a day in Bariloche I continued south on a bus whose sole occupants appeared to be escapees from a mental home. The most normal was an emaciated chain-smoking young Frenchman who told me that the French philosopher Jean Baudrillard had made him obsessed by the idea of deconstructing 'the phantasm of the end of the world'. An agitated ferociously faced Japanese backpacker was sitting on the opposite side of the aisle to a tramp-like old man with a football strip, a green walking stick and a collection of plastic bags through which he was constantly shuffling. Behind me a myopic young man periodically broke the silence by ringing up his mother to tell her in a high-pitched voice that he loved her.

A stormy late-afternoon sky just outside Bariloche cast a metallic light on a mountain whose spire-like forms had earned it the name Cathedral Peak. The storm came and went, and there was a clear evening sky when we reached Esquel, the town at the end of Paul Theroux's journey through South America. He described the landscape as having a prehistoric look, like that which 'forms a painted backdrop for a dinosaur skeleton in a museum'. He was almost surprised to be still alive. He had suffered since Boston from what was for him the worst and most constant fear of solitary travel: 'a fear of death'. 'It is impossible to spend months travelling alone and arrive in Patagonia and not feel as if one has done something very foolish . . . and thoroughly pointless.'

Theroux had avoided 'the Tyrolean fantasy of Bariloche' so as to travel to Esquel by steam train from a lowland town four hundred kilometres to the east called Ingeniero Jacobacci. The steam train, dubbed by him 'The Old Patagonian Express', functions today along a greatly reduced stretch of line and purely for the benefit of tourists and train buffs. The town, under bare, ochre slopes, seemed on passing quickly through it like a Wild West theme park. I took the last bus of the day to the nearby but much smaller community of Trevelín, whose tourist image was based instead on Welshness. I arrived there late on a night so cold that everyone was indoors. Outside the only open hotel was a pipe which had burst and turned an adjacent shrub into an explosion of icicles. I waited until morning to see more of the town.

Chatwin's *In Patagonia* had given me little idea of what I might find in Trevelín, other than the normal line-up of Patagonian eccentrics. He had turned up early in the morning and had been initially distracted by some timber buildings belonging to a Bahai community comprising 'a very muscular negro from Bolivia' and a physically less appealing Iranian. He had then gone on to meet the son and granddaughter of the town's founder, John Daniel Evans. These people all lived in a town that had 'an ordinary Victorian mill' and a lot of glinting tin.

I walked out of the hotel after breakfast to find crisp views over a flat landscape looking towards the forests and snowy mountains bordering the frontier with Chile. There was little else immediately striking about Trevelín. The place was essentially one long and monotonous street, like somewhere in the middle of the Ohio plains.

Everyone in Trevelín of Welsh ancestry appeared to have the name Evans. The first Evans I met was Lola Evans, who met me outside the Welsh chapel founded by her grandfather, Thomas Dalar Evans. Lola was a chirpy redhead who spoke only Welsh and Spanish.

The chapel, in the middle of a field, was in an austere Welsh Methodist style, with undecorated brickwork and simple wooden pews. An old photo showed the Welsh community early in the last century, with dozens of boys and girls in their Sunday best posing in rows. Lola's grandfather Thomas was at the back. He was one of the colonists who had accompanied John Daniel Evans on an expedition into the heart of Patagonia in 1885. The Welsh had originally settled near the region's eastern coast, twenty years earlier, but a series of bad harvests had encouraged the search for a place that would be agriculturally more profitable. They knew they had found the right location as soon as they came to this valley, which they dubbed Cwm Hyfryd ('Pleasant Valley').

Near the chapel was a doll-like brick cottage with a white wooden porch. This was the school that was trying to keep the Welsh language and customs alive. Inside we interrupted a class being given to four young children by a young woman called Clare. Clare was part of a scheme whereby native speakers from Wales were being paid by the Welsh education authorities to come and teach in Patagonia. Later I visited Clare in the house she rented with another teacher from Wales, Helen. The two of them were amused by the quaintly old-fashioned Welsh that was spoken here and by the strength of local Welsh nationalist feelings, which they themselves did not share.

The Victorian mill mentioned by Chatwin was the one that had given the town its Welsh name of 'Town of the Mill'. It was now a twee local museum, full of cast-iron kitchen implements and inscriptions in faux Victorian lettering. On the outskirts of Trevelín a ginger-haired man called Mervyn Evans had constructed a traditional mill that was now a popular tourist attraction. While showing me the mill, he proudly told me how the Welsh were the first to see the possibilities of growing wheat in a region which Darwin had dismissed as unsuitable for cultivation of any kind. The wheat grains, imported from Ukraine, had done particularly well in the Trevelín area, which had the ideal conditions for wheat growing – much light during the day and very cold nights. Twenty-two mills had once flourished here. Sheathes of wheat had been incorporated into the regional coat of arms. However, all this had changed in 1949, thanks to an Argentinean government ruling that gave all the subsidies to wheat growers in the north of the country and decreed that farmers south of the Río Colorado should devote themselves instead to sheep rearing. The wheat industry was abandoned in Patagonia.

Mervyn interpreted this not just as an example of bungling interference on the part of a centralized government but also as an insult to his people. He spoke about the Welsh with a patriotic fervour I had rarely found in Wales itself. He talked about how his ancestors in Patagonia could not abide the sound of English, how they had come to Patagonia in search of liberty and how they had always enjoyed wonderful relations with the Telhueches, who had thought of them as too good and too tolerant to be Christians. He also showed me in the dying light of the day a near-completed full-scale reproduction of an old biplane he was making. Naturally it bore the Welsh colours.

It was already night when I finally made contact, as Chatwin had done, with Clery Evans, the granddaughter of the legendary John Daniel Evans. She and her mother lived in a wooden house dwarfed by trees. In 1884, one year before settling in Pleasant Valley, John Evans had accompanied an expedition into the Patagonian interior in search of gold. Despite the understanding between the Welsh and the Indians, the latter had attacked John Evans and the three Welshmen with him. The Indians wanted revenge for atrocities committed during the War of the Desert. They mutilated John Evans's three companions and placed their excised sexual organs in their mouths. John Evans managed to escape this fate by getting his horse Malcara to leap over an enormous gully. In Evans's large garden was a small memento-filled cabin, outside which a boulder commemorated the burial spot of Malcara.

Clery Evans's grandfather, she explained, had gone on to play a leading role in the signing of a plebiscite at Trevelín in 1902 determining the Chilean-Argentinean frontier. According to watershed rules, Pleasant Valley should have belonged to Chile, but John Evans had persuaded the Welsh that they would be better off under Argentina.

Clery was a woman of energy and passion. She spoke of people who had passed through Trevelín and had got to know her family. Aimé Tschiffely, for instance, had come here to see the tomb of Malcara, several years after the journey in the 1920s that had made his own horses international celebrities. Butch Cassidy and the Sundance Kid had also stayed in Pleasant Valley, where they had rented a farmstead. A detective from America's Pinkerton Agency, the forerunner of the CIA, had tracked them down here by 1905 and had got employment as their gardener. When the two gangsters discovered his real identity, they shot him and buried his body in the garden. Soon afterwards their shared mistress, as a public relations exercise, invited members of Clery's family to tea, including Clery's blind great-aunt. The great-aunt's dog dug up the detective's hand, and excitedly brought it into the sitting-room as everyone was eating their scones. Butch Cassidy and the Sundance Kid headed off soon afterwards towards Bolivia.

'And what about Chatwin?' I asked. I had yet to hear a good word about him in South America, though he had merely done in Patagonia what travel writers generally do: exploit confidences, publish material without permission, misrepresent, misquote, exaggerate for literary effect, use people, and promise to stay in touch and then go away, never to be heard of again.

The anger Clery felt about Chatwin had obviously been building up for years. She, as a bookish and sophisticated person, had every reason to feel upset by Chatwin's portrayal of her father as a coarse drunken buffoon who called out for 'Horse piss!' every time he wanted another beer. She told me that Chatwin's grasp of Spanish was so poor that he got everything wrong.

'But what was he like as a person?' I continued. 'Insignificant,' she replied without hesitation, 'a small, insignificant man, dull and charmless. He was interested in people only if they could help him, or supply picturesque material. Or if they had good bodies like the Bolivian.'

Freezing temperatures were predicted over the coming days and a strong possibility of snow. Padre Leonardo, the Italian Salesian priest from Lake Titicaca, had told me of colleagues of his who had been trapped for weeks in isolated Patagonian communities. The thought excited me, but added an extra element of insecurity to my plans for travelling southwards. I had already discovered at Bariloche that all public transport south of Esquel on the celebrated Route 40 stopped running after April. This meant that the only way of following the Andes from this point onwards was to cross back into Chile and join up with the Carretera Austral, the unpaved continuation of the Pan-American Highway.

The Carretera Austral had the appeal of a road that came eventually to an abrupt end amidst the glaciers and mountainous fjords that indent the south-western coastline of the continent. During my first stay in Chile I had spent time in the archipelago of Chiloe and had sailed from nearby Puerto Montt down to the edge of Tierra del Fuego, journeying in and out of fjords and around the multitude of islands into which the Andes are finally shattered. Looking across the sea towards this empty ragged shore of forests, snows, mountains and waterfalls, I had often wondered about the road that ran behind it.

To reach the Carretera Austral from Trevelín I had to get to the Chilean mountain village of Futaleufú, from where, in the winter months, there was a weekly bus connecting to that road. This was supposed to coincide with another irregular service all the way down the Austral to Coyhaique, a town that had been almost completely cut off from the rest of Chile until the late 1980s.

The next bus from Trevelín to Futaleufú was not due to leave for four days, but the owner of my hotel managed to find me a lift to Futaleufú. It was already dusk by the time we got there. A full moon was rising above a snowy crest. Around us was forest. A thermometer recorded minus fifteen degrees centigrade.

Futaleufú, a tiny summer resort frequented by hikers and fishermen, seemed off-season a small cozy village, with none of the blatant commercialization to which it would probably have been subject in Argentina. I stayed in a B&B run by a teacher at the local school. She was originally from Valparaíso, but had moved to Futaleufú after the death of her husband. She wanted to spend her years of widowhood in a place that was quiet, remote and safe. I would think of her one year later, when a volcanic explosion led to the evacuation of the entire area and an endlessly lingering cloud of black ash.

The frost at dawn was like snow. The crispness of the air was clouded only by the breath of the six passengers waiting for the bus to take us to the yet smaller village of Villa Santa Lucía, on the Carretera Austral, from where I hoped to catch a minibus to take me to Coyhaique, the capital of this most isolated of Chilean regions.

The journey to Coyhaique was eight hours of pure enjoyment, a spectacle put on for the benefit of half a dozen passengers, four of whom were asleep. The journey was through landscapes shrouded for most days of the year in fog and rain, but now forming a brilliant Andean idyll of limitless forests, full of the sequoia-like *alerces*, overlooked by rocky summits dripping with snow.

Coyhaique, a town dating from the 1920s, was once connected to the rest of Chile only by plane and the occasional boat from the port of Puerto Aisén. The ex-husband of my Bolivian friend Marbel Garrón was from Coyhaique and had spent his early childhood there. His descriptions of the place in winter had haunted me. For those three months of the year, he said, the town's inhabitants hibernated. Fog, snow and freezing temperatures kept people at home and prevented them leaving the town.

Much of Coyhaique resembled a large rustic suburb, tucked away in a forest clearing, radiating from an octagonal landscaped square, dark and empty at night. I found a small room in a white wooden house popular with guest workers, and warmed only by a dining-room chimney, a large Aga and a solitary gas stove on the upper floor. Rogelio, the owner, with his dyed black hair and bright rosy cheeks, was someone from a Christmas tale. Solicitously attending to his guests with a red apron and a constant smile, he offered me quick snippets of tourist advice as he hurried from table to table with a marionette-like skip. The warmth of his manner compensated for the coldness of my room. The condensation on my window ledge froze during the night. I had to sleep fully clothed.

The temperature had sunk to twenty degrees below zero, Rogelio cheerfully informed me over breakfast the next morning. He advised me to 'cover up warmly' and visit a local nature reserve about an hour's walk away. The sun was shining again as I trod over leaves still crisp with frost. As it was a Saturday and the weather was so beautiful, I imagined the reserve would be full of hikers and families, but there was not a single other person. I took what was promoted as a five-hour trail, through a dense forest of conifers, past frozen lakes to observation towers with panoramas towards further forests spreading up cliffs of rock and snow. Every half-hour or so there would be a wooden panel pointing out aspects of the natural history of each section of the reserve. One panel alerted visitors to their being in 'the typical habitat' of the puma. 'Though you might not be aware of the pumas, they will certainly be observing you.'

At night, on Rogelio's recommendation, I went to a local dance hall, where a live band was playing traditional tunes. The Bavarian-style hall was filled with single middle-aged men and women sitting at separate tables. This was, I soon realized, a last chance for the lonelier of Coyhaique's inhabitants to find a partner to last them through the winter months. Two of the women invited me to come and join them. One of them was Rogelio's ex-wife; the other had known him since they were children. Everyone knew everyone in Coyhaique. Outsiders were very much in demand. They wondered if I was a mining engineer. They were disappointed I was only passing through. They tried to persuade me to stay on a few more days, a few more weeks, until the winter was over. I walked back to the hostel through the season's first flurries of snow.

A few centimetres of snow fell during the night. The landscape at breakfast was white and grey. I told Rogelio I was going to spend the day at Puerto Aisén, the scene a few weeks back of Chile's last major earthquake. Chile has more earthquakes than any almost any other country in the world, as well as 2900 volcanoes, eighty per cent of which are active. The region I was in, the XI Region, was not especially known for its seismic activity, though the fact that almost no one lived here until the last century probably means that many of its earthquakes in the past have gone unrecorded. The earthquake that shook Puerto Aisén on 22 April 2007 was one of the region's worst in living memory. Only a dozen people died, but the continuing tremors and the prospect of some worse catastrophe to come had depleted the town's population by almost a quarter.

'People are leaving all the time,' said Rogelio, 'the ground is always trembling, something strange is happening. They say that a new volcano is being born under the sea.'

The snow turned to sleet and then to rain as the bus to Puerto Aisén descended towards the coast. Puerto Aisén was like many of the poorer Chilean communities I had seen, a grid of low dwellings in tin, timber and plasterboard, with some monkey-puzzle trees along the sidewalks. Over the past few days the trembling had apparently calmed down and was now unnoticeable. Following Rogelio's advice I went straight to the local radio station, which looked like an East London mini-cab office, with dark greasy walls and old furniture in need of re-upholstery.

The only person there was a long-haired young man who was reading out the weather report when I came into the room. He gestured to me to take a seat. While waiting for the commercial break, I read through a local government leaflet stapled to the wall. It was all about earthquake activity. It was an attempt to prevent people needlessly evacuating a region that was probably less dangerous than most other places in Chile: the main advice was to stay calm.

The young man came to talk to me, and expressed his disbelief that so many people were leaving the town. 'Nowhere in the Andes is safe. Nowhere in the world is safe.' Then he contacted on his mobile someone called Basilio, who had been with some of the victims of the last earthquake seconds before they had been swamped by a tsunami. Basilio turned up soon afterwards, offering to drive me to the scene of the disaster. Looking like a sea captain, with his dark-blue pullover and weathered face, he seemed a man of cheery philosophical resignation. He told me that he had been head of the local police force and that one of his main duties had been organizing rescue missions.

The drab grey sky was being broken by the sun after we had left Puerto Aisén and driven the few kilometres to the town's small port of Chacabuco, which was situated on what now seemed an idyllic bay, with a ring of snowy mountains and forests coming straight down to the water's edge.

Basilio stopped the car next to the rusting hulk of a large fishing vessel. He got out to show me, on the other side of the bay, a tiny cove accessible only by boat. Then he produced from a folder a large blown-up photo. The photo, he said, was taken minutes before the tsunami had come, late on the morning of 22 April. It had been an unseasonably sunny April day and several of his friends and acquaintances had come to the cove on an outing. A man could be seen in the photo stirring the coals of a barbecue, while another was carrying an ice-box from a boat. A few children were playing on the shore.

'A few minutes later,' said Basilio, 'all the people you see here were swept away by the tsunami. Just before it all happened I had the same strange feeling I had had in 1991, when I had seen a landslide caused by another earthquake. I knew I had a matter of seconds to make it to the top of that rock over there. When I looked down to the shore, absolutely nothing was left. I was completely on my own.'

Basilio's outlook on life had been moulded by his experiences as a witness to disasters. He was a man of scientific instincts whose empirical observations had led him to find an explanation for the mysterious boulders dotted around the area: originally encased by snow and ice, they had been dislodged from the summits of mountains. Yet, for all his faith in science and reason, he was also someone sensitive to the inexplicable and the supernatural, such as the time when, late on a summer evening, alone on the empty coast, he could hear from the sea the sounds of phantasmal rowing. He had recorded this in a short story.

He had brought some of his stories with him. They were heavily based on his experiences travelling to remote places around Puerto Aisén, searching for survivors, organizing the removal of dead bodies, seeing ghosts.

It was snowing again on my return to Coyhaique and it continued snowing for much of the night, briefly threatening my journey south. Even without the snow there were no buses at this time of year to take me to the southernmost end of the Carretera Austral, from where, in the summer months, the only way onwards was by horse to the shores of a lake known on the Chilean side as O'Higgins and on the Argentinean side as San Martín.

The sun and snow ploughs had cleared the roads by late morning, allowing me to cross into Argentina by another lake, the Lago Buenos Aires. I embarked late in the evening on a weekly ferry. There were only five passengers and a cargo of cows.

The boat pulled out into the lake just after sunset, when the mountains around us were reduced to a black silhouette whose line was shaped like that of a cardiogram. Towards Argentina the line straightened out and descended to the level of the water. A ferocious wind was building up, rocking the boat and agitating the frightened cows on the deck. Two of the passengers pointed to a puzzling light in the sky that was neither a star nor a plane.

I sat almost on my own at the top of the overnight bus to a town on the Atlantic coast called Comodoro Rivadavia. Thanks to the virtual closure in winter of Route 40, my journey to the far south of Argentina was going to involve massive detours across a landscape as featureless and horizontal as the pampas, but with barely any traces of human presence.

Darwin's initial impressions of the plains that occupy most of Patagonia were prosaic and negative. He judged this giant empty space to be boring and useless, sadly limited in its flora and fauna and unsuitable for development. Yet on his return to England, when expanding his notes into a travel book, he romantically transformed this emptiness (where 'death and decay prevail') into a world memorably conducive to profound introspection.

'No one can stand unmoved in these solitudes,' he wrote, 'without feeling that there is more in man than the mere breath of his body. In calling up images of the past, I find the plains of Patagonia most frequently cross before my eyes. Yet these plains are pronounced by all most wretched & useless . . . Why then, and the case is not peculiar to myself, do these arid wastes take so firm possession of the memory?'

I saw an illuminated sign marked 'Perito Moreno' and a few surrounding lights but little else during the seven-hour journey to Comodoro Rivadavia, from where I set off on another double-decker to another coastal town, Río Gallegos, far to the south and a further twelve hours away. I tried staring at the flat coastline, with its occasional low cliffs. At the small town of Caleta Olivia, the other passengers all got off and the bus headed inland.

Little changed except for the clouds, which repeatedly gathered and dispersed across a flat, deep-ochre landscape as unnaturally clear as a Pre-Raphaelite painting. The road seemed always the same, running in a straight line towards a horizon that never got any closer; but this apparent monotony, viewed on your own, in complete silence, free from all other distractions, made you more fascinated still by each detail and slight variation – a solitary ostrich, a distant rainbow, a couple of vicuñas, a dried-up riverbed, a tiny hill, a pale band of blue shining towards evening over Río Gallegos.

Río Gallegos is a town that bus travellers to the far south cannot avoid. Most tourists would like to. They think of it as an obligatory purgatory you have to pass through on your way to and from the sublime glaciers and peaks of El Calafate and El Chaltén. I found the place suggestive of a drab English coastal town from my child-hood, full of grey and white chalets, Formica-decorated tearooms, old-fashioned signposting and poorly stocked supermarkets. There was a good reason for its Englishness. The town had been a major meeting place for Patagonia's English community. Many of the English had come to Patagonia to breed sheep, an activity which damaged the region's delicate ecosystem while being ultimately doomed to collapse. The other English were mainly merchants who regularly sailed from here to the Falkland Islands.

The winter of 2007 marked the twenty-fifth anniversary of the Falklands War and masses were being held in Río Gallegos to com-memorate the Argentinean victims. The town was also in conflict with its most famous native son, the country's President Nestor Kirchner. Kirchner, politically moderate, anxious to maintain good relations with Chávez and Morales, had been a welcome change after the corrupt former president Carlos Menem and the horrific military dictatorships of the 1970s and eighties. Argentina under him – as with Chile post-Pinochet – had come to enjoy political sta-bility and increasing prosperity. The troubles at Río Gallegos were among the first signs that all was not well. Local unions were demanding increased salaries; all public employees were on strike; the rubbish had not been collected for weeks; and the town had been affected by roadblocks. I could have been back in Bolivia.

A large nocturnal demonstration passed outside the town's British Club as I sat having a solitary supper in the club's wood-panelled dining-room. The waitress told me that the club was the place where Kirchner and his family always came to when in town. Kirchner's sister had been eating here only the other day, before a much-publicized incident when an angry demonstrator had thrown flour over her.

There were fortunately no protesters blocking the road to El Calafate the next day. There was almost no traffic either. I sat back on a late-afternoon bus, to relish another three hours of travelling alone through the flat solitudes, towards what could eventually be identified, just before nightfall, as a distant line of snow-brushed mountains, shaped and whittled by the winds.

Staying a few years before on the Chilean side of these mountains, in the dramatically contoured national park of the Torres del Peine, I had envisaged El Calafate as a wild frontier destination frequented as much by gauchos as by tourists. I had now been long enough in Argentina to know what I could more realistically expect, especially since the recent construction of the town's airport.

As I walked at night through the amorphous suburban spread that had grown up behind the flat eastern shores of the Lago Argentino, I began to be almost nostalgic for Río Gallegos. I passed several large gabled hotels, countless luxury gabled residences and a main street lined with gabled tourist agencies selling glacier tours monopolized by a single company, Hielo y Aventura ('Ice and Adventure').

None of the few people left in El Calafate for the winter knew of the cheap hostel where I had booked a bed. I spent most of my first night looking for it. The one person who had heard of the Hostal Lago Azul was convinced that the old man who ran it had died several years ago. When I found the place, down a dark side-street, it certainly looked closed. It was little more than a plasterboard cabin outside which was a wooden board marked in faded handwritten letters. But a faint light penetrated a crack in a shutter.

A bald man with a moustache and sweetly smiling face opened the door. He introduced himself as Don Horacio, and said he had almost given up waiting for me. He said he was ninety-one years old. His hostel consisted of two tiny dormitory rooms, both of which had been empty since the end of the season. His main room was the kitchen, which was dominated by an Aga. He invited me to a cup of tea. 'Now let me tell you a story,' he said.

He had been born in 1915 in Río Gallegos, where his father had moved from Buenos Aires. His father was a salesman who later settled in El Calafate. 'In those days the town was just a shelter for wool traders. There was a hotel, a couple of houses, a doctor and little else.'

Don Horacio had spent most of his life here, working latterly on the large estates, irrigating the fields and shearing sheep. Before that he had been what he called a 'carter', transporting food, wool, skins and mail on a horse-drawn cart all the way to Río Gallegos. He had slept at night on his cart, stretched out on sheepskins. The journey used to take him between forty and fifty days. 'And now it takes only three hours,' he laughed.

He was old enough to remember the Telhueches. He used to carry trinkets to sell to their women. Once he had been terrified by the sight of a group of Indians dancing in a circle, waving lances and making terrible shouts. He thought they were intending to kill him, but it turned out that they were behaving in this way because their cacique, their native chief, had just died and they believed the devil had been responsible. They destroyed all the cacique's possessions, pierced his corpse with their lances and covered him tightly in a shroud. The body was then buried in a secret location.

'And on that note I better be off to bed,' he said, getting up to shuffle towards his room. I had been listening to the memories of one of the last survivors of the pioneer era.

I was back in the morning to the world of streamlined tourism, signing up for one of the tours organized by Hielo y Aventura. It was my only way of getting close to one of South America's largest glaciers, the one named after Perito Moreno.

The woman who sold me the ticket was suitably icy, while the tour itself kept the adventure element to a minimum. The bus spent the first hour picking up various passengers from El Calafate's widely scattered hotels. The bored young tour guide from Buenos Aires recited a few facts as the bus followed the shores of the Lago Argentino. There were some condors standing around nonchalantly by the roadside, as if tamed by the spirit of modern Argentinean tourism.

Slowly the rising sun began to light up the dark blues of the lake and to inflame the russets of the bare snow-covered slopes above.

The sudden appearance in this landscape of the Perito Moreno glacier was like the sounding of some climactic chords of music. At the glacier's further end, where the sun was now shining, it was an expanding mass of silvery white disappearing behind a world of towering white peaks. At its nearer end, still cast in shadow, it was an eerie expanse of turquoises and greys rolling into a giant frozen wave.

The guide plied us with statistics as we got nearer. It was one of only three Patagonian glaciers that were not receding today. It was thirty kilometres long and covered an area of 250 square kilometres. It had a depth of approximately 700 metres at its deepest part. It was constantly in motion, like all glaciers. The movement of its softer lower layers resulted in the regular creation of crevasses and the repeated sounds of infernal groans and creaks.

A fragment as large as Don Horacio's hostel collapsed as we were watching it, to the great applause of our group. This gave an extra excitement to the next part of our outing: 'mini-trekking' across the glacier. We were equipped with crampons and given brief instructions on how to walk with them. We were told to circumvent the crevasses with care; it was almost impossible to rescue someone who has fallen in.

The glacier at close quarters seemed as strange as from afar – a landscape of glistening pale-blue silhouettes looking at times like glossy Styrofoam. The guide chipped off bits of it for us to drop into glasses of whisky.

As I trudged back clumsily towards our starting point, I began looking at the glacier with the eyes of an explorer. I could understand now the desire to trek westwards along it and into what was still one of the barely touched Andean wildernesses – a land where forty-eight glaciers had gone into the making of the world's biggest extension of continental ice after Greenland and Antarctica.

A naturalist called Federico Reichart had been the first actually to enter the Hielo Patagónico, as late as 1914: he had got thirty kilometres inland before being forced to turn around. In 1928 the

German aviator Gunther Plüschow, a First World War hero famed for his daredevil exploits, had realized the area's daunting extent by flying over it.

In 1931 the land was crossed from east to west by an Italian Salesian priest, Padre Alberto de Agostini, a man who saw God on Andean summits and whose obsessive Patagonian wanderings earned him the nickname 'Padre Patagonia'. In 1960 an Englishman, Eric Shipton, became the first person to lead an expedition across the Hielo from north to south. In 1985 an Italian, Giuliano Giongo, claimed to have done this same journey alone and in the middle of the winter. In 1998 the first full trek along the whole of the ice-field's 350-kilometre length was achieved by a Chilean team. Not until 2008 would work begin on the task of properly demarcating the Chilean-Argentinean frontier across the Hielo. There is still a stretch of fifty kilometres that remains undefined, within sight of Mount Fitzroy, to the north. From the top of this mountain's craggy peaks, once considered invincible, the Hielo is said to resemble on clear days a fantastical city of ice. There is even a theory that the legend of the City of the Caesars had its origins in such sightings of Patagonia's frozen expanses.

From El Calafate I went north for the day to El Chaltén to see Mount Fitzroy, the peak named after the *Beagle*'s captain. The only other passenger on the bus was a short, talkative and slightly scatty young Argentinean woman called Mariana. She was originally from Bariloche. She had moved to El Calafate in search of greater isolation; but then El Califate had started turning into another Bariloche and she had had to move on to El Chaltén. The sky was cloudy but clear, and the winds stronger than ever, as we drove through the Patagonian steppes, finally to turn and face the distant Lago de Viedma and the snowy mountains behind it. The bus driver stopped for me to get out and take a photo. The foreground was an enormous flat expanse of stony earth covered by ochre tufts of grass. The sun fleetingly appeared to light up beyond a strip of blue water.

The winds blew sufficiently to expose for a few moments the summits of a group of peaks that stood out from the faraway line of mountains. The shape of Mount Fitzroy was unmistakable. I thought I was seeing Gaudí's Sagrada Familia covered in snow.

El Chaltén was like a place at the start of a gold-mining boom, with log cabins going up everywhere to accommodate the growing crowds of tourists. Mariana walked with me through the still-unpaved streets, stopping to introduce me to the nephew of Jimmy Radboone, whose adventurous life as a pioneer had inspired the book *El Jimmy, Outlaw of Patagonia*. Further on she showed me the still-intact house of the first and most famous of the area's settlers, the Dane Andreas Madsen.

Madsen was someone whose life I began to think about after Mariana had left me at the start of my six-hour walk up into the forested mountains. He had been a model to all those who had come to the Andes to get away from the rest of the world. The son of Danish peasants, he had travelled to South America as a sailor and then became the cook on Perito Moreno's Patagonian expedition of 1902. Finding in the Fitzroy area the land of his dreams, he returned to Denmark to fetch his fiancée, with whom he settled by the banks of the river I could now see through breaks in the forest. The beauty of this valley never ceased to astonish the deeply religious Madsen. He considered it a gift of Creation.

With his wife and four children he enjoyed the sort of quiet and simple Andean life my grandfather had briefly imagined for himself and his beloved Sophie. However, no paradise can exist without some threat to its survival. Madsen was conscious that the solitude he so craved was likely to be disturbed by the arrival in Patagonia of what he called 'the damned woollies' – the sheep-rearing companies he saw as capable of destroying everything for the sake of profit.

A gentler invasion into his world was that of the growing number of mountaineers and explorers who came to the area, including Padre Agostini, who stayed with him in 1931. Madsen was unfailingly hospitable and helpful towards these adventurers, but 'for love of God, not mountain-climbing'. He thought it almost sacrilegious to want to scale Patagonia's peaks, in particular the one named after Captain Fitzroy.

Often known simply as 'The Tower', this rocky needle crowned by an ice cap became one of the great challenges of modern mountaineering. Several of the early names associated with the peak belonged to a group of Italian alpinists calling themselves 'The Spiders of Lecco'. They became fixated on Patagonia after 1955, when one of them, Carlo Mauri, joined Padre Agostini in a climb up Tierra del Fuego's Mount Sarmiento and was told about the 'impossible' Mount Fitzroy.

Two years later an Italian expedition made the first attempt on this mountain. The expedition's leader concluded afterwards that it was truly impossible. But another of the Italians who took part in the climb, Cesare Maestri, made a further attempt on the peak the following year, together with one of the best Austrian climbers of his generation, Toni Egger. Maestri said that he and Egger reached the summit, but no one believed him. The evidence should have been provided by photographs taken by Egger, who, unfortunately, was struck on his descent by a falling rock and pushed off the precipice. His body was found nearly twenty later, but not his camera.

Many other failed and fatal attempts were made, until finally Maestri got to the top in 1970, aided by a motor drill weighing nearly a hundred kilos. His achievement, though derided by climbing purists, was hailed in the Italian media as almost comparable to reaching the moon.

I climbed through the forest up to a clearing that had an unimpeded view of Mount Fitzroy, whose crags and glaciers, partially obscured until now by the shifting clouds, finally emerged in their entirety, their terrifying silhouette outlined against a patch of blue. This was as near to the mountain as I wanted to get. 'I have struggled and lived for this moment,' Maestri wrote in his diary after supposedly attaining Mount Fitzroy's summit in 1958. 'Was it worth it? Never have I understood so clearly that no mountain is worth a life. I loathe this summit. The wind, the pictures that were taken, the registered signatures, everything makes me sick! No, it wasn't worthwhile.'

On my return that night to El Calafate I met a Mexican psychiatrist who said she specialized in death. She was regularly present at the bedsides of the dying before that proverbial moment when your whole life passes before you. She had also spoken to mountaineers who had fallen off peaks and survived. Their testimonies were proof of how much went through the mind in just a few seconds.

Thoughts of fatal Andean moments took up much of my last morning along the shores of the Lago Argentino. Don Horacio had talked to me over breakfast about the death in 1931 of Gunther Plüschow, one of the many daring aviators compulsively drawn to Patagonia.

The slowness of land transport through Patagonia led to the employment of several of the early aviators in the local postal service. An Italian, Mario Pozzati, piloted the first such flight in 1921, between the Chilean town of Punta Arenas and Río Gallegos. Later in the 1920s the French writer Antoine de Saint-Exupéry flew regularly over Patagonia while delivering mail, usually at night. In his novel *Night Flight* (1931) and in his memoir *Wind, Sand and Stars* (1939) Saint-Exupéry evoked all the magic of flying and the extraordinary sense of vulnerability of being up in the air in a tiny and fragile machine, prey to the sudden extreme Patagonian winds.

While Saint-Exupéry became the great aviator of the Patagonian plains, his German contemporary Plüschow developed a passion for the Patagonian Andes. In 1928 he flew across the Hielo Patagónico ('wherever I go, I only see ice, ice, and more ice'), and carried out the first postal flight between Punta Arenas and Argentina's southernmost town, Ushuaia. Later, financed by the Germans (for whom he was probably working as a spy), he concentrated his flying activities in Patagonia on cartography and aerial photography.

In the days immediately before his fatal crash of 28 January 1931, Plüschow had other brushes with death, one of which he described in terms of being 'thrown more than five hundred metres' towards a landscape of 'ice and threatening walls of rock', and then having to descend in a glide 'with the petrol gauge marked empty'. 'What I have lived through and seen can never be taken away from me,' he wrote on 25 January, three days before the cable connected to the rudder of his greatly weakened plane snapped. Both his and his co-pilot's parachutes failed and the two men were thrown into the Lago Argentino, watched by some of El Calafate's horrified inhabitants.

Don Horacio was the first to arrive at the scene of the accident. He found the fragments of the plane's fuselage, now displayed in El Calafate's small and neglected local museum along with numerous photos relating to the crash, one of which was of the good-luck charm always worn by Plüschow, a pendant inscribed with the number thirteen.

As I looked at the relics of Plüschow's ambitions, I began thinking about another crash which took place on the way to this same lake, only a few years ago. Ever since being in Patagonia, I had been coming across references to it. It had affected me profoundly, perhaps because it reflected the whole history of the fatal attraction of these mountains.

Among its ten victims were three of the Argentinean authors whose books on Patagonia I was carrying with me in my rucksack. One of them was the mountaineer José Luis Fonrouge, the first Argentine to climb Mount Fitzroy; another was Adrian Gimenez Hutton, who wrote a book following in Chatwin's Patagonian footsteps; the third was the Buenos Aires-based journalist Germán Sopeña, a man obsessed by Patagonia, the frontier issue with Chile, the Hielo Patagónico, and the life and work of Perito Moreno.

These various passions of Sopeña coalesced in a project to plant an Argentinean flag at the spot near the Lago Argentino where one had been left by Perito Moreno, the lake's 'discoverer'. This desire to pay homage to Moreno must have seemed a just and necessary tribute to an Argentinean hero who had died in 1919 neglected and in poverty. Moreno, despite having been rewarded in 1903 with a vast tract of Patagonia (which he gave away three months later for the creation of a national park), reached old age without 'so much as a square metre of land to give my children to bury my ashes'.

On 4 April 2001 Sopeña fulfilled a long-held ambition by giving an illustrated talk on Moreno and Patagonia at London's Royal Geographical Society. He was particularly pleased to be there because Moreno himself had lectured on Patagonia at that very lectern over a hundred years earlier. An additional and unexpected satisfaction was the presence in the audience of the granddaughter of the person who had presented Moreno to the Society, Charles Darwin's son George.

Three and a half weeks later Sopeña and his friends gathered just before dawn at Buenos Aires to fly to El Calafate. Fonrouge had brought along his wife and daughter, all three of whom would be shown smiling and embracing on the back jacket of his posthumously published *Vertical Horizons in Patagonia*.

I could picture them all getting on to the small plane, pleased to be together again, excited at the imminent prospect of flying over Patagonia's icy expanses, united by a deep love for the mountains they would never see again. The plane crashed in rugged farmland 160 kilometres south of Buenos Aires.

The bus from Río Gallegos to Punta Arenas was full of schoolboys on a football outing to Chile. I was sitting in an isolated seat at the front, feeling as if I were a child again. The boys behind me offered me a gob-stopper and a sherbet fountain. Punta Arenas was the first Chilean town my grandfather had seen; it was the last place I had visited when retracing his footsteps. It had struck me as remarkably similar to my grandfather's native Yorkshire town of Hull, where I had begun my sentimental journey. It was cold, windy and grey, with monolithic civic buildings eloquent of the confidence of another era.

529

This time I was only passing through. I was heading now to my final destination, the southernmost community in the world, Puerto Williams, capital of the Chilean Antarctic Province. Flights to this remote island town had been suspended for the season, but there was an occasional boat, carrying mainly cargo, that left Punta Arenas for Puerto Williams.

The boat was scheduled to leave the evening after my arrival at Punta Arenas. I had time to visit the site of Spain's first settlement in the extreme south of the continent, a place known originally as the Ciudad del Rey Don Felipe.

The taxi took me through a barely rolling landscape of woods, fields and peat bog, with views across a wide stretch of the Straits of Magellan towards the gentler northern end of Tierra del Fuego. A strong wind was blowing below a clear grey sky, exposing distant mountains and momentary patches of blue. We were driving almost to the very end of the southernmost road in mainland South America. The forested mountains on the promontory ahead of us, though lower than one thousand metres, had summits thickly covered in snow. Far to the south, across a choppy foaming sea, the white cone of Mount Sarmiento, Tierra del Fuego's highest peak, briefly emerged above its encasing clouds.

My driver, Luis, shared his knowledge of the area and showed me places he thought would be of interest – the monument from where all distances in Chile are measured; the reconstructed fortified settlement of Fuerte Bulnes; the beechwood cross marking the burial place of Fitzroy's predecessor as captain of the *Beagle*, Pringle Stokes, who 'died from the effects of the anxieties and hardships incurred whilst surveying the western shores of Tierra del Fuego'.

After a few hours together, Luis confided that his only child had turned up a few days ago from her home in Puerto Montt. She had fallen in love with a Frenchman and was going to live with him in France. Tonight she was going to have a farewell dinner with her parents. Luis doubted if he would be seeing her again in the next two or three years.

'I'm going to miss her so much,' he sighed, his eyes beginning to water. We had left the main road and were descending to the bleak bay where the Ciudad del Rey Don Felipe had once stood. The sun had made its last appearance of the day and the dull ochres of the boggy sloping shores were made sadder by the greyness of the sky.

Darwin had studied the bay and its surroundings in 1834, when the *Beagle* had been anchored here. 'I never saw a more cheerless prospect; the dusky woods piebald with snow, could be only indistinctly seen through a drizzling hazy atmosphere.' Of the area in general he had written: 'Death, instead of Life, seemed the predominant spirit.' One day he had climbed to the top of Mount Tarn, one of the snowy summits visible from the Punta Arenas road. 'In the deep ravines, the death-like scene of desolation exceeded all description; outside it was blowing a gale, but in these hollows, not even a breath of wind stirred the leaves of the tallest trees. So gloomy, cold and wet was every part, that not even the fungi, mosses, or ferns, could flourish.'

He made no mention of the Spanish settlement which had given the bay its present name of Port Famine. The Spaniards had come here in 1584, with the intention of protecting the Straits of Magellan from foreigners such as England's 'Pirate Drake'. The man in charge of the colonizing mission was the Castilian-born Sarmiento de Gamboa.

He had arrived in the New World in 1555, basing himself at first in Mexico and Guatemala and then in Peru. In Lima he had fallen foul of the Inquisition for three separate crimes: for his claims to have a magical ink that assisted him in the writing of love letters; for necromancy; and for having shown the lines of his palm to an old woman. He was banished initially to Cuzco, where he got to know the Inca Túpac Yupanqui, who supposedly told him of the existence of the Solomon Islands. He organized an expedition in 1571 to Vilcabamba to capture the last of the Inca leaders Túpac Amaru I.

He arrived in the Straits of Magellan at the end of December 1583 and established the settlement of Nombre de Jesús in the February of the following year. In March he founded the nearby colony that was named after the Spanish King Felipe II. He stayed in the Cuidad del Rey Don Felipe long enough to supervise the construction of several wooden buildings, including a church 'of very fine timber', but in May he went back to Nombre de Jesús, to see how the settlers were getting on. On trying to proceed to the city of Don Felipe, he was forced by continual storms to sail on to Río de Janeiro, from where he continued to Spain. He was captured on the way by English pirates and later held by Huguenots. He never returned to the Straits of Magellan.

Two months after Sarmiento had deserted his settlements, the inhabitants of Nombre de Jesús travelled overland to the city of Don Felipe. In January 1587, the English privateer Thomas Cavendish landed there to find a hanged man in the square, numerous corpses and only a single survivor. The place was renamed Port Famine after the manner in which most of its inhabitants had died. No attempt was made to resettle the area until 1843.

A hideous small monument in pebbledash concrete was the only sign today that a colony had ever existed at Port Famine. It was erected in 1984 to commemorate the fourth centenary of the city's foundation by Sarmiento. The bulk of the monument was a sturdy table intended apparently to suggest that the settlers had died of hunger. A bronze panel on the base explained that these brave men and women had attempted to bring to this remote spot 'the civilizing presence of Spain'.

The pathos of this sad monument was heightened by a wreath of dead flowers and by an inscription in bold lettering attached to one of the table's sides. There were just three words: SPAIN WAS HERE.

## 26

# WHERE THE ANDES END

The *Bahía Azul*'s horn sounded as it pulled out at dusk into the Straits of Magellan. Long black clouds streaked the sky and an icy wind was blowing. A few stars emerged. The lights of Punta Arenas glowed along the barely receding shore. The ship chuntered on into the darkness, towards the islands where the Andes end.

The ship seemed tiny and old. A couple of cars and two large containers took up most of the cargo deck. Four cabins, a small eating area and a lounge with reclining seats formed a tight row to the side of this. Above was the bridge, and little else.

There were six passengers and a crew of seven. A bookshop owner at Punta Arenas was on a biannual trip to sell his books at Puerto Williams. A shy young man was going there for the first time to take on a job as a carpenter. A young German woman, completing a doctoral dissertation on the island's minks, was returning with her Mapuche boyfriend. I shared a cabin with a boyish-looking forty-year-old called Manuel Araneda.

Manuel was from Santiago. We felt immediately we had something in common. I was not surprised to discover that he had known my friend Gonzalo Donoso for over twenty years, and I took it almost for granted that he was another restless traveller with a passion for Humboldt. He was a designer currently employed on the new layout of Puerto Williams' modest local museum, 'a modern cabinet of curiosities'. He showed me on his laptop a chart he was preparing featuring all the great Andean explorers. He had strong opinions about all of them. For instance, he disliked Perito Moreno, whom he blamed for Chile's loss to Argentina of many of the most beautiful parts of the Patagonian Andes. And he hated Darwin, whom he considered a 'racist'.

He was going to include a long quote by Darwin in the section of the museum devoted to the original inhabitants of Chile's Antarctic Region, the Yaghans. The latter were described by Darwin as the most hideous and miserable human beings he had ever seen, stunted in their growth, with entangled hair, greasy and filthy skin, discordant voices and violent gestures: 'Viewing such men one can hardly make oneself believe that they are fellow creatures placed in the same world.'

The journey to Puerto Williams would take about thirty-six hours, unless the weather took a turn for the worse. Manuel did not anticipate doing much sleeping. He almost twitched at times with repressed energy. He had done the trip once before, and had been kept awake almost continually. He had not been affected by the ship's manic rocking, but by the constant drama of the landscape. This time he had brought with him a state-of-the-art digital camera so that he could record almost everything.

We stood outside on the gangways long after the lights of Punta Arenas had disappeared. The sudden showers, the growing cold and the ever rougher sea had persuaded the other four passengers to go indoors but Manuel resisted doing so, even though it was almost too dark to photograph anything. Whenever I looked towards him, he was adjusting the zoom of his camera, rushing from one end of the ship to the other, scaling ladders, always moving. Once I turned around to find him photographing me from a distance. He had caught me at the back of the ship, watching the seagulls dive in and out of the wake. I had been deep in thought.

I had been thinking about the labyrinth of islands and channels at which we were aiming. I had realized for the first time how appropriate it was that South America should end in this way. I had begun reflecting on Bolívar's disillusioned last years and his feelings of having entered a labyrinth from which there was no escape.

Bolívar had gone back to Greater Colombia in 1826 to try and prevent his dream of a unified South America from shattering. He declared himself president for life in 1828 and survived an assassination attempt a few weeks later. He had resigned from the presidency in April 1830 and was planning to exile himself to Europe at the time of his painful death from tuberculosis a few months later. He had been staying at an estate outside the Colombian coastal town of Santa Marta.

'How do I get out of this labyrinth?' he had reputedly uttered, moments before dying.

The ship's purser, Victor, came to say that supper was ready. We went down into the eating area and joined the passengers at one of the two tables. The captain, grey-featured and morose, was sitting at the other with the fresh-faced and smiling Victor and a member of the crew known affectionately by everyone as 'Vega'. I felt a special sympathy for Vega, a short and plump bachelor who was continually making jokes, and being the butt of them.

The bookseller and the carpenter returned to their reclining seats and the captain to the bridge. I offered the others a glass of rum from a bottle I had bought at Punta Arenas. I imagined that this was what people drank at sea.

The bottle was consumed within an hour, by which time the Mapuche had fetched a banjo to sing us some songs. His girlfriend, the German, talked in the meantime about minks. Minks, she said, were not native to Puerto Williams' island, the Isla Navarinho, but had swum there recently from the mainland and were now flourishing in the area. There were no predators to attack them.

'Well, almost no predators,' smiled the Mapuche in a pause between singing. 'There are the wild dogs.' In recent months a pack of these dogs had been reported wandering deep in the island's interior. Now that the winter had set in they would be getting hungrier and more savage.

The bunk below me was already empty at four in the morning. Manuel had slipped out on deck after less than two hours' sleep.

'You're just in time,' he said, as I climbed up onto one of the gangways to see the boat gliding towards the dark ghostly forms of mountainous islands. 'This is where the excitement begins.' We had spent the night crossing the widest stretch of the Straits of Magellan and were now approaching a landscape that had seemed to the twelve-year-old Francisco Coloane, the future 'Chilean Melville', 'to be the work not of nature but of some Cyclopean god'. Coloane confessed that this was a world whose 'primitive force' was beyond his 'youthful understanding'.

The dawn was blustery and unsettled. When it was light enough to see more clearly, we could make out rocky peaks dusty with snow, and dense forests of *lenga* beeches and white *coihue*, whose bark looked as if it had been twisted by the wind. We were sailing towards a shore that opened up at our approach, so that ahead of us lay not land but a channel between islands, beyond which were further channels, further islands. We were in the labyrinth.

The clouds parted and closed, like the curtains in a theatre. The intermittent sun was like a giant spotlight throwing into sharp focus the dramatic features of a landscape that came and went with the clouds. I turned in one direction to see a cascade falling through a patch of sunlit forest. I turned in another to see a silvery streak of snow outlined against a black sky. At other moments a rainbow would suddenly appear, eventually forming a full half-circle, like an illusionist completing a trick.

When the rain became too persistent, Manuel and I took shelter on the bridge, where we spoke to the pilot and one or two of the sailors. We were taught the functions of the different nautical instruments and were shown our progress on charts as unfathomable to me as the maze around us.

The drama of the scenery and the weather made the day pass quickly. As night fell we saw the first sign of human habitation in almost twenty-four hours – a faraway light that was getting nearer. The captain told us we were making a delivery to a lighthouse keeper and his family.

Closer by the shore, we saw a small cottage backed by a steep forested slope crowned by snow. The keeper, in full naval uniform, walked down to the jetty to meet us, together with his young son. He told me that they got visits once a month, unless the weather was so stormy that a ship could not land. His wife and young daughter rushed out of the house to say hello as well. The ship moved away. The family stayed cheerfully waving by the jetty as we headed off again into the dark water. Some time after midnight we entered the Beagle Channel. A vague glow in the distance was identified by Manuel as the first of the glaciers that went right down to the sea's edge. At three in the morning, lying in my cabin, I parted the curtains to see the lights of Ushuaia, at the southern end of Tierra del Fuego. It was a largish Argentinean town now living mainly off its tourist reputation as the place 'at the end of the world'.

Jean Baudrillard, the French post-structuralist, had been there in 1998 and predictably found it a place like any other: 'You think you have left the world behind, but with its faxes, technology, motorcycles, videos, and duty-free, it got here before you. To come here is to dream of a possible end of all things – and of thought. But we confirm here that the world's only extremity is the extremity of endless circulation. Wherever you are, you are hostage to the global network. It is impossible to cut the umbilical cord.'

I sensed that my reaction to Puerto Williams would be different from Baudrillard's to Ushuaia. Manuel had convinced me of this.

On the opposite shore of the Beagle Channel to Ushuaia, and thus nearer still to the end of the world, it was a far smaller place than the Argentinean town, far poorer, far more inaccessible and far less visited. It had a population of around fifteen hundred, including the occupants of a naval base. It was smaller even than my Andalusian village of Frailes.

We dropped anchor at eight in the morning. I had less than a day before the ship sailed back to Punta Arenas. I soon regretted not having more time. The island's two policemen drove us from the harbour to the street where Manuel stayed. When I told them that I was thinking of walking up to the top of the mountain behind the town, they advised me to pass by the police station, to 'register' my intention of doing so. Manuel and I both looked surprised. They explained that there had been recent heavy snows. And that a pack of wild dogs, living on the other side of the island, was thought to be moving closer to the town.

Puerto Williams looked like a decayed suburb, with only two shops and rows of cabin-like houses with corrugated roofs, painted timbers and wooden fences. Manuel rented an ochre house from a woman who ran a blue B&B next door. He called this woman 'his wife in Puerto Williams', but said that he would be happy to lend her to me.

Her name was Pati. She had kindly eyes, and took a motherly concern in all those who entered her establishment. She made Manuel and me a hearty breakfast, and then sat talking to me after Manuel had gone home to have a shower. She had been living here, she said, for the past ten years. She had been working until then in Santiago but city life had started getting her down, especially after she had become a single mother. She had wanted to move to the remotest place possible in Chile, and had been tempted at first by Coyhaique. But Puerto Williams was 'remoter still'. She had never had any regrets about settling here.

Manuel reappeared to say that he had decided to take the day off so as to come with me on my walk up to the Cerro Bandera. He had always put off doing the climb during his previous stays in the town. The idea of the snows and the wild dogs had now piqued his curiosity so much that he felt he could not hold out any longer.

We did not stop beforehand at the police station. We were given a lift to the walk's starting point by an employee at the local museum who recommended that we turn back if it started snowing. A tourist had recently been caught out by a snowfall and had almost died of exposure. The walk began near a forest shrine marking the miraculous apparition of the Virgin Mary. It was painted blue and pink and half-buried by ex-votos and fallen leaves. Beside it was a rushing forest stream. We trampled over leaves and boggy ground as we tried following a narrow ascending path. The forest was so dense that it apparently blocked out most of the light during the summer. We came to a solitary tree know as *canelo* after its resemblance to a cinnamon tree. Its scientific name was *Drimys Winteri*. It was the sacred tree of the Mapuches. Its leaves and berries were applied to wounds and used for the treatment of cancer. Its branches were symbols of peace. It was a cosmic axis whose intersection with the horizontal line of the Earth defined for the Mapuches the centre of the world.

Higher up we had our first views down to the Beagle Channel, its shores lined with snowy mountains stretching into a far distance now lit up by a growing patch of sunlight. The path ahead, barred occasionally by trees blown down by the wind, was partially hidden by virgin snow. Above the tree level the path disappeared under a blanket of boot-deep snow that left only a few tufts of grass exposed.

We struggled through the snow up to a Chilean flag placed on the mountain's cairn. The Beagle Channel, under a now enormous expanse of blue sky, appeared like the vault of heaven. The panorama to the south was no less exciting. The snow rolled over a great plateau towards further heights, promising better views still of the Isla Navarinho's untouched interior. We were so elated that we continued walking, heedless of our laborious progress through snow that now came up over our boots.

We reached a viewpoint from which we saw the full indented profile of the island's highest peaks, the Dientes de Navarinho. We reached a cliff from where we could look down into a long deep valley covered in forests and snow. We persisted through the unending whiteness, like excited children embarking on a great adventure. I was remembering the snowy winters of my childhood, setting off with my brother on what we pretended were expeditions into the Himalayas or to the polar regions.

'Whenever I come to Puerto Williams,' Manuel said, 'I feel as if I was beginning my whole life again.' He told me that he had a sister who was a psychiatrist and had spent the last fifteen years researching a book on happiness. She herself was on constant medication for nerves and depression. 'I tell her that she should come here, to Puerto Williams. This is what happiness is all about.'

'I've often dreamt of ending up in a place like this,' he continued, 'far from everywhere, forgotten by everyone, in debt to no one.' Of all the Andean explorers we had been talking about over the past two days, only Bonpland had achieved this aim. Bonpland had never settled happily back in Europe, as Humboldt had done. He had always hoped to experience once again the sense of wonder that the tropics and the Andes had awakened in him. Eventually he had gone back to South America to explore the centre of the continent. He had been thrown into a Bolivian prison for ten years, but he stayed on in South America after his release in 1831. Unable to envisage life as an aged celebrity in Europe, he died in obscurity in a remote village on the edge of Paraguay. 'I picture him in the end as a happy man,' said Manuel.

Manuel, photographing continually as he talked, was now directing his camera to our tracks in the snow. We noticed simultaneously some tracks that were not ours. They were the tracks of a large animal. They could have been those of a wild dog. Manuel took out his binoculars. He thought he saw a mastiff on the horizon. He joked that Chumberry had managed to track me down to the end of the world. I imagined her rushing towards me, her tail wagging

with excitement. I had a brief vision of homecoming. I stared distractedly into the distance and saw a horizon suddenly darkened by
snow clouds. We turned and retraced our way back to the forest.
We made it just as the blizzard started.

The snow had turned to sleet as I walked at dusk towards an area
of Puerto Williams just along the coast from the harbour. I had said
goodbye to Manuel, who had retired exhausted to bed. I was going
to sleep on the ship. But before returning on board, I needed to visit
the district of Villa Ukika, where the Yaghans had lived.

On the outskirts of the district was a large battered tent intended
to remind visitors of a traditional Yaghan dwelling. The Yaghans
had occupied cruder versions of these when Captain Fitzroy first
landed on the Isla Navarinho in October 1830. He probably thought
of the Yaghans as little more than animals but unlikely to be trou-
blesome and he was disappointed when a group of them stole the
boat which one of his sailors had used to go ashore. In the hope of
being told where the missing boat was, he took four Yaghans
hostage. He perceived them as examples of savages who were not
quite noble and saw their potential as curiosities back in England.

The four Yaghans were given silly names. One was called Boat
Memory, another York Minister and a third Jemmy Button. The
sole girl among them, a nine-year-old, was named Fuegia Basket.
On their arrival in England, they were kept in rural isolation. The
vaccinations they received were sadly insufficient to prevent Boat
Memory from dying soon afterwards of chickenpox. The others
were presented at the Court of St James. Queen Adelaide gave
Fuegia Basket one of her hats and rings and a small sum of money.

By 1831, the curiosity value of these Yaghans was waning and
Fitzroy decided to take them back with him when the *Beagle* sailed
again to South America, accompanied this time by Darwin. Darwin
found them quaintly amiable but could not understand how anyone
who had had contact with western civilization could possibly want
to go back to a primitive lifestyle.

*The Beagle* at the foot of Mount Sarmiento', illustration from Charles Darwin,
*Voyages of the Adventure and the Beagle*

Returned to the Isla Navarinho, Fuegia Basket was married off by an English missionary to York Minister and Jemmy Button went on to have three children with a local woman. The last that was heard of any of them was a report of Button's death at the age of about forty-seven during an epidemic of measles introduced to the islands by westerners. Half the Yaghan population died with him.

To discover the final fate of the Yaghans I had come to Villa Ukika in the hope of talking to a woman called Cristina Calderón. Her district was made up entirely of houses hastily assembled with nails and bare timbers, many of which were rotting. I knocked at her door. A friendly old man welcomed me into a tiny sitting-room lit by a kerosene stove. He went off into the kitchen to get Cristina, who turned out to be not the Cristina I was looking for, but her daughter. The daughter said that her mother had gone to see a friend in the town and would not be home until later. She suggested I came back the next morning. I said I was sailing at dawn to Punta

Arenas. I was still thinking of Manuel's parting words to me: 'You're a strange man,' he said. 'You go all the way to the end of the world, and you stay only a day.'

Young Cristina offered me a cup of tea all the same and showed me a photograph of her mother, an austere 78-year-old. She confirmed what I had been told by Manuel and had not quite believed: that her mother was the very last of the pure-blooded Yaghans and the only person left to speak the Yaghan language. Two nineteenth-century English missionaries, Thomas and Lucas Bridges, had brought out an English–Yaghan dictionary but no one had recorded its grammar. With Cristina Calderón's death, the civilization of the world's southernmost hunters, fishermen and gatherers would die as well.

The sound of the ship's horn got me quickly to my feet. I ran to the harbour to find the ship on the point of sailing out into the Beagle Channel. Harbour regulations obliged it at night to be moored at sea. The crew had been waiting for my return. I had been invited by Vega to the traditional barbecue held by the ship's crew on their last night before sailing home. My rucksack was filled with all the rum I had been able to buy at Puerto Williams. I smelt grilled meat as I jumped onto the ship moments before the tow-ropes were uncoiled.

I looked back at the lights of Villa Ukika as the ship slipped out into the sea. I had missed my opportunity to talk to the last of the Yaghans. The thought made me sad.

Dawn came without a break in the dark sky. The crew were half hung-over, the captain nowhere to be seen. The ship briefly returned to Puerto Williams to pick up the new passengers – a large group of crab fishermen and the only six tourists to have been staying on the island over the past two weeks. The sole passenger from before was the bookseller.

The sea was much rougher than it had been on the way out, and conditions were worsening. A young American lawyer standing

543

alongside me on a gangway voiced his concerns about the ship's lack of safety regulations. He was worried also about his wife, who was downstairs in the lounge, trying to stay calm. She was expecting their first child. He soon went to join her. He was succeeded by an earnest German, who asked me if the book I was writing was going to have a happy ending. Then he too went indoors. None of the passengers remained outside, except for the bookseller. He stayed next to me, holding tight against the railings, watching the waves as they broke against the bow, covering us with spray. He was a man of few words. He said that this was 'just the beginning'.

I went to the bridge, where the ancient barometer indicated a severe storm ahead. The captain had finally appeared and was sitting with a half-drunk bottle of rum by his feet. He took regular swigs from the bottle, as he told me ominously that this was his last journey, he was to retire next month, he had had several scrapes with death during his long life at sea and he had once been on a cruise ship which had crashed against an iceberg.

Victor arrived, as cheerful as ever. He switched on the radio and searched for some music. He told me that the winds had already reached a speed of fifty-five knots and were predicted to go up to seventy. The captain was still speaking to no one in particular. He said he had recently been with Vega to see the tomb of Captain Stokes, and that he had later heard that Captain Fitzroy, on his return to England, had also shot himself.

We were already five hours behind schedule. I had been waiting to see in daylight three of the great glaciers that fall into the Beagle Channel. But the sky was so overcast and the evening so fast approaching that Victor reckoned I would be able to see only the first of them. The glacier announced itself as a distant blue glow. I went back outside to watch it as we swayed closer. Its frothing blue mass, erupting in the colourless dusk, looked terrifyingly supernatural.

Back on the bridge, the drone of the engine and the horrific roar of the wind were competing with an exhilarating sound I had barely heard since Venezuela and Colombia. It made me feel for a moment as if I were at the beginning of my Andean journey. Salsa music was being played at full volume.

The captain held the rum above his head until the final drop of liquid fell into his mouth. The pilot was making constant adjustments to the steering to try and cushion the impact of the bigger waves. And Victor was dancing, cheered on by Vega. He timed his movements to the rocking of the ship. His face was full of joy and his energy untiring. Large blocks of ice were bobbing up and down on the turbulent sea in front of us. But Victor was unconcerned. His spirit was thousands of miles away, and he succeeded in taking Vega and me with him, so that, as death loomed on the horizon, the three of us were imagining ourselves in the tropics, absorbing the life force.

I woke up in a world of unexpected calm. The wind had died down and we were navigating through a narrow channel touched occasionally by the early-morning sun. The memory of last night's storm was manifest in the scattered books and clothes on my cabin's floor.

I walked up to the bridge, where Vega told me that the sea had become so dangerous that we had done something only a small ship like ours could do. We had left the main route back to Punta Arenas, to follow one which would take us through the smaller channels of the Tierra del Fuego archipelago. To do this you usually needed permission from the maritime authorities, but we had not bothered with this formality. 'We have become pirates,' smiled Vega, 'off the radar.'

We made our illegal way from one island to the next, meandering between forests, rocks and snows so close you felt you could touch them, until we were back in the Straits of Magellan, free from the labyrinth, heading across an open stretch of water towards Cape Froward.

Moss and lichen coloured a massive outcrop of dark rock rising above the water. The rock was crowned by a cross, silhouetted against white crags. I could picture a priest holding up a cross to the sky to try and ward off a primitive force beyond his comprehension.

The cross was the simple ending I had been looking for. It marked the end of the South American mainland, the point where the world's longest mountain range reached the ocean at last. I wanted to wave goodbye.

A rainbow appeared out at sea as the ship rounded the headland. I saw the bookseller framed against it on the opposite side of the deck. He noticed me looking at him and gave me the thumbs-up sign and pointed towards the horizon. He was shouting out something but I could not hear his words. The sky was darkening.

We continued sailing towards a distant light.

# FURTHER READING

## GENERAL

Corral Vega, Pablo, and Vargas Llosa, Mario, *Andes*, 2001
Lamb, Simon, *Devil in the Mountain: A Search for the Origin of the Andes*, 2004
Wilson, Jason, *The Andes*, 2009

## ARCHAEOLOGY

Burger, Richard, *Chavin and the Origins of Andean Civilization*, 1995
Burger, Richard L., and Salazar, Lucy C. (eds), *Machu Picchu: Unveiling the Mystery of the Incas*, 2004
Reichel-Dolmatoff, Gerardo, *San Agustín: A Culture of Colombia*, 1972
Reinhard, Johan, *The Ice Maiden: Inca Mummies, Mountain Gods and Sacred Sites in the Andes*, 2005
Rostworoski de Diez Canseco, María, *History of the Inca Realm*, 1999
Stone-Miller, Rebecca, *Art of the Andes: From Chavín to Inca*, 1995

Von Hagen, Adriana, and Morris, Craig, *The Cities of the Ancient Andes*, 1998

## HISTORY

Andrien, Kenneth J., *Andean Worlds: Indigenous History, Culture and Consciousness under Spanish Rule, 1532–1825*, 2001

Gorriti, Gustavo, *The Shining Path: A History of the Millenarian War in Peru*, 1999

Griffiths, Nicholas, *The Cross and the Serpent: Religious Repression and Resurgence in Colonial Peru*, 1996

Harvey, Robert, *The Liberators*, 2000

Hemming, John, *The Conquest of the Incas*, 1970

Hemming, John, *The Search for El Dorado*, 1978

Honigsbaum, Mark, *Valverde's Gold: A True Tale of Greed, Obsession and Grit*, 2005

Manthorne, Katherine Emma, *Tropical Renaissance: North American Artists Exploring Latin America, 1839–1879*, 1989

Moss, Chris, *Patagonia: A Cultural History*, 2008

Starn, Orin, and Degregori, Carlos Iván, and Kirk, Robin (eds), *The Peru Reader: History, Culture, Politics*, 2005

Whitaker, Robert, *The Mapmaker's Wife: A True Tale of Love, Murder and Survival in the Amazon*, 2004 (contains an excellent account of the eighteenth-century Geodesic Expedition)

## BIOGRAPHIES AND MEMOIRS

Anderson, Jon Lee, *Che Guevara: A Revolutionary Life*, 1997

Bingham, Hiram, *Lost City of the Incas* (with an introduction by Hugh Thomson), 2002

Botting, Douglas, *Humboldt and the Cosmos*, 1973

Browne, Janet, *Charles Darwin, Vol.1: Voyaging*, 1995

de Caldas, Francisco José, *Un peregrino de las ciencias* (ed. Jeanne Chenu), 1992

Desmond, Adrian, and Moore, James, *Darwin*, 1991

Feinstein, Adam, *Pablo Neruda: A Passion for Life*, 2004

Holl, Frank (ed.), *Alejandro de Humboldt: Una nueva visión del mundo*, 2005

Jones, Bart, *¡Hugo! The Hugo Chávez Story from Mud Hut to Perpetual Revolution*, 2008

Lynch, John, *Simón Bolívar: A Life*, 2006

Martin, Gerald, *Gabriel García Márquez*, 2008

Navas Sanz de Santamaría, Pablo, *The Journey of Frederic Edwin Church Through Colombia and Ecuador, April–October, 1853*, 2008

Moorhead, Alan, *Darwin and the Beagle*, 1969

Mutis, José Celestino, *Viaje a Santa Fe* (ed. Marcelo Frías Nuñez), 1991

Parrado, Nando, *Miracle in the Andes: 72 Days on the Mountain and my Long Trek Home*, 2006

Simpson, Joe, *Touching the Void*, 1988

St Aubin de Terán, Lisa, *The Hacienda: My Venezuelan Years*, 1998

Tristán, Flora, *Peregrinations of a Pariah (1833–1834)*, 1986

## TRAVELLERS' ACCOUNTS

Chatwin, Bruce, *In Patagonia*, 1977

Darwin, Charles, *Voyage of the Beagle*, 1995

Guevara, Ernesto 'Che', *The Motorcycle Diaries*, 2003

Humboldt, Alexander von, *Mi Viaje por el Camino del Inca (1801–1802): Antología*, 2004

Isherwood, Christopher, *The Condor and the Cows: A South American Travel Diary*, 1949

Jacobs, Michael, *Ghost Train Through the Andes: On my Grandfather's Trail in Chile and Bolivia*, 2006

Nicholl, Charles, *The Fruit Palace*, 1985

Parris, Matthew, *Inca-Kola: A Traveller's Tale of Peru*, 1990

Theroux, Paul, *The Old Patagonian Express*, 1981

Thomson, Hugh, *The White Rock: An Exploration of the Inca Heartland*, 2001

Thomson, Hugh, *Cochineal Red: Travels through Ancient Peru*, 2006

Tschiffely, A.F., *Tschiffely's Ride: Being the account of 10,000 miles in the saddle through the Americas from Argentina to Washington*, 1933

Whymper, Edward, *Travels Amongst the Great Andes of the Equator*, 1892

# ACKNOWLEDGEMENTS

I am especially indebted to the support and friendship over the years of George Miller, who commissioned the book, and without whose excellent editing it would have been much longer than it actually is. I have also been wonderfully looked after by the present staff of Granta Books, and am enormously grateful to the insights and enthusiasm of Bella Shand and Amber Dowell. Caroline Knox acted as my unofficial agent for this book and supplied as always much invaluable advice.

My travels around South America were hugely enhanced by the tolerant and stimulating companionship of Manolo Caño and Chris Stewart, both of whom also experienced some of the remarkable warmth, hospitality and generosity I encountered generally in the Andes. I completed the journey more convinced than ever of the saying I learnt in Colombia: '*Los buenos somos más*' (see page 126).

Among those who have made specific contributions to this book, I would like to acknowledge the following: Pablo Abad, Gastón Acurio, Lucía Acurio, Boris Albornoz, Patricia Alcira Guanúco, Olga Alfaro, Rori Alejandra Cedeño Jaury, Ramón Alirio Contreras, General Laercio Vicente Almeida Rodríguez, Isabel Álvarez, Susana Anchorena, Manuel Araneda Castex, Ana María Araya, Betty Andrade, Lourdes Barragán, Humberto Barrón Rafael

Martínez, Basilio Becerra, Diego Bonifaz, Gabriela Bonifaz, Carlos Borneo, Clara Bravo, Ernesto Bustamante, Yesica Calderón Alfaro, Francisco Carrión Mena, Cristóbal Cobo, Pablo Corral Vega, Marco Cruz, Pepe Dávila, the late Gonzalo Donoso Yañez, Gonzalo and Geraldine Donoso, Francisco 'El Pájaro' Febres Cordero, Horacio Forster, Joaquín Gallego, Mariana García, Marbel Garrón, Oswaldo Garrón, Padre Leonardo Gianelli, Oswaldo Hayo, Andrea Kroehne, Annemique de Kroon, Rafo León, Dick Mahoney, Embajador Cancio Mamani, Raúl Marca, Robert McCrum, Belkis Mira, Gustavo López Moreno, Jimmy Nelson, Silvia Octavia Pizza Tito, Achiles Ortiz, Carlos Pérez, Mariana Pérez, Inés del Pino Martínez, Mignon Plaza, Rosa Puga, Milena Ramírez, Ricardo Ramón Jarne, Agustín Rey, Federico Reyes, Carolina Rodríguez, Padre Lorenzo Sacinetti, Juan Fernando Sálazar, Alejo Sánchez, Hernán Santiváñez, Nelson Santos Pachao, Genaro Sea, Bolívar Silva, Nelson Eduardo Socorro, Jorge Sobia, Lilian Soto, Juan Eladio Susaeta, Boyd Tonkin, Kohki Toyama, Patricia Ureta Cardenas, Delia Velarde, Violeta Vinoeza, Rosa and Patricia Vintimilla, Michael White, Fausto Wilson Cabrera Apaza, Padre Stanislao Wrobel and Rod Wooden.

My thanks also to Colombia's Proexport for sponsoring my time in Cartagena de Indias and Bogotá, and to the directorship of the Hay Festival for providing me with many opportunities to expand my knowledge of the Hispanic literary world. During the writing of this book in Frailes and London I have been sustained by numerous friends, some of whom have discussed aspects of South America with me and supplied invaluable contacts in South America. I must thank in particular: Buki Armstrong, Jon Lee Anderson, Carlos Calvo, Marius Florentin Ciobanu, Cristina Fuentes, Merce García, Mamen Garrido, Bob Goodwin, Carolyn Hart, Stella Kane, Ayub Khan Din, Gina Marsh, Daniel Mordzinski, Inma Murcia Serrano, Manuel Ramos, Manuel Ruíz López ('El Sereno'), Manolo Ruiz, Ana Stewart, Carmen Suárez, Hugh Thomson, Magdalena Torres Hidalgo, Cecilia Vargas and Jason Wilson.

## ACKNOWLEDGEMENTS

As always my greatest debt has been to Jackie Rae, whose role as guardian angel came home to me during the last stages of the terrifying bus journey to Celendín, when, averting my eyes from the abyss, I glimpsed a roadside bar called the Jacklynn. I knew then that the bus would make it.

# ILLUSTRATION CREDITS

p. 2    Hugo Chávez with a portrait of Simón Bolívar, REUTERS/Kimberly White.

p. 228  'The Heart of the Andes' (engraving) by Church, Frederic Edwin (1826–1900) © Butler Institute of American Art, Youngstown, OH, USA/The Bridgeman Art Library. Nationality/copyright status: American/out of copyright.

p. 261  F.G. Weitsch, 'Humboldt and Bonpland High in the Andes of Ecuador' Stiftung Preußische Schlösser und Gärten Berlin-Brandenburg/Jörg P. Anders.

p. 256  Illustration of the differing types of vegetation at different altitudes (colour litho) by French School, (19th century). Bibliotheque des Arts Decoratifs, Paris, France/ Archives Charmet/The Bridgeman Art Library. Nationality/copyright status: French/out of copyright.

p. 431  Quaint Picture of the Toilers in the Mines of Potosi, from Gottfried's 'Historia Antipodum', pub. in 1655, from 'The Romance of the River Plate', Vol. I, by W. H. Koebel, 1914 (engraving) by German School, (17th century) (after) Private Collection/The Bridgeman Art Library. Nationality/copyright status: German / out of copyright.

p. 542 '*The Beagle* at the foot of Mount Sarmiento', illustration from Charles Darwin, *Voyages of the Adventure and the Beagle*. Reproduced with permission from John van Wyhe ed., The Complete Work of Charles Darwin Online (http://darwin-online.org.uk/)

# INDEX

557

complete book of
# yoga

# complete book of
# yoga

## Vimla Lalvani

hamlyn

# Contents

# Introduction

The aspects of yoga tradition are vast and varied, and people correspondingly come to yoga for a variety of reasons. Some people suffer from stress-related conditions and have realized that yoga exercise is one way to release stress in the nervous system; some want only to tone their body and keep it youthful, while others aim to alleviate ailments such as migraine, backache, arthritis and rheumatism; some seek to develop their sexual relationships on a new plane; and some wish to use the principles of yoga philosophy to enrich their spiritual life. No matter what reason you are attracted to yoga you will reap all the benefits. You do not even need to believe in its philosophies - all you need to do is to practice it in order to gain the true benefits of this ancient science.

## What is yoga?

Yoga is a holistic concept that unifies the physical, mental, spiritual, and emotional aspects of the self so that the person who practices it feels in total balance and in harmony with others as well as with his or her environment. It is an Ayurvedic science that teaches us how to live and function in life successfully.

The Vedic Scriptures are the oldest written verses ever recorded. Written thousands of years ago, they describe an ancient science that teaches us how to live life in harmony with the universe. From them are derived Ayurvedic medicine, a traditional Indian science of healing now increasingly popular in the West, and yoga *asanas* that help us purify our system and unite us to the cosmic Source.

Yoga is a Sanskrit word which means the union of mind, body, and soul. It follows from this that the individual person is a whole and must be viewed as such; the total integration of the mental, physical, emotional, and spiritual self is necessary in order to have a balanced life. There are five paths of yoga discipline, of which *Hatha* yoga is the first stage. The philosophy states that before you can discipline your mind in the art of meditation you must discipline your body first, Nirvana or spiritual enlightenment being your final goal. *Karma* yoga teaches us that good deeds bring us closer to God; *Bakti* yoga is devotional prayers and dedication of one's life to spiritual growth;

*Gyana* yoga is studying the philosophy of yoga and understanding the power of spiritual wisdom; and *Raj* yoga is the art of meditation that links us directly to a spiritual union with the Cosmic Energy. No matter which form of yoga that one chooses to practice the result will be the same; an understanding and belief in universal law and a deep understanding of the self. Even though your goal might not be a spiritual one you will find that you will feel more compassionate towards other people as well as being in tune with your environment.

This book is concerned with *Hatha* or physical yoga, which teaches us *asanas* or postures that discipline the mind and body. *Ha* means the sun, which represents masculine energy, and *Tha* means the moon, representing feminine energy. Each person, no matter which gender, has both masculine and feminine energies within himself or herself. *Hatha* yoga teaches us how to balance these energies in order to be in harmony with the universe. The *asanas* are held for as long as possible in order to build stamina as well as alter the energy in the body. We have seven chakras or energy centers in our torso and head that need to be unblocked so the energy flows evenly throughout the system. Twisting and turning the body forward, backward, and sideways stimulates all the nerves and internal organs and unblocks the chakras.

Breathing correctly as you perform the *asanas* constitutes a vital part of *Hatha* yoga. The *Pranayama* (breathing technique) increases the lung capacity, balances the masculine and feminine energies within the body and boosts energy levels. It calms and soothes the nervous system and acts as a natural tranquilizer so the person feels calm and relaxed.

**A modern plague**

There is a disease that is endemic in our society today: stress. Its effects range from making people tense and unhappy to causing irritable bowel syndrome, migraine, asthma, allergies, high blood pressure and heart attacks, as well as many other illnesses. It is even believed to contribute to cancer. Stress is not necessarily a bad thing: kept within bounds, it provides us with excitement, stimulation and motivation. However, in the modern world it often accelerates to dangerous levels. The major causes of stress are counted as bereavement, divorce, moving house and redundancy, and while bereavement was ever present in our lives family breakup and job losses, both forms of bereavement in themselves, are now commonplace. Add to that the sheer noise of life today, where a single home may have four televisions blaring in different rooms, burglar alarms on the house and car, a constantly ringing telephone and perhaps a flight path overhead and it's no wonder that stress levels become unbearable.

Yet even in these conditions, yoga can offer deep peace and relaxation. Just the deep breathing emanating from the diaphragm that yoga teaches has a tranquilizing effect, while the twisting and stretching of the *asanas* improves the circulation and sends fresh oxygen to the exhausted brain. Visualization and meditation techniques help to calm and focus the mind, providing a necessary distance from day-to-day worries. While a doctor may prescribe antidepressants or tranquilizers to help the individual cope with stress, this is but a short-term fix which may in itself have ill effects. Yoga, on the other hand, offers a life-long solution that brings with it a supple and toned body as a bonus.

Because of genetic differences, stress affects different people in different ways. It will manifest itself wherever there is a weakness in the system, so it is of utmost importance that each organ in the body receives an equal amount of blood and fresh oxygen in order to function properly. The deep breathing techniques in yoga send a fresh blood supply which revitalizes and rejuvenates all the internal organs, and combining this with twisting and turning the body into various positions assists the liver, kidney and spleen to eliminate harmful toxins which deplete energy and reduce the body's chance of functioning properly. If stress is not reduced or released from the internal organs, disease and decay set in, and as it is very difficult to reverse diseases it important to learn survival techniques to prevent illnesses from ever occurring to upset the natural balance of the body. However, where it is already too late to use yoga as a preventive measure for common ailments, remedial yoga offers practical quick fixes for instant relief.

## Exploring the Tantra

There is nothing more rewarding in life than a truly loving relationship between two people, but when sexual problems or frustrations set in, even the best relationship in the world will suffer. Conversely, when the mind, body, and soul are truly integrated in each partner, sexual union is joyous and fulfilling. This ecstasy spills onto every level of the relationship and enhances not only a positive mental attitude for each person but boosts self-confidence and self-esteem. Both partners radiate love and happiness and there is an inner calm that permeates into all other relationships within the family, the workplace and social relationships.

Sexual energy is the most powerful energy in the body because it is this fundamental energy that creates life. When the base or first chakra is blocked, sexual tension can explode in a negative or violent way. It is important to release tension in the pelvic region and raise the energy to the highest or seventh chakra. When this is complete enlightenment is possible. Religious leaders often describe a spiritual union with God as divine bliss. The techniques of Tantric yoga teach you how to unblock all the energy centers so you reach a state of orgasmic ecstasy similar to a divine union with God.

Not only do the techniques of Tantra intensify the senses and sharpen sexual awareness, the practice of yoga also helps to resolve the emotional and psychological problems that are the usual underlying cause of sexual dysfunction. Yoga philosophy considers the sexual union of man and woman to be sacred, a part of universal love, and the spiritual ecstasy of yoga intensifies the physical thrill of sex.

## The search for eternal youth

Since the beginning of time, the human race has been obsessed with searching for the fountain of youth. For centuries, elixirs and potions have been drunk and magical rituals have been practiced in order to ward off the ageing process. Today, millions of pounds are spent each year on cosmetics and cosmetic surgery with the hope that this will reverse the signs of ageing – but success is only limited.

However, even though we cannot stop the ageing process altogether we can certainly learn a way to outwit it so we can live longer and have better health. The secret of staying young is oxygenation. In yoga, breathing from the diaphragm increases the fresh oxygen that enters the bloodstream to purify and regenerate all the cells. This rejuvenates the entire system so the internal organs are functioning perfectly.

As you age, your metabolism and hormonal levels start to slow down and change. Practicing yoga exercises will help to maintain the same levels so your weight and your hormones remain stable. Added to this, the *asanas* improve circulation, tone the entire body, strengthen the back, energize and rejuvenate the entire system and maintain youthfulness so that you will feel fit and young. While yoga is used as a preventive measure to the signs of ageing it also relieves age-related conditions such as arthritis, rheumatism and osteoporosis. It helps to cure the insomnia and depression that often attend them as well as building the immune system to prevent further illness.

The mental attitude of people who are ageing is important – the saying that you are as old as you feel has a lot of truth in it. When someone is described as youthful you expect to see an invigorated person with boundless energy, sparkling eyes and a clear complexion. This is just what yoga can bring, with the exercises keeping your body supple, your skin toned and your mind alert.

**Basic yoga principles**

Stretching is the best way to achieve top-to-toe fitness as well as reducing stress in the muscle groups. In yoga exercise stretching is an integral part of each movement. The muscles are stretched lengthways, thus elongating them. This process eliminates the fat around each muscle so that it becomes toned, and this also helps to reduce the appearance of cellulite. People who practice yoga on a regular basis have long, lean muscles rather than bulk and always appear youthful and full of energy.

Perfect posture is an integral part of each movement and the yoga exercises are fluid and graceful. Imagine you are a dancer as you move smoothly from one exercise to the next. Never force or jerk your body – instead, allow the natural weight of the body to help you increase the stretch. Every single muscle in the body is working even as you stand tall. Visualize a string pulling you upwards from the top of your head and extend your arms from the shoulder blades as you stretch your arms out.

Yoga breathing begins from the diaphragm. As you inhale through the nose the stomach extends and as you exhale the stomach retracts. This method of breathing increases the lung capacity to its fullest so energy levels are increased instantly. A shallow breath does not circulate through the organs in the way that an intense breath is able to, and during yoga exercises the breath actually moves into the specific organ that is being stimulated. The end result of correct yoga breathing is thus a calmer mind and a relaxed and oygenated body.

Yoga is a discipline, so you must set a routine for yourself in order to achieve its benefits. Choose a time of the day when you can shut yourself off from the rest of the world. The postures might seem challenging at first, but with continued practice you will find yourself becoming more flexible so there will be a sense of joy as you tackle even the most difficult poses. As you become more advanced in your yoga practice you will feel a total feeling of inner calm. You will feel happy, healthy, and in total control of your destiny.

# How to use the book

The book is divided into four sections, starting with a general one that introduces you to classic yoga *asanas* and moving on to three that focus on a particular aspect of life where yoga can bring you benefits.

**Classic Yoga** takes you through a beginners' course in which the exercises are very gentle, slow and easy to follow, as you learn to move and breathe in a new way. Once you are comfortable with these you can move onto the intermediate and advanced *asanas*, which will demand greater levels of stamina and suppleness to perform.

When you are suffering from stress your energy levels are depleted, so the **Yoga to Relieve Stress** section offers *asanas* for boosting your energy as well as for providing deep relaxation that will enable you to replace tension and anxiety with harmony and peace. Our most stressful moments often come outside the home, so there are simple five-minute *asanas* that can be done in the office and while travelling, as well as more complicated ones to do at home.

**Yoga for Better Sex** begins with a section that prepares the physical body for lovemaking and the mind for inner calm. The *asanas* here will tone your body, giving you increased stamina and flexibility so that you can embark upon the poses of the *Kama Sutra* without worrying about any physical strain. The *asanas* in the Prelude are designed to help you and your partner prepare together for physical union, equalizing your energy and attuning to one another by means of slow, flowing movements. These are followed by the Love Poses section, which shows you some of the classical movements from the *Kama Sutra* and describes them in detail so that you will find them easily achievable, leading you to fulfilling lovemaking.

The last part of the book, **Stay Youthful with Yoga**, presents a six-day workout that can be used lifelong to help you avoid many of the syndromes that come with advancing age. They are designed for specific areas and can be combined or just used according to your particular needs. Finally, there are remedial exercises you can do to alleviate some common age-related problems.

# SAFETY NOTE

# classic
## yoga

This opening chapter includes specifically designed yoga sequences based on different levels of fitness and experience. The main objectives are to teach you the basics of yoga and to guide your progress through to an advanced level. The initial exercises provide a foundation course for total beginners, teaching the importance of breathing and alignment. These exercises are gentle, slow and easy to follow, and will teach you to move in a new way. The exercises progress to more dynamic poses which call for increased strength, stamina and suppleness. As you move into these more challenging yoga *asanas* you will feel a sense of elation in your ability to tackle difficult poses; you will become energized and motivated yet your mood will be calm. However, yoga is a discipline so only continued practice will show results. With dedication, the outcome can be dynamic: an invigorated body, increased stamina, improved muscle tone and a feeling of total harmony and calm.

# Getting Started

No matter how unfit you are, you can safely begin the practice of yoga. Unlike modern exercise regimes, which are sometimes harsh and demanding, yoga will take you forward at a pace that your body can adjust to. However, as with all exercise, you should begin with a general warm-up so that your muscles are warmed and loosened, ready for stretching.

As you progress with yoga, you will find that your outlook on life becomes more positive. You will no longer experience serious mood swings or depression. As your concentration improves, you will be more organized and you will find yourself able to handle several tasks at the same time equally well.

Yoga philosophy offers people a scientific way of transcending their problems and suffering. It does not conflict with any religion or faith and can be practiced by anyone who is sincere and willing to discipline their life and search for truth. Little effort will bring immense returns like wisdom, strength and peace. As your awareness of your body increases, you will learn to listen to your 'higher self'. *Hatha* Yoga is the first step to spiritual enlightenment. However, the philosophy states that before you can discipline your mind and master the techniques of meditation, you must first discipline your body.

Many pupils of yoga find that they develop an interest in their own spiritual development; others do not. While some people concentrate only on balancing the mind and body, others find that they develop an insatiable need to go further. Each person is different and should follow their own inclinations. As you learn the positions and exercises in this book, you can decide for yourself how far you want to take your study of yoga.

# Posture

Most people do not realize how important it is to stand and sit correctly. Bad posture is the main cause of chronic back pain and contributes to painful ailments such as slipped discs and sciatica. Invariably, people with bad posture lack energy and vitality. Their chests are slumped, and they do not breathe correctly as they use only a small portion of their lungs.

Yoga poses are designed to stretch the spine constantly and build the muscles in the lower back, enabling you to achieve perfect posture. You may think that you are standing or sitting correctly, but you may not understand your own body alignment. Indeed, pregnancy or either weight gain or loss can unbalance you.

Whether you are standing, kneeling or sitting, imagine that a string is pulling you upward from the top of your head. Push your shoulder blades down and lift the chest naturally. When you are in perfect posture, you will feel 'centered'. It is rather like placing building blocks on top of each other. If they are not evenly placed, they will tumble down.

The exercises in this book frequently refer to first and second position. In first position stand with your feet together and touching each other. Open the toes evenly and press your heels down. In second position stand with your feet approximately 30cm (1ft) apart. The feet should be positioned below the hips with the toes pointing forward.

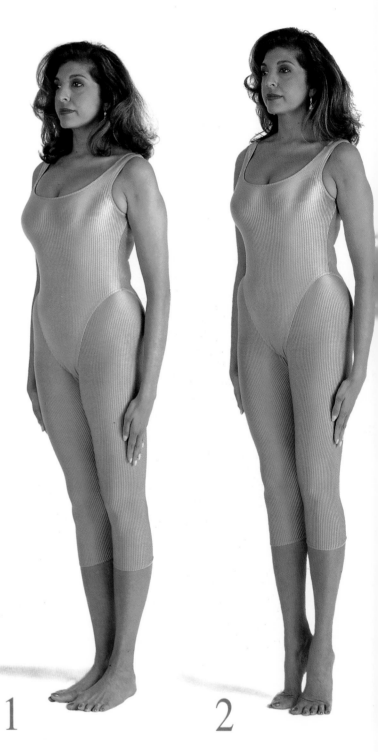

1

Stand as tall as you can with your feet together, keeping your shoulders down and your stomach and tail-bone tucked in.

2

Raise your heels and balance on your toes. If you do not fall forward or backward you are in perfect posture.

*In Steps 1 and 2, test yourself for perfect standing posture. (In Step 1, it is important to distribute your weight evenly.) Steps 3 and 4 demonstrate correct posture when kneeling and sitting.*

## 3

Sit on your heels and place your hands on your knees. Now raise your spine, straightening your elbows.

## 4

Sitting cross-legged, lift the spine as far as you can. This centers your balance, creating a positive mental attitude.

# Breathing

Breathing correctly is an integral part of yoga. All the movements you perform, if they are to be beneficial, require correct breathing. To breathe correctly means breathing through the nose from the diaphragm throughout all the exercises in this book, unless instructed otherwise. As we exhale from the diaphragm, our lung capacity increases and more oxygen reaches the bloodstream. This rejuvenates and revitalizes the cells, resulting in increased energy levels and a strong, healthy body.

When you are breathing correctly, you should breathe fluidly and evenly like a wave in the sea, flowing in natural rhythm. Take a few seconds to inhale and exhale. As you inhale the stomach extends outward and as you exhale the stomach contracts inward. As you practice you will notice that your breathing pattern increases in depth and duration and becomes very quiet.

In yoga you will use breathing techniques, known in Sanskrit as *pranayama*, that will balance the energies and focus the mind. Within the body there are seven energy centers known as chakras. *Pranayama* techniques unlock blockages so that

1

Place both hands on your stomach just below the waist and inhale slowly and evenly through your nose from the diaphragm. Feel your stomach distend as the diaphragm expands. Do not move your chest and shoulders.

the stream of energy flows smoothly from the base of the spine up to the top of the head to connect with the universal energy. When the subtle *prana,* or energy, is controlled, the body also comes under the mind's control and all imbalances are destroyed. If the body is strong and healthy, the energy flows freely.

Alternate Nostril Breathing (see page 149) shows you the difference between the masculine and feminine principle of energy. The right nostril is stronger, more fiery and more intense, i.e. masculine; the left is softer, cooler and more gentle, i.e. feminine. The alternate nostril technique combines the masculine and feminine energies to balance the entire system.

Deep breathing techniques act like a tranquilizer, calming the nervous system. The deeper you breathe, the stronger the effect and the more able you are to combat stress. *Pranayama* not only teaches willpower and self-control but also improves concentration and encourages spiritual development.

2

Exhale slowly and evenly and feel your stomach shrinking as your diaphragm contracts. As in Step 1, remember to resist moving your chest and shoulders.

# Total Body Warm-up

A sedentary lifestyle and poor eating habits make many people feel lethargic. In addition, stimulants such as alcohol, caffeine and cigarettes clog up the system. The body needs help to eliminate these toxins. The Total Body Warm-up is devised to combat lethargy and cleanse the system.

This warm-up consists of ten gentle stages to awaken the body slowly, starting with movements which loosen and relax the muscles in the neck and shoulders. This sequence quickly restores energy and vitality, improving and strengthening every muscle in the central part of the body, especially the abdomen. The flexibility of the spine improves and circulation to the brain is increased. The waist, hips, abdomen, buttocks and thighs are all toned.

The stretches release tension in the muscle groups and prepare the body for the exercises that follow. As you perform the various steps, concentrate on exhaling, as this helps to relieve stiffness. Having completed the Total Body Warm-up you will feel calm, your eyes will glow and you will be filled with a sense of inner peace.

1

Stand tall with your feet together and your tail-bone tucked in. Inhale and raise your clasped hands above your head.

2

Breathing normally, balance on your toes with your eyes fixed ahead of you. Hold for 5 seconds, then return to Step 1.

4

Take your weight onto your heels, grasping the floor with your toes. Look up, thrusting your chest forward with all your strength. Inhale deeply.

3

Exhale and release your hands so that your arms are parallel. Hold for 5 seconds, then clasp your elbows behind your back.

5

Exhale. Push your hips forward and curve your spine backward. Open your chest and relax your throat and face muscles.

23

## 6

Inhale and exhale and stretch forward, leading with your chin. Keep your spine flat by lengthening from the tail-bone.

## 7

Holding your stomach muscles in, exhale and relax further and further forward, keeping your spine straight.

## 8

Breathing normally, release your arms from behind you, place your hands around your ankles and hold for 5 seconds.

## 9

Inhale deeply then slowly exhale as you stretch forward, resting your forehead on your knees. Try to place your torso as close as possible to your thighs. Hold for 5–10 seconds.

## 10

Part your feet to hip-width and straighten your spine from the tail-bone. Hold your elbows and stretch forward. Breathing deeply, hold for 10 seconds.

# The Head Roll

The Head Roll relieves stiffness in the neck and shoulders. The exercise consists simply of rolling the head slowly in a circle without missing an inch. When the spine is not aligned properly you will experience tightness in the neck, shoulders or back. If this is the case, hold your position and breathe deeply to help the body return naturally to balance.

**1** Keep your spine straight and drop your head forward, resting your chin on your chest. Breathe normally.

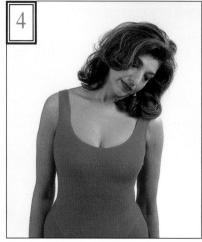

**4** Exhale and slowly roll your head to the left. Try to keep your shoulders down to allow freedom of movement.

**2** Roll your head gently up and round to the right. Try to keep your ear as close as you can to your shoulder.

**5** Complete the circle by rolling your head down toward your chest. Repeat the exercise in the opposite direction.

3

Continue the circle by rolling your head back. Relax the neck and throat and soften the face muscles, especially about the eyes.

# Head and Shoulders

After releasing tension in the neck with the Head Roll, move on to this exercise which includes the shoulders and relieves stiffness throughout the entire length of the spine. The Head and Shoulders exercise can be done either standing or kneeling.

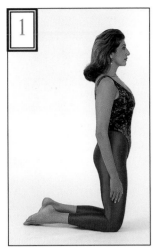

Kneel on the floor facing forward and inhale and exhale normally.

Drop your head forward, keeping your spine straight. Inhale.

Lift your elbows up behind you, resting your hands in the small of your back.

4

Exhale. Tilt your head back and, looking up at the ceiling, rotate both shoulders backward together. Repeat the exercise 6 times.

# Salute to the Sun

This is a traditional Yoga warm-up, which has a wonderful, rejuvenating effect. The slow, gentle movements exercise and tone every muscle in the body and improve the body's flexibility, stamina, poise and

suppleness. When performing Salute to the Sun, keep the energy flowing as you move from one position to another. Pay particular attention to your breathing pattern, as it is most important for increasing energy levels and vitality. Once you have managed to build up your stamina, you should aim to perform the

Breathe normally. Looking ahead, stand tall in perfect posture with palms together and shoulders down.

Inhale and step to the right. Fling your arms over your head and reach back behind you.

Exhale as you bring your feet together and relax down. Clasp the ankles and try to touch your knees with your forehead. Bend your knees slightly, if you wish.

Inhale and take the left leg back as far as you can with the toes tucked under, then flatten the leg as in Step 11. Raise your arms, with palms together. Breathe normally.

whole sequence ten times on each side.

As with all the previous exercises, Salute to the Sun should be performed with a graceful flow of energy. As you familiarize yourself with the sequence, you will eventually be able to move from one position to the next with confidence and fluidity, like a dancer.

Extend both legs behind you and raise yourself onto your hands and feet, keeping your arms straight.

Drop to your knees and keep your gaze straight ahead. Try not to make any unnecessary movements.

Sit back on your heels and stretch your arms forward to release your spine.

Inhale and dive forward like a serpent, with your chin sliding close to the floor. Bend your elbows.

9

Still inhaling, straighten your arms, swing forward with your hips and curve your spine, looking up.

10

Exhale, raise your hips, and drop your toes and heels down onto the floor, stretching the entire spine.

11

Inhale and bring your left leg forward, extending your right leg back (as for left leg in Step 4). Raise your arms, with palms together. Breathe normally.

12

Exhale and return to the position in Step 3 by leaning forward and bringing your right foot to join the left, clasping the ankles, then straightening the knees.

## 13

Inhale and step to the left. Stretch back,
looking up at the ceiling to release
tension in your back.

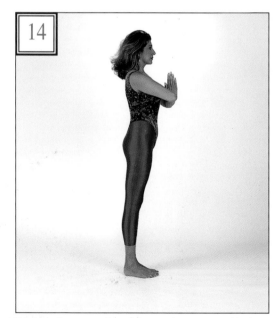

Exhale and return to Step 1. Repeat the sequence, this time
taking the opposite leg back in Steps 4 and 11.

# The Jump

The Jump is a wonderful exercise that energizes and rejuvenates the entire body. Jumping increases the heartbeat and circulation, leaving you with a feeling of youth and vitality. Because this exercise is fairly strenuous, it is important to keep your breathing regular. Remember to always breathe through the nose.

**1**

Begin by standing tall in second position with arms raised above your head and fingers together, pointing up. Breathe normally.

**2**

Inhale, bend your knees, throw your arms forward and prepare to jump. Keep the knees parallel in line with your feet.

**3**

Exhale and jump as high as you can, throwing your arms back and with feet together. Repeat the exercise 6–12 times.

# Beginners

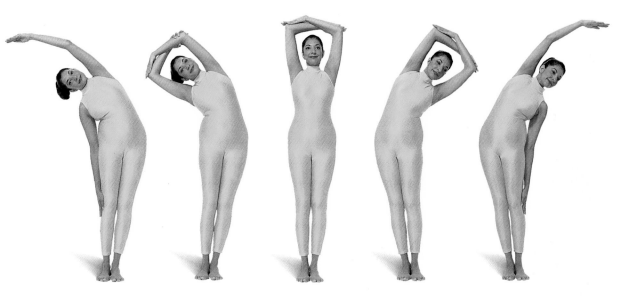

This section of the book is a foundation course for total beginners. It will teach you to balance your mental and physical energies and increase your flexibility and muscle tone, while improving your body shape and relaxing your nervous system.

Yoga is a science of movement: you should always begin with the Total Body Warm-up (page 22), and the exercises must be followed in their exact order. Here you are introduced slowly to the system with easy poses and stretches which will familiarize you with the yoga way of movement; you should pay

special attention to details such as hand and feet positions.

Remember that even if you feel motionless, yoga is never static. Physical exercises like aerobics require a lot of energy, as every violent move burns it up; lactic acids are formed in the muscle fibers and this tires the muscles. The slow movements of yoga waste no energy; deep breathing allows more oxygen absorption and muscles suffer no fatigue.

Concentrate on what your body is doing. This is the first step toward disciplining the mind and body.

# Head to Knee

This Head to Knee exercise lengthens the spine forward and is an excellent way to increase your body's flexibility and release unwanted body toxins. It helps soothe the nervous system, and will also relax the brain. You should never force your body forward, but as you increase the depth of your breathing you will be able to ease into the joy of deep stretching. It is very important to stretch forward from the waist. At the same time keep your back flat and don't round your shoulders. You might feel a pull in your hamstrings or some stiffness in the lower back. If this happens and you feel a bit dizzy, stretch your spine forward halfway, put your palms on a wall and keep your feet slightly apart.

1

Begin the exercise by standing up straight. Bend your knees slightly and place your hands on your waist.

2

Inhale and throw your arms forward, putting your head down between your arms. Bend your knees deeper and keep your head in line with your back.

Exhale and then throw your arms out straight behind your back, in line with your shoulders, but still keep your body in the same bent position.

Take your hands down and hold your ankles from behind, moving your head down toward your knees. Breathe normally for 5 seconds.

Now straighten your knees as much as you can. Pull your stomach muscles in, and drop your head down to your knees. Hold this position for at least 5–10 seconds. You'll feel the energy flow in a circular motion from your toes up the spine to your head. Uncurl and relax.

# Dog Pose

This exercise is wonderful for stretching the whole body. Not only does it increase blood circulation, it also helps to tone and strengthen the legs and arms as well as curing fatigue and increasing your vitality. As with all the downward poses, it calms the nervous system and can be used as a relaxation pose if you're tired. Breathe deeply and evenly throughout the movements and relax your neck to release any tension in the shoulders.

Sit back on your heels with your toes curled under. Stretch out your arms in front of you and straighten your elbows. Place your forehead on the floor.

Inhale and kneel up, keeping your hands balanced out in front of you. Exhale and breathe normally. Stretch your fingers evenly on the floor, and keep your knees under your hips.

# 4

Now flatten your heels on the floor and move your thighs outward. Lift up your knees and stretch your spine upward. Straighten your arms and keep your shoulders down. Relax your face and neck, and breathe deeply for 30–60 seconds. As you gain flexibility, hold for longer. Relax and slowly stand upright.

# 3

nhale, push the palms down and raise your hips pward. Stretch high onto your toes, pushing the shoulder blades down. Open out the chest and elease the neck and shoulders. Bring your head n line with your spine and push your hips back. Hold for 10 seconds, while breathing normally.

# The Tree

This pose focuses your mind and helps you learn how to concentrate and balance steadily on one leg. By balancing properly, you challenge your mind and you can unite your mental and physical energies. It also teaches you the importance of distributing your weight evenly between your heels and toes.

**3**

Now stretch your arms right up, while holding your balance for 5 seconds. Feel the energy move from your heels through your legs, into the spine and then through your arms and fingertips. Repeat on the other side.

**1**

Stand up straight. Place your right foot on your inner left thigh or close to the ankle or knee. Push out your hip but keep your hips square. Place your left hand on your left hip. Lift your standing leg as high as possible by stretching the muscle above the kneecap.

**2**

Look straight ahead and try to balance comfortably. When you are absolutely still, place your palms together and hold for 5 seconds. Grip the floor firmly with your toes so that the ankle does not move from side to side.

# Side Stretch

Stretching to the side is an exercise that improves every muscle, joint, tendon and organ in the body. It also revitalizes the nerves, veins and body tissue by increasing the flow of oxygen to the blood. It helps cure sciatica, lumbago and other lower-back ailments. The body's strength and flexibility is heightened by the deep stretching, especially in the hip joints, waist and torso.

1

Stand up straight and place your feet about 1m (3ft) apart. Stretch out your arms with your palms facing down. Keep them in line with your shoulders. Breathe normally.

2

Turn in your left foot slightly and point your right foot 90° to the right. Inhale and stretch to the right. Keep the spine straight and do not tilt forward. Breathe normally and hold for 5 seconds.

3

Place your right hand on your right ankle and extend your left arm up in a straight line with your palm facing forward. Look up toward your arm, keeping your head up. Relax your face and shoulders, and hold for 10 seconds.

**-4-**

Take the left arm over and bend to the right to feel the additional stretch. Turn your head forward and keep your weight on your back heels to maintain an equal stretch on both sides of the torso. Hold for 5 seconds.

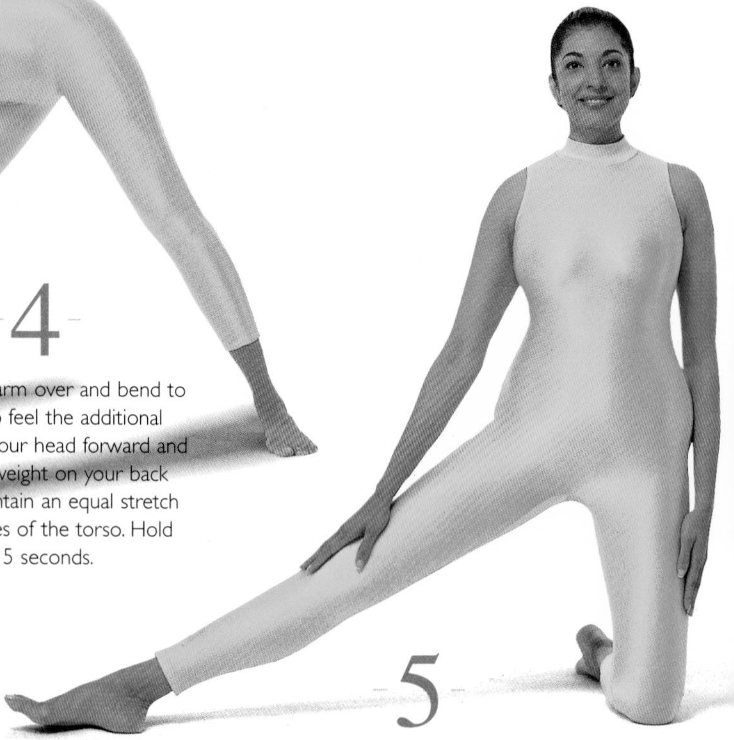

**-5-**

Return to Step 1. Bring your arms to your sides, placing your right arm on your right leg. Kneel on your left knee. Stretch the right leg out, pointing the toes. Balance evenly.

**-6-**

Inhale deeply and stretch out the right leg as far as possible without tilting forward. Stretch your left arm over to the right and feel the pull in your side. Keep your head balanced between your arms. Exhale and breathe normally.

**-7-**

Now sit on the floor, stretch out your right leg and fold your left leg in front, placing your foot on your inner right thigh. Clasp your right hand around your right foot and flex your thumb. Bend your right elbow and stretch forward toward the knee.

## 8

Inhale, take your left arm over your head and try to reach your right thumb with your fingers. Keep turning your upper torso to the side and keep your head evenly balanced. Increase the stretch and hold for 5 seconds.

## 9

Exhale and relax your head and arms down over your right knee. Keep your right foot flexed and, as you breathe normally again, relax your body further down toward the floor.

## 10

Lift your head up and stretch your legs out as wide as possible. Inhale and as you exhale stretch forward with your arms to reach your heels, or just reach for your thighs, knees or ankles. Stretch with your spine straight. Breathe deeply and hold for 10 seconds.

## 11

Now relax your head down toward the floor. Stretch your arms out, while keeping the toes flexed. Breathe normally and turn your knees upward, but push down. Hold for 15 seconds. Repeat on the other side.

# The Warrior

The Warrior pose is dynamic in its approach, and its aim is to develop a positive mental attitude and to give you physical control over your body. The Warrior is the basis for all standing postures, so the exact positioning of your spine, arms, legs and feet is very important. Hold your spine very straight as you open out your chest.

-1-

Stand up straight, feet together, and bend your knees slightly in preparation to jump. Bring your arms up to shoulder level and place your fingertips together.

-2-

Jump to open your legs wide – they should be about 1.2m (4ft) apart. Make sure your toes are pointing forward and stretch both your arms out sideways.

-3-

Turn your right knee and foot to the right. Lean your body backward and push your hips and stomach forward. Now bend your right knee, keeping your spine straight. Bend further until there is a 90° angle between your thigh and the floor. Repeat on the other side.

# The Eagle

The Eagle exercise focuses your mind so that you can concentrate on attention to detail. It grounds your energy and improves your balance. It can help to eliminate any cellulite and extra fat around the thighs, and also tones the leg, arm, and calf muscles. As you do the exercise, always keep your eyes fixed ahead on one spot to help you maintain your balance.

Stand up straight. Hold your left hand, facing upward, in front of your nose and stretch out your right arm. Focus on one spot straight ahead. Breathe normally.

Bend both your knees and wrap the right leg around the left. Try to wrap the right foot around the left ankle. The deeper you bend the easier it is to wind your leg.

3

Bring your right arm under your left, crossing them at the elbows, but keeping your shoulders down. Twist your right hand toward your left palm in front of your nose and press palms together. Keep your shoulders even, but press down to open the chest. Breathe normally, holding as long as possible. Repeat on the other side.

# Sitting Twist

If you practice these twisting movements regularly, any pain that you are suffering in your lower back will rapidly diminish. The muscles of your neck will also be strengthened, especially when you look over the shoulder (not shown) and any tension is released from your spinal system. Your liver and spleen are activated by the movements and the size of your abdomen is reduced in the twisting position.

1

Sit on the floor and bend your left leg flat in front of you with your knee in direct line with your left hip. Take your right leg over your left leg, placing your right heel in front of your left knee. Take your left elbow over your right knee and twist to look over your right shoulder. Place your right hand lightly on the floor for support. Sit upright to twist your spine further.

2

Repeat the exercise on the other side. Make sure the palm of your raised arm is facing up with the fingertips together.

# Toe Pull

This Toe Pull exercise stretches the body forward from the hips, helps to strengthen the leg muscles and increases the flexibility of the hamstrings and the spine. The movement stimulates the kidneys, liver and pancreas as you pull in the abdominal muscles. It also helps to flatten the stomach.

Sit upright with your legs out in front of you. Flex both feet and raise your arms over your head. Hold onto your elbows, keeping your shoulders down. Breathe normally.

Bend forward from the hips, keeping the back flat. Try not to curve your spine. Hold up your chin, keeping your head balanced between your arms. Hold for 5 seconds.

Reach further forward and try to grasp two fingers around your big toes. Flex the thumbs and keep the elbows straight. Inhale and exhale, and hold for 5 seconds.

Bend your elbows and stretch forward, pointing your chin. Keep your back flat and your head out in front. Breathe deeply and hold for 10 seconds.

# Flat Twist

The Flat Twist relieves any tension that gets trapped in the neck and shoulders. It also alleviates lower back pain and is a really good stretching exercise for your spine. Remember to keep both shoulders flat on the ground and always look in the opposite direction to your feet to increase the body stretch.

## 1

Lie flat on the ground and take your arms out to the side, placing your palms facing down. Put your left heel on top of the toes of the right foot. Breathe normally.

## 2

Inhale and as you exhale twist both feet to the right and look over your left shoulder. Hold the position for 5 seconds.

## 3

Bend your knees into your chest to increase the stretch, keeping legs and feet together. Inhale as your legs come up and then exhale and twist to the left. Relax onto your back and repeat on the other side.

# The Fish

When you do the Fish exercise you'll tone the stomach and leg muscles as well as releasing tension in the neck and shoulders. It also improves circulation to the face and slows the ageing process. These movements strengthen the lower back and open out the chest, increasing your lung capacity, which improves conditions such as bronchitis and asthma.

Lie on the floor with your arms out and point your toes. Inhale and raise your chest, resting your weight on the crown of your head. Feel the stretch in your neck and face. Exhale and breathe normally, holding for 3 seconds.

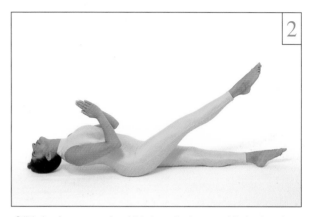

Still balancing on your head, inhale and raise your right leg, keeping your hip on the floor. Place your palms together above your chest, holding for 3 seconds. As you exhale, lower your leg slowly. Relax to the floor, if necessary, before Step 3.

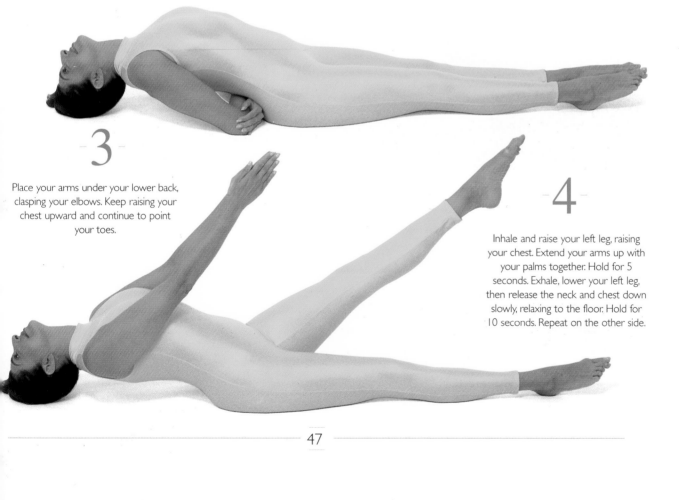

### 3

Place your arms under your lower back, clasping your elbows. Keep raising your chest upward and continue to point your toes.

### 4

Inhale and raise your left leg, raising your chest. Extend your arms up with your palms together. Hold for 5 seconds. Exhale, lower your left leg, then release the neck and chest down slowly, relaxing to the floor. Hold for 10 seconds. Repeat on the other side.

# Back Bend

All back bends strengthen the spine and open out the chest cavity to improve deep breathing. The movement increases blood circulation and raises energy levels. Even though back bends are strenuous to do, it is very important to keep your face relaxed and free of tension throughout. You will feel exhilarated in Step 4 as your whole body, especially your arms and legs, is strengthened. The deep breathing technique will also give you a feeling of complete calm.

2

Inhale and sit up tall, stretching your arms upward in line with the side of your head. Stretch out your legs slightly, but keep your feet together. Breathe normally.

1

Lie flat on the floor and bring your knees up. Place your feet as close to your body as possible. Stretch both your arms out behind your head and breathe normally.

**3**

Keeping your feet flat on the floor, balance your arms behind you. Place your palms in opposite directions to your feet to support your body weight. Inhale and lift your buttocks, keeping an even line between your knees, hips and shoulders. Look up, exhale and breathe normally for 5 seconds.

**4**

Inhale, extend your legs and straighten your knees. Drop your head back and relax the neck and face. Keep pushing your hips upward. Breathing normally, hold for 5 seconds.

# The Cobra

The Cobra strengthens and tones the lower back muscles. It alleviates back pain and prevents other common back ailments. The action of the Cobra tightens the buttock muscles and increases the intra-abdominal pressure which tones the uterus and ovaries. It also regulates the menstrual cycle and helps the thyroid and adrenal glands to work more effectively.

**1**

Lie flat on your stomach with your feet together. Point your toes, bend your arms close to your body, and place your palms flat under your shoulder blades. Point your chin downward.

**2**

Inhale and raise your head off the floor. Place your hands on the floor with your elbows inward. Keep your chin up and make sure your hip bones stay on the floor. Breathe normally and hold for 10 seconds. On the last exhalation, slowly lower yourself to the floor and return to Step 1. Repeat.

**3**

Return to Step 1, but this time place your hands under the breastbone and point your elbows outward.

**4**

Inhale, push down and lift your body off the floor. Look upward, keeping your shoulders down and your hips just off the floor. Breathing normally, hold for 10 seconds. On the last exhalation, slowly lower yourself and relax.

# Back Lift

This exercise is rather strenuous to do and your body needs to be correctly aligned to achieve the right results. Not only does this type of lift tone the legs, buttocks, and stomach muscles, it also strengthens the lower back to enable you to sit and stand with perfect posture. Both your hip bones and shoulder blades should remain on the floor to stop you moving from side to side throughout the exercise. As a beginner you need not worry about the height of your leg lift, but as you gain strength and continue practicing, your hips will become more flexible and you will be able to lift your legs even higher.

1

Lie on the floor face down. Keep your back straight and place your arms by your sides, holding your hands as fists. Inhale and raise your left leg, keeping your hips square. Breathe normally and hold for 6 seconds. On the last exhalation slowly lower the leg, then inhale and repeat on the other side.

3

Inhale and raise your legs. Place your forehead on the floor. Keep lifting, breathing deeply, for as long as you can. On the last exhalation lower both legs. Repeat, then turn your head to one side and relax.

2

With your feet together, raise your hips slightly off the floor with your elbows resting under the hip bones. Keep your hands in fists, balanced under the thighs for support.

# Soles of Feet

This Soles of Feet movement opens up the hips and increases flexibility in the hip joints, knees and thighs. Rotating the legs outward helps to increase the body's suppleness and also improves overall posture and mobility of the spine. It is an ideal exercise to do in preparation for giving birth, but take care not to bounce or jerk the spine.

**1**

Sit up tall on the floor with your legs in front of you. Bring the soles of your feet together and reach forward to place your hands around your ankles.

**2**

Bring the heels closer into your body and sit upright. Relax your shoulders, then stretch up from the pelvis and open out the chest.

**3**

To increase the stretch of the hips, thighs and knees, place your elbows over the knees. Bend over, curving your spine and keeping your shoulders down. Inhale, and as you exhale push your knees to the floor. Breathe and relax into the stretch, slowly lowering your head to your feet.

# Intermediate and Advanced

By now you have become familiar with the general style of yoga exercises and you have gained more flexibility, strength and stamina. You are now ready to twist your body in various ways, remembering, of course, to start with the Total Body Warm-Up (see page 22).

Intermediate and advanced poses are more physically and mentally challenging. The exercises are dynamic and you will experience the energy flowing from one position to another. The muscles, joints and blood vessels will all be stretched, so that the blood is equally distributed to every part of the body and more energy flows into the relaxed muscles.

Try to hold the postures for longer with a calm and still mind. This gives time for the mind to focus and the body to cleanse, purify and build the system.

# Vinyasa

Vinyasas are a series of different movements done in an active and dynamic style. Their function is to increase the stamina and strength of the body and to have an aerobic effect on the heart. Consequently, they are meant to be strenuous in nature and I have specifically designed this series to challenge your skill and to encourage you to develop grace through dynamic movement. Pay attention to the exact postures and do not rush. Breathe deeply and evenly through each of the positions.

## 1

Stand tall with your feet in second position directly under your hips and your knees bent. Inhale and throw your arms forward in parallel position.

## 2

Exhale, place your hands on the floor and jump, taking your feet out behind you. Stretch your spine and keep your legs and arms straight. Breathe normally.

## 3

Inhale, lift your heels and rise onto your toes. Change your foot position and balance on the front of your toes. Lower your hips toward the floor and raise your spine. Keep your shoulders down and look up. Breathe normally.

**5**

Exhale and place your left arm back down to the floor and swing your hips toward the floor. Tuck your toes under and point both hands forward, under the shoulder blades. Breathe normally.

**4**

Keeping your body in a straight line, turn your right hand to the front and your legs and feet together to the side. Raise your hips to maintain the straight line and raise your left arm, palm facing forward. Breathe deeply and hold for a few seconds.

**6**

Drop to your knees and begin to relax your spine. Breathe deeply.

**7**

Take your hips all the way back to your heels. Stretch your arms out in front of you. Breathe deeply and relax for a few moments.

## 8

Keeping your hands in the same
position, inhale and dive down,
leading with your chin and moving
your chest smoothly as close to the
floor as possible.

## 9

Exhale, sweep the spine
forward and come up
into the Cobra pose.
Breathe normally.

## 10

Inhale and return to the one-
arm balance as in Step 4,
but on the other side. Make sure
your alignment is correct.
Breathe normally and try to
hold still for as long as
you can.

## 11

Exhale and return to Step 5. Inhale and return to Step 2. Breathing normally, increase the stretch.

## 12

Inhale and raise your right leg in a straight line behind you. Point the toes, hold, and breathe deeply. Repeat on the other leg.

## 13

Walk your hands back to your feet. Bend your knees and balance on your toes. Straighten your spine and hold for a few seconds. Return to standing position and repeat the entire series.

# Half Lotus

This exercise is a wonderful challenge because it combines balance with concentration. In all difficult standing postures it is essential to keep the weight-bearing leg absolutely still when progressing through the various movements. Make sure the leg is pulled up as high as possible by gripping the floor with your toes and lifting the muscle above the kneecap.

## 1

Stand up straight. Lift your right foot up and bring your heel as close as possible to the left hipbone. Breathe normally.

## 2

Push your right foot against your left leg and balance your weight on your left leg.

**3**

Bring the palms together to help focus your attention. Make sure your shoulders are down and your face is relaxed.

**4**

Twist to the right and look over your right shoulder if you can. Having reached your maximum stretch, take your right hand around the back and reach for the right foot. Breathe normally and hold for a few moments.

**5**

Release the foot and return to center position. Change legs and repeat on the other side.

# Leg Extension

This position gives you more flexibility of the spine and builds strength in your lower back and legs. It opens the hips and makes you slimmer around the hips. It is also a difficult balancing exercise that focuses your concentration. The final position is quite hard to master, but don't be discouraged if you can't get your forehead right down to your knee.

### -1-

Stand up straight with your feet together. Bend forward and grasp your ankles. Breathe normally.

### 2

Place both hands on the floor in front of you and focus on one spot on the floor. Inhale and pull your stomach muscles up, while raising your left leg as high as possible. Keep the knee straight and point your toes. Breathe normally.

## 3

Still concentrating hard, take your hands to your right ankle and keep lifting the kneecap up. Open your toes and grip the floor. Breathe normally.

## 4

Keep stretching your leg out behind you as you pull your head toward your knee. Try to hold for as long as possible, pointing your toes upward, then slowly return to an upright position. Repeat on the other side.

# The Tower

This series of movements increases the strength in your legs and also makes your spine more flexible. It expands the chest, helping you to breathe more deeply and improving your lung capacity. The exercise also helps to relieve any stiffness in the neck and shoulders and make them more supple. At the end of the Tower, when your head is resting on your knee, the abdominal organs are toned and cleansed. This is because your deep breathing has pumped fresh oxygen into the blood, increasing the circulation and revitalizing and purifying them.

Stand upright with your feet about 1m (3ft) apart and your toes pointing forward. Take your arms up so that your palms face each other and straighten your elbows, keeping your shoulders down. Breathe normally.

Turn your left foot to a 90° angle, while moving the right foot slightly inward. The heel of the left foot should be in line with your right instep. Keep your head evenly balanced between your arms.

Bend your left leg so that your thigh is parallel to the floor. Throw your arms up and cross your thumbs with your palms together. Look upward and arch your spine. Breathe deeply and hold for 8 seconds.

## 4

Straighten your head between your arms and move your body forward with your weight on your left leg. Keep your leg, spine and arms in a straight line. Breathe deeply and hold for 8 seconds.

## 5

Relax down to the floor and place your hands on the floor. Drop your head to your knee. Keep breathing normally.

## 6

With your head still at your knee and with your palms on the floor, inhale and straighten the knee as much as possible. Breathe normally and hold for 8 seconds. Return to Step 1 and repeat on the other side.

# Deep Lunge

The Deep Lunge exercises every muscle and tendon in the body. The intensity of the side stretch trims the thighs, hips and waistline, invigorates the internal organs and soothes the nerves. The position of the spine in relation to the hips helps to balance the endocrine system – the pituitary gland, thyroid, gonads and pancreas, all of which are glands that secrete hormones – as well as releasing toxins that build up in the system.

-1-

Adopt the Warrior pose (page 42), making sure your left leg makes a 90° angle and the back of your knee is in line with your heel. You can take the right leg further out to increase the lunge. Breathe normally.

-2-

Take your left hand down to your left ankle, turn your upper body and look over your right shoulder, twisting as much as possible. Place your right hand on the inner left thigh to increase the twist. Breathing deeply, hold for 8 seconds.

## 3

Place your left palm down on the floor and extend your right arm, elbow straight, close to your ear. Keep looking upward. Breathing deeply, hold for 8 seconds.

## 4

Inhale and raise your body, keeping your spine in the same position. Clasp your hands together over your head and stretch upward. Breathing deeply, hold for 8 seconds, then return to Step 1. Straighten the knee and repeat on the other side.

# Side Lunge

This series of movements increases flexibility of the spine, improves balance and tones and cleanses the abdominal organs. You may feel dizzy or nauseous during the exercise, but this is a good sign – it means you are releasing toxins in the system. Just stop if you feel in any way uncomfortable and breathe deeply to regain your equilibrium. Always stretch from the tail bone and keep your hips and torso square to the side.

Exhale and, keeping your spine straight and your chin up, lower yourself to a 90° angle to the floor.

Still exhaling, bend and rest your forehead on your knee. Keep both legs straight – lift the muscles above the kneecaps to maintain balance. Breathing normally, hold for 6 seconds.

-1-

Follow feet positions in Steps 1 and 2 of Side Stretch (page 39). Place your palms together behind your lower back or toward the mid-back. Push the elbows toward each other and open the chest. Look up and bend back as far as possible. Inhale deeply.

Bend your left knee and lunge forward. Drop your head down on the inner side of the knee. Breathe deeply and hold for 6 seconds.

Straighten your knee, relax your arms down and place your hands on the floor, palms down. Breathe deeply and hold for as long as you can.

Inhale and raise your body so that your back is flat, with your arms back and upward. Breathing normally, hold for 6 seconds.

-7-

Return to an upright position, take your feet and arms through the center as in Step 1 of Side Stretch and repeat on the other side.

# Front Lunge

This exercise is beneficial both mentally and physically. Stretching forward from the hips calms and soothes the central nervous system, lifts fatigue, refreshes the mind and invigorates the blood circulation. The flexibility of the hamstrings, hips and spine is improved and the leg muscles are toned. Make sure that you always stretch forward from the tail bone and hold your stomach muscles up. Keep your spine straight throughout the exercise and breathe deeply from the diaphragm in order to increase the relaxing effect.

1

Stand tall with your feet 1.2m (4ft) apart. Place your hands on your hips. Inhale and as you exhale move your torso forward to flat-back position, keeping your chin up.

## - Tips -

+ Pay attention to your breathing, and take care not to hold your breath.

+ Push your weight onto your heels and grip the floor with your toes in order to steady your balance.

+ Keep your fingertips together in Step 4.

+ Whenever you straighten your legs, lift the leg muscles above the kneecap in order to avoid injury.

Still exhaling, relax forward, placing your hands on the floor. Push your weight to your heels, raise your hips back, grip the floor with your toes; open your fingers and stretch your spine.

Walk your hands back and distribute your weight evenly between your heels and toes. Lift your chin and keep your back straight.

# 4

Inhale and raise your arms evenly on both sides. Keep your elbows straight and your fingertips together. Breathe deeply and hold for 6 seconds.

Relax your arms and drop your forehead down toward the floor.
Breathe normally.

6

Inhale and clasp your hands around your
ankles. Exhale and stretch your forehead
down toward the floor. Breathe normally
and hold for 6 seconds. Make sure your
arms and legs are straight.

Inhale and jump. Breathe normally and balance on your toes. Steady yourself by placing your fingertips on the floor. Straighten the legs first, then the spine, and stand in perfect posture.

7

Bend your elbows and relax your knees. Push your palms down on the floor and prepare to jump into first position.

# Standing Bow

This graceful exercise, called the Standing Bow because of the curve of the spine, will give you a sense of elation and power when you hold the pose as long as possible. The energy is continuously flowing in a circular pattern and as you increase the stretch your breathing pattern will quicken. Breathe deeply from the diaphragm to increase energy levels. This exercise will rejuvenate your spine and give you a sense of joy. Your circulation will be greatly improved and your whole body toned.

## 1

Stand up straight with your arms at your sides. Take your right leg behind you and hold the inner side of your foot. Straighten your elbow.

## 2

Take your left arm up close to your ear. Keep both shoulders down and look straight ahead. Breathe normally and steady your balance.

**4**

Move your upper body forward smoothly and keep stretching your back leg upward. Breathe deeply. Imagine you are an elastic band and continue to stretch until the toe of your raised leg is directly above the top of your head, or until your energy snaps and releases. Repeat on the other side.

**3**

Inhale, lift the right leg up from the hip as high as possible and then extend the left arm forward. Breathing normally, stretch in opposite directions.

# The Letter T

Performing Letter T is very challenging and builds
up your strength and stamina. It is a powerful and
dynamic stretch and is the only asana that should
not be held longer than 10 seconds. It increases
your pulse rate and you will feel
your breath coming more
quickly.  The stretching
also firms your buttocks
and upper arms.

3

As you exhale stretch out from your tail
bone in both directions. Keep stretching
your spine forward and keep pointing
your toes behind you until you reach a
perfect Letter T. Deepen your breathing
and hold the position for up to
10 seconds. Repeat on the other side.

**1** Stand up straight with your feet together. Raise your arms above your head. Place your palms together and straighten your elbows. Push your elbows back behind your ears, keeping your shoulder blades down. Breathe normally.

**2** Inhale deeply and point your right leg out behind you. Keep both your right knee and your spine straight as you stretch out. Focus on one spot in front of you to help you to keep your balance.

## -Tips-

+ It is important to breathe deeply from the diaphragm during the final position to increase your energy levels and vitality.

+ Point your toes as much as possible. This will help you to keep your knee and foot in a straight line.

+ Keep pointing your toes and stretching your arms forward at the same time. Imagine you are a rubber band being stretched in opposite directions.

# Shoulder Stand

This is one of the most important asanas in classical yoga. Its benefits are many, the most important being that it stimulates and regulates the thyroid and parathyroid glands. Because of the chinlock, menstrual cycles regularize and weight remains stable. Healthy blood flows through the neck and chest, curing respiratory ailments and preventing sinus troubles and colds. Daily practice of this exercise cleanses the bowels and eliminates toxins.

## 2

Exhale and raise your legs to a 90° angle with your body, pointing your toes.

## 3

Inhale and take your legs over your head until your toes touch the ground. Inhale and exhale.

## 1

Lie flat on the floor with your arms at your sides. Inhale and bring your knees into your chest.

## 5

Bend your knees and bring the soles of your feet together.

## 4

Inhale and raise both legs as high as possible – the aim is to straighten the spine completely. Lock your chin, point your toes and place your hands in the small of your back to support your spine. Hold for 30 seconds, breathing normally.

▶

## 6

Straighten both legs behind you.
Tuck your toes under and, breathing deeply,
walk both feet to the right
side of your head.

## 7

Drop both knees as close to your right ear
as possible. Straighten both legs and walk
your feet to the left, then drop your knees as
close to your left ear as possible.

## 8

Bring both legs directly behind your head. Point your
toes. Inhale and raise both legs directly parallel to the
floor. Breathe normally.

-9-

Bend both knees and change the position of your hands, so your thumbs are on your tail bone and your fingers are on your waist.

-10-

Straighten your spine and split your legs, creating a 90° angle with your left leg. Repeat on the other side.

▶

# 11

Return to the classic
Shoulder Stand and
hold for 10 seconds.

# 12

Bend your right leg and place
the outer side of your foot
against your left thigh just
above your knee.

**14**

Return to the classic Shoulder Stand and hold for 10 seconds.

**13**

Bring your right heel toward your left hipbone. Push the knee back so that it is square with the left hip. Return to Step 11 and repeat 12 and 13 on the other side.

17

Twist the entire spine to the left. Return to center and rotate to the right side.

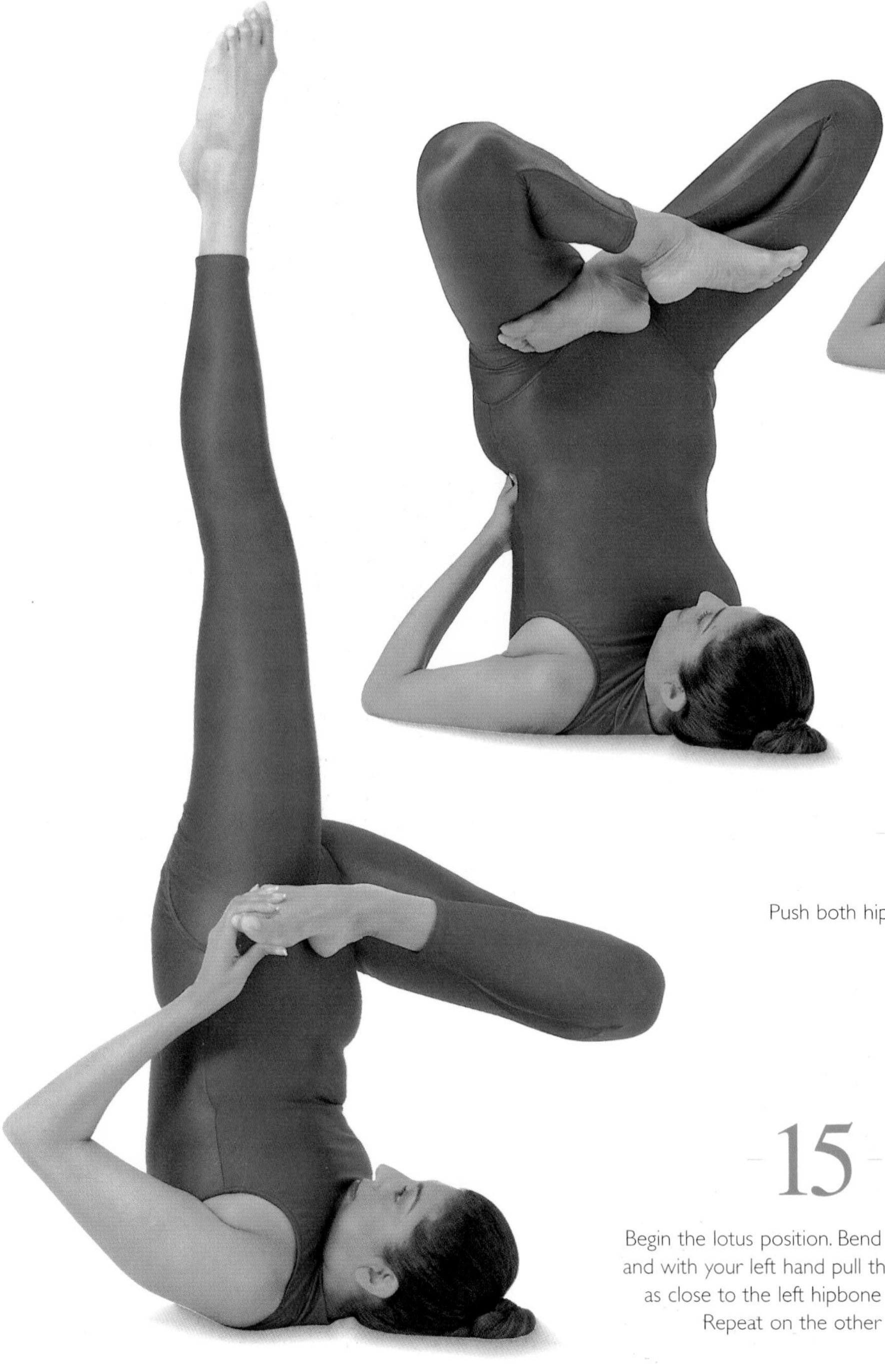

16

Push both hips back so they are square.

15

Begin the lotus position. Bend your right leg and with your left hand pull the right foot in as close to the left hipbone as possible. Repeat on the other side.

## 18

Return to the classic
Shoulder Stand. Hold for
5–10 seconds.

## 19

Repeat Step 10 but extend the right leg.
Point the toes of both feet.

## 20

Drop your left foot to the floor and point your right leg upward.

## 21

Bend your right knee and place both feet on the floor. Raise your hips as high as possible. Breathe normally.

## 22

Take your hands down to
the floor and continue to
raise your hips.

## 23

Exhale slowly and, working from the top of
the spine, slowly lower one vertebra at a
time until your spine is completely flat
on the floor.

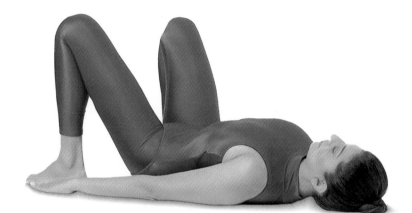

## 24

Relax your legs down to the floor and
release your spine into the deep relaxation
or Dead Man's pose. Relax for 5 minutes.

# The Wheel

The Wheel, Bow (page 92) and Camel (page 93) are intense back bends that invigorate the spine, alleviate back pain and increase lung capacity. We rarely stretch backward and these positions release fear and bestow a positive outlook on life. All three asanas release energy in the body's cells, glands and organs. The Wheel also builds muscle tone in the legs, hips, shoulders, arms, wrists and hands. Holding the position will build strength and give stamina to the spine and limbs.

Lie flat, knees bent and in line with your hips, and feet flat and as close to the buttocks as possible. Inhale and raise your buttocks as high as possible. Try to hold on to your ankles. Breathe normally. Lower down and repeat.

Keeping your feet in the same position, lift your hips and buttocks and take your arms over your head with palms facing downward. Push up and rest on the crown of your head. Breathe normally and hold for 5–10 seconds.

3

Lift as high as possible, balancing on your toes and hands. Straighten your elbows and, breathing normally, hold for as long as possible. Return to Step 2, lift your head toward your chest and lower your spine, one vertebra at a time, with your tail bone last.

# Uddiyana

In Sanskrit, 'Uddiyana' means 'flying up'. In this exercise the air is drawn up from the lower abdomen and moves under the ribcage toward the head. This movement tones the abdominal organs, increases the gastric juices and eliminates toxins in the digestive tract. It is a wonderful way to exercise the muscles of the stomach, thereby making it flatter.

Kneel down on all fours. Keep your spine straight and place your hands and feet in a direct line. Inhale through your nose and exhale through your mouth until all the breath is out of your lungs.

Pull the stomach muscles up and curve your spine slightly. Without taking a breath, contract and release the muscles to massage the internal organs. When you tire, inhale and exhale normally for a few breaths. Repeat the whole exercise up to 20 times.

# Ultimate Twist

These two twists are classic positions to increase circulation in the spine and the abdominal organs, especially the liver and spleen. Twists cleanse and purify the system and are essential to the digestive system. Elimination is regulated, the kidneys are toned, and the blood circulation releases toxins that build up in the internal organs. When you are practicing twists you will find that every time you begin the pose it will be a different experience. As the flexibility of your spine increases you will be able to twist even further. Sluggishness will be replaced by higher energy levels and you will experience a feeling of youthfulness.

Sit with knees together and feet flat on the ground. Place your right elbow on the outside of your left knee and put your left hand on the floor in the opposite direction to your feet. Push against your knee and look over your left shoulder. Keeping your chin level and breathing normally, continue to stretch around. Hold for as long as you can. Repeat on the other side.

Sit with your left leg over your right leg. Take your right hand to the left knee and twist, looking as far over your left shoulder as possible. Place your left hand on the floor in line with your left leg. Breathe normally and continue to twist. Repeat on the other side.

# Leg Pull

The Leg Pull increases the flexibility of the hamstrings and tones muscle in the knees and legs. It also tones the spine and massages the abdominal wall; blood flows around the navel and rejuvenates the genital organs. Never lift the knee that is resting on the floor – if there is too much of a pull on the kneecap do not extend your chin all the way to your knee.

Sit with both legs extended in front. Bend your left knee and bring your heel to your hip. Place your fingertips on the floor on either side of your body. Breathe normally.

Bend your right knee and clasp your first two fingers around your big toe. Flex your thumb and right foot and prepare for the stretch.

Keeping your spine straight, inhale and stretch the leg up in front of you. Hold your ankle and pull your leg towards you. Breathing slowly and evenly, hold for 20 seconds. If you can, place your chin and forehead to the leg. Repeat on the other side.

# Sitting Balance

The Sitting Balance is an excellent test for checking your alignment – you will be unable to carry out this exercise if your spine is not in the correct position. Imagine your spine to be a group of children's building blocks; if you do not place each block evenly on to the next the whole building will come tumbling down. By the same token, if you do not lift your spine upright you will keep rolling back down to the floor. Concentrate on your stomach muscles because it is equally important to pull them in at the same time as you lift your spine.

2

Still sitting upright, bring your legs up to form an exact right-angle with the body.

1

Sit upright and bring your knees up with your feet flat on the floor. Clasp your elbows under your knees. Keep your spine straight and breathe normally.

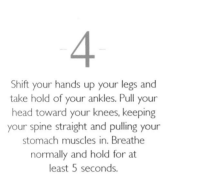

## 4

Shift your hands up your legs and take hold of your ankles. Pull your head toward your knees, keeping your spine straight and pulling your stomach muscles in. Breathe normally and hold for at least 5 seconds.

Straighten both legs up in front of you and hold the position absolutely still for at least 5 seconds, breathing normally.

# The Bow

1

Lie on your stomach and lift your legs up behind you. Hold on to your ankles and point your toes. Place your chin and nose on the floor. Breathe normally.

This exercise is called the Bow because of the beautiful bow shape that the spine creates. The back muscles and internal organs are massaged and the latter invigorated. Because of the position of the abdomen, this asana helps to cure digestive and bowel disorders such as gastroenteritis and constipation. It also stimulates the appetite, aids digestion and reduces fat along the stomach and middle of the back. As a result of the increased suppleness it gives to the spine every cell in the body is rejuvenated and revitalized, giving you renewed vitality and a more youthful appearance.

2

Inhale and lift your body up in one movement. Balance on your hip bones and keep stretching upward, trying to get your head in line with your feet. Breathe deeply and hold for as long as you can.

# The Camel

The Camel tones the entire spine as well as every muscle group in the body, building strength in the lower back and alleviating back ailments, especially sciatica and slipped discs. It is also a wonderful stretch for the face and neck – the increased circulation helps to prevent the signs of ageing. Every time you do this exercise, feel your body giving way into the stretch and relax and open the throat and chest; do not allow any weight into the thighs or leg muscles. Always push upward from the hips to increase the intensity of the back stretch and breathe deeply throughout. If you experience a sharp pain in the lower back, stop immediately and relax in Step 3. A dull pain means you are using muscles around the spine that need toning.

Kneel down, spine straight and hips directly above your knees. Hold on to your elbows behind your lower back. Inhale, push your hips forward and drop your head back. Breathe normally.

Continuing to push your hips forward, take your hands to your heels. Open your chest and throat and relax your face, neck and shoulders. Say 'Aah' to check that your facial muscles are relaxed. Breathe normally and hold for as long as possible.

To release the spine, reverse the position by relaxing your head down to the floor with your palms facing up. Breathe normally and repeat the exercise.

# The Rabbit

The Rabbit allows fresh oxygen into the blood supply, which stimulates and invigorates the brain cells. The upside-down position of the head has a beneficial effect on the pituitary gland and thyroid. It wards off senility, clarifies the mind, regulates the metabolism and strengthens the immune system. It also has a calming effect on the nervous system. A preliminary exercise to the Head Stand (opposite), the Rabbit improves the elasticity and mobility of the spine.

2

Inhale and as you exhale curl your spine and place your forehead on the floor as close as you can to your knees. Breathe normally.

3

Roll on to the top of your head. Straighten your elbows and raise your hips. Breathe deeply and hold for 20 seconds. Return to Step 1 and repeat the exercise.

## 1

Kneel on the floor, toes tucked under your haunches. Clasp your hands to your heels and sit up tall. Breathe normally.

# Head Stand

**1**

Kneel on the floor. Interlock your fingers, cross your thumbs and place your arms on the floor. Breathe normally.

The Head Stand is called the king of all yoga asanas because it stimulates the pituitary and pineal glands. These are the glands that control the brain, the seat of all wisdom, intelligence, discrimination and reasoning power. Without a healthy brain you cannot function. The inverted position of the Head Stand allows the blood to flow freely to the brain and feeds the brain cells with fresh oxygen. It gives you clarity of mind and wards off senility as you age. The brain also controls the entire nervous system and during the practice of the Head Stand all the nerves and cells are being rejuvenated. Health and vitality are restored and when you practice it on a regular basis you will develop the body, discipline the mind and broaden the spirit.

**2**

Making sure your elbows are directly under your shoulder blades, place the top of your head down on the floor just in front of your hands.

**3**

Tuck your toes under and spring up onto your toes with your legs straight. Walk your feet toward your head until your spine is straight.

▶

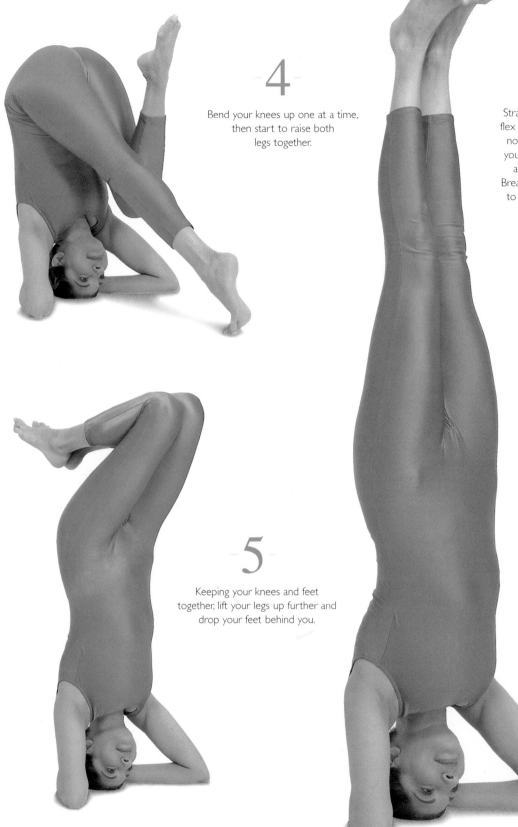

# 4

Bend your knees up one at a time, then start to raise both legs together.

# 5

Keeping your knees and feet together, lift your legs up further and drop your feet behind you.

# 6

Straighten your legs and flex your toes. You should not feel any weight on your head as your arms are supporting you. Breathe normally and try to hold still for as long as possible.

### 7

Open your legs to
second position, keeping
your feet flexed. Hold for
10 seconds.

### 8

Bend your knees at a
right angle.

### 9

Slowly bring your knees forward, curving your
spine, and return to the floor. Stay in this
position for 10 seconds. If you come up
suddenly you will feel dizzy.

# Total Stretch

This stretch is very controversial – some people find it excruciating, while others feel it to be the most marvellous of all the classic stretches. The truth is that the more flexible you are the easier the pose. It stretches every muscle in the thighs, knees and ankles, as well the entire spine. If you feel any pain in your back, place a pillow under the small of the back and open your chest. If you feel your knees are strained place a small pillow under the back of your knees. The most important thing to remember is to relax in the position. Breathe deeply and evenly and feel the chest and hips open.

1

Sit upright and bring your knees together. Spread your feet and rest them either side of your hips, with your buttocks on the floor. Place your palms facing forward on your feet.

2

Drop your body back down, taking your weight on your elbows, and feel the stretch in your legs and abdomen.

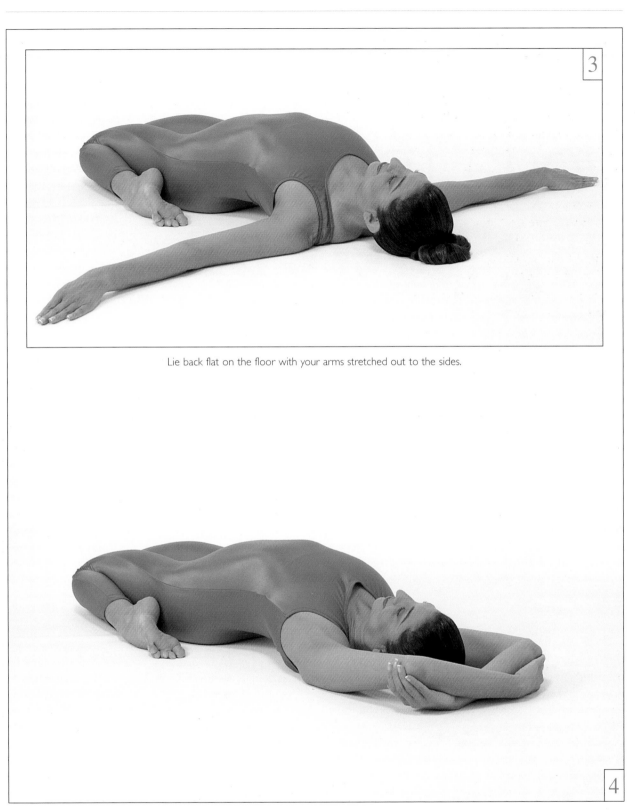

3

Lie back flat on the floor with your arms stretched out to the sides.

4

Clasp your elbows. Continue to breathe deeply and relax the entire body and mind. Try to hold this position for as long as possible – with practice you will be able to sustain it for 10–15 minutes.

# yoga to relieve **stress**

The aim of yoga is to unify the entire system through breathing techniques, gentle exercise and mind control. This combination of practices produces an inner calm and tranquility that goes deep into the mind and body. The result is a feeling of peace and harmony that translates in the way you think and react to certain situations. When you are relaxed and in control of your thoughts and emotions you are better able to cope with even the hardest problems. Most people panic when faced with difficulties and this increases stress levels immediately. Simply learning to breathe from the diaphragm acts as a natural tranquilizer that calms the nervous system instantly. In addition, the gentle movement and deep stretching of yoga improves the circulation and releases tension in the muscle groups. Another aspect of yoga is the visualisation and meditation techniques, which help to train and focus the mind. Although there are five different schools of yoga, all concentrate on the philosophy of reaching spiritual enlightenment through uniting mind and body. Yoga transforms people's lives by teaching them a new way of thinking and viewing the world, providing an anchor in an increasingly frenetic age.

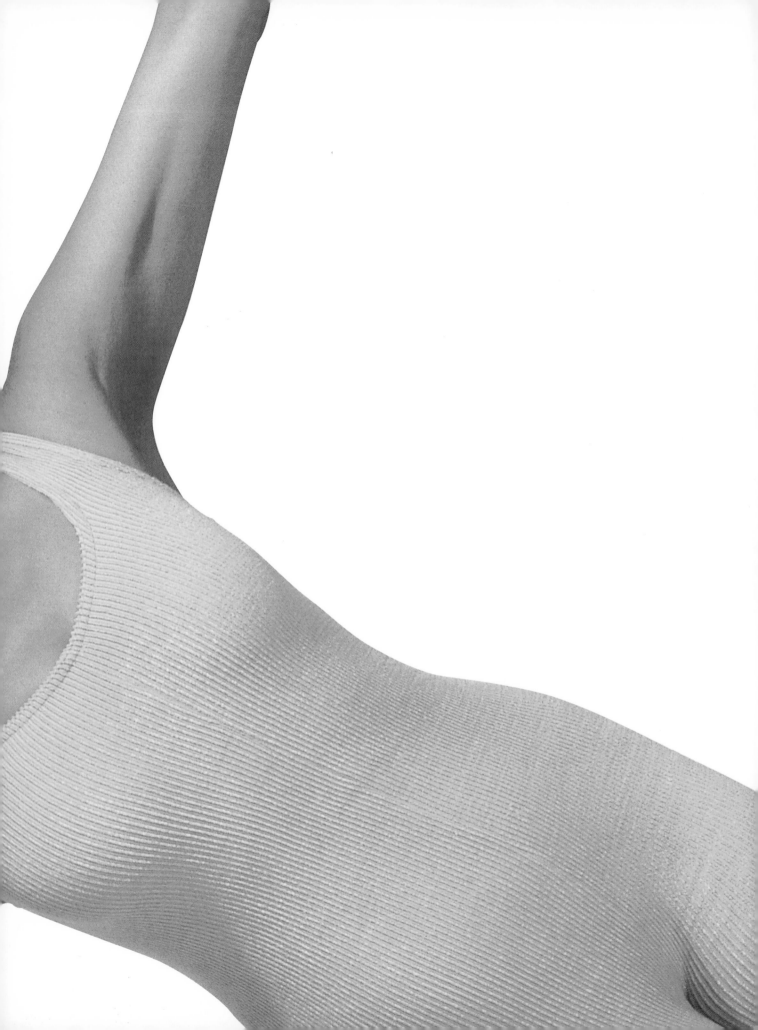

# Energy Boosters

People who suffer from stress complain of fatigue, depression and generally feeling unwell. They usually lead sedentary lives with little exercise and seem to have no joy in anything they do; lack of energy affects their mental health and erodes their self-esteem. Acidic foods, diets containing stimulants, and medication also deplete the body of energy. Yoga exercise is the best way to boost the body by releasing tension in the muscles as well as improving blood circulation and lymphatic drainage. Deep breathing, combined with stretching, increases the oxygen in the system and rejuvenates all body cells, giving you more energy. When stress is deeply rooted in the muscle groups, any jarring movements can cause injury. Yoga, with its gentle approach, will slowly ease the stress in the body while increasing stamina and strength. Stress can also cause stiffness in the ligaments and joints, and bending forward, backward and sideways can increase your body's flexibility and energy flow. Twisting movements release toxins from the organs, and inverted positions soothe the nervous system. Yoga exercises also lubricate the joints and arteries and build muscle tone as you age. In this chapter I have developed a gentle, easy, safe exercise program for people of all ages to release tension, increase energy levels and tone the body. There are also shorter energy boosters for home, work and travel to lift your spirits and rejuvenate you.

# Forward Stretch

Stretching forward lengthens the spine and helps to calm the nervous system. It opens out the hips and tones up the leg muscles. It is important to lift the muscles above the knees to increase your balance and to enable you to grip the floor with your toes. Always extend your body from the base of your spine while you tighten your abdominal muscles. Some people can feel slightly dizzy because of the increased oxygen in the system, but it passes quickly as you learn to deepen your breathing. As you push your elbows back you will open your chest and release any tension in the neck, shoulders and upper back. In the final position try to concentrate on one point on the floor and keep your back flat in a straight line from the neck to the tail bone.

Stand up straight with your feet 1–1.2m (3–4ft) apart and toes pointing forward. ▸ Place your hands on your waist and open out your chest. Inhale deeply and look upward, drawing the elbows toward each other. ▸ Lean forward and point your chin, stretching from the hips and tailbone to straighten the spine. ▸ As you continue to inhale, pause with your back straight and your hips, shoulders and head at a 90° angle. Exhale and hold this position for a few seconds while you breathe normally. ▸ Inhale again and continue stretching downward, exhaling when you have reached as far as you can. Breathe normally and hold this position for 10 seconds. As you deepen your breaths, try to stretch even further without forcing or jerking your body.

*When you reach the final position, continue with the exercise on pages 106–7.*

# Head to Knee Side Twist

This exercise increases your spine's flexibility, releases toxins from your internal organs and helps back ailments such as sciatica and lumbago. When you take your head forward it helps to soothe your nerves, making you feel calm and relaxed. Suppleness of the spine is essential for good circulation and this exercise combined with deep breathing increases the blood flow through the arteries to boost your energy. When you start to twist, try to turn as far as you can. The final position releases any stiffness you are experiencing in the lower back, neck and shoulders, and also helps to build muscle strength so that you can sit and stand tall.

Continuing from the previous exercise, inhale deeply and as you exhale reach down to your feet, clasping your hands around your ankles. Inhale and exhale deeply for a few seconds to increase the stretch. ▸ Now take both of your hands over to the right ankle. If you cannot reach your ankle, take your hands down your right leg as far as you can. ▸ Inhale and take your right arm out to the side in a straight line. ▸ Continue to inhale as you start to twist your body around to the back. ▸ Look over your right shoulder and continue to twist as far as possible. Exhale and hold this final position for 10 seconds. Return to the start position and repeat the exercise on the other side.

# Spinal Stretch

This spinal stretch increases your blood circulation and the flow of oxygen to the brain, helping to relieve tension. It also tones and increases the flexibility of the hamstrings, hips and spine and tones the leg muscles. As you take your arms over your head your breathing pattern becomes shallower, so you have to breathe more deeply to sustain an even pattern. This increase in breathing rejuvenates the body's cells and helps to purify the internal organs. You will experience a tingling sensation in your toes and fingertips as your energy flow is increased. Also your face will glow when you can hold the final position for some time.

Stand upright with your feet slightly apart, then take hold of your ankles and gently stretch down toward your legs. ▸ Cross your arms, holding onto your elbows. Inhale deeply and pull in your abdominal muscles as you begin to stretch your arms over your head. ▸ Keep your spine straight and push your hips back behind you. To maintain your balance, shift your weight back onto your heels and grip the floor with your toes. ▸ Holding your stomach muscles taut, bring your arms up to your head with your head, neck, shoulders and hips in a straight line. Exhale and breathe deeply, holding this position for 30 seconds. You will feel energized and calmer as you breathe more deeply. To release the stretch, relax your spine and drop your head down toward your feet. Hold for a few seconds, then slowly raise yourself upright.

# Deep Bend I

This bending posture promotes total body health because it allows the energy to flow through the entire system. Not only does the exercise soothe the brain but harmful toxins are also eliminated from the body's organs as the head bends forward. The spine becomes more flexible and supple, which gives you a feeling of elation. This posture also stimulates the sciatic nerve and strengthens the muscles of the lower back. Always gently lengthen the spine forward – never force your body or jerk into the pose. Breathe deeply as you relax forward, eventually trying to stretch out your entire spine as you clasp your ankles.

Stand up straight and bring your feet together, then lean down and hold onto your ankles with both hands, keeping your elbows straight. ▸ Pulling your tummy muscles in, inhale deeply, bend your elbows and slowly stretch your forehead toward your knees. ▸ Exhale and pull your head further down. ▸ Breathing deeply and slowly, lengthen your spine as you try to touch your knees with your forehead. Hold the position for 30 seconds. Do not become discouraged if you cannot reach down very far. With continued practice you will be amazed at how far down you can reach.

*Think of your spine as circles of energy around the vertebrae and not a solid mass. This will help the way you approach this position as you ease softly and gently down.*

# Perfect Posture

It is vital to understand good body alignment and to learn how to sit and stand in perfect posture. Bad posture leads to back ailments, a negative mental outlook and depleted energies. When you are standing and sitting correctly you can breathe properly to your full lung capacity. Most people with bad posture never experience the joy of feeling full of vitality. Stretching in perfect posture aligns and balances the muscles and corrects the tilt of the pelvis. It allows the spine to stay erect so that the body's energy flows freely. By stretching your arms over your head you open out your chest and your hips are free, giving more space for the internal organs to function properly.

Stand upright with feet together and big toes touching and try to balance. Distribute your weight evenly between your heels and toes and grip the floor with your toes. Place your hands on your ankles with your head tucked in. ▸ Inhale deeply, straighten your arms and pull up halfway. ▸ Then bring your arms out in front of you close to your ears, tightening your tummy and buttock muscles. ▸ Keep stretching your arms outward with a straight spine as you stand up. ▸ Lift your arms above your head, exhale and breathe normally. Keep your head lifted, your neck extended and your breastbone stretched upward. Then lift your diaphragm, rib cage and abdomen, and tuck in your tail bone; tighten your leg muscles. Release your arms down and stand for 30 seconds, drawing your energies into yourself.

*As you stretch up do not hyper-extend your knees by pushing them backward, but lift the muscles above your knees.*

# Deep Bend II

Flexible hip joints help to correct any pelvic imbalance and improve mobility as we get older. This stretch looks simple to do, but it really is a dynamic movement which creates poise and confidence. Keeping your spine upright in perfect alignment while you bend helps you breathe more deeply, but holding the pose can be quite strenous. As you lunge sideways, make sure your knee does not extend right over your foot as this can cause knee strain. The movement should create a 90° angle from the upper body to the back of the knee and heel.

Stand upright with your feet 1.2m (4ft) apart, your toes pointing forward and both hands on your waist. Turn your left foot to the left, keeping the instep of the right foot in line with the left heel. Place your left hand on your left leg with your fingertips on the inner thigh above the knee. Keep your spine straight and hips square, and remember to breathe deeply and evenly throughout the exercise. ▸ Bend your left knee to turn the thigh and hip joints. If the knee moves beyond the foot, take the right leg out further to create a 90° angle. ▸ Now extend the lunge further by pushing the pubic bone down toward the floor, keeping the right leg straight. Push the right foot down toward the floor, tightening the muscle above the knee. Keep your pelvis straight and your breastbone lifted. Enjoy the elation of the stretch, while holding for 10 seconds or more. To release the pose return to the start position and repeat the exercise on the other side.

# Cat Stretch

This is a wonderful exercise to relieve all the tension that accumulates in the spine. It also helps to calm the brain and relaxes the neck and shoulders. If you suffer from headaches and backaches caused by stress, you will find that if you place your head down on the floor in this curved position it will help to alleviate the pain. Combined with deep breathing, this exercise soothes your central nervous system and helps you to restore harmony and balance to your life. It slows down your pulse rate and gives you time to escape from any mental anxieties by relaxing the brain so that you find inner calm.

Begin by kneeling down on all fours on the floor and stretch your arms out in front of you. ▸ Inhale deeply and begin to drop your hips back toward your heels. ▸ Exhale and push your hips all the way down so that your chest rests on your knees, bending your elbows and dropping your head forward to the floor. ▸ Breathing in and out deeply, slide your arms back toward your heels. Curl your spine and relax down onto your forehead, sliding your hands back beyond your heels with your palms facing up. Hold until you feel totally relaxed. Do this exercise to rejuvenate yourself if you are feeling tired or lethargic, or use it to shut yourself off from the rest of the world. You can drift into peaceful sleep by turning to one side and rolling over to stretch out your legs.

# Home:
## *Body Rolls*

When your body stiffens and tenses with stress your spine feels locked. Your normal mobility is blocked and you experience aches and pains throughout your body. The best exercise to relieve this stress is body rolls, as the movements release tension and boost energy levels. Combined with correct breathing the exercise increases your vitality and improves your circulation. While you are breathing deeply and moving your body in a circle the fresh oxygen moving through your body revitalizes, cleanses and purifies the internal organs. Some people feel dizzy in this pose because they have too many toxins in their body. Body rolls are easy to do at home, improve your balance, and encourage a sense of wellbeing.

Stand up straight with your feet pointing forward 1m (3ft) apart. Take your hands to your waist and open out your chest. ▶ Inhale and stretch your body to the right, keeping your knees straight. Do not drop your head but keep it in line with your neck. ▶ Still inhaling, push your hips forward and extend your head backward, relaxing your neck and shoulders. ▶ Exhale and stretch your body to the left. ▶ Now flatten your spine and turn your body toward the floor, looking downward. ▶ Still exhaling, move forward between your legs and extend down toward the floor. Inhale and return to the start position. Repeat the exercise on the other side. Some people have more tension and stiffness than others, so continue the rolls until you feel your body starting to rejuvenate with energy.

# Work:
## *Slow Stretching*

Many people spend their working day slouched over a desk and consequently suffer from backache, fatigue, boredom and a sense of failure if they cannot cope with their workload. The best way to change these reactions is to boost the energy levels and calm the nervous system. Tension and stress stay in your body until they are consciously removed. If left, your body will seize up and your spine will become immobile. The way to avoid these symptoms is to find a suitable place in your office to do this exercise to release tension and restore mental harmony. Stretching up releases muscular tension in the neck and shoulders and bending forward soothes and revitalizes the nervous system.

Stand up straight with feet together, inhale deeply and throw your arms above your head with palms facing. Keep your shoulders down and your head centered between your arms. Exhale and hold briefly. ▶ Cross your arms, hold onto your elbows and push your elbows behind your ears. ▶ Inhale and as you exhale stretch over to the left from the waist with hips and feet forward. Breathe normally and hold briefly. Inhale and return to the center again. ▶ Exhale and stretch over to the right in the same way. Breathe normally. ▶ Then, with your back straight, extend your spine forward. ▶ Relax down by breathing more deeply and bring your head to your knees. Close your eyes, holding for 10 seconds. Inhale and return to the start position. Repeat the exercise.

# Travel:
## *Hands and Feet*

When you have to sit still for a long period while travelling on a plane, coach or train, your body stiffens up and you begin to feel lethargic and tired. Because you are in a confined space it is difficult to move and stretch your aching muscles without causing disturbance to the other passengers. This exercise will help to release any tension you may suffer in the sciatic nerves in your back and will also improve your blood circulation while you are forced to remain static. Gently moving your feet will alleviate any numbness or the 'pins and needles' that many people experience when they have to sit in a cramped position for any length of time.

While you are seated, extend your legs forward and flex your toes upward. (If space is too limited to do this, you can perform the exercise in the normal sitting position.) ▸ Point your toes and move both feet in a circle, first to the right and then to the left. ▸ Still pointing your toes, cross your ankles, roll onto your left hip and twist as far as you can. ▸ Move back to the center and roll onto your right hip, twisting as far as you can. ▸ Release your feet and sit up straight, taking your arms over your head with your elbows bent. Now shake your arms and hands to release any tension and improve your circulation. ▸ Keep shaking both arms around your body until your hands come down to your hips. Repeat the exercise as necessary.

# Art of Relaxation

Learning to soothe your nerves and calm your nervous system is the aim of the exercises in this chapter. Stress gets locked in the physical body and the goal is to release this muscular tension gently through a series of flowing movements. Stress can cause stiffness, especially in the neck, shoulders and lower back, leading to bad posture. Tension and stress are held in the body unconsciously and the moment people are made aware of their physical condition they will instinctively try to relax and find balance, as this is the natural state. Yoga is ideal for relaxation because it teaches you to shut yourself off from the rest of the world and go into the deeper realms of your mind to find lasting inner peace. When you relax deeply your nerve endings are rejuvenated and your nervous system functions better. The purpose of the exercises in the first part of this chapter is to release tension in specific muscle groups. The inverted postures, such as the modified shoulder stand, will calm the nervous system. Whenever the head drops forward, a sudden feeling of calm will prevail. In the dead man's pose your body metabolism slows down. Make sure you are in a warm, quiet room wearing unrestricted clothing when you exercise. By doing these exercises you will bring peace to your body and mind at will.

# Shoulder Shrugs and Rolls

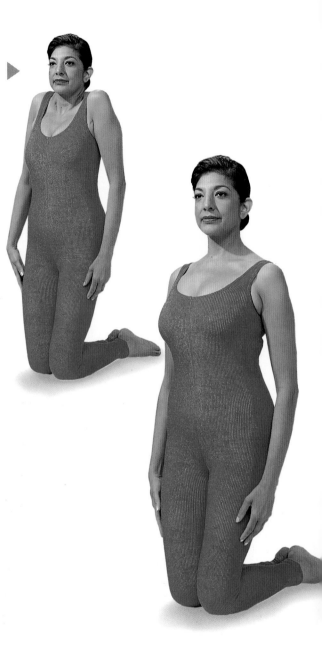

When people are very stressed and wound up, tension accumulates in the body, especially in the neck and shoulders. The only way to release this stiffness is to exaggerate the movement between the neck and shoulders while breathing deeply and evenly. When you do this exercise it is very important to keep your head straight and in correct alignment to your back and neck. As you inhale, focus your attention on the stiffness in your muscles and when you exhale imagine all the muscular tension leaving your body. Every person is different and will hold tension in certain weak spots. Visualize and concentrate on these areas and you will be amazed at how quickly you can feel relaxed.

Kneeling on the floor, inhale and take your shoulders up high toward your ears. ▶ As you exhale drop your shoulders down and push your shoulder blades together, opening out your chest. Repeat a few times until the stiffness starts to leave your body. Breathe deeply to help shift the tightness. ▶ Now inhale and repeat the shoulder shrug. ▶ As you exhale, move your shoulders back in a circular motion. ▶ To repeat the exercise, inhale and take your shoulders forward and up, then exhale as you take them back and down. Keep all your movements fluid and graceful. Return to the start position. As you exercise, keep still, concentrating on your neck and shoulders.

127

# Back Roll

When you really need to relax this back roll releases any stress and strain from the tail bone of the spine right up to the top of the neck. By taking your legs over your head you calm the nervous system and soothe the nerves. If you suffer from backache this is the easiest and safest exercise to relieve any pain. Also, when your body is feeling exhausted and needs a quick boost, this exercise combined with some deep breathing rejuvenates your entire system. You may find it hard in the beginning to take your legs right over your head, but just let the force of your natural body weight allow your legs and spine to roll over gently. At first you may need to push your palms down to the floor to help you roll over, but with practice you will soon realize that a supple spine is the main key to success.

Lie down on the floor with legs outstretched and arms at your side. Breathe deeply and evenly and feel your whole body relaxing. Draw your feet back, cross your ankles and place your palms upward, keeping your eyes closed. ▸ Bring your knees toward your chest and hold onto your toes, keeping your elbows straight. ▸ Inhale and slowly bring your knees and thighs down to your chest. ▸ Pull your tummy muscles in and start to take your legs over your head. ▸ Roll over completely and stretch your spine as far as possible. Keep your knees as close to your ears as possible and relax your neck and shoulder muscles. Exhale, and breathe deeply in this position, holding for at least 30 seconds. Repeat the exercise a few times until your body feels totally calm and relaxed.

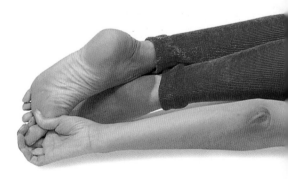

# Modified Shoulder Stand

The shoulder stand helps to regulate your metabolism and balance your hormones. People who suffer regularly from stress often experience mood swings and weight fluctuations. This exercise helps to stabilize your temperament and weight and calms your mind. Two of the most important glands in the body are the pituitary and thyroid. According to the yogic texts, locking your chin into your chest stimulates your thyroid gland to help it function normally. When you are inverted with your legs above your head the blood flows downward to all your organs, replenishing and oxygenating the cells. This increased blood flow rejuvenates and relaxes your whole body.

Lie on the floor, legs outstretched and arms at your side. Bring your knees up, put your feet on the floor and place your palms facing down.
▸ Inhale deeply, pushing your palms down, while bringing your knees up to your chest. ▸ Keep pushing your palms down and lift your spine off the floor. ▸ Take your hands to your waist to support your back and lift your legs up. Lock your chin into your chest. Exhale, and breathe normally while holding this position. Try to hold still for 30–60 seconds. To come down, inhale, and while exhaling slowly lower your back and legs to the floor. Keep breathing deeply and evenly. If you experience any back discomfort do the Back Roll (pages 128–9).

# Knee Twist

This simple knee twist exercise helps to strengthen the spine as well as releasing toxins from the system. The more flexible your spine is, the more you will be able to twist around. It is very important to sit upright to lift your spine correctly. Some people who have weak backs might feel a dull pain in the lumbar region. As you build up these muscles you will feel uncomfortable if you are not sitting upright. The intensity of the twist is felt when the spine is the only part of the body that is moving as the hips stay immobile and in line. The most wonderful thing about twists is that there is no final position. Challenge yourself and try to twist even further every time you do this exercise.

Start the twist sitting on the floor with your legs outstretched in front of you. Sitting up as tall as possible, flex your feet upward. ▸ Bend your left knee and bring your foot in as close as possible, holding onto your leg with both hands. Make sure you do not collapse your spine at this time. If you feel your back caving in, place your foot further out. ▸ With your right arm, hold onto your left leg with your right elbow in front of your knee for a tighter grip. ▸ Take your left hand and place it on your lower back with your palm facing up. Inhale and twist as far as possible, looking over your left shoulder. Exhale and breathe normally as you deepen the twist. To release the spine, gradually unwind and return to the front, still holding your leg, and then return to the start position. Repeat the exercise on the other side, and then do twice on each side.

# Dead Man's Pose

Relaxing is a technique that needs to be learned in order to maximize your capability for relaxation at will. Yoga is ideal because it allows your mind to shut out useless thoughts and relax the brain at a deeper level. This achieves stillness of the mind which helps to clarify thoughts and emotions. This exercise can rejuvenate your energy by relaxing every body nerve, and it can help cure insomnia. Find a quiet place and, because your body temperature will drop, make sure you feel warm and comfortable.

Lie flat on the floor, knees up and arms at your side. If you wish to, you can put a small pillow under your head. Breathe deeply and evenly through your nose, mouth closed. Relax your face until you feel calm. ▶ Slowly relax your legs down onto the floor. ▶ Sink your tail bone into the floor, taking your arms out at your sides with palms facing upward. Leave your feet apart and your throat open. Keep breathing deeply and slowly. Now concentrate on each muscle group, beginning with the tummy, buttocks, thighs, knees, ankles, feet and toes. Inhale and tighten each section. Hold for 5 seconds. Exhale and release. Then work on the back, arms and hands. Tighten your fists to release tension. Now do your neck. Inhale, taking your shoulders up to your ears. Exhale and release. Repeat. Take your head from side to side and then let it drop. Relax your face. Keep still for 5–15 minutes. ▶ To release, turn to one side, bringing your knees into your chest. Rest until you feel like getting up.

# Home:
## *Knee Twists*

These simple knee twists are excellent to release tension throughout the body. As you ease your hips from side to side you can sometimes feel the muscles click into place to realign the spine. The movement also gives relief for backache. The blood supply to the discs and nerves is boosted, and the spine becomes toned. To twist laterally with safety, the pelvis should be the only region that moves; twisting from the shoulders and ribs can strain the lower back. Keep the movement graceful and fluid and use the tummy muscles to help control the action of twisting from one side to the other.

Start the exercise lying flat on the floor with your legs outstretched and your arms at your sides. Inhale and bring your knees toward your chest, stretching your arms to the sides with palms facing downward in line with the shoulders, as in position 3. Exhale and keep your neck and head in line with your spine. Inhale and as you exhale take your knees down to the floor on the left, while twisting your head in the opposite direction. ▸ Inhale and bring your knees and head gradually back to the center. ▸ Exhale and take your head to the left as you twist your knees to the right. Inhale and return your knees and head to the center. Exhale. Repeat the exercise from side to side until you feel that all your tension has been released and you are totally relaxed. Return to Dead Man's Pose position 3 and 4 (pages 134–5).

# Work:
## *Eyes, Jaw and Neck*

Though space is often limited in the workplace, it is still important to release any stress that builds up during the day due to the pressures at work. The first tension spots are the eyes, jaw, neck and shoulders, and this exercise is the most effective way of releasing all the stiffness in these areas quickly. You will feel relieved immediately and be able to face the rest of the day knowing that you have an instant solution if the problem reoccurs. During the exercise, breathe as deeply as possible to help movement and calm the nervous system.

Sit on a chair or on the floor and cross your legs at the ankles. Sit up tall and clasp your hands behind your neck. Open out your elbows in line with your shoulders and push your shoulder blades down. ▶ Inhale deeply and slowly bring your elbows together. Exhale and return your elbows to position 1. Remember to keep your head straight in line with your neck and shoulders. Repeat. ▶ Now look upward as high as possible without tilting backward. Inhale, and bring your elbows together as before. Drop your head back and as you exhale open the elbows as much as possible. Open your mouth to release your jaw, and close. Repeat this jaw action twice and return to position 1. Repeat this section. Now release your arms and continue to sit upright. ▶ Rub your hands together to generate heat and blow into your palms. ▶ Place both palms over your eyes. This soothes the eyes and helps reduce pounding headaches. Breathe deeply and hold for as long as you can.

# Travel:
## *Hands and Feet*

Whenever you sit still in one place for a length of time, as happens in travelling, your circulation becomes blocked. Also, some people feel panicky when they are confined to a small place where they cannot move around freely, and indeed many people have a real fear of travelling. Trying to keep calm and relaxed is the best solution to these insecurities. Breathing from your diaphragm acts as a natural tranquilizer to your nervous system, so the deeper you breathe the calmer your mind will become. During these stressful travel situations, start to lengthen your breaths and soon you will be taking deep breaths naturally.

Start by sitting upright in your plane or train seat or when you are taking a break from driving. Take your left hand around the back of your neck and open out your elbow. ▶ Inhale and twist your neck and head to the right, bringing your elbow down into your chest to increase the stretch. Exhale, and return to position 1. Repeat 2–3 times. Now take your right hand around the back of the neck and repeat the exercise 2–3 times. ▶ Return to position 1 and take your right hand to hold your elbow behind your head. Stretch both elbows back. Breathe normally, and repeat on the other side.
▶ Now clasp both elbows with your hands over your head and take them back behind your ears. Breathe normally and hold for 5–10 seconds.
▶ Relax forward, placing your forehead down on your knees or table. Relax deeply, breathing evenly, and feel the stress leave your spine.

# Meditation and Visualization

Meditation is a skill that clarifies and focuses the mind. Mastery over the mind is achieved through yoga meditation because it teaches you to concentrate on one subject in the first stage and calm your mind in the second. Mental breakdowns caused by stress can be greatly alleviated. Through meditation a person can observe their symptoms and reactions objectively, and change their attitudes toward their ailment. Meditating will bring them back to harmony and restore the balance that was lost. The yoga student can use meditation for practical purposes or move ahead into the deeper realms of the mind to discover universal truths and spiritual bliss. We begin with breathing exercises to calm the mind, as deep breathing acts as a natural tranquilizer. The meditation poses are all sitting positions to keep your spine erect. The true position is the lotus, because your tail bone nearly touches the floor, allowing the energy to move freely through the body's energy centers to the crown chakra in the head to connect with cosmic energy. Visualization is another technique to help train your mind for meditation. To start visualizing, sit in a meditation pose and think of a happy experience when you were close to nature. Observe your surroundings, emotions and reactions to the environment to stop your mind wandering.

# Breathing

Learning how to control your breathing is fundamental to training and controlling your mind. In this exercise we learn how to contract and release the abdominal muscles to regulate the flow of *prana*, or energy. Because of these movements the abdominal organs are toned and internally massaged and the gastric juices are stimulated, which aids digestion. The exercise helps to eliminate toxins in the digestive tract as well as regulating the bowel. The contraction and release action helps to trim excess fat from the stomach and flatten the tummy. It is always best to do this *bandha* or breathing technique on an empty stomach. Allow 4–6 hours after eating a heavy meal, but a light beverage such as tea can be taken 30 minutes before. The more you do this exercise, the more you will notice the benefits. At first you might find it difficult to regulate your breathing correctly, but with practice you will understand why this breathing technique is taught to maintain good body health.

Start the exercise kneeling on the floor with your hands directly in line with your knees. Inhale deeply and then exhale quickly through your nose so that air is forced from your lungs in a rush. ▶ When all your breath is totally released, hold your breath and contract your abdominal muscles upward behind your rib cage toward your spine. Hold for 5 seconds. ▶ Still holding your breath, release your muscles and rib cage. Hold for 5 seconds. ▶ Inhale again and drop your spine down. Exhale and breathe normally. Repeat the whole exercise twice and build up to 10 times or more.

# Pranayama

It is important to learn how to breathe properly, so set aside a regular time in a comfortable, airy space each day to practice *pranayama* techniques. *Pranayama* is the science of breath control. This particular breathing exercise is a simple one and helps you understand how to regulate your breathing pattern. At first you might find it difficult to lengthen your breath and exhale in a controlled way. Look at your posture, your breathing rhythm, and the way in which you breathe. When you exhale, your ribcage should expand forward and sideways, but the area below your shoulder blades and armpits should expand only forward. The thumb and finger contact signifies the symbol of knowledge. The thumb is the universal soul and the index finger the individual soul; together they form the seal of wisdom.

Sit cross-legged, hands on the floor, with a straight spine and your head in line with your neck. Relax your muscles, especially in your face. Close your eyes to calm your mind. Breathe deeply and evenly. Take your thumb and index finger together. Inhale deeply through your nose and drop your head back without moving your spine. ▸ Open your mouth slightly and form the letter 'O'. ▸ Slowly exhale through your mouth as you drop your head until your chin rests on your chest. ▸ Do not cave in your chest or spine, and exhale evenly. The longer you exhale the better, so when you are practiced in the technique, exhale for 5 seconds, building up to 10 seconds. Repeat at least 5 times.

# Pranayama
## *(nostril breathing)*

Alternate nostril breathing is an advanced breathing technique. The energies of the body, whether male or female, have both masculine and feminine properties. The right side signifies the masculine energies, while the left side is the feminine. Alternate nostril breathing harmonizes these energies to restore balance to mind and body. The even breathing strengthens your nerves and encourages a balanced temperament and sound mind. Keep your breaths long, steady and deep. If you cannot maintain an even breathing rhythm, stop immediately in case you strain your lungs and diaphragm, and check your technique.

Sit crosslegged on the floor. Lift your spine up, but keep your shoulders down. Keep the thumb and index finger together on your left hand and rest it on your left knee. Bend your three main fingers into your right palm, but stretch up your thumb and little finger. Block your left nostril with your little finger and breathe deeply through your right nostril. Close your eyes, relaxing your face and body muscles. Inhale for 5 seconds and exhale for 5 seconds. Repeat 10 times on the right nostril and then block the right nostril with your thumb and repeat 10 times on the left. ▶ Then inhale from the right for 5 seconds, hold your breath for 3, blocking your nostril with your thumb, and exhale through the left for 5 seconds. ▶ Inhale from the left nostril for 5 seconds, hold for 3, and exhale through the right for 5 seconds. Repeat the exercise at least 10 times.

# Chakras and Candle Gazing

'Chakra' is a Sanskrit word meaning 'wheels' that radiate energy in a circular pattern through the spine's vital centers. Just as antennae pick up radio waves and turn them into sound, chakras pick up on cosmic vibrations and distribute them through the body's energy centers. To maintain good health it is vital to keep the centers generating equal energy through the body. If a chakra is blocked with too much or too little energy the body becomes unbalanced. Acupuncture uses needles placed in the energy centers to restore balance, and in yoga we learn *pranayama* (breath control) to ensure that the correct energy flows evenly through the body. Candle gazing (see page 153), a technique to train the mind to focus on one thought, helps to restore harmony to the mind and body by keeping the chakras balanced. There are seven chakras. The first is in the pelvic region and relates to the sexual organs and procreation. The second is in the belly button, controlling emotions. The third is in the solar plexus, ruling the stomach and digestive tract. The fourth is the heart chakra, which relates to love. The fifth, in the throat, relates to communication. The sixth is the third eye (the spot between the eyebrows) that rules higher consciousness. The seventh chakra is the crown chakra, which unites the person with the cosmic universe.

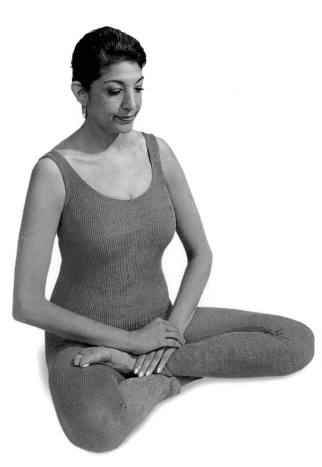

# Meditation Poses

All meditation poses are sitting positions that vary only in how the legs are placed. Whether you are sitting cross-legged, in half-lotus or full lotus position, or with your heels together, your back must be erect from the base of your spine to your neck and be perpendicular to the floor. There should be no strain on the body. Keep your tongue still and your eyes closed. In meditation the brain is passive, but alert. If your organs are not functioning correctly the brain will send warning signals immediately. Meditation focuses the mind on one thought alone, and is useful to discipline and calm the mind. It is hard to sit still when your mind is wandering, but meditation teaches you how to shut yourself off from the world and find inner peace.

The first technique to learn is candle gazing. Place a candle in front of you so that the candle is in line with the point between your eyebrows. Now gaze at the candle and observe the flicker, the candle's size, and every aspect of it. After 30–60 seconds close your eyes. You will retain an optical image of the candle and the flicker of light in your mind. When the flicker starts to disappear, force the image to stay. This trains your mind to concentrate hard. At first it seems impossible to maintain the image but with continued practice it becomes easy. The next step is meditation. Focus your attention on the third eye and concentrate on one thought. Keep breathing deeply and notice your even breathing rhythm, while still focusing your mind on one thought.

Meditation poses

Top: Lotus
Left: Half-lotus
Right: Cross-legged
Bottom: Heels together

# Remedial Yoga

*Prana* is the Sanskrit word for the energy that flows through the body. There are seven energy centers in the body and it is vital that energy flows freely through the system for good health. When people are stressed some centers become blocked, causing an imbalance. Yoga focuses on correct breathing techniques to increase the lung capacity and bring fresh oxygen to the vital organs. It is now possible to prove scientifically the effect of remedial yoga, and clinical trials have shown its beneficial results. There are four phases of stress disorders. The first is the psychic phase, in which irritability, energy loss, sleeplessness and anxiety attacks are manifested. If unchecked the person moves to the second, psychosomatic phase and experiences hypertension, tremors or palpitations. The next phase is the somatic phase, when illness develops in the vital organs. The fourth phase is the organic phase, when the affected organ is in full-fledged chronic inflammatory change. Medical attention is now required. Yoga can help prevent the first phase, relieve the symptoms in the second phase, develop a therapy programme in the third, and with modern medicine help the body return to its normal state in the fourth phase. Remedial yoga takes the stress disorder and applies a specific exercise that will alleviate the symptoms, or a series of exercises to help cure the ailment. Here I have prescribed the *asana* specific to some common ailments. There are some that respond particularly well, such as asthma, migraine and digestive disorders.

# Head:
## *Headaches*

When your head is pounding because of tension and other mental anxieties, dropping your head forward relieves the pressure in no time. The blood rushes to the brain and soothes the nervous system. Many people find this uncomfortable at first and may even feel dizzy and nauseous. In fact, it will probably feel as if the pain is increasing rather than decreasing. But do not panic, just give yourself time to get used to this sensation. Just breathe deeply throughout the exercise and the pain and panic will soon subside. Make sure you keep your weight evenly distributed between your heels and toes to maintain your balance. Keep your movements fluid and try not to pause between the positions.

Stand upright with your feet together in perfect posture (page 113). Inhale deeply and as you exhale drop your body forward. Bend your knees, relax your head and neck, shake out your arms and take your hands to the floor with your palms facing upward. Relax every muscle in your body. Hold for 30 seconds, breathing deeply. ▶ Slowly inhale and lift your body slowly upward, still keeping your head and arms forward. ▶ Now push your hips forward and drop your shoulders down. Then shift your weight to your heels, open out your chest and drop your head all the way back. Exhale, and breathe normally while you hold the position for 5 seconds. Lift up your head again and return to the start position. Repeat the whole exercise.

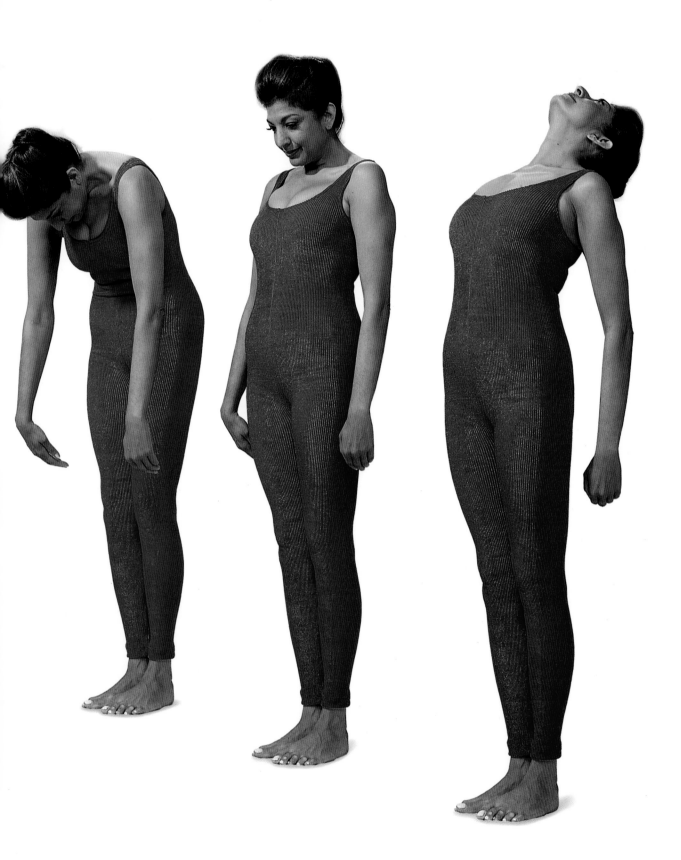

# Head:
## *Mind*

When people suffer from stress they can find it difficult to focus their mind for any length of time. Their thoughts are often confusing and conflicting. By doing balancing exercises you can help to focus your mind and improve your concentration. The concentration needed to stand on one leg can help you push distracting or negative thoughts from your mind. These exercises are quite challenging and at first you might think that you are incapable of balancing on one leg, but with perseverance you will soon reach your goal.

Stand up straight, feet together, in perfect posture (page 113). Breathe normally and draw your energies into yourself. Hold for 5 seconds. Place your right foot with your heel and toe in line with your left ankle. Place your palms together in front of your chest. Hold for 5 seconds. ▶ With your right hand lift your right leg and place it on your inner left lower leg, knee, or inner thigh according to your flexibility so that your knee is at right angles to the straight leg. Palms together, take your arms over your head and balance. Hold for 5–10 seconds and focus on an object in front of you to aid concentration. Repeat on the other side.

The one leg balance (see right) is more difficult. Stand upright with feet together. Take both hands to the floor to balance, clasp your right ankle anywhere on your leg and focus on one spot on the floor in front of you. ▶ Inhale, pull your tummy muscles in and lift your left leg up high without twisting your hips. Exhale and breathe normally. Repeat on the other side.

158

# Circulation:
## *Toxins*

In yoga exercises, bending forward, sideways and backward allows every nerve, tissue and vein in the body to be replenished with fresh blood and oxygen. This purifies the system, releasing any harmful toxins that have become trapped. When you do this dynamic exercise you might think that you are simply perspiring, but you are actually eliminating toxins from your body. Some people may feel ill while exercising because drinking alcohol, using drugs, stress and bad eating habits all contribute to toxin buildup. If toxins are not removed, the immune system can break down, leading to serious illnesses.

Stand tall with feet 1–1.2m (3–4ft) apart. Inhale and bend your right knee, pushing your left foot firmly down to help you balance. Exhale. Inhale and take your hand down to the floor in front of your right foot. As you exhale, twist your body around so your shoulders are in line. ▸ Inhale, take your left arm up in the air with your palm facing back and continue to twist, looking over your left shoulder. Exhale and breathe normally. Straighten your arm and look upward toward the palm. ▸ Turn back toward your right leg, straighten your knee and clasp both elbows behind your back. Drop your forehead down to the knee. Breathe deeply and hold for 5–10 seconds. ▸ Inhale, and bring your body up so that your back is flat. Exhale, and breathe deeply for 5–10 seconds. ▸ Inhale, and bring your body up, then drop your head back to release your neck. Exhale, breathe normally and hold for 5 seconds. Repeat on the other side.

# Circulation:
## *Joints*

This simple swinging of the arms and body helps to increase circulation, particularly in your joints, hands and fingertips. If you suffer from stress-related rheumatism and arthritis, this exercise will ease the pain because the circular swing gradually loosens the joints. Yoga with its gentle approach will help shift the stiffness while relaxing the muscle groups through correct breathing. If your hip, knee or elbow joints are acutely inflamed, never try to force any movement. Just gently ease into the swing, breathing deeply to relax your mind and mobilize your entire body. Keep your feet still as you move the body around from one side to another.

Stand upright with your legs 1m (3ft) apart, your toes pointing forward and your arms at the side. Turn your body to the right and look over your right shoulder with your arm in line with the shoulder. ▸ Inhale and bring your right arm down. ▸ Exhale and begin to swing your arm across the front of your body in a circular motion and back up until it is in a diagonal line to your head, stretching to the left as you do so. While swinging, relax your knees and release your hips so that you have a wider swing. ▸ Inhale, then as you exhale keep stretching to the left, while twisting your spine. Breathe normally and hold for 10 seconds. Repeat the whole exercise on the other side. Practice the swing on both sides a few times until you feel that all your joints have been loosened.

# Back:
## *Muscles*

People who suffer from back pain are often worried that by exercising they will damage their backs even further. On the contrary, it is vital to strengthen back muscles in order to prevent strain and alleviate pain. Yoga provides a natural solution because of its emphasis on posture and correct alignment of the spine. While exercising you constantly build these muscles while noticing at all times the natural position of the spine. In order to stand or sit in perfect posture the muscles of the lower back must support the rest of the spine. Sciatica and slipped discs are a result of weakness in the back, and a strong, healthy back is necessary for total body health. This exercise strengthens the back while helping to increase flexibility. It also shapes the waist, hips and legs.

Start by standing tall with both feet together. Inhale, and drop your head down to your knees. Exhale and bend both knees. Inhale, simultaneously straightening your left leg directly behind you while lunging forward with the right. Point your left foot and keep your hips and torso facing to the front. Inhale, slowly twist your upper body to the left and look over your left shoulder. ▸ Now lift your left leg up and take hold of your toes. Exhale and balance for 5 seconds. Make sure that you are not balancing on your kneecap but on top of the knee to avoid any damage or strain. To release, turn to the front, place your fingertips on the floor and return to the start position. Repeat the exercise on the other side.

# Back:
## *Tension*

Twisting laterally alleviates back pain while strengthening the lower back. If you feel any discomfort you can modify these positions by bending both knees throughout. Once you have a back ailment any tension will aggravate it, so try to keep mentally relaxed at all times. All stress manifests itself in your body and backs are particularly prone to chronic conditions. Yoga in its holistic approach is one of the best ways to cope with back ailments, as relaxing and calming the mind and body eliminates emotions such as fear and anger which become trapped as tension in the muscle groups.

Start the exercise by lying flat on your back with your arms by your side. Take your arms out to the sides and put your palms face down on the floor, in line with your shoulders. Keeping your shoulders down, inhale and bend your right knee into your chest. Raise your head and, flexing your right thumb, clasp your big toe with your first two fingers. Make sure you keep your hips flat on the floor. ▶ Exhale and straighten the leg, still clasping your toe if you are able to. Hold for 5 seconds. Lower your head to the floor. ▶ Inhale again, and as you exhale take your leg to the right until it touches the floor at right angles to your body, still keeping your hips flat on the floor. Repeat the exercise on the other side.

# Abdomen:
## *Stomach*

Nervous tension in the stomach produces acidity, which can lead to gastric disorders such as flatulence, heartburn and irritable bowel syndrome. Doctors now agree that there is a direct link between the emotional balance of a person and their susceptibility to certain illnesses. People suffering from stomach aches are often emotionally upset. The stomach can seize up with muscle cramps and most people take medication to relieve their pain. Yoga relaxes the stomach cramps immediately because it teaches you to breathe through the pain in order to release it.

Lie flat on the floor. Inhale and bring both knees into your chest, lifting your head off the floor. Exhale and breathe normally for 10 seconds.
▸ Hold onto your right knee and place your left foot on the floor in front of your left hip. Inhale and bring your right knee closer in to your chest, pulling with your right hand on your knee and your left hand on your ankle. Exhale and hold for 5 seconds, breathing normally. ▸ Take both hands around the back of your right knee, inhale deeply and exhale, straightening the right leg. Breathe normally and hold for 10 seconds. ▸ Place your hands on your ankles, inhale and stretch your leg down toward your head. Exhale and bring your head up toward your leg. Breathe deeply and hold for 10 seconds, stretching until your forehead touches your knee. Release the leg down and repeat on the other side.

169

# Abdomen:
## *Hormones*

It is important to maintain a good hormonal balance during your life. During puberty, pregnancy and the menopause, hormone levels shift, causing emotional reactions and mood swings. Pre-menstrual syndrome is, in fact, more common today due to modern stress levels. Hormone replacements help, but can have side effects, whereas yoga naturally relieves the imbalance and stabilizes the hormonal levels. According to yogic texts, when the head is locked into the chest it stimulates the thyroid gland, balancing your metabolism. If you are more than three months pregnant, do not take your legs over your head as this alters the position of the uterus.

Lie flat on the floor. Bring your knees up but keep your feet on the floor with your arms at your sides. ▸ Inhale, bringing both knees into your chest, clasping your elbows under your knees. Exhale, lifting your head slightly off the floor. Breathe deeply; hold for 5 seconds. ▸ Breathe normally and straighten both legs, lifting your head up further. ▸ Take your hands to your waist for support and gently roll back, taking your legs over your head. Keep breathing deeply. Hold for 10–15 seconds. ▸ Inhale, tuck your toes under and lift your left leg up straight. Exhale, then breathe normally; hold for 10 seconds. Inhale, exhale and lower your left leg down. Inhale, and raise your right leg. Exhale, and breathe normally for 10 seconds. Release both knees into your chest and roll back down to the start position.

# Respiration:
## *Stress*

Ailments such as asthma and bronchitis are commonplace when stress factors affect the respiratory tract. Slowing your breathing down to an even pace while increasing the depth acts as a natural tranquilizer to the nervous system. Increasing your lung capacity also helps to relieve fatigue and hypertension. When people are fearful or panicky their heart races, their breathing becomes shallow and noisy, and they may pant. This exercise can help you to release tension and teaches you how to regulate your breathing pattern to reduce stress at a deeper level. You will then experience a sense of harmony and inner calm. Every time you repeat the exercise, breathe more deeply until you feel your lungs are filled to the brim.

Sit comfortably in a cross-legged position on the floor, or upright in a chair with both feet flat on the floor. It is important that your spine stays straight and your head is in line with your neck and back. Concentrate on your navel and inhale deeply, taking your arms up slowly around your body. Feel the breath moving to fill your lungs. ▸ Continuing to inhale, lift your arms up as you look upward. ▸ Clasp your fingertips together and continue to stretch upward. Exhale and drop your head back, releasing your hands in a burst of energy. Repeat this exercise 5–10 times.

# Respiration:
## *Panic*

The ability to relax and control your breathing pattern helps to reduce fear during a panic attack. The bronchial tubes allow fresh oxygen into the lungs while dispelling carbon dioxide. When an attack is imminent, the muscles in the walls of the tubes constrict the breath flow. When you are particularly active you can hear the change in your breath as you need more air to sustain your activity. On the other hand, when you are resting or sleeping, little air is required. If you feel an attack coming on, take your mind off it and calm your nervous system by breathing from the diaphragm. The muscles of the bronchial tubes will relax as you allow more breath to enter your lungs and your mental state will improve as you realize that you are in control of every reaction to the attack.

Stand tall in perfect posture (page 113). Stretch your arms high above your head, clasping your hands together. Keep your elbows straight and close to your ears. Force your shoulder blades down. Hold for 5 seconds, breathing normally. ▸ Inhale, and rise up on your toes. Breathe deeply; hold for 5 seconds, concentrating on balancing. ▸ Lift your heels higher as you bend your knees. ▸ Drop your heels down and stretch your hips backward as if reaching for a chair. The depth of your breathing will increase automatically. Keep your spine straight and your arms in line with your ears. Breathe deeply for 20 seconds. Repeat.

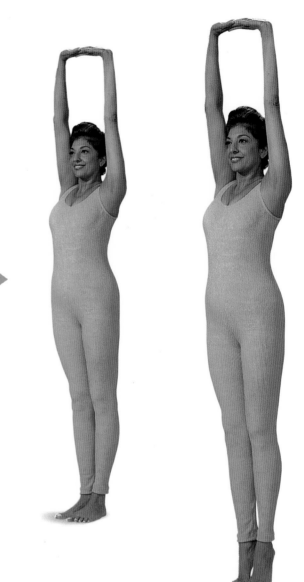

# yoga for
# **better**
# **sex**

Yoga serves as a natural aphrodisiac and sexual conditioner that unites mind, body and soul. Though not everyone shares a spiritual dimension, everyone can experience the improvement that yoga brings to one's life, including its sexual dimension. In yoga, the union of mind and body is described through physical exercises, or *asanas*, to harmonize and balance the masculine and feminine energies; in Tantric yoga, harmony and balance are achieved through the sexual union between man and women. Not only does yoga promote a calm nervous system, it gives you the suppleness and flexibility that are required in lovemaking and also teaches you how to breathe correctly, bringing extra vitality and energy to the sexual act. The exercises in this chapter are designed to improve your sexual performance by increasing your stamina and your ability to stretch. The movements are graceful and fluid, like a dancer's, and are held for a length of time in order to allow the body's energy to alter. The yogic and sexual exercises both have the same goal; when they are intelligently and properly performed they will lead to longevity, alertness, radiant health and contentment.

# Toning Your Body

These exercises are designed to build muscle tone and stamina and to increase your energy and vitality. When you stretch and twist in all directions you tone your internal organs and, combining that with correct breathing, you send fresh oxygen to each nerve and cell, rejuvenating the entire system. The sex center is located in the lower spine and by strengthening the lower back you will automatically improve your sexual performance.

There is much emphasis today on sexual accomplishment and this is one area where money, status, fame, authority, success, physical strength, and beauty are unable to play a decisive role. While these factors may offer a wider choice of partners, they cannot guarantee a good sexual performance – and unfortunately the stresses and strains which attend many of them are a contributory factor in sexual disorders.

Confidence and sound mental health remain the greatest assets in the successful consummation of the sex act. Frigidity and fear of coitus in women and lack of an erection or premature ejaculation in men are, in most cases, psychological in origin. The regular practice of yogic exercises will result in not only toning the neuro-muscular structure of the sex organs of both men and women but will rehabilitate the mind as well. Sexual performance will improve when the mind, body, and soul are integrated and the sexual partners are in total harmony with their environment.

# Balance

This balance combined with deep stretches will help focus your attention and steady your mind. Stretching is the best way to release tension in the muscle groups and this series of movements will increase suppleness and flexibility as well as building muscle tone.

Start the exercise in a wide second position.
▸ Turn your right foot to the right with your heel in line with the instep of your left foot. Take your arms behind your back with your palms facing together in a prayer position. This will automatically open the chest. Make sure your shoulders are down and your chin and head level. If you are unable to stretch your arms behind your upper back, hold onto your wrists and place them at your lower back. ▸ Inhale and drop your head back as far as possible. Relax your face and neck.
▸ Exhale and slowly lower your spine, stretching out from the waist, until your forehead touches your knee. Keep your left leg straight and pull up the muscle above your kneecap to help you maintain your balance. ▸ Keep your weight evenly distributed between both feet. Breathing normally, bend your right knee, keeping your head down to the knee. Make sure the back of your knee is directly above your heel. ▸ Release your arms from behind your back and place your right hand down to the floor in line with your shoulder to steady your balance. Fix one point on the floor and concentrate your gaze. Take your left hand to your waist. ▸ Inhale, straighten your right leg and at the same time lift your left leg up so your spine is in a straight line. Flex your left foot. Exhale and hold this position for 10 seconds. To release, return to position 5 and slowly return to the starting position with arms at your sides. Repeat the entire exercise on the other side.

# Pelvic Stretch

The pelvic stretch tones the sex organs and the kidneys, aids digestion and rejuvenates the spine. After childbirth or with advancing age, many women suffer from incontinence, a lack of tightness in the vaginal wall and a loss of sensation during sexual intercourse. Learning how to isolate and contract the pelvic muscle will greatly improve these conditions.

Kneel down on the floor, spreading your feet as far apart as you can while keeping your knees together. Place your hands behind you and sit erect. Breathe deeply and evenly. ▸ Keeping your knees together, slowly lower yourself, leaning on your elbows. You will feel a stretch in the feet, ankles, knees, thighs, abdomen, and ribs. If you feel comfortable, stretch further down to the floor, taking your arms over your head, holding your elbows. As you breathe deeply and especially during the exhalation you will feel a deep stretching sensation throughout your whole body. This intense stretch sends a fresh blood supply to the entire system and the effect is soothing, tranquil, and deeply relaxing. ▸ To release yourself from this position return to position 2, then 1. Now relax down to the floor with your arms to the side, palms facing down. Raise your knees with your feet in line with your hips. ▸ Inhale, hold onto your ankles, and raise your pelvis as high as possible. Exhale, breathe normally, tighten your stomach and buttock muscles and contract the muscles in the sex centers. Hold for 10 seconds and slowly lower to the floor by pushing down each vertebra of the spine, starting from the neck. Repeat the entire exercise, then move on to the exercises on pages 184–5.

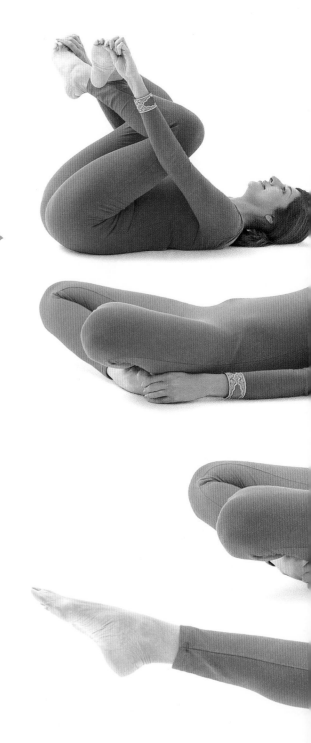

Lying on the floor, bring your knees into your chest. Cross your ankles and hold onto your feet.
▶ Inhale, and take your knees down to the floor. Exhale, and hold for 5 seconds, breathing normally.
▶ Inhale, and push up your chest until the top of your head is on the floor. In classic yoga, this pose is called the Fish; it helps corrects certain defects of the spine and sends fresh oxygen and blood supply to the brain, which soothes the nerves. Exhale, breathe normally and lower your back to the floor to return to the previous position. Repeat the exercise. ▶ Now release the legs and lie flat on the floor. Inhale, point both feet and raise the left leg up off the floor toward your head, then raise your upper body off the floor toward the leg. Lift your right leg 30cm (1ft) off the floor. Exhale, breathe normally and hold for 5 seconds. Slowly lower your back down to the floor and lift both legs in a right angle to the body. Breathe deeply and hold for 10 seconds. Inhale, lift your body up and hold onto your right ankle, stretching your head to your right knee. Exhale and lower your left leg down to 30cm (1ft) from the floor. Point both feet, breathe deeply and hold for 5 seconds. Raise your left leg until both legs are in a 90° angle to the floor. Bend both knees into the chest. Inhale, and as you exhale slowly lower the legs down to the floor. Relax for 10 seconds.

pelvic stretch

# Prelude

There is deep communication between partners who have an understanding of the philosophy of yoga, as yoga-controlled relationships achieve a high quality of cultural and spiritual life. Deep satisfaction steadies and tranquilizes the mind, and feelings of love and consideration can develop more easily; Tantric sex will accelerate these emotions and will raise the conscious level of both partners.

The techniques of Tantra were originally used by the sages and mystics to reach Nirvana, or union with God. The aim was to take the basic energy or sex energy from the base chakra and transform it into spiritual energy. Ritualistic practices were learned to raise the conscious level to a higher plane. One of the secrets of Tantra was to know how to arouse different parts of the body and play the partner's body like an instrument to create notes and sensations. So, using the arts of Tantra, two people aimed to work together to raise the sound of their bodies and their vibrations.

Even today, Tantric practices can be used by ordinary people who wish to experience mystical or ecstatic sex. One of the techniques in reaching this goal is total abstinence from sex. The couple sit directly across from one another and keep their eyes fixed on each other. As they breathe deeply their sexual vibrations unite and with meditation they begin to raise together their energy through all chakras to the crown to connect with the cosmic vibration. This gives a feeling of divine bliss and harmony with the universe.

# Double Leg Pull

The Leg Pull requires a great deal of practice to perfect as it combines increased flexibility and stamina with concentration. It is a challenging exercise and you should not be surprised if you and your partner fall down; it is always very important when you are practicing yoga to maintain your sense of humor! It is an enjoyable and exhilarating feeling to master a particularly difficult exercise and it is great fun to practice with your partner. The Leg Pull also promotes positive thinking and this attitude helps to boost the confidence and self-esteem that are necessary for a good relationship.

Begin the exercise with both partners standing together in perfect posture (page 113). ▸ Place your left hand on your waist, inhale and lift your right foot up to the inner thigh of your left leg. Exhale and hold for 5 seconds. ▸ Inhale and take your first two fingers around your toe. Exhale and hold the position for 5 seconds, standing as tall as you can. ▸ Inhale and as you exhale extend the leg outward. Keep the hips in line and try not to cave in the chest; the standing leg must remain straight. If you cannot extend the raised leg fully, keep it bent. With increased flexibility and practice you will eventually be able to hold the position for at least 7 seconds. Release, bend the right leg in a 90° angle and return to perfect posture. Repeat on the other side.

# Double Head to Knee

This pose lengthens and tones the entire spine and relaxes the brain. It opens the hips and strengthens the leg muscles. All forward bends help to release toxins that are trapped in the system and this forward action stimulates the kidneys, liver and pancreas. When you first begin this exercise you might feel disappointed that you are unable to bend very far, but with continued practice and correct breathing you will be surprised at how flexible your spine becomes. Never push or jerk your body to increase the stretch as this might cause strain to your muscles; as you increase the depth of your breathing you will automatically relax and this will loosen tight muscles in the legs and lower back and you will stretch even further. Keep your feet firmly placed on the floor and distribute your weight evenly between your heels and toes. As you stretch forward, think of moving your spine out from your tail bone. This will help to flatten and lengthen the spine.

Stand tall back-to-back with your partner and check to make sure you are in perfect posture (page 113). Breathe normally and hold hands to give each other support. ▸ Inhale, keeping your spine as flat as possible, then exhale and bend forward halfway. Hold for 5 seconds while you breathe normally. ▸ Take a deep breath and as you exhale drop your head down to your knees. Continue to breathe deeply and hold this position for 30 seconds. To release, inhale slowly, bend the knees, curl the spine and gently unroll it until you have reached the first position. Repeat the entire exercise once.

# The Locust

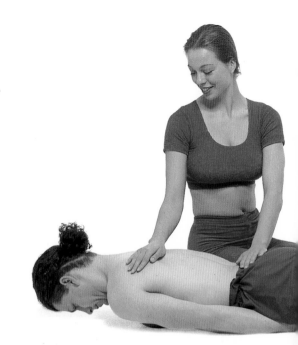

A good sexual performance demands a very strong back, especially in the ardent poses of the Kama Sutra. The Locust not only helps to alleviate back pain but strengthens the back and legs so you are able to build endurance and stamina. It also helps to improve your posture by strengthening the lower back so you are able to sit and stand for a length of time. It is important to learn to isolate certain muscle groups and in this exercise, even though every muscle is working, there is an emphasis on the stomach, legs and buttocks. Do not worry if you cannot lift your legs very high behind you – it is more important that your shoulder blades and hipbones remain on the floor to ensure that your spine is in correct alignment. As you practice this pose you will be able to lift your leg higher. Think of stretching your leg out from the hipbone and make sure you do not rock from side to side.

Begin the exercise by lying face down on the floor, your hands under your hipbones. Your partner should watch to see that your spine is perfectly straight. ▸ Inhale, and raise your right leg off the floor. Exhale, breathe normally and hold for 5 seconds. Exhale and slowly lower the leg down to the floor. Inhale, raise the left leg and hold for 5 seconds. Exhale and slowly lower the left leg. Repeat. ▸ Ask your partner to make sure both hips are down to the floor, then inhale deeply and raise both legs. Hold for 5–10 seconds. Exhale and slowly lower both legs. This is quite a strenuous exercise and your heartbeat should be racing. Relax and turn your head to one side until your pulse is normal. Repeat the entire exercise.

193

# Double Sitting Twist

All twists are excellent for increasing flexibility of the spine and eliminating toxins from the system. They are very effective in relieving backaches and headaches as well as stiffness in the neck and shoulders. As the upper body turns, the kidneys and abdominal organs are activated, aiding digestion and removing sluggishness. The beauty of twists is that there is no final position because as you become more supple your twist increases. There are many variations to the classic twist, but all alleviate back pain and inflexibility of the lower back. It is a great pleasure to hear the clicks in the spine when you release tension. You cannot be a good sex partner if you are full of anxieties and this twist eliminates the stresses and strains that build up in the body. The most important thing is your determination to rid yourself of tension. Once you have won the first battle with your mind, your body will surely follow.

Sit up as tall as possible with your legs extended in front of you, side-to-side but facing slightly away from each other. ▸ Both of you then bend the outermost leg to create a 90° angle with your knee and hip. ▸ Take the outermost arm across in front of the innermost knee and gently twist the spine. ▸ Lift the innermost leg up and place the foot in front of the outermost knee. Continue to stretch as far as possible. Breathe as deeply as you can and relax into the stretch. Hold for up to 60 seconds. Change sides and repeat.

# Leg Stretch

In lovemaking it is so important to trust your partner even if the poses are difficult. There is a healthy give and take in this pose which will give you both a sense of balancing and harmonizing each other's energy in preparation for the sexual poses that follow. This stretch increases the flexibility and suppleness of the spine and strengthens the legs and back. It also stretches and tones the internal organs. Because you are putting your full weight onto each other you are helping your partner stretch forward without strain while you are working on stretching your entire body backward and opening the chest. In yoga, the importance of opening the chest is to steady the emotional center or heart chakra that lies just below the physical heart. The final position opens this center and stabilizes emotional disturbances. The mind becomes still as if you were in a meditative pose.

Sit tall back-to-back with your legs outstretched, pointing your toes in front of you. ▸ Bring your knees up while keeping your feet flat on the floor. Lean back onto your partner's upper back so he or she will automatically move forward. Push your feet down to the floor, raise your hips and lean back even further. ▸ Stretch your legs out fully and place your entire weight onto your partner's spine, arching your back. Take your arms over your head to increase the stretch. This movement will help your partner stretch forward, placing the forehead down to the knees. If your partner finds this uncomfortable, modify the pose by taking some of the weight yourself. Change positions with your partner and repeat the entire exercise.

# Half Lotus Side Stretch

This pose is an excellent exercise for toning your entire body and calming your central nervous system. In yoga exercises you are continually moving your whole body in every direction: forward, backward, sideways. This twisting and turning of the spine strengthens the nerves and helps build the immune system. A healthy sex life is based on good health generally and when you feel well you will perform better. As you stretch to the side and front in this exercise, try not to collapse your spine. Always stretch from the tail bone and elongate each muscle to eliminate the fat around each muscle group. The result will be a lean, muscular body that is tight and firm.

Begin these stretches by sitting back-to-back as you did in the Leg Stretch (pages 196–7). Breathe normally. Place your right foot on the left thigh or left foot on the right thigh in the Half Lotus and twist your spine to look at your partner. Slide your bent leg down to the floor, keeping your knee in line with your hip. ▸ Inhale and stretch over the outstretched leg. Take your upper arm over your head close to your ear and lower your other arm to the floor. Exhale and take your fingertips to clasp your feet. Breathe normally and hold the position for 10 seconds. ▸ Now face your extended knee. Inhale, and stretch forward so your forehead touches your knee. Exhale and clasp your hands together behind your feet. Breathe deeply and evenly and hold this position for 10 seconds or for as long as you feel comfortable. Change sides and repeat the entire sequence.

# Back Arch

This Back Arch immediately restores vitality and energy to the system and relaxes the brain. It also allows you and your partner to help each other improve your suppleness. When your back is arched and your head dropped to the floor behind you, the blood rushes to your brain, revitalizing and replenishing your brain cells. It is impossible to be a good lover when your sex drive is low or there is a lack of enthusiasm, and this exercise is an excellent tonic to refresh your mind when you are feeling lethargic and tired. It also allows you to move intimately with your partner which will set the mood for lovemaking. When you are helping each other to stretch, be aware of each other's capabilities – in many cases the flexibility of the couple may not be equal. Never force or push your partner; remember that yoga is non-competitive and everyone should always work at their own pace. With continued practice and patience you will see how fast you progress.

Begin by sitting facing each other and hold one another in a gentle, loving manner. Take your legs over each other's thighs and bring both feet together. ▸ With your partner holding your lower back for support, inhale, arch your back and lift up as high as possible to rest on the top of your head. Exhale and breathe normally. This improves circulation to the face and neck and you will feel the blood flow into the brain. Hold for 5–10 seconds. ▸ Inhale, release the neck and have your partner help you back up. Exhale and relax your spine forward as your partner arches the spine and relaxes backward. Repeat the exercise 5 times with a back-and-forth motion.

# Heart Chakra

It is very important in lovemaking to be in tune mentally and emotionally with your partner. Tantric sex unites your energy centers and it is vital that these centers remain unblocked. There are seven chakras in the body and the heart chakra lies in the center of the chest. It is the energy center that rules compassion and unconditional love, and blocked energy here leads to psychological and emotional disturbances. This exercise balances all seven centers from the base or pelvic region, through the navel into the solar plexus, through the heart into the throat, and through the third eye (between the eyebrows) into the top of the head or crown to unite with the cosmic or universal energy. This technique is used as a ritual in Tantra to arouse sexual passion and heighten sexual pleasure.

Begin by sitting cross-legged, facing each other, with enough distance between you to prevent you from touching each other. ▶ Sit up as tall as possible and clasp your hands together, palms facing outwards. ▶ Concentrating on your base chakra, inhale deeply and slowly raise your arms, moving through each chakra until you raise your arms high over your head. Keep the breath even and continuous as you slowly fill your lungs with air. Exhale and slowly bring the arms back down to position 1. Try to match the exact pace of your partner while performing the exercise. Repeat up to 10 times.

# Love Poses

Sexual positions, or Kama *asanas*, bring variety and excitement to the sex act. In the *Kama Sutra*, the great sage Vatsyayana describes the ways to achieve pleasure through a systematic and scientific approach to the anatomy of the body and the reactions of the mind. While the sex urge is a natural and powerful phenomenon, it can be disciplined by the gift of yoga. Within these sexual poses it is important to prolong the sex act and to increase pleasure by observing and understanding it. If you are already acquainted with the yoga positions you should not find the *Kama Sutra* poses illustrated here difficult, and the benefits you gain will be enhanced when you achieve the fulfilment of Kama or sexual bliss. To condemn knowledge of sex as a sin, and to glorify ignorance as bliss, merely promotes misery, incompetence, fear and damage to the psyche. No man should think of sexual intercourse as the supreme test of his manliness, nor should a woman regard it as her badge of femininity. If you feel an act of sex to be a test or competition, the spontaneity and the naturalness of the situation will be destroyed. Embrace it as a wonderful and integral part of a healthy and rounded life and enjoy the pleasure that is a fundamental right for each human being.

# Splits Love Pose

This beautiful love pose is a perfect blend of a dancer's grace and poise combined with the flexibility of the hips and groin. To achieve this pose it is important for the woman to practice the Half Lotus Side Stretch (page 198–9) and Double Sitting Twist (pages 194–5) to release stiffness and help open up the hip area.

The man kneels down on the floor with his knees close together and his hips touching his heels, his feet flat down behind him. The woman half kneels down close to him on his left side so their bodies are touching and their arms caressing one another, she with her right arm around his right shoulder and her left arm on his right forearm and he with his left hand on her back and his right hand on her waist. ▶ She lunges her right leg over his thighs, creating a right angle to the floor, making sure that her lunge is deep enough so her knee does not extend over her foot. She balances on her left knee and her left hand moves to her waist, covering his hand. ▶ From this position she slides her right leg in a perfectly straight line and extends her left leg behind her until her weight is fully on his body. She points both her feet and balances between her right heel and left knee. She gently lifts her spine up toward her partner so her back is leaning on his chest, reaches her arms behind her and takes her right arm around the man's head in order to twist her body toward him so she can still gaze lovingly into his eyes.

# The Swan Love Pose

In order to achieve this love pose it is important for the woman to practice the Standing Bow (pages 72–3) and the Locust (pages 192–3) in order to improve the strength and flexibility of her lower back and the Double Sitting Twist (pages 194–5) to help rotate her spine easily. Some people might find the final position too difficult to achieve and so finish with position 2 instead.

The couple begin the pose sitting down on the floor or a divan holding each other in a loving manner. The woman sits in front of the man, leaning on her left buttock with both legs tucked under so her knees and feet are together. She leans on the man and turns her back toward him so her right cheek caresses the left side of his face. He sits upright with his left leg up in a 90° angle to the floor in line with his left hip, and his right leg folded directly in front of him. He holds the woman firmly and she gently holds his hands. ▸ She lifts herself up on both knees and slides her body on to his right thigh. She extends her right leg behind her as far as possible while balancing her weight between her left leg and her partner's upper thigh.. He drops his right hand to the floor and straightens his elbow in order to support her weight. She turns her back so she can face him and puts her right hand behind his head. ▸ She reaches behind his back and lifts her right foot up and arches her spine. She holds on to her foot and twists her body closer to his body. He takes his left hand to his left leg and kisses her gently on the mouth.

# Half-Standing Love Pose

People who are relatively fit can achieve this pose without too much difficulty. Because of its simplicity it allows the intimacy of the couple to flourish as well as heightening sexual desire. The couple can concentrate fully on their sexual pleasure and balance their weight equally between them.

The couple begin by standing facing each other. The man drops to his left knee and keeps the right knee up with his foot firmly placed on the floor in a right angle to the floor. The woman lifts her left leg up and places her left foot on his right hipbone with her toes facing outward and her heel next to his groin. Her standing leg remains straight. She takes her right arm around his left shoulder and he takes his right hand to her left buttock. She gazes down at him and holds his right hand gently. ▸ She steps over his right thigh with her left leg and lowers herself down to his pelvis so her weight is resting on his body. Her left foot is firmly placed on the floor and her right leg is bent in order to distribute her weight evenly and allow movement between them. He grips her tightly around her waist and draws her closely toward him. She puts her left hand on his right knee for support and pulls herself closer to him. ▸ She drops down to her right knee and curves her left leg around his waist so their bodies are directly touching. She points her toes and he takes hold of her foot with his left hand. He draws her body even closer as they gaze directly into each other's eyes.

211

# Leg Hook Love Pose

This erotic love pose unites the couple with equal passion and is relatively simple to perform. Both partners need to have a similar amount of strength in their arms and legs as well as in their pelvic and abdominal muscles. The Pelvic Stretch (pages 182–3) is a good exercise to help strengthen these muscle groups and the Dog Pose (pages 36–7) is particularly useful for building stamina and straightening the arms and legs.

To begin this pose the man sits on the floor with his knees facing outward and the soles of his feet together. The woman sits on top of the man with her feet also placed soles together. Their arms are gently wrapped around each other, his at her lower back and hers around the middle of his back. ▸ The woman leans back and places both her hands to the floor with her fingers pointing to the man. She straightens her arms in order to support her weight, lifts both legs up off the floor and places them on either side of her partner's head to rest on his shoulders. Both legs are exactly parallel and she is slightly off the ground, balancing on her hands. He moves his hands to her upper back to prepare to lift her and gazes directly into her eyes. ▸ Pushing down on her palms, she extends her elbows and lifts her body off the floor. When she is perfectly steady and balanced the man lifts his legs over her shoulders around her neck and places his hands behind him in order to free his hips and give himself extra support. The heads of the man and woman are at the same level to allow freedom of movement.

# Half Plough Love Pose

This pose combines the classic Shoulder Stand (pages 76–7) for the woman and the Warrior pose (page 42) for the man. The pose is dramatic in feeling and looks as if the man is dominating the woman. In reality it is a beautiful exchange of energy that is both erotic and sensuous.

The woman begins by lying flat on the floor, legs together and arms at her sides. She bends her knees to her chest, places her hands in the small of the back to support her spine and rolls back into an inverted position so her knees are on the top of her forehead. (If the abdominal muscles are weak she can place her hands on the floor to push herself back and then replace the hands on her lower back.) She lifts both legs up so her spine is as straight as possible, points her feet and locks her chin into her chest. The man stands close and pushes his weight under her hips to help straighten her spine even further. He holds her upper thigh with his right hand and both ankles with his left hand. ▶ The woman lowers her right leg to the floor directly behind her head, pointing her foot to extend her leg in a straight line. The man checks her position to make sure that she is in a 90° angle to the floor. ▶ When he is confident that her position is correct he lunges his left leg over her groin in front of her right leg and lowers himself. His left hand moves down to her inner thigh and his right hand holds on to her left ankle. He is now at a perfect angle to look into her eyes.

# Side Love Pose

The beauty of this pose lies in its simplicity and truth. As the pose requires little movement it is a perfect opportunity for the couple to connect with each other's energy flow. In the Heart Chakra pose (pages 202–3) the energy contact flows through the chakras to unite at the level of the crown. Meditate on this thought and feel as if you are uniting sexually to connect with the universal cosmic flow of energy. Keep the eye contact constant and you will have a feeling of floating into divine bliss.

The man begins this pose by sitting comfortably on the floor, his legs outstretched in front of him and his spine erect. The woman sits sideways on the left side of his lap so her legs and feet are together alongside his right hip. The man takes his arms lovingly around her hips and the woman places her arms around his shoulders. They gaze deeply into each other's eyes. ▶ The woman leans back and places her left hand on the floor to support her weight. She bends her left leg and wraps it tightly around the man's waist. She lifts her right leg and points her foot over his left shoulder so her leg is in a straight line. The man takes his right palm to the floor to support the change in the woman's movement. They are still looking directly at each other. ▶ With his right arm, the man grasps the middle of the woman's back to draw her closer. She places her left foot on the floor to support her weight and give herself freedom to move. She takes her right arm around his shoulder so she can grip on to his body, and points her toe harder to straighten her knee. They continue to gaze lovingly at one another.

# stay
# youthful
## with
## yoga

The quest for eternal youth is universal. Even the earliest records of human civilizations provide evidence of elixirs and potions used to preserve youth and beauty, while numerous scientists today are engaged in a search for new techniques with which to hold the ageing process at bay. Millions of pounds are spent by the public each year on anti-ageing creams and body treatments and some people resort to cosmetic surgery to restore the appearance of youth. There is a proverb in yoga philosophy that says that the day you begin your yoga practice the age clock stops. Yoga can counteract the effects of time by regulating your metabolism, balancing your hormonal levels and raising your energy reserves, focusing your mind and keeping your spine supple. As the spine becomes more flexible, energy flows more freely throughout the system, increasing vitality, while correct breathing rejuvenates the entire body and mind. Yoga is more than mere exercise. It can boost the immune system and help to stop ill health occurring in all age groups. If ailments do occur, yoga can help to alleviate the symptoms and in some cases can even eliminate the condition.

# Daily Exercises

This section of the book offers six exercise routines with different objectives, each taking about 10 minutes to do. Day One improves the circulation to prevent stiffness in the joints; Day Two tones the parts of the body that show the first signs of ageing; Day Three strengthens the lower back to alleviate back pain; Day Four opens the chest area to unblock trapped energy in the spine; Day Five energizes the entire system; and finally Day Six teaches correct breathing to rejuvenate the system.

# Day One:
## *Circulation*

People who have good circulation feel robust, happy and healthy, while those with poor circulation may feel constantly depleted of energy and this affects their mental attitude. Fear of immobility and of growing old plagues even the happiest of people from time to time and so it is important to keep the body active and circulation flowing evenly. Poor circulation is a common complaint which can lead to various illnesses, so in this section I have designed a series of movements to boost your energy levels, raise your spirits and reoxygenate your entire system. You will notice that you are moving and twisting in every direction, which will stimulate all the internal organs and nerves, and combining this with deep breathing to release tension in the body.

Stand with your feet together in perfect posture (page 113). Take your hands onto your shoulders, keeping the elbows up in a straight line to each other. ▸ Inhale and bring your elbows in toward each other. Exhale, and push the elbows back as far as possible to open the chest. ▸ Looking upward, clasp your hands behind your head, lifting your elbows up as high as possible without lifting the shoulders. ▸ Inhale and bring your elbows toward each other, keeping your arms as close to the head as possible. ▸ Exhale and open your elbows wide, keeping your elbows in line and the shoulders down. ▸

223

Place your feet 1–1.2 m (3–4 ft) apart, toes pointing forward. Standing tall with your spine erect, place your right hand on your waist and take your left arm to the side in an exact line to the shoulder. Turn your palm upward and gaze toward your hand. ▸ Inhale and in a fluid movement take your arm in a circular movement over your head, stretching as far as possible to the right side. Inhale and exhale and hold for 10 seconds. Release the body, stand tall, place your left hand to your waist and repeat to the other side. Keep your breathing deep and even as you stretch further to the left. ▸ Take the left hand down to the right ankle and twist, looking over the right shoulder. Repeat on the other side. ▸ Return to standing position. Cross your arms in front of your chest with your palms facing toward you. ▸ Inhale, and with a graceful movement bring your arms down in line with the hips and up in a straight line to your shoulders. ▸ Push your shoulders down and extend your arms as much as possible. Make sure your fingertips are together and your palms facing down. Exhale, breathe normally and hold for 5 seconds. ▸

225

Bend your left elbow, inhale and as you exhale reach down to your right ankle. ▶ Place your left hand on your right ankle and twist, looking over your right shoulder. If you are unable to reach the ankle, place your left hand anywhere on your right leg. Inhale and exhale deeply as you increase the twist. Hold for 7 seconds. ▶ Return to standing position with arms outstretched to the side then take your right hand to your left ankle and repeat the twist on the other side.

▶ Release the twist and take both arms down in front of you, keeping your hands parallel in line with your shoulders.

▶ Inhale and slowly reach forward from the tail bone, bringing your arms upward over your head, palms facing each other. Exhale, breathe normally and hold for 3 seconds. ▶ Keeping the arms in the exact position, turn your right foot to the right and left foot slightly inward. Make sure your right heel is in a direct line to the instep of your left foot. Turn your body all the way to the right so both hips are facing to the right. ▶

227

Bring your palms together in prayer position and cross your thumbs. Bend your right knee, making sure it does not overextend the right foot. ▶ Inhale, straighten your right leg and point your left foot as much as possible. This will help your left leg to remain straight. ▶ Exhale and lift your left leg up behind you, balancing on your right leg. Keep your arms in line with your head, close to your ears. Breathing deeply, continue to stretch in both directions so your spine is in a straight line with your arms and foot. Hold the position for 10 seconds and deepen the breath as the pose increases in intensity. ▶ To release, bend your right knee and take your left foot back to starting position. Straighten your right leg and

place both hands behind your lower back in prayer position, fingers pointing upward. Inhale and take your head back, pushing your chest and hips forward. ▶ Exhale and, leading with the chin, stretch forward from the tail bone so your spine remains in a straight line. Breathe normally and hold for 5 seconds. ▶ Inhale, drop your head forward and stretch down toward your right knee. Exhale, breathe deeply and hold for 5 seconds. Inhale, release the spine and continue to stretch forward, keeping your spine straight. As you return to the starting position, push your hips forward and drop your head backward. Exhale, breathe normally and straighten your spine. Repeat the entire exercise on the other side.

229

# Day Two:
## *Toning*

As we age our muscles begin to sag and it is vital to tone and strengthen them. Stretching is the best way to achieve top-to-toe fitness and yoga stretches the muscles lengthways, reducing the fat around each muscle and producing a long, lean, streamlined body. It also increases the flexibility and suppleness of the spine so that your movements are more fluid and graceful. A further benefit is that deep stretching stimulates lymphatic drainage which helps to eliminate cellulite, a common problem for women of all ages. The exercises in this section tone the areas of the body that show the signs of ageing first – legs, thighs, buttocks and tummy. The twisting movements help eliminate toxins from the system and the deep stretching movements increase circulation.

When toning the body it is very important to concentrate on the muscle groups you wish to firm. When you stand in perfect posture make sure every muscle in the body is working by lifting each muscle upward, especially the muscle above the kneecap. Tighten your tummy muscles and tuck your tail bone under while you imagine a string pulling you upward from the top of your head. Place your feet 30 cm (1 ft) apart, directly in line with your hips. Cross your arms in front of your chest, holding on to your elbows. ▸ Focus your attention on a spot in front of you. Rise up on your toes, lifting your heels up as high as possible. ▸ Now, keeping your spine in a straight line, bend your knees, lifting your heels up in a right angle to the floor. Hold the position, breathing deeply and evenly, for at least 10 seconds. You will find this position very challenging because you are combining balance with deep breathing. ▸ Now take the legs in a wide second position with your feet 1–1.2 m (3–4 ft) apart. Take your arms out to the side, in line with your shoulders. ▸ Turn your right foot to the right, making sure it is in an exact line to the instep of your left foot. Look over your right hand while keeping your spine upright. ▸

232

Leading from the tail bone, stretch out to the right as far as possible. ▶ Take your right hand down to your ankle and take your left arm upward in a straight line. Make sure your fingertips are together and your palm is facing forward. Breathe deeply and normally as you hold for 7–10 seconds. ▶ Take your left arm over your head close to your ear in a straight line to the spine. Keep looking upward as you inhale and exhale deeply for 10 seconds. ▶ Bend your right knee in an exact right angle so the back of the knee is in line to the right heel. Take your right palm to your instep and as you stretch diagonally take your left arm in an exact line to your left leg. Hold the pose for 10 seconds. ▶ Now take your right arm to join your left arm in a parallel line and hold the position while your breath deepens. Hold for 5 seconds. ▶ Clasp your hands together as you increase the stretch. Hold the position and breathe as deeply as possible for at least 10 seconds. ▶

Lift your spine in a straight line as you clasp your hands over your head. Deepen the stretch as you lift your spine upward to be as tall as possible. Inhale and straighten your knee and turn your body forward. Release your arms and take them to your sides. ▸ Lie back on the floor and relax your whole body, keeping your arms next to your body on either side. Inhale and lift your left leg upward in an exact 90° angle to the floor. Clasp your hands together behind your knee and point your toes upward. Hold for 5 seconds. ▸ Bend your right knee and bring your heel in as close to your right buttock as possible. ▸ Inhale and stretch your head to your left knee, keeping your leg in a straight line. Hold for 7 seconds, breathing deeply and evenly. Slowly lower your spine and then release your left leg down to the floor. Relax your right leg

so both legs are down to the floor. Repeat the exercise on the other side. Inhale and exhale as you relax down. ▸ Bring both knees up, keeping your arms to your sides. ▸ Concentrate on your hips and tighten your buttock muscles as you lift your hips as high as possible. Breathing deeply, keep lifting the buttock muscles upward. Hold your ankles if you are able to reach them – if not, hold anywhere along the leg that is comfortable. Draw your chin into your chest as you continue to lift your hips upward. You are now in a perfect circular pose. To release, isolate the spine by pushing each vertebra down from the top of the spine so the tail bone is last to return to the floor. ▸

Release your hands from your ankles and relax your legs down to the floor. Inhale and exhale deeply for 5 seconds. ▶ Bring your legs together and point your toes down. Take your arms to your sides, palms on the floor. Inhale, push down on your elbows and raise your chest as high as possible so you are able to balance on the top of your head. Exhale, breathe normally and hold for 5–7 seconds. This is called the Fish pose and is an excellent stretch for the neck and chin. ▶ Turn over onto your stomach and place your chin on the floor. Place your hands in fists at your sides.

▶ Inhale, point your left foot to help straighten your knee and raise your left leg off the floor, keeping both hipbones down. Exhale, breathe normally and hold for 5–7 seconds. On an exhalation, slowly lower your leg. Repeat on the other side. ▶ Take your arms out to the side and rest on your elbows, fingers pointing inward. ▶ Inhale and simultaneously lift both legs and your chest off the floor, taking your arms behind you. Exhale, breathe deeply and hold for at least 10 seconds. This is an excellent exercise for toning and lifting the buttock muscles. Repeat and hold for 12–15 seconds.

# Day Three:
## *Strengthening the Back*

People who suffer from chronic back pain often believe that they should refrain from doing any exercise. In fact, it is vital to strengthen the muscles in the back to alleviate pain and prevent further back injuries. The exercises in this section are designed to eliminate the fear of moving the spine forward and backward. They will remove any muscular tension trapped in the back, relieve stiffness in the neck and shoulders and strengthen the muscles in the lower back to enable you to sit and stand in perfect posture. Pay special attention to all the muscles in the spine and perform slow, deliberate movements, taking deep and even breaths throughout. A dull pain in the spine merely indicates that your muscles are working, but if you feel any sharp pain stop the exercises immediately.

Stand with your feet together in perfect posture, arms to the side. Inhale and lift your arms up in front of you in line with your shoulders. Make sure your elbows are straight and your palms are facing down. Exhale, breathe normally and hold for 3 seconds. ▸ Concentrate on the area of the lower back and reach forward from the tail bone, keeping your spine straight and tightening your tummy muscles as you stretch down. ▸ Using your natural body weight combined with deep inhalations and exhalations to loosen the spine, stretch right down so your hands reach the floor. Do not force or jerk your body down. You will be surprised how supple your spine will soon

238

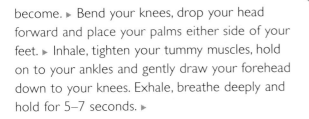

become. ▸ Bend your knees, drop your head forward and place your palms either side of your feet. ▸ Inhale, tighten your tummy muscles, hold on to your ankles and gently draw your forehead down to your knees. Exhale, breathe deeply and hold for 5–7 seconds. ▸

239

Release your hands and begin to uncurl your spine slowly, keeping your knees straight. ► Pull your tummy muscles up, tighten your buttock muscles, drop your shoulders and lift your head up. ► When you are standing tall, take both arms behind your lower back, holding firmly on to your elbows. ► Inhale and push your hips forward as much as possible. Keep your knees straight, open your chest and drop your head back. Exhale, breathe normally and relax your neck and jaw. Hold for 5–7 seconds. Slowly release by returning to standing position and relax forward to counteract the back bend. ► Relax down to the floor with your legs outstretched in front and arms to the side. Inhale, point your toes and bring your knees into your chest. Stretch your arms out in line with your shoulders. ► Exhale and take both knees to the right as you twist your spine to the left side and look over your left shoulder. ►

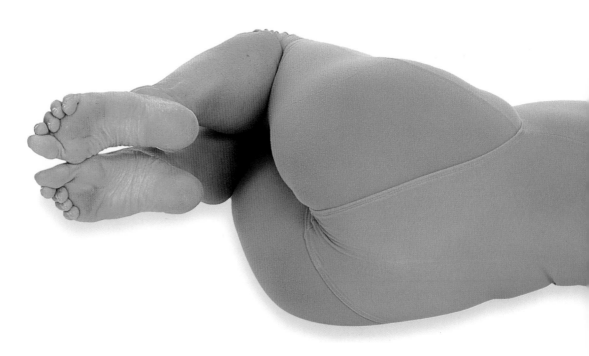

Inhale and return to the starting position. Exhale, take both knees to the left side and twist your spine and head to the right. Inhale and return to the starting position, then repeat the sequence.
► When you finish, draw your knees into your chest, pushing the small of your back on to the floor, keeping your head straight. ► Take your arms to your sides and push your palms down on the floor as you lift your legs up and over your head. ► Tuck your toes under to increase the stretch. Do not worry if you cannot reach the floor behind you. ► Hold on to your hips for support and with continued practice you will be able to stretch further backward. This motion stimulates the thyroid gland, which regulates the hormonal levels and metabolism in the body.
► Inhale and lift the left leg up in a straight line to the body. Exhale, relax the foot and breathe normally for 5–7 seconds. While you are holding the pose you will feel all the blood rush down the leg into the internal organs. This will replenish all the cells with a fresh blood supply. Lower the left leg and repeat on the other side. ►

Slowly bend both legs and lower your knees to your forehead. ▸ When you reach a 90° angle to the floor, straighten your legs and hold the position, breathing deeply and evenly, for 10 seconds. Using the tummy muscles, slowly lower your legs to the floor. Relax. ▸ Turn over, place your hands directly under your shoulders and push your hips back so you are sitting on your heels. Stretch your arms out in front. Inhale and dive forward with your chest so

your hips are up and your chest is in line with your head. ▸ In a circular motion, lift your spine and look upward as you balance on your hands. ▸ Relax down to the floor. Bend both knees and take hold of your ankles. Place your chin on the floor. ▸ Inhale, lift your legs and head and balance on your hipbones. Exhale, then breathe deeply and evenly as you continue to stretch upward. Hold for 5 seconds then release slowly.

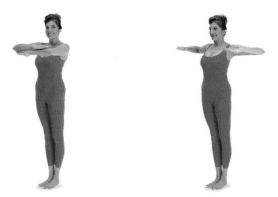

# Day Four:
## *Opening the Chest*

In yoga there are considered to be seven energy centres, or chakras, which relate to different parts of the body. These spinning wheels of energy must be flowing smoothly and evenly before a person can be balanced and centered, and this can only occur when the mind, body and soul are in total harmony and balance. The fourth chakra is related to the heart, which controls loving emotions. People who have suffered bad experiences will tend to close their heart to protect themselves from further pain. Opening the chest will help you to gain a more positive outlook on life in general; you will feel empowered and have the confidence to face the world with a brave heart.

Stand tall with your feet together. Take your arms up in front of your chest and bend your elbows, placing the right forearm over the left. Keep your arms level with your shoulders. ▸ Inhale, take your elbows back and open your chest. You will feel your shoulder blades moving toward each other. Exhale and return to the starting position. Repeat the exercise. ▸ Release your elbows and take your forearms in front of you in a parallel line with the palms facing toward each other. ▸ Inhale and take your elbows back as far as possible, palms facing forward. Exhale and return to the starting position. Repeat. ▸ Stand in perfect posture. Lift your chest upward while keeping your shoulders down. Inhale and lift your left knee up. Exhale, clasp both hands around your knee and draw your leg closer to your body. Breathing deeply, hold for 5 seconds. If you are unable to balance, lean your back against a wall or use a chair for assistance. ▸

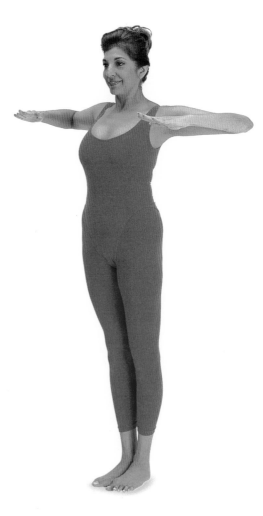

247

Still keeping your left knee up with your hips square, take your arms to the side and balance on one leg as you gaze at one point ahead of you to help focus your mind. Release your left leg and stand tall. ▸ Lift your right leg and repeat the same exercise. ▸ As you extend your arms to the side, keep your hips square and your spine straight. Return to the starting position. ▸ Take your feet 1–1.2 m (3–4 ft) apart, making sure your toes are pointing forward. Cross your arms behind your lower back, taking hold of the elbows. ▸ Before you begin to arch your spine backward, visualize yourself in the final position. Inhale, push your hips forward, open your chest, drop your shoulders down and look upward. ▸ As you exhale, relax further back so your breastbone faces upward and your neck and throat are stretched. Relax your head and release the tension in your jaw. Open your throat and say 'Aah' in a loud voice to ensure that your shoulders are down and your throat is open. Hold for 3–5 seconds. Inhale and slowly return to the starting position. Exhale and relax forward to counteract the backbend. ▸

248

Standing tall, take your arms behind your lower back with your hands in a prayer position, fingertips facing up. This allows your chest to open even further. Turn your right foot to the right, making sure that your right heel is in a direct line to the instep of the left foot. Turn your torso completely to the right, trying to keep your hips square. ▸ Inhale, push your hips forward and drop your head back. Look upward, exhale, and breathe normally for 5 seconds. ▸ On the exhalation, drop your head forward toward your right knee, leading from the tail bone. Hold for 5 seconds. ▸ Inhale, tighten your tummy muscles and raise your torso until your head, back and hips are in a straight line. Exhale, breathe deeply and hold for 5 seconds. ▸ Bend your right knee in a 90° angle so the back of your knee is in a direct line to your right heel. Make sure you do not extend your knee over your foot. Inhale, straighten up, exhale and hold for 5 seconds, breathing normally. Repeat the entire sequence on the other side. Return to standing position. ▸ Lift your right leg up behind you, taking hold of the inside of your right foot. This helps keep the hips square. Take your left hand to your waist and hold until you have perfect balance. ▸

251

252

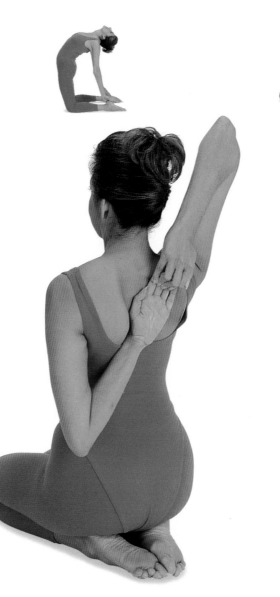

Focus your attention on a spot in front of you and begin to raise your right leg. ▶ Maintaining your balance, stretch even further, pointing your toe. Breathing deeply, hold for as long as possible, stretching in both directions. Repeat on the other side. ▶ Kneel on the floor, your knees in a direct line to your hips and arms behind your lower back. ▶ Pushing from your hips, arch backward. ▶ If you can, place your hands on your heels to increase the stretch. Continue to push your hips up, breathing deeply, and hold for 5–7 seconds. ▶ Sit on your heels and drop your head forward to counteract the pose. Lift your head and take your right arm over your right shoulder so your palm is facing your right shoulder blade. Take your left arm behind your back, palm facing outward. Inhale and try to clasp the palms together. Exhale, breathe normally and hold for 6 seconds. Repeat on the other side.

# Day Five:
## *Energizing*

Yoga is a form of exercise which constantly builds energy levels rather than depleting them. With advancing age there comes a drop in energy and some people believe that they should not do any form of exercise. Harsh and strenuous movements are harmful at any age but because yoga is very gentle on the joints even the very elderly can benefit. Try to keep the movements fluid and allow your whole body to move gracefully like a dancer. If you become short of breath during the series, take deeper breaths from the diaphragm to increase your energy flow. Repeat the section at least twice to feel the benefit and, at the end, bring your fingertips together to feel an exchange of energy from your right hand to your left.

This series of movements will energize your entire system, especially if you are feeling tired and lack energy to enjoy the pastimes you enjoy most. As you age it is more important to feel enthusiastic and full of vitality. Stand tall with your feet 1–1.2 m (3–4 ft) apart. Shift your weight to the left foot, lift the right heel off the floor and point the right foot and take both arms to the left. Extend your arms, palms facing each other, and stretch your body up, lifting your chest.
▸ Inhale and begin to swing your arms to the left in a wide circle. ▸ Bend your knees to increase the movement and take your arms down in front of you in a parallel line. ▸ Continue to swing your arms to the right and shift your weight to the right foot. ▸ As you bring your arms over to the left, exhale, and swing your body simultaneously to the left, completing the full circle. To increase the stretch, take the left arm out to the side. ▸

255

stay youthful with yoga

Curve your right arm in an
angle to the right as you lift
your left arm upward in a straight
line. ▸ Stretch over to the right as far
as possible and enjoy the feeling of
moving the entire body as a whole. ▸ Curve the
left arm and move the body toward the left.
▸ With a fluid, graceful motion, stretch over to
the left as far as possible. Breathe normally
as you move through the entire series. The
stretching from side to side rejuvenates the
whole body and lifts the spirit. Repeat the entire
sequence. ▸ Stand tall with your feet 1–1.2 m
(3–4 ft) apart, your toes pointing forward and
arms outstretched to the side. Make sure your
arms are in line with your shoulders with your
palms facing down. ▸ Turn your left foot and swirl
your body to the left, taking your left arm behind
you and your right elbow in front of your chest.
Twist from the waist as far as possible and make
sure both arms are level with each other. ▸

Turn your right foot and swing your body and arms to the right. Return to standing position with your feet together. ▸ Keeping both hips square, raise your right knee and balance on your left foot. When you have perfect balance raise both arms over your head. Clasp your hands together and hold the position for 5 seconds. ▸ Breathing normally, take your right leg up and place your right foot on the inside of your left thigh. Make sure the standing leg is straight and lift the muscle above the kneecap to help you balance. Stretch your arms over your head, keeping your elbows straight. Cross your thumbs and place your palms together. Hold for 5 seconds. ▸ Release your arms, place your left hand on your waist and take your right hand down to your right foot. Clasp your first and second fingers around your big toe and flex your thumb. As you grab hold of your foot lean toward the right, keeping your spine erect. ▸ Inhale and stretch your leg out to the side as far as possible. Exhale, breathe normally and hold for 5 seconds. If you cannot extend the right leg fully, do not worry – it is more important to keep the hips square and the standing leg straight. ▸ Release your leg and place your feet 1–1.2 m (3–4 ft) apart. Turn your right foot to the right and bend your right knee. Place your hand on top of your knee with your fingers facing the inner thigh. ▸

259

stay youthful with yoga

Place your fingertips on the floor to the right.
▶ Inhale, bend your right knee further and at the
same time lift your left leg so it is in line with your
body. Exhale, flex the left foot and keep both legs
straight. Release to the last position on page 259.
Repeat on the other side. ▶ Kneel on the right knee
and take your left leg to the side. Take your right arm
up and place your left hand on your left knee.
▶ Inhale, stretch to the left and slide your hand to

your ankle. Exhale then, breathing deeply, hold for
7–10 seconds. Repeat on the other side. ▶ Sit on the
floor, bend your left knee and place your right foot
flat on the floor so your knee is up. Place both palms
on the floor to the left. ▶ Inhale, bend your left elbow
and lift your right leg up in a 90° angle to the floor.
Clasp the two first fingers around the big toe and flex
the thumb. Exhale, breathe normally and hold for
7–10 seconds. Repeat on the other side.

# Day Six:
## *Rejuvenation*

People who practice yoga always look younger than their years; their skin is clear, their eyes are bright and they seem to glow with well-being. The difference between yoga and other forms of exercise lies in the breathing techniques. *Pranayama*, or the science of breath, is the most important aspect of yoga philosophy. In this series of exercises, concentrate on breathing deeply and evenly throughout. When you inhale, fill your lungs completely from the diaphragm. Keep your shoulders down and don't raise your chest. The movement should be concentrated only on the lower abdomen. As you exhale, let the breath out slowly as you continue with the movement. This technique can be practiced on its own or used as a warm-up to any of the exercise routines.

Stand tall with your feet together. Interlace your fingers and place your hands under your chin. ▸ Inhale deeply and lift your elbows up as high as possible while keeping your head and chin level. ▸ Drop your head back, keeping your elbows up. ▸ Exhale through the mouth, blowing the air out slowly and evenly as you bring your elbows together. ▸ Inhale deeply, lift the elbows up in line with your shoulders and repeat the entire breathing exercise 7 times. Deepen the inhalation and exhalation as you continue this rejuvenating breathing technique. ▸

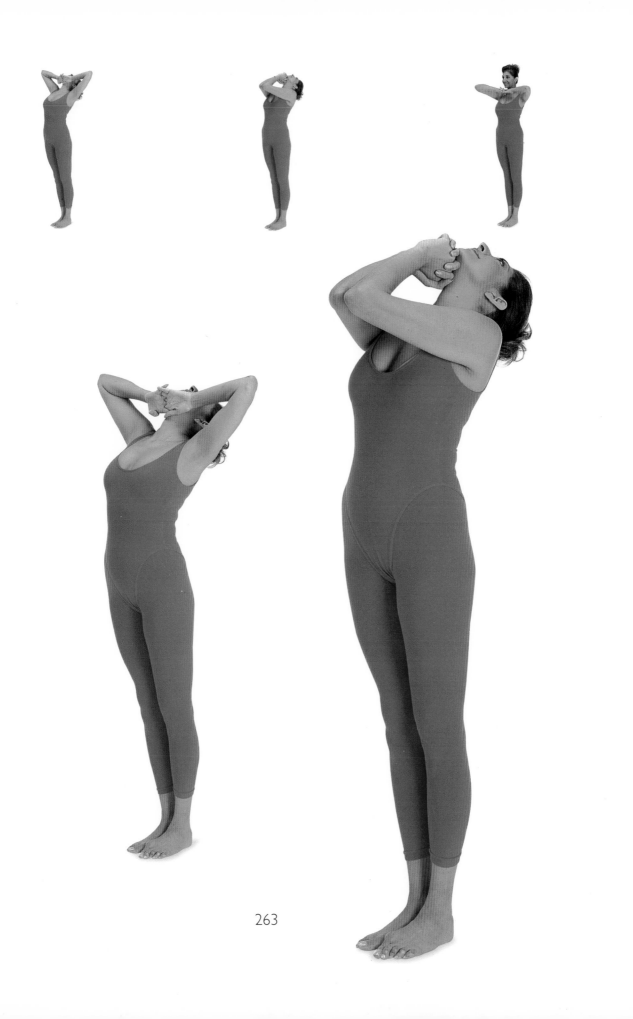

263

264

Inhale deeply and as you exhale slowly curve your spine, bend your elbows and drop your head forward, looking down to your fingertips. ▸ With a flowing movement, stretch your spine down and straighten your arms. Face your palms down toward your feet and let the natural weight of your body extend your spine further down. ▸ Inhale deeply and sweep your arms forward in a circular motion. Keep your head between your arms as you take your arms up over your head. ▸ Drop your head back and look up to your fingertips. Breathe deeply and evenly. Hold for 5 seconds. ▸ Straighten your head, bring your palms together and continue to stretch your arms up. Make sure your shoulders are down and your head is locked between your elbows. ▸ Keeping your spine straight, bend your knees, keeping your toes and heels firmly on the floor. Breathing deeply, hold for 5 seconds. ▸

265

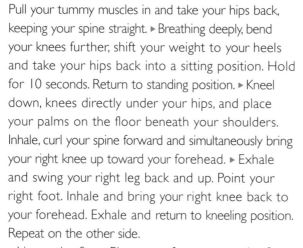

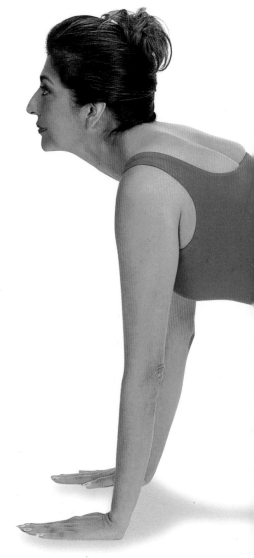

Pull your tummy muscles in and take your hips back, keeping your spine straight. ▸ Breathing deeply, bend your knees further, shift your weight to your heels and take your hips back into a sitting position. Hold for 10 seconds. Return to standing position. ▸ Kneel down, knees directly under your hips, and place your palms on the floor beneath your shoulders. Inhale, curl your spine forward and simultaneously bring your right knee up toward your forehead. ▸ Exhale and swing your right leg back and up. Point your right foot. Inhale and bring your right knee back to your forehead. Exhale and return to kneeling position. Repeat on the other side.

▸ Lie on the floor. Place your forearms on the floor and lift your head slightly. ▸ Inhale, push down, straighten your elbows and lift your spine. Keep your hipbones down and gaze upward. Exhale, breathe normally and hold for 7–10 seconds. ▸

268

Lie flat on the floor. Bring your knees up directly in line with your hips. Put your palms together and stretch your arms over your head. ▸ Inhale and as you exhale tighten your tummy muscles and bring your hands over your head to your knees, slowly lifting your head and shoulders off the floor. ▸ Sitting up further, inhale and raise your arms above your knees. ▸ Exhale, lower your back halfway down to the floor and bring your arms up in a straight line to your shoulders. ▸ Inhale and take your arms over your head as you slowly lower your spine to the floor. Exhale and lower your arms to the floor. ▸ Inhale, bend your elbows and bring your hands over the top of your head, palms together. Repeat the entire series 5 times. Keep the breathing pattern fluid as you move from one position to the next. Hold your breath for 2 seconds in each position to gain breath control.

# Maintenance

The positions on pages 272–7 constitute an exercise plan that tones and lifts the specific muscle groups that show the first signs of ageing. If your body is losing its elasticity and your muscles are beginning to sag it is important to address the problem before it becomes severe – but it is better still to keep yourself in shape and use this plan as a preventive measure. These exercises are designed to lift the entire body to restore youthfulness and suppleness; they will tone the ankles, calves, kneecaps and upper thighs, flatten the tummy, lift the buttocks and reduce the hips and waist. It is a dynamic fitness routine that can be done on its own or for increased benefit can be combined with any Day plan, depending on how much time you have or what specific areas you need to work on.

This fitness routine can also be a preface to the Remedial exercises which appear in the latter half of this section. Because the Remedial section targets specific problem areas, you will notice the results in a surprisingly short time. Doctors now agree that there is a direct link between the emotional balance of a person and their susceptibility to certain illnesses – people suffering from stomach cramps, for example, are often emotionally upset. They commonly take medication to relieve their pain, but yoga will relax the stomach cramps immediately because it teaches you to breathe through the pain in order to release it. Because yoga tones, reoxygenates and rejuvenates the entire body, it can alleviate a whole range of common problems, both physical and mental.

# Stomach Stretches

This series of movements will tighten and tone the lower abdominal muscles and flatten the tummy. Pay extra attention to the breathing pattern for the best results; breathing incorrectly may even build the muscles so your tummy actually appears larger.

Lie flat on the floor with your arms to the side. Bring your left knee up and place your left foot flat on the floor. Point your right foot and take both arms over your head. Place your palms together and straighten your elbows. ▸ Inhale and lift your right leg up to a 90° angle. Exhale, breathe normally and hold for 5 seconds. ▸ Inhale and bring your palms in toward your head. Exhale, sit up and bring your arms down in front of your face above the chest. ▸ Inhale, straighten your arms, exhale, breathe normally and hold for 5 seconds. Inhale, slowly lower your back and take your arms over your head. ▸ Exhale, lower your right leg, then your left and repeat the exercise on the other side.

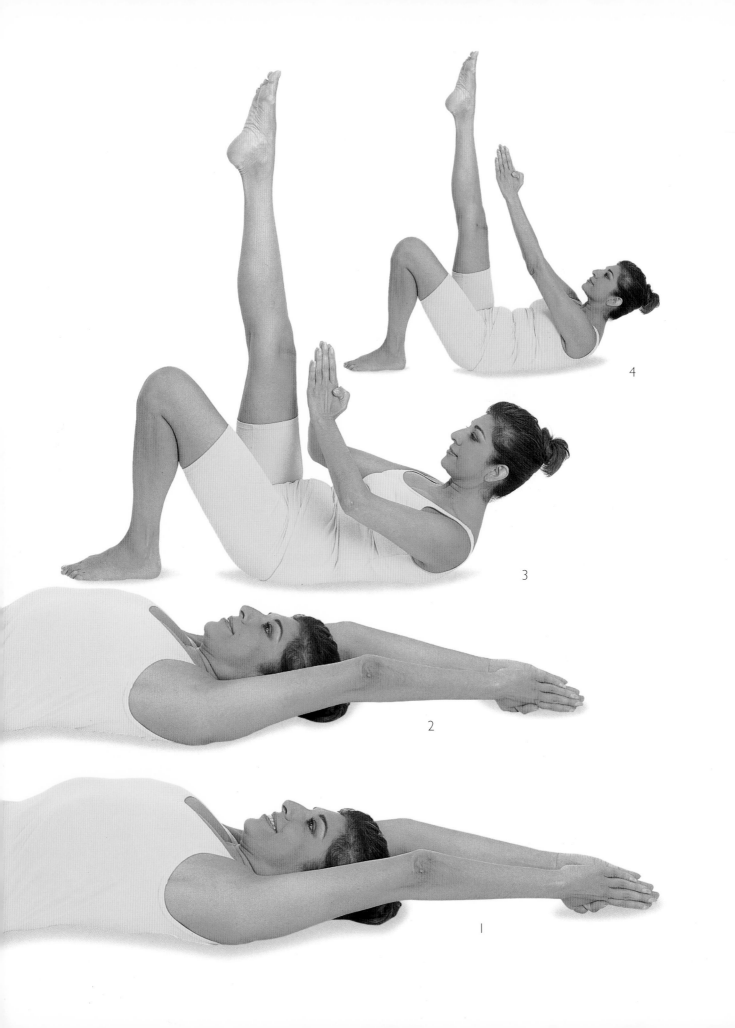

4

3

2

1

# Push-ups

2

3

This exercise will tone the upper arms, legs and tummy. The final pose requires extra stamina, so build up your strength slowly.

Sit back on your heels, tuck your toes under and stretch your arms out in front of you with your palms facing down. Leaving your hands in the same place, bend your elbows and push your palms down to the floor. Your arms will take the weight of your body as you do the next movement. ▸ Inhale, bring your chin down toward the floor and curve your spine down and up in a beautiful arch. Exhale, point your toes, straighten your elbows and lift your hips off the floor. Make sure you keep your shoulders down. Breathing normally, hold the pose for 5 seconds. ▸ Tuck your toes under and lift your whole body off the floor. Balance on your hands and feet and make sure your weight is evenly distributed between the two. Hold for 5 seconds. When you feel that you have the strength, inhale, bend your elbows and bring your entire body down to 7.5cm (3 inches) from the floor. Exhale, extend your arms and hold for 5 seconds. Repeat.

# Table Top

This exercise will tone every muscle simultaneously and requires flexibility, strength and stamina. It will help to focus your mind and give you a feeling of inner harmony. It is a challenging pose so it might take you some time and practice to master it.

Sit down with your legs outstretched in front of you. Point your toes, leave your feet flat down and bring your knees slightly off the floor in line with your waist. Lean back and take your arms behind you so your hands are hip-width apart and your fingers are facing your body. ▸ Straighten your arms, tighten your tummy and buttock muscles, inhale and lift your whole body off the floor. ▸ Exhale, inhale, and to increase the stretch, contract your buttock muscles and lift your hips higher off the floor so your body is in a perfect diagonal line. Exhale and drop your head back. Breathe normally and hold this intense stretch for 5–7 seconds. To release, sit back down on the floor.

276

2

3

# Remedial
## *Arthritis*

This exercise is excellent for relieving stiffness in the joints. At first it might feel uncomfortable but continued practice will alleviate the pain and increase circulation to the joints.

Kneel up tall then tuck the toes under and sit back on to the heels. If you feel any pain release the toes and continue. ▸ Place your hands behind you for support, fingers pointing away from you. Keep your arms and spine straight. Breathing normally, lift your hips up and push them forward as high as possible while balancing on your hands. Your weight should be evenly distributed between your arms and hips. ▸ Drop your head back, lifting your chin and hips up to create a circular shape with your spine. Hold for at least 5 seconds and repeat. When you are able to hold this pose comfortably, increase to 10 seconds.

1

2

3

# Osteoporosis

As you age your bones become brittle without extra calcium and a good supply of blood to the hip area. This twist sends fresh oxygen and a purified blood supply to the hips and increases the circulation of the entire system. It alleviates painful conditions like sciatica as well as strengthening the hip joints.

Stand tall with your feet 1–1.2 m (3–4 ft) apart. Turn your left foot to the left and make sure your left heel is in a direct line with the instep of your right foot. Take your arms out to the side in line with your shoulders. Bend your right elbow so it is in line with your left knee. ▶ Inhale, put your right hand on the floor, exhale, twist your spine and look up over your left shoulder. Breathe deeply and hold for 5–7 seconds. Keep your arms in a straight line. If you are unable to touch the floor with your hand hold any part of your left leg. Repeat on the other side.

2

1

# Immune System

Stress weakens the immune system and makes the body vulnerable to all kinds of health problems. It is hard to eliminate stress from our lives but we *can* boost the immune system in order to prevent ailments from becoming chronic.

Sit sideways on the floor, leaning on your right hip. Straighten your right leg and point your toe. Take your left knee up so your left foot is flat on the floor behind the right knee. Place your right palm on the floor about 30cm (1ft) from your right hip. Place your left hand near the upper thigh of your right leg. ▶ Inhale and push yourself up, balancing on your right hand and right foot. Exhale, keeping the legs parallel and your right arm fully extended. Your left arm should be pointed straight up in the air in line with your right arm. Breathe deeply and hold for as long as you can. Repeat on the other side.

# Thyroid

**This exercise keeps the thyroid stabilized and helps with menopausal symptoms.**

Lie flat on the floor, legs outstretched. Inhale and bring the knees to the chest. Exhale, push your palms down on the floor and roll your legs over your head. Breathe normally and hold your lower back to support your weight. Take your knees to the floor on either side of your head, close to your ears. ▸ Tighten your tummy muscles, place the soles of your feet together and create a triangle with your legs. ▸ Inhale, straighten your legs, tighten your buttock muscles and point your toes. Breathing deeply, hold for 20 seconds. To release, slowly bend your knees toward your forehead. Lower your spine, pushing each vertebra down to the floor. Lower your legs to the floor and relax for 20 seconds.

3

2

I

# Depression

1

Our mental state affects us physically, so it is vital to keep a positive outlook. This is not always easy, but keeping the mind alert and the body mobile will prevent depression. When you are in this inverted position the blood rushes to the brain and nourishes the cells.

Kneel on the floor, tuck your toes under and sit on your heels. Interlace your fingers, make a triangle with your arms and place your elbows under your shoulders. ▶ Place the top of your head on the floor, fingertips touching the back of your head. Inhale, straighten your legs and balance on your toes.
▶ Exhale, push your shoulders down and straighten your spine. Breathing normally, hold for 5 seconds. Bend your knees to the floor. Hold for 5 seconds and repeat, this time holding for 10 seconds. Sit back on your heels, your forehead on the floor. Relax for a few moments and lift your head slowly.

2

3

# Eye Strain

As people age the eye muscles become lax. These exercises are designed to strengthen the eye muscles so vision is improved.

Sit up tall in a comfortable cross-legged position. Straighten your index finger and place it in front of your nose. Stretch your right arm out in front of you and stare at your finger for 5 seconds. ▸ Keeping your eyes focused on your finger, slowly bring it toward you until it touches the tip of your nose. Still keeping your eyes focused on your finger, stretch the arm out again. Rub your hands and place your palms over your eyes. ▸ Keeping your head straight, take your arm up to the right, eyes still focused on your finger. ▸ Then take your arm diagonally to the left. Repeat on the same side, then on the other side. Rub your hands together and cup them over your eyes.

1

2

3

4

# Pelvic Floor

1

2

After childbirth and with advancing age, many women suffer from incontinence and other urinary disorders. The pelvic floor must be kept toned in order for the urinary system and sexual organs to function properly. As you do the following exercise, contract the pelvic muscle to bring elasticity to the vaginal wall, which will increase sensation during sexual intercourse.

3

Lie face down on the floor, arms to the side. Place your elbows under the shoulder blades with your palms face down and your fingers together. Inhale, push your palms and elbows down and lift your head up. Make sure your hipbones remain on the floor. Exhale and point your toes. ▸ Breathing normally, lift both legs up behind you, keeping your feet together. ▸ Balancing on your right arm, reach back with your left hand and take hold of your left foot. Lift your spine and look up. Hold for 5–7 seconds. Repeat on the other side.

# Breaks and Fractures

With advancing age, old breaks and fractures can cause arthritic conditions. This simple twist improves circulation, which will help ease the pain and boost healing.

Sit on the floor, your legs stretched out in front of you. Bring your left knee up and hold on to your leg. ▶ Breathing normally, place your right hand on the floor behind you and gently twist your body to the right so you are looking over your right shoulder. Straighten your left arm, point your fingers and keep both hipbones down on the floor as you increase the stretch. ▶ Sit up tall and take your right hand behind your lower back with your palm facing forward. Reach your left arm around your left knee and clasp your hands together. Keep your shoulders down as you increase the twist. Breathing deeply, hold for 7–10 seconds. Repeat on the other side.

# Index

First published in Great Britain in 1999 by Hamlyn, an imprint of Octopus Publishing Group Limited, 2-4 Heron Quays, London, E14 4JP

ISBN  0 600 59686 9

A CIP catalogue record of this book is available from the British Library.

Printed and bound in China

The textual material in this book is an abridged version of the following titles previously published by Hamlyn: *Yogacise* (1994); *Classic Yoga* (1995); *Yoga for Stress* (1997); *Yoga for Sex* (1997); *Stop the Age Clock* (1998).

ACKNOWLEDGEMENTS

Operations Director: Laura Bamford
Executive Editor: Jane McIntosh
Project Editor: Catharine Davey
Editor: Diana Vowles
Creative Director: Keith Martin
Design Manager: Bryan Dunn
Jacket Design: Mike Moule
Designer: Stephen Cary
Photography: John Adriaan
             Gary Houlder
             Tim Ridley
Production Controller: Sarah Scanlon

JACKET PHOTOGRAPHY

Acknowledgements in Source Order:

*Front Cover*
Octopus Publishing Group Ltd/John Adriaan front cover bottom
/Tim Ridley front cover top left, front cover top right, front cover top centre, front flap

*Back Cover*
Octopus Publshing Group Ltd/John Adriaan back cover centre right, back flap
/Tim Ridley back cover left, back cover centre left, back cover right